The Student's Companion to Social Policy

Fourth Edition

Edited by
Pete Alcock, Margaret May, and Sharon Wright

A John Wiley & Sons, Ltd., Publication

This edition first published 2012
© 2012 John Wiley & Sons Ltd

Edition history: Blackwell Publishers Ltd (1e, 1998); Blackwell Publishing Ltd (2e, 2003 and 3e, 2008)

Wiley-Blackwell is an imprint of John Wiley & Sons, formed by the merger of Wiley's global Scientific, Technical and Medical business with Blackwell Publishing.

Registered Office
John Wiley & Sons Ltd, The Atrium, Southern Gate, Chichester, West Sussex, PO19 8SQ, UK

Editorial Offices
350 Main Street, Malden, MA 02148-5020, USA
9600 Garsington Road, Oxford, OX4 2DQ, UK
The Atrium, Southern Gate, Chichester, West Sussex, PO19 8SQ, UK

For details of our global editorial offices, for customer services, and for information about how to apply for permission to reuse the copyright material in this book please see our website at www.wiley.com/wiley-blackwell.

The right of Pete Alcock, Margaret May, and Sharon Wright to be identified as the authors of the editorial material in this work has been asserted in accordance with the UK Copyright, Designs and Patents Act 1988.

Wiley also publishes its books in a variety of electronic formats. Some content that appears in print may not be available in electronic books.

Designations used by companies to distinguish their products are often claimed as trademarks. All brand names and product names used in this book are trade names, service marks, trademarks or registered trademarks of their respective owners. The publisher is not associated with any product or vendor mentioned in this book. This publication is designed to provide accurate and authoritative information in regard to the subject matter covered. It is sold on the understanding that the publisher is not engaged in rendering professional services. If professional advice or other expert assistance is required, the services of a competent professional should be sought.

Library of Congress Cataloging-in-Publication Data

The students companion to social policy / edited by Pete Alcock, Margaret May, and Sharon Wright. – 4th ed.
    p. cm.
  Includes index.
  ISBN 978-0-470-65565-8 (pbk.)
  1. Great Britain–Social policy. 2. Public welfare–Great Britain. 3. Social policy–Study and teaching. I. Alcock, Peter, 1951– II. May, Margaret, 1947– III. Wright, Sharon D. IV. Social Policy Association (Great Britain)
  HN390.S78 2012
  361.6'10941–dc23
                                                                    2011035242

A catalogue record for this book is available from the British Library.

This book is published in the following electronic formats: ePDFs 978-1-119-96080-5; ePub 978-1-119-96081-2; Mobi 978-1-119-96082-9

Set in 9.5 / 11.5 pt Minion by Toppan Best-set Premedia Limited
Printed in Singapore by C.O.S. Printers Pte Ltd

4   2014

Contents

Notes on Contributors

Pete Alcock is Professor of Social Policy and Administration at the University of Birmingham and Director of the ESRC Third Sector Research Centre. He has been teaching and researching in social policy for over thirty years. He has written widely on social policy, the voluntary sector, social security, poverty and social exclusion, and anti-poverty policy.

Hilary Arksey is a consultant and freelance researcher. Her main research interests lie in the area of community care, particularly informal or family caregiving. She has both published extensively in this area and undertaken studies for governmental and other agencies.

Rob Baggott is Professor of Public Policy and Director of the Health Policy Research Unit at De Montfort University, Leicester. He is the author of many publications on health policy. His research interests include health care reform, public health, and patient and public involvement.

Marian Barnes is Professor of Social Policy in the School of Applied Social Science at the University of Brighton. Her main areas of research include: user involvement and user movements, public participation, citizenship and new forms of democratic practice, policy and practice interfaces, mental health, older people, carers, and care ethics. She has written widely in these areas and has undertaken participative research with service users and carers.

Saul Becker is Head of the School of Sociology and Social Policy and Professor of Social Policy and Social Care at The University of Nottingham. His main research interests include informal family care (particularly children who are carers – 'young carers'), vulnerable children and their families, and research methodology in social policy. He has published extensively in these areas.).

Fran Bennett is Senior Research Fellow (half time) in the Department of Social Policy and Intervention at the University of Oxford. Her interests include social security policy, gender issues, and poverty, income distribution, and participation. She is also an independent consultant, writing on social policy issues for the UK government, European Commission, NGOs, and others.

Alice Bloch is Professor of Sociology at City University London where she teaches in the areas of migration, forced migration, race and ethnicity, and research methods. Her research interests are in the areas of migration, forced migration, and asylum policy.

Catherine Bochel is a principal lecturer in Policy Studies in the School of Social Sciences at the University of Lincoln. Her research interests include participation, the policy process and local government, on which she has published widely. She teaches on a range of policy-related courses.

Hugh Bochel is Professor of Public Policy at the University of Lincoln where his teaching includes the impact of ideology on social policy, social difference, and understanding and analysing the policy process. His wide-ranging research interests across social and public policy come together around concerns with the policy process and the politics of welfare.

Edward Brunsdon is Honorary Research Fellow in the School of Social Policy and CHASM at the University of Birmingham. His research and publication interests include: pension policy and asset management, occupational welfare, and human resource management.

Michael Cahill is Reader in Social Policy at the University of Brighton. He is the author and editor of a number of books on social policy and the environment and has written on new approaches to the study of social policy. His most recent work has been on transport and social policy.

Claire Callender is Professor of Higher Education Policy both at Birkbeck and the Institute of Education, University of London. Her research has focused on issues about student funding and finances in higher education and she has published widely on these topics. Her research has informed the deliberations of government-commissioned inquiries into student funding.

John Clarke is a professor of Social Policy in the Faculty of Social Sciences at the Open University. His research and writing has explored questions of welfare reform, both in the United Kingdom and internationally. He has written extensively about the impact of managerialism and consumerism on the transformation of welfare states and public services more generally. He has a continuing interest in the role of ideas, knowledge, and discourses in the politics of welfare reform.

Jochen Clasen is Professor of Comparative Social Policy in the School of Social and Political Science at The University of Edinburgh where his teaching centres on European social

policy and the political economy of the welfare state. He has researched and written widely in the areas of social security, labour market policy, and cross-national analysis of welfare states, particularly across European countries.

Bob Coles is Senior Lecturer in Social Policy at The University of York. He has a long-standing interest in youth policy and developed a degree specializing in children and young people at York. He helped establish youth policy as a sub-area within social policy and developed links between policy, research, and practice. His research has focused on vulnerable young people.

Guy Daly is Professor and Dean, Faculty of Education, Health and Sciences at the University of Derby. His areas of research include local governance, social care, and housing policy, including research for DWP, ODPM, local authorities, and health service organizations.

Howard Davis is Director of The Local Government Centre, Warwick Business School, at The University of Warwick. He has long experience of advising on and/or evaluating local government and local public services including projects on ageing society/later life and on governance, performance, innovation, and inspection.

Alan Deacon is Professor Emeritus of Social Policy at the University of Leeds. He has written widely on welfare reform in Britain and the United States, and was a member of the ESRC Research Group on Care, Values, and the Future of Welfare.

Hartley Dean is Professor of Social Policy at the London School of Economics. Before his academic career he had worked as a welfare rights worker in one of London's most deprived multicultural neighbourhoods. His principal research interests stem from concerns with poverty and social justice.

Peter Dwyer is Professor of Social Policy at the University of Salford. His main research and teaching interests are in social citizenship and international migration and welfare. Key themes explored in this work include, the changing mix of welfare provision, conditionality, and membership. He has published a wide range of books and articles on these issues.

Nick Ellison is Professor of Sociology and Social Policy at the University of Leeds. Research and teaching interests include welfare politics, welfare state change, and the impact of 'globalization'.

Jane Falkingham is Professor of Demography and International Social Policy and Director of the ESRC Centre for Population Change at the University of Southampton. Her research interests include demographic change and its implications for well-being, poverty, and health and span both developed and developing countries, with a particular focus on Central Asia and the United Kingdom.

Tony Fitzpatrick is a reader in the School of Sociology and Social Policy at The University of Nottingham. He has published many books and articles dealing with the relevance to social policy of new technologies, environmentalism, and social democracy, among other social and political theories.

David Gladstone is currently Honorary Visiting Fellow in the School for Policy Studies at the University of Bristol. An historian by training, his teaching and research interests are in aspects of, and the interrelationship between, British social policy past and present. He has authored and edited several books, collections of documentary sources, and book series.

Jon Glasby is Professor of Health and Social Care and Director of the University of Birmingham's Health Services Management Centre (HSMC). A qualified social worker by background, he leads a national programme of research, consultancy and teaching to support more effective inter-agency working between social care and the NHS.

Caroline Glendinning is Professor of Social Policy in the Social Policy Research Unit, University of York and Associate Director of the School for Social Care Research. Her research interests are in adult social care, infor-

mal care, and comparative long-term care policies. She has published widely in these and other areas.

Howard Glennerster is Professor Emeritus of Social Policy at The London School of Economics and a Fellow of the British Academy. He has specialized in research on the finance and economics of social policy and its post-war history. He has made a special study of social policy in the United States where he spent several sabbatical periods at American Universities. He has published widely on the history and finance of the British welfare state.

Jackie Gulland is Lecturer in Sociology in the School of Applied Social Science at the University of Stirling. Her research and teaching interests include socio-legal studies, citizens' disputes with the state, social security policy, ageing, and disability. Before entering academia, she worked in the voluntary and local authority sector as a welfare rights adviser and trainer.

Linda Hantrais is Emeritus Professor in the European Social Policy in the Department of Politics, History and International Relations at Loughborough University. She has served on a number of European committees as expert adviser. Her main research interests are in international comparative research theory, methodology and practice, with particular reference to socio-economic change and social and family policy in European countries.

Bernard Harris is Professor of the History of Social Policy at the University of Southampton. In addition to the history of social policy, he has also conducted research into different aspects of the history of health, height, morbidity, and mortality and has edited book series in the history of medicine and the relationship between gender and well-being.

Tina Haux is a senior research officer in the Institute for Social and Economic Research at the University of Essex. Her research interests include family policy, lone parents, welfare-to-work, comparative social policy, policy design, and microsimulation.

Michael Hill is Emeritus Professor of Social Policy of Newcastle University and a Visiting Professor in the Personal Social Services Research Unit at The London School of Economics. His research interests range from policy-making, public policy processes and current developments in welfare benefits and services to comparative social policy, on all of which he has published widely.

John Hills is Professor of Social Policy and Director of the Centre for Analysis of Social Exclusion at The London School of Economics. His research interests include the distribution of income and wealth, the distributional effects of public policies, pensions and social security more generally, housing finance and the impact of social policies across the life cycle. He has written on the evolution of social policies and their impacts in different phases over the past three decades and on inequality.

Chris Holden is Senior Lecturer in International Social Policy in the Department of Social Policy and Social Work at The University of York and Honorary Lecturer in Global Health at the London School of Hygiene and Tropical Medicine. He has published widely on the relationships between the global economy, international trade, transnational corporations and health and social policy.

Shona Hunter is RCUK Academic Fellow in Governance in the School of Sociology and Social Policy at the University of Leeds. Her research and teaching interests span a range of critical social policy. She is particularly interested in the reproduction of white masculinities and femininities in welfare arrangements.

Rana Jawad is Lecturer in Social Policy in the Department of Social and Policy Sciences at the University of Bath. Her main research and teaching interests are the role of religion in social policy and social policy in Middle Eastern Societies. She has a special interest in social policy in the Arab countries and Islamic welfare on which she has published widely.

Jeremy Kendall is Senior Lecturer in Social Policy in the School of Social Policy, Sociology and Social Research at the University of Kent. His research and teaching interests include the social policy process; social care, especially on older people; civil society and the third sector, especially theory and policy, international comparisons, and the role of the European Union. He has published a wide range of books and articles on these areas.

Patricia Kennett is Reader in Comparative Policy Studies, Head of the Centre for Urban and Public Policy Research and Co-ordinator of the research programme on Comparative and International Policy Analysis in the School for Policy Studies at the University of Bristol. Her research and teaching interests include international comparative social policy, with a particular focus on Europe and East Asia, governance, citizenship and social policy, global political economy and public policy, and cities, housing and social change.

Hilary Land is Emeritus Professor of Social Policy in the School for Policy Studies at the University of Bristol. She has had a long-standing interest in family policies using both historical and comparative perspectives as well as in feminist theories and social policy. She is currently studying changes in how responsibilities for both child-care and elder-care are shared between the generations as well as between men and women.

Ruth Lister is Emeritus Professor of Social Policy in the Department of Social Sciences at Loughborough University and a member of the House of Lords. Her main research interests are poverty, citizenship, and gender.

Stephen McKay is Professor of Social Research at the University of Birmingham and Director of their ESRC Doctoral Training Centre. He conducts research on poverty, inequality, family change, and the effects of social security policies. Much of his research involves quantitative analysis of large-scale datasets.

Suzi Macpherson is Research Manager with the Equality and Human Rights Commission.

Her interests focus on equality and social justice, particularly the relationship between socio-economic inequality and identity inequality critical interests. Her chapter has been written in a personal capacity.

Kirk Mann is a senior lecturer in the School of Sociology and Social Policy at the University of Leeds. His research interests are in: the relationship between social divisions and welfare, including occupational and fiscal welfare; and policies aimed at activating older people, retirement rights and pensions on all of which he has published widely.

Nick Manning is Professor of Social Policy and Sociology, and Director of the Institute of Mental Health at The University of Nottingham. His recent research interests include unemployment, poverty, ethnicity and health in Russia and Eastern Europe, and medical sociology and mental health policy. He has written books on health care, social problems, and comparative social policy.

Gabrielle Mastin is currently undertaking a PhD in the School of Sociology and Social Policy at the University of Leeds. Her research explores care services for older people and their role as users in setting service provisions.

Margaret May is Honorary Research Fellow in the School of Social Policy and CHASM at the University of Birmingham. Her research interests include employment policy, occupational welfare, human resource and welfare service management, and comparative social policy.

Jane Millar is Professor of Social Policy at the University of Bath and Pro-Vice-Chancellor for Research. Her research interests include social security and tax credits, family policy and the policy implications of family change, poverty and social exclusion, gender and social policy, and international comparative research.

David Mullins is Professor of Housing Policy at the University of Birmingham's School of Social Policy, leading research on service delivery for the ESRC Third Sector Research Centre. He has published widely on UK housing policy, specializing in the role of housing associations,

including the first evaluation of stock transfers from local authorities.

Alan Murie is Emeritus Professor of Urban and Regional Studies at the University of Birmingham, and has been a leading contributor to housing research and policy debates for more than twenty years. His research interests include the privatization of public housing, the residualization of social rented housing, differences within the home ownership sector, and changing demand for housing in the United Kingdom.

Tim Newburn is Professor of Criminology and Social Policy at The London School of Economics where he teaches sociology and criminology to undergraduate and postgraduate students. His major areas of research interest concern policing and security, youth justice, and comparative criminal justice and penal policy.

Robert M. Page is Reader in Democratic Socialism and Social Policy in the School of Social Policy at the University of Birmingham. His main current research interest is in the political history of the British welfare state since 1940.

Richard Parry is Reader in Social Policy in the School of Social and Political Studies at The University of Edinburgh where he teaches on Scottish, UK, and European social policy and on public policy and management. His major research projects have been on the role of the Treasury in social policy, the impact of devolution on the civil service throughout the United Kingdom, and a cross-national comparison of public sector employment.

Ruth Patrick is a postgraduate research student at the University of Leeds. Her research interests include welfare-to-work, disability, citizenship theory, and qualitative longitudinal methods. She is currently conducting research into the lived experiences of welfare reform.

Lucinda Platt is Professor of Sociology at the Institute of Education, University of London and Director of the Millennium Cohort Study. She has published widely in the areas of ethnic inequality and child poverty, and is particularly interested in longitudinal analytical approaches. She also leads the ethnicity strand of Understanding Society: the UK Household Longitudinal Study.

Martin Powell is Professor of Health and Social Policy in the Health Services Management Centre at the University of Birmingham. His main research interests and publications are in the areas of historical and geographical aspects of social policy, health policy, new social democracy, partnerships, decentralization, and equality.

Mark Priestley is Professor of Disability Policy and Director of the Centre for Disability Studies (University of Leeds) and Scientific Director of the Academic Network of European Disability experts (ANED). He teaches disability studies and has published extensively in the disability policy field. His current research focuses mainly on disability policies in the European Union and its member states.

Carol Propper is Professor of Economics at Imperial College and Professor of the Economics of Public Policy at the University of Bristol. She is also a founding member of CMPO, Bristol University and Research Associate at the CEPR. Her research interests include the use of market and financial incentives to enhance quality, productivity, and innovation in health care and the long-term impact of children's health on later life outcomes.

Tess Ridge is a senior lecturer of Social Policy at the University of Bath. Her main research interests and publications are in childhood poverty and social exclusion, especially from the perspectives of children themselves. She also has a keen interest in the role of policy, especially welfare and economic support, in the lives of children and families.

Karen Rowlingson is Professor of Social Policy at the University of Birmingham and also Director of the Centre on Household Assets and Savings Management (CHASM). Her research interests lie in the financial security of individuals, families, and households includ-

ing: assets and asset-based welfare; poverty, wealth and inequality; social security policy; financial capability, inclusion and education.

Rob Sykes is Principal Lecturer in Politics in the Department of Psychology, Sociology and Politics at Sheffield Hallam University. He teaches courses on public policy, globalization, and international politics and society both in the United Kingdom and in Hong Kong. He has published in the areas of globalization and social policy, and European studies.

Peter Taylor-Gooby is Professor of Social Policy at the University of Kent. He chairs the British Academy's New Paradigms in Public Policy programmes and directed the ESRC Social Contexts and Responses to Risk and Economic Beliefs and Behaviour and the EU Welfare Reform and the Management of Societal Change programmes. He has published widely on theoretical approaches, cross-national comparative issues and social attitude research.

Athina Vlachantoni is Lecturer in Gerontology in the Centre for Research on Ageing at the University of Southampton. Her research interests combine the areas of ageing, gender, and social policy.

Anne West is Professor of Education Policy in the Department of Social Policy at The London School of Economics and Political Science. She is also Director of the Education Research Group. Her research focuses on education policy, in particular market-oriented reforms in schools and their impact on equity, financing education and accountability. She has published many articles in the field of education policy.

Noel Whiteside is Professor of Comparative Public Policy at The University of Warwick where she teaches historical perspectives on developments in British and European welfare. Her recent research has focused on urban public services in late nineteenth century European cities and on the current crisis and Europe's pension systems (Her most recent books cover the pension crisis in Britain and European employment policy.

Sharon Wright is Lecturer in Social Policy at the University of Stirling. Her interests include poverty in the context of inequality and wealth, social security and governance. Her recent research focuses on in-depth studies of welfare reform and the implementation of employment services, comparing the United Kingdom with other European countries and Australia.

Nicola Yeates is Senior Lecturer in the Department of Social Policy and Criminology at The Open University. She has researched and extensively published on global social policy, care migration and social protection, and has worked with the International Social Security Association, the World Bank, UNICEF, UNRISD, and UNESCO.

Acknowledgements

As editors we are very grateful for the work put into this volume by the contributors. The *Companion* first set out to produce a collection of chapters written by some of the most distinguished teachers and lecturers in social policy in the United Kingdom, and in this fourth edition we have followed this with an expanded range of contributions. We asked all our contributors to write in as accessible a way as possible, while introducing complex issues in a short space. Authors in social policy are no different from other authors, however; some write sharply and clearly, others are more difficult to follow and pack difficult ideas together. This collection reflects the range of styles of writing and the array of ideological and political positions that students of social policy are likely to encounter. All the chapters, of course, also only provide a short summary of a wide range of issues and information in their area. The aim therefore is to encourage readers to investigate further and read more widely.

We were successful in persuading our authors to contribute to the *Companion* because of its long-standing links with the Social Policy Association (SPA) – the professional association for academics in Social Policy (see Appendix). While we, as editors, made the difficult and contentious decisions about what should be left out, what should be included, and who should be asked to write, the SPA's support was again highly valuable. We should also like to thank Justin Vaughan and Ben Thatcher at Wiley-Blackwell for their support in the production of this new edition, and the anonymous reviewers of the proposals for revision who all gave us such helpful advice. We hope that what we have produced is worthy of all this support and will continue to be of value to the social policy community as a whole. Any shortcomings in the collection as a whole are, however, our responsibility.

Pete Alcock, Margaret May,
and Sharon Wright

Introduction

Pete Alcock, Margaret May, and Sharon Wright

This *Student's Companion to Social Policy* is a resource book that will be of practical use to students of social policy throughout their undergraduate or postgraduate study of the subject. It aims to acquaint students with the study of social policy by covering all the main themes and issues likely to be included in any curriculum in the United Kingdom, and indeed in many other countries. Readers are introduced to current theoretical and ideological debates, historical developments, service areas, key policy issues, and the broader international context. Each chapter includes a short guide to further sources, which points to some of the literature that pursues the issues addressed in the chapter in more depth and also alerts readers to major web-based sources. The *Companion* will be of value to students studying social policy on its own, as part of another undergraduate or postgraduate programme (for instance, sociology, politics, applied social science, or management studies), or as part of a professional course in a related field (for instance, social and care work, nursing and health studies, public and voluntary sector management, or criminology).

This fourth edition of the *Companion* has been much expanded and updated from the previous editions. A section covering the evolution of social policy in the United Kingdom from the nineteenth to the early twenty-first century has been included. New chapters have also been added to take account of recent developments and debates and changing political and economic configurations, and existing authors have updated their contributions. In some cases previous authors have been replaced with others leading in research and teaching in those areas.

As in the last edition we have asked contributors to provide readers with a short bullet point summary of key points at the beginning of each chapter and to conclude with some brief speculation on emerging issues. To provide further support for readers the fourth edition also includes end of chapter review questions and is accompanied by a new dedicated web site www. wiley.com/go/alcock. This provides a range of supplementary resources designed to facilitate further reading and reflection and enable students to make the most of the text and their study of social policy. These include:

- Internet links to web sites referred to in each chapter.
- Guides with internet links to key UK governmental, international, and other useful resources.
- Help sheets and case studies.
- Guidance on managing the main forms of assignments in social policy including examples from the end of chapter questions.
- Careers advice.
- A glossary.

The Student's Companion to Social Policy, Fourth Edition. Edited by Pete Alcock, Margaret May, Sharon Wright.
© 2012 John Wiley & Sons, Ltd. Published 2012 by John Wiley & Sons, Ltd.

The glossary is based on and links to *The Blackwell Dictionary of Social Policy*. This is a sister volume to the *Companion*, offering short definitions of all key terms and concepts and longer discussion of major items and, as with previous editions, we hope that readers will be able to use the two together.

There has also been a change in the editors for this edition. Karen Rowlingson has taken on other responsibilities since the third edition was produced and has been replaced as third editor by Sharon Wright. The current editors and the publishers would like to thank Karen for all her work on the previous edition. We are pleased that Sharon has been able to join us, and her role has meant that the editorial process has been able to remain much the same for this latest edition.

All the contributors to this book, both old and new, are scholars and teachers in the forefront of social policy studies in the United Kingdom. They were selected on the basis that their expertise in their particular areas would provide readers with an authoritative introduction to a range of thinking and scholarship. As the book has been prepared as a handbook and guide, rather than as a single text that focuses on one or two main themes, not all readers will necessarily want to read it from cover to cover. Indeed, most readers are likely to use it as a source of reference for consultation; and so the chapters have been written so that they can be read in any order, separately, or in groups.

■ Part I introduces students to the concepts and approaches that underpin the study of social policy – and its (inter) relationship with other disciplines. These include a brief history of the development of the subject and the ways in which it is studied and researched, together with discussion of a number of the key concepts which students are likely to encounter in their studies.

■ Part II provides readers with a guide to the theoretical and ideological context of social policy. Readers are introduced to the central themes and perspectives that provide the intellectual foundations to debates about the focus and aims of the subject.

■ Part III surveys key themes and issues in the historical development of social policy in the United Kingdom including consideration of nineteenth century welfare arrangements, the growth of state welfare in the first half of the twentieth century and the policies of recent Conservative and Labour administrations.

■ Part IV explores the social, political, and economic context in which policies are developed and implemented, including key issues such as demographic change, the economic context, the role of religion, social divisions, family structures, and political processes.

■ Part V focuses on the provision and delivery of social policies. The different providers of welfare are examined by looking at the five main sectors of welfare – state, commercial, occupational, voluntary, and informal – setting these in the context of a brief examination of the ways in which welfare is financed and how citizens are able to secure access to it.

■ Part VI provides a discussion of different dimensions of the governance of welfare, including management and delivery and the role of users in determining welfare policy. The different geographical organization of welfare within the United Kingdom is explained, as well as the role of supranational agencies, including in particular the European Union.

■ Part VII comprises chapters that examine the key areas of welfare service provision, with each providing up-to-date summaries of policy developments, planning, and current debates.

■ Part VIII focuses on the provision of services to particular social groups, and analyses the extent to which these groups are advantaged or disadvantaged by different aspects of policy provision.

■ Part IX explores the international context of social policy. There is an introductory chapter on key issues in comparative analysis, followed by a number of chapters summarizing the differing policy experiences of different groups of nations across the world.

PART I
Concepts and Approaches

1

The Subject of Social Policy

Pete Alcock

▪▪

Overview

- Social policy is an academic subject which both overlaps with cognate subjects and has a discrete disciplinary base.
- It has changed its name from 'social administration' to 'social policy' to reflect a broadening concern with the theory as well as the practice of welfare.
- The welfare reforms in the United Kingdom in the period following the Second World War were critically important in establishing the policy context for subsequent policy development.
- Social policy analysts adopt a range of different theoretical perspectives, leading to differing conclusions about the viability and desirability of different policy measures.
- Much social policy has been developed by national governments, but policy also has local and supranational dimensions.

▪▪

What Do We Study?

The study of social policy is one of the academic social sciences. It is different from other areas of social science such as sociology, economics, and politics, however, because it is based upon a distinct empirical focus – support for the well-being of citizens provided through social action. In fact the term 'social policy' is not only used to refer to

academic study, it is also used to refer to the social actions taken by policy-makers in the real world. So social policy refers both to the activity of policy-making to promote well-being and to the academic study of such actions.

In doing this, social policy draws on the methods used and the understanding developed across the social sciences. Thus, although on the one hand we can see social policy as a discrete

The Student's Companion to Social Policy, Fourth Edition. Edited by Pete Alcock, Margaret May, Sharon Wright.
© 2012 John Wiley & Sons, Ltd. Published 2012 by John Wiley & Sons, Ltd.

academic *discipline*, which is studied and developed in its own right; on the other we can recognize that it is also an interdisciplinary *field*, drawing on and developing links with other cognate disciplines at every stage and overlapping at times with these in terms of both empirical foci and methods of analysis. To put this another way, the boundaries between social policy and other social science subjects are porous, and shifting; students and practitioners of social policy may also be working within or alongside these other areas or co-operating closely with others who do.

Thus students studying social policy may well find themselves in the same departments, or on the same degree programmes, as others studying different subjects such as sociology or they may be studying social policy as part of professional education and training, for instance in social work. This variety and collaboration are to be welcomed, and students on these different courses will learn much from each other through learning together; but this does not mean that social policy can be subsumed within sociology or social work. Similarly, those engaged in social policy research often work alongside others such as economists or statisticians; but the focus of their concern is distinct – on investigating the development or delivery of policy.

The later chapters in this book explore in more detail some of the key concepts and perspectives which have underpinned the study of social policy, the major issues which inform policy development, and the important areas of policy practice. Much analysis of social policy focuses on the policies and practices of national government. Within the United Kingdom, however, the devolution of policy-making and the local development and administration of significant aspects of welfare provision are of major significance, as discussed in Part VI. In Part IX the book also explores the international context of policy development and the importance of comparative analysis and global trends to any understanding of social policy in the one country. Here, however, we will focus on the development of social policy as an academic subject in the United Kingdom, for it has a particularly interesting history, involving even a change of name from *social administration* to *social policy*.

The Development of Social Policy

The development of social policy as distinctive element of policy planning in the United Kingdom can be traced back over 100 years to the end of the nineteenth century. Its history is closely linked to the development of the *Fabian Society* and to the influence of Fabian politics on policy development in Britain. The Fabian Society was established in 1884 and was strongly influenced by the work of Sidney Webb a civil servant who later became a Labour MP. The Fabians developed critical analysis of the social and economic problems found in late nineteenth-century British capitalism and campaigned for the introduction of social protection through the state to combat these. Fabian politics were closely linked to the establishment and growth of the Labour Party in Britain, which Webb and others saw as the political vehicle through which policy innovation and reform could be achieved. The early development of Fabian social policy thinking also drew on new research evidence emerging from some of the earliest empirical studies of social problems in the country by people like Booth and Rowntree, whose research revealed that the extent and depth of poverty in Britain at the end of the nineteenth century was both serious and widespread. This challenged conservative political assumptions that economic markets could meet the welfare needs of all and the Fabians used it to argue that policy intervention through the state was needed to provide those forms of support and protection which markets could not.

In fact, of course, it was some time before the Labour Party did achieve political power in Britain, and important reforms were introduced before this by the Liberal governments of the early twentieth century. The context for these reforms was influenced significantly by a review of the *Poor Laws*, the mainstay of nineteenth-century welfare policy, by a Royal Commission established in 1905. The work of the commission was an important step in the development of debate about social policy reform in Britain, in part because the commissioners themselves could not agree on the right way forward and so produced two separate reports:

■ a *Minority* Report, which was largely the work of Beatrice Webb, married to Sidney and herself a prominent Fabian; and

- a *Majority* Report, which was largely the work of Helen Bosanquet, who with her husband Bernard were leading figures in the Charity Organization Society (COS), a body which co-ordinated voluntary action to relieve poverty.

Both reports stressed the need for policy reform to improve welfare provision; but, while the minority Fabian report saw the public provision of state services as the means of achieving this, the majority COS report envisaged a continuing central role for voluntary and philanthropic activity. This debate about the balance between state and non-state provision of welfare continued to influence the development of social policy throughout the rest of the twentieth century, as the chapters in Part V of this book reveal; and the concern to secure the appropriate mix between public and voluntary provision remains a key element in social policy planning.

What is particularly significant for our purposes about the policy debate between the Webbs and the Bosanquets, however, is that this did not only influence the development of social policy reform, but extended also into the study and evaluation of policy as it developed. Despite their political differences both the Webbs and the Bosanquets were concerned to promote the study of social policy as well as the development of welfare reform. This took concrete form with the establishment, by the Webbs, of the London School of Economics (LSE) and the incorporation within it of the COS's School of Sociology to form a new Department of Social Sciences and Administration in 1912. This was the first, and most important, base for the study of social policy. Its first new lecturer was Clement Attlee (later prime minister in the reforming Labour government after the Second World War). Later members included Beveridge (architect of the modern social security system), Tawney (who developed theoretical analysis of poverty and inequality), and T. H. Marshall (whose idea of 'social citizenship' has been used by many as a theoretical basis for understanding the development of social policy in modern society).

The LSE has continued since then to provide a leading base for the study and evaluation of

social policy. In 1950 they appointed Richard Titmuss as the first Professor of Social Administration in the United Kingdom, and during the twenty three years before he died he became a leading figure in the academic study of social policy throughout the developed world. Titmuss's major contributions to the development of the study of social policy have now been collected together in a single volume (see Guide to further sources), and his writing remains at the centre of academic debates about theory and practice today. Some of the contributors to this *Companion* come from the LSE's current Department of Social Policy; but the study of social policy has now extended much further than this. Over the past fifty years social policy teaching and research has spread to most other universities in Britain, and has been taken up more widely in schools and colleges too. There are also major research centres in a number of universities, and other independent agencies and think-tanks providing specialist research and consultancy in particular fields or from different perspectives.

What is more, as we shall see shortly, this wider development of teaching and research has promoted debate and controversy over the aims and methods of study and over the direction of, and priorities for, research and policy reform – and this has provided a challenge to the Fabianism which dominated debate within social policy until the 1970s.

Much of the early teaching of social policy was geared to the training of social workers and others to act as providers within existing welfare services – it was focused upon how to administer welfare, rather than upon what welfare should be administered. Much of the early research work concentrated on measuring poverty and other social problems in order to provide evidence of the need for policy intervention – it was focused upon measurement of social need, rather than upon definitions of need or debate about the appropriateness of seeking to respond to it.

These broader questions became much more important as social policy expanded and developed in the latter quarter of the twentieth century. However, in the middle of the century such questions seemed to a large extent to be answered by the introduction of a 'welfare state' by the Labour government of 1945–51. At this stage the debate about the direction of reform appeared to have been won conclusively by the Fabian supporters of state welfare, and the focus of academic study upon the training of state welfare workers and the empirical measurement of new welfare needs appeared to have been established as the orthodoxy for all.

The Welfare State and the Welfare Consensus

The creation of what has come to be called the welfare state in the years immediately following the Second World War remains the major development in social policy in the United Kingdom and is central to the study of it, although in fact the depiction of these reforms as a 'welfare state' is a controversial and contested one. It begs questions about what we mean by this and why these particular reforms should be seen as achieving it; and these questions are matters of significant debate and disagreement. Nevertheless, the post-war welfare state thesis has been widely promulgated – and for important and obvious reasons.

Part of the reason for the electoral success of the Labour government in 1945 was its manifesto commitment to introduce state provision to meet major welfare needs and to do this on a comprehensive basis, replacing the piecemeal and partial provision which had been developed in the earlier part of the century. This message had been prefigured in Beveridge's famous report on the need for comprehensive social security reform, published in 1942 and included in Labour's manifesto promises. Beveridge had written about the *Five Giant Social Evils* which had undermined British society before the war: ignorance, disease, idleness, squalor, and want. He argued that it was in the interests of all citizens to remove these evils from British society, and it was the duty of the state, as the representative body of all citizens, to act to do this.

In the years following the war, comprehensive state provision to combat each was introduced:

- free education up to age 15 (later 16), to combat ignorance;
- a national health service (NHS) free at the point of use, to combat disease;

- state commitment to securing full employment, to combat idleness;
- public housing for all citizens to rent, to combat squalor; and
- national insurance benefits for all in need, to combat want.

All of these required the development of major state services for citizens and they resulted in a major extension of state responsibility – and state expenditure. Many of the reforms were enacted by the post-war Labour government; but despite their Fabian roots they were not supported only by Labour. Indeed, the state education plans had been introduced by a Conservative member of the wartime coalition government (R. A. Butler) in 1944, and the Conservative governments of the 1950s supported the spirit of the reforms and maintained their basic structure. This cross-party consensus on state welfare was so strong that it even acquired an acronym – *Butskellism* – comprised of the names of the Labour Chancellor (Gaitskell) and his Conservative successor (Butler).

For Fabian social policy, therefore, the post-war welfare state could be seen as the culmination of academic and political influence on government, after which analysis and debate focused more on the problems of how to administer and improve existing state welfare than on the question of whether these were appropriate mechanisms for the social promotion of well-being. However, this narrow Fabian focus within post-war social policy did not last for long. It was soon under challenge from other perspectives which queried both the success and the desirability of state welfare.

Theoretical Pluralism

From the 1970s onwards the focus of the study and analysis of social policy began to move beyond the narrow confines of Fabian welfare statism. This was symbolized most dramatically by a change (at the annual conference of the academic association in 1987) in the name of the subject from social administration to social policy, primarily because it was felt that *administration* was associated too closely with a focus upon analysis of the operation of existing welfare services, whereas *policy* encompassed a more general concern with analysis of the political and ideological bases of welfare provision. This change was representative of more general trends within academic and political debate to embrace a wider range of conflicting perspectives challenging the orthodoxy of Fabianism, and to move academic study towards a more open theoretical pluralism in which questions of *whether* or *why* to pursue state welfare became as important as questions of *how* or *when*.

The New Left

The predominant focus of Fabianism on the success and desirability of state welfare was challenged in the 1960s and 1970s by critics on the Left. Drawing on Marxist analysis of capitalist society, they argued that welfare services had not replaced the exploitative relationships of the labour market; and that, although they had provided some benefits for the poor and the working class, these services had also helped to support future capitalist development by providing a secure base for the market economy to operate. Unlike the Fabian socialists of the early twentieth century, these New Left critics did not necessarily see the further expansion of the existing state welfare base of social policy as resolving this dilemma. Indeed for them state welfare was in a constant state of contradiction, or conflict, between the pressure to meet the welfare needs of citizens and the pressure to support the growth of capitalist economic markets.

The New Right

In the 1970s and 1980s rather different criticisms of state welfare began to appear from the right of the political spectrum. Right-wing proponents of free market capitalism, most notably Hayek, had been critical of the creation of the welfare state in the 1940s, but at the time these had been marginal voices in academic and political debate. In the 1970s, as the advent of economic recession revealed some of the limitations of state welfare, these voices became both more vocal and more widely supported – especially after the move to the right of the Conservative Party following the election of Margaret Thatcher as leader in 1975. The essence of the New Right critique is that the

development of extensive state welfare services is incompatible with the maintenance of a successful market economy, and that this problem will get worse as welfare expands to meet more and more social needs. For them the desirability of state welfare itself is called into question.

New social movements

The failings and limitations of state welfare also came under challenge in the late twentieth century from perspectives outside the traditional Left/Right political spectrum. Most significant here was the challenge by feminism to the unequal treatment of men and women in the development and delivery of welfare services. As feminists point out, the provision of welfare is 'gendered'. Others have also challenged traditional analysis of state welfare to address a wider range of social divisions and social issues in analysing social policy. Anti-racists have pointed out that welfare services can be discriminatory and exclusive; disability campaigners have suggested that the needs of certain social groups can be systematically ignored; and environmentalists have argued that existing service provision is predicated upon forms of economic development which cannot be sustained.

The new pragmatism

The new radical voices which began to influence social policy towards the end of the twentieth century have widely varying, and sometimes mutually conflicting, implications. They challenged state welfare and the orthodoxy of Fabianism, but they were also critical of the New Left and the New Right. At the beginning of the twenty-first century these differing perspectives have resulted in a theoretical pluralism which has not only transformed academic study but has also shifted the focus of policy-making itself. The Labour governments at the beginning of the new century openly eschewed the policy programmes of the Fabian Left and the New Right, and appealed instead to a 'Third Way' for social policy combining private and public provision in a 'mixed economy' of welfare rather than a welfare state. They also argued that rather than policy being determined by theoretical or ideological preferences, it should be based on empirical evidence of the impact of policy measures – captured in the phrase 'what counts is what works'. The more pragmatic approach to policy development has also been embraced to some extent by the new coalition government, itself a product of political compromise; so there has been something of a return to pragmatism, rather than principle, across the theory and politics of welfare.

Emerging Issues: The Future of Social Policy

At the beginning of the twenty-first century, therefore, social policy has developed from its Fabian roots at the LSE and its support for the welfare state reforms of the early post-war years to embrace a wide range of diverse – and conflicting – theoretical debates about both the value and the success of public welfare provision and a wider conceptualization of the policy context as the product of local and global action as well as national politics. Social policy is now characterized by theoretical and geographical pluralism. It is also characterized by 'welfare pluralism': the recognition that state provision is only one feature of a broader mixture of differing forms and levels of welfare service – captured by the notion of a shift from the *welfare state* to the *welfare mix*. What is more, future policy direction will continue to change as will the focus of analysis and debate in academic social policy:

- There will be further moves away from state-based public services, to embrace partnerships between the state and other providers of welfare and a focus on the role of the state as a contractor, a subsidizer, or a regulator of the actions of others
- There will be further moves away from the 'provider culture' focus on who delivers welfare services, towards a greater emphasis upon analysis of the access to services for citizens and the transfer of power to service users through mechanisms such as personal budgets and co-production
- There will be further moves beyond the analysis of policy-making within the nation state to embrace also the importance of global forces and global actors in shaping social policy development, and to address the

impact of devolution of policy-making and trends towards greater localism in the development and delivery of welfare services.

All these, and other developments, are discussed in the later chapters of this Companion.

Guide to Further Sources

There are no textbooks dealing with the history and development of the discipline of social policy, but M. Bulmer, J. Lewis and D. Piachaud (eds), *The Goals of Social Policy* (London: Unwin Hyman, 1989), is an interesting review and history of the work of the leading department at the London School of Economics (LSE).

The major work of Titmuss, undoubtedly the founding father of the subject, is now gathered together, with commentaries, in P. Alcock, H. Glennerster, A. Oakley and A. Sinfield (eds), *Welfare and Wellbeing* (Bristol: Policy Press, 2001).

More recently, however, a number of authors have sought to provide introductory guides to the discipline. The most well established is M. Hill and Z. Irving, *Understanding Social Policy* (8th edn, Oxford: Blackwell, 2009), which provides a service-based review of welfare policy. P. Alcock, *Social Policy in Britain* (3rd edn, Basingstoke: Palgrave, 2003), takes a broader approach covering also key questions of structure, context and issues. The 4th edition is due in 2012.

J. Baldock, N. Manning, S. Miller and S. Vickerstaff (eds) *Social Policy* (3rd edn, Oxford: Oxford University Press, 2007), is a collection which covers both contextual issues and service areas. K. Blakemore (2007) *Social Policy: An Introduction* (3rd edn, Maidenhead: Open University, 2009) uses key social policy questions to provide a different perspective on provision in different service areas.

The Policy Press publishes a major series of textbooks on social policy in their *Understanding Welfare* series, edited by Saul Becker.

Finally the Social Policy Association and the Policy Press also produce an annual collection of topical essays, *Social Policy Review*. A useful web site providing introductory material on social policy is maintained by Paul Spicker: www2.rgu.ac.uk/publicpolicy/introduction/main.htm.

Review Questions

1   What is the difference between social *policy* and social *administration*?
2   To what extent did the Majority and Minority reports of the 1905 Royal Commission offer different visions for the development of social policy in the twentieth century?
3   What was *Butskellism*, and how did it shape post war policy development in Britain?
4   To what extent did the New Left and the New Right agree that the 'welfare state' had failed?
5   What is *welfare pluralism*, and how accurately does it describe current social policy planning?

Visit the book companion site at www.wiley.com/go/alcock to make use of the resources designed to accompany the textbook. There you will find chapter-specific guides to further resources, including governmental, international, think-tank, pressure groups, and relevant journals sources. You will also find a glossary based on *The Blackwell Dictionary of Social Policy*, help sheets, and case studies, guidance on managing assignments in social policy and career advice.

2

Approaches and Methods

Saul Becker

Overview

- Social policy is a research-informed and research-orientated academic subject.
- Research methods and approaches, and research evidence, form an essential part of the foundation on which the subject's knowledge and practice base is built.
- Students of social policy need to have a good understanding of the wide range of approaches and methods in social policy research, including how to read critically and make judgements about the quality of published research and how to conduct their own investigations.
- Social policy draws from the full range of social science research approaches, quantitative, qualitative and mixed methods, and research designs, with established procedures for how to review the existing literature, and for collecting and analysing data, within an ethical framework.
- There is no universally superior research design or research method – they are only as good as their suitability to the research question(s) being asked.

The Research Foundation for Social Policy

Social policy, as an academic subject and as a field of social action and practice, requires the rigorous linking of theoretical analysis with empirical enquiry. Thus, social policy is research informed and research orientated. The research methods, designs and approaches used in social policy, and the evidence generated from research enquiries, are the foundation on which the subject area (its multilayered analysis, theory and knowledge) and its application (policy-making, implementation, action, social change, evaluation) are built. The

The Student's Companion to Social Policy, Fourth Edition. Edited by Pete Alcock, Margaret May, Sharon Wright.
© 2012 John Wiley & Sons, Ltd. Published 2012 by John Wiley & Sons, Ltd.

Social Policy Association's *Guidelines on Research Ethics* (SPA 2009) argue that social policy research has four features which differentiate it to some extent from other social science disciplines:

- it tends to address both academic and policy/practice questions;
- it engages with users of welfare services;
- it works with a range of disciplines and research methodologies; and
- it has a responsibility to disseminate results to a range of audiences, both academic and policy/practice.

Social policy is to a large extent the study of policy practice in order to contribute to policy reform. It combines both descriptive and prescriptive elements. For social policy analysis and practice to be robust and trustworthy there is a need – as in all academic subjects and areas of practice – for knowledge and action to be based on a foundation of reliable research evidence generated through the appropriate application of research designs and methods of data collection and analysis, collected within an ethical framework.

Students of social policy are expected to have a good knowledge of research methods and approaches (QAA 2007). They need to:

- be aware, and make use of, the more significant sources of data about social welfare and the main research methods used to collect and analyse data;
- seek out, use, evaluate and analyse qualitative, quantitative and mixed methods data derived from social surveys and other research publications;
- understand the strengths, weaknesses and uses of social research and research methods;
- develop a critical ability to assess, summarize, synthesize, and comment on different forms of research evidence; and
- undertake investigations of social questions, issues and problems, requiring skills in problem identification; collection, storage, management, manipulation and analysis of data; the construction of coherent and reasoned arguments and the presentation of clear conclusions and recommendations.

While there are other important sources of 'evidence' that contribute alongside research to the knowledge and practice base of social policy, knowledge that is generated from research is the only 'way of knowing' that provides a systematic procedure for establishing the reliability and trustworthiness of the knowledge base and for assessing the superiority of one claim over another (Becker and Bryman, 2004). While welfare service users' experiences (Chapter 40) and service providers' perspectives have an important place alongside research in the policy-making and analysis process (because they tell us how policy is experienced in the real world by those on the receiving end of policy and by those implementing policy), there is nonetheless debate as to whether these perspectives carry the same authority as research evidence when it comes to laying the foundations for social policy as an academic subject.

Research evidence, then, unlike other forms of knowledge, can be systematically tested, refuted or verified using long-established research procedures. To 'count' as research an enquiry must be conducted in a systematic, disciplined and rigorous way, making use of the most appropriate research designs and methods to collect and analyse data and to answer specific research questions. These transparent and systematic procedures, and the evidence they generate, distinguish research knowledge from other ways of knowing (such as views founded on personal experience, or beliefs based on ideology or religion). Sources of 'experiential' knowledge, from welfare service users, providers of welfare and others, can themselves be subjected to rigorous research enquiry and scrutiny, to determine the extent, representativeness and reliability of the views and their appropriate place within the knowledge base for social policy and practice.

To this end, social policy research needs to test actively existing and alternative forms of knowledge in circumstances where they are most likely to be challenged or refuted. Where research conducted to the highest standards of enquiry cannot prove that these other sources of evidence are wrong then the social policy knowledge base can be considered to be stronger, more robust, and more reliable than before. That is why social policy locates research and research evidence at the centre of its activities: research informs teaching, analysis, theory-building, policy-making, practice and further research.

A distinction is sometimes made between research *for* policy, and research *of* policy, although much social policy research is simultaneously of both types. Research *for* policy is concerned to analyse, understand and inform the various stages of the policy process (from before the formulation of policy through to its implementation). Research *of* policy is concerned with how social problems and issues are defined, agendas set, policy is formulated and decisions are made, and how policy is delivered in the real world, evaluated and changed.

Approaches, Methods, and Designs

Social policy draws from the full range of approaches, research designs and methods that are used in the social sciences. In terms of *approaches*, these can include, for example, feminist research, service user-led research, action research, evaluation research and post-structuralist approaches to research. These approaches each have their own assumptions about the nature of the social world and the researcher's and research participant's place within it, and about knowledge creation and the research process itself. These assumptions help to inform the way in which the research is carried out, the selection of methods, the data analysis techniques and the way in which research is written up and reported. Some research-based publications give an explicit statement of the approach and assumptions that are being adopted while in other publications this is far less transparent.

A *research method* is a technique for gathering data, like a questionnaire, interview or observation. A *research design* is a structure or framework within which data are collected (for example, an experimental or longitudinal design). Research methods can serve different designs. Thus, a method of data collection such as a questionnaire can be employed in connection with many, if not all, research designs. Decisions about appropriate research methods are in a sense subsidiary to decisions about an appropriate design, since it is the research design that provides the framework for answering research questions.

Whatever the approach, design or methods used in a study, *all* research needs to be conducted in a systematic and rigorous way if it is to be a reliable knowledge base for social policy analysis and practice. There are established procedures in the social sciences and social policy by which research ideas and questions are formulated, for reviewing the existing body of knowledge on a subject, and for collecting and analysing data and drawing conclusions. The choice of research design and method(s) will also be critically informed by what is already known about an issue and what still needs to be found out.

An early stage of the research process involves a review of the available literature. This needs to be as comprehensive as possible – there may be answers here already to the questions that are of current concern. It is important to have some explicit and transparent way of distinguishing between different publications and for deciding which to include in the literature review, not least because of the sheer volume of information that is now publicly available and the need to recognize that not everything can or should be read or included. Researchers need a way of distinguishing between existing studies based on 'quality' and other criteria. 'Systematic reviews' are one way of conducting literature searches and reviews. These are comprehensive literature reviews with studies chosen in a systematic way and summarized according to explicit criteria. These forms of review are valued highly in medicine and health care research and are increasingly being used, in developing forms, within social policy.

Depending on the specific research question(s) to be addressed, in some cases just one research method may be used within an overall design or approach. This could be a quantitative method, such as a large-scale questionnaire survey, or a qualitative method, such as in-depth interviews. In other cases there may be an integration of different methods, which can bring with it specific research advantages and improve the comprehensiveness of the data and analysis. This multi-strategy research is commonly referred to as a 'mixed methods' study, and it is important to give a coherent rationale for why different methods are being integrated in the way that they are rather than the alternative of using a single method or other approach. Mixed methods research has become more accepted, common and popular in social policy and has helped to bridge the gap that has sometimes divided quantitative and qualitative researchers in other social science subjects.

Each research design and method, or combination of methods, has its own strengths and limitations, and those conducting research, and students of social policy, need to be aware of the appropriateness or otherwise of the approaches, designs and methods used in any published enquiry. Students need to develop a critical ability to 'read' research-based publications, not just for their findings and conclusions, but also to make judgements about whether or not the research design and methods are appropriate for the research question(s). Which studies are the most trustworthy? Which studies are of the highest quality? In answering these and other questions, students need to know about quantitative, qualitative, and mixed methods and what counts as quality in social policy research.

Quantitative, Qualitative, and Mixed Methods Research

Quantitative and qualitative research approaches each have a distinctive cluster of concerns, preoccupations, and assumptions. *Quantitative* research adopts an objectivist position with respect to the nature of social reality. This means that social phenomena and social reality are generally construed as 'out there' for social actors, as entities that confront them as out of their scope of influence. In thinking of social reality in an objectivist manner, quantitative researchers display a commitment to a natural science model of the research process, since the natural order is frequently conceptualized as a pre-existing phenomenon awaiting the analytic tools of the scientist. Thus, there is a commitment to provide rigorous measures of concepts that drive the research and an interest to demonstrate causal relationships between variables. Statistical tests are commonly used. There is also a concern to allow generalization from the research to a wider population, and for the study to be replicable by others seeking to confirm or to refute the findings. The approach taken by quantitative researchers also typically involves a deductive approach to the relationship between theory and research,

involving the drawing of research questions from an established body of existing knowledge which are then tested for their soundness. Finally, quantitative research has well-developed and internationally understood criteria that are sometimes employed for assessing the quality of research, centring on reliability, validity, generalization, and replication. While these are widely regarded as important principles they are not, however, universally observed. It is rare for published social policy research to discuss these criteria explicitly.

By contrast, *qualitative* research tends to be associated with a constructionist position, which pays greater attention to the role that individuals play in constructing their social networks and their influence over them. There is a strong focus on actors' meanings: qualitative researchers aim to understand the behaviour, values, beliefs, and so on of the people that they are researching from the perspective of the participants themselves. There is an emphasis on description, context, and process. There is also a degree of flexibility in the way in which the research is conducted. Qualitative research adopts an inductive approach to the relationship between theory and research whereby concepts and theory are generated out of the data, rather than as in the quantitative approach, whereby concepts and theoretical ideas often guide the collection of data. Finally, while there are criteria for determining the quality of qualitative research, there is less agreement about these than is the case with quantitative research.

The decision as to whether to conduct a quantitative, qualitative, or mixed methods study in social policy will be determined by many factors, most importantly what it is that needs to be found out and the specific research question(s) to be addressed. How a social issue or social problem is perceived, and the social policies in place (or not in place) to respond to it, will also influence the type of research that will be conducted.

Where an issue has not yet been defined widely as a social issue or social problem, then other research approaches will need to be used to highlight the issue, perhaps for the first time. Qualitative studies are particularly appropriate here, as they can take us inside a 'hidden world', give a voice to those who are invisible and raise the profile of this issue among policy-makers, the media and others. In the case of new or emerging social issues, it is often difficult to conduct a large-scale survey and would be virtually impossible (and inappropriate) to utilize an experimental research design. At other times, secondary analysis of existing large-scale datasets (when researchers re-analyse data that they did not necessarily collect themselves) can help to quantify the extent and characteristics of a problem or even enable it to be reconceptualized.

Research data, particularly expensive resources, need to be archived systematically for their potential to be fully exploited through secondary analysis or by future generations of researchers wanting to build upon former findings. It is important that publicly funded research has systems in place to archive data for future interrogation and use.

Ethical considerations underpin all social policy research. For example, it is unacceptable to conduct research that would harm research participants or place researchers themselves in danger. Data must be collected and stored in a way that is safe and secure, and which protects the anonymity of participants. Participants should give their informed consent to taking part in research rather than being coerced, bribed, or misled. The Social Policy Association have developed a set of ethical guidelines, which sit alongside those of other learned bodies (for example, the British Sociological Association) and relevant research groups (the Social Research Association), but ethics can be controversial and the SPA guidelines have generated dissension among some social policy researchers. Students need to be aware of the ethical implications of their own studies and be able to recognize good or poor ethics in published reports.

'Quality' and 'Hierarchies' in Social Policy Research

If research is to provide a reliable foundation for social policy teaching, analysis and practice, then it goes without saying that the quality of that research must be of a high standard. There is some debate, however, about what counts as 'quality' in social policy research (Becker, Becker, Bryman, and Sempik 2006). There are some criteria of quality that command widespread support and consensus among social policy researchers and research users, while for other criteria there is considerable dissension. However, most social policy researchers do place a high value on research evidence that is written in a way that is accessible to the appropriate audience, has a research design which clearly addresses the research question(s), that is transparent in explaining the ways in which the data were collected and analysed, that gives an explicit account of the research process, that makes a contribution to knowledge and that includes confirmation that informed consent and the safety of participants have been assured.

In social policy, unlike medicine, health care, and research in some other natural sciences, there appears to be little consensus or support for a discipline-based 'hierarchy' of research designs or methods, whereby the quality of research can be inferred simply from the method or design used. In medicine and much health care research, systematic reviews of randomized controlled trials, meta-analyses, and randomized controlled or quasi-experimental trials are regarded as 'gold standard' approaches to research, commanding status and authority, and forming the research foundation for these subjects' knowledge-base. Certainly, experiments can contribute to the kinds of knowledge that academics, policymakers, professionals and the public are interested in. Reliable information about the effectiveness of social policy and social interventions is hard to come by using other means, because experiments offer a robust design for assessing 'cause and effect'. There is a growing interest in the use of experiments in social and public policy as seen in the expansion in the number of social researchers who are committed to developing the use of these approaches.

However, in social policy generally there is less reverence for experimental designs or for statistical meta-analyses, and there is little agreement that these methods and approaches are by themselves indicators of high quality. What this indicates is that different research methods are regarded differently across disciplines, and within social policy itself there is considerable debate about which methods and approaches, and criteria, are indicators of high quality. The important message from this is that there is no universally superior research design or research method – they are only as good as their suitability to the research question(s) being asked.

Emerging Issues

Social policy will continue to develop and mature as a subject area with research, and knowledge from research, being central to these developments and transformations. There is likely to be a growing interest within social policy to develop and highlight research approaches and methods that might be seen as more 'social policy specific', for example, cross-national research techniques and comparative welfare state studies. There will also be an interest to devise appropriate criteria to help to judge the quality of published social policy research studies. These criteria may include a list of 'things to look out for' when reading research publications (for example, evidence that informed consent was given by participants, that the research is ethical, and so on), which students of social policy would also no doubt find of use when 'reading' published studies or conducting their own research.

There is likely to be some challenge about the weight that social policy gives to research evidence as a foundation for the subject, vis-à-vis other forms of knowledge, including welfare service users' perspectives. In other academic areas, such as social work, service users' perspectives are permeating throughout, including in direct teaching to students and representation on ethics or other committees. To what extent social policy goes in this direction remains to be seen. Meanwhile, students of social policy will be encouraged in their degree programmes to develop their own research knowledge, skills, critical analysis, and evaluation, particularly as these are transferable and will be valued highly in the marketplace.

Guide to Further Sources

There are literally hundreds of textbooks on research methods in the social sciences, but very few that have been specifically developed for social policy students.

The main text is S. Becker and A. Bryman (eds), *Understanding Research for Social Policy and Practice: Themes, Methods and Approaches* (Bristol: Policy Press, 2004), which provides an overview of all the main research methods and approaches, with research examples and illustrations from a wide range of social policy areas. The volume was thoroughly updated and revised for its 2012 edition, with new narratives and examples drawn from social policy and social work research (S. Becker, A. Bryman, and H. Ferguson (eds), *Understanding Research for Social Policy and Social Work: Themes, Methods and Approaches* (Bristol: Policy Press, 2012).

A superb 'generic' research methods text is A. Bryman, *Social Research Methods* (3rd edn, Oxford: Oxford University Press, 2008), and a very accessible and useful guide is B. Matthews and L. Ross, *Research Methods: A Practical Guide for the Social Sciences* (Harlow: Longman, 2010).

For those interested in issues around how to determine 'quality' in social policy research, then S. Becker, A. Bryman, and J. Sempik's report, *Defining Quality in Social Policy Research* (Lavenham: Social Policy Association, 2006) provides the first study of how social policy researchers conceptualize 'quality' and offers a framework for discussion. It can be downloaded free from the SPA web site www.social-policy.com. These three authors have explored further 'quality' and related issues in social policy research with a series of articles: 'The quality of research evidence in social policy: Consensus and dissension among researchers', *Evidence and Policy*, 3 (2007): 407–23; 'Quality criteria for quantitative, qualitative and mixed methods research: A view from social policy', *International Journal of Social Research Methodology*, 11/4 (2008): 261–76; 'Advocates, agnostics and adversaries: Researchers' perceptions of service user involvement in social policy research', *Social Policy and Society*, 2010, 9(3): 355–66. The SPA web site www.social-policy.com has other useful research resources including the SPA's *Guidelines on Research Ethics* (2007) www.social-policy.org.uk/downloads/SPA_code_ethics_jan09.pdf. The subject benchmark for social policy, the QAA's *Social Policy and Administration* (2007) at www.qaa.ac.uk/Publications/InformationAndGuidance/Pages/Subject-benchmark-statement-Social-policy-and-administration.aspx, identifies what research skills and knowledge students need to possess.

Review Questions

1 Why should social policy draw on research evidence as a 'way of knowing'?

2   What are some of the main characteristics and preoccupations of social policy research?
3   Why are mixed methods studies becoming increasingly attractive to social policy researchers?
4   Why is it important to consider ethical issues?
5   What criteria would you use to define 'quality' in social policy research?

Visit the book companion site at www.wiley.com/go/alcock to make use of the resources designed to accompany the textbook. There you will find chapter-specific guides to further resources, including governmental, international, think-tank, pressure groups, and relevant journals sources. You will also find a glossary based on *The Blackwell Dictionary of Social Policy*, help sheets, and case studies, guidance on managing assignments in social policy and career advice.

3

Social Needs, Social Problems, and Social Welfare and Well-being

Nick Manning

Overview

- An examination of the growth and structure of social welfare provision.
- An identification of some basic definitions of need.
- A review debates about need, and the way it is used in practice.
- A discussion of ideas about social problems.
- A brief introduction to social problems, needs, and well-being.

The study of social policy focuses on the way in which social welfare is organized to meet the needs of individuals and groups, for health care, for shelter, food, clothing, and so on. It is also concerned with the way in which social problems are recognized and dealt with. In this chapter I will examine the growth and structure of social welfare provision; introduce some basic definitions of need; review the debates that have developed about this concept; and examine the way it is used in practice. I will also discuss ideas about social problems; the way these are related to needs and to social welfare provision; and the considerable debates about this. Finally there is a brief introduction to the idea of well-being.

What is Social Welfare?

Social welfare refers to the various social arrangements that exist to meet the needs of individuals and groups in society and to tackle social problems. Our use of the term social policy in modern times implies that social welfare means government welfare. This is not at all the case. Welfare for most people is still provided through other social mechanisms than the state. In addition to the state there are three other types: family and friends, the market, and non-governmental organizations such as voluntary and charitable organizations (VCOs) and mutual associations. Social policy as an area of study is concerned with

The Student's Companion to Social Policy, Fourth Edition. Edited by Pete Alcock, Margaret May, Sharon Wright.
© 2012 John Wiley & Sons, Ltd. Published 2012 by John Wiley & Sons, Ltd.

Box 3.1 Types of Social Welfare
Institutions

- Family
- Market
- Voluntary and Community Organiza-
  tions (VCO)
- The Welfare State

the way in which all these institutions affect the
welfare of individuals and groups, and is taken up
in more detail in some of the chapters in part IV.

Social policy is a branch of social science.
From this point of view, the basic conditions for
the existence and survival of individual people
are necessarily social. No individual, however
resourceful, could survive for long in isolation.
Human beings, in contrast to many other animals,
are not capable of mediating directly with nature
without mechanisms of co-operation and a division of labour between individuals. This is illustrated well by the long period of dependence that
children need for them to become adults. The
family, then, may be taken as the archetypal social
welfare institution, both in fact and as an ideal.
Markets, governments, and VCOs are by comparison modern developments.

The modern family provides less welfare than
it did 200 years ago. Hospitals, schools, shops,
workplaces, transport, and leisure facilities have
developed to fulfil a variety of functions which
mean that social welfare provision has become a
more complex and mixed system than it used to
be. Much of this change occurred in the nineteenth century, when hospitals, schools, shops,
and factories came to prominence. Two rival
mechanisms underlay these changes: the market
and VCOs. The market developed in two senses
relevant to social welfare. The first sense is the
market in labour as individual workers shifted
increasingly from agriculture towards industrial
wage labour. The vicissitudes of this means of
livelihood threw up new insecurities whenever
the availability of, or ability to, work stopped. The
second sense is the market in goods and services,
such as food, clothes and medical care, that
accompanied these changes, and through which

families increasingly met their various needs
rather than through self-provision. Inability to
pay could have disastrous consequences for a
range of needs of family members.

Alongside the market, and very often in
response to its failures to either provide adequately waged work, or adequately priced goods
and services, VCOs developed. However, this was
not always for humanitarian reasons. On the one
hand, for example, mutual associations such as
friendly societies were indeed designed for the
mutual benefit of members when social needs
arose. By contrast, however, the settlement house
movement for the 'improvement' of working
class lives was also motivated by fear that upper-
middle-class organizers had about the consequences for all social classes of poverty life styles,
such as the spread of disease. In addition there
were also concerns about the costs of market
failure, not to individual victims, but to those
who might have to pick up the pieces. For example
in the later part of the nineteenth century the
provision of education was motivated by the
employment needs of industrialists, and the provision of agreed compensation for industrial
accidents was designed to avoid more expensive
court proceedings.

For a while the market and VCOs enjoyed
considerable independence from the attentions
of government, but there was a growing concern
by the end of the nineteenth century to regulate
their activities. In the twentieth century, regulation led on to the provision of financial support
and eventually to state provision of welfare services. Motives for this were again mixed. Genuine
humanitarian concern for the meeting of social
needs coexisted with the fear of social problems
threatening the wider social order, and the realization that the costs of social reproduction (both
the biological production of children for the
future workforce and the daily replenishment of
the capacity for work) might be better organized
by the state. The climax of this process was the
establishment of the British welfare state by the
labour government of the 1940s.

All of these institutions of social welfare,
family, market, state, and VCO continue to
coexist, but with regular changes in their functions and scope, most recently under the impact
of the new coalition government, and its commitment to the 'big society', whereby families and

VCOs are being encouraged to provide more welfare, alongside a reduction in state provision. This extends the previous New Labour government's growing emphasis on privatization and market mechanisms to the point where social welfare was increasingly thought of as a consumption good. Nevertheless the level of state expenditure on social welfare has remained at about 25 per cent of gross national product (GNP), albeit covering a steadily changing mix in favour of social security and health services, and away from education and housing.

What are Social Needs?

While I have suggested that there were mixed motives for organizing social welfare institutions, the meeting of social needs remains their central concern. We must therefore review the definition of this crucial concept. A useful starting point is to distinguish needs from two related notions: wants and preferences. There are two important senses in which wants and needs differ. First, wants are more inclusive: we may want things that we do not need; indeed marketing experts make great efforts to persuade us to do so. Second, we may need things which we do not want, either through ignorance or our dislike of them. Medical intervention can often be of this type. Both of these distinctions from want suggest that needs are more basic or essential to us than wants.

Preferences, a concept frequently used in economic analyses, differ from needs and wants in the sense that they are revealed only when we make choices, usually in the act of buying goods or services as consumers. The argument here is that it is difficult to really know what people need or want unless they act in some way to try to secure for themselves the things in question. This action component however has its limits, for of course wants cannot be revealed in the market if we do not have the money to pay for things, and needs cannot be revealed by individuals where they are not aware of them, or there are no services to meet them. Needs, then, may well have to be discovered by those other than the individual concerned.

We should also make a distinction between needs and social needs. Needs (and problems and welfare) are 'social' in the sense that they are not

Box 3.2   Needs, Wants, and Preferences

- ■ Needs
  - ■ felt need
  - ■ expertly defined need
  - ■ comparative need
- ■ Wants
- ■ Preferences

merely concerned with, for example, individual causes and experiences of illness and poverty, but also with the amount and distribution of illness and poverty in different social groups; the reasons for this that arise out of the shared conditions of life for those social groups; and the social structures and processes through which they might be ameliorated. For example, it is only necessary to vaccinate a proportion of the population to stop the spread of infectious disease. In this case, the population can be seen to have a need, but any specific individual may not necessarily feel, or be defined by others as, in need. Waiting in line for an injection, we may have all felt this way as children!

These considerations enable us to make some simple classification of types of need. First are those needs which we are aware of ourselves, felt needs. These are obvious when we feel ill, or have an accident. The second type of need is defined for us by others, usually experts or professionals, such as doctors or teachers, but also importantly by family and friends. The third type of need is partly an extension of the second, to focus on needs as revealed, perhaps in surveys, in comparison with other people in the same social group. Here an individual can be said to be in comparative need because others have something that they do not.

An important aspect of needs, shared by all three types, has given rise to many debates in social policy. This is the question of how needs can be measured, particularly when we move away from the obvious examples such as major medical emergencies. The classic case is that of poverty. How much income do we need? One approach, drawing on the second type of need as defined by experts, is to think about the basic essentials, such as food, clothing, shelter, and to work out the amount of money needed to buy the cheapest minimal provision of these, and to define anyone with less money as poor, or in need.

However any close study of the way in which poor people live reveals that the notion of 'basic essentials' or 'cheapest minimal provision' varies with the way of life of the particular family and community in which an individual lives. Is television or Internet access an essential? Is meat eating essential? What cultural prescriptions about dress codes are essential?

An alternative approach is to use the first type of need, and merely to ask poor people what they feel they need. However where this has been done, it seems that poor people often adjust to their circumstances and feel less in need than they 'ought' to, especially if they are older people; while others can feel poor where they 'ought' not to. Finally, we could merely define as poor those people with less than others as in the third type of need, comparative need, for example by ranking incomes and identifying, say, the bottom 10 per cent as poor.

This problem of measurement has resulted in an oscillation in social policy debates between those who favour an objective interpretation of what is 'basic' or 'essential', for example in terms of the ability of an individual to remain alive, and to retain the capacity to act as a 'person' in society; and those who argue that needs are really more subjectively defined by individuals themselves, experts, and government agencies and others who provide services designed to meet needs.

What is a Social Problem?

Social welfare institutions are also concerned with social problems, which are related to, but not the same as social needs. For example, as C. Wright Mills famously observed, one person suffering from unemployment may be in acute need, but it is only when unemployment becomes a more widely shared experience in a community that there may be said to be a social problem. Social problems then are to be distinguished from individual need.

A further distinction should be made between the mere existence of a shared set of social misfor-

> **Box 3.3** Elements and Types of Social Problems
>
> - Elements of social problems
>   - social conditions
>   - perceptions
>   - judgements
>   - solutions
> - Types of social problems
>   - open/contested
>   - closed/uncontested

tunes in a community, whether or not they have been defined as needs, and three further elements of a social problem: the extent to which they are perceived; the judgements made about them and the values they threaten; and the actions recommended to deal with them. Needs can exist whether or not they are known about by anyone. Social problems cannot. They exist within the public domain rather than private experience. The perceptions, judgements, and recommended actions are in the broadest sense of the term part of the political process of a society or community.

Perceptions of social problems can occur through the eyes of experts or the general public. In the case of experts, social problems are typically defined in relatively objective terms for example the incidence of divorce, where the rate of change is a crucial issue. However, since many social issues are less amenable to objective measurement, for example the effects of family neglect on children, experts can differ widely in their claims about the objective state of a social problem. In these cases the general public, community groups, pressure groups, and so on may have widely varied views, such that a social problem is more subjectively defined. Social problems, in the extreme version of this view, become merely 'what people think they are'. Since most of our experience of and knowledge about social issues is indirect, the mass media are an important influence not only on our knowledge of social issues, but also the way in which they are framed, judged and dealt with.

These perceptions are heavily influenced by judgements about the kinds of values felt to be under threat. This brings us to the heart of defining a social problem, since it is the sense that something is wrong that motivates any attempt to put things right. There are two aspects of this that we have to consider. First is the issue of whose values are threatened. Some issues command widespread consensus, for example that threats to life are unacceptable. The judgement that the spread of disease such as HIV-AIDS is a social problem from this point of view is relatively uncontested. Other issues however may be the site of sharp value conflict, for example the relevance of people's sexuality to family life in various ways.

However, a second important aspect of value judgements in definitions of social problems can sharply modify the effects of these value concerns. This is the issue of who is to blame for the problem. In the case of HIV-AIDS, what might have been an ordinary medical issue was transformed in this regard by very sharp dissensus over the judgements of blame made about gay men, and therefore about the nature, status, and solution to the problem. Where problems are the site of value conflict, or blame is attributed, we can speak of contested or open social problems, the solutions to which are far from clear. Where consensus and lack of blame are typical we can think of social problems as closed or uncontested.

The solutions proffered to social problems have an intimate connection to perceptions and judgements made about them. Indeed, it has been argued that often the solution may in fact tend to determine these other aspects. An example of this process has been the development since the 1970s of the social problem of hyperactivity (ADHD) among children, at a time when a drug treatment to calm them down became available.

The UK coalition government's approach to solving social problems illustrates the subjective nature of the perception and definition of social problems. It has defined state welfare itself as the problem. The deficit is too large, it is argued, and resources have been wasted on 'bureaucracy' (e.g. in the NHS) while popular concerns have been ignored (e.g. in school provision). The solution is to roll back state provision and regulation, and to encourage a 'big society' whereby increased VCO and market provision will deliver greater efficiency and at the same time address popular concerns.

Conclusion

Social welfare institutions have evolved in their current form alongside the development of industrial society. As industrial societies change, so do their welfare institutions. This is most clearly observed in the countries of Russia and Eastern Europe, where a variety of neo-liberal social policy innovations have been developed, and already modified in response to economic and political forces. Western societies have not been immune to such influences, with the ubiquitous assumption of globalization used to justify significant debates and changes in the trajectory of social policies for the twenty-first century. While they are chiefly oriented to meeting social needs and tackling social problems, this has not been the only motive. The German chancellor, Bismarck, and Winston Churchill classically argued in favour of social welfare institutions as a buttress against the attractions of socialist ideas.

Social needs and social problems are subject to contested definitions. In both cases a major debate concerns the relative weight to be given to objective or subjective definitions. Can needs and problems be scientifically measured in some absolute sense, or are they inescapably subject to the relative social circumstances of both those in need, and the particular interests of the definers? The genomic revolution, which seems to offer so many tantalizing health benefits, and yet to raise an even larger number of ethical uncertainties, illustrates well the interaction between industrial and scientific developments and public concerns. Public debate has never been more wide ranging, buttressed through public opinion surveys, focus groups, and the development of professional committees and academic departments of ethics.

These points lead us back to the nature of social policy as a subject. The word 'policy' implies that it is a part of the political processes and institutions of modern society, and that social needs, social problems, and social welfare are similarly political. While some observers have come to anticipate the decline of the nation-state in the wake of an increasingly globalized world, discussed further in Chapter 22, social policy issues have in reality grown in importance in regional affairs, whether at a subnational level, or more widely in multicountry regional welfare 'blocks', most noticeably in the development of a European social model, alongside the distinctive American or Asian patterns of welfare development.

Emerging Issues: From Needs to Well-being

With the steady expansion of consumer and individualist definitions of the 'good life' that have emerged with the economic growth of recent years, a new definition of needs in terms of our individual well-being has also developed. For example, health care is now focused on developing and sustaining good health as well as treating disease. The 2010 UK coalition government's public health White Paper aims to 'nudge' us to stop smoking, eat wisely, and take exercise. This emphasis has also spread into concern for our personal relationships and mental health, such that stress generated by domestic or employment factors has become central to both public health and trade union actions. Economists have noted that the level of personal satisfaction reported in public surveys has risen very little over the past twenty five years despite record levels of income and wealth, and there is a growing call for more balanced measures of well-being than the gross national product. However the arguments that we have reviewed in relation to defining needs and problems apply equally here. Well-being is a contested concept, open to subjective, objective, political and comparative definitions, and subject to the pressures of both professional and mass media fashions.

Guide to Further Sources

Web sites that include many examples of discussions about the way in which social policies should be organized, what legitimate social needs are, and how to tackle social problems can be found among think-tanks such as: Centre for Social Justice, www.centreforsocialjustice.org.uk; The Big Society, www.thebigsociety.co.uk; The Fabian Society, www.fabian-society.org.uk; Demos, www.demos.co.uk; The Young Foundation, www.youngfoundation.org; and The Fawcett Society, www.fawcettsociety.org.uk.

On social welfare institutions see D. Fraser, *The Evolution of the British Welfare State* (London: Palgrave Macmillan, 2009). This is the fourth edition of a comprehensive and balanced account of the growth of the British welfare state. J. R. Hay, The *Origins of the Liberal Welfare Reforms 1906–1914* (London: Macmillan, 1983), is a short book that gives a very clear account of the variety of different reasons for the rapid development of state welfare in the early twentieth century.

On social needs there are three classic statements on need. J. Bradshaw 'The concept of social need', *New Society*, 30th March (1972). This article was a milestone statement about different types of social need. D. Piachaud's 1981 article 'Peter Townsend and the Holy Grail' *New Society*, 10 September presents a strong argument for the impossibility of finding an objective definition of need. L. Doyal and I. Gough's 'A theory of human needs', *Critical Social Policy*, 10 (1985): 6–38 represents a cogent argument for returning to an objective basis for the definition of needs. A completely up-to-date and accessible treatment of need is provided by Hartley Dean, *Understanding Human Need* (Bristol: Policy Press, 2010). This book asserts the case for the centrality of the concept of need, and presents a comprehensive discussion of the many subtle ways of classifying it.

On social problems, an early discussion in the United Kingdom is presented in N. Manning (ed.), *Social Problems and Welfare Ideology* (Aldershot, Gower, 1985). This book offers a detailed review of the theory of social problems, together with a range of case studies. In a more North American tradition is the seventh edition of a key textbook which presents a detailed analysis of seven different models of social problems: E. Rubington and M. Weinberg, *The Study of Social Problems: Seven Perspectives* (Oxford: Oxford University Press, 2010).

Review Questions

1 What are the main sources of a person's welfare in modern society?
2 How does industrial development shape welfare states?
3 How can we establish what someone's needs are?

4   What is the difference between needs, wants, and preferences?

5   Who defines social problems and how?

Visit the book companion site at www.wiley.com/go/alcock to make use of the resources designed to accompany the textbook. There you will find chapter-specific guides to further resources, including governmental, international, think-tank, pressure groups, and relevant journals sources. You will also find a glossary based on *The Blackwell Dictionary of Social Policy*, help sheets, and case studies, guidance on managing assignments in social policy and career advice.

4

Equality, Rights, and Social Justice

Peter Taylor-Gooby

Overview

- Equality, rights, and social justice are all political slogans, endlessly contested, endlessly renewed.
- The main contrast in relation to equality is between the increasingly popular Centre-Left ideology of equality of opportunity and the traditional Left conception of equality of outcome.
- Rights have been based on needs, capabilities (the opportunities actually available to people), and deserts. The question of how far people should take responsibility for meeting their own needs and when they merit state support attracts increasing attention.
- For justice the big division is between those who base just allocations on individual contribution and circumstances and those who take social factors into account.
- In a more fluid, flexible, diverse, uncertain, and globalized world the opportunities for making claims based on these concepts multiply while the capacity of governments to achieve them directly, through tax and spend, diminishes.

Meanings and Definitions

'Equality', 'rights', and 'social justice' have been prominent among the rallying cries of those calling for radical reforms, whether to promote recognition of the equal value of women as human beings (De Beauvoir, see George and Page 1995, ch. 14), to support social investment to meet the needs of future generations (Goodin 1998: 237), or to argue that rich nations have

The Student's Companion to Social Policy, Fourth Edition. Edited by Pete Alcock, Margaret May, Sharon Wright.
© 2012 John Wiley & Sons, Ltd. Published 2012 by John Wiley & Sons, Ltd.

a moral responsibility to the poor (Sen 2009: part IV).

Equality

In mathematics, equality refers to a relationship whereby two distinguishable elements have equal value. Note that claims about equality for elements that are the same in every respect are uninteresting – if they are completely identical you cannot distinguish them anyway. Similarly, no serious reformers who use a language of equality have argued for social uniformity, although detractors sometimes wish to treat them as if they do. The egalitarian claim of welfare reformers has been that different groups should be treated as of equal value in social policy. In practice this has led to demands for equality in entitlement to benefits and services, in treatment by welfare authorities, and in participation in decision-making.

Issues arise in two main areas. First, there is a problem in setting limits to the range of egalitarianism. Views on the scope of equality will depend on theories about what influences people's behaviour. The view, associated with neoclassical economic theory, that people are inclined to maximize their individual utility, implies that egalitarianism may undermine work incentives and kill the goose that lays the golden egg. If being a victim of inequality gets you welfare benefits, why bother to be anything else? The view that individuals are more influenced by culture, social relationships, and behavioural norms suggests that the impact of equalizing policies will depend much more on the social framework within which they operate (Rothstein 2005: ch 2; Gintis *et al.* 2005; Taylor-Gooby 2009: chs 5 and 6).

The second point concerns the practical rather than the moral scope of inequality. Many policymakers have distinguished between 'equality of outcome' and 'equality of opportunity'. Policies directed at the former must aim to put people in positions of equal value, while those seeking the latter are more modest. The objective is simply to give individuals an equal starting point in an unequal society. Egalitarianism in this sense is entirely compatible with wide divergences in people's life-chances. As globalized capitalism increasingly dominates the societies in which welfare states exist and equality of outcome recedes as a practical policy goal, the main practical application of egalitarianism has been in the area of equal opportunities.

The notion is immediately relevant to education and training, and to policies in relation to the acknowledged social divisions of sex, disability, and ethnicity. It has been particularly influential in the rhetoric surrounding New Labour in the early twenty-first century. It is thus surprising that the disturbing evidence of declining social mobility does not attract more attention in policy debate.

Different groups have struggled to ensure that particular divisions are recognized as meriting equal opportunity intervention. Issues of sexuality, of age, of disability, of region, of linguistic facility, of faith, of ethnicity, and sometimes even of social class are discussed as areas where equal opportunities policies should apply. As the range of dimensions across which equality is deemed relevant expands and as globalization, migration, and international media bring people ever more closely together, the problem of deciding which merit intervention presses. One outcome is that equality becomes increasingly a terrain of political debate.

Rights

Right is essentially a juristic concept referring to the legitimacy of an individual's claims. In the context of social policy the question is whether claims to social benefits and services should be backed by state force, so that social rights become an element in citizenship in the modern state.

Claims in the welfare area can be legitimated as rights in a number of ways. In practice, ideas about need, about capability, and about desert are most important (see Box 4.1).

Arguments about 'desert' are typically linked to normative systems. In our society two are paramount: the family ethic, with its attendant claims about the gender division of labour, the spheres of childhood and adulthood, and appropriate forms of sexuality; and the work ethic, and assumptions about individual responsibility to provide for oneself, stigmatizing dependency among those deemed capable of paid work. These ethics are subject to modification, and the growing diversity of UK society adds extra impetus to this process. Ideas about the desert of particular groups are of considerable importance

Box 4.1 Three Bases for Rights Claims

- *Need-based* arguments maintain that a class of human needs can be identified, which provides the justification for an obligation on government to ensure that these are met, so far as the current stage of development allows. There are a number of problems in this approach, not least in establishing a bed-rock of human needs that is secure against relativist reduction. The human needs approach has offered some of the most profound arguments for the legitimation of welfare as an ineluctable duty of government (see Plant, 1991, chapter 5).

- The *capability-based* approach, developed in the path-breaking work of Nobel Laureate economist Amartya Sen (2009) understands well-being in terms of the capabilities a person has, 'the substantive freedoms he or she enjoys to lead the kind of life he or she has reason to value'. Poverty can be understood as the deprivation of capabilities. The onus lies on government to remedy this, if possible.

People's access to capabilities can be established by comparing what more or less privileged groups are able to do or enjoy in a society. The approach underlies the construction of the widely used UN *Human Development Index*, which, broadly speaking, seeks to compare the achievement of a range of capabilities in different countries. It has been expanded to support demands from systematically disadvantaged groups such as women and disabled people (Nussbaum 2000).

- *Desert-based* claims are founded on the view that some quality of, or activity by, a particular group imposes an obligation on society to provide them with certain services. Examples of such arguments are claims that motherhood or contribution through work or in war is deserving of social support, and that the duty to provide it should come home to the state. Such claims are typically linked to functional or reciprocal arguments or are part and parcel of a normative system.

---

in relation to social rights and the way in which they are put into practice (see Box 4.2).

The assertion of a right provides powerful support to the political claims of exploited groups. However there are limitations: mechanisms for enforcing rights are often in practice weak and favour those with the best access to the courts, they have failed to mitigate inequalities within rich nations, let alone between the global North and South and they may even entrench existing divisions.

The needs-based approach is particularly vulnerable to the problem of choosing between diverse competing needs. Capability approaches are criticized because they assume that people are autonomous, independent, reflective actors, not members of a complex society with vulnerabilities, interdependencies, and social needs. They fail to take seriously the differing needs of various social groups for support and for access to a public realm to articulate and debate risks. Desert-

Box 4.2 Entitlement through Desert

- Entitlement to social insurance benefits based on work records is more secure and, in practice, less subject to official harassment than entitlement to means-tested benefit based on need.

- Support services designed to help those caring for frail elderly people are sometimes effectively rationed by reference to the status and the access to employment of the carer; receipt of the services is influenced by gender and age.

- Allocation of social housing of particular quality may involve the grading of tenants as suitable for higher or lower status estates.

based approaches entrench assumptions about the social worth of particular activities and the corresponding damage stemming from others.

For these reasons, recent debate has stressed the importance of politics alongside rights and opportunities to press home the needs of the most vulnerable against the privileged (Lister 2003: ch. 6; Dean 2010: ch. 9).

Social justice

Social justice is concerned with who ought to get what. Resource allocation in most welfare states is dominated by market systems which rest on the idea that goods are property to be owned, valued, bought and sold, and by normative systems of distribution closely linked to kin relationship. Arguments about rights and about equality have provided a basis for claims about justice which often cross-cut market and kin allocation. The most important positions of recent years have been those of Nozick and Rawls, and these illustrate the way in which individualistic and social approaches to social justice may be developed (see Box 4.3).

Both approaches have been extensively discussed and criticized. Nozick's position rests on a particular individualism in relation to labour which is not compelling. Production in modern society involves the interlinked activity of many people. The correct allocation of credit for work is highly controversial and is carried out in practice mainly through market institutions. Nozick's approach legitimates the market order and reinforces the work ethic.

The Rawlsian approach is attractive in that it rests on negotiation free from the biases that social position, class, gender, tenure, age, employment opportunities, state of health and so on, generates in the real politics of social policy. However, there are severe problems in deciding *a priori* what allocation of benefits and services people who were abstracted from their social circumstances would agree. There is nothing irrational in favouring a grossly unequal world and hoping to come out as a winner; or, if one felt more charitable, in supporting the highest average standard of living, providing the worst off are not too hard hit. It is difficult to devise approaches to social justice which both take seriously the autonomy of individual citizens and lay down the

Box 4.3 Individualist and Social Approaches to Social Justice

- Nozick argues that the core of just claims is labour – people have a right to what they have 'mixed their labour with', that is, improved by their work. As a matter of strict justice, it is a violation of individuals' autonomy to appropriate or redistribute the goods that people have gained through their work, although individuals may as a matter of charity choose to surrender property to those they view as needy and deserving (Plant, 1991: 210–13).
- Rawls's approach rests on the notion of a 'veil of ignorance'. The central idea is that just arrangements are those which people would agree on if they did not know what position in society they themselves would come to occupy, if they had no vested interests themselves (Plant, 1991: 99–107). He goes on to argue that it is in principle possible to 'second guess' the kinds of choices about the allocation of goods (and bads) that individuals would arrive at under these circumstances. Uncertain whether they would end up at the bottom of an unequal and exploited society, they would prefer a social order in which the only permitted inequalities were those that improved the position of the worst off; for example, by raising living standards throughout the community.

definitive policies a society must follow if it is to be labelled just – to put the seal of social justice on particular welfare arrangements.

Equality, Rights, and Justice as Ideology

Equality

In the post-war decades of confident welfare state expansion the advancement of equality – in the sense of equality of opportunity – was often used to justify policy, particularly in relation to educational reform. Crosland's influential book *The Future of Socialism* (see George and Page 1995: 131–2, 144) argued that technical and economic change squared the circle. Meritocracy was both rational and just. Both class struggle and class privilege were outdated by the requirement to get the best people in the right positions in an internationally competitive economy. From this perspective, it is equality of opportunity, not of outcome that matters.

The remaking of Conservative policy from the mid-1970s resulted in a vigorous commitment to free market principles and to a traditional family ethic. Egalitarianism has no place in this doctrine. Equal opportunity policies are seen as a corrupt and unfashionable 'political correctness'. Reappraisal on the Left after four successive election defeats led first to the programme of the Commission on Social Justice (Franklin 1999: ch. 2), which deprecated egalitarians as backward-looking 'levellers' and defined justice in terms of 'the need to spread opportunities and life chances as widely as possible', and more recently to the conception of a 'Stakeholders' Britain' in which equality of opportunity again plays a clear role but in which there is also a strong emphasis on individual responsibility to contribute to society. Policy trails behind these principles in many areas, for example discrimination between asylum-seekers and the home-born in citizen rights, the promotion of divisive and selective schooling and the acquiescence in yet greater concentrations of wealth and power among the super-rich.

The philosophy of the coalition government places further emphasis on individual responsibility, and this has provided a justification for the harsh cut-backs in social spending and a restructuring of local government services, the NHS, and much of education designed to encourage a shift to private provision to be implemented between 2011 and 2015. In short, the Right in politics prioritizes rights, derived from market and family, over claims based on considerations of equality. The Left has regarded equality as important, but as only one policy objective among several. The commitment is increasingly to equality of opportunity (with an obligation to group opportunities) and to the linking of welfare to social contribution.

Rights

Individual rights are closely linked to notions of social justice. Equality has been one of the principal foundations of rights claims in social policy debate, so that citizenship in itself is seen to justify rights to welfare. The other major foundation has been the notion of desert. In policy debate, ideas about desert, linked to work and family ethics have become increasingly important, so that rules of entitlement to benefit are drawn more stringently, the mechanisms for ensuring that able-bodied people are pursuing employment have been strengthened and obligations to maintain children after the end of a relationship have been codified. Much reform has also been concerned to reduce state spending, in line with the general emphasis on property rights which requires collective spending decisions to be justified against a stricter criterion than is applied to individual spending.

The emphasis on desert is a central pillar of right-wing approaches to welfare. However, recent arguments about stake-holding on the Left have also been concerned to emphasize individual contributions as part of a move towards more active policies. These are characterized by concern to expand opportunity and also to give due weight to individual responsibility for outcomes, rather than simply provide maintenance as in the passive receipt of benefits.

Social justice

Developments in relation to social justice follow largely from the above. The key shift is towards a more active notion of how social entitlements should be structured, in keeping with the move away from an egalitarian approach and towards one influenced by meritocracy or by ideas about property- and family-linked desert.

The impact of the New Labour approach has been to shift debate on the Left from rights justified by equal citizenship to rights justified by desert. Benefit rights for unemployed people, for example, are ever more tightly linked to appropriate behaviour as 'job-seekers' or to participation in New Deal programmes. Similar requirements are being extended to single parents and some categories of sick and disabled people.

Emerging Issues

Debates about equality, rights, and social justice have become both broader and narrower. On the one hand, increasing social diversity, more fluid patterns of family life and of employment, and struggles for the recognition of the rights by a broader range of groups have extended the range of claims for social policy interventions that can be made on the grounds of social justice. On the other, the ideological pressure justifying allocation on market and family-ethic principles and promoting individual rather than state responsibility is stronger than it has been for half a century. One view requires government to expand social policy, the other to spread welfare interventionism more thinly.

More recently there are indications of a move towards democratization. Citizenship needs and social rights (Taylor-Gooby 2009: ch.11; Dean 2010: ch.9; Lister 2003) are increasingly seen as issues of public context and debate. The demand is for a broader and more vigorous public realm open equally to all and in which the principles underlying policy can be justified to the satisfaction of policy-users, rather than policy-makers.

Social policy is overshadowed by concerns about the impact of population ageing, technological un- or sub-employment, growing international competition, tax revolt, the weakening of kinship care networks, international migration, general distrust of big government, and the future sustainability of Western welfare states. The climate of policy-making is one of austerity and of scepticism about how far government can resolve social problems. Under these circumstances it is hardly surprising that conceptual debates turn away from a highly interventionist concern with the promotion of equality of outcome towards the nourishing of more equal opportunities. Moral arguments point out that equal opportunity policies may damage the interests of the most vulnerable unless we develop effective systems to protect rights. Equally, we can only determine whether the final outcomes are morally acceptable by comparison with standards of social justice.

Equality, rights, and social justice remain central to social policy, especially in a more globalized, diverse, and uncertain social world. They underlie many of the political struggles about what states should do for their citizens and this is increasingly recognized by social policy writers who repeatedly call for more inclusive democratic engagement so that disadvantaged groups can play a stronger role in determining outcomes. The next few years will see severe cuts in benefits and services bearing harshly on the most vulnerable groups. This can only reinvigorate the appeal of social justice as a rallying point for the defence of the welfare state.

Guide to Further Sources

The best (and most clearly written) guide to the main relevant currents in contemporary political philosophy remains R. Plant *Modern Political Thought* (Oxford: Blackwell, 1991) especially chapters 3 to 7.

R. Goodin, *Reasons for Welfare* (Princeton, NJ: Princeton University Press, 1998) covers similar ground in more detail (see chapters 2, 3, and 4). This book also reviews the moral aspects of exploitation and dependency and develops a principled case against New Right arguments.

Part III of A. Sen's *The Idea of Justice* (Cambridge, MA: Harvard University Press, 2009) summarizes the capability approach. Part IV discusses the implications for democracy. This book is particularly valuable since it is written from a global rather than a national perspective. See Polylog, http://them.polylog.org/3/fsa-en.htm, for a typically readable and incisive article relating his work to other writers on social justice.

M. Nussbaum's *Women and Human Development: The Capabilities Approach* (Cambridge, UK: Cambridge University Press, 2000) points the relevance of the approach to gender inequality, from which it is a short step to embrace other dimensions of difference.

R. Lister, *Citizenship: Feminist Perspectives* (Basingstoke: Palgrave, 2003) provides a detailed analysis of citizenship rights. An excellent discussion of social need and human rights approaches is provided by H. Dean *Understanding Human Need* (Bristol: Policy Press, 2010). The focus of J. Foley's *Sustainability and Social Justice* (London: IPPR, 2004) is extended to include issues of sustainability, environmentally, cross-nationally, and intergenerationally.

P. Taylor-Gooby, *Reframing Social Citizenship* (Oxford, Oxford University Press, 2009) analyses welfare citizenship and social justice in a globalized world, paying particular attention to trust.

J. Le Grand in *Motivation, Agency and Public Policy* (Oxford, Oxford University Press, 2003) discusses theories of human agency (why people do what they do) and argues that social policy should be deliberately designed to respect diversity in values and motives.

In *Social Traps and the Problem of Trust* (Cambridge, UK: Cambridge University Press, 2005) B. Rothstein argues that trust and social cohesion are central to ensure that a moral social policy can be sustained.

Moral Sentiments and Material Interests (Cambridge, MA: MIT Press, 2005) by H. Gintis *et al.* is hard going, but rewarding: a principled critique of the view that we can understand how people behave in society simply by assuming that they follow self-interest.

In *Modern Thinkers on Welfare* (Upper Saddle River, NJ: Prentice Hall/Harvester Wheatsheaf, 1995) editors V. George and R. Page provide succinct accounts of the views of major policy commentators and critics.

The value of T. Fitzpatrick's *New Theories of Welfare* (Basingstoke, Palgrave, 2005) is that it provides an up-to-date review of theoretical concepts in social policy that includes new developments in areas such as genetics, information and surveillance.

For the UN Human Development Report, influenced by Sen's work on capability see Human Development Reports web site, http://hdr.undp.org/, where the United Nations Human Development Reports can also be found. Probably the best overall web resource on political ideas is Richard Kember's page at the University of Keele: www.psr.keele.ac.uk. Further material on the capability approach can be found at the Human Development and Capability Association, www.capabilityapproach.com/index.php. The Centre for the Study of Social Justice at Oxford has useful working papers and web-links athttp://social-justice.politics.ox.ac.uk/.

Review Questions

1   What is the value of considering ethical issues such as equality, justice, and desert in relation to practical social policy issues?

2   Dean argues that 'human needs must be satisfied in the context of our interdependency with others' (2010: 85). What does he mean? Is he right?

3   Retirement pensioners, single parents, single unemployed people without dependents, and disabled people all receive different levels of state benefits. Is this fair? Why?

4   Equality, rights, and social justice are issues of political contest, not of rational debate: do you agree? How far can deliberation take us in this field?

5   In an increasingly diverse world it is impossible to devise principles of social justice that can be applied between all groups across the planet: do you agree? Suggest some possible principles and point out their strengths and weaknesses.

Visit the book companion site at www.wiley.com/go/alcock to make use of the resources designed to accompany the textbook. There you will find chapter-specific guides to further resources, including governmental, international, think-tank, pressure groups, and relevant journals sources. You will also find a glossary based on *The Blackwell Dictionary of Social Policy*, help sheets, and case studies, guidance on managing assignments in social policy and career advice.

5

Equalities and Human Rights

Suzi Macpherson

Overview

- Debating equalities and human rights involves reflecting on a number of conceptual ideas relating to freedom, rights, recognition, redistribution, and social justice.
- Policies to promote equalities in the United Kingdom have progressed in a piecemeal way, leading to significant variance in the legal protections available to different social groups.
- Human rights are of a different order than other rights; they are unassailable rights that are held by all people which are upheld and protected rather than being enacted through legislation.
- Approaches to achieving equality vary and are influenced extensively by the values of those with responsibility for implementing policy and practice to promote equality.
- The current political and economic environment calls into question the future direction of policy activity to promote equality and human rights and the extent to which these issues will be prioritized in an environment of significant public sector cuts.

Historical Context

Debates on equalities and human rights have explicitly come to the fore with the establishment in the United Kingdom of the Equality and Human Rights Commission in 2007. The Commi-ssion brings together the previous Commission for Racial Equality, Equal Opportunities Commission, and Disability Rights Commission to create a single equalities and human rights organization with powers to tackle discrimination and promote equality around seven protected characteristics:

The Student's Companion to Social Policy, Fourth Edition. Edited by Pete Alcock, Margaret May, Sharon Wright.
© 2012 John Wiley & Sons, Ltd. Published 2012 by John Wiley & Sons, Ltd.

gender, age, disability, sexual orientation, gender identity, ethnicity, and religion or belief, as well as having a duty to promote and monitor human rights in Britain. The setting up of the new single equalities Commission was part of a shift in Britain's approach to equalities, involving a widening of the remit to new protected groups and encouraging greater attention to the interrelationships between equality issues recognizing that some people face multiple forms of inequality and discrimination.

Human rights

Human rights principles can be traced as far back as the Magna Carta in 1215, when the King of England was required to renounce certain rights, respect certain legal procedures, and accept that his will could be bound and limited by law. Social revolutions in France and the United States of America highlight the important role that human rights play in people's lives; that it is unacceptable for the rights of some people to be overlooked for the benefit of the few.

The human rights protections now available to people in the United Kingdom emerge from a number of international developments, notably the development of the United Nations Declaration of Human Rights. In response to the atrocities that took place during the Second World War, the United Nations was created and world leaders made a commitment to guarantee the rights of individuals everywhere. The UN Declaration was the result of this work, setting out a number of fundamental human rights and freedoms to which all men and women, everywhere in the world, are entitled. While the Declaration has no legal standing, it has become a powerful framework through which rights are recognized and human rights legislation has been developed. The UN Declaration is the foundation stone for modern human rights legislation and policy, with eighty international conventions and treaties, as well as numerous regional and domestic conventions, bills, and legislation emerging from it.

The European Convention on Human Rights was adopted in 1950 with the aim of protecting human rights and fundamental freedoms of individuals. The Convention established the European Court of Human Rights. Any person who feels that their human rights have been violated at state level can take a case to the European Court. The decisions of the Court are binding. Until the Human Rights Act 1998 was established in the United Kingdom, people in the United Kingdom had to take human rights cases to the European Court. Human rights cases can now be heard in UK courts. The Human Rights Act applies to all public bodies in the United Kingdom, including central government, local authorities, and other bodies exercising public functions.

Equalities

Concern with promoting equalities first emerged through the Treaty of Rome in 1957. The Treaty established the European Community, which made an explicit commitment to promote 'equality of opportunity' – seen explicitly through Article 119 which introduced the principle that women and men should receive equal pay for equal work. In the United Kingdom, legislation to promote equalities has developed in a piecemeal fashion with the late 1960s seeing the first legislative measures to tackle racial discrimination. Throughout the 1970s there was a flurry of legislation focusing on equalities issues, including the Equal Pay Act 1970, the Sex Discrimination Act 1975, and the Race Relations Act 1976. The Sex Discrimination Act led to the setting up of the Equal Opportunities Commission, while the Race Relations Act led to the setting up of the Commission for Racial Equality.

Legislation to tackle disability discrimination did not come until much later, with the introduction of the Disability Discrimination Act 1995. Through this legislation the National Disability Council was set up and was in 1999 replaced by the establishment of the Disability Rights Commission. It has only been relatively recently that legislation has been introduced to promote equality on the grounds of sexual orientation (2003), religion or belief (2003), gender identity (2004), and age (2006). This piecemeal approach to the development of equalities legislation meant variance in legislative provisions available to specific equality groups. The introduction of the Equality Act 2010 has addressed this by providing a single legal framework with clear streamlined law to effectively tackle discrimination and promote equality.

Conceptualizing Human Rights and Equalities

Human rights

Human rights are associated with freedoms that all humans are entitled to hold. In contrast with needs, wants, preferences, or resource claims, human rights do not need to be assessed by the state or society as being valid or justifiable before we can claim them. Rather, it is the duty of the state to ensure that people's human rights are safeguarded. This means that public bodies must respect human rights and the government must ensure that there are laws in place to protect them. A number of the human rights set out in the European Convention on Human Rights, which are now protected under UK law are listed in Box 5.1.

There are a number of guiding principles surrounding human rights protections. First, human rights belong to *everyone* regardless of sex, race, nationality, socio-economic group, political opinion, sexual orientation, or any other status.

Second, they are *universal*, held by everyone simply on the basis of being human. Third, they are *inalienable*, they cannot be removed from people. They can only be limited in certain tightly defined circumstances. Some rights, such as the prohibition on torture and slavery, can never be limited. Finally, human rights are *indivisible*, you cannot pick and choose the rights you will endorse and those you will not. Many rights also depend on each other to be meaningful. For example, the right to free speech must go hand in hand with the right to assemble peacefully.

This conceptualization of human rights is both universalist and egalitarian. Human rights involve acceptance of both natural rights and legal rights (see Box 5.2).

Building on this framework, Drake (2001) highlights a distinction between dependent rights and unassailable rights. Dependent rights get their meaning from the settings within which associated ideas of liberty, equality, and justice are framed. Unassailable rights have three qualities that cannot be: eroded over time; removed or relinquished; overridden or superseded. Human rights are principally seen as unassailable; with breaks in human rights doing harm both to the individual and to the wider community.

Promoting human rights involves recognition of both negative rights and positive rights.

Box 5.1   Human Rights Principles

Article 1 of the First Protocol: Protection of property
Article 2 of the First Protocol: Right to education
Article 3 of the First Protocol: Right to free elections
Article 2: Right to life
Article 3: No torture, inhuman or degrading treatment
Article 4: No slavery or forced labor
Article 5: Right to liberty
Article 6: Right to a fair hearing
Article 7: No punishment without law
Article 8: Right to a private and family life
Article 9: Freedom of religion
Article 10: Freedom of expression
Article 11: Right to protest and freedom of association
Article 12: Right to marry
Article 14: No discrimination

Box 5.2   Conceptualizing Human Rights

■ Natural rights – are not contingent upon the laws, customs or beliefs of a particular society or political context. Rather they are morally universal. The Declaration of Human Rights fits within this conceptualization of rights.
■ Legal rights – are codified through legal statute, legislation, and legal systems. Legal rights can only be called upon where there is a corresponding legal provision in place to protect those rights. The Human Rights Act 1998 fits within this conceptualization of rights.

Negative rights include civil and political rights such as freedom of speech, freedom from violent crime, and a fair trial. The emphasis is on an absence of constraint on your actions or absence of action taken against you that will have negative results. Positive rights include civil, political, social, economic, and cultural rights such as education, health care, and social security. The emphasis is on action being taken to ensure that you can achieve your rights. This echoes with distinctions between negative and positive freedoms – with negative freedoms ('freedom from') concerned with minimal state/political intervention and positive freedoms ('freedom to') promoting a more significant role for the state (e.g. in providing education and health services) to ensure that people can take up a range of life opportunities.

Equalities

Equality has been a central topic of debate in social policy analysis for many years, framing the development of the welfare state and playing out as a more or less central point of debate by political leaders on both the Left and Right since (Coffey 2004). However, equality means different things to different people and is as contested as other central topics in social policy including rights, freedom, and social justice (see Chapter 4).

White (2007) highlights five forms of equality (Box 5.3)

As well as different forms of equality, there are also different reasons for promoting equality. For example, economic equality may be valued to reduce poverty and low income, while political equality may be valued in order to achieve status equality (an element of social equality) via each person having an equal right to vote. The reasons for promoting equality, and the type of equality promoted, will be influenced by a range of economic, political, social, and ideological values.

Debates on equality within social policy have tended to highlight a distinction between equality of opportunity and equality of outcome. A minimal approach emphasizes merit, with equality in access to opportunities in education, employment, and so on. A broader approach recognizes people's different histories and ensures equal chances on this basis. A third approach involves offering fair chances and taking affirma-

> ### Box 5.3   Forms of Equality
>
> - Legal equality – having equal protection and treatment by the law.
> - Political equality – having equal opportunities to play a part in political life, including voting and standing for political office.
> - Social equality – having status equality with other social groups and an absence of domination of one group over another.
> - Economic equality – having opportunities to access economic resources, with recognition of the role played by the state in intervening to achieve this.
> - moral equality – recognizing through the organization of society, people's morally significant interests in relations to freedoms, resources and so forth, that different people have equal claims in relation to their respective interests.

tive action (e.g. quotas) to address disadvantages. Finally, significant intervention comes through positive action, which can be used as a means of achieving proportionality in participation in public life and employment. Positive action involves favouring candidates from underrepresented groups where they meet the core requirements for the role. Moving from minimalist to maximalist interventions corresponds with a move from concerns with promoting equality of opportunity towards measures that more directly influence equality of outcomes.

Three different approaches to promoting equality have identified and are shown in Box 5.4.

These approaches were initially developed in analysis on gender equality, but are recognized as offering a valuable framework for promoting equality for a number of social groups (Squires 2005).

Social justice

Equality and rights concerns are often intertwined with social justice concerns. In part this

Box 5.4   Approaches to Equality

■ Sameness: focuses on treating everyone the same way. This would mean
that we neither see particular group
characteristics (for example, ethnicity,
disability, gender, sexual orientation)
as being relevant to someone's abilities, nor would we recognize these
characteristics as meaning that a
person is entitled to adaptations to
current policies or practices.

■ Difference: focuses on recognizing
and accommodating differences. This
would mean recognizing that different
people have different needs and adapting policies and practices to take
account of these differences.

■ Transformative: focuses on fundamental change within policy and
practice. A much more significant
change to relations between groups is
emphasized, with concern to design
equalities issues into policies and
practices rather than adapt or offer
adjustments to meet the needs of specific groups.

Equalities and Human Rights: Making Links

Just as there are important conceptual links
between equality, rights, freedom, and social
justice, there are also important links between
these issues that can help frame our approach
to promoting equalities and human rights.
Promoting human rights involves progressing
freedom and equality as well as dignity, respect
and autonomy. Promoting equality involves progressing freedom, social justice, and rights. The
extent of policy intervention to achieve these
aims, and the intended outcome of intervention
(a minimalist or a maximalist approach, for
example) will differ depending on the values of
those promoting these goals. The capabilities
approach offers a conceptual approach bringing
together equality and human rights within a
social justice framework.

The capabilities approach

The approach to equality promoted in the
Equalities Review (2007) builds on the human
rights principles developed by Amartya Sen
through the capabilities approach, recognizing
the equal worth of every individual:

> An equal society protects and promotes equal,
> real freedom and substantive opportunity to live
> in the ways people value and would choose, so
> that everyone can flourish. An equal society rec-
> ognizes people's different needs, situations and
> goals and removes the barriers that limit what
> people can do and can be (Equalities Review
> 2007: 6).

relates to the centrality of concerns with resource
distribution which impacts on the delivery of
these objectives (Drake 2001). However, feminists, notably Nancy Fraser, point out that cultural recognition has displaced socio-economic
redistribution as the main remedy to promote
social justice and so deal with social inequality in
modern society (Fraser 2008). While egalitarians
have long been concerned with tackling socio-
economic injustices, Fraser argues that there is
another equally important injustice in society,
with cultural domination by some groups leading
to the interests of specific social groups being
ignored, disregarded, disrespected, or treated
with hostility. This focus on cultural injustice (or
lack of recognition) sits well with the legislative
concerns that have framed the approach to tackling group based discrimination and inequality in
the United Kingdom.

The capabilities approach provides an overarching structure for understanding and measuring
equality using human rights principles. It focuses
on what matters most to people, recognizes
diverse needs, draws attention to the structural
and institutional barriers framing life chances,
and recognizes that people have diverse goals.
Capabilities are the important things people can
do or be in life, which make their lives go well.
Capabilities in this context do not refer to the
internal skills or capacities of a person. Rather,
the lack of a capability indicates a failure by

society to provide real freedom for people (Burchardt and Vizard 2007).

Martha Nussbaum's (1999) theorizing on social justice and human rights builds on Sen's capabilities approach. By virtue of being human we are entitled to be treated with equal dignity and worth no matter what our social or economic position. The primary source through which we can articulate our worth is through our abilities in making choices that allow us to plan our lives in accordance with our own intended aims and outcomes. People should have fair claims to treatment by society and policy/politics, involving choices and respect to promote the equal worth of all persons. The value of the capabilities approach is seen through the move beyond the more traditional egalitarian focus on resource distribution, with resources recognized as only being valuable where people can turn these resources into functions. However, critics highlight the limitations of its individualistic focus, arguing that it is incomplete in its current form and it is potentially unworkable in practice.

Emerging Issues

A significant number of policy developments to promote equality and human rights were progressed under the Labour leadership during the period 1997 and 2010 widening the range of issues and groups whose rights are protected through legislation and promoted by public authorities. On 1 October 2010 much of the piecemeal legislation that had been developed since the late 1960s was brought together into one single piece of legislation, bringing together and rationalizing the legislative protections available to equality groups. This is a significant development for legislation and policy in Britain, but only time will tell how this new legislative framework is received by those charged with implementing the policy activity that emerges from it.

While this has been a landmark period in the development of equalities legislation, the direction of policy on equality is now quite uncertain as a result of the current political climate in the United Kingdom. At the time of writing this chapter in 2011 the coalition government have been in power a matter of months; but they have already outlined major cuts in public spending to take effect over the next five years. These cuts will inevitably impact on the lives of specific equality groups, for example disabled and older people; and any cuts in voluntary sector funding that occur through cuts in public sector funding will also mean that a range of services delivered to ethnic minorities, lesbian, gay, bisexual, and transgender people could also be lost. It is also recognized that reducing public sector services will significantly impact on women, disabled people, and ethnic minorities as these groups are the majority of those in public sector employment. Now more than ever there is a need to ensure that equalities and human rights concerns are kept centre stage; these issues are at risk of de-prioritization in current policy planning and analysis as service providers try to manage these more austere times.

Guide to Further Sources

There are a number of textbooks that look at human rights as a social science concern. A good starting place might be M. Freeman, *Human Rights: an interdisciplinary approach.* (Cambridge, UK: Polity Press, 2002) or R. Morgan and B. Turner (eds), *Interpreting Human Rights: Social Science Perspectives* (London: Routledge, 2009). On equalities there are a wide range of books to choose from. A good starting place might be S. White *Equality* (Cambridge, UK: Polity Press, 2007). R. Drake's *The Principles of Social Policy* (Basingstoke: Palgrave, 2001) offers contributions to debates on equality, justice, freedom and rights, while A. Coffey, *Reconceptualising Social Policy: Sociological Perspectives on Contemporary Social Policy* (Maidenhead: Open University Press, 2004) reflects in Chapter 5 on the relationship between equality and difference debates within social policy. J. Squires has made a critical contribution to debates on equality policy through her work on mainstreaming, see, for example, J. Squires, 'Is mainstreaming transformative?: Theorizing mainstreaming in the context of diversity and deliberation', *Social Politics: International Studies in Gender, State and Society*, 12/3 (2005): 366–88.

A number of text are now available on the capabilities approach, including A. Sen, *The Idea of Justice* (Cambridge, MA: Harvard University

Press, 2009), M. Nussbaum, *Women and Human Development: The Capabilities Approach* (Cambridge, UK: Cambridge University Press, 2000) and M. Nussbaum, *Sex and Social Justice* (Oxford: Oxford University Press, 1999). For more practical application of the capabilities approach in the modern policy context see T. Burchardt and P. Vizard, *Definition of equality and framework for measurement: Final Recommendations of the Equalities Review Steering Group on Measurement*. CASE Paper 120 (London: London School of Economics, 2007) and Equalities Review, *Fairness and Freedom: the final report of the Equalities Review* (London: Cabinet Office, 2007). Finally, N. Fraser, *Adding Insult to Injury: Nancy Fraser debates her critics* (London: Verso, 2008) is an excellent source to explore recognition and redistribution as critical debates within social justice.

Web sources include: Equality and Human Rights Commission, www.equalityhumanrights.com/; Government Equalities Office (UK government), www.equalities.gov.uk/; Information on the Equality Act 2010, www.equalities.gov.uk/equality_bill.aspx; United Nations Human Rights information, www.un.org/en/rights/; Scottish Human Rights Commission, www.scottishhumanrights.com/; Northern Ireland Human Rights Commission, www.nihrc.org/; Northern Ireland Equalities Commission, www.equalityni.org/site/default.asp?secid=home.

Review Questions

1   What possible advantages and disadvantages are there of bringing together concerns with equalities and human rights into one policy arena?

2   Concern about equality, rights, freedom, and social justice share critical features, notably being open to multiple definitions. What would be the key advantages of promoting a maximalist approach to achieving equality? And what risks might arise from doing so?

3   Nancy Fraser argues that a just society relies on both recognition and redistribution. What are the key features of each? Why are both important? Can both be achieved?

4   How might the capabilities approach be turned into a practical tool to promote equalities and protect human rights? What are the limitations of this tool?

5   Some people are critical of the move towards a single equalities focus. What reasons might people give for this critique and what possible reasons might be given for promoting a single equality focus?

Visit the book companion site at www.wiley.com/go/alcock to make use of the resources designed to accompany the textbook. There you will find chapter-specific guides to further resources, including governmental, international, think-tank, pressure groups, and relevant journals sources. You will also find a glossary based on *The Blackwell Dictionary of Social Policy*, help sheets, and case studies, guidance on managing assignments in social policy and career advice.

6

Efficiency, Equity, and Choice

Carol Propper

Overview

- Economics provides a framework to analyse the production and use of welfare services.
- Economic analysis begins from the assumption of scarcity – we cannot have everything we want. So people and society must make choices.
- The appropriate cost of these choices to society is the opportunity cost – the resources forgone if the choice is made.
- Economic efficiency means making the most of scarce resources. Economic efficiency occurs when the opportunity cost of using resources in a particular activity is equal to the sum of everyone's marginal benefits from that activity.
- Efficiency is not the only goal. Other goals include fairness and choice. These goals may clash with efficiency.
- Economists see markets and choice as one way of delivering efficiency, responsiveness in public services.

Introduction

Economic ideas and concepts are widely used in public policy. The domain of social policy is no exception: 'effective' and 'efficient' are adjectives frequently cited by politicians and policy-makers as goals for those responsible for delivering public services. Yet the ideas of economics are considerably more than buzz words. Economic analysis provides a framework which can be – and is – used to analyse questions about behaviour as diverse as worker participation in unions, the relative welfare of nations, the tendency of bureaucracies to grow, the behaviour of politi-

The Student's Companion to Social Policy, Fourth Edition. Edited by Pete Alcock, Margaret May, Sharon Wright.
© 2012 John Wiley & Sons, Ltd. Published 2012 by John Wiley & Sons, Ltd.

cians, or why increasing wealth does not appear to bring us happiness.

Terms such as efficiency and effectiveness have rather more precise meaning within economics than when used by politicians or policy-makers. Economists see efficiency, equity, and (sometimes) choice as ends – and ends which may be achieved through a number of possible means. These means include the market, the state, and a mixed economy. This chapter presents these key economic concepts and illustrates their applicability to social policy (see also Chapter 29).

Scarcity and Choice

Economic analysis begins from a single fact: we cannot have everything we want. We live in a world of scarcity. One way of seeing this scarcity is to notice that no one can afford all the things he or she would really like. This is obvious in the case of the homeless, but it applies equally to the carer who works part time and would like to have more time to devote either to her work or to the person she cares for, or to the rich rock star who goes on giving concerts in order to buy yet one more Caribbean island. It equally applies to governments who have a larger budget than an individual but can never spend as much on health services or education as the voters would wish.

Faced with scarcity, be it of money or time, people must make choices. To make a choice, we balance the benefits of having more of something against the costs of having less of something else. As resources are finite, in making choices we face costs. Whatever we choose to do, we could have done something else. So, for example, the carer with limited time can choose between working more or looking after the person she cares for. Or a society which invests in building roads uses up time and material that could be devoted to providing hospital facilities. Economists use the term 'opportunity cost' to emphasize that making choices in the face of scarcity implies a cost. The opportunity cost of any action is the best alternative forgone. So if building a hospital is viewed by society as the next best thing to building a road, the cost of building a hospital is the opportunity cost of building a road.

In many situations the price paid for the use of a resource is the opportunity cost. So if a road costs £1 million to build, then if the materials and labour used in road construction would be paid the same amount were they used in construction of something else, £1 million is its opportunity cost. However, market prices do not always measure opportunity costs and nor are all opportunity costs faced by an individual the result of their own choices. For example, when you can't get on to a train at busy times of day, you bear the cost of the choice made by all the other people who did get on the train. This is not a price that is quoted by the market and nor it is one that the other people on the train take into account when they get onto it.

Efficiency

Efficiency has a specific meaning in economics. When deciding how much of a good or service should be produced we need to take into account that having the good or service gives rise to both benefits and costs, and how those benefits and the costs vary with the amount that is produced. In general, benefits are desirable and costs are to be avoided. Given this, it would seem sensible to choose that amount of the good at which the difference between total benefits and total costs is largest. When society has selected this amount of the good and allocated resources of production accordingly, economists call this is the efficient level of output of this good, or alternatively say that there is an efficient allocation of resources in production of this good.

In determining the level of output which is efficient, we need to take into account both the benefits from the good and the opportunity costs of producing it. As an example consider the consumption and production of something simple – ice cream. The same analytical framework can be equally applied to hospitals, schools, social work services, and nuclear power stations.

Benefits of consumption

We would expect the benefits from eating ice cream to vary according to the amount eaten. In general, for someone who likes ice cream we would expect the total benefit to rise the more is eaten. However, this total benefit may not rise proportionately with each mouthful consumed.

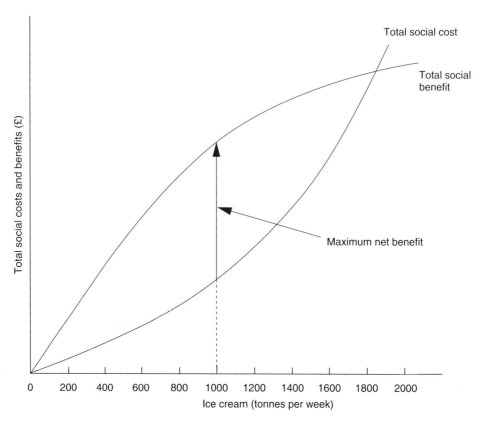

Figure 6.1   The total social benefit from ice cream consumption.

Let us consider the first spoonful. If the eater is really hungry the first spoonful will give considerable satisfaction. But, as the amount eaten is increased the satisfaction derived from each additional spoonful will begin to fall. By and large, we would expect to find that the benefit derived from each additional spoonful falls the more has been consumed. If we define the last spoonful as the marginal spoonful, we can say that the marginal benefit falls as the quantity of ice cream eaten increases. Either you become full, or because variety is nice, you would rather eat something else.

This analysis can be applied to society as a whole. Defining society's benefits as the sum of the benefits received by all individuals from ice cream, we can add up across all individuals to get the total social benefit. Similarly, we can add up each person's marginal benefit at each amount of ice cream eaten to get the marginal social benefit. This is the increase in total social benefit as we

increase society's consumption by one unit. We assume that we can add up the benefits received by different people. Often we can do this easily because benefits are measured in a single unit, say pounds. However, in some cases there may be measurement problems: for example, when it is hard to value a good, or when £1,000 is worth much more to one person than another.

Both the total social benefit and the marginal social benefit can be drawn on a graph. Figure 6.1 shows the total social benefit from ice cream consumption. The amount of ice cream consumed is on the horizontal axis and the benefit from this in pounds is on the vertical axis. Total social benefit rises as consumption increases, but it rises at a falling rate. It rises at a falling rate precisely because the marginal social benefit of consumption falls as more ice cream is eaten.

Figure 6.2 shows this marginal social benefit of ice cream consumption. The total amount consumed is shown on the horizontal axis and is

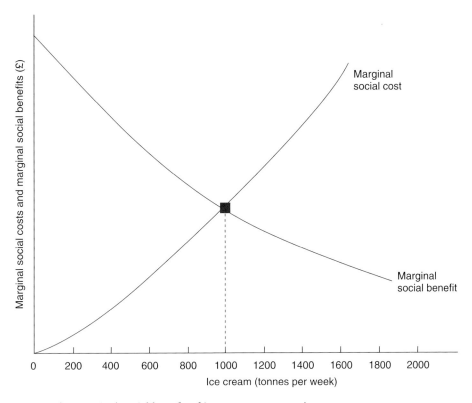

Figure 6.2 The marginal social benefit of ice cream consumption.

measured in the same units as in Figure 6.1. On the vertical axis we show the value in pounds of the marginal benefit. The marginal benefit curve slopes downwards from left to right, showing that the marginal social benefit falls as consumption of ice cream increases.

Costs of production

To determine the efficient level of production and consumption of ice cream we also need to consider the costs of production. Typically, the more of a good that is produced the more costly it is to produce – so total costs increase with production. However, what is required to establish efficiency is the cost of producing an extra unit of output, known as the marginal cost. Studies of production generally show that there is a level of production beyond which it becomes increasingly costly to expand output. This could be for a variety of reasons: firms may have to pay overtime or use less productive machinery, or the costs of co-

ordinating production or delivery rise as the amount of good produced rises. So the marginal cost of production increases as output increases.

Assuming that ice cream production has the same pattern, we can add up the total costs of production across all producers. This will be the total social cost. We can also add up all the marginal costs to obtain the marginal social cost for each unit of output. The total social cost of Figure 6.1 shows the way that total social cost rises with output of ice cream. The corresponding marginal social cost of production is shown in Figure 6.2.

The efficient level of output

We can use the information on how social benefits and social costs of ice cream consumption and production vary with output to identify that level of output at which the difference between total social benefits and total social costs (net social benefit) is at a maximum. This is the efficient level of output. From Figure 6.1 we can identify this as at 1,000 tonnes per week. Looking at Figure 6.2 we can see that this is the point at which marginal social benefits equal marginal social costs. This is no coincidence. As long as the marginal social cost is below the marginal social benefit, society will gain by producing and consuming more ice cream. Conversely, if the marginal social benefit is below the marginal social cost, society would do better by putting its resources to other uses and consuming and producing less ice cream. Only when the marginal social benefit is equal to the marginal social cost will it be impossible to increase net social benefits.

The analysis of the efficient amount of ice cream output is relevant to all goods and services. So we can define the socially efficient output of hospitals, home helps, education, or cars in exactly the same way. We may have more problems in measuring the benefits and costs, but the principle remains the same: the socially efficient amount of the good or service is produced at the point where the marginal cost and benefit are equal.

An efficient level of production is thus a desirable end: if all goods are produced in their efficient quantities then net social benefit cannot be increased by reallocating resources. Conversely, if the level of production is not efficient, then net social benefits can be increased by producing more (or less) of one good and less (or more) of at least one other. Given that resources are always finite, efficiency is thus an important social objective.

Efficiency and effectiveness

Although efficiency and effectiveness are often used synonymously by policy-makers, they are different. Effectiveness means producing something in the best possible way technically, and is sometimes called technical efficiency. We can check whether a production is technically efficient by seeing whether, given the current technology, more output could be produced from the present inputs. As an example consider the delivery of meals on wheels by one person with one van. One service might visit houses by order of number. If all the even houses are on one side of the street and all the odd numbers on the other, this will mean crossing the road between each delivery. This is likely to be less technically effi-

cient than delivering meals to all the odd numbered houses and then to all the even ones.

Efficiency goes further than (and encompasses) effectiveness. To know whether a production process is efficient we must first check that it is effective. Then we have to see whether its current technology produces the output in a cheaper way than the alternatives. This requires looking at the prices of inputs, whereas effectiveness does not. So in our example it may be that once costs are taken into account, it might be found that it is better to change the amount spent, and so to employ two people and one van. Then we must check that consumers cannot make themselves better off by choosing to buy other goods. Finally, we must check that all the costs and benefits involved have been taken into account. (Technically, this is known as checking that there are no external costs and benefits. In the train example given above, there were external costs – those imposed by train users on others. In some activities, for example, smoking cigarettes or the use of fuels which pollute the atmosphere, these external costs may be large.)

So before we can say that something is efficient we must first ensure that it is effective; hence the drive toward effectiveness in the use of scarce medical resources, for example. However, just because a production method is effective, it does not mean it is efficient. We need to know the costs and the benefits of the service and of alternatives to know that. For many areas of social policy, we are still at the stage of establishing effectiveness and not efficiency.

Efficiency versus Other Goals

Equity

Even though efficiency is a desirable end it is not the only one. An efficient outcome is not necessarily a fair or equitable one. An efficient output is one for which the sum of all individuals' marginal valuations equals the marginal social costs of production. But each individual's valuation of a good or service – and so the sum of these valuations – will depend on the resources he or she has. So the efficient level of production will be defined in relation to the existing distribution of resources. If initial resources are distributed in a way that is judged as unfair, there is no reason why an efficient allocation of those resources should be fair.

An example may make this clearer. Suppose there are only two members of society, Ms A and Ms B. Given their initial resources, their likes and dislikes and the production methods available to them, the efficient level of production of ice cream is four tubs per week. These tubs could all go to Ms A, or all to Ms B, or they could share them equally. Each of these divisions of the total production is possible, but not all will be judged as fair or equitable. On the other hand, if each received only one tub, this allocation might be judged as fair, but it is not efficient. It is not efficient because we know that the efficient level of production is four tubs. If only two tubs were produced, net social benefit would be increased by producing more and in so doing we could make both Ms A and Ms B better off.

There are many possible definitions of equity or fairness – for example, minimum standards or equal distribution for all – but we do not discuss them here. The points to note are: first, that efficiency is not the same as fairness; second, that there is often trade-off between the two (a fair allocation may be one which is not efficient); third, that efficiency embodies a value judgement just as definitions of fairness do. The value judgement underlying the definition of efficiency is that some distribution of income (often the existing one) is legitimate.

Choice

Choice is seen as an important mechanism by economists. By making choices, individuals can indicate their valuations of goods and services. If valuations are known then the production of those services which have greater net (marginal) value will be increased and the production of others decreased, and so the outcome will be more efficient. Choice is often linked to competition: competition is one means by which individuals can exercise choices. To see this, consider the case where there is no competition in the supply of a service because there is only one supplier. In this case individuals cannot choose the type of service they prefer as there is only one on offer.

Of course, there are costs to making choices – individuals have to decide which product they

prefer and this will mean finding out about each possible option. In some circumstances it could be the case that very small differences between goods do not merit the costs of trying to choose between them. In others, the amount of information required to make informed choices may be very high. It has sometimes been argued, for example, that the level of medical knowledge required to make informed choices in health care is too large for individuals to make good choices. The same argument has been advanced in debates about giving greater choice in pension arrangements. However, in general, more choice is judged to be better than less.

In the field of social policy, where choice has often been limited, increasing choice – and the allied goal of increasing responsiveness of suppliers to users' wishes – is viewed as an important goal. From an economics perspective this is viewed as a move in the right direction. However, this does not mean that the benefits of increasing choice necessarily outweigh the costs. This will depend on the particular service.

The Means of Delivering Efficiency and Choice

All societies have had methods of trying to get the most out of limited resources. In large-scale societies, two dominant mechanisms of allocation have been used. These are allocation by the government and allocation by the market. Under the former system (the so-called command economies), planning and administration were used to decide what and how goods should be produced, and to whom they should be allocated. Under the latter, allocation decisions are made by the decisions of large numbers of individuals and private firms.

Markets are seen as desirable by economists since – in the absence of market failure – they will lead to an efficient allocation of resources without the need for coordination mechanisms and the costs of planning. In practice, of course, not all decisions in a market system are made by individuals, and not all ownership is private. Government has a large role in all market economies. However, the market mechanism currently has dominance: command economies have largely abandoned their structures in favour of freer markets.

Emerging Issues

In the provision of public services, choice and competition have been introduced into systems where previously allocation was by means of administrative decision. Politicians from the Left and the Right see choice as a way of allowing greater parental say in where their child goes to school or of where individuals are treated for medical care. In health care, education, social care, and social rented housing in the United Kingdom (and elsewhere), competition in supply has been introduced as a means of increasing choice, responsiveness, and efficiency. Services which were previously delivered by government monopoly have been opened up to competition. So private firms collect rubbish, build houses for low income tenants, and run prisons. Private suppliers compete to provide care for the mentally handicapped, and not-for-profit public education providers compete for contracts to provide education. In some countries – Canada is one – while health care is financed by the state, all provision is private. Thirty years ago these arrangements would have been seen in the United Kingdom as the wrong way to provide services: today, many go without comment.

On the other hand, in health, education, and transport (among other services) there is still considerable debate about the role for the private sector as a provider, for the role of individual choice, and for competition between suppliers. Research findings make it clear that the precise institutional arrangements of choice and competition in public services matters: a reform that works well in one context cannot be transposed without adaptation to another. Nevertheless, if choice and efficiency are important goals, market mechanisms have their uses in welfare services as in other parts of the economy.

Guide to Further Sources

J. Le Grand, S. Smith, and C. Propper *The Economics of Social Problems* (4th edn, Basingstoke: Palgrave Macmillan, 2008) provides an economic analysis of social policy issues and assumes no previous knowledge of economics. A more advanced textbook, designed for those already studying economics, is N. Barr, *The Economics of* *the Welfare State* (4th edn, Oxford: Oxford University Press, 2004). For a book also aimed at economics students which discusses these issues in a US context, see J. Stiglitz, *Economics of the Public Sector* (3rd edn, New York: W. W. Norton, 2000). For a review of recent evidence on the use of competition in health care markets see S. Burgess, C. Propper, and D Wilson (2006) 'Extending choice in English health care: The implications of the economic evidence', *Journal of Social Policy*, 35/4 (2006). For a review of the evidence on choice in education, see Burgess *et al.*, 'The impact of school choice in England: Implications from the economic evidence', *Policy Studies* 28/2 (2007): 129–43. A non-technical review of a range of issues in the economics of the provision of public services is provided in P. Grout and M. Stevens (eds), 'Financing and Managing Public Services', *Oxford Review of Economic Policy*, 19/2 (2003). For a discussion of the role of economic motivation in the behaviour of those who provide public services, see J. Le Grand, *Motivation, Agency, and Public Policy: Of Knights and Knaves, Pawns and Queen* (Oxford: Oxford University Press, 2005). For an analysis of the economics of health see S. Morris, N. J. Devlin, and D. Parkin, *Economic Analysis in Health Care* (Chichester: John Wiley and Sons, 2007).

Review Questions

1   The concepts of social cost and social benefit involve the summation of individual benefits and costs. Explain why. What problems does this procedure pose?
2   The specification of an efficient allocation of resources, unlike the definition of an equitable distribution, does not involve value judgements. Do you agree?
3   Explain the concept of opportunity costs and how it relates to an efficient allocation of a good or service. Give examples where the private opportunity cost of an activity does not equal the social opportunity cost. In these cases, what tools may be used to make the private opportunity cost equal the social cost.
4   Explain why technical effectiveness is not the same thing as efficiency. Which is more difficult to achieve in your view?

5 Explain why economists value choice. Give examples of policies to improve choice in the provision of at least two public services. What are the advantages and disadvantages of increasing choice in the provision of public services?

Visit the book companion site at www.wiley.com/go/alcock to make use of the resources designed to accompany the textbook. There you will find chapter-specific guides to further resources, including governmental, international, think-tank, pressure groups, and relevant journals sources. You will also find a glossary based on *The Blackwell Dictionary of Social Policy*, help sheets, and case studies, guidance on managing assignments in social policy and career advice.

7

Altruism, Reciprocity, and Obligation

Hilary Land

▪▪▪

Overview

- ▪ Differing assumptions about human nature underpin the principles and practices upon which social policies are based.
- ▪ Understandings of family relationships are based on assumptions about reciprocal commitments to love and care. Their gendered nature has been challenged in particular by feminist critics.
- ▪ The collective obligations which underpin social policy are based on a mixture of altruism and self-interest.
- ▪ Policies based more directly on self-reliance and self-protection were promoted by neo-liberals towards the end of the twentieth century, supported by the rise in sociobiology.
- ▪ Support for altruism and reciprocity in the future may require a fundamental review of the obligations and rights of citizenship.

▪▪▪

Human Nature

Resources in societies, in the form of cash, kind, or services, are claimed by and distributed to individuals and households within a variety of institutions. The family, broadly or narrowly defined, is important in all societies as a system for allocating resources between the generations as well as between men and women. In market economies, alongside the market itself, there may be state welfare systems, voluntary societies, charities, and religious institutions. The relative importance of each of these varies over time and between countries. For example, in England,

The Student's Companion to Social Policy, Fourth Edition. Edited by Pete Alcock, Margaret May, Sharon Wright.
© 2012 John Wiley & Sons, Ltd. Published 2012 by John Wiley & Sons, Ltd.

charities, religious organizations, and voluntary societies play a much smaller role now than they did in the nineteenth century or than they do today in Italy. The principles underlying the distribution of resources in each of these systems are often different because some claims are based on 'desert', others on 'need' – both highly contested concepts. Some are enshrined in law as obligations, which one person owes another and which the courts can enforce, punishing those who fail to honour them. These also change over time and differ between countries. In the United Kingdom, for example, until 1948 grandparents could be obliged in law to maintain their grandchildren. That is still the case in Germany. Others are less well defined and are in part the product of a society's history and culture, or what the sociologist O'Neill (1994: 92) calls 'rituals of reciprocity that celebrate exchanges between society, nature and God, involving a covenant between them as a model of all other civic reciprocities between individuals, neighbours, families, communities and the state'.

The assumptions about human nature on which these principles and practices are based also differ. Some assume that individuals are motivated primarily by self-interest and selfishness, others by altruism and concern for others. Adam Smith, one of the founding fathers of political economy, recognized both but is more often quoted in support of the former view, particularly by those on the right of the political spectrum. In 'An Inquiry into the Nature and Causes of the Wealth of Nations', published in 1776 he wrote,

It is not from the benevolence of the butcher, the brewer or the baker that we expect our dinner, but from their regard to their own interest. We address ourselves, not to their humanity but to their self-love, and never talk to them of our necessities but of their advantage. (cited by Sen 2010: ix)

Smith also recognized that not all human activity could be interpreted in this way. Amartya Sen points this out. The opening sentence of all the editions of his first book The Theory of Moral Sentiments, last revised in 1790 stated: 'How selfish so-ever man may be supposed, there are evidently some principles in his nature, which

interest him to the fortune of others, and render their happiness necessary to him, though he derives nothing from it except the pleasure of seeing it' (cited by Sen 2010: x). Smith also recognized altruism to be particularly important within the family. However, by and large, political economy placed the family outside its domain and concentrated instead on developing models of human society comprising solitary and independent (male) individuals acting rationally and freely making contracts in pursuit of their own self-interest. As the philosopher Mary Midgley has pointed out, this model derives from seventeenth-century physics, in which the ultimate building blocks of matter were conceptualized as hard, impenetrable atoms. It is a model, she writes, in which 'all significant moral relations between individuals are the symmetrical ones expressed by contract' (1985: 151). However, there are other ways of thinking about human relationships. Midgley explains,

(If) . . . we use a biological or 'organic' model, we can talk also of a variety of asymmetrical relations found within a whole. Leaves relate not only to other leaves but to fruit, twigs, branches and the whole tree. People appear not only as individuals, but as members of their groups, families, tribes, species, ecosystems and biospheres and have moral relations, as parts, to these various wholes. (1985: 151)

In this model people are not independent but interdependent, and relationships cannot be specified with reference to a contract. The distinguished Nigerian writer Chinua Achebe suggests that the philosophical dictum of Descartes 'I think therefore I am' 'represents a European individualistic ideal' (2010: 166). He contrasts it with a Bantu declaration which represents an African communal aspiration: 'A human is human because of other humans.' In other words: 'Our humanity is contingent on the humanity of our fellows. No person or group can be human alone' (Achebe 2010: 166).

Family Relations

Family relationships have always been perceived to be different from those of the marketplace and not subject in the same way to rational calculation. Reciprocity within families is informed by love or altruism rather than narrow self-interest. Many economists treat the family or household as a 'black box' and have developed models which assume a household can be treated as if it were an individual – a male individual – with identifiable interests or 'joint utilities', to use the jargon. Gary Becker is one of a minority of economists who has shown a sustained interest in the family and in altruism, arguing that

> Families in all societies, including modern market oriented societies, have been responsible for a sizeable part of economic activity – half or more – for they have produced much of the consumption, education, health and other human capital of the members. If I am correct that altruism dominates family behaviour, perhaps to the same extent as selfishness dominates market transactions, then altruism is much more important in economic life than is commonly understood. (1993: 303)

However, Becker accepts women's willingness to invest in the 'human capital' of their husbands and children rather than in their own, using a rather circular argument, namely that since on average they enter marriage with less education, training, and marketable experience (i.e. less human capital) than their partners, it is rational from the point of view of maximizing the family's interest for them to use their time and effort in this way. Families invest less in the human capital of their daughters than their sons because they are expected to devote at least part of their adulthood to marriage and children, and so the cycle is repeated.

The assumptions about women's availability to care have been challenged since the 1980s as education and employment opportunities for girls improved and marriage became more risky. As Nancy Folbre, a feminist economist, explained,

> As long as male individualism is counterbalanced by female altruism, as long as rational economic man is taken care of by irrational altruistic woman, families play a particularly important (and unfair) role. But when women gain the freedom to act more like men, pursuing their rational self-interest, the price of caring labour goes up. (1994: 119)

The rise in female employment has challenged the male breadwinner/female housewife model on which the British post-war social security scheme was built. Today, the models underpinning European welfare states are developing into individual worker models. 'Work' means paid work. Women as well as men have an obligation to take it, thus becoming 'active' citizens and avoiding poverty and dependence on the state. Care and its costs have become more visible and the provision of formal childcare services became explicitly linked with EU employment policies in the 2000s. The formal and informal social care of older adults is also becoming a policy issue across the European Union as the retirement ages for all are being raised in order to reduce the cost of pensions. However, in Britain, formal services to enable older carers to combine care with paid employment have yet to attract the additional resources that child-care services have received in recent years.

Distinctions between care in the formal labour market and the 'informal' care system remain. In England and Wales child-care and social care services continue to attract charges according to means, although the Labour government in its last few months in 2009 attempted but failed, to introduce some free personal care for all frail or disabled adults living in their own homes. The devolved Scottish government introduced free personal care in 2001. This experience showed that, contrary to official expectations, families do not care less if the state provides more, although many care differently.

Family Obligations

Finch and Mason (1993) have looked at how the meaning of responsibility or obligation is understood and practised in families. They challenge the concept of 'fixed obligations' associated with a genealogical link and argue that 'in reality the responsibilities which people feel and acknowledge towards their relatives have more complex and more individual roots' (1993: 180). Obligations between spouses may be more fixed in character but those between parents and adult children can be very variable. They argue for seeing responsibilities as commitments which are built up between specific individuals over time, perhaps over many years.

This is done through contact, shared activities and particularly through each giving the other help as it is needed. This process of reciprocity – accepting help and then giving something in return – is the engine which drives the process of developing commitments. Although people do not work with a simplistic balance sheet, reciprocal help given and received over time is a crucial factor in understanding how family relationships operate. (Finch and Mason 1995: 54)

These commitments between the generations can survive divorce, although women are more successful than men in maintaining relationships with both their children and their former in-laws. This may have consequences for men's care in old age. Finch and Mason warn policy-makers against attempting to enforce obligations which are not consistent with the ways in which families practise and understand their obligations. For example, the failure of the Child Support Act, 1991, to ensure that absent fathers paid maintenance for all their biological children is explained in part by the shift in the obligation to maintain children from the legitimate or social father with whom they were living to the biological father. This was contrary to deeply held beliefs about family responsibilities.

Collective Obligations

The relationship of state welfare policies to both the market and the family has always been the subject of debate. Some have argued that the development of market economies has damaged the family's capacity to support its members. When many Western industrialized nations were debating the future of their welfare systems, Alva Myrdal, in an influential book, *Nation and Family* (1947) argued that 'collective devices' were necessary to substitute for the security once provided by families. Richard Titmuss, writing later, held similar views. He also saw state welfare as a mechanism for compensating individuals and families who were damaged by economic growth. Those who benefited from a thriving and expanding economy had an obligation to share these benefits with the less fortunate. For Titmuss, welfare policies were mechanisms for extending altruism beyond the family:

The ways in which society organizes and structures its social institutions – and particularly its health and welfare systems – can encourage or discourage the altruism in man; such systems can foster integration or alienation, they can allow for 'the theme of the gift' – of generosity towards strangers to spread among and between social groups and generations. (1971: 225)

Titmuss studied blood donors in the NHS as an example of a willingness to give to strangers – moreover, strangers never encountered. He found that it stemmed from a sense of obligation to a wider society and confidence in future unknown strangers, who in their turn would give their blood should others, including themselves, ever need it.

William Beveridge, regarded as one of the principal architects of the British post-war welfare state, proposed a social insurance system based on a clear contract between employers, employees, and the state. The risks of unemployment, sickness, and old age were pooled. He embedded in his social insurance and social assistance schemes rules to ensure that men's obligations to take paid work in order to support their families, and women's obligations to provide domestic services for their husband and children, were carried over from earlier social security systems. In the last resort, prison faced men who refused work and failed to support their families. However, Beveridge also wanted to encourage altruism within the wider society. This he called 'a sense of Divine Vocation'. Unlike many social policy analysts at the time – or since – he noticed women's altruism: 'Serving, exhausting oneself without thought of personal reward – isn't that what most women do most of their lives in peace or war?' (1943: 38) Forty years later, Land and Rose (1985) found many social policies were still based on taken-for-granted assumptions about women's willingness and availability to care for other members of their families, so much so that it was only remarkable when it did not happen. Women's altruism within the family was therefore more accurately described as 'compulsory'.

Self-reliance and Independence

In contrast to the early years of the post-war welfare state, recent debates about social welfare in the United Kingdom have been dominated by those who believe that state welfare provision undermines both the efficient working of the economic market and obligations within the family. This is coupled with a view that only the poor need state welfare provision – the middle classes and the wealthy can look after themselves.

This view of society comprising self-seeking, individualistic people has been strengthened by the rise of sociobiology as well as by the global dominance of neo-liberalism which, since the late 1970s has framed the debates about the welfare state in Western industrial societies. Eugenics, which underpinned the belief in the naturalness of inequalities and hierarchies in the first half of the twentieth century, was influential in the social policy debates of the time in Britain and the United States. Sociobiology is now providing a similar ideological basis for undermining the arguments for a universalistic welfare state. Genetic determinism and reductionism serve to turn attention away from the environmental and structural causes of inequalities, fail to recognize the interdependence of individuals within society or of societies across the globe and so support the view that a minimal welfare state is not only desirable but all that is possible.

From the early 1970s, its proponents have been arguing that prime among the traits inherent in our nature is selfishness. Richard Dawkins claimed that everything organisms do is done out of self-interest. In the preface to his first bestselling book he wrote: 'We are survival machines– robot vehicles blindly programmed to preserve the selfish molecules known as genes.' Thus he argued, 'at the gene level, altruism must be bad and selfishness good . . . The gene is the basic unit of selfishness' (1976: 38). In this model women's greater commitment to child rearing follows from the belief that women and men must adopt different strategies to maximize opportunities to spread their genes into future generations. Altruism is explained away.

This form of genetic determinism has been challenged within the biological sciences. Iain McGilchrist, an experienced psychiatrist and philosopher by drawing on a vast body of brain research has examined the relation between our two brain-hemispheres and the connection between the structures of the brain and the divided nature of thought itself. He is concerned that the precise, categorical thinking associated with the left hemisphere has been encouraged in Western European thought especially since the Enlightenment, at the expense of background vision and experience which is associated with the right hemisphere. It is now distorting our lives as well as our thinking. He challenges the notion of 'selfish genes' and is not convinced that biology justifies the jettisoning of 'altruism'. He writes,

> Altruism in humans extends . . . beyond what is called 'reciprocal altruism', in which we behave 'altruistically' in calculated expectation of the favour being reciprocated. It is not a matter of the genes looking after themselves at the expense of the individual, either; human beings co-operate with people with whom they are not genetically related. It is also far more than co-operation based on the importance of maintaining one's reputation; we co-operate with, and put ourselves out to help, those we may barely know, those we may never meet again, and those who can in no way reward us. The possibility of future reciprocation may of course influence decisions, where it operates, but it is not fundamental to the phenomenon.
>
> It is mutuality, not reciprocity, fellow-feeling, not calculation, which is both the motive and the reward for co-operation. And the outcome, in utilitarian terms, is not the important point: it is the process, the relationship that matters. (McGilchrist 2009: 147)

This understanding of reciprocity and altruism is broader than that of David Willetts, a member of the first coalition government elected in the United Kingdom in May 2010. He states: 'Reciprocity involves empathy, being able to put yourself in someone else's shoes even when their feet are a different size. Sympathy is feeling for someone else. Empathy is making the leap to understanding someone else even if your emotions are not directly involved' (Willetts 2010: 98). He points out that he uses 'empathy' to mean something similar to Smith's meaning of 'sympathy' for both involve the imagination and emotions as well as rational calculation. Stable families within which we first experience reciprocal exchanges, are therefore important as are all institutions 'with long and stable histories where we can be confident of rewards and indeed penalties out into the future' (2010: 152). Social contracts based on 'reciprocal altruism' as distinct from 'direct reciprocity' or exchange are possible because, as Smith (1790) also argued, individuals care about their public reputations and fear the penalties associated with a 'bad' reputation. He argues that women 'have borne more of the burden of maintaining such contracts because they live longer and so are likely to be recipients of more informal care later' (1790: 96). Willett's book contains much evidence that the older generation are far from a 'burden' on their children for there is a substantial flow of resources from older to younger generations. Nevertheless he fears that the larger size and selfish attitudes of the British 'baby-boomer' generation will undermine 'the intergenerational contract'.

Emerging Issues

As populations across the European Union age and greater numbers live beyond their eighties the cost of pensions and their growing need for care will place unprecedented demands on intergenerational contracts both within families and in the wider society. Raising retirement ages for all may make the reconciliation of care and work more difficult for older workers, especially women who have caring responsibilities for grandchildren or frail parents. In those countries where child-care and social care services have become collective responsibilities, demonstrating a public commitment to solidarity between the generations as well as between rich and poor, it is easier to reconcile paid work and care.

As 'choice' and 'competition' are increasingly used as mechanisms for allocating resources within twenty-first-century welfare states, cash payments replace directly provided services and the public are encouraged to think of themselves as independent 'consumers' rather than as 'citizens', a fundamental review of the obligations and rights of citizenship is becoming more necessary.

Guide to Further Sources

R. M. Titmuss's *The Gift Relationship* (London: Allen and Unwin, 1970) has remained an important contribution to the literature on altruism and reciprocity. J. Finch and J. Mason, *Negotiating Family Responsibilities* (London: Routledge, 1995) studies the processes by which family members meet the obligations between them. N. Folbre, *The Invisible Heart* (New York: New Press, 2001) analyses the importance of the values of love, reciprocity and obligation which underpin our society and economy. J. O'Neill, *The Missing Child in Liberal Theory* (Canada: University of Toronto Press, 1994) argues for a renewal of the social contract between the generations and criticizes a political economy which emphasizes individualism and ignores social responsibility. M. Midgley, *Evolution as Religion: Strange Hopes and Stranger Fears* (New York: Methuen, 1985) gives a philosopher's perspective on these concepts and provides an excellent critique of sociobiology. Amartya Sen's introduction to the Classic Penguin edition (2010) of Adam Smith's (1790) *Theory of Moral Sentiments* lucidly discusses Smith's views on both self-love and sympathy for others. D. Willetts, *The Pinch: How the Baby Boomers took their Children's Future and Why they Should Give it Back* (London: Atlantic, 2010) is a provocative analysis of changing obligations and reciprocities between the generations in the United Kingdom.

Other useful publications include:

C. Achebe, *The Education of a British-Protected Child* (New York: Alfred A. Knopf, 2010); G. Becker, *Treatise on the Family* (Cambridge, MA: Harvard University Press, 1993, first published 1981); W. Beveridge, *Pillars of Society* (London: Allen and Unwin, 1943); R. Dawkins, *The Selfish Gene* (Oxford: Oxford University Press, 1976);

H. Land and H. Rose, 'Compulsory Altruism for Some or an Altruistic Society for All?' in P. Bean, J. Ferris, and D. K. Whynes (eds), *In Defence of Welfare* (London: Tavistock, 1985), pp. 74–96; I. McGilchrist, *The Master and his Emissary, The Divide Brain and the Making of Western Thought* (New Haven, CT: Yale University Press, 2009); and A. Mydral, *Nation and Family: The Swedish Experiment in Democratic Family and Population Policy* (London: Kegan Paul, 1947).

Review Questions

1 As welfare state provision is cut in response to the economic crises of 2008–9, will reci-

procity between the generations be enhanced or subverted in future?

2 What are the limits of market mechanisms in the provision of health and social care?

3 What are the limits to state support in the form of cash payments and what else is needed?

4 What obligations will individuals have for their own welfare and that of their families in a welfare state more narrowly targeted on 'the poor'?

5 As individuals rely more heavily on the market, their families and fellow citizens rather than the state, will we be living in a more or less altruistic society?

Visit the book companion site at www.wiley.com/go/alcock to make use of the resources designed to accompany the textbook. There you will find chapter-specific guides to further resources, including governmental, international, think-tank, pressure groups, and relevant journals sources. You will also find a glossary based on *The Blackwell Dictionary of Social Policy*, help sheets, and case studies, guidance on managing assignments in social policy and career advice.

PART II
Key Perspectives

8

Neo-liberalism

Nick Ellison

Overview

- Neo-liberal ideas pose a significant challenge for supporters of extensive systems of public welfare because they believe these systems are expensive, inefficient, and unnecessary.
- Neo-liberalism has its roots in classical liberal thinking and in the writings of Adam Smith in particular. Core ideas have changed little over time with the belief in individual freedom and the free market continuing to underpin neo-liberal ideals.
- Late twentieth-century neo-liberalism is closely associated with the work of Friedman and Hayek, the latter refining ideas of 'negative liberty' and the role of free market to challenge socialist and social democratic conceptions of 'social justice'.
- For neo-liberals, public welfare systems need to be cut back to: eliminate bureaucratic waste, reduce taxation, and allow greater choice through private service provision.
- For all its apparent elegance, neo-liberal thinking contains critical flaws. The conception of 'negative liberty' is unduly restricted and the faith in pure market solutions may be misplaced.

The Neo-liberal Challenge

Neo-liberal ideas are immensely challenging for those who believe that the state has a central role to play in the organization and delivery of 'welfare' in economically developed societies. Why? Because neo-liberals fundamentally question the need for the majority of publicly funded, state-delivered, or state-regulated institutions that, taken together, comprise a 'welfare state'. As they developed from the 1960s onwards, the core beliefs and principles of neo-liberalism are best understood as a concerted attack on the comprehensive systems of social protection that emerged in Western Europe and the United Kingdom in the immediate post-war period, as well as on

The Student's Companion to Social Policy, Fourth Edition. Edited by Pete Alcock, Margaret May, Sharon Wright.
© 2012 John Wiley & Sons, Ltd. Published 2012 by John Wiley & Sons, Ltd.

socialist and social democratic assumptions about the importance of social equality and social justice that underpinned them.

Two important arguments stand out. First, neo-liberals believe that nation-states were undermined economically during the post-war period (roughly 1945–80) because governments diverted resources away from productive, entrepreneurial firms and individuals operating in the free market to the systematic state-based protection of vulnerable sections of their populations. The high taxation required to sustain levels of welfare provision that went beyond a basic 'safety-net' for the worst off reduced the scope for private sector investment. Second, neo-liberals argue that comprehensive social protection does not work anyway. For one thing, public money is wasted on vast welfare bureaucracies that appear keener to preserve their own budgets than to provide a good level and choice of services to those in need; for another, welfare recipients tend to become 'welfare dependent' and so fail to act as responsible individuals earning in the marketplace and looking after themselves and their families.

These claims about the damaging effects of state welfare will be examined in more detail below. It is worth noting here, however, that, whether or not neo-liberal ideas are considered valid, they force those who engage with them to think hard about their own values and beliefs. How 'responsible' should individuals be for their own welfare and well-being, for example? How far should the state intervene to support the lives of vulnerable individuals and groups? Conversely, should the free market and individual freedom be regarded as the key organizing principles of human societies? A brief historical survey of classical liberalism and its contemporary – neo-liberal – variant will show how perennial these questions are and how relevant they remain to modern social policy.

From Classical Liberalism to Neo-liberalism: A Historical Survey

The roots of neo-liberalism lie in the particular understandings of the nature of the free market and individual freedom developed by liberal political economists in the late eighteenth and nineteenth centuries. Although writing in political, social, and economic circumstances very different from his modern-day counterparts, Adam Smith (1723–90) is regarded as the founding figure of a philosophy that considers the free market to be the main organizing feature of society and believes state intervention in market activities to be inherently destructive. Smith argued that the market could secure individual *and* social welfare, and, most importantly, human liberty. It could create these benefits in his view because, paradoxically, individuals' self-interested pursuit of wealth naturally leads to *collective* prosperity. Simply put, the selfish desire to prosper and make a profit is constrained by competition in the marketplace because free competition among producers inevitably leads to falling prices and thus a 'natural' balance between supply and demand. So long as this self-correcting mechanism is allowed to function unhindered prosperity would be assured. Indeed, the only justification for interference in the marketplace, so far as Smith was concerned, was precisely to preserve its freedom. A legal framework for market operations is important, for instance, as is the provision of certain public goods like law and order and public health.

This basic set of beliefs was endorsed and extended by successive generations of liberal thinkers in the Victorian era – with one interesting twist. While Smith and early Victorian thinkers like Ricardo were primarily concerned with the role of the free market and the place of free individuals within it, their later Victorian counterparts took the further step of elevating this economic individualism into a political creed that stressed the virtues of individual responsibility, hard work, and 'self-help'. As Heywood (2003: 53) has noted, Samuel Smiles' popular volume *Self-Help* (1859) 'begins by reiterating the well-tried maxim that "Heaven helps those who help themselves"'.

These ideals of individual liberty, the free market, and the minimal state, with the added element of self-help, make up the classical liberal legacy. Neo-liberals like Friedrich von Hayek and Milton Friedman writing in the post-war period more or less reproduced these ideas in their own thinking – but enhanced particular aspects in their sustained attack on the failings of twentieth century state collectivism embodied in the 'Keynesian welfare state'.

Neo-liberalism in the Late Twentieth Century

Friedman is best known for his commitment to limited government and the conviction that individuals' natural initiative and drive can only be released if they are allowed to compete freely in the marketplace (Friedman 1962). He was particularly critical of Keynesian economic policies designed to stimulate demand in periods of economic recession because the government borrowing that this entailed only served to fuel inflation. Friedman argued that governments should restrict their activities to controlling the amount of money in the economy at any time – expanding or contracting money supply depending on the balance of inflationary and deflationary tendencies, but otherwise keeping taxes and spending low so as not to distort market outcomes.

Hayek's ideas pushed beyond economics into a developed neo-liberal political philosophy. The free market and minimal state were cornerstones of this perspective, but Hayek also built on the ideal of human liberty proposed by Smith and

---

Box 8.1 Key Principles

Human liberty – the freedom of individuals to act as they choose providing only that their actions are consistent with the liberty of *others.*

A competitive market economy – kept as free as possible from state interference.

Preservation of the rule of law – a constitutional framework that limits state powers and institutionalizes rules of property and contract.

Minimal public provision – applying only to those goods like public health that markets are unable to provide efficiently.

'Safety-net' security – for older people and others unable to work in the marketplace.

---

others. In particular he used a concept of 'negative freedom' to underpin an approach to politics and society that proved particularly influential for a generation of neo-liberal thinkers that emerged in the late 1970s and 1980s in the United Kingdom and United States. For Hayek (1990: 12), freedom meant 'independence of the arbitrary will of another'. Individuals were 'free' so long as they were not coerced into decisions or actions that they would not otherwise take. Indeed, like Smith, the only form of 'coercion' that Hayek would countenance was from a minimal state dedicated to ensuring, through an agreed impersonal legal framework, that private individuals could not arbitrarily limit others' actions and choices.

This understanding of liberty is 'negative' because it argues that individuals should be free *from* constraints – what individuals do with their freedom is a private matter. Hayek believed that human liberty and the free market, working through a process of 'catallaxy', would create a natural, spontaneous socio-economic order more efficient and less coercive than the interventionist systems produced by Keynesian-social democratic forms of governance. Attempts to interfere with this natural order – however well meaning – would only increase coercion and reduce liberty. Hayek (1990: 385) was especially critical of efforts to 'limit the effects of accident' through policies designed to produce greater 'social justice', arguing that policy-makers and others could not possibly possess the necessary levels of information to ensure a better distribution of justice than that achieved in the marketplace – indeed it was a 'conceit' even to try. This conviction that the organization of society should approximate closely to the 'natural order' produced by the market inspired the neo-liberal attack on state welfare systems in the 1970s and 1980s.

Neo-liberalism and Welfare

For neo-liberals, 'welfare states' with their large, complex public welfare bureaucracies are inherently coercive. Coercion comes through monopolistic state provision of social services, which has the effect of 'squeezing out' private and voluntary alternatives, thus limiting both consumer choice and the freedom of individuals to supply welfare

Box 8.2 Two Concepts and Five Remedies

Two concepts
- Bureaucratic over-supply – key public servants will devise budget-maximizing strategies to increase salaries and prestige as opposed to dispensing high-quality services to client populations.
- State coercion – state welfare services are monopolistic and therefore restrict choice.

Five remedies
- Reduction of state welfare provision – reduced state activity will allow private and voluntary organizations to enter the welfare marketplace, cutting the costs of public sector bureaucracy.
- Greater choice of services – new service-providers will allow welfare consumers greater choice of provision.
- Negative income tax – the state should subsidise low earnings through NIT to ensure continued participation in the labour market.
- Safety-net welfare – individuals should be encouraged to insure against risk. The poorest will need public support, but income should be provided at subsistence level and services delivered through voucher schemes.
- Tax cuts – savings from the closure of monopolistic state bureaucracies should be returned to individual earners through tax cuts.

interest in expanding the size of their budgets 'because their salaries and frills of office vary directly with the size of the budgets they administer' (Seldon 1987: 7). This tendency is compounded by politicians, who collude with budget maximization strategies because they believe that voters respond positively to public spending on key services. Unfortunately, according to neo-liberal thinkers, politicians are less keen on raising the taxes required to pay for these services with the result that 'bureaucratic over-supply' inevitably leads to unmanageable public sector deficits and budget crises.

Taken together monopolistic behaviour that crowds out alternative service-providers combined with civil servants' tendencies to protect their own budgets are perhaps the worst evils of state welfare for neo-liberals. However, Seldon lists a number of other features that exacerbate the problem. For example, the high taxation required to fund extensive public welfare systems depresses incentives and therefore reduces risk-taking in the marketplace. Again, owing to lack of competition, state-supplied services tend to neglect quality, while public sector employers and (unionized) employees can be resistant to change, thereby compromising innovation in terms of both choice and quality of service. Finally, Seldon makes the point that the real losers in the welfare game are the poor. Low-income groups lack the resources to contest bureaucratic decisions and pay a higher proportion of their earnings in taxation to fund poor-quality services. Moreover as Murray (1984) argues, lack of choice leads to welfare dependency and failures of personal responsibility because families on low-incomes are not encouraged to take active decisions about the goods and services they require, or to budget to meet their costs.

So neo-liberals clearly have a different conception of 'welfare' to that prevailing in many of the developed economies in the post-war period. As Minford (1991) argues, the waste associated with monopolistic provision and over-supply can be reduced through privatization strategies, which would widen individual choice and encourage individuals to understand that many services should be paid for. In his view, the state should provide only a minimal 'safety-net' for the poorest, provided through a Negative Income Tax (NIT) to subsidize low wages and maintain work

goods and services. The fact that most people in the United Kingdom have to obtain medical care from the state-run National Health Service and education from state comprehensive schools constrains choice, according to neo-liberals, and thus restricts human liberty.

In addition to the problem of state coercion, neo-liberal thinkers like Seldon and Minford in the United Kingdom, and Public Choice economists such as Niskanen and Tullock in the United States, have argued that civil servants have an incentives. This system would replace costly means-testing with effectively one 'payment' covering housing costs and other recognized needs associated with, for instance, family size. Elsewhere, health and education services would have to be 'paid for' by vouchers, which could be exchanged at surgeries and schools of choice. For Minford, there would be no extra help for vulnerable groups like retired people, who should have made provision for their old age during their working life. Echoing Murray's views, support for single parents should be minimal because 'there is a trade-off . . . between alleviating distress and encouraging the conditions for more distress' (Minford 1991: 79). Finally, savings made from the reduction of state welfare services would be handed to individuals in the form of tax cuts so they can use a greater proportion of their earnings to buy services of their choice.

Neo-liberalism and Welfare: A Critique

Although neo-liberal arguments about the size, power, and expense of state welfare systems are compelling, they have certain conceptual difficulties (see also Box 8.3). Four key criticisms question the core assumptions that underpin the neo-liberal approach. First, might it be that the definition of human liberty employed by Hayek and others is too narrow? It focuses exclusively on *individuals* and, as mentioned, is conceived negatively as 'freedom from' constraint. This understanding dismisses a 'positive' conception of liberty cast in terms of various social groups' 'freedom to' enhance their potential and prospects. Women, disabled people, and minority ethnic populations, for example, typically have less access to resources and suffer from greater discrimination than others. To offset these disadvantages, it may be that they need to pursue specific political objectives and demand particular policies that can increase their *collective* opportunities, thus adding to the liberties of individual members.

Second, as Plant (1990) argues, neo-liberals do not distinguish between 'freedom' and 'ability'. For Plant, the free market distributes income and resources neither fairly nor equally, and those with less earning power and few other advantages have less *ability* to use their liberty than wealthier individuals. Lacking access to particular goods (the best education and health care) they are not in a position to make the most of their notional freedom.

Third, state institutions are not necessarily more coercive than their private sector counterparts. *Any* organization can be insensitive to the needs of its 'customers' – and state welfare agencies are certainly no exception. Nevertheless, private sector service providers can also 'coerce' consumers by creating price cartels, thus restricting choice, or by providing 'selective information' about the benefits of their products. In each case, providers are able to circumvent the supposedly price-reducing environment of the competitive market. Arguably, too, state institutions can at least be called to account through the democratic process if service provision is unsatisfactory. Where neo-liberal objections about bureaucratic over-supply are concerned, critics would argue that executives and managers in the private sector appear no less successful at expanding salaries and budgets than their public sector counterparts.

Finally, on taxation and incentives, comparative analysis suggests that expectations about tax levels vary greatly in different countries. The United States and the United Kingdom favour low taxation on the grounds that it stimulates entrepreneurial behaviour and encourages personal responsibility. Scandinavian countries, however, despite some adjustments in recent years, tax highly and provide comprehensive social services as a basic citizenship right. High tax rates and an extensive welfare state do not

Box 8.3 Four Criticisms

Neo-liberals fail to:

- appreciate the potential of 'positive' freedom,
- distinguish between freedom and 'ability',
- appreciate that privately run institutions can also act coercively, and
- understand that the socio-cultural dimensions of welfare are important.

appear to have reduced Swedish economic competitiveness or created high levels of welfare dependency. Might it be that attitudes to taxation, incentives, and responsibility have a sociocultural dimension, which influences individuals' decision making and the kind of rationality they deploy?

Emerging Issues: Neo-liberalism in the Twenty-first Century

Neo-liberal thought has undoubtedly had an impact on economies and welfare systems in countries like the United Kingdom and the United States, and will continue to do so. Looking back over the thirteen years of New Labour governments in the United Kingdom, for example, these governments broadly accepted the free market as the principal system of resource allocation for the economy in a way that 'Old Labour' simply did not. It is true that New Labour's 'social justice agenda' saw a dramatic expansion of state services during the period with greater attention being paid to enhancing equal opportunities (if not equality) and reducing social exclusion. However, these concerns never hindered the enthusiasm for market solutions. Even in core areas of social provision like education and health care, where free market principles do not entirely hold sway, Labour governments, like their Conservative predecessors, mimicked market behaviour by creating 'internal markets' within publicly funded services. And 'welfare' certainly got tougher, with more conditions attached to benefit receipt, more means-testing, and greater official endorsement for the view that salvation for all but the most vulnerable groups lies in finding paid employment in the marketplace.

This verdict on New Labour leads to a particular conclusion about the influence of neo-liberalism. Although ideas alone are by no means the sole influence on policy making, they provide a basic 'road map' to preferred objectives and priorities. If neo-liberal ideas have not been implemented by governments (including Conservative governments) in any *pure* form, they have nevertheless provided the sustained ideological support required to ensure that demands for greater equality and social justice are understood *as subordinate to* the free market.

Looking ahead to the likely policies of the new Conservative–Liberal Democrat coalition government elected in the United Kingdom in May 2010, this order of priorities is set to persist. Adherence to market principles is the government's central article of faith – and with the public sector shouldering much of the financial burden generated by the banking crisis of 2008, concerns about social justice are set to become the preserve of the voluntary and community sectors, and private social enterprise (Cameron 2009, 2010). Meanwhile, in the words of the current UK Chancellor, the economy requires 'low tax rates and a simple tax system to attract and retain mobile capital and talent . . . light touch regulation to keep down costs and avoid stifling innovation [and] a flexible labour market that allows employers to respond to fast changing market conditions' (Osborne 2008: 1–2).

Guide to Further Sources

The 'classic' economic case for the free market and limited government is made by M. Friedman, *Capitalism and Freedom* (Chicago: Chicago University Press, 1962). For a more philosophical account of neo-liberal ideas, see F. Hayek, *The Constitution of Liberty* (London: Routledge, 1960). Essential reading for an understanding of the neo-liberal approach to state welfare is P. Minford, 'The role of the social services: A view from the New Right', M. Loney et al. (eds), in *The State or the Market: Politics and Welfare in Contemporary Britain*, eds (London: Sage, 1991), pp. 70–83. See also A. Seldon, *The New Economics*, Study Guide No 2 (London: Libertarian Alliance, 1987). C. Murray, *Losing Ground* (New York: Basic Books, 1984) provides a view from the United States.

The best short critique of the neo-liberal perspective is R. Plant, *Citizenship and Rights in Thatcher's Britain: Two Views, R. Plant and N. Barry* (London: IEA, 1990). For a general overview of liberal ideas see A. Heywood, *Political Ideologies: An Introduction* (3rd edn, Basingstoke: Palgrave, 2003).

Important speeches include: David Cameron, *The Big Society*, 10 November 2009 and *From Central Power to People Power*, 22 February 2010. George Osborne, *We Have to Mend Britain's Broken Society*, 15 July 2008.

Useful web sites include: the Adam Smith Institute (ASI), The Centre for Policy Studies, and Civitas, three neo-liberal think-tanks, run web sites that provide a wealth of information about contemporary neo-liberal thinking including current publications: www.adamsmith.org, www.cps.org.uk, and www.civitas.org.uk. Policy Exchange (www.policyexchange.org.uk) is a Centre-Right think-tank that broadly endorses neo-liberal ideas.

Review Questions

1 What are the key components of neo-liberal thought?
2 How do the ideas of Friedman and Hayek build upon Adam Smith's understanding of liberal political economy?
3 What are the key elements of the neo-liberal critique of state welfare systems?
4 What are the main criticisms that social democrats have levelled against neo-liberal ideas about welfare? How convincing are they?
5 How influential have neo-liberal ideas about the role and purposes of welfare states been over the past thirty years?

Visit the book companion site at www.wiley.com/go/alcock to make use of the resources designed to accompany the textbook. There you will find chapter-specific guides to further resources, including governmental, international, think-tank, pressure groups, and relevant journals sources. You will also find a glossary based on *The Blackwell Dictionary of Social Policy*, help sheets, and case studies, guidance on managing assignments in social policy and career advice.

9

The Conservative Tradition

Hugh Bochel

■■

Overview

- Emerging from groupings which opposed the ideas of the Enlightenment and the French Revolution, by the late nineteenth century the Conservatives were more accepting of the need for social reform, while at the same time emphasizing national unity and a strong defence and foreign policy.
- During the 1920s and 1930s a number of Conservative politicians sought to encourage the party to be more supportive of a greater role for the state in the economy and social reform.
- Following their return to government at the 1951 general election, the Conservatives maintained, and in some respects developed, the welfare state, leading some to claim that there was a cross-party consensus.
- By the 1970s the balance of power within the Conservative Party was shifting to the Right, and from 1979 the Thatcher and Major governments sought to roll back the frontiers of the state, including in most areas of social policy.
- Following his election as Conservative leader in 2005, David Cameron attempted to give the party a broader appeal, including policy proposals that appeared to indicate a move towards the political Centre, while the creation of the coalition government in 2010 led to new challenges.

■■

Conservatism

Conservatism has often been seen as difficult to define, for, as Norton has noted, 'There is no single corpus of Conservative dogma, no particu- lar text which Conservatives can hold aloft as representing the basis of their beliefs . . . [and] This in itself says something about the nature of British Conservatism' (Norton 1996: 68). Indeed, for much of the twentieth century the Conservative

The Student's Companion to Social Policy, Fourth Edition. Edited by Pete Alcock, Margaret May, Sharon Wright.
© 2012 John Wiley & Sons, Ltd. Published 2012 by John Wiley & Sons, Ltd.

Party was widely characterized as pragmatic in relation to ideas and policies, with its emphasis being on winning and exercising power, rather than ideology.

Nevertheless, it is possible to identify a Conservative outlook and Conservative beliefs. Broadly speaking, these can be seen as encompassing:

- A view which sees society as organic, as more than the sum of its individual parts, and as developing slowly and naturally, so that radical reform is often seen as potentially problematic; an acceptance of gradual change, but a scepticism about reforms which emerge from what may be passing fashions.
- A commitment to the ownership of property by individuals, with property seen as providing freedom and social stability.
- Support for the free market economy and a belief in the importance of market forces in wealth creation, with government intervention seen as inefficient, monopolistic, and damaging to individual freedom.
- A view that the wealthy have obligations, including to assist those who are less fortunate, for example though voluntary charity or through supporting a degree of social reform by the state.
- A belief that people are imperfect, and that there is a need for authority, a strong state and strong government to maintain law and order.
- A belief in the union of the United Kingdom, and key political institutions such as parliament and the monarchy.
- A willingness to be pragmatic and compromise, when necessary, including on these underlying beliefs.

While it is possible to identify many different strands of thinking within Conservatism, those which have been most widely seen as influential from the second half of the twentieth century have been One Nation Conservatism and neo-liberalism. Although some would argue that it draws upon and reflects a long strand of Conservatism, including the ideas of Disraeli and Baldwin, One Nation Conservatism is most associated with the One Nation Group of Conservative backbench MPs, which was formed in 1950, and

with the policies pursued by the Conservative governments of 1950 to 1964, which were generally supportive of the welfare state and the mixed economy. On the other hand, as discussed in more detail in Chapter 8, neo-liberalism argues that the state should play only a very limited role in economic and social affairs, seeing the market as a better way of providing and distributing goods and services.

The Development of Conservative Ideas

The Conservative Party grew out of the Tory Party, which had its origins in the seventeenth century, and which supported the monarchy, the Church of England, and the rights and interests of landowners. Toryism, and later Conservatism, tended to oppose the ideas which emerged from the Enlightenment from the late seventeenth to early nineteenth century, and many of the changes associated with industrialization. In particular, the French Revolution of 1789, and ideas associated with it, such as those of liberty, equality, and fraternity were opposed by conservative thinkers who felt deeply uncomfortable at the nature and scale of such change. For Edmund Burke and others, utopian political visions were doomed to fail because they worked against human nature, because change should come about through the organic development of society rather than through revolution, and because they contradicted the traditional framework of obligations and entitlements that they saw as underpinning British society.

Conservatism sought to maintain the economic, political, and social order against these pressures for change. Yet Conservatism was also able to accept change, and flexibility and pragmatism have continued to be key aspects of Conservatism, albeit with a preference for gradual rather than radical reform. As the franchise was widened in the nineteenth century Conservatism had to develop a new basis of support, becoming identified with the interest of property, and thus much of business, rather than simply landed property, and even seeking support from the working classes through the introduction of a degree of social reform. In the 1840s Peel's government introduced income tax as a temporary measure, creating a shift from indirect to direct taxation, and repealed the Corn Laws; under Disraeli in the 1870s, the Conservatives became the 'national party', associated with patriotism and a strong defence and foreign policy, but also displayed some early signs of a willingness to accept social reforms; and in the 1890s, Joseph Chamberlain and the Liberal Unionists sought to make the Conservatives the party of social reform, although with only limited success.

Conservatism and Social Reform

By the early twentieth century the Conservative Party was facing the challenges of Liberal collectivism and the growing strength of the Labour movement. It opposed most of the social reforms that were introduced by the Liberal governments from 1905 to 1915. However, when the Party was in power for much of the 1920s and 1930s, the paternalistic tradition and the pragmatic nature of Conservatism was obvious, particularly with the Baldwin government of 1924–9 having the avowed aim of reconciling the bitter differences in the country. The Conservatives therefore maintained the basic structures introduced by the Liberals, and indeed expanded some provision, including pensions, unemployment, and health insurance, and encouraged local authorities to develop hospital provision. However, unemployment remained high in many parts of the country, and the government made extensive use of means-testing. A strong element of concern over public morals within the Conservative Party also became evident at this time.

During the Second World War Churchill's Conservative-led coalition government introduced the 1944 Education Act, with the intention of improving educational opportunities for all, the 1945 Family Allowances Act, and published plans for major improvements in health care and social security. While the Conservatives opposed some of the key proposals of the Beveridge Report during the 1945 general election campaign, they retained a generally positive approach to social and economic intervention, including a commitment to high levels of employment, and promises to build at least 220,000 homes in the first two years in office, to develop a compulsory National Insurance scheme, and to create a comprehensive

health service with no one excluded from treatment because of an inability to pay. However, when Labour swept to victory in 1945 some more progressive Conservatives called for a clearer statement of principles and for a clearer vision for the Party in the post-war era.

In 1950 a group of nine backbench MPs came together to form the One Nation Group, the publications and ideas of which have frequently been seen as underpinning the Conservatives' approach to social policy through the 1950s and into the 1960s. The extent to which this was actually the case, and the extent to which there was a consensus between the political parties on the future of the welfare state from 1951 to 1979, is perhaps debatable, but as with the Liberal reforms of the early twentieth century, the Conservatives, particularly under Macmillan's premiership, maintained a commitment to full employment, an incomes policy, and social welfare, including developing further some parts of the welfare state.

However, when Macmillan resigned as prime minister on health grounds in 1963, and with the Conservative Party's defeat at the 1964 general election, the strength of the One Nation strand within the Party was arguably in decline and the door open for the growing influence of neo-liberal thinking.

Conservatism and Neo-liberalism

While the Heath government of 1970–4 saw some shifts in emphasis towards the free market policies associated with neo-liberalism, high levels of unemployment saw these abandoned, and it was not until 1976, when Margaret Thatcher became leader of the Conservative Party, that the shift within the Party moved markedly in favour of the 'New Right' wing of the Party and their neo-liberal views, including on free market economics and the responsibility of individuals and families for their own welfare.

This was a period when the Conservative Party sought to 'roll back' some elements of the expansion of the state that had taken place since the end of the Second World War, but at the same try to ensure that when government did act, it would be able to do so effectively. The concern was therefore with smaller, although not necessarily weaker, government, and a greater role for the market and market forces. Although 'Thatcherism' was, in some respects, complex and even contradictory, there were a number of ideas which were visible across government activities during the period from 1979–97, some of which have continued to impact upon Conservative Party policies up to the Cameron government.

Drawing upon neo-liberal ideas, from 1979 there was an emphasis upon:

- Monetarism – the idea of tackling inflation through controlling the money supply, rather than trying directly to limit price and wage increases was fundamental to Thatcherism, although the Thatcher governments frequently missed their money supply targets and later played down the idea. Monetarism has also been credited with substantially increasing unemployment during the 1980s, although this in itself might have had some impact on reducing inflation.
- Privatization and competition – the Thatcher governments' preference for the market was illustrated by the privatization of state-owned industries and utilities (including electricity, gas, and telecommunications), as well as the sale of council houses, often at substantial discounts, to tenants. Compulsory competitive tendering was introduced for many ancillary services, such as hospital cleaning and laundry provision. Even where it was not possible to introduce private sector providers the Conservatives sought to create market-type systems, such as 'parental choice' of schools, and a split between 'purchasers' and 'providers' in health care
- Trade union reform – through a series of seven Acts between 1979 and 1990 the rights of trade unions were gradually restricted, making collective action through unions much more difficult. At the same time the government also sought not to become openly involved in trying to resolve disputes.
- Reforming government – although having come to office committed to reducing the number of quangos, the Thatcher governments shifted responsibility for many of the functions of central government to semi-autonomous agencies. While intended to strengthen the position of managers and increase efficiency, these changes also led to

a blurring of accountability. In addition, controls were introduced limiting the ability of local authorities to raise taxation (initially household rates, later the community charge ('poll tax') and then council tax).
- Cutting tax – Thatcher and her supporters believed that high taxation had been damaging to entrepreneurialism and the economy and sought to reduce the levels of taxation, including through the use of receipts from privatization and revenue from North Sea Oil, although the emphasis was primarily upon cutting income tax, while VAT, which is paid by everyone regardless of their income, was increased.

While the Thatcher governments made significant changes in some areas of social policy the extent of real cuts and change in the welfare state should not be overstated. In addition, despite the anti-state and anti-public expenditure rhetoric, the Thatcher governments were not particularly successful at cutting public expenditure, in part because high levels of unemployment led to higher expenditure on welfare benefits.

Indeed, while in many respects the Thatcher governments did mark a significant break with what had gone before, including being more conviction-led and ideologically driven, at the same time they also displayed a significant degree of pragmatism.

Searching for Direction

Following Margaret Thatcher's resignation in 1990, John Major won the 1992 general election and continued with broadly similar approaches to social policy, albeit with a Conservative Party that was deeply divided, particularly over Europe. If part of Thatcher's legacy was to leave the traditionally pragmatic Conservative Party more ideologically driven than it ever had been, the election of the Labour Party (then branded as 'New Labour') in 1997, under the leadership of Tony Blair, posed new challenges for the Conservative Party that took many years for it to respond to successfully. Labour's shift towards the political centre ground from the mid-1990s, its apparent control over the political agenda, and the Conservatives' attachment to Thatcherism, meant that it was hard for the Conservatives to develop a new identity and approach to policies. In particular, the Party's commitment to tax cuts was difficult to square with the public's apparent desire for increased expenditure on public services.

Major's successor, William Hague, arguably sought to follow Blair by 'modernizing' the Conservatives in a similar fashion to that which had created 'New Labour'. He also sought to reach out to potential supporters with a more liberal line on some social issues, including gender, race, and sexuality. However the Conservatives remained committed to privatization and tax cuts, and failed to convince the public that public services were safe in their hands. Ultimately his period as leader was characterized by attempts to consolidate the Party's core support, including by hardening its line on Europe.

Hague was followed as Conservative leader by Iain Duncan-Smith, whose leadership followed a broadly similar pattern, with attempts to be more socially inclusive, to be more positive about public services, and to recognize the Party's past shortcomings. Like Hague, these attempts failed to generate widespread support within the Party and he resigned in late 2003. However, Duncan-Smith's vision of 'compassionate Conservatism' did find an audience among some new, young, Conservative MPs who would eventually come to prominence.

The next Conservative leader was a former Home Secretary, Michael Howard, whose leadership was seen by many as something of a return to the Thatcher and Major era, and which saw little by way of policy development.

A Return to Pragmatism?

While Hague, Duncan-Smith and even Howard did make some attempts to develop more socially liberal and inclusive approaches, each moved back to the Right over time. Following Howard's resignation David Cameron became Conservative leader in December 2005. Almost immediately he sought to move the Conservatives towards the centre ground, arguing that economic stability should take precedence over tax cuts, that the Conservatives would support action to promote social justice and combat poverty, and arguing that the Party should reach out beyond its core support.

Cameron's early years as leader could largely be characterized as ones of statement of principle from the leader, together with assertions that policies take time to develop. However, despite a relative absence of policy development Cameron was attempting to change public perceptions of the Conservatives, including through a number of symbolic and policy shifts, such as his statement in 2006 that 'there is such a thing as society, it's just not the same thing as the state', deliberately designed to set Cameron apart from Margaret Thatcher's famous claim that 'there is no such thing as society'.

He established a number of policy review groups, including on 'public services improvement', 'social justice', and 'globalization and global poverty', some of which involved people from outside mainstream party politics. These produced a series of 'Policy Green Papers' which could be seen as having a number of broadly common features including: the continued use of assessment and sanctions for benefit claimants; the commitment to greater involvement of the voluntary and social enterprise sectors in society and in the provision of public services, together with a significant role for the private sector; choice for consumers; and reductions in bureaucracy, but the retention of mechanisms such as audits and inspections.

Cameron also drew significantly on the work of the Centre for Social Justice, established by the former Party leader, Iain Duncan-Smith, including its reports on *Breakdown Britain* and *Breakthough Britain*. Indeed, the idea that society was 'broken', whether applied to poverty, family breakdown, or problems with public services, became a major theme for Cameron and the Conservatives in the run-up to the 2010 general election, as did the view that to respond to this situation there was a need for a smaller state, with some of its functions being replaced by charities, community organizations, and social enterprises, encompassed for Cameron in the term the 'Big Society'.

By the time of the 2010 general election Cameron had to some extent therefore adjusted the Conservative 'brand', and was seeking to portray a different sort of Conservatism from that which had dominated the Party for more than thirty years.

Emerging Issues

The past decade has seen significant shifts in the Conservatives' approach to social policy. Under David Cameron, in particular, there were attempts to dissociate the Party from some of the ideas and policies of the Thatcher era. However, despite such changes the Party failed to win the 2010 general election outright, and was forced into a coalition government with the Liberal Democrats an outcome which in itself was likely to have implications for the shape of Conservatism.

The new government's policies following the election help highlight the apparent continuing tensions over direction within the Conservative Party. The commitment to maintain expenditure and front line services on schools and the NHS may be seen as drawing upon One Nation ideas, yet at the same time, the depth of cuts in spending on other services (ostensibly as a reaction to the need to cut public expenditure following the financial crisis of 2008–9), the calls for a smaller state and for greater private, third sector and citizen involvement in the delivery of services, can be seen as echoing many of the neo-liberal influenced policies of the 1980s and 1990s.

Guide to Further Sources

T. Bale, *The Conservative Party: From Thatcher to Cameron* (Cambridge, UK: Polity Press, 2010) – an interesting consideration of the Conservative Party and its problems from the end of the Thatcher period to the emergence of David Cameron. H. Bochel (ed.), *The Conservative Party and Social Policy* (Bristol: Policy Press, 2011) covers the development of Conservative social policy from the 1990s with a focus on the period since 2005 and the coalition government with the Liberal Democrats in 2010. The book includes discussion of general ideas and major areas of social policy.

J. Charmley, *A History of Conservative Politics Since 1830* (2nd edn, Basingstoke: Palgrave Macmillan, 2008) provides a useful history of the Conservatives from Peel's leadership in the 1830s to David Cameron's election to the leadership in 2005. It highlights both the ideas and the individuals that have contributed to the party's development through almost two centuries. K. Hickson (ed.), *The Political Thought of the Conservative Party Since 1945* (Palgrave Macmillan, 2005) contains a number of chapters which consider not only the traditional ideological positions associated with the party, but others which focus on particular themes, such as social morality and inequality. P. Norton (ed.), *The Conservative Party* (New York: Prentice Hall/Harvester Wheatsheaf, 1996) although somewhat dated, many of the chapters, particularly in Part I, continue to provide valuable analyses of British Conservatism

The web site of the Conservative Party, www.conservatives.com, provides access to a wide range of information on the Party, particularly of a contemporary nature

In addition, the web sites of right-leaning think-tanks also contain a variety of information and publications, such as www.adamsmith.org, www.centreforsocialjustice.org.uk, www.civitas.org.uk, www.cps.org.uk, and www.iea.org.uk.

Review Questions

1 Can you identify the significant shifts in Conservative approaches to the welfare state since 1945?

2 How visible are One Nation and neo-liberal views in the policies adopted by the Conservatives since 2010?

3 To what extent is it possible to see echoes of Thatcherism in Conservative Party policies since 2006?

4 Why do neo-liberal and One Nation Conservatives take different approaches to the role of state welfare?

5 In what ways might 'pure' neo-liberals criticize the social policies of the Thatcher and Cameron governments?

Visit the book companion site at www.wiley.com/go/alcock to make use of the resources designed to accompany the textbook. There you will find chapter-specific guides to further resources, including governmental, international, think-tank, pressure groups, and relevant journals sources. You will also find a glossary based on *The Blackwell Dictionary of Social Policy*, help sheets, and case studies, guidance on managing assignments in social policy and career advice.

10

Social Democracy

Robert M. Page

Overview

- In the modern era the term social democracy has been used to describe parties, governments, or states which have sought to exert political control over capitalism in order to achieve greater equality and social justice.
- Social democratic welfare states are characterized by a commitment to egalitarianism, the maintenance of full employment, and a wide range of high quality universal welfare services.
- Although it is possible to draw fine distinctions between social democracy and democratic socialism, the terms tend to be used interchangeably.
- Modernized social democratic approaches have been adopted by some Centre-Left political parties such as New Labour.
- Public support for traditional social democratic parties appears to be in decline across Western Europe.

What is Social Democracy?

Social democrats believe that political institutions should be used to control or constrain market forces for the advantage of all citizens rather than a particular sectional interest. This is to be achieved through democratic means rather than through violent forms of revolutionary change.

Many nineteenth-century social democratic movements and political parties were supportive of class-based, economically determinist, Marxist critiques of capitalism. However, by the end of the nineteenth century, revisionists, such as the German social democrat Eduard Bernstein, expressed doubts about the inevitability of revolutionary change given that the operation of

The Student's Companion to Social Policy, Fourth Edition. Edited by Pete Alcock, Margaret May, Sharon Wright.
© 2012 John Wiley & Sons, Ltd. Published 2012 by John Wiley & Sons, Ltd.

capitalism had not, as anticipated, led to a significant decline in working class living standards. Bernstein believed that social democrats should form progressive, democratic cross-class alliances in order to curb market excesses. By the end of the First World War, a clear division had emerged between revolutionary communist parties and the more reform minded social democratic parties.

Social democracy became influential in Western Europe during the second half of the twentieth century. Indeed, Berman suggests that it became 'the most successful ideology of the twentieth century: its principles and policies under girded the most prosperous and harmonious period in European history by reconciling things that had hitherto seemed incompatible – a well-functioning capitalist system, democracy and social stability' (2006: 6). While this statement has considerable validity, it does hint at the possibility of diverse forms of social democracy. As Gamble and Wright (1999) point out, social democracy

> is not a particular historical programme or political party or interest group, or even an unchanging set of values. As a political movement its only fixed point is its constant search to build and sustain political majorities for reforms of economic and social institutions which counter injustice and reduce inequality. (1999: 2)

A broad definition of this kind can encompass those political parties or governments which believe that only modest interventions are necessary to constrain market 'failures' as well as those that believe that the pursuit of social justice requires much more extensive forms of state action. Given the lack of doctrinal purity within social democracy, such diversity is to be expected though it is far from unproblematic. There is a continuing debate among social democrats over the question of whether it is sufficient to 'humanize' capitalism or whether more far reaching changes should be pursued.

Although social democracy is not a static entity given its need to respond to the dynamic nature of capitalism, it has tended to be associated with particular patterns of economic and social intervention at specific points in time. In the second half of the twentieth century, for example, Western European social democracy has been associated with 'Keynesian' forms of economic interventionism which were designed to secure full employment and economic growth, as well as redistributive forms of state welfare. Indeed, those nation states which have been most active in their pursuit of such policies, such as Sweden, have come to be regarded as emblematic social democratic nations or regimes.

Social Democratic Welfare States

State action to protect and promote the welfare of citizens, irrespective of labour market participation, has been a hallmark of social democracy. For social democrats the welfare state has come to be regarded as a vital means of promoting social solidarity. Given the elasticity of the concept of social democracy, one would expect to find a diverse range of social democratic welfare arrangements. Moreover, it can be argued that it is possible to tackle injustice and pursue equality by diverse configurations of public, private, voluntary, and informal provision. The key feature of a social democratic welfare state from this standpoint is the willingness to use state action to achieve progressive outcomes rather than adherence to a particular principle (universalism), method (public provision), or form of government (national rather than local). This will result in many countries being classified as social democratic welfare states even though they have different histories, traditions, and organizational arrangements.

It could be argued, in contrast, that the constituent features of a social democratic welfare state need to be defined more tightly. In his book *The Three Worlds of Welfare Capitalism*, Esping-Andersen (1990) contends that social democratic welfare regimes should be distinguished from both their liberal and conservative counterparts. For Esping-Andersen, a social democratic welfare regime is characterized by de-commodified, comprehensive, universal state welfare services provided on the basis of citizenship with relatively minor or marginal roles played by the private, voluntary, and informal sectors. Social democratic regimes of this kind have flourished in Scandinavia.

Sweden

Sweden has come to be regarded as an exemplar of a social democratic welfare state. This stems in part from the fact that the Social Democratic Party has been in power in its own right or in coalition almost continually since 1932 (the exceptions being 1976–82, 1991–4, and from 2006 to the present day). In attempting to create a more egalitarian society, the Social Democrats did not pursue a class based electoral strategy. Instead, they sought, successfully, to create a broad coalition of support. Per Albin Hansson, who led the Social Democrats from 1928 to 1946, adopted the term 'The People's Home' to emphasize his party's desire to govern in an inclusive way so that the values of equality, selflessness, and co-operation could take root as they would in an 'ideal' family. The achievement of this goal required the removal of class differences, the establishment of universal social services and industrial democracy.

Although the Social Democrats were highly critical of the exploitative nature of capitalism, they believed it could be reformed through purposeful government action and by enlisting the co-operation of industrialists and property owners. Crucially, they sought to use political influence, rather than nationalization, to regulate and control the market economy. This led one influential American journalist – Marquis Childs – to assert in a book entitled *The Middle Way* (1936) that the Swedish Social Democrats were pursuing a path midway between the free market capitalism that flourished in the United States and the centrally planned economic system of the USSR.

By the late 1930s the Social Democrats' 'middle way' had begun to take shape. Under the Saltsjobaden accord of 1938, employers and trade unionists entered into an agreement to work co-operatively so that economic productivity and worker prosperity could be enhanced without recourse to damaging industrial disputes. Although the government was not expected to be formally involved in these industrial agreements it had a major role to play in creating a macroeconomic climate conducive to full employment and in pursuing active labour market policies which enabled workers to move from declining industries to those that were prospering. The govern-ment was also expected to develop high quality welfare provision and to ensure that income was distributed in an equitable way.

In the period from the 1945 to the early 1970s, the key features of the Swedish social democratic welfare 'model' were put in place. Full employment, universal state welfare provision, industrial democracy, a solidaristic wage policy (designed by two leading economists Rehn and Meidner), and an active labour market programme became defining features of Swedish society. The development of high quality day care facilities also enhanced gender equality by providing women with the opportunity to undertake paid work.

The major post-1945 expansion of the Swedish welfare state came to a halt in the late 1970s and 1980s as economic growth slowed in a period marked by inflationary wage settlements, a sharp increase in oil prices, growing unemployment, and budget deficits. Attempts to revitalize the economy while maintaining full employment in the early 1980s resulted in some cutbacks in welfare expenditure. By the 1990s more stringent reforms were deemed necessary as Sweden struggled to cope with severe international financial pressures occasioned by its decision to deregulate its financial markets in the mid-1980s.

Global economic pressures of this kind have led the Swedish Social Democrats to reconsider their approach to the welfare state. This has resulted in more diverse welfare arrangements including increased levels of non-state provision, internal markets, and user charges. Such developments raise the question of whether such changes are compatible with the central 'tenets' of social democratic thought. In exploring this question, it is useful to consider whether modernized forms of social democracy might be emerging. For example, the New Labour government in Britain (1997–2010), attempted to pursue such a strategy. In order to give some context to New Labour's approach, it is useful first to consider the approach that Labour had previously been pursuing in the post-1945 era.

Democratic Socialism and Social Democracy in Britain

Although well established in much of Western Europe, the term social democracy does not have the same resonance in Britain. It is the related 'doctrine' of democratic socialism that tends to be used in the British context. British democratic socialism has both *ethical* and *Fabian* roots. Ethical socialists believed that the operation of capitalism, underpinned as it was by a legal system which permitted wealthy property owners to exploit and control the poor, was both unfair and immoral.

To counter such exploitation, the ethical socialists supported collective action and social reform in order to create a 'better' society. The so-called Fabian socialists (whose founding members included Sidney and Beatrice Webb and George Bernard Shaw) also favoured state collectivism and social reform. Although many Fabians shared the concerns of their ethical compatriots in terms of the de-humanizing impact of capitalism, they were more concerned with the inefficiency of the capitalist mode of production. Like the Marxists, the Fabians believed that capitalism was prone to crisis and that it would inevitably be superseded by a more efficient planned economy.

Unlike the Marxists, the Fabians did not believe that the abolition of capitalism would come about through violent means. They argued that a democratically elected, reform minded government would be able to transform unjust and inefficient economic and social arrangements. This Fabian approach underpinned the 1945–51 Labour governments of Clement Attlee. Planning and nationalization were the chosen instruments in the economic sphere, while the creation of the welfare state was seen as a way of taming the 'Five Giants' (want, ignorance, squalor, disease, and idleness) identified by Beveridge in his influential wartime Report on Social Insurance.

Although Labour was in principle committed to the establishment of an egalitarian society – a so-called socialist commonwealth – they lacked a clear blueprint as to how this was to be achieved. Indeed, following the Party's electoral defeat in 1951, so-called revisionists began to sketch out a more 'reformist' economic and social strategy. For example, in his seminal text *The Future of Socialism*, Anthony Crosland (1956) argued that post-war Britain could no longer be regarded as an 'unreconstructed capitalist society' (1956: 57). He contended that capitalist power and control had been diluted by the steady advance of democ-

racy, increasing degrees of state intervention, growing trade union influence, and the emergence of a more autonomous, socially responsive managerial class. For Crosland, these developments meant that different *means* should now be employed in order to achieve greater equality. Unlike 'fundamentalists' such as Bevan, Crosland believed that more extensive public ownership was no longer necessary for the creation of a socialist society. Instead the welfare state financed by progressive taxation was now accorded a key role in the pursuit of greater equality. Crucially, however, the success of this social strategy was dependent on economic growth so that improvements in the position of poorer groups within society were not dependent on reductions in middle class living standards.

Labour's gradual acceptance of this revisionist strategy is often seen as representing a shift from a *transformative* democratic socialist strategy to a more *reformist* social democratic approach. Indeed, it has even been suggested that a 'social democratic' consensus took root in Britain between 1945 and 1979, a period in which both Labour and the Conservatives accepted the need for high levels of employment, a mixed economy, and a welfare state. While the existence of such a welfare consensus remains a matter of dispute, there is greater agreement that any such accord came to an end with the election of Thatcher's neo-liberal inclined government in 1979.

New Labour and Modernized Social Democratic Social Policy

It has been argued that Labour's long period in the electoral wilderness (1979–97) was only ended after the Party developed a 'modernized' form of social democracy, which was championed by Tony Blair (who led the Party from 1994 to 2005) and by the sociologist Anthony Giddens, who popularized the notion of a 'Third Way' (see Chapter 20). For both Blair and Giddens, 'traditional' social democracy had become outmoded in an era which had witnessed the demise of communism, the growth of global markets, changing family and work patterns, and more diverse forms of personal and cultural identity. In their view, the Left–Right division was now obsolete and the false opposites of the past needed to be put to one side.

They believed, for example, that it was possible to be supportive of *both* the free market *and* social justice. Crucially, though, this twin pursuit was deemed to necessitate reform of the welfare state. For New Labour, a modern social democratic welfare state has seven distinguishing features.

1   *Active rather than passive welfare system:* A modern welfare state should be *active* rather than *passive*. All those of working age not currently in, but capable of, paid employment should be encouraged, by a mixture of incentives and sanctions, to return to work in order to avoid the debilitating effects of long term state dependency.
2   *Diverse range of publicly funded providers:* Although key services such as education and health care should continue to be publicly *funded*, there is no automatic need for them to be publicly *provided*. Voluntary organizations, social enterprises, and private firms working in the public interest may be able to provide services in a more efficient and effective manner.
3   *Consumer focused:* A modern welfare state should focus on the needs and preferences of service users, who are likely to demand more personalized services rather than the uniform and undifferentiated services favoured by producers.
4   *A better balance between universal and selective provision:* There is no longer any ideological reason for social democrats to be wedded to the principle of universalism. A modern social democratic government should be prepared to provide some services on a universal basis and others more targeted so that the needs of both taxpayers and service recipients are met as fully as possible.
5   *A focus on equalizing opportunities rather than outcomes:* Modern social democrats should be less concerned with inequalities of outcome and focus instead on ensuring that there are opportunities for all. Particular emphasis should be given to removing socially constructed barriers to individual mobility such as poor schooling or inadequate health provision.
6   *Promoting active forms of citizenship:* Individuals should be expected to take greater responsibility for promoting their own wellbeing and be encouraged to take a more active

role in their local community. The rights of citizenship come with social responsibilities. Instead of seeing state support as an unconditional right, citizens should regard such provision as a 'gift' exchange. Accordingly, citizens are expected to respond positively to government offers of financial support and training by making themselves available for work and taking advantage of the various opportunities they are provided with.
7   *Rigorous monitoring of service outcomes:* State funded welfare services should be regularly monitored to ensure that they are securing good outcomes for service users. In contrast to 'traditionalists', modern social democrats are more sceptical as to whether welfare providers can be trusted to deliver high quality, cost efficient services. Target setting, audit and inspection are deemed necessary to ensure that egalitarian outcomes are achieved.

The question remains of whether New Labour's modern approach to the welfare state can be described as social democratic. Critics argue that New Labour's rapprochement with neo-liberalism in the economic sphere has had a negative impact on their approach towards the welfare state. Certainly, it can be argued that three key features of traditional social democratic welfarism have been undermined.

■   *First*, the use of non-state providers and the incorporation of a market vocabulary has served to undermine the non-commercial ethos of public services as well as transforming citizens into consumers.
■   *Second*, New Labour's narrow focus on opportunity barriers has led them to neglect the need for redistributive measures to counter growing inequalities of income and wealth.
■   *Third*, New Labour's decision to link 'good' citizenship primarily to labour market participation has served to devalue non-commercial forms of community involvement.

Emerging Issues: Can Social Democracy Survive?

The long-term future of social democracy has been questioned in recent decades. In particular the lacklustre electoral performance of social democratic parties in both Germany (where the SDP won only 23 per cent of the popular vote in 2009) and Sweden (where the social democrats secured just 30 per cent of the vote in 2010, thereby failing to unseat the ruling Centre/Right coalition government for the first time since 1931) has led to the suggestion that social democracy is becoming unpopular and irrelevant. Could it be that the rise of globalization (which limits the possibility of autonomous economic control at the national level) and increased cultural and ethnic diversity (which can undermine long-standing integrative social bonds) will undermine social democracy? Support for political parties which challenge market imperatives is declining. As a consequence, social democracy, or at least that variant based on universal welfare, strong economic regulation and egalitarian forms of distribution, is in a perilous position. However, writers such as Judt contend that social democracy remains the best vehicle for security, prosperity, and greater equality.

Guide to Further Sources

Two of the best places to start in understanding social democracy are Donald Sassoon's magisterial overview of developments in socialist and social democratic thought and practice – *One Hundred Years of Socialism* (London: I.B. Tauris, 1996) and Sheri Berman's lucid account of the impact of social democracy in twentieth century Europe – *The Primacy of Politics* (Cambridge University Press, Cambridge, 2006). Michael Newman's *Socialism: A Very Short Introduction* (Oxford: Oxford University Press, 2005) provides a concise overview of social democracy within a broader socialist context.

Timothy Tilton's *The Political Theory of Swedish Democracy: Through the Welfare State to Socialism* (Oxford: Clarendon, 1991) and Sven Olsson's *Social Policy and Welfare State in Sweden* (2nd edn, Lund: Arkiv, 1993) have written informative studies of the development of Swedish social democracy and the welfare state.

Anthony Crosland's revisionist text, *The Future of Socialism* (London: Jonathan Cape, 1956; London: Constable, 2006), is still regarded as the most significant contribution to British post-war social democratic thought.

Anthony Giddens has published a number of influential texts on modern social democracy including *The Third Way: The Renewal of Social Democracy* (Cambridge: Polity Press, 1998); *The Third Way and Its Critics* (Cambridge: Polity Press, 2000); *Where Now for New Labour?* (Cambridge: Polity Press, 2000); and *Over to You Mr Brown* (Cambridge: Polity Press, 2007). Tony Blair's pamphlet *The Third Way, New Politics for a New Century* (London: Fabian Society, 1998) also sets out the case for the Third Way. Patrick Diamond has co-edited two revisionist social democratic collections: *Rethinking Social Democracy* (London: Policy Network, 2003, with Matt Browne) and *Beyond New Labour: The Future of Social Democracy in Britain* (London: Politico's, 2009), with Roger Liddle.

The future prospects for social democracy are addressed by Andrew Gamble and Anthony Wright, *The New Social Democracy* (Oxford: Blackwell, 1999). Chris Pierson, *Hard Choices: Social Democracy in the 21st Century* (Cambridge: Polity Press, 2001); Tony Fitzpatrick, *After the New Social Democracy* (Manchester: Manchester University Press, 2003); and Tony Wright's *Where Next? The Challenge for Centre-Left Politics* (Lomdon: IPPR, 2010). A spirited defence of social democracy is provided by Tony Judt's *Ill Fares the Land* (London: Allen Lane, 2009).

The Social Europe Journal provides topical discussions on developments in European social democracy, see www.social-europe.eu.

Policy Network is an international think-tank which seeks to debate and promote modernized forms of social democracy, see www.policy-network.net.

Review Questions

1 What are the distinguishing features of social democracy?
2 Why do you think a social democratic welfare state took root in Sweden in the twentieth century?
3 Did a 'social democratic' consensus occur in Britain between 1945 and 1979?
4 Why did New Labour believe that social democracy needed to be modernized in the 1990s?
5 Does social democracy have a future?

Visit the book companion site at www.wiley.com/go/alcock to make use of the resources designed to accompany the textbook. There you will find chapter-specific guides to further resources, including governmental, international, think-tank, pressure groups, and relevant journals sources. You will also find a glossary based on *The Blackwell Dictionary of Social Policy*, help sheets, and case studies, guidance on managing assignments in social policy and career advice.

11

Socialist Perspectives

Hartley Dean

Overview

The socialist perspective on social policy

- ■ Argues that capitalism as a social and economic system is inherently inimical to human well-being.
- ■ Regards the welfare state as an ambiguous phenomenon that has benefited disadvantaged and working-class people while also subjecting them to social control in the interests of capitalism.
- ■ Has nonetheless played a role in the development of social policy in capitalist societies.
- ■ Has informed past attempts to establish 'communist' social and economic systems with different approaches to welfare provision.
- ■ Represents an intellectually significant critique of particular relevance to our understanding of social inequality and the practical development of alternative social policies opposed to capitalism.

Socialism as Critique

Elements of socialist thinking have been traced back to a variety of sources, from the Bible to the seventeenth-century English Levellers. However, socialism is best understood, like Liberalism, as one of the principal 'metanarratives' of the post-eighteenth-century Enlightenment era. While liberalism champions individual freedom, socialism champions social equality. Socialism emerged in Western Europe as a political critique of the capitalist economic system and its social consequences.

The Student's Companion to Social Policy, Fourth Edition. Edited by Pete Alcock, Margaret May, Sharon Wright.
© 2012 John Wiley & Sons, Ltd. Published 2012 by John Wiley & Sons, Ltd.

Essential tenets

Socialism as a creed is humanistic, collectivist, and egalitarian. Modern socialism articulated itself in opposition to industrial capitalism: its de-humanizing effects, its individualistic competitive ethos, and the ways in which it exacerbated social inequality. Early socialists were utopians who drew upon religious authority or ethical argument for their beliefs, as indeed some do today. The writings of Karl Marx (1818–83), however, offered a brand of 'scientific' socialism that crystallized its essential tenets. His central insight is that it is the ownership of the natural, physical, technological, and financial resources required for the maintenance of life (the 'means of production') that determines the structure of society. Marx's argument was that human history has been a story of struggles between dominant and oppressed classes. Under capitalism – the most recent stage in human history – the mass of humanity has become alienated from the means by which to produce what it needs to sustain its own existence. Capitalism, however, contains the seeds of its own destruction, because the oppressed class under capitalism (the working class) will in time be able to seize control of the state apparatus established by the dominant class (the property owning capitalist class). Socialism, therefore, is the project by which workers' control will be exercised, leading in time to a classless or communist society in which human needs can be fully realized and properly satisfied. Marx did not offer a blueprint for a classless society. Nor was he a theorist of the welfare state, which did not exist in his lifetime. He offered an analysis of capitalism's unjust and contradictory nature and of the relations of social and economic power on which it was founded.

The capitalist welfare state did not emerge until the twentieth century. Certain of its proponents and supporters subscribed to some kind of socialism. From a socialist perspective, however, there are various ways in which we can interpret the role of the welfare state as it has in practice developed. We can distil these into three kinds of explanation: the instrumentalist, the structural-logical, and the neo-Marxist. These explanations overlap in some respects and they all contend that the capitalist welfare state remains a capitalist institution rather than the outcome of a socialist transformation.

Instrumentalist critiques

Some critics interpret literally a suggestion made by Marx that the state behaves as the managing committee of the capitalist class. The welfare state in capitalist countries ultimately serves the interests of the capitalist, not the working class. The key positions in government and administration are held by people from relatively privileged backgrounds or those who have an underlying allegiance to 'the establishment' and/or the status quo. The welfare state, by implication, is a conspiracy against the working class.

According to this explanation, the shape and nature of the welfare state is deliberately contrived to accord with the economic requirements of capital. The welfare state has become both the handmaiden of capitalism and its henchman. Through health and education policies, the state ensures an orderly supply of workers for industry and commerce, so reducing the costs of reproducing labour power. Through a range of social services the state ensures that the costs of the weak and vulnerable do not fall on industry. Through social security and labour market policies the state manages those workers who are unemployed or temporarily unproductive. Whereas Marx had pointed to the fundamental instability of capitalism, the welfare state has not hastened its demise but smoothed over its contradictions and helped sustain it.

Structural-logical critiques

A different line of reasoning is that the functioning of the state under capitalism is not a cunning conspiracy so much as a consequence of capitalism's structural constraints or immanent logic. The state behaves like a managing committee only in a metaphorical sense. It is not necessarily a willing handmaiden or henchman. It has a degree of autonomy. And yet, well meaning reformers remain, in part at least, captive creatures of circumstance. In the last instance it is economic imperatives that determine the outcomes of social policy. This happens because in order to survive the state must acknowledge certain priorities over which it has no control. For example, it must maximize economic growth, protect profits, and maintain social order. In liberal democracies economics trumps politics. It is deterministic or functional-ist argument.

A more abstract variation is that the essential form of the welfare state is derived from or mirrors the unequal relations of power that char-acterize capitalist market relations. So, just as capitalists obscure the exploitative nature of their relationship to labour through the legal fiction of the individual wage bargain, so the state obscures the disciplinary nature of its relationship to its citizens by making welfare goods and services appear as a form of 'social wage' or democratic settlement. Not only are social welfare reforms one-sided compromises driven by economic imperatives, but the beneficiaries of such reform are being ideologically manipulated in the inter-ests of capital so they cannot see the true nature of their oppression. This gloomy scenario can be lightened using the ideas of thinkers, such as Antonio Gramsci (1891–1937), who argued that not everyone is hoodwinked by capitalist ideol-ogy, nor are they necessarily persuaded by the inevitability of capitalism's logic. Part of the socialist project has to do with whose ideological interpretations of the world will dominate. Drawing on this kind of insight social policy can be understood not as the inevitable outcome of capitalist structures, but as a distillation of the class forces in play within an enduring political struggle. Socialism can act as a counter-hegemonic force.

Neo-Marxist critiques

Finally, there is a group of academics who in the 1970s brought together elements of the above critiques to produce a distinctive over-arching 'neo-Marxist' critique. In a critical review Klein (1993) dubbed this 'O'Goffe's tale'. The epithet captured the names of three of the most promi-nent contributors to the neo-Marxist critique: James O'Connor, Ian Gough, and Claus Offe. The essence of O'Goffe's tale is that the welfare state has proved to be an ambiguous phenomenon, since it exhibits two kinds of contradiction.

First, while the welfare state has brought real benefits to the working class and the most disad-vantaged members of capitalist society, it has also played a part in repressing or controlling them. The welfare state succeeded in increasing social consumption and living standards but capital

benefited more than labour, while poverty and inequality persisted. State welfare enhanced the productivity of labour, while minimizing the adverse social consequences of the capitalist eco-nomic system. It regulated both the quantity and the quality of labour power. The development of state welfare played a necessary part in constitut-ing the modern wage labourer and by according popular legitimacy to capitalism. It also subjected the working class to new forms of administrative scrutiny and normative control – through, for example, compulsory education and the condi-tions that attach to the receipt of many welfare benefits.

The second kind of contradiction was that the stabilizing influence which the welfare state had brought to capitalism would be fiscally and polit-ically unsustainable. Capitalism could neither survive without having a welfare state, nor could it endure the costs and implications of having one. To an extent, this prophecy has been borne out since many capitalist countries sought to 'roll back' their welfare states towards the end of the twentieth century and to shift the responsibility and costs of welfare provision from the public to the private sector, from the state to the individual or, in effect, from capital to labour. At the same time many poorer countries have been persuaded in their pursuit of capitalist economic develop-ment to establish no more than limited state welfare provision.

Socialism as Practice

Socialism is concerned not only to critique capi-talism conceptually, but to challenge it politically. There are anarchistic and libertarian socialists who have envisioned a society in which human welfare would be achieved though mutuality and co-operation, without any kind of state interven-tion. However, we shall concern ourselves with two strands within the socialist perspective that have sought practically to *harness* state power as a means of promoting human welfare: the gradu-alist and the revolutionary.

Gradualist socialism

The emergence of the capitalist welfare state is attributable, in part at least, to the effects of class struggle. Class agitation and the growth of the labour movement in capitalist societies were significant factors in the way in which – from the end of the nineteenth century onwards – state social welfare provision developed, although how this played itself out differed between countries. Socialism played a key part in helping mobilize the working class movement. While some socialists saw this mobilization as a step towards the overthrow of capitalism, others saw it as transition to socialism by stealth. This, as the twentieth century progressed, was the position of Fabian socialists (a key intellectual influence within the British Labour Party) and of Social Democratic parties across Europe (especially in Scandinavia, where the most extensive capitalist welfare states have been developed).

Gradualist socialist politicians, such as Anthony Crosland, argued that the development of a mixed economy and the policies of a Labour government in the post-Second-World-War period were such that by the 1960s a country like Britain was no longer a capitalist society in the original sense. However, it can also be argued that social liberalism was probably a stronger force than gradualist socialism in the creation of the modern welfare state. 'Enlightened' capitalists were prepared not only to concede some of the demands advanced by organized labour but to promote measures that would compensate for the foreseeable failures and correct the inherent instabilities of free market capitalism. The extension of state welfare, therefore, was implicated in the transition from industrial to post-industrial or 'advanced' capitalism in which both the state and the market play a role. Capitalism has changed and, by and large, Fabians and social democrats have become effectively resigned to improving this new form of capitalism, not overthrowing it; to the further amelioration by state intervention of the effects of market forces.

There is a distinction to be made between the contemporary social democratic perspective discussed in Chapter 10 and the socialist perspective. The former seeks to reform and extend the capitalist welfare state as an end itself; the latter in one way or another to supersede it. In practice, the distinction is not necessarily evident from the names by which political parties and organizations call themselves. For example, the Party of European Socialists (with 32 affiliated parties)

and the reformed Socialist International (with 170) include a mixture of parties from across the world which describe themselves variously as 'socialist', 'social democratic', or 'labour' parties, but whose shared objectives are clearly gradualist and more social democratic than socialist in essence.

Revolutionary socialism

Revolutionary socialism aims to overturn capitalism not by gradually transforming the state, but by taking command of it so it may properly serve the interests of the oppressed and working class. Marx's contention had been that if this were achieved the state would in time 'wither away' as a truly classless society emerged. There were in the course of the twentieth century examples of socialist revolutions – most notably in Russia in 1917 and China in 1949. The societies that resulted were called 'communist' regimes, despite the fact that in none of them did the state wither away. On the contrary, what characterized such societies was a highly centralized and enduring form of state planning. The countries in which socialist revolutions occurred were not at the time fully industrialized capitalist countries and revolution was pursued not so much by the organized working class as by vanguard activists. The programmes the activists adopted were informed by visions of human progress. The social and economic arrangements they wanted would be based not on the wastefulness of unfettered competition, but rational planning and co-operation. The intention was to maximize human welfare.

Even supporters of the socialist perspective admit that such examples of 'actually existing' socialism turned out to be a failure. Not only did 'communist' regimes never reach the stage when universal human welfare could be assured without state intervention, but in many instances the socialist project was cruelly stripped of its essential humanity. Initially, under the Soviet system, for example, citizens were guaranteed work with state enterprises that offered a range of social benefits as well as wages. Prices were subsidized. Housing, education, health care, and pensions were all provided. However, the standard and nature of provision were such that it often failed to satisfy human need. There are three explanations for this. First, the ruthless idealism of the original revolutionary activists entailed a desire to reform not only society, but the human race itself: however beneficent in intent, it was 'top-down' and authoritarian in nature. Second, such idealism was easily diluted, distorted, or corrupted: for example, the Stalinist era that succeeded the Bolshevik revolution became brutal and totalitarian. Finally, it may be argued that socialism should be an international project since it is impossible to establish socialism in just one country or one group of countries: in an interconnected world, dominated by capitalist modes of economic production and by global markets, systems such as that in the former Soviet Union can end up functioning not as state socialism, but as centrally regulated state capitalism. Alternatively, a small socialist country, such as Cuba with its impressive health and education systems, may suffer reduced living standards because its capitalist neighbours will not trade with it.

The Death of Socialism?

This leads to the suggestion that socialism is now dead: that the historic 'cold war' between socialism and capitalism has ended with a global victory for capitalism. Towards the end of the twentieth century we witnessed the collapse of Soviet communism. 'Post-communist' countries are now transforming themselves into capitalist welfare states. Even communist China is rapidly adopting market-based reforms. We have, supposedly, entered a postmodern age in which the metanarratives of liberalism and socialism have been superseded (see Chapter 14).

There are two questions that the socialist perspective must now address. The first has to do with the nature of social class and the unfashionable notion of 'class struggle'; the second with the global nature of capitalism and the scope for anti-capitalist social policies.

Class versus identity?

The concept of class has been central to the socialist perspective. But as we pass from the industrial age to an information age the nature of class structures in capitalist societies has been changing. And as we pass from the age of cultural

modernity to an age of post-modernity we have become preoccupied with issues of identity, not class.

Throughout the capitalist world the 'traditional' manual working class has been declining in size. In a 'high-tech' global environment, with increasingly flexible labour market requirements, the class divisions within post-industrial societies are complex, but there is a trend for such societies to become more unequal as the gap between rich and poor increases (see Chapter 26). There is an incontrovertible and enduring association between people's socio-economic status and their life chances. From a socialist perspective conceptualizing the class divide requires some sophistication, but the concept is, or ought to be, as meaningful as ever it was. Contemporary socialist theorists argue that, while there are those in capitalist societies who occupy anomalous or ambiguous class positions, there is still a fundamental distinction to be drawn between the many who sell their labour (whether it be manual, technical, or intellectual) in order to live and the few who own or control a significant amount of capital.

If, despite this, the idea of class has lost salience, this is in part because a new politics of identity has tended to displace the old politics of class. The past few decades have witnessed the emergence of new social movements, which address issues hitherto neglected in class-based struggles over the distribution of power and resources. These movements addressed human rights, global poverty, and ecological issues, but significantly they also included second-wave feminism, the black power, and anti-racist movements and, for example, movements of disabled people, older people, gays, and lesbians. The struggles these movements promoted were not about material redistribution, but 'parity of recognition' (Fraser 1997). They were concerned with social injustices arising from social divisions other than class. None of this necessarily precludes the possibility of alliances between movements and the combination of different struggles. Feminist socialism and eco-socialism, for example, now provide their own distinctive strands within the socialist perspective. What the socialist perspective emphasizes is the extent to which the social inequalities inherent in capitalism can exacerbate or fuel all kinds of oppression and injustice.

Emerging Issues

As an intellectual critique the socialist perspective plainly is not dead. Nor is it necessarily dead in any practical sense. So long as anywhere in the world there is active resistance to capitalism, socialism is more than an atavistic curiosity. There have, for example, been recent electoral successes for left-wing presidential candidates in several Latin American countries, the most radical of who has been Hugo Chavez in Venezuela. There have also been spectacular 'anti-globalization' demonstrations mounted against the World Trade Organization and the G8 summits of rich nations, though in practice the anti-globalization movement represents an eclectic mixture of political groups, social movements, and non-governmental bodies. Nonetheless, the emergence of organizations like the World Social Forum signals the basis of what might amount to an anti-capitalist alliance. The essential demand is for a more inclusive form of globalization, rather than a world shaped by capitalist market forces.

Writers like Callinicos (2003) have envisioned a global campaign for an anti-capitalist manifesto, including distinctively socialist social policies. A transitional programme that might incorporate such things as universal basic income, progressive and radically redistributive forms of taxation, widespread reductions of working hours, and the defence of public services, none of which by themselves would be sufficient to achieve socialism, but which together amount to a fundamental challenge to capitalism. The central question raised by the socialist perspective on social policy is whether the short-term interests of capitalism are compatible with the long-term needs of humanity.

Guide to Further Sources

For accessible general introductions, see Tony Benn's *Arguments for Socialism* (Harmondsworth: Penguin, 1980) and/or the late GA Cohen's *Why Not Socialism?* (Princeton, NJ: Princeton University Press, 2009). Different types of socialism are described in Tony Wright's *Socialisms* (London: Routledge, 1996).

Introductions to classic neo-Marxist thinkers may be found in V. George and R. Page (eds), *Modern Thinkers on Welfare* (Upper Saddle River, NJ: Prentice Hall, 1995). For a critique of neo-Marxism see Rudolf Klein's 'O'Goffe's tale', in C. Jones (ed.), *New Perspectives on the Welfare State in Europe* (London: Routledge, 1993), pp. 6–15. For a social policy text by revolutionary socialists, see I. Ferguson, M. Lavalette, and G. Mooney, *Rethinking Welfare: A Critical Perspective* (London: Sage, 2002). For a contrasting 'post-socialist' account, see Nancy Fraser's *Justice Interruptus: Critical reflections on the post-socialist condition* (London: Routledge, 1997). Interesting from a social policy perspective is Alex Callinicos' *Anti-Capitalist Manifesto* (Cambridge: Polity Press, 2003.)

Potentially useful web sites include the Socialist International www.socialistinternational.org, the Party of European Socialists www.pes.org, the World Social Forum www.worldsocialforum.org, and, from the United Kingdom, *Red Pepper Magazine* www.redpepper.org.uk.

Review Questions

1 What are the defining characteristics of the socialist perspective?
2 In what ways does the socialist perspective interpret the role of the welfare state?
3 To what extent has socialism been a practical influence on the development of social policy?
4 Where does the difference between socialism and social democracy lie?
5 What relevance, if any, does the socialist perspective have today?

Visit the book companion site at www.wiley.com/go/alcock to make use of the resources designed to accompany the textbook. There you will find chapter-specific guides to further resources, including governmental, international, think-tank, pressure groups, and relevant journals sources. You will also find a glossary based on *The Blackwell Dictionary of Social Policy*, help sheets, and case studies, guidance on managing assignments in social policy and career advice.

12

Feminist Perspectives

Shona Hunter

Overview

- The welfare state, its policies and practices construct and are simultaneously constructed through gender inequalities. It provides goods and services to support women, but at the same time fixes understandings of their needs.
- Feminists have used women's experiences to challenge what is understood by welfare to include the cultural and intimate spheres.
- Recent focus on the concept of care has informed the development of a feminist political ethic of care, creating new differentiated principles for welfare which recognize care as a valid human activity sustaining various welfare activities.
- More differentiated approaches to feminist social policy analysis bring issues of masculinity and relations of power and oppression to the fore, raising questions on how to reconcile gender inequality with other inequalities.
- Feminists interact with mainstream political structures to fight for gender inequality. However, there are complexities and costs. These are particularly acute in the contexts of moves to mainstreaming and financial austerity.

Feminist Questions

What does it mean to have a feminist perspective on welfare and social policy? There is a vast and changing range of contested responses to this question. Liberal, welfare, socialist, Marxist, and postmodern feminisms (to name a few) approach this question differently. Each is concerned in different ways about women's equality, their agency, gender relations, and social justice and how these are achieved, enabled, or hindered through the arrangement of welfare.

The Student's Companion to Social Policy, Fourth Edition. Edited by Pete Alcock, Margaret May, Sharon Wright.
© 2012 John Wiley & Sons, Ltd. Published 2012 by John Wiley & Sons, Ltd.

Liberal feminism, advocating the equal partici-pation of women in the public sphere, has a long history dating back as far as Mary Woolstonecraft's *A Vindication of the Rights of Women* published in 1792. Its influence is still seen in policies for equal employment rights, including equal pay and in anti-discrimination legislation. In contrast to liberal feminism is welfare feminism's concern to improve the lives of women in the private sphere, as wives, and mothers. Forwarded by a range of social reformers such as Beatrice Webb in the early 1900s, and Eleanor Rathbone in the 1930s, it can even be seen in Beveridge's 1945 welfare reforms. By the 1970s however, radical, Marxist and social-ist feminists were critical of the connection between women's public and private disempow-erment and the assumption as to the existence of natural, biological differences between men and women. Their arguments were around the impor-tant role of welfare in maintaining the subordina-tion of women in the home, which served to support the broader material and ideological needs of labour. Thus, the gendered division of welfare was viewed as an important means to reproducing class relations and maintaining the social stability necessary for the smooth running of capitalist labour relations.

These feminist debates show the complexities of understanding gendered inequalities; where being treated the same as men causes a problem for women because of the neglect of their specific needs (as mothers for example), but being treated differently on the basis of an assumed women's specificity can lock women into unequal and dependent relations with men and constitutes the source of their inequality.

Later, in the 1980s and 1990s postmodern feminists have critiqued the universalizing and generalizing nature of earlier debates over same-ness and difference. Their aim is to think about the *differential* relationships of various groups of older, black, disabled, and heterosexual women to welfare arrangements and their varying material and social consequences. This sort of approach emphasizes the dynamic, changing, and contra-dictory processes of welfare and its *changing gen-dered relations* between men and women, rather than assuming universally disempowering conse-quences of social policies for women.

At their most radical, feminist analyses have the potential to expose and transform how we understand the very notions of welfare and the state as gendered. That is, how the state is both defined through, and defining of, broader social and cultural formations of gender. The key issue here is not to measure levels of gendered inequal-ity (though this is part of an analysis), but to explore how the social and cultural categories of gender (being a woman or a man) come to be understood and constructed through the institu-tions, practices, and policies of the welfare state. Feminists have used women's lived experiences and agency as household heads (hetero)sexually active partners, caregivers, and abortion seekers, to include matters of divorce, birth, and care for parents and in-laws as well as for children in defi-nitions of welfare. This has expanded definitions of welfare to include families and the informal sphere as well as states and markets.

Taken as a whole feminist analysis seek to rec-ognize the multidimensionality of women's expe-riences as structured through macro-institutional disadvantages, and also explores how women's agency is also supported and contested at the sub-jective, symbolic, and emotional levels within families, kinship, and organizational contexts. Together these analyses bring into question whether liberal models of welfare can ever enable gendered equality when they rely on models of risk which do not consider the cultural and emo-tional costs incurred in welfare citizenship.

Women Workers and Carers

Despite debates over the appropriate breadth of feminist concerns in welfare, the substantive focus of much work has tended to be on women's contradictory positioning as providers and receivers of welfare – that is, the marginality of women's concerns within welfare, coupled with their centrality to its formal and informal provision.

The post war welfare settlement in the United Kingdom was built upon male breadwinner model, rooted in the principle of cohabitation based on a family wage system, where benefits were paid to men for the support of their wives and children. Thus, where a woman cohabited with a man her benefits were withdrawn. This system created, supported and maintained a structured dependency between men and women.

Even when women occupied public roles within state bureaucracies, their positioning often reflected the private distribution of women's work, with women occupying lower ranks, providing domestic functions within health, child-care and personal services. One example of where this division has been most marked is within nursing, a traditionally gendered profession where women fulfil the care role in public, but within a hierarchically ordered division of medical labour and where nursing management continues to be dominated by men.

Feminist analysis coming in particular from the United States identified important variations on this male breadwinner model, highlighting maternalist, as well as paternalist roots to social policies. Whilst women in the USA lacked formal political power to shape welfare, they exerted considerable agency at key points in the early stages of welfare development through grass roots organizations and effective lobbying. This meant that even in a context of minimal state managed and funded welfare provision like the United States, these groups successfully pressed for maternal child welfare benefits, such as mother's pensions (an early form of child welfare benefit) and other protective labour legislation.

Shifts from the male breadwinner to the 'adult worker model' of welfare are related to the rise of dual earner families in western contexts. Also known as the citizen-worker model, this adult worker model moves some way to equalizing women's position vis-à-vis men in terms of treating them as economically independent, for example through the individual basis for national insurance and income taxation since the 1970s.

By the late 1990s feminists capitalized on discourses around 'social investment' to argue for the positive contribution of care and the caring role within welfare and society as a whole. So called 'Social investment states' developed more gender inclusive 'citizen-worker-carer' models directed towards investment in children and young people as the future of economic stability and growth resulting in more child, family and mother friendly policy. The Scandinavian welfare states are often considered to be the most advanced in these terms, with child friendly, work life balance policies such as paid parental leave including a period of at least one month's leave reserved for new fathers, dubbed the 'daddy quota'.

In the United Kingdom the New Labour government pursued similar policies, such as:

- the National Care Strategy committing to the universal right to child-care
- the National Carer's Strategy for those providing various forms of home care
- Sure Start support for parents and family and more generous parental leave rights.

However, there are ongoing feminist concerns around the ways in which these arrangements can continue to disadvantage women if, as in the more gender neutral versions such as the USA, there is a failure to recognize the already gendered starting points for women and men workers which impact on ability to benefit from these policies. For example men's take-up of caring responsibilities is structurally discouraged within a working context where women's work is lower paid than men's. This material discouragement is often accompanied by cultural antithesis to male involvement in child-care.

More ambitious feminist interventions around the social investment state, have sought to develop a political ethical of care to challenge established ways of conceptualizing welfare citizenship through economic or intergenerational contracts of market and welfare systems. In the United Kingdom, research into Care, Values and the Future of Welfare sought to capitalize on a renewed interest in the concept of care to argue for care for the self and for the other as meaningful activities in their own right and regardless of their value in supporting the future labour market. This concept of care is used to rethink collective human agency as rooted in interdependence, challenging individualist models of social responsibility. This sort of approach begins to fulfil the promise of more radical feminist critiques around the nature of human values and how these values are supported or denigrated through welfare systems. It considers the value of paid work and caring activities together.

Gender Relations and Masculinities

These developments in feminist theorizing on social policy along with movement towards a

Box 12.1   A Political Ethic of Care

A political ethic of care reconsiders (Williams 2002):

■ The unequal distribution of time and space between the activities of personal care, other care, and paid work, valuing all three as crucial to work/life.
■ Differences in social relationships of care, rooted in historical formations of power and identity.
■ Intimacy as broader than the traditional heteronormative family to cover the role of kith as well as kin in the form of friends, lovers, step families, and so forth.
■ Inclusive diversity to include multiple identities which create forms of belonging which cross-cut family, community, and nation.
    User voice as a core component of trust within the identification of welfare needs.

created within school to encourage boy's participation in learning. A focus on fathers and fatherhood has been prompted by concerns to stem this educational (and broader social) exclusion of boys, for instance:

■ asking schools to send children's reports to fathers who live outside the family home;
■ a drive to encourage fathers to read to their children;
■ training for professionals who work with children to communicate with fathers; and
■ the promotion of child-care services to black and ethnic minority fathers.

However, the tendency to focus on children and fathers can be at the expense of a broader analysis of the complex gendered dynamics of violence, power, and care within families. It can reproduce the invisibility of mothers and motherhood. This neglect risks the reproduction of women's disempowerment within the home through the provision of formal services.

Feminist Intersections

Feminists have long been concerned with the interconnections between, gender, class, and race. William's (1989) groundbreaking analysis of the UK welfare state as part of a racially structured patriarchal capitalism in which women were central to the reproduction of nation as well as family demonstrates the uneven and contradictory progress of post-war welfare for different groups of women. For example, the opening up of Higher Education in the 1960s benefited largely white middle-class women. While the post-war NHS had improved general health of women, it had done this less so for working-class and black women, whose contact was still regulated through immigration law.

    This analysis paved the way for a more differentiated and critical feminist analysis of welfare in the United Kingdom and other contexts, one which takes account of the struggles of a range of welfare users social movements and activists. Other UK focused critiques like Carabine's intervention 'Constructing Women' and Morris's 'Us' and 'Them'? show how mainstream feminist analysis continued to rely on heterosexual assumptions as to the primacy of mothering and the separation of women and dependent people.

'universal caregiver' model of welfare serve as a reminder of the ways in which gender in social policy is as much about men as it is about women. The rise in explicit interest in men and masculinities within social policy is manifest in a number of ways in terms of concern over men's relations to education, violence, health, and social exclusion, but in particular through a focus on father's fatherhood. Critique of monolithic hegemonic masculinity in favour of understanding multiple masculinities highlights the way male breadwinner models of welfare created hegemonic oppressive, but ultimately unattainable ways of being a man, as much as it created problematic conflations between women, care, and the home.

    Debates over men's health, such as their higher mortality rates, including suicide, and particular forms of ill health relate these phenomena to certain 'inappropriate' or risky masculine behaviours, for example the reluctance to seek medical help, or an apparent propensity to violence. Other prominent debate since the late 1990s has been over the disproportionately lower educational attainment of boys, with a variety of measures

This emphasis on differentiation within the category of woman built on debates from within the feminist movement around the reproduction of racism, heterosexism, ablism, and so on. It highlights the ways in which multiple social relations produce differential experiences of disadvantage within welfare and how different groups of women may require different support and policy in order to meet differing needs. Perhaps most importantly, emphasis on difference and differentiation serves to highlight the ways in which women can be simultaneously vulnerable and empowered within the organization of welfare through their multiple identities. For example a black woman worker suffering institutional discrimination blocking career progression as a black person, may benefit as a woman worker who is a mother from child-care services provided by that same organization, designed to enable women's career progression. Differential analysis poses challenges around how to provide for women's sometimes competing needs, and puts into question the possibility of broader feminist collective challenges to welfare services.

Gender mainstreaming policies, first developed at European Union level, seek to respond to many of these complexities. They recognize the lack of gender neutrality in normative welfare systems and the advantages accrued to a white middle-class (masculine) norm, and aim to correct this bias, rather than to prescribe ad hoc piecemeal measures aiming to develop women's position. They also dovetail the feminist language of intersectionalities and multiple social difference using the notion of human diversity as a way of considering how normative welfare systems exclude a broad range of people including some white men. However, feminists have also criticized the way mainstreaming and diversity policies have been co-opted to serve individualistic rather than collective ends.

Feminists in Public Policy and Activism

Despite their marginality within formal public policy mechanisms feminists have long played an important role in the public sphere. This contribution as activists and more recently as public intellectuals within policy-making is evidenced by the introduction of gender mainstreaming.

Even within the more paternalist context of UK welfare, feminist activism directed towards challenging economic dependency on men had early success with the introduction of family allowances payable directly to women at the same time as the introduction of Beveridge's family wage. Later the Women's Family Allowance Campaign defeated the Conservative government's 1972 tax credit proposals which would have removed this form of direct payment to women, replacing it with an indirect payment to the working father through tax breaks within the wage packet. The Women's Budget Group has also been actively scrutinizing the budgets of UK governments since the early 1990s; and the Fawcett Society, named after its founder the Dame Millicent Garrett Fawcett, has adopted a liberal campaigning role for women's equality for well over 100 years.

Much of feminism's ability to influence social policy has depended on its ability to impact on the broader social and cultural relations through which policy is established. Equal Opportunities Policies, the Equal Pay and Sex Discrimination Acts and the establishment of the Equal Opportunities Commission are all important elements of this broader cultural shift in the United Kingdom. Increasing opportunities for women to occupy positions within formal political institutions are an important dimension to women's influence.

Milestones in women's visibility in the United Kingdom have been the introduction of a Minister for Women in 1997 and the establishment of the Women and Equality Unit in 2001. However, there is considerable feminist ambivalence around these sorts of mainstream political engagements as a 'politics of women without feminists', arguing that engagement with formal systems tends to be confined to certain, largely white, middle-class women.

Emerging Issues: Post-feminism, Human Rights, and the Return to Austerity

The past ten or so years has seen debate as to whether we are entering an era of 'post-feminism', where the core arguments of feminism have become irrelevant. This debate turns on two ideas, that women's increasing visibility in public life attests to the success of struggles for gender equality and that this success has even in some circumstances been at the disadvantage of men and boys. Other developments related to main-streaming have created a move away from the specificities of women's concerns. The EOC, like its counterpart the CRE has been collapsed into the newly established Equality and Human Rights Commission (EHRC). Ostensibly created in order to integrate intersectional analysis of multiple inequality, there is an absence of strong feminist agenda within the EHRC which has been a concern to feminist campaigners. It remains to be seen how the human rights agenda adopted by the commission will play out in relation to broader feminist concerns (see Chapter 5).

The coalition government highlights some ongoing and perhaps increasingly acute problems for women. For instance, the first coalition cabinet contains only four women, from a total of twenty nine attending cabinet, and one (the only non-white member) an unpaid, unelected minister without portfolio.

The most obvious danger to come, however, is in the new government's agenda for public expenditure cuts to meet the projected budget deficit. High profile losers here are child benefit and local government services, both of which impact disproportionately on women in terms of financial provision, services, and opportunities for employment. The Women's Budget Group and the Fawcett Society have already come out as highly critical of the government's first budget in terms of its return to policies more supportive of the male breadwinner than the universal carer model. The coalition has also failed to implement fully requirements from the 2010 Equalities Act relating to reducing the ongoing gender pay gap in the private sector. Other questions remain as to how the 'Big Society' agenda will impact women and families. Will this enable the princi-ples of a feminist ethic of care to flourish, or will it reinforce the disproportionate burdens placed on women in the private sphere into broader informal contexts?

Guide to Further Sources

There is a range of textbooks and edited collec-tions which forward feminist analysis of social policy, Fiona Williams *Social Policy: a Critical*

Introduction (Cambridge: Polity Press, 1989) and Gillian Pascall's, *Social Policy: A Feminist Analysis* (2nd edn, London: Routledge, 1999) are two examples. Sophie Watson and Lesley Doyal's *Engendering Social Policy* (Philadelphia, PA: Open University Press, 1999) explicitly focuses on gen-dered social relations adopting a more postmod-ern difference focused analysis. Other books consider key social policy ideas from a feminist perspective, for example Ruth Lister, *Citizenship: Feminist Perspectives* (2nd edn, New York University Press, 2003). Fiona Williams' 2002 article on 'The presence of feminism in the future of welfare', *Economy & Society*, 31/4: 502–19, is a good introduction to ideas around a political ethic of care.

There is also a range of relevant feminist jour-nals. Most directly related to the concerns of social policy is *Social Politics: International Studies in Gender, State and Society*. *Critical Social Policy* remains a key source for current feminist debate in welfare and a good means to explore femi-nism's development within the discipline. Jean Carabine's 'Constructing Women': Women's Sexuality and Social Policy (*Critical Social Policy*, 12/34 (1992): 23–37) and Jenny Morris's 'Us' and 'Them'? Feminist Research Community Care and Disability (*Critical Social Policy*, 11/33 (1991): 22–39) are good examples of critique moving forward internal feminist debate over gendered difference and its relationship to social policy.

Used critically the web hosts a vast range of relevant feminist resources. The Fawcett Society web site, www.fawcettsociety.org.uk/, provides up-to-date information on liberal femi-nist campaigning and on equality. It includes research reports and facts and figures. The fword is a webzine including a wide range of contem-porary feminist debate and resources from a range of feminist perspectives: www.thefword.org.uk/index

Review Questions

1   How is it that social policies disadvantage as well as advantage women?
2   What are the key points of contention between different feminist approaches to social policy analysis?

3 In what ways does the idea of multiple social relations impact on feminist social policy analysis, what are the benefits and the challenges?

4 Why introduce an analysis of men and masculinities into a feminist analysis of social policy, and what does this add to an understanding of gender relations?

5 What are the complexities of feminist's involvement in formal politics and policy-making?

Visit the book companion site at www.wiley.com/go/alcock to make use of the resources designed to accompany the textbook. There you will find chapter-specific guides to further resources, including governmental, international, think-tank, pressure groups, and relevant journals sources. You will also find a glossary based on *The Blackwell Dictionary of Social Policy*, help sheets, and case studies, guidance on managing assignments in social policy and career advice.

13

Green Perspectives

Michael Cahill

Overview

- The environmental damage produced by our economic system is all too plain to see in oil spills, greenhouse gases, the loss of the rain forests, traffic pollution, and many other consequences of the industrial way of life.
- Widespread loss of life is predicted in the coming decades as global warming leads to changed weather patterns The human cost is already manifest across the globe as drought, hurricanes, and flooding have produced hundreds of thousands of 'environmental refugees'.
- Over the last quarter of the twentieth century concern for the environment moved from the province of small, uninfluential pressure groups to the agenda of the world's leading nations.
- There are many varieties of green thought but they are all united in their belief that the environment should take priority in social and political discussion.
- Climate change is persuading governments around the world to take environmental issues much more seriously than they have in the past.

The Development of Environmentalism

Widespread interest in the environment can be traced back to the publication of the *Limits to Growth* report in 1971. The authors used various computer models to see how long the world's stocks of basic non-renewables would last given population increases and continuing economic growth. Also in the early 1970s Friends of the Earth and Greenpeace were formed and began to popularize the environmental message with

The Student's Companion to Social Policy, Fourth Edition. Edited by Pete Alcock, Margaret May, Sharon Wright.
© 2012 John Wiley & Sons, Ltd. Published 2012 by John Wiley & Sons, Ltd.

imaginative and persistent campaigning. Shortly afterwards in 1973 the oil price hike by the Middle East oil producers led to widespread energy saving measures in the Western world, although this was not to endure. An environmental movement began to emerge with a growth in the membership of environmental pressure groups.

However, green political parties were in their infancy in the 1970s and did not gain some electoral success until the 1980s, particularly in Germany, with Die Grünen gaining seats in parliament, taking power in local government, and by the late 1990s forming part of the national government. In the United Kingdom it was to take much longer for the Greens to enter the national parliament with their first MP in Westminster elected only in 2010. However, it was not so much political parties or pressure groups that spread green ideas rather it was the impact of what was happening to the environment. In the late 1980s two extremely serious environmental problems were acknowledged: global warming and the discovery of holes in the ozone layer. In the 1990s the quickening pace of environmental crisis – particularly the onset of climate change – pushed the issue of the environment on to the agenda of the leading industrial countries. This was symbolized by the attention given to the United Nations Earth Summit held in Rio de Janeiro in 1992 which committed the international community to a programme of sustainable development.

Greens are united in their recognition of the fact that there are natural and social limits to material progress. These have now been reached: the planet is over-populated, the emissions from industrial and transport activity are damaging the biosphere and there is insufficient food to feed the population while species extinction proceeds apace. The green response is to call for a reduction in the burden of human activity on the planet which could have important implications for social policy. How the reduction of humankind's burden on the planet can occur is at the heart of green arguments and debate. Obviously it is of paramount importance that environmental policies do not damage the welfare of the poorer sections of the population.

There are a great many ways to classify green thinking. A basic distinction can be made between light and dark green.

■ *Dark* greens see the survival of nature and the planet as all-important. Human activity, particularly in the past 200 years, since the emergence of industrialism has despoiled the planet and threatens the existence of other life forms. This leads some greens to call for severe curbs on population. Dark greens believe that humans, in order to reduce their burden on the planet, need to reduce their consumption patterns. They are at one with supporters of animal rights in calling for an end to the second-class treatment of other sentient creatures on the planet. Rather than people from the poor world looking to the rich West for a model, 'dark' greens would have the rich world try to imitate the poor world. Lifestyle change is key to this with people adapting their way of life in order to reduce the damage they cause to planet Earth. In reply to the charge that this is not terribly attractive to generations reared on consumer products dark greens argue that if people were to reduce their consumerist lifestyle then they would gain immeasurably. A sustainable way of life involves reducing one's impact on the environment straight away and not waiting for some future government to legislate. It can be seen that 'dark' greens integrate a set of ethical beliefs with their political and social views.

■ *Light* greens are reformists: they want to work with the grain of advanced industrial societies and adopt a pragmatic approach. For them, the environmental problems of the world are not too grave or too large to be beyond the problem solving capacity of science and technology. They believe that it is possible to have continued economic growth yet solve environmental problems. Many think that it is possible to use market mechanisms to correct the environmental imbalances which abound. Various techniques can be used to weigh the claims of the environment against other factors. Forms of cost-benefit analysis, assigning a monetary value to natural resources, can be used to decide on the degree of environmental protection required. Equally, it is possible for modern industry to clean up its act and, indeed, the production of technologies to do this will be a highly profitable investment. 'Light green' thinking is not a distinctive ideological position: it prioritizes green issues within existing modes of thinking about the world's political and economic problems. It is frequently described as environmental (or ecological) modernization.

Varieties of Green Thought

Many writers dispute the claim that there can be a distinctive green ideology arguing that many of its key propositions are taken from other traditions of political and social thought. Clearly this is an important and contentious issue, for its resolution will bear upon the viability or otherwise of separate green parties. Let us now summarize some of the positions whose adherents have added the prefix 'eco' to their belief.

- *Eco-socialism* is really only as old as the green movement, although it has to be admitted that many of its decentralist arguments were anticipated by the early socialists 100 years ago. Eco-socialists link the damage wrought to the biosphere to the organization of economic life under capitalism. They are of the belief that the replacement of this economic system will lead to a society where the profit imperative will not lead to ceaseless encroachment on nature. They do not believe that large-scale production processes must disappear, only that they should be planned and controlled to prevent pollution and waste. Clearly there is a real question mark as to whether the international capitalist system would permit such a transformation to occur.
- *Eco-feminism* regards the exploitation of nature as being historically linked to the exploitation and subordination of women. It attributes many of the environmental problems of our time to the triumph of 'male' values – ambition, struggle for control, and independence – over 'feminine' values – nurturing, caring, and tending. Naturally there is some considerable doubt as to whether these values can be seen as specifically male or female. All we can say with certainty is that in the history of the modern world one

set of values has been more widespread among men than women and vice versa. Eco-feminists argue that men must become more caring and nurturing and this should be reflected in the world of work, with unpaid, caring work being given a much higher priority by men. Women, for their part, need to take from masculinity the idea of being strong and assertive. In practical terms this means sharing of the care of children and domestic work. In paid work eco-feminists would call for a retreat from a masculine ambience which devalues the emotional life; at the same time criticizing those feminisms which exalt individual autonomy and self-determination for women for seeing them as merely the female embodiment of consumer capitalism. This critique becomes more pertinent as in rich world countries increasingly women are gaining higher status and well-paid employment leaving caring work to be done by others. There is within eco-feminism a quasi-spiritual dimension exalting 'female' values but there is also a more practically based eco-feminism in the poor world which points to the importance of women's resistance in some countries to the environmental destruction wrought by industrialism.

- *Green conservatism* Traditional conservatism in England emphasized the small community and the rural village, and was, in the first half of the nineteenth century, opposed to the industrial system and urban life. In some ways this made it akin to the programmed of dark greens today. The system of market liberalism has been a powerful force which, in moulding and expressing many people's desires for greater wealth, has released enormous energies which endanger the environment. There are many ways in which a politics of 'limits' and restraints on the use of economic and technological power would be close to the traditional conservative position.

What eco-socialism, eco-feminism, and green conservatism have in common is that they emphasize certain aspects of their 'parent' ideology in order to reformulate it as a response to the environmental crisis.

The Welfare State

The welfare state divides green thinkers and reveals the strands of thought which are present in green movements. Many greens are opposed to the welfare state. Not that they are against the goods which it delivers – free education, free health care, a national minimum – rather that they object to the *state* delivering these services. However, for some greens this is tempered by the acknowledgement that inequalities in access to services and inequities in distribution are capable of being ameliorated by a state apparatus. Welfare states are welfare bureaucracies and as such become organizations which have the ability to control people's lives, and greens believe that this tendency has to be resisted. They believe that a decentralized welfare system would mean less need for welfare, as citizens would be providing these services for themselves and each other. There is a high degree of emphasis on the advantages and positive benefits of mutuality – organizations of like-minded citizens providing services for themselves in their local community.

The welfare state, in most green accounts, would be local and decentralized with a high degree of citizen participation and an important role for voluntary organizations. In discussing the future of the welfare state under a green regime one must remain sensitive to the differing green positions. Welfare does not have to be provided by the state; indeed, it will be more spontaneous and appropriate if it is not provided by the state. The neighbourhood, the voluntary organization and what form of local administration is then organized will attend to the welfare needs of the local population. One of the key problems with this line of argument is that it downplays the role of social justice and disparities in income. Admittedly, structures of welfare can be oppressive, but they are also routine and accessible. This is an important consideration for the weak, vulnerable, and isolated who rely on the local welfare state for regular support and assistance. It might also be added that there are some who will find it difficult, whatever the society, to find ready acceptance and help – they might be mentally ill or they might have a disability of some kind – and state services through their employment of professionals aim to integrate such people into the community. The role of the professional is central to the discussion of the place of welfare in a green society. Many greens are unenthusiastic about welfare state professionals, believing that they have usurped the caring and nurturing which individuals and communities ought to be doing themselves. They feel that they tend to turn their clients into passive consumers of welfare when they should be self-determining individuals.

Green Social Policies

Greens argue that the overvaluation of paid work has had destructive consequences for both society and the individual. They were among the early proponents of a citizen's income (also known as basic income) which gives, as a right to all, a weekly income. The intention here is that this will provide some recognition of the worth of unpaid work. There are many variations but essentially this income would replace all National Insurance benefits, tax allowances, and as many means-tested benefits as possible. Such an income has the attraction for greens in that it can begin the process of revaluing unpaid work – for those who do unpaid caring work will receive the citizen's income in their own right. It fits in with the green idea that there should and could be more opportunities for local employment, such as workers' co-operatives, and removes some of the disadvantage associated with the low rates of pay often attached to such work. Equally, the income would be paid to those who do voluntary work. Critics of such a scheme point out that it could bear very heavily on the taxpayers who have to fund it, especially the full blown scheme outlined here, although it is crucial, of course, at what rate the income is paid. The citizen's income has also received a fair amount of criticism for possibly removing the incentive to work, although this is a problem common to all social security provision of a safety net income and is not peculiar to citizen's income. Another telling criticism is that it would require a great deal more centralized and bureaucratic state machinery than is currently seen as necessary in most accounts of a future green society.

In this green society the locality is restored to its place as the centre of people's lives. Another way, therefore, in which greens believe that the volume of unpaid work can be recognized is through the spread of local employment trading schemes (LETS). These are token economies where people trade their skills with one another and are usually computed on the basis of so many hours worked. The tokens earned, however, remain a local currency and this ensures that the local community benefits from this activity. The advantages of LETS are obvious. They enable a deal of 'economic' activity to go on without the need for conventional employment. They enable those who are poor (that is, without cash income) to obtain goods and services outside of the cash economy.

At the national level environmental modernizers argue for a taxation regime which moves away from taxes on individual income towards taxes on pollution. These eco-taxes would need to take many forms in order to deal with the various unsustainable activities prevalent in an advanced economy. For example, a resource depletion tax would try to ensure that a certain resource was only extracted to an agreed level. Pollution taxes could be levied on goods which have deleterious consequences for the environment in order to promote the sale of benign products. In like manner these goods can be zero rated for some taxes in order to encourage their consumption. Climate change has concentrated the minds of governments on the need to reduce carbon emissions with a variety of carbon taxes being proposed which would encourage a reduction in behaviour which produced carbon. Admittedly this is a 'big ask' given that the global economy is premised on mobility of goods, people, and capital.

Sustainable Development

Following the United Nations Earth Summit in 1992, which pledged the world's leading nations to a programme of sustainable development, the UK government committed itself to sustainable action across all policy sectors. Sustainable development was defined as development that meets the needs of the present without compromising the ability of future generations to meet their own needs. The Labour government elected in 1997 linked sustainable development to issues of social policy. Its sustainable development strategy gave sustainable development objectives across

government and contained indicators upon which progress could be judged. These indicators are a mix of social, economic, and environmental: including air pollution levels, populations of wild birds, river water quality; but also unfit homes, crime levels and educational levels among many others. UK governments are committed to promoting economic growth as well as sustainable development and some environmental critics feel that wherever there is a conflict between the two then it is usually the perceived needs of the economy which prevail.

Ever since someone coined the slogan 'think global, act local' the local has been central to green and environmental thinking. The recognition that one's local environment was important has been seen in sustainability projects sponsored by local authorities throughout the United Kingdom. Most people will not have heard of the word sustainability but they will be concerned about their local environment: dog dirt on the pavement, graffiti, a lack of safe play space for their children and so on. All sections of the population can relate to issues around their local environment and will have views on what needs to be done. The 'big society' theme of the coalition government may be a way of encouraging and expanding local environmental action.

Environmental Justice

There is accumulating evidence that poor people tend to suffer disproportionately from pollution. To give some examples, the bulk of vehicle exhaust pollution generated by commuter motorists driving into and out of urban centres affects those in low-income areas living adjacent to major roads. The major polluting factories tend to be sited close to low-income areas. Children in social class five are five times more likely than children in social class one to be killed in road accidents. These are examples of environmental injustice where poverty is compounded by a poor environment and a greater exposure to environmental hazards. When Hurricane Katrina hit the US mainland in August 2005, leaving 180,333 dead in its wake, the majority of the residents of New Orleans and the other urban areas were able to flee by car. Those who were left behind, for example in the Superdome Football Stadium in

New Orleans were without access to personal transport and predominantly black. Too often the poor do not enjoy the benefits which produce these environmental hazards: those on the lowest incomes are the least likely to own a car, for example. In a society where mobility is important for the maintenance of social networks then this can be a significant handicap.

Emerging Issues

This chapter has outlined various green social policies which would be part of a future society where green values were dominant. In the shorter term the emerging issues in the area of environment and social policy are likely to be debated within a light green or environmental discourse. These are likely to include:

- Environmental taxation will increasingly be resorted to by government and has the capacity to make goods and services more expensive for those on the lowest incomes. In dealing with climate change right through to road pricing, mechanisms will need to be put in place which will protect the poorest.
- If it is accepted that the standard of living and way of life enjoyed by the populations of rich world countries are not sustainable for the entire population of the planet then we in the rich countries will have to live more simply and with much less use of energy. Sustainable consumption is likely to become a significant issue.
- As it is recognized that consumer societies are bad for the health of the planet there will be an increasing focus on well-being and the quality of life.

Guide to Further Sources

There are a number of books which explicitly examine the links between the environment and social policy. Michael Cahill's *The Environment*

and Social Policy (London: Routledge, 2002) is an introductory text. For more extended discussion see the essays in Michael Cahill and Tony Fitzpatrick (eds), *Environmental Issues and Social Welfare* (Oxford: Blackwell, 2002) and Tony Fitzpatrick and Michael Cahill's (eds), *Greening the Welfare State* (Basingstoke: Palgrave Macmillan, 2002). For the environmental and social impact of transport see Michael Cahill's *Transport, Environment and Society* (Maidenhead: Open University Press, 2010). The most comprehensive account is now Tony Fitzpatrick's (ed.), *Understanding the Environment and Social Policy* (Bristol: Policy Press, 2011).

Informative and useful web sites include: Local Exchange Trading Schemes at www.letslinkuk.net; New Economics Foundation publishes a number of useful pamphlets, particularly on well-being at www.neweconomics.org/gen/; Citizen's Income at www.citizensincome.org; and the UK government's sustainable development site at www.sdcommission.org.uk/.

Review Questions

1 Why is the idea of limits so important in green thinking?
2 To what extent can green ideas be successfully accommodated within existing political ideologies?
3 Can there be a green welfare state?
4 How would a citizen's income promote a green society?
5 Are environmental inequalities inevitable?

Visit the book companion site at www.wiley.com/go/alcock to make use of the resources designed to accompany the textbook. There you will find chapter-specific guides to further resources, including governmental, international, think-tank, pressure groups, and relevant journals sources. You will also find a glossary based on *The Blackwell Dictionary of Social Policy*, help sheets, and case studies, guidance on managing assignments in social policy and career advice.

14

Postmodernist Perspectives

Tony Fitzpatrick

■■■

Overview

- Postmodernism articulates a disillusionment with traditional social and political theories, one which makes room for new approaches and ways of thinking.
- Post-structuralism also departs radically from previous philosophies, though it is more theoretically and methodologically precise, drawing attention to the instabilities of identity and meaning.
- As postmodernism and post-structuralism have themselves become established features of the intellectual landscape many have queried their importance or significance. In some respects they appear distant from the 'bread and butter' issues of social policy, yet in others they articulate changing social realities with which social policy must get to grips.
- Other social changes include increased attention to the concept of risk and its relevance to contemporary notions of citizenship and well-being.
- Some also believe that we must look to a wide variety of social movements to understand the dynamics of recent social developments.

■■■

Theories of the Postmodern

Postmodernism was *the* intellectual fashion of the 1980s and like all fashions it attracted zealous supporters and equally zealous critics. Yet postmodernism's legacy has confounded both sides.

It did not sweep away traditional schools of thought, as its supporters had anticipated, nor yet has it proved to be an empty, transitional fad, as its critics had hoped. This is because, with its roots reaching far into the history of ideas, postmodernism reinvented some old themes within

The Student's Companion to Social Policy, Fourth Edition. Edited by Pete Alcock, Margaret May, Sharon Wright.
© 2012 John Wiley & Sons, Ltd. Published 2012 by John Wiley & Sons, Ltd.

new social, political, and cultural contexts. Therefore, whether we agree with postmodernism or not, we cannot ignore its recent influences. By the time social policy took an interest in postmodernism, the latter had already nurtured the intellectual soil upon which the former depended.

The turn towards postmodernism was largely inspired by a disillusion with traditional forms of politics and social philosophy. The 'rediscovery' of Marxism in the 1960s inspired the Left to believe that alternatives to consumer capitalism were both imaginable and achievable. By the 1970s, however, many activists and intellectuals had become disenchanted with Marxism and began to rethink the meaning of emancipation and progress.

Jean-François Lyotard contended that we can no longer cling to 'metanarratives'. A metanarrative is any system of thought that attempts to understand the social world within a single, all-encompassing critique. Marxism is one such 'grand narrative' by trying to explain all aspects of society in terms of material production and class struggle. This is like trying to step beyond the social world and understand it from the outside. But Lyotard, like Wittgenstein before him, insisted that there is no 'outside' to which we can ascend; since we are enmeshed within language there is no space beyond language that would enable us to map the world in its entirety. Therefore, knowledge must proceed from 'the inside', from within our language-using communities: knowledge is always contextualized and particular rather than absolute and universal. Lyotard defines postmodernism as an 'incredulity towards metanarratives' and so a rejection of the view that emancipatory politics can rely upon a single explanatory model or system (see Box 14.1).

Box 14.1 Lyotard

In contemporary society and culture – post-industrial society, postmodern culture – the question of legitimation of knowledge is formulated in different terms. The grand narrative has lost its credibility . . . regardless of whether it is a speculative narrative or a narrative of emancipation. (Jean-François Lyotard 1984: 37.)

Jean Baudrillard goes even further. Marxism may have been appropriate in an age of production but we now live in societies of signs and codes. Indeed, so ubiquitous are these signs and codes that they no longer symbolically represent reality; instead, the philosophical distinction between reality and representation has collapsed into a 'hyperreality'. Whereas we could once distinguish between original objects and their copies, hyperreality implies that only copies exist and no originating source for those copies is identifiable. Ours, then, is an age of simulations that endlessly refer only to other simulations. The infinite circularity of these self-references is what Baudrillard calls the simulacra: everything is a reproduction of other reproductions. Society implodes in on itself and we cannot liberate ourselves from the simulacra: ideologies of progress are just another form of seduction to the system of codes.

These ideas came under considerable attack from other theorists. Jürgen Habermas alleges that postmodernism is a philosophical justification for social and political conservatism. By taking progress to be impossible and undesirable, postmodernism resembles a conservative defence of the *status quo*. Habermas charges postmodernist theorists with depending upon the very philosophical premises and assumptions that they claim to have dispelled.

However, there are some who, while not supporting postmodernism *per se*, insist that its emergence and popularity reveal something very important about recent social change. Fredric Jameson describes postmodernism as 'the cultural logic of late capitalism' in that it accurately describes the fragmentation and heterogeneity of contemporary life. This is because of developments within capitalist production and consumption. Our cultures are pervaded by surfaces, hybrids, repackaging, parody, pastiche, and spectacle because this is now the most effective way of valuing, circulating, and consuming commodities. Capitalism dominates by seeming not to dominate, by fragmenting both itself and the objects it dominates. So Jameson is insisting that postmodernism *can* be utilized by those committed to a progressive politics of the Left.

Postmodernists reject the idea that values, judgements and principles can apply universally across space and time. For critics of postmodernism like

Box 14.2 Postmodernism summarized

Postmodernists
- reject universalism
- believe truth to be contextual
- abandon foundationalism and essentialism
- avoid binary distinctions
- support identity politics, and
- celebrate irony and difference.

Christopher Norris this leads inevitably to relativism, the idea that there are *no* universal standards of morality and truth. This, he argues, tempts postmodernists into intellectual absurdity, such as Baudrillard's 1991 claim that the Gulf War never happened.

However, as a defender of postmodernism, Richard Rorty argues that it is the futile search for absolute truth which creates relativism, so if we stop searching for that which is unobtainable then we can transcend the sterile distinction between universalism and relativism. This does not leave us unable to speak about truth, it means that truth is contextual, that is, dependent upon the frame within which truth-claims are made. As Chantal Mouffe observes, ideas are rooted within particular traditions and there is no 'God's eye view' which is external to all traditions.

Postmodernists also reject foundationalism and essentialism. Foundationalism is the notion that knowledge and belief are based upon secure foundations that can be discovered, for example, through science. Postmodernists argue that there are no such foundations as we can never fully justify any knowledge- or belief-claim. Understanding is always a matter of interpretation and interpretation is never complete. Essentialism is the idea that objects have essences which define and explain that object, for example, the essence of humans is 'human nature'. For postmodernists, though, all objects and their supposed essences are merely social constructs.

Postmodernists insist that we should avoid thinking in terms of binary distinctions, hierarchies and structures, for example, nature vs. culture. Postmodern feminists like Judith Butler argue that this way of thinking reflects masculinist assumptions about the world – that the world is divisible into parts which relate to one another in relations of higher and lower, superior and inferior. For postmodernists there are no edges and peripheries or, rather, *everywhere* is an edge *and* a periphery! Instead, they prefer to emphasize the importance of centreless flows, fluidities, networks, and webs.

Postmodernism is often taken to prefer a form of identity politics based around culture and the self. Oppression and discrimination is not just about a lack of resources but also about a lack of recognition and status, about not being able to shape the norms which define and exclude you. Yet identity – of individuals, groups, societies – is never fixed but is in a state of indeterminate flux, being constantly renegotiated and redefined. Identity implies not only 'resemblance to' but also 'difference from'.

Finally, postmodernism embodies a playful, ironic stance: postmodernists often refuse to take anything too seriously, including themselves! Yet rather than being self-indulgent this playfulness is meant to be a celebration of diversity, hybridity, difference, and pluralism. For Rorty, philosophy is not the 'mirror of nature' but a means of devising new vocabularies and descriptions. Rather than debating which description is real our job is to assist each other in endlessly deconstructing and reconstructing our understanding of the social world. Solidarity, rather than truth, is the proper object of enquiry.

Postmodernism and Social Policy

Many social policy theorists and researchers are quite critical towards postmodernism.

For instance, if social policy is concerned with welfare then we must be able to distinguish between higher and lower forms of well-being in making interpersonal, historical, cross-national, and cross-cultural comparisons. Yet it is precisely these judgements that postmodernism might disallow. By embracing contextualism, anti-foundationalism, and anti-essentialism, postmodernists undermine notions of truth and social progress and so efforts to create greater freedom, equality, and community. But if these notions should *not* be dismissed – as their enduring popularity might suggest – then perhaps we should reject postmodern ideas because their political and social consequences are likely to be damaging.

Take one example. Social policy is arguably based upon the view that there is a human nature consisting of basic needs. The task of welfare systems is to enable those needs to be fulfilled. But if human nature is a modernist fiction, as postmodernists claim, and if needs are constructed through language rather than being natural, then the rationale of state welfare may be undermined. This is just one reason why some social policy commentators are very suspicious of postmodernism, accusing it of providing an intellectual justification of anti-welfare state politics.

Others, though, insist that postmodernism and social policy need not be so hostile. Traditionally, social policy has been concerned with class, that is, income and occupation. Yet although our identities are undoubtedly constructed in terms of socio-economic relations there may be other forms of relations that are also important: gender, ethnicity, sexuality, religion, disability, nationality, and age. Therefore, social policy must take account of these additional categories and perhaps postmodernism might assist the subject in doing so. Yet this is where disagreement kicks in, for how should we weigh class against non-class divisions? For some, class is still of central importance and postmodernism therefore an unwelcome distraction. For others, there has to be a more equitable balancing of class and non-class categories.

Nancy Fraser suggests that social justice requires both redistribution and recognition, not only material questions of distribution but also cultural questions of status and respect for different groups. If we place too much emphasis on economic justice and redistribution we may neglect the extent to which discrimination is about symbolic exclusions, the denial of status, and disrespect. Conversely, if we place too much emphasis on cultural justice and recognition we potentially ignore the role which class continues to play in shaping social institutions and the distribution of opportunities and liberties. We need both. Therefore, by drawing attention to the importance and complexity of social identities, postmodernism has arguably performed an important service.

Another form of rapprochement between postmodern themes and social policy is outlined by Zygmunt Bauman. Bauman believes that we now live in a postmodern world, one which has been individualized, fragmented and, through the flows of globalization, speeded up. Yet, in their rush to celebrate this, postmodernists themselves often neglect the role of deregulated, global capitalism in bringing that state of affairs about. Postmodern capitalism, says Bauman, empowers the wealthy by disempowering the poor. Collective systems of welfare – though also the victims of global capitalism – are the means by which we recognize our interdependency and reassert the importance of common values and needs.

The influence of postmodernism may also extend to the delivery of services. Social policy has been characterized by a debate between universalists and selectivists, with the former resisting the means-testing advocated by the latter. A postmodern slant on this debate suggests the provision should be universal but that, within this framework, there must be a greater sensitivity to the particular needs and demands of certain groups. For some, this will imply market-driven, consumerist forms of local empowerment. Yet a progressive postmodernism stresses the importance of non-market types of participative inclusion and deliberation.

So although some believe postmodernism and social policy to be irreconcilable opposites, others think that both contribute to our understanding of self and society.

Post-structuralism

Post-structuralism agrees with postmodernism that we cannot transcend the traditions in which we are embedded. For post-structuralists, what we call reality is no more than a temporary effect of discourse and signification, with no stable reality beyond the play of language. Truth is therefore discursive, that is, there is no such thing as 'Truth', merely a series of truth-claims that have to be understood in terms of the subjectivities expressing them. What we call truth is just another face of power and there are no structures of reality lying beneath the social surface. Power has endless faces and there is no real one underpinning all the rest.

Michel Foucault focuses upon the conditions (the discourses) through which knowledge and ideas are generated. He sets out to understand discursive practices through a 'genealogical' approach which closely traces the history and operation of power within a number of institutional settings, for example, prisons, asylums, clinics. For instance, in the nineteenth and twentieth centuries madness was medicalized, redefined as mental illnesses that require specialized treatment by medical practitioners eager to assert their influence. Other discourses, for example, the religious emphasis upon mania, possession and exorcism, were thereby dispelled. Foucault analyses the extent to which medicalization incarcerates the mentally ill in another normative framework, not necessarily superior to any of the earlier discourses (such as the religious one). 'Madness' enables the rest of us to define ourselves as healthy and normal (see Box 14.3).

So Foucault identifies the 'panopticon' as the essential metaphor for all modern forms of discipline and normalization. The panopticon was a design for a prison that would use the least number of prison officers to survey as many prisoners as possible. The prisoners would not know when they were being observed and so would need to act as if they were under constant surveillance. Using these ideas we can understand welfare systems as discourses, as the disciplinary mechanisms of normative surveillance. To be a subject is to be constantly policing oneself. Post-structuralism does not offer manifestoes for welfare reform. Instead, it is a kind of 'spring-cleaning' exercise, a way of undermining our commonly held assumptions.

Many within the social policy community reject these ideas, however. If truth-claims dominate, if power is everywhere, what happens to the struggle for universal emancipation, progress and justice? Ironically, just as some Marxists interpret everyone as a representative of their class, so post-structuralists often treat agents merely as the embodied spaces of discourses flowing in and around them. I may believe in progress and rationality *as* a white, Western, middle-class male, but that does not mean I hold those beliefs *because* I am a white, Western, middle-class male. Perhaps truth is not simply another face of power.

Yet Foucault has been highly influential and, like postmodernism, post-structuralism has contributed to contemporary debates regarding identity, agency, governance, regulation, and surveillance.

Risk Society

There are other theorists who, while believing that modernity has changed, do not allege that the modern period is over. Ulrich Beck argues that we have reached the beginning of a *second* modernity. The first modernity was an age of industrial progress where all political and social institutions were designed to generate 'goods' (welfare, economic growth) in a world that was taken to be stable, knowable, and scientifically calculable. By contrast, the second modernity is a risk society characterized by the attempt to limit, manage and navigate a way through a series of 'bads', anxieties, and hazards. For instance, nuclear and industrial pollution undermines the simple class hierarchies of the industrial order, affecting the ghettoes of the rich as well as those of the poor (see Box 14.4).

Box 14.3   Madness/Normality

The judges of normality are present everywhere. We are in the society of the teacher-judge, the doctor-judge, the educator-judge, the 'social worker'-judge; it is on them that the universal reign of the normative is based; and each individual, wherever he may find himself, subjects to it his body, his gestures, his behaviour, his aptitudes, his achievements. (Michel Foucault, *Discipline and Punish* (Harmondsworth: Penguin, 1991), 304.)

Box 14.4   Risk Societies

Risk societies are *not* exactly class societies; their risk positions cannot be understood as class positions, or their conflicts as class conflicts. (Ulrich Beck 1992: 36)

One implication is that whereas state welfare was once thought of as a protection against collective risks, for example, through social insurance provision, the welfare state has now become a principal source of risk. Tony Giddens agrees with much of Beck's thesis and insists that welfare reform must be based upon a notion of 'positive welfare' in which people are equipped with the skills needed to navigate their way through the new social environments of insecurity, transforming risks-as-dangers into risks-as-opportunities.

The risk society idea has proved to be very influential but has attracted many criticisms. Some reject the sociological assumptions upon which it is based. The contrast between the first and second modernities may be too crude and the suggestion that class structures have become less important has been condemned as naïve. Also, Beck may neglect the extent to which risks have been produced politically by those opposed to welfare state capitalism.

Social Movements

Nevertheless, the idea that class is less salient now than in the past has also appeared in other debates. Some argue that society is best understood as consisting of social movements. A social movement is a process of collective action, a network of interrelated actors who share similar values, identities and objectives in a given socio-historical context.

Social movement theories emerged in the 1960s when those such as the civil rights, the feminist, the green, and the gay/lesbian movements arose to challenge specific forms of injustice and promote the values of their identities. Those theories do not necessarily replace a class analysis but they certainly demand that class analyses be re-thought.

In terms of social policy we could regard the 'new' social movements, listed above, partly as a product of the welfare state. With rising prosperity, increased educational opportunities, and the growth of the public sector, new social movements emerged as traditional distributive conflicts begin to subside. For instance, as the middle class expands in size and influence then conflicts related to culture and lifestyle appear

and lead to new conceptions of politics and social organization.

This means that new social movements may also bear implications for the welfare policies of the future. They offer new perspectives on what it means to be a citizen and user of the welfare state. So as well as providing for basic needs and aiming at the goal of social justice, perhaps social policy should also try to fulfil other imperatives, ones that are less material in nature and related more to quality of life. This is the point that Fraser seems to be making (see above). Some, though, resist these ideas, arguing either that society should not be thought of in terms of social movements or that the existence of the latter should not distract us from the fundamental questions of distributive justice.

Emerging Issues

All of the ideas reviewed above deal with three main themes that show no sign of declining in importance. First, whether we should describe ourselves as still living in a period of modernity. Second, whether class is the main organizing principle of contemporary society. Finally, how we should try to understand society and judge the best means of reforming it and its welfare institutions. Social policy debates in the twenty-first century continue to revolve around these themes and these new directions.

Guide to Further Sources

A comprehensive survey of the key figures in postmodernism is provided in Hans Bertens and Joseph Natoli, *Postmodernism* (Oxford: Blackwell, 2002). An excellent, comprehensive anthology of the greatest philosophers, which traces key debates about modernity across the centuries, can be found in L. E. Cahoone, *From Modernism to Postmodernism: An Anthology* (Oxford: Blackwell, 2003). For useful and accessible discussions of postmodernism in relation to social policy see: John Carter (ed.), *Postmodernity and the Fragmentation of Welfare* (London: Routledge, 1998); Peter Leonard, *Postmodern Welfare* (London: Sage, 1997); John Rodgers, *From a*

Welfare State to a Welfare Society (London: Macmillan, 2000).

Good introductions to post-structuralism can be found in: C. Belsey, *Poststructuralism: A Very Short Introduction* (Oxford: Oxford University Press, 2002); A. Finlayson and J. Valentine, *Politics and Post-Structuralism: An Introduction* (Edinburgh: Edinburgh University Press, 2002).

For a wide-ranging application of the risk society literature to questions of social and public policy, see D. Denney (ed.), *Living in Dangerous Times: Fear, Insecurity, Risk and Social Policy* (Oxford: Blackwell, 2009). For an engaging introduction to social movements and their significance within the history of social policy and welfare reform, see J. Annetts *et al. Understanding Social Welfare Movements* (Bristol: Policy Press, 2009). Also see Jean-François Lyotard, *The Postmodern Condition* (Manchester: Manchester University Press, 1984); (Ulrich Beck, *Risk Society* (London: Sage, 1992).

Web resources include EpistemeLinks www.epistemelinks.com/; Everything Postmodern www.ebbflux.com/postmodern/; Internet Modern History Sourcebook www.fordham.edu/; Stanford Encyclopaedia of Philosophy http://plato.stanford.edu/entries/postmodernism.

Review Questions

1   Is postmodernism merely a critique of modernity or does it present alternative forms of social organization?
2   Are concepts such as 'needs', 'rights', 'class', and 'truth' nothing more than constructs of Western discourse?
3   To what extent are our social identities cultural rather than material?
4   What would a 'postmodern welfare state' look like?
5   What are the disadvantages of using post-structuralist ideas to understand the significance for social policy of risks and of social movements?

Visit the book companion site at www.wiley.com/go/alcock to make use of the resources designed to accompany the textbook. There you will find chapter-specific guides to further resources, including governmental, international, think-tank, pressure groups, and relevant journals sources. You will also find a glossary based on *The Blackwell Dictionary of Social Policy*, help sheets, and case studies, guidance on managing assignments in social policy and career advice.

PART III
Historical Context

15

History and Social Policy

David Gladstone

Overview

- It is easy to argue that a present- and future-centred subject like social policy has little need of an historical perspective.
- By contrast, this chapter suggests that an understanding of welfare in times past is important in providing an awareness of changes and continuities in relation to risk, resources, and responsibility.
- New environmental hazards, demographic patterns, and working practices may suggest new threats to welfare. But a view over time suggests that continuity as well as change is important in understanding threats to well-being.
- Resources – or responses to risk – show a considerable variety of agencies at work in the past as well as in the present. Together they comprise what is often called the mixed economy of welfare.
- There are also long-standing historical continuities in the ideological debate about who should be responsible for responding to risk. Should it be individuals themselves or government action?

The Value of History

Chapters 16 to 20 highlight changes and developments in Britain's welfare arrangements over the past two centuries. By way of introduction, this chapter suggests the importance of an historical perspective in terms of risk, resources, and responsibility. It does so aware that those who study social policy are often more concerned with the present and the future than with the past. They engage with current issues about the supply and distribution of welfare. They discuss how

The Student's Companion to Social Policy, Fourth Edition. Edited by Pete Alcock, Margaret May, Sharon Wright.
© 2012 John Wiley & Sons, Ltd. Published 2012 by John Wiley & Sons, Ltd.

social policies might be improved and made more effective and efficient in the future. Why, then, study the past? What can a historical perspective contribute to Social Policy as an academic subject and as a programme for action? Those themes are central to this chapter.

Personal and Public History

Each of us has our own personal history: a timeline of events and experiences that, to a greater or lesser extent, define who we are and how we may act in the ever-present now. Memory is complex and may be distorted over the passage of time. That said, however, it often plays a significant role in reminding us as persons of our previous experience and understanding of welfare:

- times of risk, hardship and need;
- times as a user of welfare services;
- times of working as a paid professional in the health and welfare sector; and
- times of giving in voluntary organizations or in personal tending care to a relative, friend, or neighbour.

Our personal histories may help us to understand the central concerns of Social Policy. However, it is public history which has most engaged those interested in the study of welfare. Whereas public history used to be the study of kings and queens, battles, wars, and great national events, it is now a much more multifaceted view of the past which is itself the product of increasing specialization among academic historians. One of the most significant developments in that specialization over the past half century has been the growth of social history. Once crudely defined as 'history with the politics left out', social history provides a distinctive perspective on the past: how people lived and worked and thought and behaved towards each other

The history of welfare is an important ingredient of that perspective: for it addresses issues of risk and responsibility as part of the way in which state and citizen, men and women, parents and children, people of different social classes, ethnic origin and economic and political power, behaved towards each other in time past. Public history enables us to describe the changes and continui-

ties in the supply of welfare over time. But, in addition, it also helps us to explain them by highlighting the factors predisposing towards change in the balance of welfare agents and agencies over time, and those countervailing forces favouring the status quo.

Not only has there been an increasing specialization among historians. There has also been a great widening of the sources which they use to research and understand the past. These now include interviews (often tape recorded) in which individuals recall experiences and events in their own past and that of their communities, as well as a whole variety of visual and material artefacts. Jordanova (2000) lists a wide range of examples: maps, photographs, drawings, prints, paintings, costume, tools and machines, buildings, town plans, films: many of them, in her phrase, 'transparent windows onto past times.' For those interested especially in the history of welfare, children's toys, the legacy of the large barrack-like buildings in which 'the poor', 'the mad', and 'the criminal' were incarcerated, and the class-segregated housing developments of towns and cities provide such transparent windows onto past times. The past, in other words, is not confined to the written records of previous centuries or generations. It is, in a variety of ways, all around us as a component of our present.

For all that increasing diversity, however, documentary sources and written records remain an important ingredient of historical research. We are now, however, much more aware that the documentary evidence that has survived from the past was generally written and recorded by those in powerful positions of authority. As such, it is official history. Thus, for example, while much documentary evidence exists concerning the Poor Laws, one of the key suppliers of evidence about past British social welfare, there is comparatively little recording of the experiences and reactions of those who were on the receiving end of its policies as paupers, whether living at home or in a workhouse. The sources of historical evidence are thus more often 'top down' records of policy-makers and administrators rather than 'bottom up' accounts of the impact of their decisions on the lives of ordinary people.

Investigating the past is more than ever complex, specialist, and challenging: with postmodernism simply the latest challenge to attempts to reconstruct the past of human experience. Furthermore, we have to recognize that there are a variety of perspectives on the past, partly as a result of the ideological and experiential baggage which individual scholars bring to their historical enquiry and research. As a result it is often said that there is not one history, but many histories. Yet for all that, the past remains a central feature of the way in which we understand and make sense of the present, not least in welfare and social policy. Present day ideological and political debates about rights and responsibilities, organizational and administrative arrangements and demarcations between service sectors, as well as the language and terminology of welfare all resonate with echoes of the past. The past may be, in L. P. Hartley's phrase, 'a foreign country', but the historical perspective is one which no present day explorer can afford to ignore. Those who are ignorant of history, as George Santayana observed, are doomed to repeat it.

Themes in Welfare History

It is possible to identify three distinct yet interrelated themes in the historical approach to welfare – *risk*, *resources*, and *responsibility*. These themes also link past and present in the study of social policy.

Risk

■ What were the risks or threats to their wellbeing to which individuals were exposed in the past? How similar or different are such threats to welfare today? The historian Johnson defines social risk as 'the probability weighted uncertainty that derives from the changing and dynamic world in which people live.' In other words, it constitutes what the Social Policy tradition tends to define as social problems. Johnson's analysis highlights four categories of risk. Each will now be examined in turn.

■ *Health* It is now well established by demographic historians that death rates only began to fall significantly from the beginning of the twentieth century. In the preceding century there was a high level of infant deaths (until 1900 about 150 in every 1000

children died in their first year), an average life expectancy of forty years, and a much greater risk of premature death for those living in the expanding industrial towns and cities. The contrast with present day statistics suggests a considerable improvement or reduction of risk measured by nineteenth-century standards, an improvement which historians explain in different ways. Some see it as the consequence of a general improvement in the financial and material conditions of the population; others as the result of more comprehensive and accessible health services, public and environmental health improvements and the wider range of medical and clinical treatments that are now available.

■ *Life course* In this category Johnson highlights the vulnerability of large families with several dependent children and the poverty of old age consequent on declining physical powers and enforced withdrawal from the labour market. Both of these categories of risk were identified by Rowntree, one of the early social investigators at the beginning of the twentieth century, in his discussion of the life cycle of poverty based on his research in York. With the high infant mortality of the nineteenth century, a large number of children represented an insurance for care of their parents in old age; while as life expectancy improved so too did the poverty that invariably accompanied the final phase of the life course. The abolition of child and family poverty was one of the priorities of the New Labour government elected in 1997; a target that remained unfulfilled when they left office in 2010. Similarly, it is now generally recognized that there are two nations in old age: those who have the benefit of occupational pensions (even where the calculation of the final pension settlement is subject to change, as is happening now in many such schemes) and those who are dependent on the state retirement pension (where the age of payment is set to rise later this decade).

■ *Economic and occupational* Economic risks are very much determined by the availability and remuneration of paid employment. In the second half of the nineteenth century, on average some 4.5 per cent of male workers were unemployed, but of greater significance at that time was underemployment. Workers in many trades and industries were hired and paid by the day on a casual basis. Such irregularity of employment had considerable effects on household finances which became more precarious when the main wage earner was ill, became disabled, or died. Though the unemployment rate has fluctuated in recent years, the experience of unemployment still impacts on an individual's self-worth, the economic and social well-being of the household unit, and the national economy.

■ *Environmental* The final type of risk in Johnson's analysis is that which results from living in a physically hazardous world. This category ranges, therefore, from all types of accidents to industrial pollution and environmental hazard on a grander scale such as that occasioned by climate change. It has been observed recently that 'it is those near the bottom of the social scale who are most exposed to hazards at work': something which accords very closely with the historical evidence on the nineteenth century. One study of coal mining, for example, notes that between 1869 and 1919 one miner was killed every six hours, seriously injured every two hours and injured badly every two or three minutes.

Resources

Historians have not only researched the risks and threats to welfare in the past: they have also mapped the strategies of survival and sources of available support. Their evidence shows the existence of a mixed economy welfare in the nineteenth century in which a developing diversity of agencies – formal and informal – played an often overlapping role.

Household strategies, often initiated by women who deprived themselves to maximize the well-being of their husbands and children, were an important resource, as were the earnings of children even after the introduction of compulsory elementary schooling in 1880. Mutual support networks existed in working class communities and faith-based organizations – like the Jews and the Salvation Army, for example – also provided financial and material support. Self – help organizations, such as savings banks and

commercial insurance, provided a means for those with a regular and reliable income to save against the eventuality of hazards and risks. This was especially important at a time when most medical treatment required payment and when the accident or death of the principal wage earner could create considerable financial difficulties for the household unit. The trade union movement and the Friendly Societies, controlled by the working class themselves, provided a range of benefits for their members and their dependents at times of unemployment, ill health, or death which were based on the payment of weekly subscriptions – although the benefits of membership were limited to those who were able to pay the weekly dues. Membership of such organizations thus became one of the defining characteristics of the so called *respectable* working class.

Philanthropic charity expanded dramatically during the nineteenth century, co-ordinated to some extent by the Charity Organization Society. Philanthropy encompassed housing schemes, schools, and specialist hospitals (such as Great Ormond Street Hospital for Sick Children), as well as many of the voluntary societies which still exist today (such as the children's charity Barnardo's). At the time some critics deplored the unorganized spread of philanthropic endeavour, seeing it as an encouragement to dependency and pauperization; although more recent criticism has stressed the intrusions made into working class households by the middle class 'lady' visitors of many local charitable associations.

The state – both centrally and locally – became more proactively involved in aspects of welfare during the course of the nineteenth century. The long established system of state-provided financial assistance – the Poor Law – was reformed in the interests of the emerging industrial society in 1834, and parliamentary legislation was also introduced in relation both to public health and elementary education. Despite the activity of the encroaching state, the level of intervention and public spending remained small and much welfare provision remained largely localized and amateur.

By contrast the twentieth century was characterized by more extensive state provided welfare and a growing professionalization of welfare activities. A variety of social legislation passed by the Liberal government between 1906 and 1914 encompassed the provision of school meals, school medical inspection, and Old Age Pensions, as well as the creation of a National Insurance scheme of sickness and unemployment insurance which was progressively expanded during the inter-war years. But it was the classic welfare state developed between 1944 and 1948 in legislation passed by the wartime coalition and post-war Labour government that provided a more comprehensive coverage of risks – from the cradle to the grave – for the British population. The Appointed Day for the introduction of the National Health Service and the schemes of post-war social security and financial assistance was 5 July 1948. It was described by the prime minister, Clement Attlee, as 'a day which makes history.'

The introduction of a more comprehensive system of state-provided welfare meant something of a readjustment in the roles of other suppliers in the mixed economy of welfare. Although their roles may have been redefined over the past sixty years in relation to changing state activity, each of the sources of formal and informal assistance and support continue to operate; and Britain's welfare system today is made up of a diversity of responses to risk, just as in the past.

Responsibility

Historians do not only describe change, they also seek to explain it. In that task, Britain's welfare system is a fertile area for investigation both of particular policy changes as well as more general and significant transformations. At the general level is the comparative historical study which locates the development of welfare states in Europe and America in the context of political mobilization (the voter motive in the conditions of mass democracy) and specific levels of economic development (i.e. when sufficient resources are available to yield the tax revenues necessary to fund public welfare services), whereas more detailed studies of particular policy changes indicate a wide range of change agents. In the middle are theories drawn from a number of historical case studies which explain change in more conceptual terms such as:

■ Legitimacy – is this an area in which government is legitimately involved?
■ Feasibility – is the proposed change feasible in terms, for example, of resources?

■ Support – is the change in question likely to enhance rather than diminish support for government?

Such a framework indicates the inevitably political and value-laden nature of welfare state change and takes the historian into the history of ideas and political debate. What a historical perspective suggestively indicates is that current discourse around the respective welfare responsibilities of state and citizen is in fact by no means new. Political discussion has been around for the past century and more, and over that time a number of distinct ideological positions have been developed, many of which still influence policy debates today. These different ideological positions raise important questions for the historian about the changing role of the state in welfare and the factors which can explain the greater comprehensiveness of the classic welfare state of the 1940s, the much discussed 'crisis' of the welfare state in the 1970s which provided the springboard for the Thatcherite agenda of rolling back the frontiers of the state, and the austerity agenda proposed by the coalition government elected in 2010.

One final issue that needs to be considered in the context of responsibility is the objective of state welfare. Whereas earlier writers on Britain's welfare past tended to portray it as an essentially beneficent activity, more recent critical commentators have emphasized the functional necessity of public welfare in a capitalist economy, and its role in regulating the poor, especially those receiving increasingly conditional and selective benefits.

Emerging Issues: New Developments in the History of Welfare

Early studies written in the aftermath of the creation of Britain's classic welfare state in the mid-twentieth century, with titles such as *The Coming of the Welfare State* tended to be *Whiggish* in character – that is they characterized the emergence of comprehensive state welfare as a unilinear progression from the 'darkness' of the nineteenth century Poor Law to the 'light' of the Beveridge Plan of 1942 and the post-war welfare state. These Whiggish accounts saw comprehensive public welfare as part of a generally beneficent process, although, as we mentioned earlier, more modern commentators would dispute that welfare provision has been an unqualified benefit for all.

Such a 'welfare state escalator' view of history has therefore largely been replaced in more recent accounts by the mixed economy approach. This recognizes the continuance of the diversity of welfare suppliers, the growth of state intervention as well as the changing role of the state (from direct service provider to financier and regulator of other agencies) and the moving frontier between providers that has characterized both the present and the past of welfare.

Increasingly too, more recent studies of welfare have pushed back beyond the nineteenth and twentieth centuries. The Poor Law, it is true, has a long history dating from the sixteenth century and historical studies of welfare have ranged over its total time frame. There is now much more attention to a wider range of risk and resources in earlier historical periods which encompass households and families, philanthropy, community, and informal networks.

Furthermore, the British experience is now increasingly set within a wider geographical context of comparative study. Such research has challenged both the notion of the primacy of Britain's welfare state (itself a German term of the 1920s) and located the British experience within a broader discussion of welfare state regimes. It is appropriate, therefore, to end with Lewis's observation that

> Rather than seeing the story of the modern welfare state as a simple movement from individualism to collectivism and ever increasing amounts of (benevolent) state intervention, it is more accurate to see European countries as having had mixed economies of welfare in which the state, the voluntary sector, employers, the family and the market have played different parts at different points in time. (Lewis 1999: 11)

Guide to Further Sources

The Pursuit of History (Harlow: Longman, 2009) by John Tosh and *History in Practice* (London: Arnold, 2000) by Ludmilla Jordanova provide stimulating introductions to the study of the past.

The volumes by Martin Daunton – *Progress and Poverty* (Oxford: Oxford University Press, 1995) and *Wealth and Welfare* (Oxford: Oxford University Press, 2007) locate welfare in the context of British social and economic change between 1700 and 1950, while *No Turning Back* (Oxford: Oxford University Press, 2010) by Paul Addison takes the story to the beginning of the twenty-first century.

Johnson's essay referred to in the text provides a useful framework for understanding both changes in risk and response. P. Johnson, 'Risk, redistribution and social welfare in Britain from the poor law to Beveridge', in M. Daunton (ed.), *Charity, Self Interest and Welfare in the English Past* (London: UCL Press, 2000).

See also Jane Lewis, 'The voluntary sector in the mixed economy of welfare', in David Gladstone (ed.), *Before Beveridge: Welfare before the Welfare State* (I.E.A. Health and Welfare Unit, 1999), p. 11.

The most relevant web site is that of History & Policy, www.historyandpolicy.org. The Institute of Historical Research's web site, www.history.ac.uk, contains good links to other sites and sources.

Review Questions

1   What characteristics differentiate public from private history?
2   Do we need more than documentary sources to understand the past?
3   Why do you think Social Policy needs a historical perspective?
4   Give some examples that link the present and the past in terms of risk, resources, and responsibility.
5   Identify some emerging trends in the study of welfare in past times.

Visit the book companion site at www.wiley.com/go/alcock to make use of the resources designed to accompany the textbook. There you will find chapter-specific guides to further resources, including governmental, international, think-tank, pressure groups, and relevant journals sources. You will also find a glossary based on *The Blackwell Dictionary of Social Policy*, help sheets, and case studies, guidance on managing assignments in social policy and career advice.

16

Nineteenth-Century Beginnings

Bernard Harris

Overview

- During the nineteenth century, people sought protection against the risks of poverty and poor health with the aid of their families, friends and communities, through charities, and by joining mutual-aid associations.
- In England and Wales, the main form of statutory provision was the Poor Law, which originated in a series of Acts passed during the sixteenth century. Scotland possessed a much more rudimentary system of poor relief and a poor law was only introduced in Ireland in 1838.
- The English and Welsh Poor Laws experienced a major transformation in 1834. The Poor Law Amendment Act aimed to make poor relief less accessible to able-bodied men, and further efforts to 'tighten up' the Poor Law were introduced in the 1870s. However, there were also indications of a more flexible attitude to welfare provision during the final decades of the nineteenth century.
- The century also witnessed important developments with regard to the improvement of working conditions and the introduction of new housing standards, together with the provision of health care.
- In England and Wales, government grants to educational bodies were introduced in 1833, and School Boards assumed responsibility for the provision of elementary schools after 1870. The first Public Health Act was passed in 1848, and local authorities intensified their efforts to improve the standard of public health from the 1870s.
- Despite considerable progress during the final part of the nineteenth century, there was also growing anxiety about the need for further reform, and this contributed to the introduction of the Liberal welfare reforms after 1906.

The Student's Companion to Social Policy, Fourth Edition. Edited by Pete Alcock, Margaret May, Sharon Wright.
© 2012 John Wiley & Sons, Ltd. Published 2012 by John Wiley & Sons, Ltd.

Introduction

As José Harris observed, 'all political regimes have social policies of some kind, even if such policies consist simply in leaving the pursuit of welfare to the family or the local community or the corporation or the market' (quoted in Harris 2004: 17). However, nineteenth-century Britain also witnessed a series of changes which had a major impact on the scale and scope of public welfare provision. This chapter summarizes these developments, while also recognizing the role of other providers within the overall framework of a 'mixed economy of welfare provision'.

In the late eighteenth century, Britain was still a largely agricultural society. Although 29.7 per cent of workers were employed in manufacturing, mining and industry, nearly 36 per cent were employed in agriculture, forestry, and fishing. Only 34 per cent of the population lived in towns or cities containing more than 2,500 inhabitants. However, during the first half of the nineteenth century, the proportion of workers engaged in agricultural occupations fell to 21.7 per cent and the proportion employed in industry rose to 42.9 per cent and by the end of the century 78 per cent of the population was classified as 'urban'. The number of people in England, Scotland, and Wales increased from 10.5 million to 37 million over the course of the century.

Throughout this period, families, friends, and neighbours played a central role in meeting social needs. In his pioneering analysis of family life in early industrial Lancashire, Michael Anderson argued that when an individual migrated to a town 'it was advisable, or well-nigh essential, to make every effort to keep in contact . . . or enter into reciprocal assistance with kinsmen, if life chances were not to be seriously imperilled (quoted in Harris 2004: 77), and Marguerite Dupree drew similar conclusions from her study of the mid-nineteenth-century Potteries. Other writers have also highlighted the importance of friends and neighbours. In 1911, Margaret Loane concluded that many older people would have been unable to maintain themselves without 'valid and recognised claims on the services of neighbours or relatives earned by former kindnesses and exertion' (quoted in Harris 2004: 78).

Many people also relied on the support of charities and mutual-aid organizations. As Frank Prochaska has argued, a great deal of working-class charity was of a type – local, spontaneous and independent – which left little trace in official records, but more institutional forms of charity also helped to build bridges between different social groups, creating an infrastructure of support for education and health care, developing different forms of housing provision, and giving financial and other kinds of support during periods of crisis. In Coventry, seven appeals for the relief of distress were launched between January 1837 and April 1860, and a national appeal was initiated in November 1860. The Lord Mayor of Manchester appealed on behalf of Lancashire cotton workers and their families in 1862, and the Lord Mayor of London issued emergency appeals in 1866 and 1886.

Historians have become increasingly interested in the role played by friendly societies and other mutual-aid organizations in the development of a range of social-protection schemes. Although many friendly societies claimed great antiquity, the movement 'took off' during the mid-eighteenth century. Members paid money into a common fund in return for support during periods of sickness and old age and following their deaths. By the end of the nineteenth century, more than four million individuals (of whom the vast majority were male) belonged to a friendly society, while many others belonged to trade unions (many of which also offered welfare benefits), collecting societies (a specialized form of friendly society offering funeral benefits), co-operative societies, savings banks, and building societies. However, despite these provisions, many people continued to rely on the assistance provided by public welfare authorities, such as the Poor Law, at different stages of their lives.

Poor Relief

Although several authors have argued that the development of state welfare was directly related to the process of industrialization, the earliest form of statutory welfare in Britain predated the emergence of an industrial society by more than two centuries. During the late fifteenth and sixteenth centuries, Parliament passed a series of Acts, known as the Poor Laws, which allowed local magistrates to: punish vagrants and return them to their own homes; issue licences to 'deserving paupers' to enable them to beg; outlaw 'indiscriminate almsgiving' and set vagabonds to work; make arrangements for the apprenticeship of pauper children; and establish weekly collections for the relief of the 'impotent poor'. These Acts culminated in the passage of the Elizabethan Poor Laws of 1597 and 1601. These Acts gave the churchwardens and overseers of each parish the power to levy a tax, or poor rate, on the local population and to use the proceeds to 'set the poor on work', maintain those who were unable to work, and board out pauper children as apprentices.

Despite a series of modifications, the essential features of the Poor Law remained unchanged for the next 230 years. However, during the second half of the eighteenth century, critics argued that they undermined work incentives, weakened social ties, encouraged population growth, and exacerbated the poverty they were designed to ameliorate. In 1795, the Conservative philosopher, Edmund Burke, sought to distinguish between those who were 'poor' because they could not support themselves without working, and those who were 'genuinely poor' because they were unable to work. His views were echoed by the Utilitarian philosopher, Jeremy Bentham (best known for his maxim that 'the greatest happiness of the greatest number . . . is the measure of right and wrong'), and the social commentator, Patrick Colquhoun, and their ideas had a major impact when a Royal Commission was appointed to investigate the Poor Laws in 1832.

The Royal Commission on the Poor Laws was one of the most important investigative bodies in the history of British social policy. Although it recognized that some form of provision was necessary, it also argued that 'in no part of Europe except England has it been thought fit [to apply this] . . . to more than the relief of *indigence*, the state of a person unable to labour, or unable to obtain in return for his labour, the means of subsistence. It has never been deemed expedient that the provision should extend to the relief of *poverty*, that is, to the state of one who, in order to obtain a mere subsistence, is forced to have recourse to labour' (quoted in Harris 2004: 46–7). It sought to enforce this distinction by ensuring that only those who were genuinely destitute would be willing to apply for poor relief. The key

to this policy was the workhouse test. The Commission argued that if claimants were told that relief would only be made available inside a 'well-regulated workhouse', those people who were capable of supporting themselves outside the workhouse would prefer to do so.

The Poor Law Report provided the foundation for the Poor Law Amendment Act of 1834. However, this Act did not compel Poor Law authorities to establish workhouses or to abandon the payment of 'outdoor relief' (i.e. the provision of assistance to individuals outside a workhouse). Its most important innovation was the establishment of a central body, the Poor Law Commission, with the power to make and issue rules for the management of the poor throughout England and Wales and to create combinations of Poor Law parishes, known as Poor Law Unions, to administer the Poor Law in each area. The Commission could only order Unions to construct workhouses if it obtained the written consent of a majority of the Poor Law Guardians, or the support of a majority of the ratepayers and property-owners who were eligible to vote in Guardians' elections.

Historians have often disagreed in their assessment of the Act's impact. Although many traditional Poor Law practices survived the advent of the 'New Poor Law', workhouses were constructed in most parts of the country and the vast majority of parishes had been reorganized into Poor Law Unions by the end of the 1850s. Karel Williams argued that the main aim of the New Poor Law was to deter able-bodied men from seeking poor relief. He also pointed out that the real test of the workhouse as a deterrent institution was not the number of people who entered a workhouse, but the number who were discouraged from applying for relief by the fear of entering one. Judged by this standard, the establishment of the New Poor Law appears to have led to a substantial reduction in the number of able-bodied male paupers, but the Poor Law authorities continued to support large numbers of non-able bodied men, as well as women and children, and the majority of these people were relieved outside the workhouse.

Contemporaries also debated the impact of Poor Law reform. While many people thought that the New Poor Law was too harsh and was failing in its duty to provide for the most vulnerable, others believed that the original principles of the 1834 reform had been diluted and that its deterrent functions were being undermined by 'indiscriminate' charity. In 1847, the Poor Law Commission was replaced by the Poor Law Board and in 1869 the Board's president, Viscount Goschen, advised London's Poor Law authorities to work more closely with private charities and to restrict the flow of statutory relief. This policy continued when the Poor Law Board was itself replaced by the Local Government Board in 1871, and this led to what became known as the 'Crusade against Outdoor Relief'. The 'crusade' led to sharp reductions in the numbers of both male and female paupers throughout the decade.

However, despite the 'crusade', other evidence suggested that approaches to poverty were moving in a different direction. This was reflected in measures such as: the use of income scales to identify parents who might qualify for the remittance of school fees following the introduction of the Forster Education Act in 1870; the removal of restrictions which prevented men who claimed outdoor medical relief from voting in Parliamentary elections in 1885; the authorization of public works schemes during periods of unemployment between 1886 and 1893; and the democratization of Guardians' elections and the appointment of the Royal Commission on the Aged Poor in 1894. Attitudes to poverty were also shaped by the results of two major surveys of poverty in London and York between 1887 and 1901. Many of these developments contributed to the adoption of new approaches to the prevention and relief of poverty by the Liberal governments of 1906–14 (see Chapter 17).

Public Services

Although the Poor Law provided the bedrock of public welfare services during the nineteenth century, the period also witnessed major developments in other aspects of the state's welfare role. These developments were reflected in the introduction of measures to regulate living and working conditions as well as the establishment of new kinds of public service.

As we have already seen, the late eighteenth and early nineteenth centuries saw a significant increase in the scale of industrial employment, including the growth of factories and workshops.

During the late eighteenth century, reformers such as Thomas Percival highlighted the conditions under which children were employed in these establishments and this led to a series of attempts to regulate conditions of employment for children and, subsequently, for women and, eventually, men. The earliest Acts included the Health and Morals of Apprentices Act (1802) and the Factory Acts of 1819, 1820, 1825, and 1833, and they were followed by more wide-ranging pieces of legislation such as the Ten Hours Act (1847), the Factory Acts of 1867 and 1874, and the Factory and Workshops Acts of 1878 and 1901.

Local authorities and central government also tried to establish minimum standards for the construction of new housing and to improve the quality of the built environment. Many of the earliest measures took the form of Local Improvement Acts and were largely ineffective, but the pace of reform quickened after the Municipal Corporations Act allowed the larger towns and cities to establish single unitary authorities after 1835. Local authorities acquired the power to prosecute the owners of 'filthy and unwholesome' properties and demolish 'ruinous or insanitary buildings' in 1846 and 1847 respectively. The Public Health Act of 1848 allowed local boards of health to prohibit cellar-dwellings, regulate common lodging houses, ensure that all new buildings were connected to sewers, and make arrangements for the removal of 'nuisances', such as refuse piles and unclean privies. The Artizans' and Labourers' Dwellings Act (1868) and the Artizans' and Labourers' Dwellings Improvement Act (1875) gave local authorities the power to demolish insanitary dwellings, but little effort was made to provide affordable forms of replacement housing for displaced tenants. However, the Housing of the Working Classes Act of 1890 allowed local authorities to construct new houses for more affluent workers and encouraged hopes that this would reduce the pressure of demand at the bottom of the housing market. Although the Act had relatively little effect on total housing stock before 1914, it anticipated the first large-scale experiments in council housing after 1919.

The nineteenth century also saw important changes in the development of medical services. The traditional divisions between physicians, surgeons, and apothecaries became increasingly blurred, and a more unified medical profession began to emerge. At the start of the century, most people preferred to be treated in their own homes, but by the end of the century they were more likely to seek hospital care for more serious forms of treatment. In 1891, approximately 25 per cent of hospital beds were located in charitable, or voluntary, institutions and the remainder were in the public sector. The majority of these were located in Poor Law infirmaries, but a growing number were housed in more specialized institutions administered by local authority public health committees.

There was also a rapid increase in the number of people who lived in urban areas, and many contemporaries feared that the pace of urbanization and the concentration of health problems in towns would undermine the health of the population as a whole. In 1848, Parliament passed the first of a series of Public Health Acts (other Acts followed in 1872, 1875, and 1936). In addition to the housing clauses which have already been described, the Act led to the creation of the first central government health department, the General Board of Health, and gave it the power to examine the sanitary condition of any area where more than 10 per cent of ratepayers requested such an enquiry, or where the local death rate averaged more than twenty-three deaths per thousand living over a seven-year period. The General Board of Health was also empowered to create local Boards of Health if such a measure seemed appropriate. However, despite this legislation, it was not until much later in the century that many local authorities began to take concerted action to improve sanitary conditions. The expansion of public health activity after 1870 had many causes, but one of the most important was the provision of central government support for the appointment of local Medical Officers of Health from 1872.

At the start of the nineteenth century, many observers were afraid that the expansion of educational opportunities would foment unrest, and it was left to a number of religious societies, including the Non-Conformist British and Foreign Schools Society and the Church of England National Society, to take the lead in establishing new schools. However, in 1833 the government granted £20,000 to these societies to enable them to build more schools in northern England, and both the scale and scope of public educational funding expanded rapidly after 1840. During the 1860s, many commentators expressed concerns about the number of children who were not attending recognized elementary schools, and this led to the Elementary Education Act in 1870. The new Act aimed to 'fill the gaps' in the existing system of voluntary education by creating School Boards in areas where the level of provision was supposed to be inadequate. Although the Act did not make education compulsory for children across the whole of England and Wales (separate legislation applied to Scotland), it allowed School Boards to make education compulsory for children between the ages of five and ten in areas where they were established, and this was extended to other areas in 1876 and 1880. Elementary school fees were abolished in 1891, and the School Boards' powers were transferred to Local Authority Education Committees in 1902.

Emerging Issues

As this chapter has shown, the nineteenth century witnessed many important changes in welfare provision. Although the Poor Law Amendment Act was designed to restrict the extent of welfare support, especially to able-bodied men, a more expansive attitude to the relief of poverty became apparent from the 1870s onwards. The state's role also expanded in other ways. These included the introduction of a series of Acts to regulate the employment of women and children, establish minimum standards of health and safety at work, improve the quality of new housing, protect the population against the spread of disease, and provide new educational services.

However, despite these measures, many Victorians approached the start of the new century with growing unease. During the 1880s and 1890s, surveys by two independent researchers, Charles Booth and Seebohm Rowntree, appeared to show that the extent of poverty was much greater than previously thought, and Rowntree's findings in particular helped to fuel concerns that a significant proportion of the working-class population was living below the standard of 'merely physical efficiency'. These fears were compounded by suggestions that the health of the population was being undermined by continuing urbanization and by the high proportion of prospective army recruits who were rejected on grounds of physical unfitness. The established political parties – the Liberals and Conservatives – faced a growing challenge from an increasingly organized labour movement (the Labour Representation Committee was formed in 1900), and concern over Britain's failure to keep pace with the emerging economic powers of Germany and the United States continued to mount. Many of these anxieties were reflected in the background to the new welfare measures which the Liberal government introduced after 1906.

Guide to Further Sources

There are a number of general texts dealing with the history of British social policy since 1800. This chapter is largely based on B. Harris, *The Origins of the British Welfare State: Society, State and Social Welfare in England and Wales, 1800–1945* (Basingstoke: Palgrave, 2004). Other general texts include D. Fraser, *The Evolution of the British Welfare State* (4th edn, Basingstoke: Palgrave, 2010) and P. Thane, *The Foundations of the Welfare State* (2nd edn, London: Longman, 1996).

For more specialized introductions to individual topic areas, see: A. Kidd, *State, Society and the Poor in Nineteenth-Century England* (Basingstoke: Palgrave, 1999); K. Williams, *From Pauperism to Poverty* (London: Routledge, 1981); G. Finlayson, *Citizen, State and Social Welfare in Britain, 1830–1990* (Oxford: Oxford University Press, 1994); J. Burnett, *A Social History of Housing, 1815–1985* (London: Routledge, 1996); A. Wohl, *Endangered Lives: Public Health in Victorian Britain* (London: Methuen, 1984); and W.B. Stephens, *Education in Britain, 1750–1914* (Basingstoke: Palgrave, 1998).

Review Questions

1 How important were charity and mutual aid in helping working-class people to support themselves during the nineteenth century?
2 Why was the Poor Law 'reformed' in 1834 and what were the consequences?
3 How might we explain the growth of state welfare intervention in Britain before 1900?
4 To what extent did attitudes to the relief of poverty change in Britain after 1870?
5 How did the development of social policy during the nineteenth century contribute to the origins of the modern welfare state and what lessons, if any, should contemporary policy-makers draw from nineteenth-century developments?

Visit the book companion site at www.wiley.com/go/alcock to make use of the resources designed to accompany the textbook. There you will find chapter-specific guides to further resources, including governmental, international, think-tank, pressure groups, and relevant journals sources. You will also find a glossary based on *The Blackwell Dictionary of Social Policy*, help sheets, and case studies, guidance on managing assignments in social policy and career advice.

17

The Liberal Era and the Growth of State Welfare

Noel Whiteside

▪▫▪

Overview

- ▪ In the late nineteenth century, growing international economic rivalry and rising pauperism created fears about social degeneration and imperial decline.
- ▪ New social scientific and medical analyses created fresh debates on the causes (and prevention) of poverty.
- ▪ A more radical organized labour movement threatened the political hegemony of Britain's two-party system.
- ▪ The Liberal governments of 1906–14 introduced extensive controversial new legislation principally designed to promote the health of the rising generation and to organize urban labour markets.
- ▪ While in some respects prescient of the future British welfare state of the late 1940s, the impact of this legislation was undermined by opposition and the mass unemployment of the inter-war years.

▪▫▪

Context

In the late nineteenth century, social welfare began to emerge as a national issue requiring national solutions. This modified *laissez faire* liberal sentiments and a Poor Law orthodoxy that understood poverty as a sign of personal fault and moral inadequacy. Why did this happen? And

why did the Liberals – the political party most closely associated with industrial interests and the free market economy – emerge as the champion of welfare reform? What were these reforms like and what did they set out to achieve? With hindsight, this period represents the zenith of Britain's imperial and industrial power. Extensive areas in global maps were tinged pink, the pound sterling

The Student's Companion to Social Policy, Fourth Edition. Edited by Pete Alcock, Margaret May, Sharon Wright.
© 2012 John Wiley & Sons, Ltd. Published 2012 by John Wiley & Sons, Ltd.

was the global trading currency, and Britain's merchant marine dominated international commerce. In the face of all this prosperity, it seems an odd time for issues of poverty and its effects to attract the attention of government.

Yet Britain's manufacturing and commercial centres were causing increasing public concern. By 1900, Britain was no longer the sole industrial power. Domination of world trade had been easy when few countries were industrially developed. However, others were catching up; rivalry from the United States and particularly from Imperial Germany threatened Britain's supremacy. While the United Kingdom had been a world leader in the first and second industrial revolutions (based on water and steam power respectively), it trailed others in the third, based on electricity and petrochemical industries. German rates of growth outstripped Britain's own, industrialization in Germany took place behind the safety of tariff barriers (while Britain remained committed to free trade) and, thanks to innovations in the realm of social insurance, poverty in Germany appeared far less problematic than it was in Britain. The promise that a free market economy would create prosperity for all seemed to be contradicted in Germany where industrial development lay at the core of state policy.

The example set by German social legislation proved particularly influential. By 1900, Germany was Britain's chief industrial competitor and, of all countries in Europe, the one whose urban and economic profile most closely matched Britain's own. Germany's state-sponsored social insurance against the risks of accident, ill health, and old age, introduced in the 1880s, excited a mixture of admiration and hostility: admiration for the protection these schemes afforded: hostility towards German authoritarianism and the heavy handed bureaucracy that most British critics assumed underpinned these measures. Germany, however, was not the only nation that attracted attention. Other countries offered alternative solutions. The German system of contributory old age pensions, for example, was readily compared with the New Zealand – and later Australian – schemes, which offered tax-based support to all elderly citizens. In the event, the latter examples were more significant in shaping the British Old Age Pensions Act (1908). Then, as now, measures adopted overseas informed discussion about possible British responses to the 'social question, which is discussed in the next section.'

The Social Question and the Threat of Economic Decline

Late nineteenth century social investigation revealed the poverty dominating Britain's inner cities and reawakened fears of mass pauperism. Widespread destitution caused rates of pauperism to rise, adding to the ratepayer's (local tax payer's) burdens. Thanks to the expansion of major industrial centres and the flight of the middle classes to the suburbs, inner city boroughs found themselves unable to raise the money required to meet their social obligations without pauperizing yet more residents. Places like Poplar in East London (a notorious example) required loans from the Treasury to make ends meet – loans that could never be repaid. This mismatch between local needs and local financial resources proved one of the most compelling reasons to promote national solutions to welfare issues – leading eventually to a national welfare state.

The causes of destitution and the rising burden of pauperism were ascribed to an overstocked labour market, under-employment, poor diet, overcrowding, and disease – all fostering economic inefficiency. The results were manifest in the numbers of casual or intermittent workers and domestic workers employed in 'sweated' (underpaid) occupations. During the economic slumps of 1884–7, 1888, and 1892–5 the situation degenerated further. In the eyes of potential reformers, the 'regular' worker who lost his place had no more right to state support than the most hopeless casual. In hard times, the respectable man would be forced to compete for work with such riff-raff; insecure employment, poor diet, and exposure to the 'rougher' end of the job market would eventually undermine both his willingness to work and his capacity for it. Unemployment thus bred unemployability, added to the casual 'residuum' and damaged those with working skills and experience essential for economic recovery. If treated like a pauper, the 'respectable' unemployed man became one: demoralized and incapable of self support. So, to prevent this cycle of impoverishment that threatened the working population, state intervention was considered necessary.

This construction of the 'social question' fed fears of economic and imperial decline. Growing international competition led to falling commodity prices and profits; this in turn produced more aggressive management strategies designed to raise productivity and to cut labour costs. As a result, established modes of industrial relations – based on mutual understanding between employer and employed – deteriorated. In the 1880s and 1890s the number of strikes grew as 'new', militant trade unions organized unskilled workers. The successful London Dock Strike of 1889 epitomized the shift from co-operation to confrontation which this climate invoked. For contemporary observers, these developments appeared to threaten Britain's economy and, with this, the security of Empire. First, strikes disrupted production and trade union resistance delayed the introduction of key technologies, damaging entrepreneurship and economic growth. Second, inner cities were a breeding ground for social and mental degenerates. Inefficient workers formed a growing burden on the industries they served and the communities they lived in, thanks to irregular working habits and a perpetual reliance on poor relief. In brief, the free market economy was not working in the manner its supporters suggested it should. The need for reform was winning support on all sides of the political spectrum.

The Social Question: Diagnostics and Analysis

At the same time, social analysis was changing, to become based on rather different premises from those that had originally informed Poor Law reform. The focus shifted from individual failings and towards environmental and social factors. In the work of Henry Mayhew and Charles Booth, who analysed poverty of London's East End in the 1840s and 1880s respectively, we witness this changing approach. Mayhew's account of the street sellers and mud larks focused on personal stories: individual accounts of poor people's lives. Booth, a founding member of the Royal Statistical Society, developed social scientific methods, later refined by A. L. Bowley and Seebohm Rowntree,

to distinguish poverty caused by age, infirmity, or unemployment from that due to drink, criminal tendencies, or laziness. Such social categories, based on reasons for destitution, have subsequently provided a lasting foundation for poverty analysis.

Social science was not alone in creating a new diagnosis of the 'social question'. Led by Galton and Pearson, early eugenicists claimed inheritance explained the larger part of poverty through the perpetuation of mental, moral, and physical weakness. They demanded that 'unfit' paupers be sterilized and that official inspection be required prior to marriage before the happy couple be permitted to wed and breed. Such ideas, later elaborated in Hitler's Germany, carried heavy racist overtones and appealed to imperial sentiment through references to quasi-Darwinian theories concerning 'the survival of the fittest'. Socially indiscriminate breeding, endemic in inner cities, threatened the pre-eminence of the British race, eugenicists argued, and, in consequence, undermined British industry and Britain's Empire. The solution lay in reversing population decline among the middle classes (who, thanks to Marie Stopes, could now control family size) and restricting the reproductive capacity of the degenerate poor. This approach was vigorously opposed by Fabian social scientists led by Sidney and Beatrice Webb (the latter having worked on Charles Booth's London enquiry). For the Webbs, solutions to the problem of poverty lay in the correct application of professional knowledge appropriate to the cause of destitution. The Poor Law, by incorporating all destitute without regard for the causes of their situations, was a demoralizing and inappropriate instrument and should be abolished. Instead, professional analysis should inform the provision of state services appropriate to cure poverty: medical care for the sick, residential care for the old, work for the unemployed, disciplinary camps for the 'workshy', and so on.

The debates stimulated by such conflicting views were revealed in the many official enquiries into causes of industrial unrest, of physical degeneration, and of Poor Law problems that took place in the quarter century before 1914. Such investigations bear witness to the degree of official concern that emerged during these years about the well-being of the British population – embracing industrialists and defenders of Empire as well as philanthropists, Poor Law officials, and the labour movement. How the issue was apprehended determined how it was to be tackled – and to the political dimension of the question we now turn.

The Social Question: Politics and Reform

Urban degeneration carried political consequences. Radical organizations, like the Social Democratic Federation (SDF), recruited extensively among the unemployed. In the 1880s and early 1890s, the SDF organized demonstrations in major British cities; demonstrations which degenerated into riots and looting. Socialist ideas also informed the strikes perpetrated by the 'new' trade union organizations; the TUC (Trades Union Congress) began to create its own reform agenda. In 1900, trade unions and socialist groups (not only the SDF, but the Independent Labour Party and the Fabian Society) combined to form the Labour Representation Committee, later the Labour Party. Such developments threatened the political status quo, encouraging both the main political parties to propose remedial action.

By the turn of the century, many philanthropists also recognized that poverty would not be solved through the medium of social casework and self-improvement, but required state intervention. Prominent politicians in the main political parties were also convinced of the need for action. Following the near disaster of the Boer War (1899–1902), when many potential military recruits had to be turned away as physically incapable of bearing arms, concern for physical, economic, and general national efficiency reached new heights. Within the Conservative Party, Joseph Chamberlain had established a reform agenda including the provision of extensive public works for the unemployed, to be funded by tariffs on imported goods. In the General Election of 1906, the Conservatives were heavily defeated as voters rallied in support of free trade and the Liberals. The newly formed Labour Party did particularly well and subsequently sponsored private members' bills to help poor school children and to promote the Right to Work. If the Liberal government was to retain the support of working class voters, it had to produce its own programme of reform.

This was not easy; the Liberal party was the natural base for industrial interests and for classic liberal principles of minimal government. These Liberals were neither natural allies of left-wing socialists nor would they support reforms that, to their eyes, undermined Poor Law principles. The idea of state help for poor children, for example, contravened the basic tenet that fathers should be held responsible for the well-being of their families and that failure to provide should be punished by incarceration in the workhouse. From this perspective, provision of free medical care or school meals rewarded parental indolence and vice and should be opposed. In consequence, the Liberal programme did not go as far as some of its supporters would have liked. Such compromise, however, papered over divisions of principle that eventually tore the Liberal party apart. After the First World War, the Left turned to the Labour Party and the Right to the Conservatives as the Liberals entered a long period of political decline.

Before 1914, however, the uneasy political alliance held together. In 1908, the prime minister, Campbell Bannerman, unexpectedly died and Asquith, the leader of the party's reforming wing, took over the premiership, supported by Lloyd George (a radical land reformer and future wartime prime minister (1916–24)) as Chancellor of the Exchequer and the young Winston Churchill as President of the Board of Trade (and in charge of labour market policy). The reforming alliance was augmented by the rise of civil servants of Fabian conviction and reforming persuasion in major Whitehall departments. The agenda for reform revolved around two main issues: the organization of the labour market and the social welfare of the next generation. Both invoked an increased role for the state.

High levels of infant mortality and evidence on the impact of poor diet on physical and mental development presented to the Interdepartmental Committee on Physical Deterioration in 1903–4 focused official attention on children. In 1904 the then Conservative administration had allowed Poor Law authorities to fund meals for poor children, but this pauperized the parents and take-up rates were very low. The first parliamentary bill sponsored by a backbench Labour MP in 1906 concerned the feeding of school children. Two years later the Liberal government added compulsory school medical inspection (but not treatment) and legislation providing for trained health visitors, midwives, and infant welfare centres. The object was to protect infant life, by offering trained attendance at childbirth and professional instruction to new mothers on infant care. Thanks to their internal political divisions, the Liberals made the provision of such services permissive, not obligatory. Local authorities could, if they wished, raise a rate to provide school meals, or fund infant welfare; compulsion was only introduced after 1918.

The labour market formed the focus for more concerted attention. The main objective was to concentrate the provision of work in the hands of the most efficient workers, to raise industrial efficiency, and promote economic growth. This required the separation of those who could not work regularly (due to age, incapacity, or illness) from those who would not (the incorrigible idlers in Poor Law parlance) to offer support to the former and punitive correction to the latter. The agency for sorting the sheep from the goats was the labour exchange: promoted by the young William Beveridge who met Winston Churchill through the Webbs. The idea of the labour exchange was directly adopted from German cities that Beveridge visited in 1907. The project in the United Kingdom was taken one step further by his vision of a national network, linked by the latest technology (the telephone) to allow labour to be sent where required from any part of the country. That year (1908) Lloyd George piloted the first United Kingdom old age pensions through Parliament. Independent of the Poor Law and available to all over seventy on a means-tested basis, tax-funded supplementation to reduced income allowed women (widows, then as now the vast majority of aged poor) to claim in their own right while helping the aged and infirm to leave the labour market.

Finally, the National Insurance Act (1911) covered working people on or below a stipulated minimum income per year. The first part provided health insurance, to be administered by the myriad voluntary friendly and collecting societies offering protection against sickness (Chapter 16) and industrial insurance companies who had long sold life policies to the poor. Again inspired by German example following Lloyd George's visit to that country in 1908, a tripartite contribution from employer, employee, and the state funded a weekly sickness payment and the right

to basic medical treatment for workers (but did not cover their families). This aimed to remove another source of inefficient labour and to prevent the sick being forced, by threat of poverty, to continue working – thereby exacerbating their condition and becoming chronic (pauperized) cases. Unemployment insurance, the second part of the 1911 Act, covered workers in construction, shipbuilding, engineering, and associated metal trades. It was compulsory, involved similar tripartite contributions and offered unemployment benefit for up to fifteen weeks per year. Long-term unemployment was not recognized; on exhausting benefit rights the claimant ceased to be 'unemployed' and rejoined the pauper class.

With hindsight, we can see that these reforms were the antecedents of what later, extended and modified, became the welfare state; their legacy is still discernible today. The trained midwives and health visitors, the protection of child health and nutrition are still considered public obligations. Although health insurance has been replaced by the National Health Service, unemployment insurance cover was extended in 1920 and 1946: its principles are still discernable in today's Jobseekers Allowance. Labour exchanges are the evident ancestors of current Jobcentre Plus offices and means-tested, tax funded old age pensions are still with us. Above all, we can discern a shift away from local discretion in the provision of help to the poor and towards a national policy based on categories derived from social scientific precepts with rights to welfare that are not based on destitution alone.

Far from being hailed as the dawn of a new age at the time, however, reform generated hostility. The costs of tax-funded pensions provoked a major budget crisis in 1911, led to a confrontation with the House of Lords, and a constitutional change permanently reducing their Lordships' powers. While the extension of child services was popular on the Left, its breach of Poor Law principles provoked opposition from both Conservative and traditional Liberals. Both sides of industry viewed labour market reform with distrust, hating compulsory insurance contributions and seeing labour exchanges as an unwelcome intervention by officialdom into private business, while trade unionists feared their use for breaking strikes. Even members of the Liberal Cabinet found the reforms distasteful. The President of the Local Government Board described the results as creating 'a race of paupers in a grovelling community ruled by uniformed prigs'; his opinion was hardly unique.

Aftermath

It remains to evaluate these initiatives: did they succeed in securing social harmony and prosperity for all? In general, historians have concluded that their impact was marginal – certainly well removed from their original objectives. The principle reason, as indicated, stemmed from the hostility they provoked, an opposition that reformers had been prone to ignore.

The First World War offered the chance for the advocates of central labour market co-ordination to prove their case. Total war required tight labour market controls, to prevent industrial conflict disrupting war production and to apportion scarce manpower according to war priorities. In the 'scientific' analysis of labour markets, policy solutions would be found and enforced by impartial administrators. The results were disastrous. Unofficial strike action rocketed; an attempted extension of unemployment insurance to all war workers collapsed as those covered refused to comply. Union leaders and management alike found Whitehall inefficient, uninformed, and arbitrary. By 1918, the trend towards central regulation of the labour market, visible before the war, had been abruptly halted and, when peace was restored, was thrown permanently into reverse.

The inter-war years of mass unemployment in old industrial centres undermined the logic on which Liberal policy had been based: far from rationalizing the labour market, it became desirable to spread work among as many people as possible. Nor could unemployment benefits be confined to fifteen weeks per year. Instead, constant modifications allowed most unemployed men (but not women) to claim benefit in advance of contributions, creating 'the dole' on which the long-term cases relied. As unemployment worsened during the Slump years of the 1930s (the Devil's Decade according to the journalist Claud Cockburn) ever stricter means tests were applied to contain public expenditure – stimulating the Hunger Marches and renewing debate about the association of poverty with deformity and disease. The experiences of this decade explain the huge acclaim that greeted the Beveridge Report (1942) with its promises of total state protection 'from the cradle to the grave' (see Chapter 18).

In the meantime, constraints on public expenditure took their toll in cuts to schools, school medical and meals services, local infant welfare, public sector salaries, and the new housing programmes ('homes fit for heroes' promised by Lloyd George). In spite of wartime inflation, old age pensions were not raised, forcing older people to supplement their income by recourse to means-tested assistance. Then, as today, the solution to poverty was presumed to lie in reducing state intervention to allow the free market economy to create new prosperity and new jobs through economic growth. Then, as now, such growth was sporadic and failed to benefit all sectors of society. The birth of Keynesian economics, advocating the redistribution of wealth, underpinned the later creation of a welfare state. As this solution is now repudiated, we may ask what alternatives are available to prevent a return to those grim inter-war years.

Guide to Further Sources

The texts by Harris, Fraser, and Thane cited at the end of Chapter 16 include sound accounts of the Liberal reforms of 1906–14. A more detailed description of their causes can be found in J.R. Hay, *Origins of the Liberal Welfare Reforms* (London: Macmillan 1975). More specialist texts include a close interrogation of policy development in Jose Harris, *Unemployment: A Study of British Politics* (Oxford: Oxford University Press, 1971) and, for real enthusiasts who want to unravel the problems social welfare posed for local government finance, Avner Offer, *Property and Politics 1870–1914* (Cambridge: Cambridge University Press, 1981). An excellent detailed description of the interrelationship of British and German welfare reforms can be found in E.P. Hennock, *The Origins of the Welfare State in England and Germany, 1850–1914* (Cambridge: Cambridge University Press, 2007).

Review Questions

1　How was 'the social question' in Britain understood in the early twentieth century?

2 How did new forms of scientific knowledge inform Liberal welfare policies?

3 Were the Liberal governments' social policies socialist in intent, or were they capitalism's answer to the problems of capitalism?

4 Did the reforms of 1906–14 form the foundations of a welfare state?

5 Why did the Liberal welfare reform programme split the Liberal party and what principles were at stake?

Visit the book companion site at www.wiley.com/go/alcock to make use of the resources designed to accompany the textbook. There you will find chapter-specific guides to further resources, including governmental, international, think-tank, pressure groups, and relevant journals sources. You will also find a glossary based on *The Blackwell Dictionary of Social Policy*, help sheets, and case studies, guidance on managing assignments in social policy and career advice.

18

The Post-war Welfare State

Robert M. Page

■■■

Overview

- The decision of the Labour Party to join Churchill's Conservative-led wartime coalition government in 1940 and the publication of the Beveridge Report on Social Insurance in 1942 resulted in renewed emphasis being given to social policy and post-war reconstruction. The coalition government introduced a landmark Education Act in 1944 and published a series of influential White Papers on employment, social security, and health care.
- The Labour governments of 1945–51 are often credited with creating the modern welfare state. Two of their major reforms were the National Insurance Act of 1946 and the establishment of a National Health Service in 1948.
- Following their second post-war General Election defeat in 1950, the Conservative Party attempted to persuade the public that they were fully supportive of the welfare state. The One Nation Group played a significant role in developing a modern Conservative approach to social policy.
- There is continuing debate as to whether a welfare 'consensus' between the two major parties occurred in the post-war period.
- Looking ahead it remains to be seen whether the 'classic' welfare state can survive in the twenty-first century.

■■■

Context

Labour's success in the 1945 General Election has been attributed to increased social solidarity during the war and the emergence of more positive public attitudes towards the role of the state in terms of preventing the return of mass unemployment and of ensuring 'fair shares for all'. With 48 per cent of the popular vote and an overall majority of 145 seats Labour sought to carry out its manifesto pledge to create a socialist society which would be 'free, democratic, efficient, pro-

The Student's Companion to Social Policy, Fourth Edition. Edited by Pete Alcock, Margaret May, Sharon Wright.
© 2012 John Wiley & Sons, Ltd. Published 2012 by John Wiley & Sons, Ltd.

gressive [and] public-spirited'. This would involve the nationalization of key industries, state regulation of the economy, progressive taxation, and the introduction of an egalitarian welfare state.

The idea that the Attlee governments (1945–51) created the welfare state is questioned by some commentators who point to the significance of earlier welfare reforms (see the discussion in Chapters 16 and 17). However, those who favour the notion that it was indeed the post-war Labour government that gave birth to the welfare state argue that these previous reforms were of an ad-hoc, piecemeal nature and lacked any clear ideological or transformative vision.

Before examining Labour's post-war reforms in more detail, it is useful to consider the welfare agenda pursued by the wartime coalition government, not least because influential historians such as Addison (1977) have argued that it was this administration that laid the foundations of the post-war welfare state.

The Wartime Coalition Government

The Labour ministers who joined Churchill's Conservative-led coalition government in 1940 following Chamberlain's resignation were given significant responsibilities on the 'home front' not least in making plans for the reconstruction of society after the war.

Labour members of the coalition such as Clement Attlee, Herbert Morrison, and Ernest Bevin pressed for the introduction of more egalitarian economic and social policies in the sure knowledge that many Labour MPs and grassroots party activists would regard such initiatives as ameliorative at best. This underlying tension came to a head following the publication of William Beveridge's influential *Report on Social Insurance and Allied Services* in 1942. Beveridge sought to protect citizens from the financial insecurity associated with predictable risks such as unemployment, ill health, and old age through a comprehensive system of social insurance. Despite popular acclaim (over 100,000 copies of the report were sold within a month of publication) the coalition government decided to delay implementing the various recommendations because of Conservative concerns about the cost

of the new scheme and fears that its introduction would detract from the war effort. As a consequence, ninety-seven Labour MPs defied their own party leaders and supported a motion condemning the government's lukewarm response to the report in February 1943.

One of the consequences of this backbench revolt was the establishment of a Ministry of Reconstruction in November 1943 which ensured that welfare reform in areas such as social security, education, and health moved up the political agenda. While many Labour supporters viewed some of the compromise agreements on social policy that emerged after this time – such as the White Papers on Social Security (1944) and the National Health Service (1944) – as half hearted, they were more supportive of the Education Act of 1944, which aimed to provide free secondary education for all up to the age of fifteen, and Family Allowances, which were introduced in 1945. Although the coalition government achieved workable compromises over a range of social policies the lack of an ideological consensus limited the progress that could be achieved.

The General Election campaign of 1945 demonstrated the continued ideological divide between the Conservatives and Labour. This was never better illustrated than by Churchill's provocative comment in a General Election broadcast in June 1945 that Labour would need a 'Gestapo' to push through its socialist programme. In terms of economic policy the Conservatives favoured a return to a free enterprise economy while Labour pressed for greater state intervention in the form of increased public ownership, planning, and controls. Although the Conservatives recognized the need to respond to the public mood for change by promising to introduce a National Insurance scheme, comprehensive health provision, and a house building programme, these were widely perceived as limited, pragmatic measures. In contrast, Labour's transformative welfare agenda chimed with the 'never again' ethos of the electorate and the party swept to power.

The Labour Governments 1945–1951

Despite inheriting a war damaged economy and having to adjust to the abrupt ending of the favourable Lend-Lease agreement with the United States (financial credit provided by the United States since March 1941), as well as the subsequent fuel and currency convertibility crises of 1947, the newly elected Labour government pressed ahead with its ambitious plan to create a post-war welfare state. It aimed to banish the five giant evils identified in the Beveridge Report – want (poverty), squalor (homelessness), disease (illness), ignorance (educational disadvantage), and idleness (unemployment). The welfare state, together with the nationalization of key industries, state regulation of the economy and progressive taxation, were to be the key elements in the creation of a more egalitarian and solidaristic society.

The introduction of a comprehensive social security system was one of Labour's most significant welfare initiatives. Under the universal National Insurance Act of 1946 contributors were entitled to claim unemployment benefits, sickness benefits, dependants' allowances, maternity payments, retirement pensions, and a death grant at time of need. The National Assistance Act of 1948 provided means-tested allowances for those ineligible for National Insurance payments.

Although Labour's reforms drew significantly on the proposals contained in the Beveridge Report, there were some notable differences. Labour decided to introduce full retirement pensions immediately rather than phase them in over a twenty-year period as recommended by Beveridge. In contrast, Beveridge's proposal for an open ended entitlement to unemployment benefit was rejected by the incoming Chancellor, Hugh Dalton, as being too generous. Accordingly, entitlement was restricted to a period of six months. Although the National Insurance benefit rates that Labour introduced were of a higher monetary value than those proposed in the coalition's White Paper of 1944, the rise in inflation meant that they were less favourable than those advocated by Beveridge. As a consequence it proved extremely difficult to guarantee that those claiming insurance benefits would be living above the 'poverty line'. By 1948, some 675,000 recipients of National Insurance with higher than average housing costs had to claim additional means-tested benefits (which included a full rent allowance) in order to maintain a basic standard of living.

While Labour's social security reforms represented a significant step forward, it was recognized that there was room for improvement in terms of benefit levels, eligibility criteria, and the administration of the means-tested scheme.

The introduction of the National Health Service in 1948 is generally regarded as the finest achievement of Labour's first post-war government. Aneurin Bevan's decision to nationalize the voluntary hospitals represented a major departure from the coalition's health policy. Although Bevan was able to secure the co-operation of consultants in this venture by granting them significant influence in shaping the new service as well as generous forms of remuneration, his negotiations with General Practitioners were far from straightforward and more acrimonious. Many General Practitioners only agreed to sign up to the new service following an eleventh hour agreement guaranteeing them that they could retain their professional autonomy by contracting in to the NHS rather than becoming state employees. Although Bevan has been accused of granting too many concessions to the medical profession in his drive to establish a universal, comprehensive, tax funded health service based on medical need rather than ability to pay, it could be argued that the ends justified the means.

Labour's achievements in the areas of housing and education were, arguably, less successful. In terms of the former, Labour's General Election manifesto commitment to 'proceed with a housing programme with the maximum practical speed until every family . . . has a good standard of accommodation' proved difficult to implement (*Let Us Face the Future*, The Labour Party's General Election manifesto of 1945). Wartime bombing had resulted in half a million homes being destroyed or made uninhabitable at a time of growing demand from those returning from military service. In addition, there was an acute shortage of both building materials and construction workers. Although Bevan (whose ministerial responsibilities covered housing as well as health) oversaw the completion of some one million new homes by 1951, this proved to be far fewer than were needed. This 'failure' has been linked to Bevan's 'ideological' preference for the construction of high quality public sector houses for rent rather than what he regarded as 'inferior' private sector initiatives.

In the sphere of education, Labour saw no reason to introduce any major changes to the 1944 Education Act, which they had helped to bring on to the statute book. The new education minister Ellen Wilkinson (1945–7) and her successor George Tomlinson (1947–51) supported the 'different but equal', tripartite schooling system of schooling (grammar, technical, and modern) in which children were allocated to schools on the basis of their skills and aptitudes rather than their social background. They devoted their attention to practical matters such as securing the necessary resources for the new buildings that would be needed as a consequence of the raising of the secondary school leaving age. This 'pragmatic' approach proved disappointing to the more radical wing of the party who believed that the government should have pushed ahead with the creation of comprehensive schools, particularly in the light of growing concern about limited working class access to the more prestigious grammar schools, which were seen as conferring the greatest long-term advantages to their pupils In addition, leading members of the Attlee government showed little appetite for reforming the 'public' (fee paying) schools, which many of them had attended and retained strong attachments to. Although it was acknowledged that these schools ensured that those from privileged backgrounds maintained a stranglehold on elite positions in British society, particularly in professions such as law and medicine, it was believed, optimistically, that rapid improvements in state education would soon neutralize any remaining advantages bestowed on privately educated pupils.

By the end of 1948, the Attlee government's democratic socialist 'crusade' appeared to run out of steam. The party seemed to have no clear plan of how to build on their first term reforms. Although the party reiterated its commitment to the creation of a new social order in its General Election manifesto of 1950, it was the theme of consolidation, rather than further advance, which came to dominate the agenda. Although Labour won this election, its majority was cut to just five seats. Attlee sought a fresh electoral mandate a year later in far from ideal circumstances. He had had to cope with internal disunity (Bevan, who was by then Minister of Labour, had resigned over the proposed introduction of prescription charges in his beloved NHS), balance of pay-

ments problems, growing industrial unrest, and the Persian oil crisis. Despite achieving a slightly higher proportion of the popular vote than their Conservative opponents (48.8% to 48.1%), it was the latter that was returned to office with a 17-seat majority.

Modern Conservatism and the Welfare State

Following their sizeable defeat in the 1945 General Election the Conservatives had made strenuous efforts to convince the public that they were not hostile to the welfare state. In a series of influential policy papers such as *The Industrial Strategy* (1947) and *The Right Road for Britain* (1949), it was stipulated that the Conservatives were fully supportive of the 'new social services', which they sought to portray as the fruition of earlier Conservative initiatives in this field. It was not, however, until after the party's defeat in the 1950 General Election that the party began to map out a more distinctive approach to the welfare state. It fell to the One Nation Group (ONG) of newly elected MPs (including Iain Macleod, Enoch Powell, and Edward Heath) to chart a way forward in a highly influential pamphlet entitled *One Nation. A Tory Approach to Social Problems.* Significantly, the ONG sought to construct a modern welfare strategy that would complement traditional Conservative concerns such as sound finance, efficiency, lower taxation, thrift, self-reliance, voluntarism, and charitable activity. This involved distancing the party from what they regarded as Labour's costly, unduly generous, egalitarian approach. According to the ONG, egalitarian social spending should not be allowed to take priority over economic stability, and social services should be targeted on those in the greatest need (selectivity) rather than provided on a citizenship basis for all (universalism).

Following their electoral success in 1951, the Conservatives' commitment to the welfare state was quickly put to the test in the light of mounting economic pressures. Although a number of cost containment measures were introduced including NHS charges and cut backs in the school building programme, the new Chancellor, R. A. Butler opposed any major reduction in spending levels. He believed that it was necessary to ensure that any modifications in the area of social policy should be introduced gradually in order to reassure the public that the Conservatives had no secret plans to dismantle the welfare state. One of the ways in which the new government attempted to persuade the public that it was committed to the welfare state was by pressing ahead with its election pledge to build 300,000 new homes each year (albeit of a lower 'quality' than had been the case under Labour).

Although the modern Conservative approach to the welfare state became more fully entrenched under Eden (who led the party to a further electoral victory in 1955) and Macmillan (who secured a 100 seat majority over Labour in 1959), it proved difficult in practice to balance the party's traditional quest for economic stability with their newly found commitment to the welfare state and full employment. In particular, the Treasury continued to call for expenditure constraints and reductions in the scope of service provision. This issue came to a head in 1958 when the then Chancellor, Peter Thorneycroft, resigned from the government after his Cabinet colleagues refused to sanction a range of welfare cuts he deemed necessary to curb inflation and restore confidence in sterling. Although politically damaging, these internal disagreements were rarely over the question of the desirability of spending reductions but rather their extent. In general, the modern Conservatives attempted to constrain the growth in social expenditure by low key measures, such as increases in social security contributions and council house rents, rather than by more controversial forms of targeting.

A Welfare Consensus?

The fact that the Conservatives proved willing to make an accommodation with Labour's welfare legacy throughout their lengthy period in office from 1951 to 1964 has led to the suggestion that a welfare consensus or settlement emerged during this period. In 1954, for example, *The Economist* introduced its readers to the composite figure of Mr. Butskell, in order to highlight the perceived similarities between the economic policies being pursued by the then Conservative Chancellor, R. A. Butler and his Labour predecessor, Hugh Gaitskell. The possibility of an emerging post-war economic

and social consensus based on support for the mixed economy (private and public enterprise), 'Keynesian' interventionism, and the welfare state was given added weight by the growing influence of revisionist thinking within Labour circles. In particular, Crosland's contention that government regulation and intervention were more suitable mechanisms than nationalization for ensuring that market activity complemented broader egalitarian social objectives, served to narrow the gap between Conservative and Labour thinking on economic matters (see Chapter 10).

The question as to whether a welfare consensus developed during the 1950s and early 1960s remains a contentious one. It should not be assumed, for example, that the decision by a newly elected government to continue with some of the previous administration's welfare agenda, despite commitments to the contrary in their election manifesto is indicative of an underlying cross-party ideological consensus. It is more likely to be the case that the postponement of reform will be due to an unexpected downturn in the economy, insurmountable administrative problems or unanticipated public antipathy to a specific policy initiative.

Certainly, there is insufficient evidence to argue that there was an ideological consensus during the first two decades after the war. For example, there remained a fundamental disagreement over the question of equality. While One Nation Conservatives supported equality of opportunity, they were, unlike Labour, diametrically opposed to the use of greater state power to bring about greater equality of outcome.

Emerging Issues

In the decades following Labour's creation of the post-war welfare state there have been continuous debates between the two main parties about its purpose, scope, and cost. The election of the first Thatcher government in 1979 signalled the emergence of a more overtly hostile Conservative approach towards the welfare state. Fundamental questions were raised about the way in which the protection offered by the welfare state to those outside the labour market was having an adverse effect on work incentives and the performance of the economy. In addition, the effectiveness and efficiency of state intervention in areas such as health, housing, and education was deemed problematic. Although the welfare state survived this onslaught, its 'legitimacy' was undoubtedly damaged. Indeed, subsequent New Labour governments (1997–2010) did not display the same enthusiasm for the 'classic' welfare state believing that it needed to be 'modernized' in order to meet the challenges of a changing global economic and social environment. This resulted in attempts to improve the performance of the welfare state by encouraging private and voluntary involvement in service delivery, more stringent expectations for providers and the encouragement of a consumerist, as opposed to citizenship, mindset on the part of service users.

Guide to Further Sources

There are a number of very useful accounts of the wartime coalition including: Paul Addison, *The Road to 1945* (Jonathan Cape: London, 1997); Kevin Jefferys (ed.), *War and Reform: British Politics During the Second World War* (Manchester: Manchester University Press, 1994); and Stephen Brooke's *Labour's War: the Labour Party During the Second World War* (Oxford: Oxford University Press, 1992).

Martin Francis' volume *Ideas and Policies Under Labour 1945–1951* (Manchester: Manchester University Press, 1997) is an extremely readable and accessible account of the post-war Attlee governments which provides extended commentary on social policy issues. Other wide-ranging, accounts of the Attlee years are to be found in Kenneth Morgan (1984) *Labour in Power, 1945–1951* (Clarendon: Oxford, 1984); Peter Hennessy, *Never Again: Britain 1945–1951* (Vintage: London, 1993); and Stephen Brooke (ed.), *Reform and Reconstruction: Britain After the War, 1945–51* (Manchester: Manchester University Press, 1995).

Texts by Rodney Lowe *The Welfare State in Britain Since 1945* (3rd edn, Basingstoke: Palgrave Macmillan, 2005); Howard Glennerster, *British Social Policy 1945 to the Present* (3rd edn, Oxford: Blackwell); and Robert Page, *Revisiting the Welfare State* (Maidenhead: Open University Press, 2007) provide useful overviews of social policy issues and developments during the post-war era from 1945 to 1964 (including discussions of the post-war consensus). Paul Bridgen and Rodney Lowe's *Welfare Policy Under the Conservatives 1951–1964* (Lonodn: Public Records Office, 1998) provides a forensic examination of Conservative social policy from the early 1950s to the end of the Douglas-Home government in 1964.

Accessible information about the post-war welfare state can be found on the following the BBC web site www.bbc.co.uk and the National Archives web site www.nationalarchives.gov.uk.

Review Questions

1 How significant were the coalition government's (1939–45) welfare policies?
2 Did the post-war Labour governments create the welfare state?
3 What were the distinctive features of the modern Conservative approach to the welfare state?
4 Was there a welfare consensus between 1945 and 1979?
5 Why did the 'classic' post-war welfare state come under attack in the late 1970s?

Visit the book companion site at www.wiley.com/go/alcock to make use of the resources designed to accompany the textbook. There you will find chapter-specific guides to further resources, including governmental, international, think-tank, pressure groups, and relevant journals sources. You will also find a glossary based on *The Blackwell Dictionary of Social Policy*, help sheets, and case studies, guidance on managing assignments in social policy and career advice.

19

Crisis, Retrenchment, and the Impact of Neo-liberalism (1976–1997)

Howard Glennerster

Overview

- Neither 'economic crises' nor the resulting 'retrenchments' are new. But the neo-liberal ideas that took root during the oil price triggered crisis of the mid-1970s have had a lasting influence. They convinced many governments to change their approach to social policy.
- The outcome was not to dramatically reduce the size of modern welfare states in the subsequent thirty years. They continued to grow, albeit at a slower pace. One reason lay in the failure of the neo-liberal theorists to accept the fact that many of the problems they saw facing state welfare institutions faced their private alternatives to an even greater extent.
- However, these ideas did prompt a major *restructuring* of welfare institutions worldwide, not least in the United Kingdom between 1979 and 1997.
  - Governments were convinced it was necessary to limit social benefit generosity and duration and encourage a faster return to work.
  - Competition between state run providers and new private entrants to the welfare marketplace was designed to improve service efficiency.
  - Public service providers were given productivity targets. Failing to reach them was publicized and punished.
- The scale of the recent credit crisis provided the opportunity for the Conservative–Liberal coalition at Westminster to drive through a series of policies that derived from this body of ideas with even greater determination than Mrs Thatcher – the Conservative prime minister from 1979 to 1991.

The Student's Companion to Social Policy, Fourth Edition. Edited by Pete Alcock, Margaret May, Sharon Wright.
© 2012 John Wiley & Sons, Ltd. Published 2012 by John Wiley & Sons, Ltd.

Neo-liberal Theory

The scale of inflation in the 1970s, over 20 per cent a year at one point, rapid public spending growth, public resistance to tax increases, resulting government deficits, and extensive public sector strikes provided fertile ground for a fundamental reappraisal of the 'post war settlement', that is, government support for full employment, a universal safety net, and free and growing public services (see Chapter 18).

American neo-liberal writers beginning with Milton Friedman (1962) and younger followers like William (Bill) Niskanen (1971) challenged the core belief that social welfare institutions had emerged in response to revealed human need – child poverty, for example. Not so, claimed these authors:

■ Those who press for extensions in social provision are merely seeking to advance their own monetary gain or power by increasing the size of their agencies' budgets. This was Niskanen's key argument. Public employees and professionals are importantly driven by their own financial gain.

■ Once established public sector institutions tend to become monopolies. They do not face competition from other schools or health providers, for example. In consequence their employees can draw 'monopoly rents' by being more lazy, inefficient or incompetent than they would be if they faced competition. Public organizations are run in the interests of their employees not users, Friedman claimed.

■ Though cash benefits to those in need have a place in society, the rules that governed their administration had become lax. Over the long term 'good behaviour' and the desire to work and marry, had been undermined. It was now possible to live without work or a partner and depend on the state. These changes in behaviour had only taken root slowly but after forty years of welfare statism 'bad behaviour' was becoming the norm. The popularizers of this view were American writers notably Lawrence Meade (1986) but they entered the formal economics literature through a Swedish economist Assar Lindbeck (1995).

■ Productivity gains are achieved in the marketplace by entrepreneurial companies. The financial gains are partly shared with their employees in higher wages. This drives up real wages. The need for public service operators to sustain the quality of their labour force and trade union activity leads public sector wages to rise in line with those in the private sector over the long term. Public social services are incapable of achieving productivity gains. So the relative price of these services tends to rise. The faster productivity in the private sector grew the faster the relative price of public services would rise. This analysis was shared by many on the Left – the Marxist parallel to the neo-liberal argument (Gough 1979).

■ The population was living longer and birth rates were falling so the tax burden falling on the working population was growing. The tax claims on working families were leading to excessive wage claims in an attempt to pass on the tax burden to the employer (Bacon and Eltis 1976). This was destroying 'productive' jobs.

Taken together this set of arguments amounted to a formidable critique of post-war social and economic policy and they were largely accepted by the incoming Conservative government of 1979.

A Neo-liberal Programme

The preliminary stage in the new programme was initiated by the Labour government following the visit of the International Monetary Fund in 1976 and its conditional support for the pound. The steady rise in the share of public spending in the economy was checked and the then prime minister, Callaghan, accepted the neo-liberal contention that it was wrong to seek to maintain levels of full employment in the face of rising inflation.

However, it was not until the election of a Conservative government in 1979 that the full set of related measures was introduced driven by the diagnosis outlined above. This did not happen all at once but over the following eighteen years all its elements found their way into statute or government practice.

In its first public spending White Paper in 1979 the new government declared that excessive public expenditure and state ownership were the main reason for the United Kingdom's poor economic performance. Public spending was to be reduced as a share of total economic activity. This led to a review of all aspects of social spending.

One of the early measures (1982) of the new Conservative government was to stop increasing the level of benefits annually in line with the earnings of the average worker. Instead, benefits were to rise in line with prices. This meant that benefits fell further and further behind wages. The theory was that this would force people to return to work faster, stop 'scrounging', and save money. As time went on it did, indeed, do the latter on a large scale. However, as unemployment was allowed to rise to 'cure' inflation the benefits bill still rose in the short term. Much later the government began to take some tentative measures to introduce sanctions on those who were not 'actively seeking work'. This was to be taken much further by the successor Blair and Brown governments (see Chapter 20).

Another significant change was that all the extensive nationalized industries of the time were privatized step by step; electricity, gas, coal, railways, buses, and water. Tenants of council houses were given the right to buy their own dwellings at low prices depending on the length of time they had been living in them (1980).

Mrs Thatcher also toyed with the idea of privatizing schools and hospitals along with many local authority services. In the end she confined her major acts of social service privatization to social care. Local authorities were encouraged to use privately run homes for older people, not employ staff in their own residential care services. In 1980 65 per cent of all places in residential care were provided by local authorities and their staff. By 1997 the share had fallen to 20 per cent and is now less than 10 per cent. The same policy was adopted for services caring for people in their own homes.

Mrs Thatcher also wanted to develop private health insurance, subsidizing it for older people, and funding health care by a mix of social and private insurance. She soon realized that this was a political step too far and opted instead for a 'quasi market' in health services. Hospitals were to compete for custom from local health authorities and general practitioners who would receive their funds from the central exchequer. This

major reform was launched in a White Paper published in 1989 and driven through under her successor John Major. Hospitals, it was argued, instead of acting like sluggish monopolists, knowing they had a captive set of customers, would have to compete to gain contracts.

Mrs Thatcher also wanted to introduce state funded 'school vouchers' for parents that could be cashed in at any school, state or private, as Milton Friedman had advocated. Here, again, she realized this was too radical and opted instead for confining this policy to state schools in a modified form. They would compete for pupils and once a pupil was accepted a sum of money would automatically follow paid by the local authority. Parents would be able to judge how well the school was doing by requiring all pupils to take tests based on a National Curriculum at 7, 11, and 14. Along with GCSE and A-levels these results had to be published nationally. Making teachers publically accountable in this way would be an antidote to sloth and incompetence. These measures were introduced in the 1988 Education Reform Act, though the exams at 7, 11, and 14 were only fully implemented by all schools in 1996.

Loans were introduced to cover student maintenance costs (1990) – a partial implementation of an idea Milton Friedman had again advocated. Universities at first faced reduced funding for student places but, then, as more qualified school leavers were denied places universities were told they could expand if they were willing to be paid much less for each additional student they took. They responded with enthusiasm, numbers of students rose sharply and the resources available to teach each of them fell by about half in real terms between 1979 and 1996. This was, officials argued, clear proof that universities, like any public bureaucracy, were more concerned about their overall budgets than the product they were producing!

The changes of this period are described in more detail in Glennerster (1997) and Chapters 8 and 9. But they all conform to a surprisingly common and clear view of how public institutions and those in them work.

What was Wrong with the Neo-liberal Diagnosis?

While the diagnosis of the problems facing public sector services had some validity what most of the literature failed to mention was that the same problems applied even more strongly to human services in the private sector. Private sector human services typically offer higher staffing standards. The relative price of their services has therefore risen faster than in the public sector since 1980.

Another difficulty was that rising life expectancy affected the funding of private pensions and long-term care even more disastrously than the state alternatives. Occupational private pension schemes underestimated the rise in longevity and not only began closing more generous defined benefit schemes but employers reduced their contributions to the defined contribution schemes that replaced them. Faced with a collapse of public confidence in the private pensions market the state had to step in and underpin the declining role of private pension provision (see Chapter 56).

A key persistent problem with the use of market forces in social policy is that people do not necessarily act rationally when faced with risks that may occur many years later. We put off action to fund these risks until it is too late. This is true of pensions and long-term care in old age. We call this 'market failure' which is discussed in Chapter 35.

With the reduction of state support the private alternatives failed to materialize and the state had to step back in to promise to improve the standard of the National Health Service, to reduce child poverty, and rescue the pension system as the next chapter describes.

Critics of the use of competition and choice as ways to improve standards argued that

- There was actually little opportunity for new entrants or other state providers to enter local health or education markets. Few did so.
- If they did enter they would merely cream off the easy or cheap cases or the clever children.
- Competition would be about the wrong things – cutting standards to appear cheaper.
- It would infuse public services with a competitive mentality and destroy the sense of social solidarity and support for local institutions in which everyone felt they had a stake.

Emerging Issues

As a set of coherent arguments, however, neo-liberalism is still a force to be reckoned with. It was certainly the dominant framework underpinning the Conservative–Liberal coalition approach to social policy in the United Kingdom in 2010 when it assumed power and produced a string of policy pronouncements on the health service, schools, and welfare benefit reform. The major cuts in social spending announced in the spending review of October 2010 will continue every year until 2014/5 and indeed beyond. This new fiscal crisis was only partly forced by the banking crisis. However, it it has put the long-term financing of social policy and the very future of welfare states at the centre of political debate. It adds to the already major problems posed by an ageing population. The future of social policy as we have known it is now in doubt. However the logic that drove the creation of welfare states remains if anything more powerful than ever.

The weakest part of the theories, in their 1980 form, was, as we have seen, their refusal to accept the scale of market failure (see Chapters 35 and 36). Modern behavioural economics provides a new and empirically grounded challenge to many of these ideas. People do not act with foresight or efficiency in making judgements about risk or insurance. They may lack information but even if they do not they tend to put off action. To counter such 'behaviour failure' does not necessarily require state provision but it does require major state involvement in shaping and incentivizing private markets and funding others.

Unregulated and unsupported private action has simply proved incapable of responding to the needs of an ageing population, for example. But there have been serious government failures too. It is difficult not to accept that unrestrained and unchallenged market power in the public as well as the private sector is a bad thing. Evidence is beginning to amass in favour of the view that choice and competition do improve quality if they are combined with published results of service standards (see Guide to Further Sources). Much more work and debate will be needed before a consensus emerges though – if it ever does.

In the coming five years these questions should emerge at the centre of political debate:

- Are the scale of cuts being carried through in the United Kingdom justified by the 'crisis' or is it merely an excuse to carry through a long-held neo-liberal agenda that did not get implemented in the 1980s? Are they, indeed, making things worse?

■ What will be the likely long term effects of an attempt to 'roll back the frontiers of the state' as far as social policy is concerned? Who will gain and who will lose most?

■ How far will service user reaction cause governments to rethink crisis driven cuts?

■ Will the electorate lose hope and do what the reformers of the 1980s expected – give up hope in public services and go private? Will this cause a steady downward spiral in social service quality with less taxpayer support breeding worse services and more exits from them? What might be done to reverse such a trend?

■ What should those who study social policy do about this situation?

Guide to Further Sources

Much of the original theoretical literature, for example W. Niskanen, *Bureaucracy and Representative Government* (Chicago: Aldine Atherton 1971) is sometimes difficult for the non-economics student to follow, though the basic ideas are very simple. Milton Friedman's *Capitalism and Freedom* (Chicago: University of Chicago Press, 1962) and *Free to Choose* (Harmondsworth: Penguin Books, 1980) are, however, beautifully lucid. One of the best expositions, and criticism, of the self-interested public bureaucrat model is to be found in Patrick Dunleavy's *Democracy, Bureaucracy and Public Choice* (New York: Harvester-Wheatsheaf, 1991) chapter 8.

For a social policy endorsement of the case for choice and competition see J. Le Grand, *Motivation, Agency and Public Policy: Of Knights and Knaves, Pawns and Queens* (Oxford: Oxford University Press, 2003).

The argument that welfare benefits had undermined 'good behaviour' is best expounded by a Swedish economist A. Lindbeck. 'Welfare state disincentives with endogenous habits and norms', *Scandinavian Journal of Economics*, 97/4 (1995): 477–94. It is to be found more influentially expressed in the work of the American Lawrence Meade, *Beyond Entitlement: The Social Obligations of Citizenship* (New York: Free Press, 1986).

An influential version of this set of ideas can be found in two Oxford economists' writing,

Robert Bacon and Walter Eltis, *Britain's Economic problem: Too Few Producers* (London: Macmillan, 1976). A Marxist treatment of the reasons for the crisis can be found in Ian Gough's book *The Political Economy of the Welfare State* (London: Macmillan, 1979)

I have described the measures taken in this period in more detail in *British Social Policy 1945 to the Present* (Oxford: Blackwell, 2007) Chapters 8 and 9.

For a critical account of the way the neo-liberal prescription has been followed in different countries see N. Ellison, *The Transformation of Welfare States?* (London: Routledge, 2006). See especially the summary chapter 8.

A very thorough attempt to measure the impact of choice and competition on the English Health Service is M. Gaynor, R. Moreno-Serra and C. Propper, *Death by Market Power: Reform, Competition and Patient Outcomes in the National Health Service*, Working Paper No 10/242 (2010) available at http://www.bristol.ac.uk/cmpo/. A paper by the same institute looks at the consequences of the Welsh Assembly decision to give up publishing test results in Welsh schools – S. Burgess, D. Wilson and J. Worth, *A Natural Experiment in School Accountability: The Impact of School Performance Information on Pupil Progress and Sorting*. Working Paper 10/246 (2010).

Review Questions

1 What were the key points made by the neo-liberal writers of the 1970s and 1980s?

2 What impact have their ideas had on social policy in the United Kingdom?

3 What in your view are the major strengths and weaknesses of their case?

4 What current social policies seem to be inspired by neo-liberal thinking??

Visit the book companion site at www.wiley.com/go/alcock to make use of the resources designed to accompany the textbook. There you will find chapter-specific guides to further resources, including governmental, international, think-tank, pressure groups, and relevant journals sources. You will also find a glossary based on *The Blackwell Dictionary of Social Policy*, help sheets, and case studies, guidance on managing assignments in social policy and career advice.

20

Modernization and the Third Way

Martin Powell

Overview

- It is difficult to define the Third Way, but it is best represented by the US Clinton Democratic (1992–2000) and UK Blair/Brown New Labour (1997–2010) administrations.
- The Third Way can be examined in terms of discourse, values, policy goals, and policy mechanisms.
- The Third Way in practice shows a wide variety of new policy goals and mechanisms, which increasingly seem to draw upon neo-liberalism.
- In many areas, the rhetoric of the New Labour government was not matched by delivery, and so 'third order' or 'paradigmatic' change was limited.
- The New Labour legacy is probably less influential than those of the Attlee Labour (1945) and Thatcher Conservative (1979) governments.

Context

The Third Way was the 'big idea' of the New Labour governments of 1997–2010. The Third Way was generally associated with the writings of Anthony Giddens (e.g. 1998, 2007) and the policies of the Democrat administrations of Bill Clinton in the United States (1992–2000) and of the New Labour governments of Tony Blair and (to a lesser extent) Gordon Brown in the United Kingdom. Giddens (1998) claimed that it was new and distinctive from both traditional social democracy (see Chapter 10) and from neo-liberalism (see Chapter 9), but stressed that it is a renewed or modernized social democracy: a left of centre project. In historical terms, the Third Way can be seen as a third or middle way between the 'classic welfare state' of 'Old Labour'

The Student's Companion to Social Policy, Fourth Edition. Edited by Pete Alcock, Margaret May, Sharon Wright.
© 2012 John Wiley & Sons, Ltd. Published 2012 by John Wiley & Sons, Ltd.

(1945–51; 1964–70; 1974–9) and Conservative (1951–64; 1970–4) on the one hand and the restructured welfare state of the Thatcher and Major Conservative governments (1979–97). For a few years around the millennium Third Way left or left of centre governments were in power in many countries in Europe. However, the Left lost power in many countries such as Germany and Sweden. The United Kingdom Blair government is a rare exception of a Left party that remained in power for a long period. Blair was the longest serving Labour prime minister in British history (before being replaced by Gordon Brown in June 2007), and the New Labour government secured a historic third term, winning General Elections in 1997, 2001, and 2005. During this period in office New Labour attempted to 'modernise the welfare state' (Powell 2008). However, as we shall see, many critics argued that the Third Way increasingly blurred with neo-liberalism (see Chapter 8). The Third Way is now history having given way to a Conservative/Liberal Democrat coalition with its own 'big idea' of the 'Big Society'.

This chapter aims to provide a brief introduction into these large and complex debates. The first part examines the dimensions of the Third Way, arguing that it is useful to unpack the concept with a focus on discourse, values, policy goals, and policy mechanisms. The second part discusses the broad features of the Third Way in practice, concentrating on the social policies of New Labour in England (as Chapter 42 shows, there are some differences between the administrations in London, Belfast, Cardiff, and Edinburgh). The final part aims to sum up the New Labour legacy.

The Essence of the Third Way

Much has been written about the Third Way, but its essence or main 'dependent variable' remains unclear, with many critics dismissing it as vague and amorphous. The problem in examining the Third Way is that the term was used in very different senses. A number of commentators suggested broad characteristics or themes of the Third Way or new social democracy. However, this conflated different elements such as means and ends. As an explanatory device, it is useful to distil these into separate discussions of discourse, values, policy goals, and policy means or mechanisms.

The Third Way generated a new discourse or a new political language. Clinton and Blair shared a number of key slogans or mantras such as being 'tough on crime, tough on the causes of crime', 'a hand up, not a hand out', 'hard working families that play by the rules', and 'work is the best route out of poverty'. In addition to new phrases, there was a redefined language where old words had new meaning. For example, the Third Way vocabulary or 'New Labour Speak' includes terms such as 'full employment' and 'equality', but they have very different meanings to their traditional usage.

The new discourse does not simply consist of new terms, but also emphasized the relationship between them. The Third Way was a political discourse built out of elements from other political discourses to form, in Blair's term, political 'cross-dressing'. The language of the Third Way was a rhetoric of reconciliation such as 'economic dynamism as well as social justice', 'enterprise as well as fairness'. They were not deemed antagonistic: while neo-liberals pursued the former and traditional social democrats the latter, the Third Way delivered both. For example, it was claimed that the 'new right' promoted economic growth at the risk of large social inequalities, while the 'old Left' attempted to 'level' inequalities at the risk of reducing growth. However, the Third Way claimed that it was possible to increase the size of the 'economic cake' while sharing it more equally. The more radical claim was of 'going beyond' or transcending such themes: it was not simply about managing the tension between the promotion of enterprise and the attack on poverty, but claiming that they were no longer in conflict. However, it does seem difficult to achieve a reconciliation of some terms such as inclusion and responsibility. Should the 'irresponsible' be 'included' even if they fail to carry out their obligations such as to look for work? The carrot of inclusion can be dangled in front of all, but there must be some stick with which to beat the 'irresponsible'.

Some commentators suggested a number of core values for the Third Way. These included CORA (community, opportunity, responsibility, and accountability) and RIO (responsibility, inclusion, opportunity). However, the values of the Third Way remained problematic. This is mainly for two reasons. First, adequate understanding of values required more than one word treatments. Terms such as 'equality' as essentially contestable concepts, mean different things to different people (see below). It follows that values must be more clearly defined and linked with goals (see below).

Second, and linked, it is not clear whether the Third Way was concerned with 'old' values, new or redefined meanings of old values, or new values. The best known accounts argue the first position. For example, Blair claimed that the Third Way is concerned with the traditional values of social democracy. However, critics disputed that Blair's values – equal worth, opportunity for all, responsibility and community – adequately summed up traditional socialism in Britain. Moreover, some terms were redefined. For example, the old concern with equality of outcome and redistribution was diluted. A few 'new' values also appear to have been smuggled in. Positive mentions of terms such as entrepreneurship were rarely part of the vocabulary of traditional social democracy in Europe before the Third Way period.

Blair claimed that policies flow from values. In this sense, goals or objectives may be seen as a more specific operationalization of values. For example, 'equality' was often referred to as a value, but this may result in very different policy objectives such as equality of opportunity or equality of outcomes. It follows that advocates of 'equality' might desire very different goals such as a reduction of inequalities of income, wealth, health status, and educational qualifications or merely that there must be an equal opportunity to enter a race with a large gap between rich prizes for the winners and nothing for the losers.

It was claimed that traditional values and goals must be achieved by new means. In some ways this had parallels with 'Croslandite revisionism' (Chapter 10). The British Labour politician and theorist, Anthony Crosland, whose classic text appeared in 1956, separated the means and ends of socialism, suggesting that the Labour Party means of nationalization was not the best way of achieving the end of equality. Similarly the 'Third Wayers' such as Blair and Giddens claimed that the 'new times' of the 1990s called for new policies. They argued that the world had changed and so the welfare state also had to change. For example, in the period of globalization it is no longer possible to think of a 'job for life'. Governments cannot protect jobs, but can only ensure that individuals who lose jobs have skills to apply for new ones. However, new solutions were not based on outdated, dogmatic ideology. There was a new emphasis on evidence-based policy-making, with a key phrase of this new pragmatism being 'what works is what counts'.

Table 20.1 presents a necessarily rather stylized account of the Third Way that has been distilled from a variety of sources. It does run the risk of some rewriting of history, caricaturing the old Left, the new right, and the Third Way that has been a feature of both advocates and critics.

The Third Way in Practice

This section develops some of the themes of policy goals and means from Table 20.1. New Labour emerged during the long period of opposition to the Conservative government of 1979–97. The Labour leader of the time, John Smith, set up the Commission on Social Justice which flagged up many elements of the Third Way in its report of 1994. It rejected the approaches to social and economic policy of the 'Levellers' (the Old Left) and the 'Deregulators' (the New Right), and advocated the 'middle way' of 'Investor's Britain'. This approach featured in much of the discourse that became central to New Labour: economic efficiency and social justice are different sides of the same coin; redistributing opportunities rather than just redistributing income; transforming the welfare state from a safety net in times of trouble to a springboard for economic opportunity; welfare should offer a hand-up not a hand-out; an active, preventive welfare state; paid work for a fair wage is the most secure and sustainable way out of poverty; and the balancing of rights and responsibilities. An investor's welfare state is proactive, emphasizing prevention, and stressing causes rather than effects: attacking the causes of poverty rather than its symptoms, preventing poverty through education and training rather than simply compensating people in poverty. For example, Blair once stated that a large expenditure on out-of-work benefits was 'bad' rather than 'good' as it would be better to help to lift people out of poverty by giving them

Table 20.1 Dimensions of the Third Way in social policy.

Dimension	Old social democracy	Third Way	Neo-liberalism
Discourse	Rights	Rights and responsibilities	Responsibilities
	Equity	Equity and efficiency	Efficiency
	Market failure	Market and state failure	State failure
Values	Equality	Inclusion	Inequality
	Security	Positive welfare	Insecurity
Policy goals	Equality of outcome	Minimum opportunities	Equality of opportunity
	Full employment	Employability	Low inflation
Policy means	Rights	Conditionality	Responsibilities
	State	Civil society/ market	Market/ civil society
	State finance and delivery	State/private finance and delivery	Private/state finance and delivery
	Security	Flexicurity	Insecurity
	Hierarchy	Network	Market
	High tax and spend	Pragmatic tax to invest	Low tax and spend
	High services and benefits	High services and low-ish benefits	Low services and benefits
	High cash redistribution	High asset redistribution	Low redistribution
	Universalism	Mainly universal services and mix of universal and selective benefits	Selectivity
	High wages	Minimum wages and tax credits	Low wages

employment skills rather than paying them to remain workless.

New Labour probably set itself more targets than any previous British government. However, despite the claim of SMART (specific, measurable, accurate, relevant, timed) targets, many were vague and difficult to operationalize. In broad terms, it set targets on increasing educational qualifications, reducing child poverty, and health inequality but not, crucially for 'old Labour' critics, income equality. New Labour rejected a simple, fiscal equality to be achieved through the tax and benefit system. It claimed that it sought a more ambitious and dynamic redistribution of assets or endowments. In short, instead of compensating people for their poverty with transfer payments, it aimed to increase opportunities by increasing poor people's levels of health and education. Critics who argue that *all* of New Labour's *aims* are less radical than Old Labour were wide of the mark. Old Labour would be proud of the child poverty and health inequality targets. However, they were long term, and were not met.

As Toynbee and Walker (2010: 196) put it, 'Blair once said that if he did not leave behind a fairer Britain, he would have failed. He failed'.

In terms of policy instruments, New Labour emphasized conditional or contractarian welfare. Rights were not 'dutiless' but tended to be given to those who fulfilled their obligations. The main obligations were connected with work, but others were concerned with housing and checking a baby's progress with a health professional. For example, if allowances are given to 'job seekers', then individuals who cannot demonstrate that they are seeking jobs should have some sanctions imposed in the form of benefit reduction. At the extreme, this can be seen as a change from a patterned to a process-driven distribution: distribution does not depend simply on people's need, but on their actions and behaviour.

Services were still largely financed by the state, but were increasingly delivered by private or voluntary bodies in a 'purchaser/provider split' – rather than hierarchies, or markets, coordination and collaboration through 'partnerships' or networks were stressed. New Labour ended the old 'class war' with private education and health providers, and worked with them through agreements or 'concordats' in which NHS patients were treated in private hospitals. The government encouraged new 'independent' (for profit) centres to treat NHS patients, and allowed patients to choose a private hospital under its 'choose and book' scheme. Moreover, many hospitals and schools were built and run under a revamped Conservative Private Finance Initiative (PFI), which Labour termed 'privatization' in opposition. However, in some cases there was some 'privatization of risk' where the state expected people to provide more of their own resources towards contingencies such as old age. Tax and service levels were pragmatic rather than dogmatic, with a tendency to prioritize services such as health and education that can be preventive in nature and increase human capital over reactive, passive, 'relief' cash benefits. Redistribution was 'for a purpose' and based more on endowments rather than in terms of transfer payments, although there has been some 'silent' or 'back-door' fiscal redistribution especially to families with children.

Paid work was central to Third Way approaches to welfare. Key policy goals were seen in the slogans of 'work for those who can; security for those who cannot' and 'making work pay'. The Third Way stressed 'full employment', but this was to be achieved in terms of 'employability' through the 'supply-side' than by 'old' style Keynesian demand management. Paid work was more 'flexible', with an increase in part-time and temporary employment. The Third Way's work-centred social policy had a mix of carrots and sticks. On the one hand, it may have emphasized carrots in the form of giving information about job opportunities, preparing CVs, and job interviews. The slogan of 'making work pay' included a national minimum wage, in-work benefits of tax credits (or fiscal welfare), and increasing the availability of high-quality affordable child care. On the other hand, critics argue that there was an element of US policy that tended to 'starve the poor back into work' through low or time-limited benefits.

Debates about universalism versus selectivity were not dogmatic. On the one hand, inclusion through universal services or civic welfare was stressed. On the other hand, there was increasing selectivity in cash benefits such as targeting the poorest pensioners and new area based policies.

The New Labour Legacy

It is difficult to examine the New Labour legacy for three main reasons. First, the Third Way was difficult to pin down, with the original 'Third Way' looks like more like a 'blurprint' than a 'blueprint', or indeed a 'Blairprint'. Second, it is difficult to find a clear analytical template. Third, it is probably a little too early to detect long-standing legacies.

A number of commentaries appeared at the time of Blair's resignation (Powell 2008). These were broadly positive on social policy, although some questioned the gaps between rhetoric and delivery, and between spending and results. It might be said that in terms of achievements, to use Tony Blair's own words, 'a lot done; a lot still to do' – an ambitious policy agenda has only partially been delivered. Like Bill Clinton, Blair campaigned in poetry but governed in prose. In his resignation speech, Blair claimed that 1997 was

> a moment for a new beginning, for sweeping away all the detritus of the past. Expectations were so high. Too high. Too high in a way for either of us. However, only one government since 1945 can say all of the following: more jobs, fewer unemployed, better health and education results, lower crime, and economic growth in every quarter' (in Powell 2008: 259).

Some of this changed with the brief and unhappy period of Gordon Brown premiership (2007–10) which saw the scandal of MP's expenses, a banking crisis, an economic crisis, and the need to sharply reduce public expenditure and the national debt. In short, boom turned to bust, and Brown was – in cricket terms – playing on the back foot. Brown's mistaken claim that he had 'saved the world' (not saved the banks – by a vast injection of public money) did not save his job as prime minister. There is some uncertainty among commentators about Brown's influence on social policy. Some see a partial return to some 'Old' Labour themes, while others detect a becalming of policy. However, it is difficult to see a distinctive Brownite agenda on social policy.

Toynbee and Walker (2010: 298, 303) write that the good that Labour did and the bad they avoided make an impressive list. Public services measurably improved, but there is a sense of disappointment that the government lost much direction after their first term ended in 2001, and in overall terms it wasted the extraordinary opportunity of ten years of economic prosperity and a secure parliamentary majority. The New Labour period of government saw a number of significant changes in social policy. First, there was a significant increase in public spending and employment after about the year 2000. For example, the NHS saw a large increase in expenditure that brought it more into line with the spending levels of other European health systems. Second, new instruments and institutions were set up. For example, the National Institute of Clinical Excellence (NICE) advised on cost-effectiveness in the NHS. However, a 'snooze' of regulators (such as the Health Care Commission and the Financial Services Authority) tended to sleep through vital warning signs in the NHS and in finance respectively. Probably the most important legacy is whether a government changes the political landscape for future governments, making it almost impossible to return to previous agendas. There was potentially significant change in the areas of welfare pluralism (increasing the private funding and provision of social policy), conditionality (reducing rights if work obligations are not carried out), and the promotion of choice and consumerism (e.g. choosing hospitals). However, with some important exceptions (such as the vast future 'mortgage' bill associated with the Private Finance Initiative), these were generally more significant in terms of rhetoric rather than delivery or impact. In this sense, there were probably few paradigmatic changes for three reasons. First, many of New Labour's themes built on earlier Conservative reforms (especially the later rather than the earlier years of New Labour). As former Conservative prime minister John Major put it in 1999 – 'I did not appreciate at the time the extent to which Blair would appropriate Conservative language and steal their policies. The attractive candidate was to turn out to be a political kleptomaniac' (in Powell 2008: 267). Second, it is difficult to specify the 'counterfactual': what Labour would have done if it had been re-elected in 2010. It would probably have cut public expenditure, although probably not as quickly and not as steeply. Third, there was no clear linear policy development over time as policy changed in a series of phases with some u-turns. There were many changes over time. If we had 'New Labour' and the 'Third Way' in 1997, perhaps we had in later years 'New New Labour'; 'Even Newer Labour', or the 'fourth way'. For example, New Labour initially stated that it wished to 'abolish' the market in the NHS, only to later reinstate a stronger market. However, two very broad trends involved the 'New Labour shuffle', a complex dance involving one step backwards and then two forwards towards markets and choice; and the 'New Labour ventriloquist', talking left but acting right.

Putting all these factors together, New Labour promises of 'welfare reform', 'world-class public services', and a 'modern welfare state' have only been partially delivered, resulting in an incomplete New Labour legacy. Blair's legacy is probably less far reaching than Attlee's (1945) or Thatcher's (1979), in the sense that their governments made it almost impossible to return to previous policies. It is also possible to examine the New Labour legacy in England as compared to the other nations which were governed by different governments and produced different policies. For example, hospital waiting lists appear to have fallen more sharply in England, but Scotland produced different policies on student finance and continuing care (see Chapter 42).

Emerging Issues

The influence of the Third Way in the future shape of British social policy is difficult to detect. There is clearly some shared ground between New Labour and the coalition. It is likely that elements such as 'active' and 'positive' welfare, consumerism, obligations, and a more pluralist welfare state are here to stay, and it is very doubtful that there will be a return to the traditional social-democratic welfare state. The coalition government appears to be tackling the crisis in a harder, faster, less progressive, and less apologetic manner. On the other hand, in the final analysis when all the 'spin' has been stripped away, it is likely that millionaire footballers and bankers will derive more benefits from both the 'Third Way' and the 'Big Society' as compared with poorer people.

Guide to Further Sources

G. Bonoli and M. Powell's (eds), *Social Democratic Party Policies in Contemporary Europe* (London: Routledge, 2004) sets the United Kingdom in the wider European context. A Giddens' *The Third Way* (Cambridge: Polity Press, 1998) is an influential original source written by the leading academic proponent of the Third Way. Giddens' *Europe in the Global Age* (Cambridge: Polity Press, 2007) restates and updates his view on the Third Way, with Chapter 4 (From Negative to Positive Welfare) being of greatest relevance to social policy. An exploration of the Third Way in the United Kingdom and internationally is provided by J. Lewis and R. Surender (eds), *Welfare State Change. Towards a Third Way?* (Oxford: Oxford University Press, 2004). M. Powell's (ed.), *Modernising the Welfare State: the Blair Legacy* (Bristol: Policy Press, 2008) examines the impact of New Labour up to Blair's resignation in 2007. *The Verdict. Did Labour Change Britain?* by P. Toynbee and D. Walker (London: Granta, 2010) provides material on the three terms and thirteen years of the Labour government.

Review Questions

1 What do you understand by the 'Third Way'?
2 In what ways is the 'Third Way' a new and distinctive approach, which differs from both the 'old Left' and the 'new Right'?
3 Examine how the main themes of the 'Third Way' apply to different services and benefits.
4 Examine how the 'orders of change' apply to individual services and benefits.
5 What are the continuities and discontinuities between the 'Third Way' and the 'Big Society'?

Visit the book companion site at www.wiley.com/go/alcock to make use of the resources designed to accompany the textbook. There you will find chapter-specific guides to further resources, including governmental, international, think-tank, pressure groups, and relevant journals sources. You will also find a glossary based on *The Blackwell Dictionary of Social Policy*, help sheets, and case studies, guidance on managing assignments in social policy and career advice.

PART IV
Contemporary Context

21

Demography

Jane Falkingham and Athina Vlachantoni

Overview

- Changes in the size and composition of the population are the result of the combined effects of changes in mortality, fertility, and migration. However, the most important driver behind population ageing is the decline in fertility rates.
- The key demographic changes in the United Kingdom over the past century include a declining fertility rate, a fluctuating but generally low mortality rate, and the shift from the United Kingdom as a country of emigration to a country of predominantly inward immigration.
- The United Kingdom today can be described as an aged society, where the proportion of older people (aged sixty-five and over) increasingly represents a greater part of the total population.
- Changes in mortality, fertility, and migration in the United Kingdom have been taking place alongside an increasing diversity in the ethnic composition of the population and changes in family structures and living arrangements.
- Understanding demographic changes is a key part of designing and implementing social policies for a constantly changing population.

Population Change

A basic understanding of the drivers and consequences of population change is essential for all students of social policy. This is because demographic trends determine the number of children and others requiring education, the composition of families requiring housing and social benefits, and the size of the current and future older population who will rely on pensions in later life.

The Student's Companion to Social Policy, Fourth Edition. Edited by Pete Alcock, Margaret May, Sharon Wright.
© 2012 John Wiley & Sons, Ltd. Published 2012 by John Wiley & Sons, Ltd.

Demographic changes also impact the demand for, and supply of, health and social care, with improvements in mortality meaning more people will survive into old age. At the same time, changes in patterns of family formation and dissolution mean that a greater number of older people may continue to live with a partner in later life, but more will also have experienced a divorce and may be estranged from their adult children and grandchildren. However, the relationship between demography and social policy is not one-way, as social policies may also impact on demography. For example, the introduction of sanitation into Britain's burgeoning cities during the nineteenth century contributed to the reduction of the death rate, while the introduction of midwives towards the end of the same century led to improvement in infant mortality (see Chapter 16). Today, family policies such as parental leave, child care, and cash benefits can impact women's employment and fertility behaviour, and international migration flows are directly regulated by migration policies. This chapter explores recent changes in the key demographic variables of fertility, mortality, and migration, as well as trends in marriage and divorce and their implications for changing family structures. All of these changes are set in the context of an ageing population.

A Century of Population Change in the United Kingdom

The last century witnessed a transformation of the UK population. In 1901, the total population of the United Kingdom was 39.3 million; by 2001 it had reached 59 million. In 1901, the total fertility rate, which is the average number of children a woman could expect to bear over her lifetime if current birth rate rates prevailed during her entire reproductive lifespan, was 3.5; by 2001 it was 1.7 children. Similarly, in 1901 the average life expectancy in the United Kingdom for a man was forty-five years and for a woman it was forty-eight years, but by 2001, this had increased by thirty years to seventy-five for men and seventy-eight for women. The improvement in mortality across the past one hundred years is equivalent to three years in every decade of the twentieth century, or 3.6 months in every year, or 2.1 days

> **Box 21.1   The Drivers of Population Change**
>
> The size and age structure of the population at any one time is determined by the population in the previous period plus births and minus deaths. If the population is an 'open' population it is also important to take into account migration, adding the in-migrants and deducting the out-migrants.
>
> The formula to calculate the population is known as the *balancing equation*, and is expressed as:
>
> $$Pt2 = Pt1 + B + D + I - E$$
>
> Where:
>
> Pt2   Population at time t2
> Pt1   Population at time t1
> B   Births
> D   Deaths
> I   In-migration
> E   Out-migration (or emigration)

in every week, or seven hours in every day. The advance in survivorship should be seen as one of the greatest achievements of the twentieth century, but it also has important policy implications which are discussed further below.

Figure 21.1 shows the annual number of births and deaths registered in the United Kingdom since 1901. There are several things to note in this figure. First, in all years (except 1976) births exceeded deaths, resulting in a positive rate of natural increase in the population. The gap between births and deaths shows the growth in the population, excluding migration. Second, the two baby boom cohorts following the end of the two World Wars are clearly visible in the peaks in births 1920 and 1947, as is the more extended baby boom of the 1960s. Finally, the peaks in deaths around the World Wars are also visible. Over the century, the annual number of deaths has risen, reflecting the growth in the overall size of the population. The year-on-year trend has also become more stable as the impact of epidemics and infectious diseases has reduced.

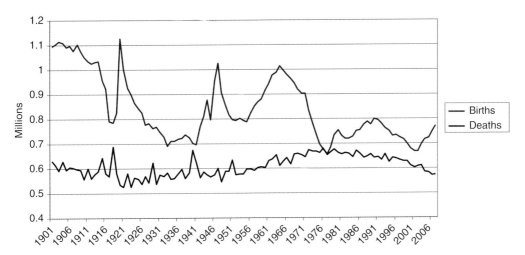

Figure 21.1 Births and deaths, UK, 1901–2007.
Source: National Statistics web site: www.statistics.gov.uk. Crown copyright material is reproduced with the permission of the Controller of Public Sector Information (OPSI).

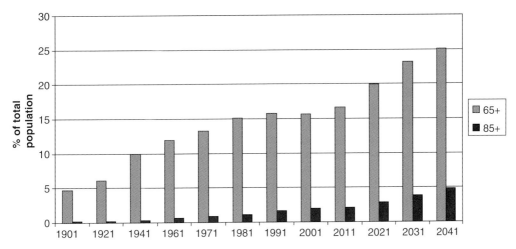

Figure 21.2 Proportion of Britain's population aged 65+ and 85+ (%), 1901–2041.
Source: National Statistics web site: www.statistics.gov.uk. Crown copyright material is reproduced with the permission of the Controller of Public Sector Information (OPSI).

An Ageing Population

One of the main consequences of the changes in fertility and mortality across the past century has been a dramatic shift in the age structure of the population. Figure 21.2 shows the percentage of Britain's population aged sixty-five and over, and eighty-five and over. We can see that the share in the total population of those aged sixty-five and over has increased dramatically. In 1901, around 5 per cent of the population were aged sixty-five and over, by 1941 it had doubled to 10 per cent and by 1981 it had reached 15 per cent. This share has been fairly stable between 1981 and 2011. However, over the coming twenty years, we can expect to see a significant rise in the percentage of those aged sixty-five and over, as the baby boom cohorts (those born in the late 1950s to mid-1960s) begin to enter retirement. In 2021, 20 per cent of the population will be aged sixty-five and over, and this will rise to 23 per cent by 2031 and 25 per cent by 2041. The graph also indicates the ageing of the elderly population itself, reflecting an increase in the proportion of the 'oldest old'. The proportion of those aged eighty-five and over was only 0.2 per cent in 1901. Today, the 'oldest old' account for about 2 per cent of the total population, which numbers 1.4 million people, and by 2041, this will have more than doubled, reaching 3.5 million and accounting for 5 per cent of the total population.

How does a population age? It is important to distinguish between individual ageing and population ageing. Individuals age inevitably from birth to death. Although there is a debate about physiological ageing and slowing the pace of ageing, nevertheless technology has not yet been successful in the quest to reverse the ageing process. In contrast to individual ageing, which can happen only in one direction, populations can become older or younger depending upon the proportion of the population in different age groups. An ageing population is one where the proportion, rather than the absolute number, of elderly people is increasing (generally taken as those aged sixty-five and older). The age of a population is generally measured in one of three ways: the proportion of the population aged under sixteen; the proportion aged sixty-five or over; or the median age of the population. Britain today may be said to have an 'aged' rather than an 'ageing' population, in that a significant rise in the proportion of older people has already taken place.

The age structure of a population is determined by fertility, mortality, and migration. The most important factor in determining the proportion of elderly people in the population is not the improvement in the ability to survive to older ages, but rather changes in the sizes of all age groups. More particularly, whether a national population is relatively young or old depends on the numbers of children born, because the level of fertility determines the numbers of people entering the population at its base. As such, high fertility populations tend to include a larger proportion of children relative to adults of parental age, while low fertility populations tend to have few children relative to current parents, who in turn are not numerous relative to their parents. Falling fertility leads to fewer younger people in the population and hence a rise in the proportion who are elderly. Thus, the main engine driving

the ageing of the United Kingdom population has been the decline in births across the twentieth century. However, that is not to say that mortality is unimportant. Decreasing mortality rates and increasing life expectancy lead to an increase in the proportion of people who can expect to survive to old age. Moreover, mortality decline at older ages is particularly important for the ageing of the elderly population itself thereby increasing the proportion of the 'oldest old'. The projected increase in the proportion of those aged sixty-five and over, and aged eighty-five and over, raises challenges for the design of social policies in the future, as older people will comprise a larger part of the total 'client' population of the welfare state (see Chapter 56).

However, this postponement of mortality (or simply put the delay in death), does not come without a cost. According to the Office for National Statistics, between 1981 and 2006, life expectancy (LE) for both women and men has increased more than healthy life expectancy (HLE) and disability-free life expectancy (DFLE), which means that the proportion of our life that we can expect to live in a good health state has decreased. Although LE, HLE, and DFLE are higher for women than for men on average, the gender gap has narrowed over the past two decades or so. These changes are taking place alongside other demographic and socio-economic changes affecting the quality of life of older people. For example, the proportion of obese people aged sixty-five to seventy-four increased from 21 to 30 per cent between 1995 and 2007, and 61 per cent of women aged 75 and over compared to 34 per cent of men in the same age group lived alone in 2007. Although later life is not always synonymous with deteriorating health for older people, nevertheless these changes can have implications for the amount and kind of support older people can be expected to require in the future and for the organization of long-term care provision (see Chapter 51).

Migration

Across the whole of the twentieth century more people emigrated from the United Kingdom than immigrated, with the net exodus from the United Kingdom being just over 15 million. Without this net out-migration, the growth in the size of the population would have been even higher.

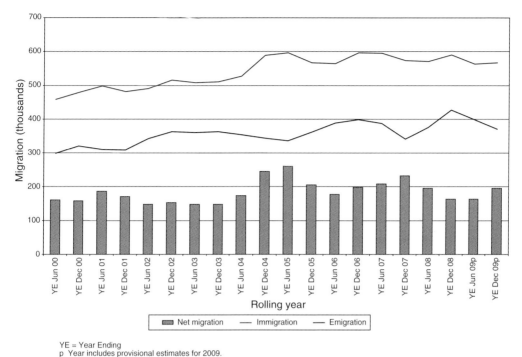

Figure 21.3   Long-term international migration, UK, 2000–2009.
Source: National Statistics web site: www.statistics.gov.uk. Crown copyright material is reproduced
with the permission of the Controller of Public Sector Information (OPSI).

However, as we will see below, today the United
Kingdom is a country of net in-migration. Figure
21.3 shows trends in international migration to
and from the United Kingdom over the past
decade. Much has been written in the press concerning the increase in migration, particularly following the accession of the A8 countries (Czech
Republic, Estonia, Hungary, Latvia, Lithuania,
Poland, Slovakia, Slovenia) to the European
Union in 2004. The United Kingdom was only one
of three European countries which fully opened
their borders and labour markets to migrants
from such countries. However, although there was
a clear rise in net migration in 2004 to 2005, net
migration was already at around 175,000 in the
early 2000s. Moreover, through the decade significant numbers of people have continued to emi-
grate. Emigration peaked at over 400,000 in 2008
while immigration has been relatively constant
since 2004, with a slight decrease since November
2008, when the government introduced a Points-
Based System (PBS) aimed at managing migration for work or study in the United Kingdom.

Some of the rise in births since 2001 shown in
Figure 21.1 is due to the increase in the number
of births to non-UK born mothers. In 1999, 14.3
per cent of births were to non-UK born mothers;
by 2009 this had risen to 24.7 per cent. Both the
rising birth rate and the growing share of births
to non-UK born mothers have implications for
the provision of school places and support for
children with English as an Additional Language
(EAL). Data from the 2010 School Census show
that in maintained primary schools, the first language of 16 per cent of all pupils at compulsory
school age or above was other than English, while
in state-funded secondary schools this proportion was 11.6 per cent.

An Increasingly
Diverse Population

One outcome of extended periods of migration to
the United Kingdom is the country's increasingly
diverse ethnic composition. Figure 21.4 shows

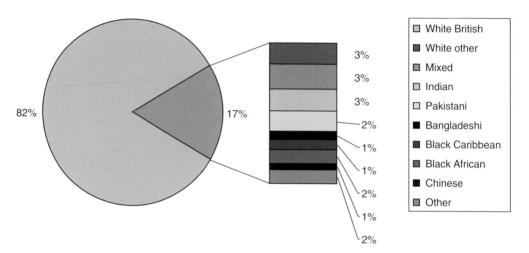

Figure 21.4 Ethnic composition of population aged 15–19, 2007, England.
Source: National Statistics web site: www.statistics.gov.uk. Crown copyright material is reproduced with the permission of the Controller of Public Sector Information (OPSI).

that in 2007 just under a fifth of all young people aged fifteen to nineteen in England were from a background other than white British.

The number of older people from a black and minority ethnic background is still relatively low. According to the 2001 Census, people from minority ethnic groups comprise about 6 per cent of the total population aged fifty and over in Britain, and the largest minorities within this group are of an Irish, Indian, black Caribbean, or Pakistani origin. However, as the cohorts who came to Britain from the early 1970s onwards move through the life course and enter into retirement, this proportion will increase. The implications for the design and delivery of social services are already being considered in government policies, for example the National Service Framework for Older People, which was introduced in 2001, established standards of health and social care provision for older people and promoted greater equality of access regardless of a person's age or ethnic origin.

Changing Patterns of Partnership and Family Formation

The past thirty years have seen significant changes in patterns of partnership and family formation. Figure 21.5 shows the percentage of women who have experienced various life course events according to the year of their birth. For example, among women born between 1943 and 1947, three-quarters (75 per cent) had married by age 25, and this contrasts with just under a quarter (24 per cent) of women born thirty years later, between 1973 and 1977. Although the number of marriages has declined across successive birth cohorts, this does not indicate a rejection of partnership per se, as the percentage of women cohabiting has increased. However, the rise in cohabitation has not been sufficient to offset the fall in marriage, and overall fewer young women are entering partnerships, and those that do, tend to enter partnerships later.

Alongside the delay in partnership, the average (mean) age at childbirth has also increased steadily since the late 1960s. The delay in child bearing is clearly visible in Figure 21.5 with just 30 per cent of those women born between 1973 and 1977 having had a child by age twenty-five, compared with over half of women at the same age who were born between 1943 and 1947. In 2007, the average age at first birth among women in England and Wales was 27.5 years compared with 23.7 years in 1970. It is, however, important to bear in mind that this is an average, and that the United Kingdom still tops European league tables for the highest teenage pregnancy rate. In 2009, there were twenty-six live births

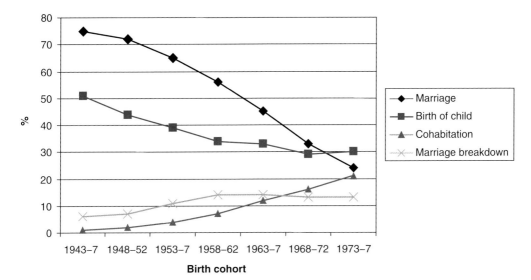

Figure 21.5 Percentage of women who have experienced various life events by age 25 by birth cohort. Source: National Statistics web site: www.statistics.gov.uk. Crown copyright material is reproduced with the permission of the Controller of Public Sector Information (OPSI).

per thousand women aged under twenty in the United Kingdom. Rates of teenage births in the United Kingdom are seven times those in the Netherlands, double those in France, and more than twice those in Germany (United Nations Statistics Division 2010: online). In February 2010, the government published a policy document entitled *Teenage Pregnancy Strategy: Beyond 2010*, which set out a series of measures to tackle the high teenage pregnancy rate, including improving the quality of sex and relationship education in schools and increasing access to online advice.

The decline in marriage is reflected in the increasing proportion of children who, according to their birth certificate, are born outside a legal marital union. In the nineteenth century, the percentage of all births outside a marriage hovered at around 7 per cent. This rate persisted through the twentieth century, apart from a small rise during both World Wars. However, since the 1970s there has been a consistent and steep increase, and in 2008, 45 per cent of all children were born to parents who were not legally married.

Many parents do still go on to marry after the birth of a child, but the combination of declining marriage and increasing partnership breakdown

has meant that the proportion of dependent children in the United Kingdom living with married parents has fallen from almost three-quarters (72 per cent) in 1997 to less than two-thirds (63 per cent) in 2009. In contrast, the proportion of dependent children living with cohabiting couples rose from 8 per cent to 13 per cent, and the proportion of dependent children living with lone parent families rose from 22 per cent to 23 per cent.

The number of dependent children living in different family types has implications both for the way in which services and benefits aimed at children are provided, but also for the future availability of informal care from kin. It is an open question whether children will be willing to provide care for a step-parent or for a natural parent that they may not have grown up with. Similarly, it is unclear whether women and men in mid-life will be willing to care for their former parents-in-law.

Emerging Issues

Changes in the timing of demographic events such as partnership and childbirth, combined with an increasing average life expectancy, have resulted in a continuous restructuring of the life course into the future. For example, according to projections by experts at the Max Planck Institute for Demographic Research, half of all the children born in the United Kingdom in 2007 will live to age 103. Such remarkable demographic changes have been taking place alongside other social and economic changes, for example the economic recession which started in 2008 has impacted on patterns of immigration into the United Kingdom, as a decrease in employment opportunities has forced many migrants to return to their home countries. The extent of demographic changes over the past few decades has also meant that it has become more difficult to predict what kind of lifestyle, work, leisure, and family roles individuals may be engaged in at a particular chronological age. Finally, we can expect the increasing diversity in the composition of the younger population in the United Kingdom, for example the ethnic diversity of the teenage population described in Figure 21.4, to be reflected among the older population as this cohort moves through the life course.

One of the key questions facing policy-makers is how to accommodate for these demographic changes in order to continue tackling social problems, satisfying social needs and maximizing well-being across all age groups (see Chapter 3). A key part of designing social policies to take demographic changes into account is understanding population change, the various forms it takes, its dynamic nature, and what it means in terms of policy implications.

Guide to Further Sources

An excellent source of information on the UK population and on families and households is the annual publication *Social Trends* published by the Office for National Statistics. Since 2010 *Social Trends* has been published online and the latest issue is available from www.statistics.gov.uk/socialtrends/stissue/.

Another valuable source of data and commentary on demographic changes is the Office for National Statistics (ONS) journal *Population Trends*. This journal is published quarterly and contains peer-reviewed articles as well as tables on key demographic variables such as births, deaths, migration, marriage and divorce. Current and past editions are available online at www.statistics.gov.uk/populationtrends/. The web site of the ONS includes current and historical population projections, as well as statistics on specific subject areas, such as life expectancy, living arrangements, and the older population. Other useful web sites include the ESRC Centre for Population Change's www.cpc.ac.uk.

Comparative data on countries in the European Union is available through the *European Statistics* (Eurostat) portal http://europa.eu/documentation/statistics-polls/index_en.htm and useful comparative data and research findings on demographic trends in Europe can also be found on the web site of the *Population Europe* partnership www.population-europe.eu/. Finally, international comparative data is available from the *United Nations Statistics Division* at http://unstats.un.org/unsd/demographic/default.htm and the *Population Reference Bureau*, www.prb.org/, which is based in the United States but contains useful articles and resources on global trends.

Review Questions

1 What are the key drivers of population change?
2 What have been the most important demographic changes in the United Kingdom over the past century?
3 What causes population ageing?
4 How can we measure population ageing?
5 What are the some of the implications for social policy of population change and population ageing in particular?

Visit the book companion site at www.wiley.com/go/alcock to make use of the resources designed to accompany the textbook. There you will find chapter-specific guides to further resources, including governmental, international, think-tank, pressure groups, and relevant journals sources. You will also find a glossary based on *The Blackwell Dictionary of Social Policy*, help sheets, and case studies, guidance on managing assignments in social policy and career advice.

22

Economic Policy and Social Policy

Rob Sykes

Overview

- What is economic policy?
- Why is the relationship between economic and social policy considered problematic?
- What have been the key features of British governments' economic policies since 1945, and how were they linked to social policy provision?
- Why and how has the international context become increasingly important for economic and social policy-making? What is all the fuss about competitiveness?
- Does the process of globalization imply that governments can no longer make autonomous decisions about the economic and social policies?

Economic Policy and Social Policy: The Issues

Given the recent furore about public spending and its impact upon the British economy, it might seem that the central issue about economic policy and social policy is self-evident. As Figure 22.1 indicates, in 2010 the majority of UK government public spending was on Pensions, Health, Education, and Welfare spending, comprising some £327 billion from a total central government expenditure of nearly £496 billion, or 66 per cent of the total. Put another way, according to the government's own figures (UK Treasury PESA 2010) spending on these same categories comprised just over 22 per cent of gross domestic product (GDP) from a total of central government spending that formed 33.63 per cent of GDP. This means that social policy and welfare spending are a major part of the UK economy; and this is true of most other advanced industrial nations, as discussed below.

The Student's Companion to Social Policy, Fourth Edition. Edited by Pete Alcock, Margaret May, Sharon Wright.
© 2012 John Wiley & Sons, Ltd. Published 2012 by John Wiley & Sons, Ltd.

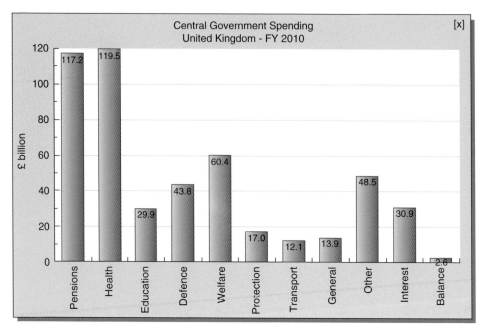

Figure 22.1 Central government spending by function 2010.
Source: HM Treasury, Public Expenditure Statistical Analyses 2010, www.hm-treasury.gov.uk/
pespub_pesa10.htm.

Just what is the relationship between the economy as a whole and its welfare provision? Is spending on the various areas of welfare simply a cost to citizens and companies via taxes, and to governments in terms of their public expenditure? How do governments try to manage their economy as a whole and, in so doing, what are the links between the economic and social policies they pursue? Furthermore, why and how far does it matter whether the economy is competitive with other national economies and to what degree is national government policy affected by developments outside its shores, either in Europe or in the global economy as a whole? Does the process of globalization now mean that national governments are very limited in the economic policies, and in order to compete they must severely reduce their welfare provisions? These are the questions that analysis of economic policy must address, even if it cannot answer them.

What *Is* Economic Policy?

Before looking more closely at the relationships between economic policy and social policy it

makes sense to be clear about exactly what is meant by the term *economic policy*. Although there is often an overlap between the two sorts of policy, as for example in policies to do with employment and taxation, we can broadly define economic policy as government activities in the economic field focused, *inter alia*, on the following sorts of activities and topics.

- Industrial policy, for example, promoting manufacturing industry with grants or tax benefits.
- Managing trade with other countries, for example, through tariffs or trade agreements.
- Securing economic growth of the economy as a whole i.e. seeking to produce more goods and services in the economy
- Redistribution of income, property, and wealth between different groups in society, for example, through taxation policies.
- Employment policies, for example, trying to manage the rate of unemployment, or managing shifts of employment from one sector, say manufacturing, to another, say services, in the economy.

When considering these and other economic policy interventions it becomes apparent that there are many areas where it is difficult if not impossible to distinguish between economic and social policy. For example, housing policy may be both targeted at securing decent housing for a country's citizens and thus their welfare through the promotion of house building, but increased house building activity will not only contribute to increasing the housing stock, it will also generate business for house builders and associated trades, and have an impact upon the financial sector dealing with home loans and so on, thus affecting the economy as a whole. Similarly, changes in taxation may be primarily designed by governments to manage the economy and increase revenue and/or dampen demand and thus keep the rate of inflation manageable, but taxes also have social consequences. Increasing rates of Value Added Tax (VAT), for example, as the coalition government did in January 2010, may increase government revenue and slow down sales of goods. But it will also have welfare implications for different groups in society since VAT is recognized to be a regressive form of taxation that affects those with lower disposable incomes ('the poor') more than those with higher disposable incomes ('the rich').

It is possible, and indeed helpful when looking at the changes in government policies over time, to recognize the three major types of economic policy. These are

fiscal policy – the management of government revenue (income) and pending (expenditure);
monetary policy – the management of interest rates to affect the cost of borrowing money and rewards for saving and the supply of money in the economy; and
regulation – laws that affect the way that individuals or businesses can act in the economy.

A focus on one or more of these types of policy has characterized British governments' economic policy interventions in the past sixty or so years. Different governments, whether Conservative or Labour have targeted different objectives for their economic policies and tended to rely on one or more of these policy types, as we shall summarize in the next section. What, however, has become more apparent in the latter twenty years or so is

that national governments, whether the British, other European countries, or countries in other parts of the world such as China and the United States, have discovered that both their economic and social policy options have become more and more constrained by the increasingly international character of the economy. We need to consider now whether national governments can act autonomously from international and global networks in determining their economic or social policies, or whether all are inevitably forced to respond to the 'global economy' by maintaining international competitiveness through paring back the costs of welfare. In other words, whether international economic pressures in practice prevail over national policy planning.

This idea of the dominance of economic over social policy is not new, however. It is often assumed that the essential relationship between economic and social policy in capitalist societies has to be one where economic imperatives predominate – unless the economy is healthy then there can be no meaningful financial basis for public investment in social policy objectives. However, some have suggested that the converse may be true, that social policy provision is a necessary feature of a successful and competitive modern economy, especially in the context of increasing globalization (see Gough 2000). We return to this later.

British Post-war Economic Policy

Policy consensus 1940s–1970s

At the end of the Second World War the British economy was in crisis. The response to this was an economic policy based upon Keynesian principles of demand management. Both Labour and Conservative governments attempted to deal with the high levels of unemployment and economic recession by generating demand through government intervention in various forms of public works but principally, at least in the 1940s, through the development of the so-called welfare state. The unemployed, sick, and disabled, the retired, the homeless, and other groups began to receive transfer payments, or benefits, which allowed them to buy goods and services thus generating higher levels of consumer demand than might otherwise have prevailed. At the same time, the growth of welfare provision in the form of school and hospital buildings and public housing, for example, also generated demand in the building trades and associated businesses.

These methods of demand management were thus believed by successive governments both in the United Kingdom and elsewhere to be the key feature of economic policy. The advantages were that when the economy was in decline and rates of unemployment higher then benefit recipients would spend those benefits, rather than save them, and this activity would act to counter economic decline by injecting demand for goods and services into the economy. Conversely, when economic times were good and levels of unemployment low then much fewer benefits would need to be paid and the level of demand would fall, thus preventing inflation in the economy sometimes described by economists as 'too much money chasing too few goods'.

In short the relationship between the welfare state and the economy in the 1940s to 1970s period was believed by UK governments, and many other governments managing capitalist economies around the world, to be mutually beneficial – social policy was good for the economy by stimulating demand and, of course, was also good for those who needed welfare support.

During this period both Conservative and Labour governments shared the following goals in their economic policies:

- economic growth
- low inflation
- a reasonable balance of payments (i.e. between exports and imports), and
- full employment.

The mix between these goals their prioritization varied in different policies and at different times; but essentially this was a period of consensus in economic and social policies in the country. The main tools of economic policy were:

- fiscal measures for management of taxation and public expenditure;
- control of the supply of money and credit through manipulating rates of interests, that is, monetary policy; and

- regulation and other controls through such measures as incomes policies and labour market controls.

A number of factors ended that consensus from the mid-1970s onwards and changed the economic policy goals of government and tools employed to implement them.

Conservative economic policy 1979–97

Economic stagnation in the 1970s had begun to threaten the success of the Keynesian demand management model, and thus the post-war consensus on economic and social policy (see Hutton 2002). This came into sharper focus with the arrival of the first Thatcher government of 1979. Almost immediately the goal of full employment was discarded and priority was given to fighting inflation and reducing public expenditure. More generally the commitment of government shifted to reduction of government intervention in all areas of activity and the promotion of economic competitiveness rather than employment or the balance of payments. This led to the development of the new tools of economic policy that follow.

Monetarism – in the 1980s this came to mean an ideological commitment to limited government intervention focusing mainly on inflation and cuts in public expenditure rather than the control of the overall money supply.
Rolling back the public sector – cuts in public spending both at national and local government levels added to the privatization of public services and tax cuts.
A move to so-called *supply-side* policies to reduce drastically welfare spending on unemployment and focus instead on promoting labour market participation in more flexible jobs in service industries.
Deregulation in employment and labour relations, local government services, and financial investment, to improve the competitiveness of the UK economy.

In practice, many of the stated Conservative policy goals concerning both public expenditure and reducing the welfare state failed to meet their stated aims, but the terms of debate about both economic and social policies had shifted radically.

When the Labour government under Blair came to power in 1997 significant elements of the previous economic and social policies continued to feature, albeit in a different mix of New Labour rhetoric and policy initiatives.

New Labour policies 1997–2010

New Labour governments led first by Blair and then Brown were committed to what was called '*economic prudence*'. They were committed to control inflation through the setting of interest rates, but decided that this role should no longer be carried out by government, which may be influenced by electoral and other political considerations, but by a special committee of the Bank of England. Thus, a key element of economic management was devolved from government. Furthermore, monetary policy was to be subject to the 'golden rule' of no net government borrowing over the economic cycle to finance current expenditure. Any borrowing to finance capital expenditure must also meet strict rules and normally be matched by private investment.

Initially at least, these rules coupled with a regular Comprehensive Spending Review of public spending led to the reduction of public expenditure for the first time since the 1980s. New Labour also made various changes to the system of taxes, including a limited redistribution of income towards lower income earners. However, the supply-side approach remained and welfare policy was linked to economic policy via welfare-to-work programmes that targeted getting people into paid employment, rather than paying benefits.

Overall, this so-called *Third Way* aimed to avoid both the Keynesian policies of earlier years, and the more strident monetarist and anti-public sector policies of the previous Conservative governments, which led Labour to argue that their governments were successfully managing both economic and social policy. Indeed, in terms of economic growth and stability the UK economy did seem to be more successful than most other economies internationally into the early years of the twenty-first century (see Hutton 2002).

However, the British economy gradually began to suffer from a variety of internal and external problems generated in large part by changes in the international economy. Economic growth began to falter, which meant that economic activity did not meet various policy targets set for it. One result was a significant increase in government borrowing to meet public expenditure commitments into the mid-2000s. At the international level it became increasingly clear that the British economy was becoming less competitive especially against the nascent economies of the Far East and China. More and more consumer goods were imported, and the economy relied more heavily on credit to boost consumption. The banks lent increasingly large amounts to fund such purchasing and, in particular, to fund home buying.

The scene was set for the global financial crisis which began in 2007. As a result the British economy was hit by a variety of financial shocks, some transmitted from the international economy especially from the United States, some generated by internal failures of British banks and other financial institutions. As a consequence the government's economic policies were thrown even more off course, and this led to a short term return to neo-Keynesian policies of public spending to prop up ailing financial institutions and promote economic growth. However, after Labour lost the 2010 election, the new coalition government moved quickly to reduce public spending in order to remove the burgeoning public sector deficit – criticized by Labour as threatening economic recovery. As we have suggested, however, economic activity may now no longer just be determined by the actions of national governments, whatever their political colour.

Globalization, Economic Policy, and Social Policy

Important though the international financial crisis of 2007 was for all capitalist economies, the broader role of globalization and its impact upon both economic and social policies was a concern well before the crisis. Increasingly politicians blamed globalization for changes in the international economy that, they argued, limited the freedom and effectiveness of governments to manage their economies, and also rendered state welfare provision problematic if not directly damaging for their countries' economic well-being.

Put at its crudest, the argument was that the need for competitiveness in the new globalized economy means that state welfare schemes have become too costly and damaging for national economies. Those countries with expensive and extensive welfare states would therefore lose out in the global economy to those countries with less costly support. However, the relationship between globalization, economic policy, and social policy is more complex than this – and more disputed, as can be seen from the following three perspectives on globalization and its economic and welfare implications.

1   The first of these arguments is that the internationalization of the world economy implies a reduction of national government freedom to make effective policy decisions, and a reduction in their policy options. At the same time, global economic changes generate more unemployment, especially among unskilled and semi-skilled workers as the patterns of international trade and technological change diminish the demand for such work. Although such changes generate increasing demand for unemployment and other welfare benefits, the need for national economies to compete in world markets exerts pressure for continuing reductions in social expenditure by both governments and private firms. In short, so the 'hyperglobalist' argument runs, globalization limits national economic policy choices and is likely to lead to overall retrenchment and decline in national welfare states and social expenditure (see Mishra 1999).

2   However, some challenge this view, and argue that the changes in the world economy are less widespread, smaller and more gradual than the hyperglobalization thesis suggests. Even if globalization has occurred, welfare states remain compatible with this process – globalized economies need to provide some sort of social welfare and political counterbalance to the effects of economic change or else the economies will become even more unstable. Indeed some suggest that the so-called threat of globalization is more an ideological ploy of national governments wishing to restructure welfare than an unchallengeable economic force (see Pierson 2001).

3   A third argument recognizes that globalization is changing the character of the international economy and thus also changing the ways in which governments may focus their economic and social policies. However, the emphasis of this view is less on the character of globalization and more on the specific character of politics and policy in particular countries. Put simply, due to their previous economic and social policies and institutional frameworks, some countries are better able to cope with, and respond to, the challenges of globalization than others. Thus, different governments will change in different ways in their response to globalization, both with regard to economic and social policies – though all must to some extent respond (see Esping-Andersen 1996).

A variation of this 'politics matters' perspective suggests that globalization should not be seen as some sort of unstoppable external economic force constraining and limiting governments' policy choices. Rather it was the development of democratic welfare states in the advanced economies that created the conditions the deregulation of national economies and the liberalization and re-regulation of the international economy, and hence globalization. In this view national rather than international bodies remain the key decision-makers in economic policy as well as welfare policy.

Emerging Issues

There is a considerable variation between the developed economies that comprise the OECD in terms of their social expenditure. Nevertheless, there has been a trend of an increase in such expenditure over time in almost all developed countries even though some countries (such as the United States and Australia) have lower expenditures, some (such as Sweden, Germany, and France have much higher expenditures). The United Kingdom sits somewhere in between, not much above the OECD average (see the OECD Social expenditure database for more detail at http://stats.oecd.org).

The issue that confronts all such economies and governments, however, and which is a central feature of their economic policies, is how to manage this expenditure and public expenditure overall in their response to the worldwide economic crisis. The relationship between economic and social policy we have outlined above is right at the heart of this issue: how can governments manage their economies to seek recovery and economic growth with such high rates of public expenditure and indebtedness and what will be the effect on social policy? If they make sweeping cuts to welfare expenditure, which is the major part of public expenditure, then unions, political parties, and voters may well reject these policies and political instability may result. On the other hand, if they do not make cuts to expenditure in an attempt to cut economic debt and to secure economic growth, then their competitive position vis-à-vis other economies may well be affected and the national economy be weakened still further in the global marketplace. It is this conundrum that confronts governments internationally in the post-crisis years.

Guide to Further Sources

W. Hutton, *The World We're In* (London: Abacus, 2002) provides a relatively easy-to-read review of Britain's economy and its issues in the twenty-first century, linking these to the international arena. The best single source on economic competitiveness and the link to welfare is still I. Gough (2000) 'Social Welfare and Competitiveness' in id., *Global Capital, Human Needs and Social Policies* (Basingstoke: Palgrave, 2000). N. Yeates and C. Holden (eds), *The Global Social Policy Reader* (Bristol: Policy Press, 2009) provides a wide-ranging treatment of the various dimensions of globalization as they affect, and are affected by social policy: Section 4, *Globalisations and Welfare Transformations* looks most closely at economic and social policy. For exemplars of the three perspectives on globalization and welfare look at the following: Perspective 1: R. Mishra, *Globalization and the Welfare State* (Cheltenham: Edward Elgar, 1999); Perspective 2: P. Pierson (ed.), *The New Politics of the Welfare State* (Oxford: Oxford University Press, 2001); and Perspective 3: G. Esping-Andersen (ed.), *Welfare States in Transition: National Adaptations in Global Economies* (London: Sage, 1996)

Review Questions

1 Why is the relationship between economic policy and social policy considered problematic?
2 What are the main targets of government economic policy?
3 What were the main features of the so-called consensus in economic and social policy in Britain between the 1950s and the 1970s?
4 Why has the international economy in general, and competitiveness in particular, become so important for government economic and social policies in the 2000s?

Visit the book companion site at www.wiley.com/go/alcock to make use of the resources designed to accompany the textbook. There you will find chapter-specific guides to further resources, including governmental, international, think-tank, pressure groups, and relevant journals sources. You will also find a glossary based on *The Blackwell Dictionary of Social Policy*, help sheets, and case studies, guidance on managing assignments in social policy and career advice.

23

Religion

Rana Jawad

■■■

Overview

- Religious bodies were often the first providers of social welfare and social assistance and remain so in many countries round the world.
- United States and continental European analysts have paid more systematic attention to the role of religion in the development of social policy in their countries than their British counterparts.
- All world religions, including new age religions, have teachings on the nature of happiness and well-being, as well as selfless service.
- The extent to which religious welfare groups are able to solve social problems varies. Some are more focused on issues of morality and identity, but others run large-scale programmes designed to improve social and economic conditions.
- In the United Kingdom, government policy has, controversially, grown increasingly faith-friendly since the 1980s.

■■■

Religion and Social Policy: An Old–New Partnership

The role of religion in social policy can best be described as an 'old–new' partnership with emphasis in this chapter perhaps being laid on 'old'. This is important for various reasons: first it establishes that the received history of social policy as an academic subject has been somewhat incomplete because it has not always recounted the way in which religious figures, values, voluntary groups and charities, political parties, and institutions have influenced the development of social policies and welfare states across the countries of the world; second, this assertion helps to allay fears and suspicion with regard to

The Student's Companion to Social Policy, Fourth Edition. Edited by Pete Alcock, Margaret May, Sharon Wright.
© 2012 John Wiley & Sons, Ltd. Published 2012 by John Wiley & Sons, Ltd.

the apparent re-entry of religion into the public sphere both in the United Kingdom and elsewhere; and third, we begin to see that social policy and religion share some core concerns and are built on similar foundations: both aspire towards an idea of the 'good society' and are underpinned by particular conceptions of human nature.

In short, the connections between religion and social policy are intrinsic but separate in large part because social policy has come to symbolize the flagship enterprise of the secular modern nation-state dependent on science and human rationality for its flourishing, whereas religion is a cultural relic besieged by conservativism and backwardness, whose historical record is steeped in war and social oppression. There are, therefore, some very real cultural and material challenges for a constructive discussion of the role of religion in social policy.

Social Welfare in the Five Main World Religions

The eminent US sociologist Wuthnow (1988) proposes a definition of religion that emphasizes how deeply connected it is to social action. He argues that religion has as much to do with abstract moral beliefs and ideas, as it does with a sense of belonging to a community and a drive to be socially engaged in society. In this way, it is possible to argue that religious people and values have a natural role to play in public life, and indeed to speak out against social injustices. Religion need not be confined to the private sphere of life.

The five major world faiths of Hinduism, Buddhism, Judaism, Christianity, and Islam command followers totalling more than half of the world's population (around 3 billion). They also underpin the empirical studies which were handmaiden to the birth of sociology as a discipline in the early twentieth century and provide the most advanced forms of engagement with political mobilization and poverty alleviation in human history. These five religions are also the only ones to have penetrated formal state organs around the world as can be found in India, Iran, Israel, and England. Although internally diverse, we will highlight here some of their key commonalities.

What is significant in the way in which religion and social policy have intertwined throughout human history is that religiously inspired welfare has been championed not just by religious orders but also by lay intellectuals, political activists, and social reformers such as Seebhom Rowntree and William Beveridge (in Christian Socialism), Mahatma Ghandi and Rammohan Roy (in modern Hinduism), and Seyyed Qutub and Abdolkarim Soroush (in reformist Islam). Examples of political mobilization and social action by religious groups abound in the examples of the Base communities of Latin America, the Catholic Church in the 1980s Solidarity Movement of Poland, the development of socialist strands of Protestantism and Sunni Islam in the nineteenth century, the establishment of the Hindu *gram seva* (village service) in India in the early 1900s.

The relevance of religious teachings to social welfare thus lies in their overarching concern with ethics (the rules that govern correct social relationships). These translate into basic values about human life, dignity, equality, social justice, property, honest communication, law, and order. World religions do not immediately seek to prescribe what types of social structures and public institutions are needed for the good society. What they offer are moral standards for correct social relations that they see as the path to pleasing God and establishing a just social order. The *Ten Commandments* or *Decalogue* in Judaism, Christianity, and Islam and the skills required to live one's life according to the *dharma* as in Buddhism and Hinduism are key illustrations of this. Moreover, a common social welfare idea is that of (selfless) service. The main world faiths all incite believers to act selflessly and to help others in need as in the Christian story of the Good Samaritan, the Islamic injunctions to help orphans, the sick and vulnerable or pay the obligatory tax of *zakat*, the Jewish emphasis on *g'millut chassadim* which refers to selfless kindness and service and *tikkum olam* (meaning repair the world); *seva* (service) and *dharma* in Hinduism as the key inspirations to fight against social injustice.

Yet, while the main world religions have clear injunctions about social and material well-being, the primary condition of welfare is found at the level of the human being's personal spiritual wellness, thus these religions do not necessarily like big government: they caution against the evils of earthly politics and the control of elite minorities over the popular masses. However, certain strands of Christianity and Islam for example favour strong state control as the main guarantor of social equality and justice. In some cases therefore, there is mistrust of the welfare state, and this explains the tension inherent in whether or not religious believers are to embrace or detach themselves from the material concerns of earthly life – as in Max Weber's "world-affirming" or "world-rejecting" classification of religion.

Religion, Spirituality, and the Study of Social Policy

It follows logically then, that religion should make very scant appearance in histories and theories of social policy. What has tended to be the case is that many academic authors refer to religion as a social and political force in the medieval period, particularly in the European context and that by the time of the English Reformation (sixteenth century) and the Enlightenment (eighteenth century Europe) religion had lost its grip on society and science allowed mankind to take control of its destiny.

This situation contrasts North America and Continental Europe with the United Kingdom and England in particular. Continental European and North American historians of the welfare state have more readily accounted for the role of religion in the development of social policy. They cite the important role that the state religions and established churches have played, for example in the Netherlands, Sweden, or Germany in fortifying state responses to social needs and problems. In the United States, there is a rich literature about the role of voluntary religious groups and how critical their entrepreneurialism and free voting systems helped to develop social policy and democratic politics in the United States. Some historical accounts go as far as arguing that Catholic countries failed to develop the same kinds of sophisticated welfare systems as certain Protestant countries because the Catholic Church was fiercely protective of its independence and continued to uphold the subsidiarity principle

whereby responsibility for poverty was to lie outside state control, most notably within the family. Protestantism on the other hand, emphasized the work ethic and was able to align itself more easily to the secular state and therefore, to give way to its increased role in social welfare provision.

Some arguments thus posit religious welfare against modern state welfare. According to Modernization theory which states that societies will become increasingly secular with technological advancement, religious welfare has been replaced by state welfare since morality and social control are no longer the dominion of the Church or Temple but rather, that human beings are able to analyse themselves and provide rational solutions to make their lives better. In this view, social policy remains a moral endeavour but its values come from humanist assumptions about social citizenship and social rights.

But double standards in academe persist as Gorski (2003) has argued: in contrast to the academic study of so-called Third World countries, Western academics give passing tribute to the role of Christian socialism in the development of the welfare state. In these analyses, religious welfare is generally lumped with the voluntary sector with no critical discussion of how religious values inspired major social policy thinkers or political parties or as Chapman (2009) shows the ways in which religious and secular voluntary organizations compare and contrast with each other.

The relegation of religion to the private sector is thus, part and parcel of the Secularization thesis that reached its heights in the 1960s and 1970s. Yet in the 2000s, it is now argued that more people claim to be religious then the previous generation, and indeed that established state religions continue to exercise power even in the supposed heartland of secularity: Western Europe. Today, tens of thousands of religiously inspired organizations operate around the world offering a whole array of social services from cash assistance to emergency relief to education and health care. Religion has also entered the formal state apparatus and underpins the design of social policies in countries from North America to the Far East. In the latter for example, the focus on family based social welfare is directly the result of Confucianism (see Chapter 62).

Religion is no longer a factor of social and economic backwardness that academics readily consider in 'Third World' politics. It is now a major variable in sociological analyses of European and American societies for four major reasons:

1 These societies have become truly multicultural with religion playing a key role in the identity of a significant part of their populations.
2 Cataclysmic events such as 9/11 mean that religion, especially Islam and the social integration of Muslims is now seen as a government priority in the West.
3 The onward march of neo-liberalism and the withdrawal of the welfare state have made it easier for religious groups to enter the social welfare scene as private providers.
4 Empirically, there is a cultural/spiritual turn in social science research, which recognizes the failure of money-metric analyses of poverty and a real need to respond to post-materialist understandings of human well-being.

What we find therefore, is that world leaders such as Bill Clinton, George Bush, and Tony Blair actively opened the way for religious welfare associations and the promotion of religious freedoms through new legislation and welfare reforms, most notably Bush's Charitable Initiative Act in the United States.

Critics have been quick to highlight the threat which religious involvement in social welfare poses to social citizenship and civic values as the stakes run high over how best to rescue the dying ideals of social democracy. Faith-based schools are perhaps among the most hotly debated in this respect. However, major investment in research is now beginning to redefine and reconceptualize the contribution of religion to society. The scene is especially interesting and vibrant in contemporary Britain.

The United Kingdom Context

According to the 2001 census, 72 per cent of the British population considered themselves to be Christian while around 10 per cent were of other religions, primarily of immigrant origin. The Church of England, The Salvation Army, and increasingly, non-Christian groups such as Jewish Care, The Hindu Gujarati Society, The Nishkam Centre, The Faith Regen Foundation, and Islamic Relief are now among the most active and largest religious social welfare providers in the United Kingdom. Some of them operate directly under government contracts for example through the new Work Programmes that have come into operation under the UK coalition government.

Allegiance to religious welfare has enjoyed close ties within both the Conservative and Labour Parties. The Thatcher era was staunchly anti-state and brought in welfare reforms which opened the way for private (and religious) welfare initiatives. Key Conservative figures such as Iain Duncan Smith (Director of the Centre for Social Justice) have played a key role in promoting religious social action and are likely to continue to do so with more force perhaps in the policies of the UK coalition government. On Labour's side, a strong bond ties the Protestant non-conformist movement with the party and Blair's election in 1996 was a watershed for the re-entry of religion into British public life. In key speeches addressing the Christian Socialist Movement in 2001 and then Faithworks (the movement led by Rev. Steven Chalke, founder of one of the United Kingdom's most socially active Christian organizations, Oasis) in 2005, Blair seemed to embrace religious welfare as a kind of missing link in British social policy which tied the ends of the (new) political rhetoric of welfare pluralism, social capital, partnerships, and community participation. This new policy direction was supported by influential intellectuals such as Giddens who began to argue that religious identity would help fortify the disintegrating moral fabric of British society. In 2007, the then minister of state John Murphy observed that religious welfare would become a key plank of British social policy in the years to come.

In parallel, the role of the Church of England as moral patron of the nation has increasingly been put to question. After the publication of *Faith in the City* in 1985, a major report by the Church that criticized the Thatcher government and the persistence of stark social inequalities and urban poverty in the United Kingdom, the Church of England has begun to feel its role is marginalized as government funding increasingly moves towards multi-faith councils and forums. Yet, Church leaders have continued to speak out against social injustices, such as the severe cuts to welfare benefits – especially in housing – that were announced by the UK coalition government in the latter half of 2010. In his Christmas sermon that year, the Archbishop of Canterbury, Reverend Dr. Rowan Williams made a passionate plea for the burden of economic recession on the United Kingdom to be shared by the rich members of society as well.

Today, religious welfare politics remains very much in the making. There is much grey literature that seeks to pin down the contribution of religious groups to society. Some economic estimates have been offered. The National Council for Voluntary Action has also sought to classify the work of religious groups in the United Kingdom. It is thought that their annual income is close to £5 billion, a figure nowhere near total state social expenditure in the United Kingdom, but still significant nonetheless. British government policy thus sees interest in religious welfare groups in three main ways:

1   As providers of social welfare since they possess valuable resources such as buildings and volunteers.
2   As promoters of social cohesion since the United Kingdom is now a multi-ethnic and multireligious society.
3   As new actors in an ever-expanding of stakeholder politics and democratic governance particularly at local authority level.

The new discourse around the Big Society with its corresponding emphasis on community and social capital is also set to further enhance the role of religious organizations in the United Kingdom.

Yet, caution and even confusion prevail: some religious groups are suspicious of government fearing that their prophetic mission and their closeness to their local communities might be compromised if they are used instrumentally by the state as cheap and ready forms of welfare provision. Indeed, many religious groups are small and lack the professional capacity to compete for government funding and take on more bureaucratic roles. On the part of govern-

ment policy, there is an issue of 'religious literacy' broadly meaning that government officials lack knowledge about religious groups and the kind of values and language they use. Thus, there is an issue of mutual understanding and communication that needs to be resolved.

Emerging Issues

The role of religion in social policy, especially in the British context, is very much a scene to watch. There is increasing interest from policy-makers and research funding organizations in the role of religion in the public sphere, particularly after cataclysmic events such as 9/11 but also as a result of deepening neo-liberalism. There is therefore, a renewed sociological debate on the role of religion in late modern and what some have called post-materialist societies.

Consequently, there is renewed interest in the non-material and non-metric dimensions of human well-being, which is seeing a revival of interest in issues such as spirituality, social cohesion, and psycho-social interpretations of human well-being. This poses the question of the need of definitions of human need encompassing spiritual ones as well.

At the macro level, major social policy shifts in Europe and America are opening the way for religious organizations to become formally involved in social welfare provision. In the United Kingdom, the coalition government's discourse on the Big Society is taking shape and it is expected that religious welfare will form a key part in the social policies to come – though the extent of public or even religious support for this is open to question.

Guide to Further Sources

A. Backstrom and G. Davie (eds), *Welfare and Religion in Twenty-First Century Europe: Vol. 1* (Surrey: Ashgate, 2010) offers innovative empirical research on various countries in Europe. C. Milligan and D. Conradson (eds) (2006) *Landscapes of Voluntarism: New Spaces of Health, Welfare and Governance* (Bristol: Policy Press, 2006) includes several chapters on religion in the context of the voluntary sector. R. Chapman

'Faith and the voluntary sector in urban govern-ance: Distinctive yet similar?' in A. Dinham, R. Furbey and V. Lowndes (eds), *Faith in the Public Realm: Controversies, Policies and Practices* (Bristol: Policy Press, 2009) also provides a good introduction to the key debates on the role of religion in the United Kingdom.

A. E. Farnsley, II 'Faith-Based Initiatives', in J. Beckford and N. J. Demerath, III (eds) *The Sage Handbook of the Sociology of Religion* (London: Sage, 2007) discusses George Bush's Charitable Initiative in America. S. Furness and P. Gillingan, *Religion, Belief and Social Work* (Bristol: Policy Press, 2010) offers an empirical analysis of the contribution of religion from the point of view of social work. R. Jawad, *Social Welfare and Religion in the Middle East: A Lebanese Perspective* (Bristol: Policy Press, 2009) provides a review of all major world faiths in relation to social welfare and a fuller discussion of both R. Wuthnow, *The Restructuring of American Religion: Society and Faith since World War II* (Princeton, NJ: Princeton University Press, 1988); and P.S. Gorski, 'The return of the repressed: religion and the political unconscious of historical sociology' in J. Adams, E. S. Clements and A. S. Orloff (eds), *Renaming Modernity: Politics, History and Sociology* (Durham and London: Duke University Press, 2003), pp. 161–89.

For historical reviews see M. Parker-Jenkins, D. Hartas, and B. A. Irving, *In Good Faith: Schools, Religion and Public Funding* (Aldershot: Ashgate, 2005) and F. Prochaska, *Christianity and Social Service in Modern Britain: The Disinherited Spirit* (Oxford: Oxford University Press, 2006) provide historical overviews of Christian social welfare action in Britain. K. Van Kersbergen and P. Manow (eds), *Religion, Class Coalitions and Welfare States* (Cambridge: Cambridge University Press, 2009) offers a historical overview of how welfare states in Europe developed in light of their religious politics and traditions.

UK policy developments in relation to religion and faith communities can be tracked on the web site of the Department for Communities and Local Government's (CLG), www.communities.gov.uk/corporate. Analysis of such policy developments can be found on Christian think-tanks such as that of Theos, www.theosthinktank.co.uk. Information about what kinds of religious welfare organizations exist in the United Kingdom and how to contact them can be found via the Multi-Faith Centre at the University of Derby at www.multifaithcentre.org.

Review Questions

1 Do faith schools pose a threat to citizenship?
2 Should religious welfare groups be considered as part of the larger category of voluntary sector organizations?
3 How has the secularization thesis been challenged?
4 Should spirituality be considered an essential human need?
5 How might the study and practice of social policy benefit from greater appreciation of the role of religious welfare?

Visit the book companion site at www.wiley.com/go/alcock to make use of the resources designed to accompany the textbook. There you will find chapter-specific guides to further resources, including governmental, international, think-tank, pressure groups, and relevant journals sources. You will also find a glossary based on *The Blackwell Dictionary of Social Policy*, help sheets, and case studies, guidance on managing assignments in social policy and career advice.

24

Family Policy

Jane Millar and Tina Haux

■■■

Overview

- There have been significant changes in patterns of family formation and dissolution, and so in family structures, in the United Kingdom in the past half-century. There have also been changes in employment patterns, with most mothers, especially those with older children, now in paid employment.
- Family values and norms about the 'right thing to do' have become more complex and dependent on context. But this does not imply a lack of commitment to family, although these commitments are subject to reflection and negotiation.
- Family policy can be defined in relation to policy goals, to areas of activity and to institutional structures. The key areas of activity include the regulation of family behaviour, cash and tax transfers for families, and the provision of services.
- In the United Kingdom family policy has become more explicit in recent years, with a range of new policies introduced and existing provisions developed.
- Family policy is at the heart of important debates about the future direction of the welfare state, in particular in relation to the reconciliation of paid work and unpaid care.

■■■

Family Change and Social Policy

Family policy has now become a significant and accepted part of the political and policy landscape in many industrialized countries. Family policy is usually defined to include the regulation of family behaviour, cash transfers to families, and the provision of services to families. Family policy in the United Kingdom has become much more explicit, coherent, and extensive in recent

The Student's Companion to Social Policy, Fourth Edition. Edited by Pete Alcock, Margaret May, Sharon Wright.
© 2012 John Wiley & Sons, Ltd. Published 2012 by John Wiley & Sons, Ltd.

Table 24.1   Family formation and family structure in Britain over thirty years.

	Early/mid- 1970s	Late 2000s
Percentage children born outside marriage	8	46
Percentage single women cohabiting	8 (1979)	26
Median age at first marriage for women/men	21/24	30/32
Number of abortions, women aged 15–44	161,000	215,903
Fertility rate (live births per 1,000 women)	84	64
Number of divorces	79,000	141,300
Divorce rate per 1,000 married population	5.9	11.9
Percentage families headed by lone parents	8	26
Percentage one-person households	18	29
Average household size	3.1	2.4
Percentage of population aged under 16 years	25	19
Percentage of population aged over 65	13	16

Sources: *Social Trends 40* (2010); *Household Formation in Scotland* (2010); *Mid Year Population Estimates* (2009); *Birth Statistics* (2010).

years. The political discourse behind these developments stresses the role of families as the 'bedrock' of society – the basic social unit which carries values, which brings up the next generation, and which sustains local communities.

Thus, families are very much at the centre of contemporary political and policy debate in Britain. All political parties claim to have policies that support families and sustain family life. Family life and personal relationships are the focus of media attention, not only in press and television but also on Internet sites such as 'mumsnet' which attract millions of people. Academic interest in the relationship between family and state has made this a growing area of research and publication.

Much social policy is concerned with families and family life, and in the making of policy certain assumptions must be made about families and family roles. It has often been argued, for example that the provisions of the post-war British welfare state rested on a very clear model of family life, in which men were full-time workers and women were full-time carers. Families were assumed to be stable and long-lasting, and the family roles of men and women were seen as being quite distinct.

It is debatable how far real families ever conformed to this idealized model, even in the 1950s, a decade in which family structures were unusually stable and homogeneous. Families today,

however, are much more volatile and heterogeneous. Although the 1960s are often characterized as the 'permissive decade', it was really in the 1970s that patterns of family life in Britain began to change very rapidly. The 1969 Divorce Reform Act, implemented in 1971, made divorce possible for a much wider range of people. Cohabitation also began to rise at that time, as did rates of extra-marital births. Table 24.1 summarizes some key trends in family formation and structure since the 1970s. As can be seen, there have been some very significant changes over this period. Many more children are born outside marriage, more couples are cohabiting, first marriage is later, abortion is more common, women have fewer children, and there is a higher risk of divorce. As a consequence, there are more lone-parent families, more people live alone and the average household size is smaller. The population is also growing older, with a lower percentage aged under sixteen and a higher percentage aged over 65. This also includes more of the very elderly, with more people now aged eighty-five and above.

Employment patterns for families with dependent children have also changed over this time period. In the early 1970s just about half of married mothers were employed, usually women with older children, since mothers in that period typically spent several years out of the labour market to provide full-time care for their

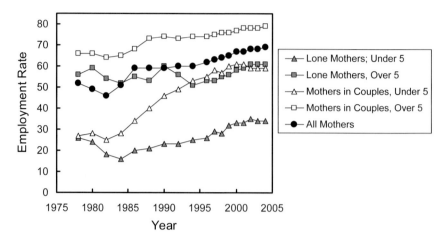

Figure 24.1   Employment rate of mothers by marital status and age of youngest child, 1977–2005. Sources: *Living in Great Britain* (1997) and Walling, A. 'Families and employment', *Labour Market Trends*, July, (2005). See www.statistics.gov.uk.

husbands and children. In 2010, around three-quarters of married mothers are employed, including over half of mothers with preschool children. As Figure 24.1 shows, employment rates remain lower for lone mothers than for married mothers, but have been rising in recent years, especially for mothers whose youngest child is under five-years-old. Many employed mothers, both married and lone, are in part-time jobs. Most women who work part time say that they prefer to do so, as it makes combining work and care easier, but part-time work does tend to be restricted to certain parts of the labour market and to be lower paid. Nevertheless, the earnings that women contribute to family income are increasingly important in maintaining living standards and preventing family poverty. The income gap between no-earner, one-earner, and two-earner families is a key factor in widening economic inequality.

These family and employment trends have been characterized as the decline of the 'male breadwinner' family that was, as noted above, at the centre of the twentieth-century welfare state. The family type of married couple with the man at work and the woman at home now accounts for less than a quarter of all families with children. It is important, however, to recognize that family situations change over time. Families form, break up and reform, and people move in and out of work. Thus, although the male-breadwinner family is a minority at any one time, it is still an important stage in the family 'life course' for many people. This is also true of lone parenthood. The women (and less commonly, men) who become lone parents do not usually stay lone parents for ever – many remarry or set up home with new partners and even if they do not, their children grow up and leave home. Lone-parenthood can therefore be characterized as a stage in the family life course, rather than as a fixed and separate family type.

The extent to which family relationships and values and norms about family life have also changed alongside changes in family structure has been the subject of much debate in the sociological literature. It is sometimes argued that family commitments have become weakened because people are now more 'individualized' and motivated by their own personal goals and aspirations. As people focus more on their individual needs and self-actualization, they become less committed to sustaining family ties. This individualization thesis has been challenged on both theoretical and empirical grounds. For example, Smart (2007: 189) argues that the concept of individualization focuses attention on 'fragmentation, differentiation, separation, and autonomy' rather than on the ways in which people 'connect' across family and other relationships, over time and place. Williams (2004) summarizes a major research programme which explored issues of personal

relationships, intimacy, family values and obligations, and love and care in family and friendship
networks. A key conclusion from this research is
that, while the 'new conditions' of more fluid and
complex family structures and work/care patterns
'have changed the shape of commitments they
have not undermined commitments itself' (2005:
83). Families, of origin and of choice, are very
important to people, but family obligations are
negotiated rather than fixed, family values are
complex and there is no simple consensus about
what is the 'right thing to do'.

Thus, it can no longer be assumed that all
families are broadly the same with the same sorts
of needs and resources. Nor can it be assumed
that everyone shares the same values about family
life. The issue of whether and how governments
should respond to family change is therefore an
issue of ongoing debate. Some people see the
welfare state as having weakened and undermined the family and call upon government to
turn the clock back and restore 'traditional' family
structures and roles. Others are more pragmatic
and argue that policy should reflect these changes
and seek to ensure that people are not disadvantaged as a consequence.

Family Policy in the United Kingdom

There is no simple way to define family policy.
Some definitions include everything that affects
families, whether intended or not. Others include
only those policies directly targeted at families,
with particular goals in mind. Hantrais, for
example, offers a definition that focuses on policy
goals: 'Families policies, in the plural, can be
characterized as policies that identify families as
the deliberate target of specific actions, and where
the measures initiated are designed to have an
impact on family resources, and ultimately, on
family structure' (2004: 132). However, as noted
above, there are very different political and ideological views as to the role of government in relation to the family. Hantrais herself goes on to
note that many governments do not explicitly
identify the family as a target for policy, nor seek
to influence family structure. It may be more
useful, therefore, to define family policy in relation to areas of activity, as in Box 24.1.

Box 24.1 Defining Family Policy

Family policy can be defined by three main
areas of activity:

1 *The legal regulation of family behaviour*:
   laws relating to marriage and divorce,
   to sexual behaviour, to contraception
   and abortion, to parental rights and
   duties, to child protection.
2 *Policies to support family income*: tax
   allowances, family and child benefits,
   parental leaves and benefits, enforcement of child support.
3 *The provision of services for families*:
   child-care provisions, subsidized housing, social services, community care,
   for example.

As noted above, family policy in the United
Kingdom has become more extensive and explicit
in recent years. In particular the Labour governments from 1997 to 2010 introduced, or extended,
family policy in several directions. Daly (2010)
summarizes these under six main areas.

1 Early education and child-care (the expansion of child-care and early years services as
   part of the National Childcare Strategy).
2 Financial support for families with children
   (the introduction of tax credits and increased
   financial support for families with children).
3 Services for young children and their families
   (the introduction of Sure Start).
4 Employment activation (New Deal for Lone
   Parents and welfare-to-work reform).
5 Work family reconciliation (the extension of
   maternity leave, introduction of paternity
   leave and right to request flexible working).
6 Parental responsibility and behaviour (greater
   intervention in family life, e.g. parenting classes).

The extent to which this represents a fundamental
shift in policy is the subject of ongoing debate
(and judgement may depend on what happens
under the 2010 coalition government, see discussion below). Daly (2010: xx) concludes that there
were changes in policy instruments but that 'the

appearance of substantial change and innovation masks deep-seated continuities'. The underlying paradigm remains that of 'a market-oriented, family policy model'. However, focusing on specific policy areas highlights more strongly the extent of change. For example, Lewis (2009) focuses on work–family reconciliation and argues that the level of expansion and innovation in this policy area has taken the United Kingdom in a new policy direction and closer to Europe (see Box 24.2). Millar (2010) summarizes the substantial changes in policy in relation to lone mothers and employment. Lister (2006) argues that the

'social investment approach', in respect of children (where all adults are or should be workers and children are workers of the future), of New Labour is indeed new. Tackling child poverty was a central feature of Labour's policy and Box 24.3 summarizes the progress in that area.

Box 24.2   The Adult Worker Model and Work–family Balance

Assumptions about families, and what families do, are an essential underpinning of the welfare state. Jane Lewis has analysed how Britain has moved from assuming a 'male breadwinner' to an individualized 'adult worker' model. Under the new mode, it is assumed that all adults have the duty and responsibility to engage in paid employment, and that such paid work can and should be carried out alongside caring responsibilities. This raises clear challenges for how care work can be combined with paid employment, and what policy measures are needed to enable this to happen.

Prior to Labour coming to power in 1997 the United Kingdom clearly lagged behind other countries in Europe with regard to policies enabling families to combine paid work and family care responsibilities. Lewis argues that there have been three dimensions to work–family policies under Labour: child-care provision, flexible working arrangements, and parental leave.

Lewis argues that this new policy package marks a new departure for family policy in Britain and places it more in line with its European neighbours. However, she also argues, that while claiming to be gender neutral and aiming to give parents more choice, the policies have, in effect, been targeted at mothers.

Box 24.3   Investing in Children: Ending Child Poverty

When New Labour came to power 3.4 million children (one in four) were living in relative poverty, making it one of the highest child poverty rates in the developed world. The announcement by Tony Blair in 1999 to cut child poverty in half by 2010 and to eradicate it within a generation came as a surprise but quickly became one of the most high profile policy targets. It has been estimated that New Labour spent 1 per cent of GDP on reducing child poverty.

Jane Waldfogel (2010) looks at the UK experience from a US perspective. She concludes that progress was made against all three measures of poverty enshrined in the target, namely relative poverty, absolute poverty, and deprivation. By 2009 relative child poverty had fallen by 16 per cent, absolute poverty by 50 per cent and deprivation by 18 per cent. The difference in the level of progress between the three targets is explained by the simultaneous increase in income disparity in the United Kingdom which meant that the relative poverty line kept moving upwards and by the fact that deprivation tends to require a more sustained improvement in income and is therefore likely to lag behind pure income measures.

Looking ahead, Waldfogel identifies five challenges for Britain in combating child poverty: addressing the poverty of families in work; workless two-parent households; the high risk of poverty of minority ethnic families; getting more lone parents into work; and addressing the overall increase in income inequality.

See the Poverty Site for a comprehensive summary of UK poverty trends www.poverty.org.uk/.

Public expenditure on families and family support has increased. The Institute for Fiscal Studies have shown that the main beneficiaries from tax and benefit reforms since 1997 have been low-income families with children or pensioners, see www.ifs.org.uk. The OECD shows the United Kingdom spending 3.55 per cent of GDP on family benefits (cash, services and tax) in 2005. This puts the United Kingdom in third place (behind France and Luxembourg) and above the OECD average of 2.33 per cent. United Kingdom expenditure on child-care and pre-primary education was at 0.6 per cent of GDP, the average for OECD countries (see OECD Family Database: www.oecd.org/els/social/family/database).

Emerging Issues

Since May 2010 the Conservative Party and the Liberal Democrats have formed a new coalition government. The coalition government set up a review on Poverty and Life Chances, a committee on Social Justice, and a taskforce on Childhood and Families. These will give a clearer indication of their plans for family policy. Three themes from the Labour governments seem set to continue, however, namely the focus on the first years of children's lives, the continuing (and deepening) activation of lone parents, and the focus on families as the 'bedrock' of society. However, the level of support, both cash and services, for families is likely to be reduced significantly as a result of substantial cuts in public expenditure from 2010 onwards. The measures introduced by the new government in the June 2010 emergency budget and the Comprehensive Spending Review in 2010 contain a range of policy changes affecting families directly through changes to benefits and more indirectly through the cut in spending on public services. Overall, families with children have been identified as the biggest losers by the Institute for Fiscal Studies. More generally, the perceived need for deep spending cuts across all government departments has re-ignited the debates over universal benefits such as child benefit versus means-tested benefits such as tax credits. Provision is likely to become more targeted on the poorest families, with less universal provision. The first example of this trend is the introduction of a means-test for child benefit. In addition, families not in work or on a low income are likely to be affected by the introduction of the Universal Credit, a single benefit that is going to replace the current, complex benefit system from 2014 onwards. The universal credit will be assessed on the basis of households rather than individuals and joint claims will be required, but with a single payment. This has implications for women's access to social security and will exacerbate the fact that women are likely to be major losers as a consequence of the current social security and tax credit cuts.

Alongside these public expenditure developments, there is also a renewed interest in early years, parenting and long-term poverty, and in the promotion of marriage in the policy agenda. Family breakdown and poor parenting are being blamed for a number of social ills, despite the evidence showing the complexity of the casual factors involved.

More broadly, key issues in family policy remain at the heart of important debates about the future direction of the welfare state. For example, Esping-Andersen (2009) provides an analysis that encompasses issues of low fertility, ageing populations, the needs of young children, the 'revolution' in the roles of women, and polarization and inequality across households. He argues that welfare states need a new approach to family policy, 'reconciling motherhood and employment', and that the lack of such policy will 'result in one (or both) of two evils: too few children and/or too few workers and too little family income' (2009: 174). The long-standing feminist arguments for the importance of state policy in enabling the reconciliation of paid work and unpaid care are thus increasingly coming to centre stage in debates about future policy.

Guide to Further Sources

M. Daly, 'Shifts in family policy in the United Kingdom under New Labour', *Journal of European Social Policy*, 20/5 (2010): 433–43 discusses the main developments in family policy under New Labour and argues that they do not add up to a paradigmatic change.

G. Esping-Andersen, *The Incomplete Revolution: Adapting to Women's New Roles* (Cambridge:

Polity Press, 2009) analyses economic, social, and demographic change and argues welfare states have not yet adapted to the revolutionary changes in the roles of women. Family policy, it is argued, should be seeking to 'accelerate the maturation of the female revolution'.

A detailed account of the emergence and success of work–family balance policies in Britain and as well as a comparison with policies in France, Germany and the Netherlands is provided by J. Lewis, *Work–Family Balance, Gender and Policy* (Cheltenham, Edward Elgar, 2009).

L. Hantrais' *Family Policy Matters: Responding to Family Change in Europe* (Bristol: Policy Press, 2004) provides an overview of debates and policies in the European Union and the twenty-five member states.

The nature and implications of the children as 'social investments' approach to family policy under New Labour is discussed in R. Lister, 'Children (but not women) first: New Labour, child welfare and gender', *Critical Social Policy*, 26/2 (2006): 315–35.

Jane Millar's 'Lone Mothers, Poverty and Paid Work in the UK', in S. Chant (ed.), *International Handbook on Gender and Poverty: Concepts, Research and Policy* (Cheltenham: Edward Elgar, 2010), pp. 147–52, summarizes the nature and impact of policies relating to lone mothers and employment.

In her discussion in *Personal Life* (Cambridge: Polity Press, 2007) Carol Smart argues for a new sociology of personal life, placing her discussion in the context not just of the sociological literature and but also her own personal life.

J. Waldfogel's *Britain's War on Poverty* (New York: Russell Sage Foundation, 2010) provides a detailed discussion of the policy measures, their intentions, limitations and successes in Britain, including lessons for the United States.

F. Williams, *Rethinking Families* (London: Calouste Gulbenkian Foundation, 2004), provides an overview of key family changes and discusses research findings about 'how people balance work, care, and commitments to family and friends'.

The Office for National Statistics gives access to social trends, population trends, and so forth and to the various data sets that can be used to create tables and charts (e.g. Table 24.1) www.statistics.gov.uk. Additional statistics for Scotland can be accessed through the government web site www.scotland.gov.uk.

Review Questions

1 What have been the key changes in family patterns in Britain over the past thirty years?
2 What are the challenges for social policy arising from increased employment among mothers?
3 Define family policy.
4 Did the Labour governments from 1997 onwards transform family policy?
5 What will determine the future of Britain's family policy?

Visit the book companion site at www.wiley.com/go/alcock to make use of the resources designed to accompany the textbook. There you will find chapter-specific guides to further resources, including governmental, international, think-tank, pressure groups, and relevant journals sources. You will also find a glossary based on *The Blackwell Dictionary of Social Policy*, help sheets, and case studies, guidance on managing assignments in social policy and career advice.

25

Divisions and Difference

Sharon Wright

Overview

- The study of the social divisions of welfare is concerned with understanding fundamental and enduring differences between social groups in their experiences of welfare provision and the type of outcomes that they receive from it.
- Key divisions have been identified as existing between men and women, disabled and non-disabled people and between people of different socio-economic classes, ethnic groups, religions, nationalities, ages, and sexualities.
- Social divisions can be complex and cross-cutting.
- Some social groups have distinct and identifiable welfare needs that are different from other categories of people. Researchers and campaigners have argued that such differences should be recognized formally and taken into account when social policies are designed and implemented.
- Social divisions are related to, but distinct from social inequalities, social justice, and issues of equity and equality.

Choice, Identity, and Difference

We are who we choose to be. This is the message conveyed by influential multi-billion dollar marketing ventures. In the twenty-first century, whole industries are directed at convincing us that we can buy the lifestyle of our choice. The implica-tion is that what we buy can help us to be who we want to be – to have the body we want, the relationships we want, the job we want, the leisure activities, or the home we want. If we don't like how we look or how we feel then we can buy a product or a service to change it. Processes of individualization, mass consumption, and the

The Student's Companion to Social Policy, Fourth Edition. Edited by Pete Alcock, Margaret May, Sharon Wright.

blurring of social boundaries can all contribute to give the impression that anyone can be anything. But, as social scientists, we are compelled to break the surface of these superficial impressions of contemporary society and probe more deeply. How much choice do we really have in determining our own prospects? Can we choose freely to be who we want to be or are our life experiences and life chances already structured by forces beyond our individual control?

The starting point for our analysis of contemporary social relations is to observe that unique individuals share aspects of their identities with other people. Shared characteristics can form the basis of group cohesion and a sense of inclusion. However, acknowledging that we belong to one group also involves highlighting that we are excluded from membership of certain other groups, for instance, as a white woman, I am neither a black woman nor a white man. This leads us to the main argument of this chapter – that there are differences between social groups and that these differences can be significant and consequential, for instance,

- You are more likely to experience poverty if you are a woman than a man.
- You could live up to ten years longer if you are a lawyer rather than a labourer.

These are examples of how experiences of well-being and life chances can be related to differences between social groups. These social inequalities provide a radical challenge to the picture of contemporary society that was painted in the opening paragraph of this chapter. We do not live a social world where anyone can be anything – far from it. We live in societies that are structured, stratified, and deeply divided. Ultimately, recognizing that substantial, long-term divisions exist between different groups within society implies that these groups may have different interests and that these interests may be the source of conflict.

The study of the social divisions of welfare recognizes the importance of understanding the different needs and experiences of social groups and argues that where these differences are fundamental and enduring, a division exists in society. The 'big three' social divisions that have received greatest attention in academic litera-

ture are class, gender, and 'race' or ethnicity. Chronologically, class was the first category of to receive sustained attention from social scientists, in the late nineteenth century and early twentieth century. Much later, in the 1970s and 1980s, feminists and anti-racist writers became more prominent in identifying different social cleavages that had, until then, been largely ignored. This gave birth to a new field of academic attention, the study of new social movements. Furthermore, a number of other divisions have been identified and explored more recently: disability, age, nationality, and sexuality.

This wider body of work is relevant for our discussion of social divisions in the sense that it sought to recognize and legitimize difference. For instance, it challenged the basic assumptions on which the welfare state had been built, such as the structure of families (the stereotypical lifelong marriage with 2.4 children no longer holds true). It became necessary to acknowledge that lifestyles, relationships, family formations, and the role of men and women had changed dramatically since the post-war period. This led to an increased awareness of issues of difference and the need to recognize the ways in which underlying policy assumptions interact differently with particular groups in society. For instance, the conditions for receiving access to council housing were found to be inherently racist because of their weighting towards those who had been resident in particular geographical areas for longest. Similarly, taxation arrangements (such as the married man's tax allowance) and inheritance laws assumed that long-term relationships were heterosexual, meaning that gay men, lesbian women, and bisexual people were excluded from financial benefits and discriminated against in terms of joint claims on property or assets.

Thus, is it essential to recognize that policies which appear to be neutral can have differential impacts upon diverse categories of people. For example, welfare-to-work policies are presented as neutral in constructing paid work as the best way to provide for welfare needs. However, on closer inspection, we can see that compelling people who receive social security benefits to look for paid work may conflict with their other responsibilities, most significantly with caring roles. For example, in the United Kingdom, it is perfectly legitimate for a married woman to stay at home to bring up her own children. But, if the same woman was to split up from her husband, she would be required to discuss the possibility of paid employment before being allowed to claim social security benefits, so her role as a full-time mother might be open to challenge.

Understanding Difference and Divisions

The experience of social divisions is related to differences between social groups. As we have already seen, each of us shares aspects of our identity with other people. The relationship between different groups is complex and variable. Social differences can (but do not always) lead to social divisions. At some points, one aspect of our group identity might be more important than others. On a rainy Saturday afternoon, for instance, being Scottish may matter more to a row of rugby spectators, as they watch their national team play against England, than being either male or female, or being working class or middle class. However, Scottish national identity may have become much less important by nine o'clock the following Monday morning when the rugby fans go back to their usual activities.

Gender is likely to have a big influence on whether or not a person is at home looking after children. For those who are in paid work, gender and class are likely to be related to the type of job they do and the amount of money they get paid for it. On average, women, for instance, earn 15.5 per cent less than men per hour for full-time work. This example provides two insights:

- First, that it is impossible to make blanket assumptions about which aspects of group membership are most important to people's identities.
- Second, we can observe that people can belong to multiple groups and that social divisions may intersect or be cross-cutting.

Ultimately, the differences between men and women or people of different classes, for instance, are of interest to us here because they are related to their command of personal and collective resources, such as wealth, status, and power. Since these are the means by which they can protect

themselves from risks such as poverty or unemployment, they bear a direct relationship to their means of meeting welfare needs.

Membership of some social categories may by dynamic, fluid, or transitional, while membership of other categories may be more fixed. Clearly, for each individual, membership of some social groups is more fixed than others – people usually retain their gender throughout their lifetime, but their age changes constantly, shifting through different phases of childhood, youth, adulthood, and older age. It is interesting to consider how these multiple, and perhaps conflicting, social identities are negotiated, reconciled, or changed. Each of us can exercise a degree of choice over membership of some social groups. We cannot choose the gender we are born with, but it is possible to change it. Similarly, we did not control the geographical place into which we were born, but we may move to another town or country; we may choose to seek an alternative national citizenship.

However, such identity and status markers are often so deeply embedded that we would never consider exercising this choice. On the other hand, we may experience a change that moves us against our will from one category to another, for example, a car accident could move us from non-disabled to disabled. So, there is a complex relationship between the exercise of individual agency, or choice, and the impact of wider structural constraints. To answer one of the opening questions of this chapter, it seems that although individuals can exercise some choice in decisions about their lives, they often do so within very powerful constraints. The value of a social divisions approach is that we can begin to understand some of the major dimensions of these structures of opportunity and constraint.

A word of caution: there is a temptation to simplify the analysis of social divisions of welfare to a discussion of 'winners' and 'losers'. Perhaps in some ways it is inevitable that discussion of different social groups and their relative positions in relation to material and social resources will slip into the terrain of moral value judgements. However, it is important to recognize the roots and limitations of such an approach. In relation to understanding social divisions, using the 'winner'/'loser' distinction does have the advantage that it allows us to demonstrate a series of processes of opportunity and constraint in education, the labour market, and social policies that reward some activities (i.e. paid work) over others (i.e. unpaid care).

On the other hand, speaking of 'winners' and 'losers' engages us in a value-based discussion that affords primacy to financial position within society. The problem with adopting such a stance is that not all human activities can be evaluated in economic or monetary terms. For instance, feeling loved is very important to personal well-being, but has very little to do with financial position or social status. Is it really adequate, for instance, to say that a lone mother who receives social security benefits has a 'worse' life than a wealthy male company director? We can certainly identify a gendered social division in their material circumstances. However, to say that the lone parent has lost out and the male executive has won is only useful up to a certain point. This position would mean that spending time bringing up children would have to be ranked below the generation of income through paid work.

Indeed, this is precisely the value judgement that many governments around the world have adopted in their design of welfare-to-work policies. Such policies encourage or compel lone parents to look for (and preferably to engage in) paid work, leaving less time available for parenting their children, who will have to be looked after by someone else during working hours. So socio-economic position is only one part of the picture and does not, in itself, tell us whether certain groups of people have a 'better 'or 'worse' life.

We cannot, therefore, over-simplify the issue of social divisions. In terms of social policy analysis, we are interested in how social divisions affect well-being. Understanding divisions and difference is concerned with the role of the state and the market in creating, perpetuating, mediating, or tempering the structures and processes that influence people's life experiences and life chances. Since social policies are designed to intervene in areas of well-being (for instance health, income, housing, or education), understanding how they impact differentially upon groups in divided societies is a crucially important task.

Studies of the social divisions of welfare have shown, essentially, that the costs and benefits of a welfare state are shared out unevenly between different groups of people. That is, the financial support (e.g. social security for disabled people) and services (such as health services) offered by the welfare state, as well as the costs of maintaining it (through paying taxes or charges), impact differentially on particular groups of people. Often this literature is based on an explicit or implicit argument that certain groups in society benefit unfairly from past and present welfare arrangements, while others are disadvantaged. People from lower socio-economic groups, for instance, have been shown to pay proportionally more of their disposable income towards the welfare state than their more affluent counterparts (however, this is a complex issue, since the taxation burden and redistributive effects of welfare vary depending on how they are measured: see Chapter 27).

The next section uses the example of class to provide a more in-depth illustration of some of the key issues involved in analysing social divisions. Class was chosen as a case study because it is one of the most fundamental divisions in contemporary society. Also, unlike many of the other categories of division and difference, class is not explicitly investigated in greater depth elsewhere in this book (for gender, see Chapters 12 and 24; for 'race' and ethnicity, see Chapters 5 and 53; for age, see Chapters 54 to 56; for disability see Chapter 57; and for religion and nationality see Chapter 23).

Class: A case study of divisions and difference

Class presents an interesting example because although it was the first social division to be recognized, it is now commonly misunderstood or overlooked. The work of classic theorists Karl Marx and Max Weber, in the late nineteenth century and early twentieth century, was extremely influential in recognizing deep divisions in societies. The main argument is that societies are stratified, or layered (like a wedding cake), with clear divisions between different social classes, who have largely separate and conflicting interests.

■ Marx believed that the struggle between social classes would drive social change.

■ Weber (although he accepted much of Marx's analysis) had a different view, that occupational classification would determine social status and life chances.

Although societies have changed significantly since this body of work was written, these approaches continue to have relevance in their recognition of class differences, and more particularly in Marx's analysis, class interests, and conflicts. This leads us to a view of individuals who are connected to wider society through processes that are political and exploitative.

Perhaps it is partly *because* of this long history of class analysis – and the socialist or communist associations that it conjures up – that it has become distinctly unfashionable to talk about class divisions in society. Some commentators have even gone so far as to announce the demise of class. Popular perceptions of class seem to be influenced by the life stories of high profile personalities like David Beckham, J. K. Rowling, or Alan Sugar. Each of these individuals, and many more like them, have tales of building massive personal wealth from humble beginnings – playing football at school, writing in a café, or selling vegetables out of the back of a van.

However, these extraordinary triumphs of personal talent over adversity, leading to multi-millionaire status, are exactly that – extraordinary and individual. The reason that they are so newsworthy is that they are exceptional. The vast majority of people living in Britain retain the social class that they were born into, much the same as a century ago. Where social mobility between classes does occur, it is generally at the boundaries between classes, rather than the extremes of rags to riches. Thus, it is possible to identify distinct social classes and it is evident that these classes are considerably cohesive.

Class divisions are reproduced over generations through subtle processes of inclusion and exclusion. For example, during the transition from childhood to adulthood, young people experience a series of opportunities and constraints as they make important life decisions like when to leave school, what sort of job to get, and whether or not to go to university.

Class-based analysis also provides a fruitful basis for reflection on the welfare state. On the one hand, it is interesting to think about the role

that class interests played in the development of state welfare. For instance, one explanation for increased state intervention in the early twentieth century and later in the establishment of the post-war welfare state, was that it was a response to 'pressure from below' – working class people (who previously had not been voters) were demanding that their welfare needs be met. On the other hand, more than half a century later, we could ask questions about why the welfare state has not made more of a difference in addressing class-based inequalities in health, education, or the eradication of poverty. Class is, therefore, very much alive as a major social division.

The precise definition of class – and what it means to people – is the source of much debate and research. The current official system (see Table 25.1) is based on occupation (with 9 major categories, 25 sub-major, 90 minor groups, and 369 unit groups). This approach is important, but also problematic. For example, one particular difficulty is presented for those who are not in paid employment. If socio-economic class is determined primarily by occupation, then how should people who do not have paid employment be categorized? The idea of a distinct class of non-workers can be traced back to Marx, who

Table 25.1 UK Standard occupational classification, 2010.

Classification	Occupations
1	Managers, directors, and senior officials
2	Professional occupations
3	Associate professional and technical occupations
4	Administrative and secretarial occupations
5	Skilled trades occupations
6	Caring, leisure, and other service occupations
7	Sales and customer service occupations
8	Process, plant and machine operatives
9	Elementary occupations

Source: Based on data from the Office for National Statistics. Contains public sector information licensed under the Open Government Licence v1.0.

identified a group below labourers that he called the '*lumpenproletariat*'.

More recently, however, the analysis of this type of group has been heavily politicized in highly controversial debates about whether or not an 'underclass' exists. This issue is not, therefore, simply a mundane matter of statistical classification. The term 'underclass' was coined by an American academic, Charles Murray, who argued that a separate and dangerous group of poor people existed, whose behaviour presented a threat to the moral fabric of society. Murray's work has been discredited in a number of ways. The research methods that he used to reach his conclusion have been exposed as deeply flawed. Furthermore, his work has been interpreted as politically motivated and biased by right-wing values and beliefs about how other people behave. Most seriously, the idea of an 'underclass' has been seen as offensive, particularly in relation to its racist undertones.

Using the label 'underclass' has, therefore, been viewed generally by sociologists as an unacceptable way of conceptualizing issues of class difference and poverty. Instead, many academics prefer to consider people who have very low incomes as 'living in poverty' or 'experiencing social exclusion'. This has the advantage of moving the analysis away from only considering individual behaviour (or agency) to also incorporating wider structural causes, such as worldwide economic recession, for understanding phenomena such as unemployment. We must also remember that 'non-workers' cannot be used as a definition for a class that is associated with poverty since it would also include a range of people who do not have jobs but nonetheless have incomes or assets from other sources (e.g. rich land-owners).

Emerging Issues

Understanding how differences between social groups affect well-being is an essential part of understanding how societies operate and how social policies affect our everyday lives. There are major differences between individuals and groups of people in relation to their life chances and life experiences. The first category to be identified by theorists was class. From the 1970s onwards,

gender, 'race', and ethnicity were also identified as key divisions. More recently, growing attention has been paid to inequalities that relate to age, religion, nationality, sexuality, health, and disability. Researchers and campaigners have argued that diversity needs to be recognized as legitimate in the design of social policies. Challenges remain for policy-makers in balancing the recognition of diversity with the provision of fair policies that produce equitable outcomes. For students and analysts of social policies, social divisions are an important way in which major axes of inclusion and exclusion can be understood.

Guide to Further Sources

Start with Fiona Williams' classic book *Social Policy: A Critical Introduction* (Cambridge: Polity Press, 1989), which is still an essential read. Williams' approach is particularly interesting because she provides a critique of the inherent gender and racial assumptions embodied in welfare policies and also reflects on the limitations and biases of the academic study of social policy.

For a broader sociological understanding of social divisions and differences there are two indispensable introductory collections: Geoff Payne's *Social Divisions* (2nd edn, Basingstoke: Palgrave, 2006), and P. Braham and L. Janes' *Social Differences and Divisions* (Oxford: Blackwell/The Open University, 2002). Both provide thought-provoking accounts from a series of different perspectives.

There are a range of excellent books that explore class, gender, and ethnicity in greater detail. Ken Roberts' *Class in Modern Britain* (Basingstoke: Palgrave, 2001) provides a comprehensive overview of class, economic change and social mobility. Also, be sure not to overlook Rosemary Crompton's *Class and Stratification* (2nd edn, Cambridge: Polity Press, 2001). Key reading in the field of ethnicity is David Mason's edited book *Explaining Ethnic Differences* (Bristol: Policy Press, 2003). For a firm foundation in gender analysis try Nickie Charles' *Gender in Modern Britain* (Oxford: Oxford University Press, 2002)

Data on social divisions can be found on the National Statistics web page www.statistics.gov.uk.

Review Questions

1 What are social divisions?
2 In which ways can gender impact on job experiences (e.g. type of job, levels of pay) and likelihood of building up wealth (through income or assets, like a house)?
3 To what extent is lifetime wealth related to job experiences?
4 Do the interests of different classes connect or conflict?
5 How do processes of inclusion or exclusion (e.g. in education) operate to reinforce positions of advantage or disadvantage?

Visit the book companion site at www.wiley.com/go/alcock to make use of the resources designed to accompany the textbook. There you will find chapter-specific guides to further resources, including governmental, international, think-tank, pressure groups, and relevant journals sources. You will also find a glossary based on *The Blackwell Dictionary of Social Policy*, help sheets, and case studies, guidance on managing assignments in social policy and career advice.

26

Poverty and Social Exclusion

Pete Alcock

Overview

- Poverty has always been a major concern for social policy researchers and policy makers.
- Academics and policy-makers disagree about how to define and measure poverty.
- Definition and measurement has more recently been extended to include also the problem of social exclusion.
- Poverty and social exclusion are complex multidimensional problems; but both began to grow in the 1980s after relatively low levels since the Second World War.
- Academic and policy concern is increasingly focused on the global dimensions of poverty and exclusion.

Poverty and Social Policy

The problem of poverty has been a key concern of social policy throughout its development. Some of the earliest policy measures introduced in the United Kingdom were concerned with poverty, including in particular the Poor Laws, which can be traced back to the beginning of the seventeenth century and provided the core of social policy provision throughout the nineteenth and early twentieth centuries (see Chapter 16).

Poverty has also always been a major focus for academic analysis and research. Some of the earliest social policy research in the United Kingdom, and indeed in the world, sought to define and to measure the extent of poverty in the late nineteenth century in London (Charles Booth) and York (Seebohm Rowntree).

Poverty has been at the centre of social policy in part because it provides a bridge between academic debate and policy action. Starting with Booth and Rowntree, academics have been

The Student's Companion to Social Policy, Fourth Edition. Edited by Pete Alcock, Margaret May, Sharon Wright.
© 2012 John Wiley & Sons, Ltd. Published 2012 by John Wiley & Sons, Ltd.

concerned to define and measure poverty, not merely as an academic exercise, but also because of a belief that, if poverty did exist, then policy-makers would be obliged to do something about it. This is because poverty is a policy problem – an *unacceptable* state of affairs, which requires some form of policy response. Debate about, and evidence of, poverty therefore is not only an academic issue it 'drives' policy development.

There has also, however, been much debate, and disagreement, about exactly what poverty is and how we should seek to define and measure it; and this is linked to its role as a policy driver. The different ways in which we define and measure poverty, and the differing extent of the problem that we therefore reveal, will lead to different demands for policy action, and different forms of policy response. The definition and measurement of poverty is bound up with the policy response to it.

Defining Poverty

The question of how to define poverty is thus at the heart of policy debate and academic analysis; and it is a question to which there is no simple or agreed answer. Academics and policy-makers disagree about how to define poverty, in large part because they disagree about what to do about it too. This was captured most revealingly in a quotation from the Secretary of State for Social Security in the Thatcher government of the late 1980s, John Moore, who sought to dismiss academic research which had suggested a growing problem of poverty in the country.

> The evidence of improving living standards over this century is dramatic, and it is incontrovertible. When the pressure groups say that one-third of the population is living in poverty, they cannot be saying that one-third of people are living below the draconian subsistence levels used by Booth and Rowntree. (Moore, Speech to Greater London Area CPC, 11 May 1989)

In the 1980s the Conservative government did not believe that specific policies were needed to combat poverty beyond the well-established provision of social security benefits; and their argument that, by the standards of the nineteenth century few people were poor, meant that there was no need for further policy action.

Since then of course the views of the governments have changed, with the Labour governments under Blair in the 1990s, identifying child poverty in particular as a serious social problem and pledging to eradicate it by 2020 (see Walker 1999). This led Labour to initiate a review by the Department for Work and Pensions (DWP) of the definition and measurement of child poverty, which resulted in the adoption of a new definition of poverty for policy purposes, with other measures developed within the devolved administrations, who also took up the commitment to eradicate child poverty. The new definition included both absolute and relative dimensions; and it is the distinction between these different approaches to understanding poverty which underpins the policy differences between Moore and Blair.

Absolute poverty is the idea that being in poverty means being without the essentials of life, and it is sometimes referred to as subsistence poverty. It is often associated with the early research of Booth and Rowntree, who were concerned to identify a subsistence level based on the cost of necessities and then to measure the numbers of people with household incomes below this level, and hence unable to provide for themselves and their families. However, in practice what is essential for life varies according to where and when one is living; and indeed when Rowntree repeated his research later on in the twentieth century he extended his list of essential items (see Chapter 5). Despite Moore's assertion, most commentators do accept that the 'draconian' levels of the nineteenth century are not a valid basis for determining what it means to be poor over a hundred years later.

Relative poverty takes up this notion of changes in the determination of poverty levels over time, and place. It has been associated in particular with the work of Townsend, who in the 1950s and 1960s developed a new definition and measurement of poverty linking income to social security benefit levels, which showed that, despite general increases in affluence and improved social security protection, a significant proportion of the UK population did not have enough to achieve the living conditions 'customary' in society. According to this approach, as overall living standards rise so to does the notion of what it means to be poor, so that any definition of poverty will be relative to the average standard of living of all within society. This is sometimes taken to be some proportion of average income levels, which, as we shall see, has in practice become widely used as a poverty level in the United Kingdom and across many other developed countries.

Defining poverty by reference to average incomes is potentially a circular approach, however. It would suggest that however much incomes rise a fixed proportion would always be poor; and it was just this illogical relativism that Moore was seeking to attack in 1989. What it means to be poor may change over time; but there must be more to the definition of poverty than simply the proportion of average income received.

Income is only an indirect measure of poverty in any event, of course. It is what we are able to buy with our incomes that determine our actual standard of living. This was recognized by Townsend, who sought to identify indicators which could be used to determine whether someone was going without essential items of living. It has since been taken further by a group of researchers led by Gordon, who have used a major social survey to identify those items which a majority of the population think to be essential for modern life and then measured the numbers unable to afford most or all of these. This was the basis of a Poverty and Social Exclusion (PSE) survey carried out at then end of the last century (Pantazis, Gordon, and Levitas 2006), and it is now being updated in a major new survey in the 2010s.

This includes both absolute (the notion of essential items) and relative (those considered necessary by contemporaries) elements of the definition of poverty. This is the way in which most debate about the problem of poverty is now conducted (see Lister 2004: ch. 1); and has been recognized specifically by government in the new measure of child poverty mentioned above and in more general policy debate on poverty and deprivation.

Deprivation and Exclusion

In developing his relative poverty approach Townsend was aware that maintaining a customary standard of living involved more than just having a sufficiently high income. He recognized that people's health, housing conditions, and working conditions would also affect living standards, and yet these might be determined by factors beyond current income levels. Townsend discussed these other dimensions of deprivation in the report of his major research on poverty (*Poverty in the United Kingdom*, 1979), and argued that it was this notion of deprivation, rather than simply income poverty which better captured the problem of an inadequate standard of living in modern society.

In the mid-1980s the contributors to a Child Poverty Action Group (CPAG) publication (Golding 1986) took up this broader approach and drew attention to an increasingly wide range of other aspects of modern life, which could lead to deprivation for those excluded from them. These included information and communication technology, banking and financial services, and leisure activities, all of which are now readily recognisable as essential elements of modern life. The CPAG book was called *Excluding the Poor* and it highlighted the notion of exclusion from social activities as an important element of the problem of poverty. It is not just what we *have*, but what we *do* (or do *not* do) which can be a problem in society; and it is this notion of social exclusion which has begun to accompany poverty as a broader conceptualization of this key driver of social policy in twenty-first century Britain.

Social exclusion has become a more central feature of UK academic and policy debate in part because of the influence of European policy-making, where exclusion has for some time been a target of EU initiatives (see Room 1995). However, in 1997 a publicly funded research centre, the Centre for the Analysis of Social Exclusion (CASE) was established in the United Kingdom at the LSE. Here the researchers (Hills *et al.* 2002) developed the idea of exclusion as non-participation in key social activities such as

- *consumption* – purchasing of goods and services;
- *production* – participating in economically or socially valuable activity;
- *political engagement* – involvement in local or national decision making; and
- *social interaction* – with family, friends and communities.

These expanded the approach developed in the CPAG book back in the 1980s; and led the researchers to focus their attention on a range of different ways of measuring social exclusion using both quantitative and qualitative approaches, which revealed that the experience of exclusion varied over time and place, with different people experiencing different dimensions of the problem at different times.

The broader approach was also taken up by the Labour government after 1998 through the establishment of a special Social Exclusion Unit reporting direct to the Cabinet Office, though it was later downgraded to a Taskforce. The unit was never intended to combat all the different aspects of exclusion mentioned above, but to focus action on a small number of key policy priorities such as rough sleeping, school exclusion, and teenage pregnancy. The hope was that it would influence policy making across government departments; however, this had limited success, and in 2010 the coalition government formally abolished it.

Measuring Poverty and Social Exclusion

Researchers have tried to develop some means of measuring the broader concept of social exclusion, taking account of some of the different dimensions involved. The Labour government developed a list of fifty-nine indicators, including school attendance, infant mortality, and fear of crime, and tracked changes in these over time; but this has now been abandoned. The Joseph Rowntree Foundation has also supported research over ten years on a list of fifty similar indicators (Parekh, MacInnes, and Kenway 2010). However, the complex and changing information that these multiple measures provide does not make it easy to establish general levels of poverty and social exclusion or track changes in these. The problem might indeed be a complex one; but there is sometimes a need for simple summary measures.

This is to some extent recognized by both academics and policy makers; and in practice there are some simple (proxy) measures of poverty and social exclusion which are widely employed by researchers and politicians and do provide important evidence of the scale of the problem.

Most important here is the data on income levels produced annually in the *Households Below Average Income* (HBAI) report, available on the DWP web site. This uses a measure of poverty based on those households with an income below 60 per cent of median average income (that is the midpoint in the income distribution). This is a widely quoted measure, it is incorporated into the official definition of child poverty, and is also adopted in many other developed countries, in particular across the European Union.

On this measure 13.5 million people were poor in the United Kingdom in 2008/09, around 22 per cent of the population, and an increase of over one and a half million over four years. This includes 3.9 million children in poverty, over 0.6 million above the initial target of a 25 per cent reduction in child poverty in five years, on the way to the 2020 target of removing it altogether. Indeed progress on reducing child poverty is now in reverse. The HBAI figures also include information about the differing risk of poverty for different social groups including those with disabilities and ethnic minorities, and for different geographical regions; and summaries of these and other recent statistics can followed on the 'poverty' web site listed at the end of this chapter.

The proportion of average incomes measure can also be used to track the changing extent of poverty and social exclusion over time. This is also provided on the poverty web site, from which Figure 26.1 is taken.

The figure also shows the proportions below 40 per cent and 50 per cent of the median and it has been adjusted to account for housing costs, as these can vary significantly across the country. As can be seen levels of income inequality rose sharply in the mid-1980s, and dropped slightly in the early twenty-first century, before starting to rise again a little over the last few years.

Of course the explanations for these changes are complex, and Hills explores some of them in his work on inequality. Nevertheless, the figures reveal that the proportions of people in poverty on this low income measure have remained high since the 1980s, with only some improvement in the early years of the new century under Labour. What is more, they suggest that the target of eradicating child poverty by 2020 will be a demanding one, and will require policy changes that go some way beyond the recent initiatives in

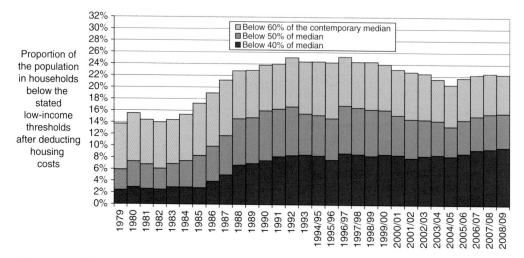

Proportion of the population in households below the stated low-income thresholds after deducting housing costs

Figure 26.1   The proportion of people in low-income households, 1979–2008/9.
Source: Households Below Average Income, DWP (1994/95 onwards) and the IFS (earlier years); UK; updated August 2010, www.poverty.org.uk/01/index.shtml?2.

tax credits and benefit increases begun under the previous government and now being cut back by the coalition as part of their deficit reduction strategies.

Emerging Issues

Despite the limitations in practice of the achievements of the previous Labour governments in eradicating child poverty and tackling the wider problems of social exclusion, there was a strong policy commitment to the embracement of anti-poverty policy and the promotion of social exclusion as core public policy goals, represented in the creation of the Social Exclusion Unit. In opposition the Conservatives were critical of Labour's record, however, and argued that despite increased government expenditure, the government had not succeeded in mending what they called 'Broken Britain'.

The new coalition government has therefore abandoned many of Labour's initiatives, such as the exclusion taskforce, and have sought to shift the focus of policy development. The coalition's primary policy commitment, of course, is the removal of the public sector deficit inherited from Labour. This means widespread cuts in public expenditure, but in particular cuts in

spending on welfare benefits, where Child Benefit is to be frozen and Tax Credits cut back. These changes are likely to increase the proportions of families on low income. The government have not formally abandoned Labour's 2020 child poverty target, however; although they do argue that the problem of child poverty, and indeed social exclusion more generally, is not primarily a function of low income, but is rather the result of wider failures in individual and family responses to social problems. The focus of policy has therefore shifted to greater emphasis on promoting employment and improving work incentives, through a simplification of benefit entitlement and stricter requirements for job search and take-up (see Chapters 45 and 46).

Whether this does lead to reductions in poverty and social exclusion remains to be seen, but at the moment, as the evidence above suggests, these have remained high in the United Kingdom in the 2000s. They also compare unfavourably with some other EU nations such as France and the Netherlands, and in 2009 the United Kingdom was just above the EU average for the proportion of low income households. Other countries have higher levels, for instance Italy and Greece, as do other countries beyond Europe, such as Japan or the United States; and to a significant extent poverty and social exclusion are major problems in all countries across the world. This is much more serious when developing countries are taken into account, however, in particular those in Africa and the Indian Subcontinent. Here poverty and exclusion are much more pressing, with millions in Africa facing starvation and early death.

Poverty and social exclusion are therefore international – or rather global – problems. This was brought starkly into relief by the *Make Poverty History* campaign in 2005, which sought to put pressure on the developed nations to make commitments to relieve poverty in Africa and elsewhere. This did lead to some promises to increase international aid for developing countries and to 'write-off' debts and trade deficits where these were preventing future economic development, though in practice not much changed following this. Earlier than this the 117 nations attending a United Nations (UN) summit on social development in Copenhagen in 1995, had committed the UN to a goal of eradicating global poverty through international action; and international agencies such as the UN Development Programme, the World Health Organization, and the World Bank have been instrumental in implementing a range of international programmes to combat poverty and promote economic development across the world.

There is an increasing recognition among leading politicians and policy-makers that poverty and social exclusion are global, and not just national, problems; and that concerted international action will be needed to address these – although the extent of the commitment and resources required, and the time taken to achieve significant results may not be fully appreciated by many. The scale of this international challenge has also now been explored by academic researchers, notably by Townsend himself, who went on to write about the need to combat 'World Poverty' (Townsend and Gordon 2002). The future policy climate for poverty and social exclusion is therefore likely increasingly to become an international one, within which national government can only play a limited role.

Guide to Further Sources

The most comprehensive general book on research and policy on poverty and social exclusion is P. Alcock, *Understanding Poverty* (3rd edn,

Basingstoke: Palgrave, 2006). R. Lister, *Poverty* (Cambridge: Polity Press, 2004) provides a convincing explanation of why poverty is a problem and how we should respond to it, as does P. Spicker, *The Idea of Poverty* (Bristol: Policy Press, 2007). Different dimensions of poverty and exclusion are discussed by the contributors to T. Ridge and S. Wright (eds), *Understanding Inequality, Poverty and Wealth: Policies and Prospects* (Bristol: Policy Press, 2008).

An overview of trends in levels of poverty and inequality is provided by J. Hills *et al.*, *An Anatomy of Economic Inequality in the UK*, CASE report 60 (London: LSE, 2010); and a review of the record of the Labour governments is provided by J. Hills, T. Sefton and K. Stewart (eds), *Towards a More Equal Society?: Poverty, Inequality and Policy since 1997* (Bristol: Policy Press, 2009). A. Parekh, T. MacInnes, and P. Kenway, *Monitoring Poverty and Social Exclusion 2010* (York: Joseph Rowntree Foundation, 2010) reports on the latest data on their list of indicators.

Early discussion of the dimensions of social exclusion can be found in P. Golding (ed.), *Excluding the Poor* (London: CPAG, 1986); G. Room (ed.), *Beyond the Threshold* (Bristol: Policy Press, 1995) contains papers from European commentators on social exclusion; and a summary of the CASE research can be found in J. Hills, J. Le Grand, and D. Piachaud (eds), *Understanding Social Exclusion* (Oxford: Oxford University Press, 2002). The extensive findings of the 2000 PSE survey are now available in C. Pantazis, D. Gordon, and R. Levitas (eds), *Poverty and Social Exclusion in Britain* (Bristol: Policy Press, 2006). P. Townsend and D. Gordon (eds), *World Poverty* (Bristol: Policy Press, 2002) contains contributions on the developing global context of poverty policy.

Government web sites are important sources of official policy and research reports, in particular that of the Department for Work and Pensions, www.dwp.gov.uk. An independent web site with up-to-date statistics on poverty and social exclusion, from which Figure 26.1 was taken, is maintained by Guy Palmer www.poverty.org.uk. The Joseph Rowntree Foundation web site, www.jrf.org.uk, contains copies of their many research reports in the area. The CPAG site, www.cpag.org.uk, includes information on campaigning activity, policy briefings, and summaries of recent statistics.

The Labour government's child poverty pledges are discussed in R. Walker (ed.), *Ending Child Poverty: Popular Welfare for the 21st Century* (Bristol: Policy Press, 1999).

Review Questions

1 Why has research on poverty been so important to the development of academic social policy?
2 What is the difference between *absolute* and *relative* poverty?
3 How did the Poverty and Social Exclusion survey seek to define and measure social exclusion?
4 How, and why, have levels of income poverty in the United Kingdom changed over the past thirty years?
5 How effective were the policies of the New Labour government 1997–2010 in eradicating child poverty?

Visit the book companion site at www.wiley.com/go/alcock to make use of the resources designed to accompany the textbook. There you will find chapter-specific guides to further resources, including governmental, international, think-tank, pressure groups, and relevant journals sources. You will also find a glossary based on *The Blackwell Dictionary of Social Policy*, help sheets, and case studies, guidance on managing assignments in social policy and career advice.

27

The Distribution of Welfare

John Hills

Overview

- The distribution of resources is central to the provision of welfare through social policy, although distribution and redistribution takes place through both state, and private and voluntary transfers.
- There is a range of different rationales underpinning the redistribution of resources to promote welfare.
- There are different ways of measuring distribution and its benefits for different groups. How it is paid for – and who pays – is very important in this.
- Much of the redistributive effect of welfare is as a sort of 'savings bank' transferring resources between different stages of people's own lives.
- However redistribution also plays a significant 'Robin Hood' role benefiting poorer sections of society most, particularly once one allows for how it is paid for.

Distribution and Redistribution

Distribution is a central issue in the appraisal of social policies; for some, it is *the* central issue. Much of the justification advanced for social policy is in terms of distribution: 'without a National Health Service providing free medical care, the poor could not afford treatment'; or 'the primary aim of social security is preventing poverty'.

Most of this chapter is about the distributional effects of government spending on welfare services. However, redistribution – and its measurement – are not only issues for government. For instance, in the 1990s the Child Support Agency attempted (not very successfully) to enforce payments by absent parents (generally fathers) to parents 'with care' (usually mothers). Similarly, under the 2008 Pensions Act, after 2012 employers will have to make a minimum contribution

The Student's Companion to Social Policy, Fourth Edition. Edited by Pete Alcock, Margaret May, Sharon Wright.
© 2012 John Wiley & Sons, Ltd. Published 2012 by John Wiley & Sons, Ltd.

towards their employees' pensions if the employee does not opt out of the pension scheme. Such payments made under state regulation could be important distributionally but are outside the 'welfare state'.

Whether redistribution is occurring can depend on when you look at it. Under private insurance for, say, burglaries, a large number of people make annual payments (insurance premiums) to an insurance company, but only a small number receive payouts from the company. After the event (*ex post*) there is redistribution from the (fortunate) many to the (unfortunate) few. But, looking at the position in advance (*ex ante*), not knowing who is going to be burgled, all pay in a premium equalling their risk of being burgled, multiplied by the size of the payout if this happens (plus the insurance company's costs and profits). In 'actuarial' terms there is no redistribution – people have arranged a certain small loss (the premium) rather than the risk of a much larger loss (being burgled without insurance).

Similarly, if you look at pension schemes over a single year, some people pay in contributions, while others receive pensions. On this 'snapshot', there is apparently redistribution from the former to the latter. But with a longer time horizon, today's pensioners may simply get back what they paid in earlier. Redistribution is across an individual's life cycle, rather than between different people.

Assessing redistribution depends on the aims against which you want to measure services, and the picture obtained depends on decisions like the time period used. The next section discusses the first of these issues, the aims of welfare services. The subsequent sections discuss the conceptual issues raised in trying to measure distributional effects, illustrate some of the empirical findings on different bases, and discuss their implications.

Aims of Welfare Services

As previous chapters have shown, there is little consensus on the aims of social policy or of government intervention to provide or finance welfare services. For some, the primary aim of welfare services is redistribution from rich to poor. Whether the welfare state is successful

therefore depends on which income groups benefit: do the rich use the NHS more than the poor, and are social security benefits 'targeted' on those with the lowest incomes?

For others, this is only a part of the welfare state's rationale. Depending on political perspective, other aims will be more important. Some of the main aims advanced and their implications for assessing distributional effects are as follows:

1 *Vertical redistribution* – if the aim is redistribution from rich to poor, the crucial question is which income groups benefit. Since welfare services do not come from thin air, the important question may be which are the *net gainers* and *net losers*, after taking account of who pays the taxes that finance welfare provision. Allowing for both benefits and taxes in understanding distribution has become even more important since the government started using 'tax credits' (which can count as reduced tax liabilities) instead of some cash benefits in the late 1990s.

2 *Horizontal redistribution on the basis of needs* – for many, relative incomes are not the only reason for receiving services. The NHS is there for people with particular medical needs: it should achieve 'horizontal redistribution' between people with similar incomes, but different medical needs.

3 *Redistribution between different groups* – an aim might be redistribution between social groups defined other than by income; for instance, favouring particular groups to offset disadvantages elsewhere in the economy. Or the system might be intended to be non-discriminatory between groups. Either way, we may need to analyse distribution by dimensions such as social class, gender, ethnicity, age or age cohort (generation), or kind of area (rich or poor neighbourhood) rather than just income.

4 *Insurance* – much of what the welfare state does is insurance against adversity. People 'pay in' through tax or national insurance contributions, but in return, if they are the ones who become ill or unemployed, the system is there to protect them. It does not make sense just to look at which individual happens to receive an expensive heart bypass operation this year and present him or her as

the main 'gainer' from the system. All benefit to the extent that they face a risk of needing such an operation. The system is best appraised in actuarial terms; that is, in terms of the extent someone would expect to benefit on average.

5   *Efficiency justifications* – an extensive literature discusses how universal, compulsory, and possibly state-provided systems can be cheaper or more efficient than the market left to itself for some activities, particularly core welfare services like health care, unemployment insurance, and education. Where this is the motivation for state provision one might not expect to see any redistribution between income or other groups. Services might be appraised according to the 'benefit principle' – how much do people receive in relation to what they pay? – and the absence of net redistribution would not be a sign of failure.

6   *Life cycle smoothing* – most welfare services are unevenly spread over the life cycle. Education goes disproportionately to the young; health care and pensions to the old; while the taxes that finance them come mostly from the working generation. A snapshot picture of redistribution may be misleading – it would be better to compare how much people get out of the system over their whole lives, and how much they pay in.

7   *Compensating for 'family failure'* – many parents do, of course, meet their children's needs, and many higher earning husbands share their cash incomes equally with their lower earning wives. But in other families this is not so – family members may not share equally in its income. Where policies are aimed at countering this kind of problem it may not be enough to evaluate simply in terms of distribution *between* families, we may also need to look at distribution between individuals; that is, *within* families as well.

8   *External benefits* – finally, some services may be justified by 'external' or 'spill-over' benefits beyond those to the direct beneficiary. Promoting the education of even the relatively affluent may be in society's interests, if this produces a more dynamic economy for all. Appraisal of who gains ought to take account of such benefits (although in practice this is hard).

The relative importance given to each aim thus affects not only the interpretation placed on particular findings, but also the appropriate kind of analysis.

Conceptual Issues

As will already be clear, there is no single measure of how welfare services are distributed. It depends on precisely what is measured, and apparently technical choices can make a great difference to the findings.

The counterfactual

To answer the question, 'how are welfare services distributed?' you have to add, 'compared to what?'. What is the 'counterfactual' situation with which you are comparing reality? A particular group may receive state medical services worth £2,000 per year. In one sense, this is the amount they benefit by. But if the medical services did not exist, what else would be different? Government spending might be lower, and hence tax bills, including their own. The net benefit, allowing for taxes, might be much less than £2,000 per year.

Knock-on effects may go further. In an economy with lower taxes, many other things might be different. Without the NHS, people would have to make other arrangements: private medical insurance, for instance. The money paid for that would not be available for other spending, with further knock-on effects through the economy. Britain without the NHS would differ in all sorts of ways from Britain with it, and strictly it is this hypothetical alternative country we ought to compare with to measure the impact of having the NHS. In practice, this is very difficult – which limits the conclusiveness of most empirical studies.

Incidence

Closely related is the question of 'incidence': who *really* benefits from a service? Do children benefit from free education, or their parents who would otherwise have paid school fees? Are tenants of subsidized housing the true beneficiaries of the subsidies, or can employers attract labour to the area at lower wages than they would otherwise have to pay? In each case different assumptions about who really gains may be plausible and affect the findings.

Valuation

To look at the combined effects of different services, their values have to be added up in some way, most conveniently by putting a monetary value on them. However, to do this requires a price for the services received. This is fine for cash benefits, but not for benefits which come as services 'in kind', such as the NHS or education. To know how much someone benefits from a service, you want to know how much it is worth *to them* - but you cannot usually observe this. Most studies use the *cost* to the state of providing the service. But 'value' and 'cost' are not necessarily the same. It may *cost* a great deal to provide people with a particular service, but if offered the choice they might prefer a smaller cash sum to spend how they like: the cost is higher than its value to the recipients. Conversely, collective provision may be much cheaper than private alternatives, so the value of the NHS, for instance, may be greater in terms of what people would otherwise have to pay, than its cost to the taxpayer.

Distribution between which groups?

Comparing groups arranged according to some income measure is of obvious interest, but so may be looking at distribution between social classes, age groups, men, and women, or ethnic groups. A related issue is the 'unit of analysis': households, families or individuals? A larger unit makes some things easier: we do not have to worry about how income is shared within the family or household. But it may mask what we are interested in: for instance, distribution between men and women. It may also affect how we classify different beneficiaries. The official Office for National Statistics (ONS) results described below examine the distribution of welfare benefits between *households*. In this analysis a family with four children 'scores' the same as a single pensioner living alone – the situation of six people is given the same weight as that of one person. Weighting each person equally could change the picture.

Distribution of what?

Depending on the question, different measures will therefore be appropriate. We might be interested for instance in gross public spending, or in net public spending after allowing for taxes financing services, or in gross public spending in relation to need.

These can give apparently conflicting answers. NHS spending may be concentrated on the poor, but this may reflect their poor health. Allowing for differences in sickness rates, the distribution of NHS care in relation to need may not favour the poor after all.

Similarly, the gross benefits from a service may appear 'pro-rich'; that is, its absolute value to high income households exceeds that to low income households, say by 50 per cent. But if the tax which pays for the service is twice as much for rich households, the *combination* of the service and the tax may still be *redistributive*, in that the poorer households are net gainers and the richer ones net losers.

Time period

In a single week fewer people will receive a service than over a year. As services vary across the life cycle, a single year snapshot will differ from the picture across a whole lifetime. But available data relate to short time periods: there are no surveys tracking use of welfare services throughout people's whole lives. To answer questions about lifetime distribution requires hypothetical models – the results from which depend greatly on the assumptions fed into them.

Data problems

Finally, research in this area is based on sample surveys: whole population surveys like the Census do not ask the questions about incomes and service use required. Even the sample surveys may not be very specific, asking, for instance, whether someone has visited a GP recently, but not how long the consultation lasted, whether any expensive tests were done and so on. Results assume that GP visits are worth the same to all patients. But this may gloss over the point at issue: if GPs spend longer on appointments with middle-class patients – and are more likely to send them for further treatment – the distribution of medical services may be 'pro-rich', even if the number of GP consultations is constant between income groups.

Some Empirical Results

This section illustrates some of these issues by considering findings from empirical analysis, contrasting the gross distribution of welfare services with that of the taxes required to pay for them.

Figure 27.1 shows official ONS (Barnard, 2010) estimates of the average benefits in cash and kind from welfare services received by households in different income groups in the financial year 2008/9. Households are arranged in order of 'equivalent disposable income' (that is, income including cash benefits but after direct taxes like income tax, and allowing for the greater needs of bigger households). The poorest 'decile group' is on the left, the richest on the right.

On average, households with the bottom half of incomes received 2.1 times as much from cash benefits (including tax credits) as those with the top half. Means-tested benefits such as Income Support and Housing Benefit and tax credits are most concentrated on the poorest, but even 'universal' benefits such as the retirement pension are worth more to lower than to higher income households.

The figure also shows official estimates of the combined value of benefits in kind from the NHS, state education, and housing subsidies. Sefton (2002) suggests that such figures can be qualified on various grounds, such as the omission of the benefits of higher education for students living away from home (which tends to understate benefits to high-income households), or the way in which housing subsidies are calculated (which tends to understate benefits to low-income households). Also, the assumption that people of the same age and gender use the health service equally is not necessarily correct: other characteristics affect service use too. However, even with adjustments for such issues, the general picture is similar: benefits in kind are less concentrated on the poor than cash benefits, but households at the bottom of the distribution receive considerably more than those at the top. On the ONS's estimates, these benefits in kind were worth an average of £6,400 for the poorest tenth of households in 2008/9 but only £3,300 for the richest tenth. On these estimates, the absolute value of welfare benefits and services is greatest for low-income households, and much lower than average for high-income families. Taxation,

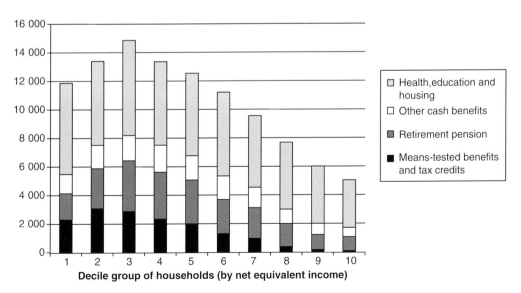

Figure 27.1   Welfare benefits and services by income group, 2008/9 (£).
Source: Based on Barnard (2010).

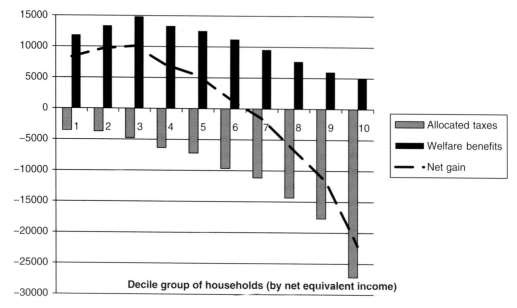

Figure 27.2   Benefits and allocated taxes by income group, 2008/9 (£).
Source: Based on figures from Barnard (2010).

by contrast, is greater in absolute terms for those with higher incomes (although it is not necessarily a greater proportion of income).

Most welfare spending is financed from general taxation, so it is hard to be precise about *which* taxes are paying for welfare: if state education were abolished, would it be income tax or VAT which would fall? Figure 27.2 compares the total of welfare benefits given in the previous figure with the ONS's estimates of the impact of national insurance contributions and an equal proportion (about 85 per cent) of each other household tax to cover the remainder of welfare spending. For the bottom six-tenths of the distribution, benefits are higher than taxes and the figures suggest a net gain; for those in the top four groups – particularly the top two-tenths – taxes are higher, suggesting a net loss.

These results suggest that on a cross-sectional basis, the combination of welfare services and, on plausible assumptions, their financing is significantly redistributive from high- to low-income groups (although they say nothing about the scale of such gains in relation to 'need', such as for medical care).

However, it should also be remembered that redistribution also takes effect over the lifetime of individual citizens. Over their lives people both receive benefits and pay taxes. Those with higher lifetime incomes pay much more tax than those with low incomes. In effect, people finance some of the benefits they receive through their *own* lifetime tax payments. However, some people do not pay enough lifetime tax to pay for all of their benefits; they receive 'net lifetime benefits' from the system. These net lifetime benefits are paid for by others who pay more than enough tax to finance their own benefits; they pay 'net lifetime taxes' into the system. Evidence on this lifetime redistribution suggests that on a lifetime basis the system does still redistribute from the 'lifetime rich' to the 'lifetime poor', but as it was in the 1980s and 1990s, nearly three-quarters of what the welfare state does is like a 'savings bank', and only a quarter is 'Robin Hood' redistribution between different people (see Hills, 2005: ch. 8 and Barr, 2000).

Emerging Issues

How welfare services are distributed has a major bearing on whether we judge them successful. The results presented above suggest that lower income households receive more from the welfare state than they pay at any one time. As a corollary, as policies try to reduce the government budget deficit that emerged after the economic crisis that stared in 2008, doing this through cutting welfare services and benefits hits those in the bottom half of the distribution harder than those at the top; doing it through tax increases takes more from those with higher incomes in absolute terms (but much the same from all groups as a share of their income). The plans of the coalition government elected in 2010 put most emphasis on spending cuts, with initial analysis suggesting that losses through reduced benefits and services will represent a much greater share of income for those with lower than those with higher incomes (Browne and Levell, 2010; Horton and Reed, 2010).

Distribution between rich and poor is not the only issue though. As the population ages, and the retired population grows in size relative to the working age population, questions are being asked about whether the age groups are being treated fairly – and whether older 'baby boom' generations have done better out of the system than younger ones will do.

Guide to Further Sources

Each year the Office for National Statistics (ONS) publishes official estimates of the distributional effect of taxation and of a large part of public spending, including social security and welfare services on their web site, www.statistics.gov.uk. The figures in this chapter come from A. Barnard, 'The effects of taxes and benefits on household income, 2008/09', *Economic and Labour Market Review*, 4/7 (2010): 36–47.

T. Sefton, *Recent Changes in the Distribution of the Social Wage*, CASEpaper 62 (London: London School of Economics, 2002), http://sticerd.lse.ac.uk/case/publications/papers.asp, looks in detail at the changing distribution of government spending on health, education, housing subsidies, and personal social services. Chapter 2 of J. Hills, T. Sefton, and K. Stewart (eds), *Towards a More Equal Society? Poverty, Inequality and Policy Since 1997* (Bristol: Policy Press, 2009) looks at the distributional effect of changes in tax and benefit policies and of the value of benefits in kind between 1996 and 2008.

T. Horton and H. Reed, *Where the Money Goes: How we Benefit from Public Services* (Online: TUC, 2010) www.tuc.org.uk/extras/wherethe moneygoes.pdf looks at a wider range of public services, including those beyond the welfare state, and looks at who will lose from their reduction. J. Browne and P. Levell, *The Distributional Effects of Tax/Benefit Reforms to be Introduced between June 2010 and April 2014: A Revised Assessment*, www.ifs.org.uk/publications/5246, looks at the combined effects of both tax rises and benefit changes being introduced as part of the deficit reduction plans.

J. Hills, *Inequality and the State* (Oxford: Oxford University Press, 2005), discusses trends in inequality in Britain in recent decades, including impacts of tax and benefit policy within a single year and across the life cycle, as well as public attitudes towards these effects. These are examined in more detail in T. Sefton, 'Give and Take: Attitudes to Redistribution', in A. Park, J. Curtice, and K. Thomson (eds), *British Social Attitudes: The 22nd Report* (London: Sage, 2005), pp. 1–32, using data from the 2004 British Social Attitudes survey.

For further analysis of life cycle issues, N. Barr, *The Welfare State as a Piggy Bank* (Oxford: Oxford University Press, 2000) examines, from an economics perspective, the way in which the welfare state distributes income across the life cycle.

The report of the National Equality Panel, *An Anatomy of Economic Inequality in the UK* (London: Government Equalities Office and London School of Economics, 2010) presents a large amount of information on differences in outcomes such as earnings, incomes, and wealth both *between* different groups (such as by gender or age) and *within* those groups: http://sticerd.lse.ac.uk/dps/case/cr/CASEreport60.pdf.

Review Questions

1   Is its success in redistributing towards the poor the only, or even, the main criterion we should use in evaluating the impact of the welfare state?

2   Does it matter that some of those with middle or high incomes receive cash benefits and use services like the NHS and state education, so

long as they pay in more for them through the tax system?

3   What does the distribution of who receives welfare benefits and services and who pays the taxes that pay for them tell us about how different ways of closing the public budget deficit would affect different groups?

4   Why does it matter what time period is used to measure who 'gains' and who 'loses' from welfare spending and taxation?

5   If much of what the welfare state does is to act as a 'piggy bank', with people paying in at one point and benefiting later in their lives, is this a safe arrangement, if, for instance, younger generations decided they no longer wanted to continue with as generous a system?

Visit the book companion site at www.wiley.com/go/alcock to make use of the resources designed to accompany the textbook. There you will find chapter-specific guides to further resources, including governmental, international, think-tank, pressure groups, and relevant journals sources. You will also find a glossary based on *The Blackwell Dictionary of Social Policy*, help sheets, and case studies, guidance on managing assignments in social policy and career advice.

28

The Policy Process

Hugh Bochel

Overview

- Studying the policy process can add to our understanding of the ways in which policies are made, implemented, and evaluated and the reasons that particular policies are or are not adopted, including how power is exercised to bring social issues and problems to the agendas of decision-makers.
- There is a wide range of models and concepts that can be used to analyse the policy process. Applying particular models to specific policies and policy areas can allow us to gain a better understanding of the role of different groups, their power relative to one another, and the motivations behind particular government actions and inactions.
- In recent years there has been a greater awareness of the complexity of the social world, meaning that new ways of analysing and understanding the policy process have emerged.
- In addition, the approaches taken by different governments to the making and implementation of policies can impact upon the type of policies that emerge, so that, for example, a preference for market-based approaches is likely to have particular consequences for the shape of policies.

Context

The term 'policy process' is used to describe the ways in which policies are made (or indeed not made), implemented, and evaluated. This is essentially a process which is 'political' in the broadest sense of the term, in that it can involve a wide range of actors and processes, and, importantly for social policy, is ultimately concerned with the ways in which power is distributed and

The Student's Companion to Social Policy, Fourth Edition. Edited by Pete Alcock, Margaret May, Sharon Wright.
© 2012 John Wiley & Sons, Ltd. Published 2012 by John Wiley & Sons, Ltd.

exercised. This is often linked to debates about the state, democracy, and the distribution of resources, with, for example, views differing about whether there is a pluralistic distribution of power with widespread opportunities for participation by the public and organized interests, or whether policy-making is slanted towards or dominated by certain interests or groups. Similarly, we can (and perhaps should) consider not only the decisions and actions of governments, but also which alternatives are excluded, and what the reasons for this might be. These are clearly of crucial importance in enabling us to understand how and why social policies are developed.

The examination of the policy process is often described as 'policy analysis', but there are many different types of policy analysis. These can be broadly, although somewhat artificially, divided into analyses *of* policy and analyses *for* policy, with the former seeking to understand policy and the latter to understand and improve the quality of policy. Where analyses of policy are concerned, much academic work is concerned with the study of policy content, seeking to describe and explain how and why particular policies have developed, consider how they were implemented, and to assess their impact. Similarly, considerable attention is often paid to policy output, with attempts to explain the different distributions of resources. On the other hand, process advocacy seeks to improve the systems of policy-making and implementation, while policy advocacy involves the use of analysis in order to provide support for a particular idea or choice in the policy process, and these would tend to fall within the category of analysis for policy.

There is a range of models that can be applied to specific policies and policy areas to gain a better understanding of the role and power of different groups in the policy process, and the motivations behind particular actions and inactions. However, it is important to recognize that while some models may seek to be prescriptive, policy-makers themselves rarely set out to use a particular model in developing policies, so that models are generally best seen as tools for analysis.

Perspectives on the Policy Process

While we use the term 'policy' frequently in our everyday language, we use it in many different ways to describe different things. For example, we may use it to describe the decisions of government, formal authorizations such as through legislation, fields of activity (education policy, pensions policy), specific programmes, and the outputs and outcomes of government actions. At the same time, policies, and the policy process, are continually interacting with and are affected by other factors, cultural, economic, social, and political, as well as other policies. We therefore need to be aware of the environment in which policies are made and implemented.

The policy process is often described and discussed in relation to a series of stages, frequently formulation, implementation, and evaluation. However, this stagist approach, with its depiction of a static, segmented process, is rather misleading. An alternative view would be one which sees the policy process as dynamic and continuous, with overlap between the stages, a constantly changing environment, and feedback which in turn affects policy development (for example, when evaluations highlight weaknesses which need to be addressed and which they impact on the refinement of existing policies or the development of new ones). While traditional views of decision-making reflected the stagist approach, seeing politicians as making decisions which were then implemented by others, the dynamic, continuous model fits more closely with perspectives which highlight the continued influence of decision-makers in the implementation of policy and the input of those who deliver policies on their formulation.

However, despite its weaknesses, breaking down the policy process into stages can help us to understand it. The initial 'stage' is usually that of 'formulation' where a policy idea is developed. For an idea to have a chance of becoming a policy it has to get on to the agenda of policy-makers. This might happen through the development of ideas by bodies such as political parties, think-tanks or the media, as responses to perceived problems, such as poverty or crime, or to particular challenges or demands, such as the pressures of an ageing population on health care or pension provision. It is at this stage that pressure groups and the media are often seen as being able to exercise influence, by bringing issues and ideas to the attention of policy-makers. However, while some have argued that in pluralistic societies there should be opportunities for a wide range of groups and interests to have input into policy-making, in practice agenda setting is often skewed towards those with the greatest power, so that some ideas may never reach the agenda. The exclusion of some issues from discussion is sometimes referred to as a 'policy silence' or a 'non-decision', and illustrates that the ability to set the agenda is a fundamental way in which power is exercised.

Once an idea is on the agenda of decision-makers it is then subject to discussion and development. Writing in the 1940s and 1950s Herbert Simon suggested a 'rational' model, intended to improve decision-making. He argued that, ideally, all possible policy options would be considered before the most suitable option to achieve the aims of the policy would be selected. Such an approach, is, however, generally unrealistic, as policy-makers are generally operating in the context of policies that have existed before, as well as within financial and administrative boundaries, while the time and resources required to explore all options would themselves be likely to be prohibitive. Policy-makers may therefore more usefully be seen as adopting a more limited approach, sometimes referred to as 'bounded rationality', taking account of factors such as existing policies and limitations on resources, and choosing from a more restricted range of options. Nevertheless, in some circumstances we can see policy-makers adopt approaches that reflect Simon's arguments, for example as happens with the use of experts for enquiries and reviews.

However, it can be argued that much government policy builds upon what has existed previously, and as such often develops only in small steps. The idea of incrementalism is closely associated with the work of Charles Lindblom, who suggested that policy-making is a process whereby policy-makers cope with problems as they arise, and that they tend to stick with the manageable and familiar, with new policies often differing only marginally from old policies. He argued that incrementalism ('muddling through') is therefore a more realistic model of policy-making than is rationalism. Perhaps importantly for social policy, critics have argued that such an approach may be essentially conservative, and that by focusing on short term change it risks ignoring fundamental issues or major policy challenges, which could mean, for example, that disadvantaged groups could continue to lose out in favour

of only small moves from the status quo. However, it can also be argued that while incrementalism may appear to work against radical policy change, a series of small steps can, over time, result in major change to policy.

The challenge of responding to new issues and demands, and the apparently increasing complexity and uncertainty of the contemporary world are perhaps some of the reasons that policy-makers seek to learn lessons from other states (sometimes referred to as 'policy transfer'). Looking to other countries to see if they have any policies that can be transferred is popular with governments as it can provide a short-cut in the creation of policies. It has been argued, for example, that the 1997 Labour government drew upon the experiences of Australia and the United States in developing its welfare reform policies. However, there are dangers in inappropriate transfer and a failure to take into account the differences between states, with the Child Support Agency, introduced by the Conservatives in 1993 and drawing upon the experiences of the United States, often being seen as an example of policy failure.

Implementation is often seen as following formulation in the policy process, although, as noted earlier, such divisions are arguably artificial. Actors from different tiers of government, and from different sectors, public, private, and not-for-profit, may be involved in policy implementation. The extent to which a policy is successfully implemented will depend upon and be affected by many factors, including the clarity of the policy itself, the number and type of organizations involved and the availability of appropriate resources. For example, if one body is responsible for implementation then, at least in theory, it should be more straightforward than if successful implementation depends upon a number of autonomous agencies, which may have different aims, values, and resources, and which may even be in competition with each other. In such instances, with high degrees of complexity, the potential for a policy to be only partially implemented increases. 'Implementation deficit' is often associated with top-down approaches to policy-making. These see policy as made by those at the top of a hierarchical structure, with those at 'street level', such as doctors, housing officials, the police or teachers, having no say in policy formulation and simply implementing policies without question. However, this is an artificial divide not only between stages, but also different actors within the policy process. Those who deliver services on the ground, sometimes called 'street level bureaucrats', also have an interest in ensuring that appropriate and workable policies are introduced, as well as frequently being able to exercise a degree of discretion and thus impact upon the ways in which policies are implemented. Top down approaches to policy-making may therefore fail to recognize that policies are likely to be dependent upon a variety of agencies and individuals for successful implementation, and that policy-making is often more of a two-way process, with flows up and down, rather than the one way system that the top-down model implies. Some argue that a more realistic and successful approach would be to take into account those who policy will affect and those who will be responsible for implementing it. From this perspective good policy-making would start at the bottom and work upwards. In recent times a variety of other approaches, such as those focusing on policy networks have also helped to highlight the complexity of policy-making and implementation and the interdependence of many actors in the policy process. Finally, it is worth noting, that not all policies are actually implemented, with governments sometimes making policy statements, or even passing pieces of legislation, that are not put into practice.

Evaluation (see Chapter 29) is often seen as the final stage of the policy process, when the success or otherwise of a policy is assessed. Together with monitoring during the implementation of a policy or programme, evaluation is generally seen as an integral part of the policy process which may lead to changes to existing policies or to the development of new policies. This view clearly relates to the idea of a dynamic, continuous policy process.

Approaching the policy process from a different perspective, recent years have seen greater attention paid to different levels of analysis, such as the macro, meso, and micro used by Hudson and Lowe (2009). Analysis at the macro level is concerned with the broad themes and issues that shape the overall contexts within which policies are made and implemented, with 'globalization' being a widely used example. However, there is

not necessarily any consensus on if and how these shape policies and outcomes. The meso level comes between the micro and the macro and considers how policies are made, how problems put on (or kept off) the policy agenda, and the institutional arrangements within which policies are defined and implemented. Finally the micro level directs our attention to the impact of individuals, whether they are politicians or civil servants, professionals providing a service, or the users of services.

Analyses have also taken on the greater complexity of politics and society, and in particular the perceived need of governments to work with a wide range of other organizations and interests if they are to successfully implement policies. In many respects these run in tandem with other intellectual and political debates, including over the shift from government to governance, the extent of and likely impacts of globalization, technological change, and the growing awareness of 'risk', both for individuals and the state, and its implications for policy-making and implementation, all of which feed into the literature on the policy process.

There are many other models and concepts that can be used to analyse policy-making, implementation and evaluation, with many of these being covered in the 'Further Sources' at the end of this chapter.

Governments and the Policy Process since 1979

The approaches taken to policy-making and implementation can also have an impact on the shape of the policies that emerge. The Conservative governments of 1979 to 1997 were strongly influenced by ideas about individual responsibility and a preference for markets rather than the state, and this in turn had an impact upon their approaches to policy-making and implementation. For example, there was an emphasis on managerialism, performance measurement, competition, and privatization in the public sector, in an attempt to improve efficiency and responsiveness to consumers, while a variety of implementation and delivery functions that had previously been undertaken by central and local government were devolved to quangos and non-departmental public bodies while allowing the centre to retain control over policy formulation.

Under the Labour governments from 1997 to 2010 considerable effort was put into attempts to 'improve' many aspects of the policy process, from formulation through delivery and evaluation. This made terms such as 'evidence based' (perhaps more accurately 'evidence informed') policy-making and 'joined up' approaches a common part of the social policy lexicon. At the same time an emphasis on 'partnership', rather than competition between agencies, became a key mechanism for the implementation of policy and the achievement of the government's objectives, a development that was particularly noticeable in many areas of social policy.

However, while attempts such as these to develop 'better' policy-making may be desirable, it is important not to understate the importance of values in determining policies, and to recognize that the aims and outcomes of policies will almost inevitably be contested. Highly technocratic approaches, or indeed market approaches, to the policy process risk depoliticizing and legitimizing decisions about the distribution of resources. However, policy-making is inevitably political, and values and value conflicts are an inevitable part of the policy process. Improvements to the policy process should therefore arguably aim to improve the quality of political interaction, rather than to replace it.

In addition Labour introduced a number of constitutional and structural changes that had implications for policy-making and implementation. These included: devolution to Northern Ireland, Scotland, and Wales, increasing further the scope for a greater variety of approaches to policy-making (and to policies) within the United Kingdom; the incorporation of the European Convention on Human Rights into UK law through the Human Rights Act 1988, enabling those who feel their rights have been infringed to pursue their grievances in the domestic courts; and reforms to local government, particularly in England, that were intended to provide greater democratic accountability and more effective policy-making, although the extent to which these aims were achieved remained questionable.

When the coalition government was formed in May 2010, like its predecessors it brought with it certain preferences which were likely to be translated into the policy process. These included a preference for a smaller state and for greater involvement by citizens, the private and not-for-profit sectors in the delivery of services, echoing in many respects the approaches taken by the Conservative governments of the 1980s and 1990s.

Emerging Issues

Not only have recent decades seen something of a shift from government to governance, but they have also seen a much greater awareness of and perhaps an increase in, complexity and risk in relation to the policy process. For example, there has been a growing awareness of the need for governments to work with a wide range of agencies and interests to successfully implement social policies. As a result it is hard now to envisage ways in which simple policies can be devised to deliver clear-cut outcomes. In addition, as events in the relatively recent past have demonstrated, particularly at the global level, such as in relation to global warming or the financial crisis of 2008/9, governments may appear relatively weak, although there are also counter-arguments that suggest that nation-states remain of major importance in making policy choices.

There have also been debates over the extent to which policies in different states may be converging over time (perhaps because many states now experience similar pressures, or use similar policy instruments, or as a result of greater use of policy transfer). However, there is no consensus on the extent of such a development, or even if it is occurring at all.

Guide to Further Sources

Although based largely on an examination of the policy process under the Labour governments from 1997 many of the ideas covered in C. Bochel and H. Bochel, *The UK Social Policy Process* (Basingstoke: Palgrave Macmillan, 2004) remain relevant.

Making Policy in Theory and Practice (Bristol: Policy Press, 2007) edited by H. Bochel and S. Duncan combines academic and practitioner perspectives in an examination of approaches to the policy process under the Labour governments from 1997, including attempts to 'professionalize' policy-making.

B. Hogwood and L. Gunn, *Policy Analysis for the Real World* (Oxford: Oxford University Press, 1984) – although written more than a quarter of a century ago this book continues to provide a useful introduction to policy analysis, covering a range of key issues in an approach that remains relevant.

J. Hudson and S. Lowe, *Understanding the Policy Process* (2nd edn, Bristol: Policy Press, 2009) draws upon and highlights a wide range of perspectives to help us understand how change occurs in social policy, focusing in particular on analysis at the macro, meso, and micro levels.

For a good discussion and critique of both theoretical and practical approaches to the policy process see M. Hill, *The Public Policy Process* (5th edn, Harlow: Pearson, 2009). It provides an accessible overview of many aspects of policy-making and implementation and draws upon social policy for many examples.

W. Parsons' *Public Policy: An Introduction to the Theory and Practice of Policy Analysis* (Aldershot: Edward Elgar, 1995) is a useful book that provides a comprehensive coverage of the development of the study of the policy process and incorporates discussion and critiques of a wide range of perspectives.

Review Questions

1 Can you identify social policies in recent years which might be said to reflect 'rational' or 'incremental' approaches to policy-making?

2 Why might the views of some groups be excluded from the policy agenda?

3 How useful might policy transfer be as a tool for governments seeking to inform the making of social policies?

4 Why might 'top-down' approaches to policy implementation appeal to decision-makers but prove problematic in practice?

5 In what ways might a shift in power from Westminster to the devolved administrations of Northern Ireland, Scotland, and Wales, and to the European Union, affect policy-making and implementation in the United Kingdom?

Visit the book companion site at www.wiley.com/go/alcock to make use of the resources designed to accompany the textbook. There you will find chapter-specific guides to further resources, including governmental, international, think-tank, pressure groups, and relevant journals sources. You will also find a glossary based on *The Blackwell Dictionary of Social Policy*, help sheets, and case studies, guidance on managing assignments in social policy and career advice.

29

Evaluation and Evidence-based Social Policy

Martin Powell

▨▬■ ▨ ▨▬■▬■▬ ▨▬■ ▨ ▨▨▬■ ▨ ▨▬▨▬■ ▨ ▨▬■▬■ ▨ ▨▬■▬■ ▨ ▨▬▨▬■ ▨ ▨▬■▬■ ▨ ▨▬■

Overview

- Both the previous New Labour and the current Conservative–Liberal Democrat coalition governments have claimed that policy evaluation and evidence-based policy-making are important.
- Different types of policy evaluation – prospective, formative, and summative – operate at different stages in the policy cycle.
- Different types of evaluation designs exist.
- There are different views about what constitutes valid 'evidence' in evidence-based policy-making.
- It is impossible to eradicate 'values' from either policy evaluation or evidence-based policy-making.

▨▬■ ▨ ▨▬■▬■▬ ▨▬■ ▨ ▨▨▬■ ▨ ▨▬▨▬■ ▨ ▨▬■▬■ ▨ ▨▬■▬■ ▨ ▨▬▨▬■ ▨ ▨▬■▬■ ▨ ▨▬■

Background

There are many different definitions and types of evaluation in social policy, but in general terms it is concerned with examining the extent to which a policy is working. Ovretveit (1998: 9) defines evaluation as: 'attributing value to an intervention by gathering reliable and valid information about it in as systematic way, and by making comparisons, for the purposes of making more informed decisions on understanding causal mechanisms or general principles'. The level of success or failure of a policy is important since this should provide some useful information that feeds back into the formulation and implementation of new or revised policies. Similarly, evidence-based policy-making (EBPM) involves basing policy on evidence of 'what works' rather than ideology or dogma. Policy evaluation and basing policy on 'evidence' has a long and sometimes inglorious history. Both the recent New Labour (1997–2010) and the current Conservative–

Liberal Democrat coalition governments claim that that EBPM should be a more important ingredient in public policy. One of the main themes of the New Labour government was 'what counts is what works' (Powell forthcoming).

Policy evaluation and EBPM fit well with the 'rational model' and 'stagist' approach to policy-making (Powell forthcoming; see Chapter 28 this volume). The 'Green Book' (HM Treasury 1997) presents a sequential model of policy-making using the acronym, ROAMEF (Rationale, Objectives, Appraisal, Monitoring, Evaluation, and Feedback). Recent governments claim that evaluation is at the heart of policy-making, with different types of evaluation (often with commentators using different terms) taking place at different stages of the policy process. Here we differentiate between prospective, formative, and summative evaluation (cf Ovretveit 1998), which differs in terms of the place of evaluation within the policy cycle, and in the type of research that is conducted.

Prospective evaluation (programme feasibility assessment, programme appraisal, option analysis, modelling and simulation, front end, ex ante, feasibility evaluation) seeks to determine what worked in similar settings in the past or elsewhere: what policy might work? This assesses whether a proposal is worthwhile, and takes place before the policy. This might involve a simulation exercise or reviewing the literature through techniques such as systematic review. The result of the appraisal may not proceed with the policy. It is difficult to fit 'pilot' studies into this scheme. They may be seen as prospective in the sense that they are intended to determine if a policy works in certain areas before rolling it out to other areas. On the other hand, it might be seen as formative or even summative.

Formative (process, bottom-up, developmental) evaluation takes place when a policy is being implemented. It examines issues of process such as to determine whether guidelines have been followed: how is the policy working? The main aim is to provide feedback which may serve to improve the implementation process. Formative evaluation often involves qualitative methods such as interviews.

Summative (impact, programme, retrospective, outcome) evaluations take place after the policy implementation and are typically quantitative. This examines the effects or impact of the policy: has the policy worked? what were its results? This is sometimes linked to policy goals. Successful policies achieve their initial goals. However, as we shall see later, this is problematic for three reasons. First, goals are often unclear. Second, the policy may have achieved its positive goals, but also with negative side effects. Third, it is difficult to attribute causality, with success being caused by other factors beyond the policy. Nevertheless, 'successful' policies are maintained or expanded, while failed policies are terminated. It is often difficult to draw a hard and fast line between the different types of evaluation as policies are often ongoing rather than terminated, and so many evaluations have some elements of 'formative' and 'summative. However, Box 29.1 gives some examples based on the dominant feature of the evaluation.

Evaluation

In this section, we examine the 'who', 'what', and 'how' issues of evaluation. First, the 'who' issue focuses on the persons carrying out the evaluation. 'Internal' evaluations are undertaken within an organization. While this has the advantage of familiarity, there is the danger of a lack of independence associated with this 'inside job'. Some evaluations are undertaken by interest groups who wish to argue a certain case, and some of these evaluations are little more than lightly disguised calls for policy changes or for more resources. 'External' evaluations are carried out by independent organizations. Many social policy evaluations are undertaken by academics commissioned by governments or charitable foundations such as the Joseph Rowntree Foundation. While such evaluations are nominally independent, there may be some pressure to arrive at the 'right answer' or at least not to be too critical of government.

Second, the 'what' issue examines the criteria of evaluation. The seemingly innocent question of what works becomes a more complex issue of what works for whom in what circumstances? (see EBPM below). Evaluations can be seen in terms of the 'production process' of inputs, outputs, and outcomes. Inputs refer to expenditure or staffing levels. Outputs (or activity)

Box 29.1   Examples of Policy Evaluation

Summative: Impact of Quality and Outcomes Framework (QOF) on GP practice, public health outcomes and health inequalities in England (A. Dixon *et al.*, SDO Project 207/2007).

The aim was to evaluate the impact of QOF on public health and health inequalities, using quantitative and qualitative methods www.sdo.nihr.ac.uk.

Formative: Employment and Support Allowances: early implementation experiences of customers and staff (H. Barnes *et al.*, DWP Report 639). This is a qualitative study that aims to explore the range of variety of experiences, conducted by interviewing thirty-eight staff and thirty-nine customers: http://campaigns.dwp.gov.uk/asd/asd5/rports2009-2010/rrep631.pdf.

Mixed: Evaluation of Phase 1 City Strategy (A Green *et al.*, DWP Report 639). The main research questions included assessing different models of partnership; assessing the effectiveness of funding; measuring the employment rate; assessing which groups can be most effectively helped; and assessing the most appropriate geographical level for the provision of employment services to disadvantaged groups. The study claims that ex-ante, formative and summative evaluation are all relevant, see http://campaigns.dwp.gov.uk/asd/asd5/rports2009-2010/rrep639.pdf.

A search on the DWP research study web site indicated sixteen mentions of 'summative', sixty-two 'formative', and seven 'ex-ante': http://campaigns.dwp.gov.uk/asd/asd5/rrs-index.asp.

between these terms gives us some basic criteria of evaluation in the so called three Es: economy, effectiveness, and efficiency.

- Economy refers to the costs of a service. The most basic input into a policy is expenditure. Although in popular debate services such as the NHS tend to be 'evaluated' on inputs (the level of expenditure), this is unwise as we do not know whether higher spending is 'good' or 'bad'. It can be a sign of purchasing more and better items (such as more expensive drugs and more complex operations) or of inefficiency and waste. It is easy to maximize economy or reduce costs. The cheapest service is to provide no service. The difficulty is to reduce costs while not reducing activity or outcomes (cutting waste or 'red tape').
- Effectiveness refers to benefits: an effective drug is one that works.
- Efficiency takes both effectiveness and cost into account. Day surgery is more efficient than in-patient care if it produces the same level of success at lower cost.

Many commentators have added a fourth E: of equality or equity (see Chapters 4 and 6). Policy-makers sometimes have to make difficult rationing decisions. Providing expensive drugs to prolong life has 'opportunity costs' in that the money could be spent elsewhere in other ways to benefit more people, so an effective drug may not be efficient in terms of society's limited resources. It is often said that there is a trade-off between efficiency and equity. It would not be efficient to provide major hospitals for every small village in remote rural areas, but this leads to unequal outcomes in terms of differential travel time to hospital. In other words, policies may succeed on some criteria, but fail on others. For example, policies may be effective, but not efficient, or effective but not equitable.

Third, the 'how' issue refers to evaluation design. Ovretveit (1998) provides a clear discussion of alternative designs:

- descriptive
- audit (goal-based evaluation)
- before–after
- comparative-experimentalist, and
- Randomised Controlled Experimental.

consist of the number of treatments (such as the number of people who are treated in hospital). Outcomes focus on issues such as the health of the nation, and issues such as whether mortality and morbidity rates are falling or rising. The links

This sets out a series of designs which ask different questions. Descriptive evaluation asks 'what happens' and aims to produce a good description of the important features of the intervention. Audit or goal-based evaluation determines whether the intervention achieved its objectives. However, the goals of a policy are often diffuse, unclear, or diverse. Moreover, the question is only worth asking if the objectives are worth achieving, and may ignore unforeseen consequences. Before–after evaluation compares change over time, but has problems in attributing causality. For example, it has been claimed that 'zero tolerance' policing reduced crime rates, but it is possible that other factors (such as changes in unemployment or the demographic composition of the population) may have been more important. It is also difficult to decide the time interval by which policy effects should be felt. Some may be felt quickly, but others may take many years. Comparative-experimentalist evaluation compares the success of two interventions. Randomised Controlled Experimental evaluation (Randomised Control Trial – RCT) seeks to determine causality by giving the intervention to one group and withholding it from another (the control group). This is often seen as the 'gold standard' in medical research, but its relevance to policy research is hotly debated (see Chapter 2; see below).

Space permits only an expansion of a few points. Perhaps the most important point relates to the distributional consequences of policies. Very few policies are 'win-win' (good for all) and are often 'good' for some but 'bad' for others. For example, a new road may be 'good' for commuter as may reduce journey time, but 'bad' for local residents as it may affect property values, and for environmentalists as it might increase road traffic and pollution. Similarly, as discussed above, policies sometimes succeed on some criteria but fail on others. The problem, which no sophisticated evaluation can solve, is how to 'weigh' the various competing values of the stakeholders.

Evidence-based Social Policy

Both recent governments claim that they wish to base policy on 'evidence', but the definition of

---

Box 29.2   Ovreteit's Golden Rules of Data Collection

Ovretveit (1998) provides some useful practical information for evaluation in his 'eight golden rules of data collection'.

- Don't collect data if it already exists.
- Don't invent a new measure when a proven one will do.
- Don't ignore what is available.
- Measure what's important, not what's easy to measure.
- Don't collect data when confounders make interpretation impossible.
- Spend twice as much time on planning and design as on data collection.
- Analysing data takes twice as long as collecting, if you have not defined clearly which data you need and why.
- Data collection will take twice as long as you expect.

Box 29.3   Ovreteit's Common Evaluation Problems

Ovretveit (1998) also discusses some common evaluation problems (with my brief explanation for some):

- vague users (criteria about goals may not be clear)
- 'gate-crashing users' (different stakeholder views)
- 'after thought' and 'by tomorrow' evaluations
- no baseline measures, and 'drop outs'
- 'fuzzy boundaries'
- 'environmental disorder'
- 'gate-crashing confounders'
- 'wobbly' interventions
- 'ghastly goals' (unclear or contradictory)
- the 'police car' effect (behaviour changes when being observed)
- missing informants and information
- problems in making valid comparisons; and
- 'distant outcomes' (long term).

evidence and EBPM is often unclear. First, the definition of EBPM is problematic. First, there may be some differences between the evidence-based 'family' members: evidence-based medicine; evidence-based management; evidence-based practice and policy. Second, a number of commentators have argued that EBPM exists only in a prescriptive rather than a descriptive sense. In the 'real world', the best that can be hoped for is evidence-informed policy. Research and analysis will only ever be one of the influences upon policy. There are many obstacles to, or 'enemies' of, EBPM. Policy-makers' ability to access evidence-based advice is constrained in a number of ways, such as time pressures, information overload, and the fact that in many cases evidence can either be incomplete, contradictory or inconclusive, adding to the difficulty of taking informed decisions rather than reducing it (see Davies *et al.* 2000; Powell forthcoming).

Second, there are debates about what constitutes 'evidence'. Many writers initially present the 'hierarchy of evidence', albeit in slightly different versions (e.g. Davies *et al.* 2000; Powell forthcoming):

- systematic review and meta-analysis of two or more double-blind randomized control trials;
- one or more double-blind randomized control trials;
- one or more well-conducted cohort studies;
- one or more well-conducted case-control studies;
- a dramatic uncontrolled experiment;
- expert committee sitting in review, peer leader opinion; and
- expert opinion.

However, while the RCT and meta-analysis is often regarded as the 'gold standard' of EBM, it does not necessarily follow that the same is true for EBPM. Becker (Chapter 2) writes that in social policy, there is less reverence for these methods, with more stress on qualitative methods, stressing a continuum rather than a hierarchy. Most commentators in social policy argue for a 'horses for courses' approach, which does not recognize universally superior research designs or methods. They are rather seen as only as good as their suitability to the research question being

asked. While some types of evidence are concerned with summative evaluations and pilot programmes (e.g. New Deal for Communities, the employment New Deals, Sure Start, and the Children's Fund), others are more concerned with formative evaluation. Some are quantitative, while others are qualitative. In short, there is no single 'gold standard' of 'positivist', quantitative, and summative EBPM (see Becker and Bryman 2004). However, evidence needs to be appraised according to some notion of 'quality'. While all evidence may be equal, some evidence is more equal than others. No doubt, some would consider me a 'positivist' for preferring to be treated by a drug that is effective according to a meta-analysis rather than because Mrs Jones said that it worked for her. Anyone who regards all evidence of equal quality cannot criticize any dossier as 'dodgy'. There are often differences between 'scientific' evidence and opinion, and between EBPM and choice. For example, many RCTs and meta-analyses claim that homeopathy does not work (and so should not be publicly funded by the NHS) but many individuals claim that it works for them.

Emerging Issues

Evaluation and EBPM have become important issues in recent years in social policy. However, they are both complex and are subject to ongoing debate. Some argue that evaluation and EBPM provide excellent opportunities for social policy analysts to influence policy. Others argue that they amount to little more than smokescreens that turn complex ideological issues into 'non-ideological' simple solutions, or give a veneer of objectivity and legitimation to decisions already taken. In other words, a 'good' evaluation provides support for the answer that funders want (the policy worked; this is the right policy direction). Despite the coalition government's rhetoric about the importance of EBPM, its future is far from clear. First, the previous Conservative government (1979–97) tended not to commission many evaluations of policy. Second, if it takes place, it is likely that evaluation and EBPM may take a rather different turn in the near future. Rather than examining maximizing the benefits of increased spending and new policies, it is possible that attention may turn to examining minimizing the costs of reduced spending and 'austerity' policies. In other words, rather than research that examines what benefits new policies and investment produce, a new type of 'misery evaluation' might ask what is the 'least worst' disinvestment policy, and what cuts in which areas might be the least painful to which people. Austerity evaluation and EBPM may not be of much comfort for either researchers or governments.

Guide to Further Sources

King's College, London hosts the journal 'Evidence and Policy', www.evidencenetwork.org/. It is an excellent source for the latest information on EBPM. It has links to the Campbell Collaboration, www.campbellcollaboration.org, the Cochrane Collaboration, www.cochrane.org/, the Centre for Reviews and Dissemination, www.york.ac.uk/inst/crd/, and the Evidence for Policy and Practice Information Centre (EPPI-Centre) http://eppi.ioe.ac.uk/cms/.

The 'Policy Hub' terms itself the 'first point of call for all concerned with policy-making' – www.nationalschool.gov.uk/policyhub/; The 'Magenta Book' has a web site on policy: www.civilservice.gov.uk/; The 'Green Book' by the HM Treasury (2007) deals with economic assessment at www.hm-treasury.gov.uk/greenbook; The DWP has produced 'Research Methods for Policy Evaluation' at http://research.dwp.gov.uk/; Saul Becker and Alan Bryman (eds), *Understanding Research for Social Policy and Practice* (Bristol: Policy Press, 2004) is a basic source book that covers research in social policy, including evaluation, EBPM and quantitative and qualitative methods.

Hugh Bochel and Sue Duncan (eds), *Making Policy in Theory and Practice* (Bristol: Policy Press, 2007) focuses on New Labour's nine principles of policy-making, which includes chapters on EBPM and evaluation.

The standard source on EBPM is Huw Davies *et al. What Works?* (Bristol: Policy Press, 2000).

For a clear and comprehensive guide that has wider relevance to social policy and focuses on health care see John Ovretveit, *Evaluating Health Interventions* (Buckingham: Open University Press, 1998).

M. Powell's 'The policy process' in J. Glasby (ed.), *Evidence-based policy and practice in health and social care: critical perspectives* (Bristol: Policy Press, forthcoming) takes a critical view both of EBPM, and the critics of EBPM.

Review Questions

1 Why should policies be evaluated?
2 What are the different approaches and methods in policy evaluation?
3 What are the main problems involved in policy evaluation?
4 How would you go about evaluating a policy such as a NHS telephone 'helpline'?
5 Should social policy be 'evidence-based'?

Visit the book companion site at www.wiley.com/go/alcock to make use of the resources designed to accompany the textbook. There you will find chapter-specific guides to further resources, including governmental, international, think-tank, pressure groups, and relevant journals sources. You will also find a glossary based on *The Blackwell Dictionary of Social Policy*, help sheets, and case studies, guidance on managing assignments in social policy and career advice.

PART V
Welfare Production and Provision

30

State Welfare

Catherine Bochel

Overview

- The role of the state in the provision of welfare grew markedly for much of the twentieth century, yet the extent and form of its involvement in social policy has always been a matter of contention.
- There have been major debates about the balance of provision between the public, commercial, not-for-profit, and informal sectors and the relationships between and responsibilities of individuals and the state, and these have been reflected in the approaches of governments.
- From the late 1970s Conservative governments sought to reduce the scope of state welfare provision and make the public sector more similar to the private sector in its operation.
- Between 1997 and 2010 Labour were much more accepting of the state playing a major role in welfare and public expenditure grew significantly.
- The policies of the UK coalition government from 2010 implied major changes in state welfare, with public expenditure cuts and a desire for greater involvement in social provision by non-statutory providers.

Defining the State

The modern state is complex and made up of diverse elements. It is difficult to define in simple terms. There are many different views and con-

ceptions of 'the state': for example, some see it as providing protection and security; for some the term has connotations of secrecy and control; while for others it is the power of the state and the ways in which this is exercised which is of

The Student's Companion to Social Policy, Fourth Edition. Edited by Pete Alcock, Margaret May, Sharon Wright.
© 2012 John Wiley & Sons, Ltd. Published 2012 by John Wiley & Sons, Ltd.

greatest importance. Clearly, views of the state are many and varied, and while they may contribute to our understanding of the state and its relationships with other entities, space requirements necessitate a more focused approach here. Suffice it to say therefore, that one of the most important reasons for studying the state is that it has enormous influence over our lives, and thus the relationships between the state and society and the state and individuals form a key underlying dimension to much of the discussion.

The state and the mixed economy of welfare

In social policy the term 'welfare state' is widely used. Given that this appears to imply that the bulk of welfare is provided by the state, an impression perhaps reinforced by the fact that the majority of services used by much of the population, such as health care and education, are widely associated with the public sector, it is perhaps unsurprising that there is a popular belief that the state is the dominant institution in the provision of welfare services. However this is no longer the case, if indeed it ever was (see Part III). Welfare services are paid for and provided by a variety of different means, including individuals and organizations from the commercial, public, not-for-profit, and informal sectors. There is therefore a plurality of providers, in areas such as health care and education, and even more so in relation to services such as child-care, housing, and pensions, a situation often referred to as 'the mixed economy of welfare'. Indeed, one of the major debates in social policy over the past three decades has been about the relative sizes and roles of the different sectors, including the role of the state in welfare funding as well as provision. The balance of responsibility for service provision has changed markedly over time, and we can see, for example, a shift from a growth in state provision from 1945 to the mid-1970s to a greater role for the private, not-for-profit, and informal sectors from the 1980s onwards. Increasingly from the late 1990s 'state' welfare services have been provided by or in partnership with organizations from other sectors, and from 2010 the UK coalition government was planning for 'non-state' providers to take on an enhanced role.

Analysing the state

Although there are many approaches to describing and analysing the state, one is to view it as a sovereign institution – it exercises legitimate power and is recognized as doing so by other states (although even here the growth of international organizations, such as the European Union, raises questions about the degree of sovereignty) – the government of which comprises a range of institutions through which laws and policies are developed and implemented.

There is also a range of different views of the state that can be used to help us understand the ways in which state power is exercised. For example, in liberal democracies, pluralist theory suggests that power is widely distributed and that many groups and organizations are able to influence policy. In contrast, other perspectives, such as those from elite and Marxist approaches, suggest that power is more restricted (see Chapter 28).

Given the difficulties of defining and analysing the state, and the particular focus of this chapter, it is perhaps appropriate to consider the functions of 'government' in respect of state welfare. In the United Kingdom the institutions that comprise government include

■ Central government – the Westminster Parliament, the prime minister, the Cabinet, and a variety of central government departments. Within these it is possible to distinguish between, for example, The Treasury, which is responsible for managing public expenditure, and 'spending departments', such as those responsible for services like education, training and skills, health care, pensions and benefits. It is also possible to make further distinctions, between, for example, departments which largely play a policy-making role, setting the direction and frameworks for services that are delivered by other organizations, and those that are more involved in the direct delivery of services, such as health care through the NHS, and the state pension and other benefits.
■ The Scottish Parliament, the National Assembly for Wales, and the Northern Ireland Assembly, each of which is able to exercise differing levels of power over welfare

policy and provision within their jurisdictions (see Chapter 42).

■ Local government – which traditionally had a central role in the direct delivery of services, but whose powers since the 1980s have been dispersed. As a result of this many services which were once delivered by local authorities are now delivered by other sectors (see Chapter 41).

■ A wide range of agencies at each tier of government variously referred to as quasi-autonomous non-governmental organizations (quangos), non-departmental public bodies (NDPBs), committees of experts, next steps agencies and extra-governmental organizations (EGOs). These are effectively organizations that perform some of the functions of government but at 'arms-length' from the departments to which they are responsible. While incoming governments frequently seek to reduce the number of such bodies, and are susceptible to reorganization and renaming, they remain both useful and significant. Examples from early 2011 include the Homes and Communities Agency, the Equality and Human Rights Commission, the Child Support Agency, Jobcentre Plus, and the Independent Police Complaints Commission.

State Involvement in Welfare

It is also possible to analyse the state in terms of the functions that it performs, such as defence, the collection of taxation, the delivery of services, and regulation. As is apparent from the discussion above, and other chapters in this book, state involvement in welfare happens in different ways (Box 30.1)

Given the variety of roles that the state plays in relation to social policy, and the existence of a mixed economy of welfare, it is unsurprising that it is possible to identify a whole range of different permutations of state involvement. For example, education can be privately delivered and funded, delivered and funded by a mix of both private and public funding, or solely publicly funded and delivered. In the case of commercial health care, it is not funded or delivered by the state, but elements of it are regulated by the state, and in some

cases the state will itself purchase commercial provision for public patients. These examples can be repeated across the variety of welfare services and provision. Clearly therefore, there is enormous complexity in the mixed economy of welfare.

The range of the discussion above, together with the numbers and types of bodies involved, serves to provide some indication of the complexity of the role of the state in relation to the production and delivery of welfare. There is considerable debate as to what the role of the state should be. For example, some argue that the number of roles and functions of the state are now so great that it has reached the point where it can no longer undertake all of them successfully, and that it is necessary to involve a range of other organizations, for example, in relation to service delivery and administration. Some believe that a large state apparatus is inefficient, bureaucratic, unresponsive to the needs of its citizens, and reduces freedom and choice. Others argue that the state should retain much of its role but that it needs to be more efficient and effective in fulfilling it. Yet others argue that there is scope for further expansion of the role of the state in social policy, particularly in relation to reducing inequalities. All of these arguments are reflected not only here, but in other chapters in this book and in wider debates in society.

The Changing Role of the State

As the historical development of the welfare state is considered elsewhere in this book (see Part III) the intention here is to provide a guide to the main changes and developments in the role of the state since 1979.

From 1979 the Conservatives, led by Margaret Thatcher and then John Major, and influenced by New Right thinking, pursued a strategy of reducing the role of the state in welfare. There was an emphasis on 'managerialism', in the belief that the introduction of private sector business methods into the public sector could make it more efficient; and from 1988, a range of different policy instruments, often termed 'the new public management', were used. These included: the greater use of markets, ranging from privatization (for example, sales of council houses),

Box 30.1   The Main State Functions in Welfare

Policy-making and the passage of legislation: the state plays an important role in formulating policy in many areas, in central government, the devolved administrations and local government, with the two higher tiers also being able, in some circumstances, to direct local authorities or other agencies to implement their policies. State institutions, legislation, and policies also provide the framework within which services are delivered.

Funding: central government funds the great bulk of state welfare. It does this in a variety of ways: as a direct provider of services, such as the NHS; through direct financial assistance to individuals, as is the case with the state pension and Child Benefit; and indirectly through local government, 'arms-length' agencies, or private or not-for-profit providers, whether this is through grants or contracts for service provision. In addition, the state also provides fiscal support for some people through tax relief, tax credits, and other forms of support such as free or subsidized prescriptions.

Delivery: as is apparent from above, the state plays a major role in providing welfare services, such as the NHS, state education, and large areas of social care, and in determining the form that they take, although responsibility for some services is channelled through local government or 'non-state' providers.

Enabling: since the 1980s the state has developed its role in enabling or overseeing

service delivery by private and not-for-profit sectors organizations rather than providing services itself.

Co-ordination and collaboration: this has become increasingly important in the delivery of welfare services, and across all tiers of government there has been an emphasis on bringing a range of organizations from different sectors together to respond to issues and deliver services in a way that is intended to be more flexible and comprehensive than would be achieved through agencies working alone or in competition with each other.

Regulation and direction: recent years have also seen a much greater awareness of the regulatory role of the state, and this has been very apparent in relation to social policy. Examples of regulatory bodies from early 2011 include: the Care Quality Commission, responsible for registering, inspecting, and reporting on the provision of social care in England; the National Institute for Health and Clinical Excellence, which provides guidance on promoting good health, and the prevention and treatment of ill health; the Office for Standards in Education (OFSTED) responsible for the standards of care and education of children and young people in England; and the Financial Services Authority, responsible for regulating the financial services industry throughout the United Kingdom.

through compulsory competitive tendering (such as cleaning services in hospitals), to the introduction of market-type mechanisms into the provision of public services (for example in health and education); the development of a view of the state as an enabler rather than a provider of welfare services, with greater provision by the commercial and voluntary sectors and by individuals themselves; and the devolution of non-essential functions, such as policy implementation and service delivery, previously undertaken by central and local government to organizations such as

quangos, non-departmental bodies, and Next Steps Agencies. Such developments served, over time, to make the organization and delivery of services much more fragmented and complex, while there was little agreement among commentators about their success or their social impacts.

Under the Labour governments from 1997 it was possible to identify a number of, sometimes overlapping, or even contradictory, elements to the relationship between the state and welfare: there was an expansion of the role of the state as an enabler of services, and greater use of non-statutory agencies as service deliverers. Partnerships took on a prominent role as a way of utilizing the perceived strengths of the private and not-for-profit sectors for social ends. The efficient and effective delivery of public services was seen as paramount and as part of achieving this aim there was increased use of a variety of mechanisms for regulation, audit, and inspection (see Chapter 39). At the same time Labour increased public expenditure in some areas of state provision, notably social protection, education, and the NHS. It also increased the use of indirect 'fiscal welfare', particularly through the expansion of tax credits aimed at lower income groups. The relationship between the state and individuals was seen as one where citizens' rights were matched by responsibilities. This was reflected, for example, in relation to work and benefits, where there were debates over conditionalities and how best to encourage those individuals who failed to meet their responsibilities to do so.

The devolution settlements for Northern Ireland, Scotland, and Wales created the possibility for increasingly different approaches to state involvement in welfare across the constituent components of the United Kingdom, with for example, the decision of the Scottish Executive in 2000 to provide personal care free for older people, the decision of the Welsh Assembly to abolish prescription charges from April 2007, and different approaches to tuition fees for higher education (see Chapter 42). Also as political control of the United Kingdom's legislative bodies changes over time, the prospects for greater divergence in social policy may increase further.

Following the formation of the UK coalition government headed by David Cameron in May 2010, there was an emphasis upon reducing public expenditure. While this was in part a response to the fiscal deficit arising from the financial crisis of 2008–10. It was also clear that for many in the new government there was an ideological impetus for a smaller role for the state. For Cameron and many in the Conservative Party the idea of a substantial shift from 'big government to Big Society' was a key part of their vision. This was underpinned by a belief that there was too much intrusion by government into the lives of people, that the role of the state in welfare had grown too large, and that the welfare state had become inefficient, wasteful, and overly bureaucratic. This view was close to that of some Liberal Democrats who sought to apply some of the ideas of economic liberalism to parts of social provision.

This combination of the perceived failings of the welfare state, major cuts in public expenditure, a desire for greater provision by the voluntary sector, social enterprises and local communities, and for a new relationship between individuals and the state implied a significant reduction, or even residualization, of the state in many areas, although the coalition government committed itself to maintaining or increasing expenditure on the NHS and school-age education, albeit through a new range of providers, who were likely to be drawn from outside the state. The idea of citizen participation and involvement in decision-making, the shaping and indeed running of services was an important part of the coalition's plans for the future. More generally, the government was seeking to open the public sector up to a greater range of providers, for example in the case of education, allowing schools to become Academies, answering directly to Whitehall rather than the local council, and creating 'free' schools, to be run by parents or other organizations.

Emerging Issues

The relationships between individuals, society, and the state have been central to the development of social policy over the past three decades. The New Right's influence on the Conservative governments of the 1980s and 1990s was reflected in attempts to reduce the role and size of the state and an emphasis upon individuals providing for themselves and their families. While there were echoes of this in some areas of social policy under Labour, an emphasis on individuals' rights and responsibilities, and citizen participation and involvement in decision-making were key dimensions of its approach, there was also a clear commitment to state welfare, and particularly state funding of welfare.

From 2010 the UK coalition government placed particular emphasis on reducing and reshaping the role of the state, with greater responsibility for the structuring and running of services being placed on individuals, community groups, voluntary organizations, and social enterprises, as part of the 'Big Society', and an expansion of 'non-state' providers in the public sector. While the government's thinking was not entirely clear, by early 2011 a range of ideas was being discussed, including the mutualization of services, the promotion of multiple and diverse providers, and the freeing up of bodies from state control. Reductions in public expenditure were also beginning to have an impact on individuals (for example, through the removal of Child Benefit for higher rate tax payers) and upon organizations, including redundancies and retrenchment in local government and pressure for savings in education and the NHS.

What appears clear is that the nature of the mixed economy of welfare is set to continue to be a central feature of social policy, and that arguments about the form and extent of the state's role that is appropriate for different sectors will remain contentious. In addition, at least in part because of the changes introduced by successive governments, including the fragmentation of systems of welfare provision and the consequent need for greater regulation and new methods of co-ordination, relationships between central government and the variety of providers from all sectors have become considerably more complex. The challenges associated with establishing a clear overview of what is happening, and in exercising control over those responsible for policy implementation, mean that accountability and regulation are therefore likely to remain key issues.

Guide to Further Sources

The book edited by M. Powell, *Modernising The Welfare State: The Blair Legacy* (Bristol: Policy Press, 2008) looks specifically at developments under Labour, while H. Bochel (ed.), *The Conservative Party and Social Policy* (Bristol: The Policy Press, 2011) considers early developments in the life of the coalition government. C. Hay, M. Lister, and D. Marsh (eds), *The State: Theories and Issues* (Basingstoke: Palgrave Macmillan, 2006)

considers a wide range of different perspectives about the state ranging from pluralism through to governance and globalization. A different and detailed approach to some of the issues considered in this chapter is taken by T. Bovaird and E. Loffler, *Public Management and Governance* (London: Routledge, 2009) which, for example, includes chapters on partnership working and the size and scope of the public sector. M. Powell (ed.), *Understanding the Mixed Economy of Welfare* (Bristol: Policy Press, 2007) is an accessible account of welfare pluralism and the book by C. Pierson and F. G. Castles, *The Welfare State Reader* (Cambridge: Polity Press, 2006) considers a wide range of different perspectives, debates, and challenges to the welfare state. Current developments can be tracked through the *Social Policy Digest* http://journals.cambridge.org.spd/action/home.

Review Questions

1   To what extent is the state the principal source of welfare provision in contemporary society?
2   How has the role of the state in the provision of welfare changed since 1979?
3   Why might the relationship between and responsibilities of individuals and the state be so contestable for social policies?
4   What do you see as the key issues facing the development of state welfare over the next decade, and how do you think these might best be tackled?
5   What should the role of the state be in a mixed economy of welfare?

Visit the book companion site at www.wiley.com/go/alcock to make use of the resources designed to accompany the textbook. There you will find chapter-specific guides to further resources, including governmental, international, think-tank, pressure groups, and relevant journals sources. You will also find a glossary based on *The Blackwell Dictionary of Social Policy*, help sheets, and case studies, guidance on managing assignments in social policy and career advice.

31

Commercial Welfare

Chris Holden

Overview

- There are many different kinds of for-profit companies that are involved in the delivery of welfare services.
- The extent and type of state welfare activity plays a key role in determining the scope for commercial welfare services in advanced welfare states.
- Recent reforms in advanced welfare states have led to a 'blurring of the boundaries' between the public and private sectors.
- The more the provision of welfare services relies on markets and private providers, the more important regulation of these becomes in the pursuit of social policy goals.

Markets and Businesses in Welfare

Commercial welfare involves the sale and purchase of welfare services and products in markets of one kind or another. The sellers of these services are usually aiming to make a profit, although not-for-profit providers such as voluntary organizations (or provident associations, which are also technically non-profit making) may also be involved in welfare markets. Even these types of providers, however, must usually try to maximize their income if they are to remain competitive. The consumers of these services are individuals, although the payers may be the individuals themselves (or their families), insurance companies (with the contributions to the insurance plan paid by the individuals or their employers), or state agencies. In principle, services necessary for the satisfaction of human welfare needs may be sold and bought in markets in the same way that

The Student's Companion to Social Policy, Fourth Edition. Edited by Pete Alcock, Margaret May, Sharon Wright.
© 2012 John Wiley & Sons, Ltd. Published 2012 by John Wiley & Sons, Ltd.

any household item may be. There are two key reasons, however, why welfare services should be distinguished from other goods and services.

The first is that welfare services are by definition so important for the meeting of basic human needs that governments often decide they should take action to ensure that all of their citizens have access to at least a certain minimum level of these. If governments did not take such action, many of their citizens would not be able to afford to meet their basic needs, leading to huge inequalities. In countries like Britain during the course of the twentieth century, this government action often took the form of direct provision by state agencies, as well as state funding and regulation of services (see Chapter 30). Direct state provision was often seen as the best way of ensuring that services would be provided to the degree and standard that the government thought necessary. In health services, for example, private provision was pushed to the margins by the creation of the National Health Service (NHS) in Britain, which was (and is) paid for out of general taxation and free to citizens at the point of use. However, as we will see, governments have increasingly begun to question the idea that the state itself should be the provider of welfare services if the needs of their citizens are to be met.

The second key reason why welfare services should be distinguished from other goods and services is that the market often does not provide them efficiently (see Chapters 6 and 35). There are many reasons why this is the case. Deciding what kind of health care you need, for example, is not the same as choosing a new television, and you are much more dependent on the knowledge of professionals. Therefore, even if markets and private providers are to play a role in the delivery of welfare services, these need to be carefully regulated to ensure that they help to meet the goals of social policy.

In most countries, commercial provision of welfare services such as health and social care, education, pensions and other financial products, and of course housing, has always continued to exist wherever firms can make a profit. However, in advanced welfare states, the extent and type of state welfare provision has tended to be the largest factor determining the scope for private provision. The less state provision there has been, the more scope there has been for private provision.

Nevertheless, in many countries (including Britain) there have always been a number of private firms that have benefited from payments by the state to provide services on behalf of the government and the number of such businesses has been growing considerably as a result of government policies. Furthermore, firms that produce goods such as medicines that are crucial for the delivery of welfare services have also benefited hugely from state funding.

Where state provision or funding of services is low, the size and shape of the market is largely determined by the degree of effective demand, that is, how much people are willing and can afford to pay for services. Since people will not necessarily have the money to pay 'out of pocket' for support when they need it, this tends to encourage the development of commercial insurance schemes. In countries like Britain with tax-funded public health services, these have tended to be taken out by those whose employers pay for health or other insurance as a non-wage benefit, or those who are relatively better off and can afford to pay, for instance, to be treated more quickly or in more pleasant surroundings than those provided by the public system.

There are in fact a large number of different types of for-profit firms involved in some way in the delivery of welfare services (see Box 31.1). Any of these companies may be entirely privately owned by one or two individuals or by a small number of investors, or they may be 'public' in the sense of being listed on the stock exchange so that people may buy shares in them. They range from small individual owners of care homes to huge multinational corporations (MNCs). Currently, the most significant multinational firms are those that produce welfare-related goods such as pharmaceuticals (rather than services), but as the provision of welfare services by private firms increases, these businesses too are likely to become more multinational, and international trade in welfare services between countries is likely to increase. Such developments will need careful study if the goals of social policy are to be safeguarded and advanced. As well as firms performing the different roles in the delivery of welfare described in Box 31.1, a variety of firms whose core business activities may have little or nothing to do with the direct provision of welfare may also exert influence on social policy. For

Box 31.1 Types of For-Profit Firms in Welfare Delivery

- Firms that directly provide welfare services to the public, including health and social care, education, and many other services. These are the most important type of firm for social policy.
- Firms that produce goods which are indispensable to the delivery of welfare services, such as medicines and educational materials. These kinds of firms have been somewhat neglected in the study of social policy, but their behaviour often has important implications for welfare outcomes.
- Firms that supply services to the organizations (both public and private) which directly provide welfare services. For example, all hospitals, whether they are run by state agencies or by private firms, rely on companies which distribute medicines to them, clean their premises and provide catering services to their patients and staff. Firms in this category may also provide consultancy or management services to direct providers by, for example, taking over the management of a state-owned school or hospital where the existing management has been deemed to have failed.
- Firms that provide insurance or financial services such as health and disability insurance, private pensions, or mortgages.
- Firms that are involved in the design, building and maintenance of the premises from which welfares services are provided, such as hospitals and schools, as well as prisons and the construction of houses. This type of firm has become much more important in Britain in recent years as a consequence of the Private Finance Initiative (PFI).
- A number of different firms that, whatever their business, provide some form of occupational welfare services to their own employees.

example, firms may participate less directly in the management of state welfare services through various types of boards or sponsorship deals, as is the case with academy schools. Firms might also take political action, such as lobbying politicians about social policy issues, in order to protect or advance their interests.

We can see then, that there has always been a huge range of different firms that are involved in some way in the delivery of welfare, often deriving a large portion of their income from the government by selling goods or services as inputs to state providers, as well as selling these goods and services directly to the public for private payment. The most important type of companies for the meeting of social policy goals are the direct providers of services. In Britain, the most rapid growth in the involvement of private firms in welfare delivery in recent years has been among these very providers.

Government Policy and Welfare Markets

We have said that the extent and type of government welfare activity is the most important factor determining the scope for commercial welfare in advanced welfare states. Paying attention to the *type* of government activity is particularly important, because it is not simply a case of the presence or absence of such activity (see Part IX). The government may choose to pay private sector companies to provide welfare services, or mandate other organizations to administer services, rather than provide them itself. Government mandated social insurance schemes are one example of this. So, for example, many European countries have social health insurance schemes, whereby citizens (or their employers on behalf of them) pay into independent funds, which are regulated by the government and pay for their health care when they need it. The government in these countries usually pays contributions for those who can't afford to do so for themselves, so that everyone has access to a minimum level of health care. This set up often means that citizens can choose to access the services of private health care providers as well as public ones, and have their bills paid by the social insurance fund. In this way, private providers make their money not simply from private payments (either private insurance or out-of-pocket), but from payments by government mandated insurance funds. Government activity in the pursuit of social policy goals may therefore support rather than undermine commercial providers, depending on the form it takes.

In the United States where the welfare state is much less extensive than in most other economically advanced countries and where many citizens can afford to pay for their needs commercial welfare is more developed than in any other country (see Chapter 61). There is therefore a huge market in health and other services, with large chains of for-profit hospitals, for example. Inequalities in access to welfare services are consequently also much greater than in most other economically advanced countries, since not everyone can afford to pay for the services they need. Even here, however, the government provides some support for its poorest citizens, with a government funded health insurance service called Medicaid for the poor and a similar scheme called Medicare for older people. People making use of Medicaid or Medicare are just as likely to be treated by private providers as everyone else, but the provider will claim back the cost of the service from the government scheme.

As already discussed, in countries like Britain, where services such as health care have mainly been provided by the state since the end of the Second World War, there has been less opportunity for commercial welfare. However, since the 1980s, that has begun to change for two reasons. First, there has been a relative shift towards individuals taking responsibility for their own needs, so that people cannot rely on the state for their pension, for example, but must make their own provision through occupational or personal private pension schemes. Second, there has been a relative shift towards the state paying private companies to provide services that it used to provide itself.

This second change has involved the introduction of 'quasi-markets' into welfare services that were previously provided almost exclusively by state agencies. Reforms to the NHS are a good example of how these changes have provided more opportunities for private providers. As prime minister, Margaret Thatcher introduced an 'internal market' into the NHS, whereby purchasing of services was separated from their provision. This involved hospitals and other services (the providers) being reorganized into independent trusts, which would then provide services under contract to health authorities and 'fund-holding' GPs (the purchasers). At this point there was very little purchasing of services from the commercial sector, but NHS trusts were expected to behave more like independent businesses 'selling' their services to the purchasers, hence the term 'internal market'.

However, the purchaser–provider split was also introduced into social care services like residential and nursing care for older people, with local authority social service departments as the purchasers and a 'mixed economy' of commercial, voluntary and state agencies as the providers. Here the market was not 'internal', but involved external for-profit providers, who soon dominated the provision of social care. Large multinational corporations moved into this new market alongside smaller private providers, making most of their profits providing care services under contract to local authorities.

The purchaser–provider split was thought by Thatcher to allow more choice for service users and to be more efficient than the old state-provided services, even though it involved extra costs in administering contracts. This new 'mixed economy of care' eventually became the model for public services adopted by subsequent Labour governments. Private providers were invited into the NHS system alongside NHS trusts, under contract to Primary Care Trusts (PCTs), the new NHS purchasers for England. The UK coalition government which came to office in 2010 planned to take these reforms even further by reintroducing GP fund-holding and widening the scope for private involvement in the English NHS. The devolved administrations of Scotland and Wales, however, have been less keen on market mechanisms.

The increasing involvement of commercial firms in welfare has also included new ways of commissioning welfare facilities such as schools and hospitals, through schemes such as the Private Finance Initiative (PFI). PFI involves for-profit consortiums financing and maintaining, as well as building, such facilities. It has been controversial because it means that these are then owned by the consortium for a period of twenty to thirty years, with welfare agencies such as NHS trusts locked into inflexible long-term leases which may not be cost-effective, despite the declared intention of making government procurement more efficient.

Equity, Quality, and the State

Bringing commercial organizations into the heart of the welfare state in these ways has led to a 'blurring of the boundaries' between the public and private sectors. This turn towards the private sector in Britain has both led and reflected a more general drift among policy-makers across the developed world towards the view that the state should 'row less and steer more'. In other words, the pursuance of social policy goals does not necessarily require the state to directly provide services; rather it is the role of the government to ensure that these goals are met through whatever means seem effective. In this view, therefore, it may be better for the government to pay for other agencies and organizations to provide the services, including for-profit companies, or to simply oblige its citizens to make adequate provision for themselves, by paying into pension funds, for example. However, it is not enough for the government to fund the services, or to make sure that citizens pay for themselves; where companies are providing services primarily in the pursuit of profit, the government needs to think carefully about two issues if it is to 'steer' services effectively.

First, where the government funds commercial provision, it needs to think about the kinds of behaviour that are encouraged by the payment system. Any kind of payment system creates its own incentives to behave in a certain way. For-profit providers, voluntary organizations and autonomous public agencies such as foundation hospital trusts will all tend to act in ways that maximize their income, even if other goals are also important to them. Markets, including the 'quasi-markets' created by governments, are premised upon and encourage this very fact. So the government needs to design its payment system very carefully in order to try to incentivize companies to act in the optimum way. It also needs to specify its contracts with providers very clearly so that they know what is expected of them.

Second, the government needs to make sure that it regulates providers properly. This means that the government must create a set of rules within which all providers must operate, monitor adherence to these rules, and apply sanctions where they are not adhered to. Different types of regulatory 'instruments' may be needed in order to ensure that different policy goals are met (see Chapter 39). For example, governments usually want to ensure that certain minimum standards are met in the delivery of services, that is, they want to ensure that quality goals are met. In a hierarchically organized service that is directly provided by a state agency, they can do this at least partly through the agency's internal management structure. However, where services are provided by independent providers, they need to set up special regulatory agencies whose job it is to monitor the quality of services, and take effective action where standards are not met. This means that they must specify clearly the standards which are expected to be met, how they will be monitored, and what action may be taken towards those organizations that fail to meet them.

However, perhaps the biggest concern about the use of markets in welfare is their impact upon equity. The principle of equity is at the heart of the welfare state, and markets may have profound implications for both equitable access to services and for equitable outcomes. Markets are based upon competition and responsiveness to incentives rather than, for example, the encouragement of a public service ethos, and will therefore tend to change the nature of the welfare system. Therefore, careful thought needs to be given to what the goals of social policy should be, and what are the most appropriate means to achieve them.

Emerging Issues

These issues of equity, quality, and regulation are of the utmost importance given that the policies of the UK coalition government are likely to increase the role of the private sector still further. On the one hand, extensive cuts to public sector spending are likely to force even more people to rely on services purchased individually in the market. On the other, the government has embarked on a substantial programme of reforms to encourage 'social enterprises' and to increase private sector involvement in a range of policy areas, including deepening markets in the NHS, allowing parents to initiate 'free schools', contracting out employment services to for-profit businesses, and establishing a series of 'responsibility deals' which give large corporations a substantial say in public health policy.

Furthermore, in the context of an increasingly liberalized and integrated world economy, welfare markets themselves are likely to become increasingly internationalized, with an ever greater movement across national borders of welfare firms, practitioners, and service users. Such developments have the potential to enhance the sharing of knowledge and skills between countries, but also make regulation of services even more difficult and have potentially even greater implications for equity, both within countries and between them. Additionally, the more these services are traded across national borders, the more they are likely to become subject to the rules and treaties of international organizations like the World Trade Organization (WTO). International trade agreements like the WTO's General Agreement on Trade in Services (GATS) are complicated and there is much debate about their implications for welfare services. However, it is increasingly likely that social policy analysts will need to engage with these implications in the years ahead.

Guide to Further Sources

M. Powell (ed.), *Understanding the Mixed Economy of Welfare* (Bristol: Policy Press, 2007) contains a number of chapters looking at different aspects of the mixed economy of welfare. K. Farnsworth and C. Holden's 'The business-social policy nexus: Corporate power and corporate inputs into social policy', *Journal of Social Policy*, 35/3 (2006): 473–94, provides a useful way of classifying types of corporate inputs into social policy, while K. Farnsworth *Corporate Power and Social Policy in a Global Economy: British Welfare Under the Influence* (Bristol: Policy Press, 2004) looks in more detail at how corporations can act politically to influence social policy.

C. Holden (2009) 'Exporting public–private partnerships in health care: Export strategy and policy transfer', *Policy Studies*, 30/3 (2009): 313–32, provides an overview of the Private Finance Initiative and analyses Britain's 'health care industrial strategy'. The main issues relating to international trade in health services, as an example of how welfare services can be traded across borders are outlined in R. Smith, R. Chanda and V. Tangcharoensathien, 'Trade in health-related services', *The Lancet* 373/9663 (2009): 593–601.

The World Health Organization has a number of resources related to trade and health at www.who.int/trade/trade_and_health/en/. Current developments can also be tracked through the *Social Policy Digest* at http://journals.cambridge.org.spd.

Review Questions

1   What distinguishes commercial providers of welfare services from voluntary and state organizations?
2   What different kinds of commercial companies might play a role in the delivery of welfare services?
3   Why have governments since the 1980s chosen to introduce a greater role for private providers in the delivery of welfare services?
4   What are the potential problems that may arise from a greater role for private providers in the delivery of welfare services?
5   What is meant by the term 'row less and steer more'?

Visit the book companion site at www.wiley.com/go/alcock to make use of the resources designed to accompany the textbook. There you will find chapter-specific guides to further resources, including governmental, international, think-tank, pressure groups, and relevant journals sources. You will also find a glossary based on *The Blackwell Dictionary of Social Policy*, help sheets, and case studies, guidance on managing assignments in social policy and career advice.

32

Occupational Welfare

Edward Brunsdon and Margaret May

Overview

- Occupational provision is a key but neglected component of the United Kingdom's welfare mix.
- It consists of the 'above-wage' elements of the reward packages supplied by employers to secure the health, safety, and well-being of their staff.
- Potentially embracing a wide range of benefits it has been revamped over the past decade in the face of changing mandatory requirements and challenging economic conditions.
- The adjustments reflect the revised calculations of the key stakeholders: employers, governments, and trades unions.
- In spite of these changes workplace schemes continue to complement UK statutory welfare provision albeit in an uneven and unequal way.

Context

Whether construed as 'fringe benefits' or simply subsumed within 'private welfare', the production and consumption of occupational welfare is largely overlooked in UK social policy analysis. This is something of a disappointment not simply because of its role in the development of the discipline (Titmuss first drew attention to employer-sponsored provision in the 1950s), but also because of its place in international welfare arrangements. In the United States and Japan it is pivotal to the employee deal and a competitive necessity in staff working conditions. It has been central to the enterprise-based systems of China and remains a key component of provision in many parts of Europe as well as the United Kingdom.

So why has it attracted so little attention here? In part this is a matter of research preference, but

The Student's Companion to Social Policy, Fourth Edition. Edited by Pete Alcock, Margaret May, Sharon Wright.
© 2012 John Wiley & Sons, Ltd. Published 2012 by John Wiley & Sons, Ltd.

it is also due to factors such as an ambiguous division of intellectual labour that treats employment practices as the subject of human resource management (HRM) and employee relations as well as social policy; the lack of good quality secondary data and the difficulties of accessing first-hand information from organizations. In spite of such obstacles, analysts persisting with their investigations have come to appreciate the significance of workplace schemes in the UK social division of welfare.

What is 'Occupational Welfare'?

While there have been variations in the past, policy researchers today tend to define occupational welfare in a manner similar to HRM and employee relations analysts, namely, as the above-wage benefits utilized by UK employers to secure the health, safety, and well-being of their staff. It includes both the *voluntary* provision initiated by organizations themselves and the *mandatory* arrangements instigated by the state. While the latter obligations apply to most organizations (requirements can vary by the staff numbers employed), the majority of interventions are either contractual or non-contractual voluntary welfare schemes that employers custom-build and choose to supply.

The Occupational Welfare Landscape

It is this bespoke nature and the fact that non-contractual voluntary provision can change rapidly that makes creating a typology of current benefits a difficult representational task. However, with these caveats in mind, UK workplace welfare can be classified into nine main types of provision (see Table 32.1 which gives examples of the possible forms of support within each).

These services have grown somewhat unevenly in the recent past. During the Blair and Brown administrations new mandatory schemes were introduced and existing ones extended, while organizations also launched independent programmes, overhauling others in the process. The most far-reaching changes occurred in occupational social security. Of particular significance

was the restructuring of pensions and the launch of mandatory employee savings. Stimulated by tax concessions and contracting-out arrangements, the former had developed into a crucial second pillar of retirement income, supplementing Britain's minimalist state pension. By the 1980s around half the workforce had such cover, mostly in the form of defined-benefit, final-salary plans.

Maintaining them as part of a broad pensions strategy was integral to Labour's welfare agenda. However, plummeting equity markets in the early 2000s and the global market crash of 2008, combined with tighter regulation, tax changes, and concerns over rising life expectancy led some commercial organizations to withdraw from pension provision and large numbers to switch new and existing employees to defined-contribution occupational schemes or other low-cost options. Public sector employers also adjusted their historically more generous arrangements. Union pressure meant amendments here were subject to protracted negotiation. But the general trend was to introduce measures controlling employers' costs and replace final-salary with cheaper career-average plans.

Concerned by the declining coverage in the commercial sector and the estimated seven million employees not saving enough for an adequate retirement income, Labour sought to boost provision through the 2008 Pension Act. Under this legislation, from 2012 employers have to enrol all eligible jobholders into a pension plan, either the new National Employment Savings Trust (NEST) or an approved scheme providing equivalent or better benefits. Tax supported, but largely funded by compulsory employer and employee contributions, NEST is targeted at moderate to low-income earners and intended to complement not compete with existing employer provision. The UK coalition government subsequently endorsed this initiative reaffirming occupational pensions as a welfare fixture. They sit alongside employer-sponsored social security developments such as the increase in the number of workplaces offering above-statutory sick-pay and, given their prominence in the current economic climate, more extensive redundancy packages with enhanced outplacement services.

A similar combination of organizational and government-driven change characterized work-

Table 32.1 Main types of voluntary and mandatory occupational welfare in the United Kingdom.

Type of provision	Examples
Social Security	Occupational pensions (retirement, survivors, ill-health retirement)
	Statutory social security contributions
	Mandatory and above-mandatory pay substitutes (e.g. sickness and redundancy payments, paid maternity, paternity and adoption leave)
	Voluntary pay substitutes (e.g. maternity and child care grants, life, critical illness, disability, personal accident insurance, and death in service)
	Voluntary pay supplements (e.g. professional indemnity insurance, interest-free loans, affinity benefits)
	Corporate individual savings plans
Social care	Mandatory and above-mandatory leave entitlements (e.g. for holidays, parents, carers, civic duties)
	Voluntary support services (e.g. counselling, pre-school, school-age, and adult care, work-life balance and pre/post retirement services, lifestyle benefits)
Health care	Mandatory and above-mandatory health and safety measures
	Voluntary 'illness services' (e.g. private medical insurance and cash plans)
	Voluntary rehabilitation services (e.g. for individuals with ongoing health problems, returning to or re-entering employment)
	Voluntary 'wellness', 'well-being', and 'healthy ageing' services (e.g. screening, diagnostic and referral services, health education and promotion)
Education and training	Mandatory and extra-mandatory health and safety and young workers' training
	Employer-provided training
	Employer support (e.g. for professional/personal development, children's education)
Housing	Employer-provided accommodation
	Voluntary financial assistance (e.g. with mortgage/rent, relocation, insurance)
Transport	Company cars
	Voluntary assistance (e.g. with car purchase/lease, congestion charges, rail tickets, driving lessons, tax, fuel, insurance)
Leisure	Organizational recreational facilities (e.g. sports grounds)
	Voluntary support (e.g. for gym access, attendance at sports/social events)
Concierge services	Voluntary provision (e.g. information and referral services, cafeterias, meal allowances/vouchers, domestic services)
Community participation	Voluntary support for employees' community activities (e.g. school governorships, committee work, fund-raising, mentoring, secondments, leave).

place health and social care. In line with EU strategy, Labour gradually increased holiday entitlements and paid maternity leave and introduced paid and unpaid paternity leave, provisions for adoptive parents and shared parental leave for new parents. Taking up the latter, the coalition promised further measures to augment paternity and shared leave. While increasingly mindful of costs, many organizations independently offered enhanced leave arrangements for parents and carers and developed support services such as child-care vouchers or elder-care assistance. Filling a major gap in state welfare, counselling, retirement planning, legal aid, and referral services also grew along with a range of preventive and curative healthcare measures including medical insurance, cash plans, rehabilitation, well-being, and health education programmes.

Education and training followed a comparable path of expansion and diversity. Large employers in particular increased their investment in staff training and development and their use of web-based provision. Some firms established them-selves as corporate universities, others offered accreditation for work-based learning. More gen-erally, public and private sector agencies enhanced their support for employees seeking qualifications, a process encouraged by the government. Labour also prompted developments focused on skills, 'train to gain' and lifelong learning measures, a policy later revised by the coalition which, while keen on meeting skills shortages, was concerned at their administrative and regulatory costs. The amendments, based on its Skills for Sustainable Growth strategy, include targeted investment in transferable skills, amendments to NVQ entitle-ments and revised apprenticeship programmes.

Of note in each of these different types of development was the degree to which employers shifted from fixed to more flexible provision. In other words, they offered a 'pick-and-mix' of ben-efits and expected employees to choose if, when, and how they took them up. This more personal-ized approach was seen as being responsive to the changing needs and life conditions of staff; there was, however, a residual concern as to whether all members of the workforce could adjust to the new landscape and shoulder the required respon-sibilities. They also increasingly offered benefits on a salary sacrifice basis where employees paid towards the costs from their pre-tax earnings and had their income tax and national insurance con-tributions reduced proportionately.

These modes of delivering occupational welfare gained in popularity in the wake of the global crisis at the end of the decade with employers, including the state, pruning and reshaping provision. Apart from pensions, the key occupational welfare areas hit by the challenging economic conditions were the voluntary provision in housing, transport, leisure, and concierge services. In some instances, benefits were withdrawn or restricted to senior employee grades in others they were allowed to decline in value in the face of increasing costs. Following the shift in taxation from mileage to CO_2 emissions and the introduction of new accounting standards forcing car-leasing costs onto company balance sheets, many companies cut their company car fleets for non-executives, providing cash or mileage allowances instead.

Sports event attendance was largely expunged as an unaffordable benefit, while mortgage/rent and relocation allowances, luncheon vouchers, and meal allowances were allowed to decline in value.

Variations in Occupational Welfare

The picture that emerges of current occupational welfare in the United Kingdom is one of com-plexity, diversity, and flux. There are, however, patterns to the variation in provision in terms of

- *Sector*: public sector organizations are more munificent than commercial or voluntary sector organizations in the level and range of provision and pursuit of equity;
- *Organizational size*: non-mandatory benefits are more widespread and more generous in large commercial and voluntary entities than their smaller counterparts;
- *Industry*: commercial organizations in finance, professional, and other 'knowledge' industries, capital-intensive manufacturing and high-end retailing invest more heavily in welfare programmes than other enterprises in the sector; and
- *Employment status*: in the commercial sector, while some benefits are provided for all or most employees, others are confined to senior staff. This difference occurs less frequently in public and voluntary organizations.

These incongruences reinforce other disparities. For instance, while women and people from ethnic minorities working in the public sector access a relatively high level of occupational welfare, the majority working in small firms and lower tiers of employment in the commercial sector are offered a much narrower range of ben-efits. The spread of salary-sacrifice schemes as a means of co-funding this type of welfare has meant that some of the lower paid have opted out of available voluntary facilities as well.

Accounting for Occupational Welfare

There are three main stakeholders contributing to the historical and contemporary configuration of occupational welfare: individual employers and employer bodies; trade unions; and (at various levels) governments. Though analytically discrete, historically their influence is complex, with the grounds for their interventions changing over time and in importance, and each frequently supporting but also capable of opposing different initiatives.

Individual employers and employers bodies

With little mandatory intervention beyond health and safety, individual employers were key to the nature and level of workplace welfare in the late nineteenth century and early twentieth century. The main drive for provision came from the larger enterprises. In some instances this was on a combination of philanthropic and business grounds, as in the case of Rowntree, in others it was simply to gain competitive advantage. The gas and railway companies, for example, built houses and hospitals and provided pensions as a way of attracting and retaining staff.

As the century progressed, companies grew and the grounds for intervention widened. During the First World War employers were encouraged to boost output and limit absenteeism and turnover by improving health and safety, engaging specialist welfare staff and providing services such as canteens and rest rooms. The inter-war years saw the growth of the employers' industrial welfare movement that, while it did little to allay the hostile industrial relations of the 1920s, promoted company welfare through pensions, sick pay schemes, life insurance, and on-site health care. Income enhancement and replacement benefits were however typically restricted to supervisory, clerical, and managerial staff. The Second World War saw a further concerted effort to expand coverage again to sustain productivity. Further growth and variation occurred in the post-war years as employee welfare developed alongside state provision and new benefits such as housing subsidies, company cars and voluntary pay substitute and supplements began to feature in remuneration packages.

There were a number of different reasons for these enhancements. The continuation of the pre-war shift to larger firms and new industries necessitated more formal HRM strategies, a process hastened by the entry of overseas com-

petitors into the United Kingdom (many of whom brought their own workplace welfare practices). Tight labour markets also placed a new value on benefits that employers felt bought allegiance and eased technological change. They became particularly important as a way of rewarding staff in the 1970s circumventing incomes policies.

While coverage remained concentrated in larger commercial organizations and public services, in the 1980s and 1990s the range of benefits was further modified through the arrival of companies from Japan and the United States and their vision of occupational welfare as part of corporate strategy. For UK establishments following their philosophy, workplace welfare added strategic and operational value not only in terms of recruitment, retention, staff performance, and exit management, but in greater control of the labour process and curbing the financial losses associated with ill health and accidents at work. There was, in other words, a strong business case for treating occupational provision as a core procedure and valuable investment.

The economic downturns at the beginning and end of the past decade threatened this vision. They forced many commercial employers to review their benefits and look for ways of maximizing what they offered while restricting costs. It was these difficult conditions that led to the revisions to pensions, the rapid development of salary-sacrifice schemes, and the rebrokering of voluntary benefit schemes on a regular basis. The public sector was largely insulated from such pressures until the UK coalition government announced the need for major spending cuts in 2010. Apart from pensions, it then followed the path of the private sector and looks likely to face the same imperatives to consolidate and reshape provision. While employers in all sectors are unlikely to engage in a comprehensive retreat from workplace welfare, they will be searching vigilantly for more cost-effective programmes.

Trade unions

Trade unions have always held a more ambivalent attitude towards occupational welfare. In the late nineteenth century and early twentieth century, for instance, they generally opposed pensions and health insurance provided by employers, viewing them as a threat to wage levels and the schemes unions and friendly societies were themselves offering. It was also clear that some employers, particularly in industries like mining and gas, were using workplace welfare to pre-empt the spread of unionization and secure acceptance of hazardous working conditions. However, the mandatory changes to health and safety along with the acceptance of unions' negotiating entitlements in many industries between the wars, led them to increasingly press for workplace benefits.

While reserving the right to oppose particular interventions, unions generally sought to protect and, where possible, improve what was becoming a significant feature of members' remuneration. Benefits were an important negotiating tool in collective bargaining particularly

■ where they were not legally or contractually provided and thus could be withdrawn by employers;
■ in response to changing working practices; and
■ as a means of offsetting low pay rises.

With the steep fall in private sector membership over the past thirty years, however, the unions' influence on provision has been somewhat skewed towards the public sector and, in the face of recent economic pressures, increasingly focused on protecting existing benefit levels rather than their enhancement.

Government

UK governments of varying political hues have contributed to the development of workplace welfare through one or combinations of

■ mandatory interventions
■ fiscal incentives and subsidies, and
■ promotional measures.

The first stretches back to nineteenth century health and safety legislation addressing issues in particular industries or workgroups; this was replaced by broader national and EU legislation in the twentieth century and early twenty-first century that spread beyond risk protection to more general employment conditions. The twentieth century also saw the use of tax relief and subsidies as incentives or ways of cushioning the expense of implementation or delivery. In recent decades, for instance, governments have used both legislation and taxation to change the course and cost of benefits such as sick pay, paid holidays, family-related leave, pensions and company cars – revisions that have not been uniformly welcomed by employers or unions.

Urging employers to adopt/develop welfare initiatives has led to more consensual growth. Whether underwritten by financial incentives or simply supported through the dissemination of good practice, recent governments have argued that employer-sponsored benefits have evolved into crucial business tools with positive national repercussions. They

■ provide a cost-effective supplement to existing state services;
■ boost employee performance, productivity, and engagement;
■ maximize employment levels (through reduced absenteeism and turnover) thus cutting sickness benefit and unemployment costs;
■ respond to the health-maintenance issues posed by an 'ageing' workforce; and,
■ contribute to the well-being of wider society through the benefits they offer employees and their families.

The Blair and Brown administrations, for example, saw voluntary provision as integral to their bid to modernize the UK economy and welfare system, improving productivity and meeting the challenges of globalization. Linked to EU directives and its Employment Strategy, they sought to increase the size of the workforce, thus reducing the numbers dependent on benefits and enabling the funding of more focused public service provision. Boosting employment, however, was contingent on extending supportive practices for working parents and carers as well as extending more general benefits. To this end, they sanctioned a clutch of employer initiatives ranging from 'work-life balance' and 'flexi-working' through to the promotion of 'wellness'. Primarily because of their relatively equitable distribution of benefits, public agencies were used as 'model' providers and 'good practice' advocates to promote further voluntaristic employer action.

It is questionable whether the nature and style of support for such schemes will continue under the UK coalition government. Seeking to reduce total expenditure, it has already lowered funding to state departments and local authorities forcing sizeable redundancies and cost-cutting. Within these confines and detached from a clear employment strategy, workplace welfare is unlikely to remain a public sector priority. More generally, the government has also increased VAT and national insurance and affirmed the NEST pension scheme, all adding to employers' welfare costs. It is also reviewing 'tax-efficient' benefits such as childcare vouchers and pensions offered via salary-sacrifice, suggesting that it may well withdraw their existing fiscal advantages.

Emerging Issues

In the current period of austerity, workplace welfare is under considerable pressure. However, given its importance to organizations in all sectors, it is unlikely to lead to wholesale cutbacks. More probable are further piecemeal adjustments to non-contractual provision. In the public sector, where equity and social inclusion hold some value, such changes can be expected to affect all employees. In the private sector, companies are more likely to calculate what they can afford and couple this with who they should invest in to provide maximum business advantage. In other words, they could well reinforce current inequities by rewarding managers and high performers rather than those in minimum- or low-wage jobs.

Guide to Further Sources

The issues raised here are explored more fully in R. M. Titmuss (1958) *Essays on the Welfare State* (London: Allen & Unwin, 1958); E. Brunsdon and M. May, 'Health, Safety and Employee Wellbeing', in W. Bloisi (ed.) *An Introduction to Human Resource Management* (Maidenhead: McGraw-Hill, 2007): 323–60; E. Brunsdon and M. May, 'Occupational Welfare', in M. Powell (ed.), *Understanding the Mixed Economy of Welfare* (Bristol: Policy Press, 2007), pp. 149–76; and E. Brunsdon and M. May, 'Commercial and Occupational Welfare', in R. M. Page and R. Silburn, *British Social Welfare in the Twentieth Century* (Basingstoke: Macmillan, 1999), pp. 271–98. Mandatory and voluntary UK initiatives can be tracked through the magazine *Employee Benefits* and the government web site www.workingforhealth.gov.uk and the Health and Safety Executive's web site www.hse.gov.uk.

Review Questions

1   What do you understand by the notion 'occupational welfare'?
2   Why is it a significant area of social policy?
3   Why have employers invested in occupational welfare?
4   Why, and in what ways, have successive governments promoted occupational welfare?
5   How will occupational welfare develop over the next decade?

Visit the book companion site at www.wiley.com/go/alcock to make use of the resources designed to accompany the textbook. There you will find chapter-specific guides to further resources, including governmental, international, think-tank, pressure groups, and relevant journals sources. You will also find a glossary based on *The Blackwell Dictionary of Social Policy*, help sheets, and case studies, guidance on managing assignments in social policy and career advice.

33

Voluntary Welfare

Jeremy Kendall

Overview

- Voluntary welfare' is nurtured and delivered through a plethora of organizations situated between the market and the state.
- The scale, structure, and diversity of these organizations is recognized in both empirical and theoretical accounts.
- Deepening interest in 'social capital' has reinforced interest in the role of associations in social, political, and economic life.
- Volunteering is increasingly understood as involving a range of motivations and structures.
- Voluntary organizations' growing proximity to the state and possible role in notions of a 'Big Society' are hotly debated.

Voluntary Welfare and Voluntary Organizations

'Voluntary welfare' – meaning the contribution of organizations between the market and the state to social well-being– embraces an extraordinarily diverse range of activities. Many of these allow needs to be met that would otherwise go unrecognized. The scope and scale of this 'sector' is remarkable – from local playgroups, hospices,

and Age Concern groups to Barnardo's and the Child Poverty Action Group on the national stage, and CAFOD and Oxfam internationally. The groups that populate it are often legally recognized as 'charities', although many organizations the public believe are charitable are not, and others – such as independent schools and some exclusive hospitals – that the public believe are not, are. Partly to rectify this confusion, the 2006 Charities Act widened the legal definition and for

The Student's Companion to Social Policy, Fourth Edition. Edited by Pete Alcock, Margaret May, Sharon Wright.
© 2012 John Wiley & Sons, Ltd. Published 2012 by John Wiley & Sons, Ltd.

the first time made demonstrable public benefit a requirement for all registered charities.

Many other countries with long track records of liberal democracy also have rich traditions of voluntarism, although its form and shape varies dramatically. In the United Kingdom policy recognition of these groups has reached such a level that they may be considered to have been 'mainstreamed' under the last government, as a prelude to even greater attention from the UK coalition government. Drivers include policy-makers' belief that voluntary organizations can be more *responsive, cost-effective*, or *responsible* than the alternatives, can exhibit greater sensitivity to the needs of *socially excluded* constituencies, and seem to be central in generating *social capital* and fostering *social enterprise*. More recently, under the coalition, fiscal considerations have been uppermost.

Some of these beliefs are well based on evidence and argument, and others less so. This is all against the backdrop of a loss of faith in market and state solutions – the sector is increasingly being promoted as a necessary additional ingredient for supposedly exhausted, narrow models of 'statism' for the political Left, and 'market dogma' for the Right. In this sense, the sector partly finds support for what it is not, as well as reflecting what it can demonstrably achieve.

Definitions and Types

An attempt to capture the diversity of this terrain has been made with the label 'a loose and baggy monster'. Its fluidity and fuzziness has led some commentators to argue that talk of a 'sector' is unhelpful or even dangerous. Especially in continental European discourse some, in principle, prefer metaphors such as 'space' or 'field', or represent our subject matter as part of (organized) civil society. Others (including this author) persist in using 'sector' pragmatically as a good enough form of working shorthand, while explicitly attending to diversity and fluidity as potential subjects of analysis rather than prior assumptions.

If one pragmatically accepts the 'sector' construct, how might this be defined? This again is contested and the appropriate formulation depends on the analysts' purpose, values, and priorities. For example, Marxists tend to deny the possibility of a durably independent sector flourishing in capitalist systems. Another route is neo-elitist, also adopting an anti- or post-positivist epistemology, but now accepting the existence of the sector – albeit as a political construct flowing from the agendas of special interests, politicians, and allied researchers.

However, if we subscribe to a liberal, positivist world-view – involving the claim that there is an organizational terrain 'out there' which can be scientifically 'discovered' – a 'structural operational' definition seems to work well for cartographic purposes. This defines into the 'non-profit sector' *formally organized* entities which are *constitutionally/legally separate* from the State, bound *not to distribute surpluses* ('profits') to owners, and demonstrably benefiting from some degree of *voluntarism* (uncoerced giving) of money ('donations') or time ('volunteering').

Once we have identified our terrain in this way, it can then be useful to differentiate organizations within it in a number of ways, for heuristic or hypothesis generation and testing purposes. 'Types' can be distinguished according to their *social functions* – such as service provision, advocacy, innovation, 'community-building' (or 'community development'), and value expressive roles. Other taxonomies refer to how leading actors' or constituents' *values, norms, and motivations* compare – usually aligned to a normative view that some are progressive/constructive/healthy – while others are not. Contrasts can also be made in terms of *resource base* (financial or human resource size and other measures of scale); and of *governance/control rights* distribution.

Also much used is the *policy field* distinction (analogous to the idea of 'industries' in economic life tailored to areas of salience for these groups). For British social policy purposes, this makes a good deal of analytic sense. We are usually interested in distinguishing in decreasing order of economic (but not necessarily social) significance: education and research; social care; development and housing; and health. Some writers would also include sacramental religion.

Finally, distinguishing associations according to whether or not they evidence significant trust-building interpersonal, face-to-face interaction is increasingly widespread in the context of renewed interest in the sector as vehicle for 'civic renewal' or social capital investment (see below). Thus 'secondary associations' – with demonstrably active memberships and apparently vibrant cultures of participation, reciprocity, and networking – are seen as more conducive to economic and political success than 'tertiary associations' – that is, passive, 'armchair', or 'cheque book' membership based bodies. (Family and friendship circles being the 'primary' form of association)

Overall, the single formulation which probably has most currency in social policy 'on the ground' in Britain, cutting across these swathes, is probably still simply 'the voluntary sector'. But the interested student of policy also needs to be aware that the UK coalition government increasingly refers to '(organized) civil society' and renamed the Cabinet Office unit with responsibility the 'Office for Civil Society' – although most reflective commentators believe 'civil society' is a more wide-ranging term. The terms 'charities' (see above) and 'social enterprise' are also used.

Theorizing the Third Sector

So far we have acknowledged the relevance of two perspectives the positivist 'discoverers' and the political 'constructors', as well as the (distinct) Marxist line of argument. As governments have become ever more preoccupied with 'performance' measurement, it is pertinent to note that this broad distinction has also appeared in the analysis of 'effectiveness'. Positivist and social constructionist tools have both been used for evaluative purposes in relation to this sector in social policy fields. But most effort in the past two decades has probably gone in to attempting to answer two further fundamental questions:

- Why do we need a third sector in developed market economies?
- What difference does it make not only in terms of economic productivity, but political performance?

This is where 'social capital' has recently come to the fore. A leading role here has been taken by economic theorization, particularly in the United States in the 1970s and 1980s. One line of thinking suggested voluntary organizations could be

seen as a response to the inabilities of both markets and states to provide 'collective goods' (services where benefits cannot be limited purely to paying customers and in which one person's consumption does not completely exclude that of other people). Up until that point, the mainstream assumption in orthodox economics was that the 'market failure' associated with public good provision traduced a role for the state.

Second, theorization on 'contract failure' pointed out how these organizations seemed to be providing output quality, under conditions of 'asymmetric information' where donors or users could not surmise it for reasons of distance or vulnerability. It was deemed they could be protected from exploitation by the non-distribution constraint – since there were no shareholders waiting in the wings, eager to profiteer at funders and users' expense. Finally, on the supply side, other analysts point to the role of ideological (including religious and political) entrepreneurs in starting and sustaining voluntary organizations.

Though influential, this thinking has been criticized as ahistorical, failing to recognize patterns of co-operation (rather than substitution) as between sectors, tending to represent state-market-voluntary organization divisions as reflecting free(ish), efficient choice and a stable demand, and privileging analysis of the 'service provision' function over others. In reaction, further more socio-political models have been developed, emphasizing some combination of macro political power; the part played by needs rather than wants, and normatively/duty-bound actors rather than sovereign consumers at the micro level.

Prominent here has been an emphasis on the welfare mix approach of Evers and Laville (2003) bringing in non-instrumental rationalities, and emphasizing the tensions at stake between market-driven, state-driven, and community-driven logics; and Anheier's (2005) social origins framework, borrowing conceptually from Esping-Andersen's welfare regime theory (see Chapter 59). The latter more institutionally specific approach attempts to account for how the strategizing of elite political groups at key moments of welfare system design formatively advantaged, or marginalized, the voluntary sector vis-à-vis the state.

Social Capital

Overlaying these approaches, the notion of 'social capital' now also influences thinking in this field. This idea is not only concerned with delivering welfare services, but more general ties, habits, relationships, and interactions in communities. These function better, it is claimed, when involving trust, reciprocity, stability, and respect. So, it also clearly relates closely to the third sector's long-standing 'functions' of 'community building' or 'community development' in Britain. What is new about contemporary community-oriented arguments is that relations of trust and norms of reciprocity are presented as not just socially constructive, but economically and politically instrumental. The word 'capital' underlines economic value – while *at the same time*, keeping in play the imagery of citizenship and public mindedness.

The work of Putnam (1993, 2000, 2002) is key here and the sector, particularly those parts which are 'secondary' (see above) and/or involve volunteers, is now highlighted as a school for fostering civic skills, an arena for rebuilding decayed 'community' values, even 'renewing' democracy itself – while simultaneously strengthening economic performance! No wonder it appeals. But can we really have our cake and eat it? The argument is intensifying, and the evidence base growing, with rounds of claim and counter-claim. This will run and run.

Voluntarism and Voluntary Welfare

Voluntarism – taken here to mean action not directly constrained by State coercion or market imperatives, and outside the informal sector (see Chapter 34) – is an explicit component of some of the theories encountered above, and implicit in others. Arguably, it should be placed centre-stage in any attempt to understand the relationship between this sector and policy. As state engagement with the sector has grown and public funds have flowed, especially into larger organizations, private donations have dwindled in relative terms to become a relatively limited form of support.

Despite much talk of a 'giving age' understood in terms of finance – with politicians, the National Council of Voluntary Organisations (NCVO) and others looking jealously across the Atlantic – in Britain as elsewhere in Europe, the main way voluntarism is manifested is through unpaid *labour*. While the global hours put in by paid workers was demonstrably similar to those of volunteers in the mid-1990s in terms of *numbers of people* involved, the latter still vastly outnumber the former. (Most paid workers, even in the voluntary sector, are full time; most voluntary workers contribute less than half a day per week). Moreover, in the key policy field of social care (see Chapter 51), even in 'full time equivalent' terms, volunteering has remained more important than paid work – and across all sectors here there are still many more volunteers than paid employees.

So, why do people volunteer? In Titmuss' time (see Chapter 1), we would have alluded to the centrality of altruism fostered by market subordination, to be contrasted with the self-interest thought to characterize paid work (prototypical of markets). But the understanding of volunteering has progressed in leaps and bounds, and a much more complex and variegated picture is now in evidence – although it is still arguably possible to discern broad distinctions between apparently more publicly and more privately oriented underpinnings.

Recognized motivations for volunteerism which mix altruism and self-interest include deliberate or incidental 'social capital' building; investment in human capital (with advantages for the individual and society in terms of training and experience useful across working life); 'intrinsic' satisfaction from the act of volunteering and the associated processes of relationship building with others; 'extrinsic' satisfaction from the results of volunteering; and the relatedly, psychic benefits, or gains in self-esteem and respect.

Obviously, pro-volunteering state policies and funding programmes may directly or indirectly help or hinder organizations' capacity to recruit and retain volunteers. But there are numerous other ways in which social policy connects with volunteering. For example, formal education policy and other educative experiences are relevant, because socialization experiences seem to impact on people's basic disposition to volunteer. Attitudes towards volunteering – and the character of opportunities to get involved – also seem to be systematically related to ethnicity, gender, and social class, and the nature of paid work and domestic sphere commitments all seem to shape individuals' willingness and ability to get involved in volunteering.

Emerging Issues

At the time of writing, the UK coalition government has high expectations that the voluntary sector can help define, construct, and defend the 'Big Society'. This term is both vague and unfamiliar. But at the most basic level is simply meant to demarcate the ideological claim that civil society, including voluntary action, can in general really flourish only in the absence of 'Big Government', which is equated in this way of thinking with over-bureaucratization, inauthenticity, intrusiveness, and inflexible policy implementation.

Accordingly, it is suggested the role of the state should be curtailed and in some fields subjected to draconian cuts, on the assumption that its interventions tend to be inherently counterproductive and are a drain on national resources: civil society can and should step in to 'fill the gap'. The idea, therefore, seems to be to retain the 'mainstreaming' emphasis of the previous administration, but to do so on the assumption that to draw out voluntary welfare's progressive potential, a self-censoring state should take a massive step back.

An ever higher public policy profile – and the greater state proximity it is bringing – raises a range of concerns about the sector's autonomy, identity, and social functioning. Marxist writers (and some influenced by the Foucauldian tradition, as well as those on the Right in principle hostile to state intervention in all its forms – see Part II) tend to read this trend deterministically or fatalistically. For them, it is necessarily leading to voluntary organizations' 'incorporation', 'co-option', or 'subordination'. However, those working from other analytic perspectives consider the issue of how state and third sector can and do co-evolve as an empirical question. As stressed before there are necessarily severe limits to generalization here because of the sector's diversity in terms of, *inter alia*, size, substantive policy field, ideologies, level of engagement with

the state, and so forth. However, we can perhaps highlight two key questions that commentators on policy in the years ahead will need to keep at the forefront of their analysis.

First, how inherited and new voluntary sector policies play out in practice – at the level of *front-line implementation* – from the perspective of the relevant organizations, and their stakeholders – not least, users/beneficiaries, and volunteers. Rhetorical acknowledgement has reached, or is close to, saturation point: what matters is the extent to which claims of policy supportiveness are followed through into concrete practice. As their relations with government get closer, are assertions, that these organizations and those involved with them will be given room to breathe and even flourish, being respected? The research to date is mixed on this point, especially in relation to the fractious financial dimension, and a very close eye will need to be kept on how the process pans out in the years ahead.

Second, are any relevant policies – including front-line practices evolving in a *balanced* way? Are institutions and relations taking shape which respect the *range* of functions and diversity of roles we have identified? Perhaps the key challenge is to ensure that the drive to increase the sector's role in public service delivery does not undermine its functioning in other dimensions – including social change oriented campaigning and community development contributions.

Guide to Further Sources

H. K. Anheier, *Nonprofit Organizations: Theory, Management, Policy* (London: Routledge, 2005) is a stimulating and attractive textbook for relatively advanced students while D. Billis and H. Glennerster's 'Human services and the voluntary sector: Towards a theory of comparative advantage', *Journal of Social Policy*, 27/1 (1998): 79–98 is still relevant, drawing on economic and organization theory to interpret the role of the sector in mid-1990s British social policy, with an emphasis on social exclusion. S. Bridge, B. Murtagh, and K. O'Neill, *Understanding the Social Economy and the Third Sector* (Basingstoke: Palgrave Macmillan, 2009), offer a more descriptive account than Anheier's, but draws a range of otherwise fragmented materials into a reasonably coherent whole. A. Evers and J.-L. Laville (eds), *The Third Sector in Europe* (Cheltenham: Edward Elgar, 2003) provides a wide ranging, rich, intriguing – although sometimes polemically anti-American overview.

J. Kendall, *The Voluntary Sector: Comparative Perspectives in the UK* (London, Routledge, 2003) is still the most systematic and up-to-date analytical account available on Britain, with a focus on the situation in England. It builds on J. Kendall and M. Knapp (1996) *The Voluntary Sector in the UK* (Manchester: Manchester University Press, 1996) (the first systematic attempt to put the United Kingdom in comparative context). W. W. Powell (ed.); and Powell, W.W. and Steinberg, R. (eds), *The Nonprofit Sector: A Research Handbook* (Yale: Yale University Press, 1st edn, 1987; 2nd edn, 2006) both editions are widely regarded as the 'bibles' of research on nonprofits in the United States. Anyone interested in social capital also needs to read, moving from the sub-national, to the national and international, R. Putnam's *Making Democracy Work* (Princeton NJ: Princeton University Press, 1993); *Bowling Alone* (New York: Simon & Schuster, 2000); and *Democracies in Flux* (Oxford: Oxford University Press, 2002). D. Halpern, *Social Capital* (Cambridge: Polity Press, 2005) is a useful UK-based compendium.

Governmental web sources are subject to change, but the best place to start is www.cabinetoffice.gov.uk/voluntary-sector.aspx. For current policy developments, briefing papers, debates and research the most helpful starter sites are www.ncvo-vol.org.uk (the web site of the main co-ordinating body for the English voluntary sector, the NCVO), www.tsrc.ac.uk/ (the site of the Third Sector Research Centre), and www.vssn.org.uk (that of the Voluntary Sector Studies Network: the primary UK academic and research association) and the *Social Policy Digest*, http://journals.cambridge.org.spd/action/home.

Review Questions

1 How do the concepts 'voluntary sector' and 'civil society' relate to one another?
2 What are the most important distinctions we should make between 'types' of voluntary welfare?
3 Why is the debate on social capital now so relevant to voluntary sector policy?
4 Does state action tend to help or hinder volunteering?
5 What are the main policy implications of the 'Bio society' agenda for the voluntary sector?

Visit the book companion site at www.wiley.com/go/alcock to make use of the resources designed to accompany the textbook. There you will find chapter-specific guides to further resources, including governmental, international, think-tank, pressure groups, and relevant journals sources. You will also find a glossary based on *The Blackwell Dictionary of Social Policy*, help sheets, and case studies, guidance on managing assignments in social policy and career advice.

34

Informal Welfare

Hilary Arksey and Caroline Glendinning

■■

Overview

- Informal care refers to care provided over and above the normal support that friends or family members give each other as a matter of course.
- Caregiving can have negative impacts on carers' physical health and emotional well-being.
- Carers can find it difficult to combine paid work with caring, but giving up employment, or reducing the number of hours worked, can have negative impacts on finances and future work prospects.
- Government policies to support carers have had only limited impact.
- The future supply of informal carers may be inadequate to support an ageing population.

■■

Informal Welfare and Informal Care

As well as services funded by the welfare state, a large number of organizations and individuals provide 'welfare', in its broadest sense, as can be seen in other chapters in Part V. An even more significant source of non-state welfare is the help given by relatives, friends, and neighbours. This help is often called 'informal' as it derives from the family and other types of relationships between individuals.

Specifically, 'informal care' describes the help given to ill, disabled, and older people by friends and relatives, as distinct from that given as part of a paid job such as nurse, care worker, or home help. Informal care refers to care provided over and above the normal support that friends or family members give each other as a matter of

The Student's Companion to Social Policy, Fourth Edition. Edited by Pete Alcock, Margaret May, Sharon Wright.
© 2012 John Wiley & Sons, Ltd. Published 2012 by John Wiley & Sons, Ltd.

course. It can involve direct 'hands on' help, including

- personal or physical care – help with bathing, toileting, managing medication, feeding, getting in and out of bed, mobility;
- other practical help – shopping, cooking, cleaning; and
- keeping someone company or making sure they avoid danger.

Another common aspect of informal care is 'managerial care'; this includes completing application forms, managing money, seeking information, discussing and arranging services for or on behalf of the disabled or older person.

Carers of disabled or older people have different experiences and needs to people with child-care responsibilities. For example, people undertaking elder care tend to be older than those bringing up children and at different stages in their employment careers and life cycle. They may not live in the same house as the person they are looking after. Informal care is less predictable than child-care; the care recipient's condition may fluctuate or deteriorate over time; and, particularly where older people are concerned, care commitments are likely to increase rather than decrease.

The support provided by informal carers is increasingly important – indeed, they are the main source of help for older people in all developed societies and carers save the United Kingdom an estimated £87 billion per year by providing unpaid care at home. But, despite carers' significant role, it is only relatively recently that this form of welfare has been recognized by the state and reflected in policy measures.

Informal Carers: Who Are They?

For the first time ever, the 2001 census asked whether citizens cared for someone who was sick, disabled, or elderly. It found that there are nearly six million carers in the United Kingdom – around 12 per cent of the adult population. Of those, 1.9 and 1.25 million people provide care for more than twenty hours and more than fifty hours per week respectively. Research suggests that three in five people will become a carer at some point in their lives. Women have a 50 per cent chance of providing care by the time they are fifty-nine, men by the time they are seventy-four.

Although people in their fifties are most likely to be providing care, as the population ages so numbers of older informal carers are also increasing. The 2001 census found that in the United Kingdom there are over 1.5 million people aged over sixty providing unpaid care. Over 8,000 carers are aged ninety and over; some 4,000 of these very elderly carers provide more than fifty hours of care per week. Older carers are often in poor health themselves. They are usually living with, and caring for, a partner, especially male carers. At the other extreme, the census showed that in the United Kingdom there were at least 175,000 children and young persons under the age of eighteen with caregiving responsibilities, just over 13,000 of whom cared for more than fifty hours per week.

Traditionally caring has been thought of as a female responsibility, and, overall, women are slightly more likely than men to be carers. However, after the age of seventy-five men outnumber women as carers and with advancing years are more likely than women to become carers.

Many carers also have paid work; about one in eight adults working full-time is a carer, as are 17 per cent of part-time working adults. Female carers are more likely than male carers to work part time. Not surprisingly, the risks of carers working fewer hours or not at all increase with the number of hours providing care. The incidence of caring is highest among unemployed or economically inactive working age adults, of whom 21 per cent are also carers. However, it is not clear how far people give up paid work because of care commitments or become carers because they are already economically inactive, perhaps because of their own poor health.

The poorer health of people from minority ethnic communities suggests that there is likely to be a greater demand for informal care among these communities. Difficulties in accessing culturally appropriate health and social services may also increase the demands on ethnic minority carers, who are also more likely to experience poverty, poor housing, lack of information, and social isolation.

The Consequences of Caring

Carers experience many of the disadvantages that contribute to social exclusion, including isolation; difficulty in obtaining help for their own health problems; and problems in obtaining other services to help them provide care. Without adequate support, caring can harm carers' health, particularly their mental health and well-being. The risks to carers' health increase with the intensity (amount of time each week) and duration (length of time) of caregiving. Nevertheless, many also report emotional rewards from being able to help someone they feel close to.

Carers who give up paid work, reduce their hours of work or are prevented from following career opportunities lose out financially compared with non-carers. Their earnings are likely to be lower than average, particularly if they spend more than twenty hours a week caring. Caring often involves extra costs (for example on transport, laundry, heating, special food, or equipment), so savings can be depleted. Welfare benefits for carers do not make up for loss of earnings. Breaks in employment or low earnings are also likely to reduce carers' pension entitlements and increase the risk of poverty in their own old age, particularly for women.

Policies to Support Carers

Carers' issues rose on the policy agenda through the successful campaigning of carers' organizations such as Carers UK and the Princess Royal Trust for Carers. Since 1995, a series of initiatives have been introduced to improve information, advice, and services for carers (see Box 34.1) and following devolution in 1999 the different countries making up the United Kingdom have followed broadly similar policies for carers, centring on assessing carer's needs, having a break from caregiving, access to/support for training and employment, and financial help for carers

Assessing carers' needs

The 1995 Carers (Recognition and Services) Act gave eligible carers entitlement to an assessment of their circumstances and needs arising from their caregiving role. Under the Carers and

> **Box 34.1   Policy Landmarks for Carers***
>
> 1995 Carers (Recognition and Services) Act.
> 1999 National Strategy for Carers.
> 2000 Carers and Disabled Children Act.
> 2004 Carers (Equal Opportunities) Act.
> 2007 Standing Commission on Carers.
> 2008 Revised National Strategy for Carers.
> 2010 Review of National Strategy for Carers.
>
> * Because health and social services became a devolved matter in 1999, some of these policy measures relate to England (or England and Wales) only.

Disabled Children Act 2000, carers' rights to have an assessment were strengthened but assessment practice and the provision of information to carers did not appear to improve significantly. The 2004 Carers (Equal Opportunities) Act had even wider ambitions, aiming to reduce the many disadvantages experienced by carers compared with non-carers. When assessing carers' needs, local authorities are obliged to consider their aspirations to participate in paid work, education, training or leisure, and must provide appropriate information, advice, and support. The 2010 review of the National Carers Strategy emphasized a whole family approach to assessment, noting that carers found accessing assessments overly bureaucratic and slow, and that they were often disappointed about the inadequacy of any subsequent service provision.

Having a break from caregiving

Having regular breaks from caregiving is crucial in helping carers to continue in their caregiving role (if that is their wish). The 1999 National Strategy for Carers introduced the Carers Special Grant, which comprised £140 million over three years for local authorities to develop innovative and flexible services to give carers a break. The 2008 revised Carers Strategy included an increase of £150 million in the amount of money available for breaks. In 2010, the UK coalition government pledged £400 million additional funding over four years for carers' breaks as part of its vision for adult social care.

Access to/support for training and employment

Many carers combine work and care but, as noted earlier, this can prove challenging and flexible working arrangements are essential for many carers to remain in paid work. The flexible working regulations included in the 2002 Employment Act gave parents of disabled children under the age of eighteen the right to request flexible working from their employer. In April 2007, this entitlement was extended to eligible carers of adults and older people; the 2010 review of the Carers Strategy included a commitment to consult on extending flexible working rights to all employees, which would benefit those carers currently not entitled to this right.

Carers can also benefit from the right of all employees to take a 'reasonable' amount of (unpaid) time off to deal with an emergency involving a dependent. A landmark decision in 2008 by the European Court of Justice in the case of Sharon Coleman, the mother of a disabled child, means that carers should have legal protection from 'discrimination by association' with disability. However carers have no entitlement to an extended period of leave to care, or to pay during that leave (although they may be able to claim Carers Allowance – see below – if they have no other income). The 2008 revised Carers Strategy did however recognize the difficulties that carers face in returning to the labour market after a period of full-time caregiving. One initiative to improve carers' access to employment and training was an investment of up to £38 million in employment services to help carers find paid work. The review of the Carers Strategy included a strong emphasis on working with employers to better support staff with caring responsibilities.

Financial help for carers

The United Kingdom is relatively unusual in providing a social security benefit directly to eligible carers. Carer's Allowance (originally called Invalid Care Allowance) was introduced for full-time

carers who have only minimal income from other sources. In February 2008, there were just under 508,500 people receiving Carer's Allowance in the United Kingdom, the vast majority of who were working-age women. Although it is very low, carers do have direct entitlement to it, in contrast to some other countries such as Germany, where carers risk being financially dependent on the person they care for.

However, Carer's Allowance remains one of the lowest benefits in the UK social security system. It provides only token replacement of the incomes lost when carers have to give up paid employment and, because of its stringent eligibility criteria, it does not encourage carers to combine work and care. Carers who spend long periods out of work altogether risk poverty in their own old age as only their minimum state pension entitlement is protected. Its low level and inflexibility have been consistently criticized over the years.

Under the 2000 Carers and Disabled Children Act, for the first time carers could receive services in their own right, or a cash 'direct payment' for themselves as carers. Direct payments offer more control and flexibility than services; for instance, carers can use them to pay for taxi fares, gym membership, training courses, help with gardening or housework. However, the number of carers receiving direct payments remains low and there are major variations between local authorities in the numbers receiving direct payments and the levels of those payments.

Key Issues and Debates

There are major questions about the adequacy and appropriateness of current policies to support carers. While the United Kingdom remains ahead of many countries, carers nevertheless remain at high risk of stress, poor health, social isolation, and poverty in both the shorter and longer terms.

Who should be supported: Disabled and older people or informal carers?

Opinion is divided as to who should be the primary target of policy – carers or disabled and older people themselves? The original (1998) National Strategy for Carers stated that 'helping carers is one of the best ways of helping the people they care for'. Practitioners and policy-makers may assume that the needs and interests of carers and the people they support are the same and can therefore be addressed by the same policies and services.

However, as public awareness of carers has increased, organizations of disabled people have argued that this overlooks *their* rights for choice, control, and self-determination. Indeed, disabled people have argued that the very terms 'care' and 'carer' imply dependency and that disabled people are a 'burden' and are less able to make choices for themselves (see Chapter 40). Moreover, a policy focus on carers has been criticized for failing to recognize the reciprocity that underpins many caregiving relationships; many disabled adults and older people also care for others at the same time as needing support with their own personal and daily activities.

Research shows that providing services for disabled and older people is the most effective way of supporting carers, because it reduces the pressures on family and friends. At the same time, replacing some of the help provided by informal carers with formal services does not necessarily reduce the support provided by relatives and friends, though it may change the nature of that support. In Scotland, increases in funding for per-sonal care services for older people have enabled carers to concentrate on providing social support, such as keeping relatives company and taking them out, rather than undertaking mundane tasks or intrusive intimate care; extra services for the older person have also helped carers to sustain caregiving for longer (see Chapter 42).

Models of informal care in policy and practice

It has been suggested that policies and health and social care professionals respond to carers accord-ing to one of four models (Box 34.2).

A fifth model has now been proposed: 'carers as experts'. In this model, carers are seen as equal partners with health and social care professionals and an integral part of the team working to support the care recipient. The 'carer as expert' model was strongly emphasized in the revised (2008) Carers Strategy, and the review of the Strategy (2010) continues this theme.

Box 34.2 Models of Informal Care

Carer as 'resource'	Main focus on care recipient. Carers treated instrumentally, as a 'taken-for-granted' resource; promotion of carer well-being is only important if it sustains caregiving.
Carer as 'co-worker'	Carers' interests and well-being are given some attention, although the care recipient remains the central focus of attention.
Carer as 'co-client'	Carers' interests and well-being are valued outcomes, and support is provided aimed at making caring easier for carers to manage.
'Superseded' carer	Services to meet all the care recipient's needs are provided, which eliminates the need for informal care.

Emerging Issues

Population ageing is a global phenomenon; most countries in the West are experiencing decreasing fertility and increasing longevity, leading to a shift in age structures (see Chapter 21). Governments worldwide are concerned about whether in future the supply of informal care will keep pace with rising demand. A number of factors affect the future supply of informal care:

■ Population ageing also affects carers them-selves: whether or not older people are able to support their partners and very elderly parents depends upon their own state of health.
■ Adult children are less likely to live with their elderly parents than in previous generations. Although there is no evidence that they are less likely to care, they are less likely to be

able to provide intensive personal care from a distance.

■ Changing attitudes may lead potential carers to want to avoid the restrictions of caregiving.

■ Disabled and older people may also demand greater choice and control over who supports them, with, therefore, the option of receiving help from informal carers or formal services.

■ Changing family patterns – divorce and remarriage – may blur traditional family obligations and responsibilities.

It has been claimed that informal care is essential for the overall sustainability of long-term care. However, based on current patterns, the future supply of informal care is likely to fall short of increases in demand. Modelling projections of likely demands for long-term care services in England for people aged sixty-five or over suggests that spouse carers are likely to become increasingly important. This raises issues about their support needs, given that spouse carers are often elderly and in poor health themselves.

Another growing area of debate is how to resolve the tensions between growing demands for informal care and the demands of the labour market. The peak age for providing informal care is forty-five to sixty-four years; many carers (including women) are therefore in paid work when older relatives begin to need substantial help. Carers who stop work do not currently receive adequate income maintenance benefits, adequate protection of their future pension entitlements, or targeted help to return to work once caring commitments cease. The Carers (Equal Opportunities) Act 2004 requires practitioners to consider carers' wishes relating to training and paid work when conducting assessments. There is still a long way to go before social services practitioners recognize the importance of carers' participation in paid work and are able to offer appropriate services that are acceptable to both the carer and the person needing support.

Personalization, whereby social and health care are tailored to people's individual needs, is a key government priority for all client groups, including carers and is also likely to become a key issue. It may relate to both the support provided to the disabled/older person and to the support provided to the carer. Given that personalization

is about giving people more choice and control over their lives, it is important that service providers give due attention to the desired outcomes of both parties – and these might not be the same. Carers' assessments, and having choice about their own support, will have important roles to play in ensuring that carers can maintain a life beyond their caring responsibilities.

The 2010 Comprehensive Spending Review saw an increase of £2 billion for social care, however, the impact for carers is unclear given the removal of ring-fencing and reductions to local authority budgets. The reductions in public spending are likely to have a major impact on carers as services for older and disabled people are cut and eligibility criteria are raised.

Guide to Further Sources

H. Arksey and C. Glendinning, 'Choice in the context of informal caregiving', *Health and Social Care in the Community*, 15/2 (2007): 165–75, review evidence about carers' opportunities for choice. L. Pickard (2004) *The Effectiveness and Cost-effectiveness of Support and Services to Informal Carers of Older People* (published online 2004) www.pssru.ac.uk/pdf/dp2014.pdf considers the evidence about 'what works' for carers of older people) and M. Hirst, *Health Inequalities and Informal Care*, Social Policy Research Unit: University of York (published online 2004), www.york.ac.uk/inst/spru/pubs/pdf/healthinequalities.pdf), looks at the impact of providing care on carers' health.

The NHS Information Centre for Health and Social Care's *Survey of Carers in Households in England 2009/10*, Survey of Carers in Households – 2009/10 England – Provisional Results (published online 2010), presents national results on the extent and nature of caring and the number of carers in England. Previously, this research was conducted at five-yearly intervals between 1985 and 2000 as part of the General Household Survey (GHS), http://tinyurl.com/carers-in-households. An analysis of the factors affecting future demand for, and supply of, informal care for older people can be found in L. Pickard *et al.*, 'Care by spouses, care by children: projections of informal care for older people in England to 2031', *Social Policy and Society*, 6/3 (2007): 353–66.

The best 'starter' electronic resources are: www.direct.gov.uk/en/CaringForSomeone/index.htm, www.nhs.uk/Carersdirect/Pages/CarersDirectHome.aspx, and www.carersuk.org.

Review Questions

1 To what extent are women and men of different ages affected by informal caring?
2 What factors should individuals contemplating whether or not to take on a caring role consider in their decision-making?
3 What is the relationship between models of caregiving and support for caregivers?
4 What is the appropriate balance between family and state responsibilities for support-

ing disabled and older people and how far have successive governments got that balance right?
5 Why is it necessary to give equal consideration to the choices and rights of carers and those of the people they are looking after?

Visit the book companion site at www.wiley.com/go/alcock to make use of the resources designed to accompany the textbook. There you will find chapter-specific guides to further resources, including governmental, international, think-tank, pressure groups, and relevant journals sources. You will also find a glossary based on *The Blackwell Dictionary of Social Policy*, help sheets, and case studies, guidance on managing assignments in social policy and career advice.

35

Paying for Welfare

Howard Glennerster

Overview

- Some of the reasons why we have come to pay for many of the most important things in life through collective state funding lie in the economic theory of market failure.
- Another reason lies in the spread of our needs throughout the life cycle.
- How we pay for these services matters not just in terms of how the burden falls on rich and poor but in taxation's impact on efficiency in the wider economy. How welfare institutions are funded also affects their own efficiency.
- Many welfare services are paid for privately both in cash and in time spent by carers.
- Governments are using new ways to respond to the challenge of an ageing population, rising expectations of service standards, and growing reluctance to pay through taxation.

Who Pays Matters

None of the ideals discussed elsewhere in this volume are attainable unless the means to achieve them are paid for by someone. Meeting socially defined needs, through some kind of welfare state, or providing for the care and education of those in one's own family, costs money. Who pays and how is of central importance to every family.

If we have a generous set of public services and yet we pay for them by imposing heavy taxes on the poor we are not helping but crippling them. If the way we tax people or means test them is a big disincentive to work or save that too is inefficient. If you, as a graduate of social policy, go to work in a human service agency, the first thing you will become aware of is its budget limit and the resources you have available to do a decent

The Student's Companion to Social Policy, Fourth Edition. Edited by Pete Alcock, Margaret May, Sharon Wright.
© 2012 John Wiley & Sons, Ltd. Published 2012 by John Wiley & Sons, Ltd.

professional task. How do schools get their cash, or hospitals or social service organizations? Your working life will not make much sense unless you can answer these questions.

What Are We Paying For?

Other contributors to this volume have discussed what social policy means in general terms. For our purposes we define it as the allocation of scarce resources necessary to human existence and well-being. We are not concerned with the economics of video recorders – at least not yet! Of course, the notion of exactly what is a basic necessity changes over time and between societies. The dilemmas about paying for the costs of such needs are, however, universal.

In this chapter we are concerned with the costs of ensuring that no one falls below an acceptable minimum standard of living, that citizens have an adequate diet, shelter, education, and health care. We are concerned to ensure that those who can no longer look after themselves because of old age or infirmity are adequately cared for. How we pay for those ideals is one of the central political and economic debates of our time.

Market failure

There is no intrinsic reason why any of these services should not be purchased by individuals for themselves, if they have the money. All are purchased privately by the rich. Many economists argue that the state should confine itself to giving poor people enough money to exist and should cease to provide such services itself. There are, however, some basic characteristics of human needs and the services that meet them that mean that they are not well suited to individual purchases in the market place. We cannot buy clean air in bottles and consume it as a private product. If the air is clean it will be enjoyed by the whole population of our own and other countries. This 'non-excludability' is characteristic of what economists call a 'public' or 'social' good. Where goods and services are like this we say that markets fail.

Nevertheless, such public goods are not free. We pay for the cost of clean air regulations in the price of goods produced in factories that have to install filters and burn smokeless fuels.

While some aspects of social policy concern the production of public goods such as clean air which cannot be produced without state action others do not. We can certainly buy medical care or education if we have the money. But we may make inefficient choices as private consumers since the information we need to buy our own medical care efficiently is not readily available. There is an inherent imbalance of information between seller and buyer. Economists call this a problem of information failure.

Furthermore, the item we may want to buy is so far in the distance that we find it difficult to take it seriously or do it at all. Worrying about our future care in an old persons' home is a good example. How many of us are exercised about that in our youth? Pensions are another, slightly different, example. People put off taking action even if they know that theoretically they should take out a private pension. This kind of market failure, studied in the new behavioural economics, is discussed in the first report of the UK Pensions Commission (2004).

Market failure, information failure, and 'behavioural' failure between them explain why, in most of the world, many human services are provided and paid for, not through ordinary private markets but through collective means of funding – taxes, insurance contributions and the like, or through compelling private action. Requiring or strongly encouraging membership of a private pension scheme is an example of the latter. None of this, notice, is a logic driven by the motive of being nice to poor people. This argument for state intervention is that it is more efficient in these special cases.

Savings bank

We collectively pay for such services for another reason too. Many things we need, such as education for our children, a new home for the family, health care, and pensions, cannot be financed very readily at exactly the time we want them. When we are ill we have little, or possibly no, income to pay high health care costs. Education and housing are very expensive and demand payment early in a family's existence before it has had time to amass sufficient savings. Only if the family has rich parents, a secure inheritance, or a secure asset like a house, will banks lend it the money to pay the bills now and repay later.

So the market may make it possible for some families to borrow now to pay later for expensive necessities but will not do so for most people and certainly not for the poor. This is called a 'capital market failure'. This is particularly important in the case of education. An able student with poor parents will not be able to get a bank loan. Her human capital will not be developed to its full extent in the absence of a loan and this too is inefficient as well as unjust. This is the case for the state to make such a loan.

Part of what social policy is doing, therefore, is to shift the time at which people pay for the services they need from periods when they cannot pay to times when they can. Social policy is acting like a lifetime savings bank much more than a simple transfer to the poor (Falkingham and Hills 1995).

Who Pays?

Despite the natural focus on public tax-financed social services in this volume, many of the human services included in social policy's remit are paid for directly out of individuals' own earnings or by private borrowing or insurance policies. In addition to this form of private welfare, firms may provide their employees with pension schemes or health care. Titmuss (1958) called this 'occupational welfare' (see Chapter 32).

Research in the 1990s calculated how much of the total costs of welfare were paid for in these different ways (Burchardt, Hills, and Propper 1999). It turns out that 40 per cent of the nation's income is spent on the broad purposes of providing human services – the long-term care of dependent elderly, health, education, pensions, and housing. Even this does not cover items not included in the nation's accounts: the care provided by a family for its own members (discussed in Chapter 34).

Of the total 'welfare activity', defined above, roughly 70 per cent is funded by the state out of taxation. That figure varies enormously between services. Roughly 70 per cent of the costs of housing are paid directly by individuals, but only 20 per cent of education and 15 per cent of health costs. This leaves a very large sum to be paid out

of taxes! More than a quarter of everyone's income has to be taxed away to pay for these services or cash benefits.

Unusually among advanced industrialized countries, the United Kingdom relies overwhelmingly on taxes raised by the *national* government to pay for its social services. Less than 5 per cent of government revenue is funded by taxes raised by local government – the council tax. Health and social security are directly provided by central government agencies in one form or another. But housing, education, and personal social services are not and there has to be a complex system of grants that rechannels the taxes raised by central government to pay local councils to provide them.

This already complex pattern was complicated further with the devolution of many social policy responsibilities to the devolved administrations and assemblies in Scotland, Wales, and Northern Ireland. These receive a block grant from Westminster to fund their devolved powers. They in turn pass them on to local governments in their areas. The Scottish Assembly has power to levy its own addition to the national income tax but has not yet used this power. Changes to the Barnett funding formula and the case for devolving more taxing powers to these devolved bodies have been made by various commissions and by the political parties concerned (see Chapter 42).

Government may tax some individuals less heavily to encourage a particular form of saving for retirement, house purchase, or giving to charity. Economists call these flows *tax expenditures*. Titmuss (1958) called this '*fiscal welfare*' (see Chapter 36).

Who Decides?

Her Majesty's Treasury is the central government department responsible for advising the Cabinet as to how much the economy can afford to be allocated to public programmes and it masterminds the complex round of negotiations between the spending departments that determine how much is to be available to, for example, the health service or universities.

Major decisions about which service gets what are taken as part of a Comprehensive Spending Review. These decisions, approved by Cabinet and Parliament, determine how much the NHS, universities, schools, and local authorities will receive. The Review published in the autumn of 2010 set the limits for public spending for the next five years.

Local councils now get a grant which must be spent on schools and a general grant which they can spend on any of their services. They also receive small specific grants which are tied to particular smaller services. What they are permitted to raise additionally from the council tax is heavily constrained by government rules. That tax is based on the value of property owned in the area. The basis of local taxation has always been politically controversial, never more than the poll tax when Margaret Thatcher was prime minister. The whole basis of local finance has been reviewed recently by the Lyons Inquiry in England and the Burt Committee in Scotland.

The Westminster government allocates money to English local health authorities and does so on the basis of a population-based formula which gives an area more money if it has more elderly or ill or poor people, because they use health services more. The Scottish, Welsh, and Northern Irish governments do the same.

Required or Encouraged Behaviour

Government can seek to encourage private individuals to act in ways that provide for their own welfare – to buy a house or save for their own pension. They have traditionally done so by giving tax relief to those who take out mortgages – no longer the case in the United Kingdom – or they reduce taxes if you invest in a private pension. The Labour government with cross-party support following the Pension Commission introduced another kind of incentive to get people to save for their retirement. We saw that young people are reluctant to take the initiative and save for retirement because the investment decisions are complex and retirement seems a long way away. However, evidence from other countries suggests that if employees are automatically opted into a private pension scheme, and if employers are required to add to those contributions, and government supplements them, then most people will not take steps to opt out. That, at least, is the

hope that lay behind the latest pension plans (see Chapters 32 and 56)

Vouchers and Quasi-vouchers

So far we have described the way grants are allocated to local authorities and then on to bodies like schools and hospitals. Some economists argue that these institutions are more likely to work efficiently if users have some sanction over them – the chance to choose another provider (see Chapter 19). It is important to recognize that giving state schools, or hospitals, money on the basis of the number of children or patients they attract as now happens in England is already a form of voucher – a 'quasi-voucher' system.

Giving

Individuals give large sums of money and time to voluntary organizations, and statutory ones too, helping to visit old people or run youth clubs. Giving cash attracts tax relief but giving time does not. In his classic study of blood donation, Titmuss (1970) showed how giving blood to the National Blood Transfusion Service without compensation was not only a tangible example of individuals contributing to a larger social whole and enriching that society in the process, but also turned out to be a more efficient process because donors had no incentive to lie about their medical history. If blood donors were paid for their 'gift' there would be more risk of infected blood entering the system and people would have more of an incentive to lie about their medical history. Feminist writers (see Chapters 12 and 34) have made us much more aware of the scale of giving that takes place within the family when women, and to a lesser extent men, undertake caring tasks. The personal social services budget would need to double if we were to pay women for these duties.

Rationing

We have seen that the Treasury essentially sets the limits to public spending on the social services, under political direction of course! The result is that the supply of these services is fixed by political decisions. Yet these services are free, or at least partly free. Prices cannot rise to levels that will equate demand with supply. The result is that service providers have to take some action to set priorities and ration care. As is also discussed in Chapter 37 this may take the form of rules and entitlement to benefit, or judgements made by professional staff working to fixed budgets.

Rationing of scarce social policy resources thus takes place in a whole range of decisions, which descend from fairly explicit judgements made by the Cabinet about what each service shall receive through explicit allocations on a formula basis to areas and, indeed, to institutions like schools. But these are followed by front-line and less explicit judgements about which child in a class or which social work client gets most of the worker's attention (Glennerster 2009).

Emerging Issues

For the past decade the share of the nation's income being devoted to social policy has been rising sharply (see Figure 35.1 and Table 35.1). This was aggravated by the recent recession but the underlying drivers were deep seated and set to grow in importance. The Labour government from 1997 to 2010 responded by increasing social spending but did not have the courage to raise taxes enough to compensate. The response of the UK coalition government elected in 2010 has been to announce big cuts in planned spending in its Comprehensive Spending Review (HM Treasury 2010). Figure 35.1 and Table 35.1 show an estimate of the scale of the cuts. However, the underlying pressures will grow and long- term measures are necessary to meet them or further regular cuts will follow. Some attempts to restructure the way we pay for our welfare state are underway and are crucial for its future.

The number of people over the traditional retirement age is rising faster than the number of families of working age. People are spending a growing proportion of their adult lives in retirement. The cost of providing health and social care for the over seventies and especially eighties is much higher than for younger age groups. The costs will fall increasingly on those of working age. This could add more than 5 per cent of GDP

to the cost of the welfare state without any improvement in standards.

As a response the Pensions Commission (2005) recommended that the length of working life should rise in line with life expectancy so that the percentage of our lives we spend in retirement should remain constant. The UK coalition government has speeded up the timing of this move. But it has also accepted the Turner Committee proposals encourage private pension saving.

A commission has been appointed chaired by Andrew Dilnot to consider new ways to fund long-term care of older people (see Chapter 51). This will become a major focus of debate.

The very small amount of local funding from locally raised taxes in the United Kingdom compared to other countries will come under scrutiny as will the form of that local taxation and the funding of social policies now devolved to Scotland, Wales, and Northern Ireland.

The Browne Review (2010) on the funding of higher education and its broad acceptance by the UK coalition government will shift most of the burden of tuition costs onto graduates away from the general taxpayer. That will be another long running debate (see Chapter 49). In short, how we pay for our welfare state is going to be at the heart of politics for the next decade.

Guide to Further Sources

T. Burchardt, J. Hills, and C. Propper, *Private Welfare and Public Policy* (York: Joseph Rowntree Foundation, 1999) covers some of the key issues addressed in this chapter in more detail especially the complex ways in which public and private funding and provision interact. J. Falkingham and J. Hills, *The Dynamics of Welfare* (London: Harvester Wheatsheaf, 1995) shows how and why the welfare state redistributes income through the lifetime. H. Glennerster, *Understanding the Finance of Welfare. What Welfare Costs and How to Pay for It* (Bristol: Policy Press, 2009) covers all aspects of the finance of social policy and theories of rationing. It summarizes the theoretical economic literature and describes the practical ways in which each of the social services receives its funding in the United Kingdom. It includes comparative material.

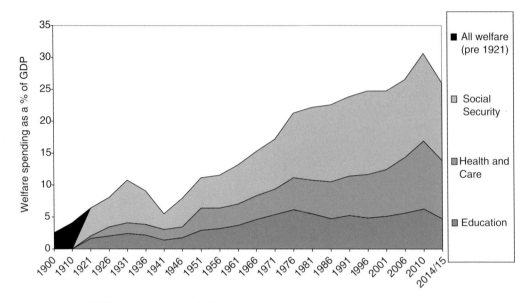

Figure 35.1 Welfare spending[a] in the United Kingdom, 1900–2015.
Sources: Glennerster 2007; HM Treasury 2010 Public Expenditure Statistical Analysis, Comprehensive Spending Review, and Office of Budget Responsibility Report November 2010.

Table 35.1 Welfare spending[a] in the United Kingdom, 1986–2015.

	1986	1996	2008/9	2010[b]	2014/15[c]
Education inc HE	4.8	4.9	5.8	6.3	4.8
Health and social care	5.7	6.8	9.5	10.6	9.1
Social Security (incl. housing benefit)	12.1	13.1	12.4	13.7	12.1
All welfare spending	22.6	24.9	27.7	30.6	26.0

[a] This includes the old Poor Law, modern social security, housing benefit and its predecessors. From 1987 some small items are included from agencies like the criminal justice system. They formed 0.5% of GDP in 1987. Social care spending has been removed from the official figures on social protection and added to health care for consistency with previous figures. Housing capital is excluded.
[b] Recession impact.
[c] Assumes a 5% increase per annum in cash GDP and takes cash limits for spending in the 2010 Spending Review. Assumes Scotland Wales and NI keep to English growth rates. Lower growth or inflation would revise the percentage figures up and vice versa. Education includes higher education.
Sources: Glennerster (2007); HM Treasury 2010 Public Expenditure Statistical Analysis, Comprehensive Spending Review, and Office of Budget Responsibility Report November 2010.

The Burt Inquiry 2006 in Scotland and the Lyons Inquiry in England 2007 and papers done for them contain a useful history of local government finance in both countries www.national archives.gov.uk. Richard Morris Titmuss, *The Gift Relationship* (London: Allen & Unwin, 1970), takes the giving of blood as a parable for the virtues of giving in modern societies. His *Essays on the 'Welfare State'* (London: Allen & Unwin, 1958) introduced the concepts of 'occupational' and 'fiscal' welfare. The Pensions Commission First Report, *Pensions: Challenges and Choices*

(London: The Stationery Office, 2004) and Second Report, *A New Pensions Settlement for the Twenty-First Century* (London: Stationery Office, 2005) provide the rationale for state encouraged and regulated private pension funding.

The Browne Review, *Securing a Sustainable Future for Higher Education* (published online 2010) www.independent.gov.uk/browne-report considers the issue of funding higher education. The UK coalition government's spending plans can be found in HM Treasury, *Spending Review 2010* Cm 7942 (2010). The Treasury web site provides up-to-date figures on public spending, the economy, and taxation www.hm-treasury.gov.uket.

Review Questions

1   What do we mean by market failures and which are important for explaining why social policies exist?

2   What are the major sources of cash income or other resources that make welfare services possible?

3   How does a local school get the income to pay its teachers?

4   Who decides how much public spending shall be and on what it is spent?

5   What are likely to be the major debates on paying for welfare in the next five years?

Visit the book companion site at www.wiley.com/go/alcock to make use of the resources designed to accompany the textbook. There you will find chapter-specific guides to further resources, including governmental, international, think-tank, pressure groups, and relevant journals sources. You will also find a glossary based on *The Blackwell Dictionary of Social Policy*, help sheets, and case studies, guidance on managing assignments in social policy and career advice.

36

Taxation and Welfare

Fran Bennett

Overview

- The tax system affects well-being but is often bypassed in social policy debates.
- Different kinds of taxes differ in the way they affect inequality; but, when combined with benefits and services, they redistribute towards those on lower incomes.
- Tax expenditures (tax reliefs and allowances) are a parallel form of welfare to public benefits and services that often give more to the better off.
- Taxation may be thought to affect behaviour, including work and family life.
- Taxation is about the civic contract – the relationship between citizen and state.

Background

Taxes, in the United Kingdom as elsewhere, are a compulsory payment to the state by individuals and businesses. Although commonly seen only as a 'cost' and a means of raising revenue, in practice they serve multiple (some potentially conflicting) purposes, operating as a means of

- economic policy/management;
- funding government expenditure;
- supporting particular groups in society;
- redistributing income and wealth; and

- encouraging/discouraging particular behaviours.

So taxes are not only the major means of paying for the welfare state; they also have effects as an instrument of social policy in their own right. For example, allowing people not to pay tax on certain elements of income is as much a social policy as giving them a sum of money, and may have similar effects on individuals, the economy, and society. Taxation may be designed to secure *vertical redistribution* (trying to ensure that those with more income pay a higher proportion of

My grateful thanks go to Adrian Sinfield, Emeritus Professor, Edinburgh University. *F.B.*

that income in tax) or *horizontal redistribution* (trying to equalize the tax position of people in different situations – such as by giving extra allowances for additional costs). It can also be used for alternative distributional, or other, purposes.

Social goals can thus be achieved via taxation, as well as via benefits and services; and taxation involves far more than simply taking money from individuals. Following Titmuss (1958), who first highlighted the ways in which individuals can be helped through tax allowances and reliefs, taxation can also be used as *fiscal welfare*. But it is a form of welfare that is less visible than direct services or benefit payments, and one often overlooked in public debates.

Recent developments have, however, drawn attention to the social significance of taxation, and changes in the role and structure of the tax system have become a matter of extensive discussion. Although the details of taxation may appear technical and sometimes esoteric, they are – as with social security benefits – important in understanding the social impact of what is being described.

The Tax System in the United Kingdom

The UK tax system, in common with those of other countries, is complex and subject to frequent change. The focus of political debate about tax is often on income tax. But there are also taxes on other things besides incomes – for example on property and on goods and services. Most writers distinguish between two main types of taxation: direct taxes, which include income tax on individuals and corporate taxes levied on company profits; and indirect taxes on goods and services. Depending on how they are structured, either type can be progressive (taking a higher percentage of the income of those on higher incomes); proportional (taking the same percentage); or regressive (taking a higher percentage of the income of those on lower incomes). Policy regarding these is set by HM Treasury and implemented by HM Revenue and Customs, with the Scottish government having some additional income tax raising powers.

Direct taxes

Forms of direct taxation

Income tax: which is levied on earnings and other forms of income (including some benefits) and, for most employees, is withdrawn by their employer through PAYE. Self-employed people and some others fill in annual tax returns. It is paid on income above a personal tax allowance, or threshold, which is usually increased annually at least with rising prices (in line with a rule known as the Rooker Wise amendment, after the politicians who introduced it). Since 1990, it has been levied on an individual basis for couples (rather than husbands being responsible for income tax on their wives' income). Its structure has typically included two or more tax rates: the basic rate (payable on income above the personal tax threshold) and one or more higher rates (levied on those above certain higher income thresholds). However, there has been a lower rate in addition.

National Insurance Contributions (NICs): some people argue that NICs – which are paid on earnings (but not other forms of income) by employees, employers, and the self-employed, and go towards benefits such as Retirement Pensions – should be seen as another form of income tax. Recent governments have increasingly aligned the two systems, but political and practical difficulties as well as issues of principle have, hitherto, prevented radical changes.

Taxes on savings and capital: income from savings is taxable above the personal tax threshold, unless it is saved in certain forms, though much income put into pensions is also tax-exempt. The major UK tax on wealth is inheritance tax, which is levied on estates above a certain value (with some exemptions) after someone dies. Individuals may also be liable for capital gains tax (a levy on the increase in value of certain assets when they are sold compared with when they were bought).

Local taxation: finances a proportion of local services. Currently this is the council tax, a modified property tax, which replaced the highly contentious individually based poll tax or community charge introduced by the Conservatives in the 1980s to replace the traditional property-based rates. (Businesses still pay rates, however.)

Corporation tax: a levy on company profits. Businesses can offset a range of costs and claim various tax allowances for instance, for investment – but also for pension contributions and other employee benefits, which often benefit high earners the most (see Chapter 32).

Income tax allowances and reliefs As noted above, one tax principle is that of horizontal redistribution. This can be achieved through tax exemptions, allowances or reliefs for particular groups or extra costs; but these can only be of benefit to those who are liable to pay income tax, which means that they may not be the best way to pursue certain social goals. Child Benefit, for example, replaced child tax allowances (and Family Allowances) in the late 1970s in order to pay financial support for children in a fairer way.

Before the introduction of independent taxation in 1990, married men had an additional tax allowance. More recently, the UK coalition government adopted Conservative proposals enabling a married (or civil) partner who could not use their personal allowance to transfer part of it to the other. This would probably be limited to couples with children. The argument was that, though modest, this was a symbolic recognition of the importance of marriage, held to be good for society, and particularly for children. To many, this appears, however, to be going back to the days before independent taxation, linking marriage (and now civil partnership) with the dependence of one partner on the other.

Tax reliefs have also been used to encourage other forms of behaviour, such as charitable donations (through the gift aid scheme) and, most extensively, saving. Employers' and employees' contributions towards occupational or private pensions, for example, have been exempt from tax for over eighty years (though now, for employees, only up to a ceiling). Such tax reliefs are often regressive – benefiting the better off more. In part, this is because traditionally relief has been given at the top tax rate that individuals would otherwise pay – so someone paying tax at 40 per cent would get twice what someone paying 20 per cent gets. Someone paying no tax cannot benefit at all.

Tax Credits

Tax credits differ from tax allowances in that once the total income tax bill is calculated certain amounts are deducted. Examples were the new (and possibly short-lived) tax credits introduced by Labour to 'make work pay' and integrate support for children with parents in and out of work (see Chapter 45). These tax credits were also 'refundable': if someone's award was larger than their income tax liability, they could receive the remainder as a payment. Labour argued that identifying tax credits with the income tax system meant that they were associated with paid employment, reducing stigma, and resulting in higher take-up – though in practice, it may also have contributed to a growing divide between those in and out of work. The UK coalition government plans to replace tax credits (and means-tested support for those out of work) with an amalgamated benefit called 'Universal Credit', the implications of which are still unfolding.

Indirect taxes

Indirect taxation includes *VAT* (Value Added Tax) on certain goods and services and *excise duties*, for instance on cigarettes and alcohol. Both add to the prices of the goods on which they are levied; but people may or may not buy such goods, or may buy differing amounts of them. In the United Kingdom, some goods (such as most foods) are exempt from VAT and others are zero-rated. At different times, governments have raised or lowered the standard rate of VAT and altered the balance between direct and indirect taxes. In the 1980s, the Conservatives, for instance, raised VAT and, together with their later income tax cuts, this led to a shift in the balance of direct versus indirect taxation. More recently, the UK coalition government's measures to reduce the deficit included raising VAT from 17.5 per cent to 20 per cent.

Key Debates

Tax and economic competitiveness

Discussions about the balance between direct and indirect taxation, and about the right level of corporation tax are part of the wider debates generated by concerns that globalization is resulting in a 'race to the bottom', with companies seeking to base themselves in countries with lower corporate and individual tax levels, and better-off individuals faced with higher tax also moving elsewhere. Looking at the evidence, the Commission on Taxation and Citizenship (2000), however, argued that other issues are equally important to companies, including a skilled workforce, trust, and good services – all of which are more likely in countries whose taxes are sufficient to fund these 'public goods'. It also argued that individuals were likely to value a wider range of factors.

Another key, related, debate is between those who contend that lower (especially lower direct) taxes stimulate private sector enterprise and individual endeavour, thus promoting economic growth, and those who argue that this relationship is not proven, and that such measures will result in a meaner welfare state and a more unequal society. These controversies are often driven by long-standing ideological differences.

There are also different views about the impact of taxation on labour market behaviour. Economists recognize two possible consequences – income and substitution effects. In other words, someone may decide to work harder to make up the income lost through taxes, or not as hard because it is no longer seen as worth their while to do so. (Another possible response is working 'cash in hand', to avoid tax altogether.)

For those on lower incomes reductions in means-tested benefits often occur alongside increased taxation. When together this process means that a high proportion of each extra pound of income is being taken away, it is called the 'poverty trap'. The 'poverty plateau' means that increasing gross income across quite a wide range would make little difference to net income and therefore could again affect labour market behaviour.

Inequality and redistribution

There is also extensive debate over the degree of redistribution achieved by income tax; the tax system as a whole; and/or the tax and benefits systems (and services) together.

Income tax is the most progressive of the major taxes in the United Kingdom today. The degree of progressivity depends on the personal allowance and the other tax thresholds at which different tax rates apply, as well as on the marginal tax rate, the rate of tax paid on the last pound of income earned. (This should not be confused with the 'average tax rate', which is the proportion of tax paid on total income.)

Some analysts argue in favour of limiting or withdrawing tax allowances and reliefs and introducing higher tax rates for higher earners. This, they contend, would raise additional revenue and also have symbolic value in gaining public acceptability for taxation. Others, however, hold that increasing the tax rate on the rich would be unlikely to raise extra revenue and would dampen enterprise.

When looking at the whole tax system, because of difficulties in allocating indirect taxes to individuals, households are usually the unit of analysis. The UK tax system is usually seen as proportional, with each section of the population paying roughly similar proportions of income in taxes once more regressive indirect taxes are balanced against more progressive income tax (though, if households are ranked by expenditure instead of income when analysing the impact of VAT, it does not appear to have the same regressive effect). Despite its implications for those on low incomes, however, a shift towards indirect taxation is not reflected in the poverty statistics, because the 'poverty line' is a percentage of median net disposable income (i.e. after direct taxes, but before indirect taxes such as VAT).

In 2008/9, income before taxes and benefits for the top one-fifth of households was £73,800 per year on average, compared with £5,000 for the bottom one-fifth – a ratio of some 15 to 1; but after taking account of taxes and benefits, the gap was reduced to 4 to 1 (Barnard 2010). This is in part because much of the income of those on low incomes is made up of benefits/tax credits, so they are net beneficiaries; but these payments are received largely because of additional needs, and so could be argued only to put people on low incomes back into the same position as others. This analysis also included the impact of benefits in kind (including services) on inequality. Services are also received disproportionately by those on low incomes, and so help to reduce inequality – with the same proviso as for benefits, explained above.

These debates about inequality and redistribution also raise issues about the taxation of wealth. This is discussed less, but can have very significant consequences. There seems to be considerable resistance to inheritance tax, which is seen as 'double taxation' by many because they see it as paying tax on earnings and then again on the product of these earnings if they are left to someone else. Indeed, inheritance tax became a party political football when the main parties outdid each other in promising reductions before the 2010 general election.

Some commentators, however, argue that wealth inequalities are more significant than income differences, and that high inheritance taxes, resulting in a position closer to everyone 'starting from scratch', would be much fairer in terms of equal opportunities. The Commission on Taxation and Citizenship suggested a capital receipts tax – a tax on the recipients of any inheritance, rather than on the inheritance itself – which would be likely to result in the wider redistribution of wealth, because it would encourage gifts to be dispersed more widely. An annual wealth tax has also been discussed for many years, but is usually seen as difficult to implement.

Tax reliefs, 'fiscal welfare', and the 'hidden welfare state'

As we noted above, social goals can be achieved via taxation, as well as via benefits and services. But different standards are often applied to tax allowances and reliefs (which reduce the tax take) compared with benefits (which result in the government spending more). 'Revenue foregone' via tax allowances and reliefs does not usually count as 'public expenditure' in international accounting practices, and these far less visible provisions are also often overlooked in public debates. Yet such fiscal welfare can have substantial distributional consequences, and is criticized by the 'Left' as regressive. So tax allowances and reliefs are purposely called 'tax expenditures' by some, to mirror public expenditure (OECD 2010). They are also, however, criticized by the 'right' for potentially distorting market behaviour.

As Sinfield (2007) notes, recent governments have limited or abolished tax reliefs such as mortgage interest tax relief (though they have also introduced some new ones), and the relative amount of tax revenue foregone has fallen not only for this reason but also because income tax rates have been reduced. (Ironically, with a progressive tax system tax reliefs are more valuable to those who would otherwise pay higher tax rates.) However, as he also notes, continuing tax exemptions for the lump sums received on redundancy cost 80 per cent more than contributory JobSeeker's Allowance, and, though Labour simplified and cut pension tax relief, it was nonetheless retained, with the main beneficiaries still being high earners.

Taxation and citizenship

The Commission on Taxation and Citizenship saw taxation as the price we pay for living in a civilized society, rather than as a 'burden'. But its research found people increasingly failing to connect taxes with their prime function: to provide the services needed for such a civilized society. Hypothecation, or earmarked taxation, is one way to make such a connection – linking a tax, or tax increase, with what it finances. This happens already with some taxes, and the Commission recommended it for others. Since it is impossible to do this for all taxes, however, other ways to achieve this connection – particularly more informed public debate – were, it argued, also essential.

Another report suggesting how to restructure the tax system, the Mirrlees Review (2010) – starting from different premises, and focusing on economic issues – was published more recently. But as the Commission's report emphasized, the functions of tax systems have long been neglected in public, especially media, discussion, and there is a strong strand of ideological antipathy to taxation. Where taxation is addressed, the focus has often been on 'stealth taxes', the 'burden' of income tax, and counterposing 'taxpayers' – usually limited to payers of income tax – to benefit recipients.

Recent governments have also placed more emphasis on the responsibilities of benefit recipients than on those of taxpayers. Yet the Institute for Fiscal Studies (IFS) has shown that in any year one-third of UK adults do not pay income tax, whilst many benefit claimants do pay both income and other taxes. In addition, other research points to the widespread use of *tax avoidance* (exploiting legal loopholes to minimize tax) and there is long-standing concern over the extent to which benefit fraud is pursued more resolutely than *tax evasion* (illegal activities to avoid tax) despite the higher sums at stake. While there is still considerable concern over benefit 'abuse', there are also signs in the current economic climate of growing public anger about 'non-doms' (wealthy foreigners residing in the United Kingdom without paying the same tax levels as UK citizens) and, more broadly, over tax avoidance and evasion by individuals and particularly companies (HM Revenue and Customs 2010).

Emerging Issues

Concern over these issues, and pressure for greater 'citizenship' by both companies and high earners in tax matters, are likely to feature increasingly in policy debates in the future. Several other key issues are also emerging.

Most immediately, controversy is likely to centre on the UK coalition government's pledge to make significant reductions in the deficit in a 'fair' way. This is because, as demonstrated above, the benefits and services paid for by taxation are central to achieving progressive redistribution in the United Kingdom, making it very difficult to achieve deficit reductions fairly if (as planned) close to 80 per cent are made via public spending cuts, and only some 20 per cent via tax increases.

Debate is also likely to centre on the phasing out of tax credits, the UK coalition government's Universal Credit scheme and its plans to simplify the tax system, including tax reliefs, and integrate national insurance and income taxation.

Beyond these lies a new set of issues relating to the further use of taxation to modify behaviour. The Commission on Taxation and Citizenship (2000) discussed taxing 'bads' such as environmental damage; and excise duties are already levied on alcohol and tobacco, and could be argued to give signals about appropriate behaviour. The UK coalition government's interest in what is sometimes called 'nudge theory', stretching across its agenda, may well take its tax policies in this direction. Imposing taxes on certain behaviours may encourage people not to indulge in them (as much). But there is then a conflict between behaviour modification and maximization of revenue raising.

Other debates also relate to issues of international concern. Activists working on development issues in particular have called for a tax on short-term foreign exchange transactions (sometimes called a 'Tobin tax' after the person who devised it, or the 'Robin Hood' tax), to be used to meet urgent global priorities. And others have drawn attention to 'tax havens' – countries in which individuals and companies can keep their income or profits and pay little or no tax. So, taxation is also an increasingly important issue of global justice, as well as a key area of debate about social justice in the United Kingdom.

Guide to Further Sources

The UK government publishes annual analyses of the distributional impact of taxes and benefits: A. Barnard, *The Effects of Taxes and Benefits on Household income 2008–09* (London: Office for National Statistics, 2010, www.statistics.gov.uk/STATBASE/Product.asp?vlnk=10336); tables which show the interaction between taxes, NICs, tax credits, and some benefits for selected households from Department for Work and Pensions (2009), *Tax Benefit Model Tables: April 2009* (published online 2009), http://research.dwp.gov.uk/asd/index.php?page=tbmt; figures on the difference between the tax collected and the amount that should be – HM Revenue and Customs *Measuring Tax Gaps 2010*); and a table (1.5) of 'Tax expenditures and tax ready reckoners' (published online 2010) www.hmrc.gov.uk/thelibrary/national-statistics.htm.

Debates over 'fiscal welfare' can be found in R. Titmuss, 'The Social Division of Welfare: Some Reflections on the Search for Equity', in *Essays on the Welfare State* (London: Allen & Unwin, 1958) and A. Sinfield (2007) 'Tax Welfare', in M. Powell (ed.), *Understanding the Mixed Economy of Welfare* (Bristol: The Policy Press, 2007), pp. 129–48. H. Glennerster, *Understanding the Finances of Welfare: What Welfare Costs and How to Pay For It* (Bristol: Policy Press, 2009) examines the finances of the welfare state, including fiscal welfare. The Organisation for Economic Co-operation and Development has published a study of tax expenditures in ten countries, including the United

Kingdom: OECD, *Tax Expenditures in OECD Countries* (Paris: OECD, 2010). Tax restructuring is considered in The Commission on Taxation and Citizenship, *Paying for Progress: A New Politics of Tax for Public Spending* (London: Fabian Society, 2000) and J. Mirrlees *et al.*, *Tax by Design: The Mirrlees Review – Conclusions and Recommendations* (London: IFS, 2010).

The Institute for Fiscal Studies www.ifs.org.uk produces analyses of the tax system and reforms. Its *Fiscal Facts* provides tax/benefit tables and summaries of tax changes. Organizations interested in tax issues and with a variety of political views include Taxaid, the Tax Justice Network, the Taxpayers Alliance, and the Low Income Tax Reform Group.

Review Questions

1   In what ways can the taxation system in the UK affect wellbeing?

2   Why do governments develop 'fiscal welfare', and what issues does it raise?

3   What is the 'poverty trap', and why is it perceived as problematic?

4   Should tax policy be used to encourage or discourage certain behaviours?

5   Why are reductions in public expenditure less likely to be progressive in their impact than increases in taxation?

Visit the book companion site at www.wiley.com/go/alcock to make use of the resources designed to accompany the textbook. There you will find chapter-specific guides to further resources, including governmental, international, think-tank, pressure groups, and relevant journals sources. You will also find a glossary based on *The Blackwell Dictionary of Social Policy*, help sheets, and case studies, guidance on managing assignments in social policy and career advice.

37

Citizenship and Access to Welfare

Ruth Lister and Peter Dwyer

Overview

- The principles governing access to welfare are, in part, an attempt to ration resources.
- A key criterion for assessing these principles is the extent to which they ensure that needs are met.
- Need may be interpreted in broad or narrow ways, drawing on principles of universal citizenship or selectivity.
- Access to welfare depends on residence status and is mediated through rights (conditional or unconditional) or discretion.
- Proposals to enhance welfare include substantive reforms to widen access and procedural or process reforms designed to ensure respectful treatment of users, the securing and enforcement of rights, and user-involvement in the development of welfare.

Rationing Resources

Definitions of social policy tend to centre on human welfare and on the societal institutions designed to promote it. A critical question both for social policy and for individuals and groups is how resources, limited by economic and political constraints, are allocated so as best to promote welfare and meet human needs. Social policy is, therefore, partly about how resources are rationed. This chapter discusses the key competing principles which govern this rationing process and

The Student's Companion to Social Policy, Fourth Edition. Edited by Pete Alcock, Margaret May, Sharon Wright.
© 2012 John Wiley & Sons, Ltd. Published 2012 by John Wiley & Sons, Ltd.

thereby the rules determining the access of individuals and groups to welfare, with particular reference to citizenship.

Different Approaches to Meeting Need

A primary criterion for assessing the different principles governing access to welfare is whether the rules derived from them are successful in ensuring that people's needs are met. The concept of need (see Chapter 3) is by no means straightforward when applied to the question of access to welfare. On the one hand it is invoked to justify an approach to social welfare which is *rights*-based and which is founded on the principle of *social citizenship*. As discussed in Chapter 4, in this formulation the principle of need is counterposed to that of the market. In theory, social citizenship overrides that of the market, in that it is argued that every citizen has a right to be able to participate fully in that society. This right has to be underwritten by the state so as to ensure that people are not totally reliant on the labour market to meet their needs. Social rights are necessary to enable people to exercise their political and legal rights. Theoretically, we are all equal before the law, in practice some are more equal than others, so that without assistance from, for example, the Community Legal Service, access to the law for people living in poverty is effectively blocked. Nor, arguably, can people be expected to fulfil their responsibilities to the wider community as citizens if that wider community is not prepared to ensure that their needs are met.

The principle of citizenship is also about equality of status. Consequently, those subscrib-

ing to it argue that everyone should have access to the same set of rights, the principle of universality, instead of dividing off people in poverty from the rest of society through the application of selective mechanisms, such as means-testing, which promote residual welfare.

Yet proponents of such selective mechanisms also appeal to the concept of need to justify their position, arguing that when resources are limited, they should be targeted upon those who really need them. Targeting can take various forms including, for instance, according to age. However, the most common mechanism, particularly in social security schemes, is means- or income-testing, whereby assistance is limited to those whose resources fall below a certain level (see Chapter 45). The use of discretion, whereby officials or professionals decide what an applicant needs and what she can have instead of the applicant being able to claim on the basis of predetermined rights, is another approach more common in the provision of services such as housing and community care. This individualized approach, it is contended, is more likely to ensure that the individual's 'true' needs will be met than one based on rigid rules. The disadvantages of such selective approaches are explored below.

In practice, the distinction between rights and discretion in meeting needs is not as clear-cut as this discussion might imply. On the one hand, officials often have to exercise judgement or discretion in applying the rules governing rights; on the other, discretion is frequently exercised on the basis of (non-legally binding) guidelines set down by central or local government. Nevertheless, as the basis for organizing access to welfare they represent two very different approaches (see Figure 37.1). Together with the citizenship versus

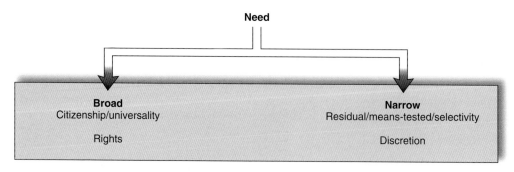

Figure 37.1   Access to welfare: interpretations of need.

residual welfare models (discussed in Chapter 59), these distinctions have implications for the welfare achieved by individuals and social groups, which are explored in the next section.

Access to Welfare

Immigration and residence status

First, we need to take a step back and consider what, for newcomers to a country, is the first gateway to access to welfare: rules which include or exclude people on the basis of their immigration or residence status. As Chapter 51 also shows, one way in which nation-states can limit the resources devoted to welfare is to limit the access of non-nationals both through restrictive immigration and asylum laws and through circumscribing access to welfare for those immigrants and asylum-seekers allowed into the country. Here citizenship is being used as a tool of exclusion rather than inclusion, overriding rather than underpinning the basic principle of meeting need.

Many Western countries are now using both immigration and welfare laws to exclude 'outsiders' from their welfare benefits and services. Behind the ramparts of 'Fortress Europe', tougher laws have been enacted to exclude immigrants and asylum-seekers. In the United Kingdom, access to welfare has been tied more tightly to immigration or residence status, thereby making it more difficult for immigrants and asylum-seekers to receive financial or housing assistance from the state. This then may have consequences for minority ethnic group 'insiders', who might be subjected to greater scrutiny when claiming welfare; some can be deterred from claiming altogether for fear that their own immigration status might be jeopardized or to avoid racist practices.

Discretion

The potential for racist or other prejudiced attitudes leading to discriminatory decision-making by those controlling access to welfare is one of the chief arguments against the discretionary approach. Its roots lie in charity, where access to welfare was as likely to be governed as much by considerations of merit or desert as of need. In the British social security system, the extent of discretion in the safety-net social assistance scheme was a major focus of debate in the 1960s and 1970s. Much of the criticism of the scheme was directed to its continued heavy reliance on discretion, which was seen as acting as a rationing system which put too much power in the hands of individual officials. Gradually, the scope of discretion was reduced, but one of the most controversial aspects of the reform of social security in the mid-1980s was its revival in the form of the social fund – a cash-limited fund paying out mainly loans to meet one-off needs such as furniture and bedding. Discretion was reintroduced explicitly as a rationing mechanism to reduce expenditure on such one-off payments. The social fund is an example of how discretion can be managed on the basis of detailed official guidelines, without giving claimants themselves clear rights. More recently, the scope for discretion in some rights-based programmes has been increasing again (see Chapter 38).

Discretion plays a more prominent role in the social assistance schemes of many other European countries and in the United Kingdom the service sector. Even if a right to a service exists, it is harder to specify how that right should be met by the statutory authorities, and professional interpretations of need come to the fore, again in the context of the rationing of limited resources. Thus, for example, the right to health care, enshrined in the British National Health Service, does not constitute a right to any treatment a user might demand; the right to treatment will be interpreted according to health professionals' assessment of the user's need.

In the field of community care, local authorities have a duty to assess the needs of disabled people, but they can then exercise their discretion as to whether and how they meet any needs that may have been identified. The exact boundaries between discretion and rights are, however, rather hazy here, as, in a few cases, the legislation has been used to require a local authority to provide a service once a need has been established. The problem is that, as long as local authorities' resources are so limited, the temptation will be not to identify the need in the first place, so that discretion again comes into play as a rationing device. The same applies to the duty on local authorities introduced subsequently to meet the separately assessed needs of carers. The power that the discretionary approach gives to professionals has been challenged by the disabled people's movement (see Chapter 57). Instead of having to rely on professional assessments of their needs, some disabled people are framing their demands in the language of citizenship rights.

Rights

The advantage of the rights-based approach to welfare is that it gives greater power to users by providing them with (more or less) clear, enforceable entitlements. Provided the criteria of entitlement are met, the claimant can refer to legal rules in support of her claim. Not all rights claims are, however, rooted in the principle of citizenship. As Figure 37.2 indicates, rights too can be selective and the citizenship principle itself can be interpreted to embrace both unconditional and conditional forms of welfare.

Residual Selectivity

The case for selective means-tested welfare – that it targets help on those in greatest need – has long been the subject of controversy. (It should be noted here that, in the United Kingdom, some means-tested benefits have been transformed into tax credits, going further up the income scale than traditional means-tested benefits.) Critics point to the significant numbers of people who fail to claim the means-tested benefits for which they are eligible. The reasons are varied, but include the sheer complexity of the benefits and the claiming process. Minority ethnic groups and older people are particularly likely to underclaim. Similarly, there is evidence that, as local authorities apply charges and means-tests to more services, some people prefer to do without.

Means-tests are also criticized for trapping people in poverty, as an increase in income reduces their benefit, and for penalizing savings. They do not necessarily provide people with genuine security, as changes in circumstances, which are common among low-income working families, can affect entitlement. They also tend to disadvantage women in couples and to reinforce their economic dependence on male partners. Entitlement is normally calculated on the basis of a couple's joint income. This means that where, as is frequently the case, income is not shared fairly within a family, means-tests may be failing to target help to the women within families who need it, with potential consequences for the welfare of children. Moreover, because of the strict rules limiting earnings while one is claiming social assistance, it is not generally worthwhile for the partners of unemployed claimants to undertake paid work.

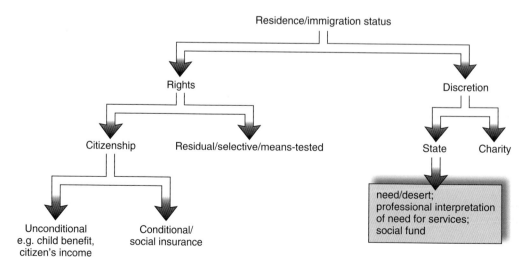

Figure 37.2 Principles of access to welfare.

Claiming a means-tested benefit all too often means admitting to the label of poverty, which can still be experienced as stigmatizing. One of the dangers of a residual welfare system, it is argued, is that benefits and services confined to 'the poor' can all too easily become poor benefits and services, as the rest of society no longer has an interest in ensuring their adequacy and quality. When access to welfare is confined to 'the poor' or nearly poor, it contravenes the principle of common citizenship.

Citizenship: Conditional and Unconditional

In the British social security system, social insurance is often held up as exemplifying the principle of common citizenship. Here, access to welfare depends primarily on having paid contributions of a specified value while in work and, for some groups, various work-related activities. However, it is, some would maintain, a conditional and limited form of citizenship which is promoted by the current social insurance scheme. Instead of overriding the market as a mechanism for distributing income, it mirrors market principles by confining entitlement to those with an adequate labour market record and, through additional earnings-related pensions, perpetuating (albeit in modified form) inequalities in earning power. Because the rules governing access to social insurance are based on male employment patterns, women, in particular, are the losers. A diminishing number of women are excluded from the system altogether because their earnings are too low to bring them into the social insurance system. Immigrants too are disadvantaged.

As part of a 'new welfare contract', the conditional nature of the social insurance (and social assistance) system is being intensified through increasingly tough and extensive rules enforcing the obligation to seek and take work, which is promoted as the best form of welfare. In addition, in certain circumstances entitlement to benefit is being made conditional on other forms of 'responsible' behaviour, for example, the possibility of reducing housing benefit as punishment for persistent antisocial behaviour has been piloted. Such policies reflected a central tenet of Labour's 'Third Way' philosophy that rights come with

responsibilities. Increasingly, conditional welfare rights are openly endorsed by UK politicians from across the mainstream political spectrum. It is the intention of the UK coalition government (elected in 2010) to build on the conditionality that underpinned the approach of their Labour predecessors. In British social security universal, unconditional, citizenship benefits are rare. There are a number of benefits which are paid to people in specific categories, such as carers and disabled people, without either a contribution or a means-test. However, the future of such universal benefits is far from certain. Previously seen as the epitome of universal benefit, the UK coalition government has decided to means test Child Benefit and from 2013 higher rate tax payers will loose their entitlement.

The social security systems of different countries combine the principles of access to welfare in different combinations, although generally with one predominating. Thus, for instance, as noted in Chapter 59, the citizenship approach is associated with Scandinavia, the residual with the United States, and the conditional social insurance with Germany. The United Kingdom, more than most, is a hybrid, but with an increased tilt towards a more residual model. Labour's principle of 'progressive universalism' – basic universal support combined with additional help for those who need it most – exemplified this hybridity in some areas of income maintenance. The citizenship principle does still operate in the NHS. However, as discussed above, it is difficult to operationalize in specific terms what is a generalized right to health care, free at the point of use. Moreover, it is an increasingly consumerist model of citizenship which dominates.

Emerging Issues

The weaknesses in current welfare arrangements have prompted a range of proposals for improvement. These can be divided into *substantive* and *procedural or process reforms*.

One area of *substantive reform proposals* aims to shift the balance of social security entitlement from residual to citizenship-based principles of access. One example is the recasting of social insurance so that it excludes fewer people and, in particular, better reflects women's employment patterns. Another is the idea of a basic or citizen's income under which every individual would receive a tax-free benefit without any conditions attached. Access would be on the basis of citizenship rights alone. The development of substantive rights to services is more difficult. One approach has been to suggest, as a first step, a framework of broad constitutional rights, partly building on the existing European Social Charter of the Council of Europe. This would provide rights to services at a generalized level, expressed as duties pertaining to government. Specific legislation would then need to develop more specific enforceable rights within such a framework.

It is easier to envisage how *procedural reforms* might improve access to welfare services. The Conservative government under John Major adopted such an approach in its Citizen's Charter. However, this was criticized as representing the principles of consumerism rather than citizenship. A more citizenship-oriented notion of procedural rights has been suggested by the Institute for Public Policy Research. Procedural rights to welfare focus on the processes through which substantive rights can be secured, on how people are treated (with dignity and respect, which is a foundational principle of a human rights approach), and the manner in which decisions are taken. An important element of procedural rights is enforceability. To access and enforce rights, people must have information about them and often need advice and assistance in negotiating with welfare institutions and taking cases to tribunals or, less frequently, the courts.

Rights to information and advocacy are also promoted by self-help groups, where users help each other without having to rely on professionals. The principle of citizenship is taken still further in the growing demands for user or citizen involvement in service development (see Chapter 40). The case is made on the grounds that welfare will be enhanced both by the greater democratic accountability of welfare institutions and by the empowerment of users. Thus, in incorporating a more dynamic and active conception of citizenship, which treats people as active agents rather than as simply passive recipients of rights, the principle of citizenship is promoted in terms of both outcomes and process. The principle of user involvement is now recognized in community care law although, in prac-

tice, it still has some way to go to avoid criticisms of tokenism. Whereas initially user involvement was developed at the level of local service delivery, more recently there have been demands for its extension to national policy-making. Increasingly, it is being argued that the opportunity to participate in decision-making about welfare should be treated as a right.

This chapter has emphasized the importance of the principles that govern access to welfare resources, highlighting the processes of rationing involved and the ways in which different principles affect marginalized groups such as women, members of minority ethnic communities, and disabled people. It has also underlined the significance of issues of process: procedural rights which assist people in claiming and enforcing substantive rights to welfare as citizens treated with respect and user involvement in the development of welfare. However, any immediate enhancement or expansion of the welfare rights enjoyed by UK citizens appears unlikely. Given the UK coalition government's stated priority to reduce the deficit in public finances, the fundamental restructuring of welfare to which it is committed may well lead to a more residual and conditional welfare state in the future

Guide to Further Sources

Many of the ideas raised in this chapter can be found in H. Dean (2002) *Welfare Rights and Social Policy* (Harlow: Pearson Education, 2002) which offers a critical exploration of welfare rights, social citizenship, and social legislation in historical and comparative context. P. Dwyer has written two introductions to social citizenship. The first, *Welfare Rights and Responsibilities. Contesting Social Citizenship* (Bristol: Policy Press, 2002) provides a discussion of the principles of social citizenship, which also includes the views of welfare users in relation to health, social security and housing. The second, *Understanding Social Citizenship* (2nd edn, Bristol: Policy Press, 2010), relates social citizenship to welfare rights, puts it in historical context and considers issues of difference. For a more detailed exploration of principles of access to social security, see R. Walker, *Social Security and Welfare* (Milton Keynes: Open University Press, 2005) and a number of chapters in J. Millar (ed.), *Understanding Social Security* (2nd edn, Bristol: Policy Press, 2009). A robust case for universal welfare can be found in T. Horton and J. Gregory, *The Solidarity Society* (London: Fabian Society, 2009).

Review Questions

1   Outline the key ideas underpinning the notion of citizenship.
2   Consider the implications of *broad* and *narrow* interpretations of need for social citizenship.
3   How might an individual's immigration and residency status impact on their access to welfare provisions?
4   Define 'discretion' and consider its implications in relation to citizens' welfare rights.
5   What kind of substantive or procedural reforms could enhance welfare provision in the future?

Visit the book companion site at www.wiley.com/go/alcock to make use of the resources designed to accompany the textbook. There you will find chapter-specific guides to further resources, including governmental, international, think-tank, pressure groups, and relevant journals sources. You will also find a glossary based on *The Blackwell Dictionary of Social Policy*, help sheets, and case studies, guidance on managing assignments in social policy and career advice.

PART VI

Welfare Governance

38

Managing and Delivering Welfare

John Clarke

Overview

- The processes of managing and delivering welfare are not merely technical matters.
- Managing welfare involves dealing with conflicting priorities.
- Delivering welfare involves managing demanding, difficult, and unstable relationships with the public.
- Delivering welfare increasingly involves welfare recipients in do-it-yourself delivery.
- Welfare delivery is moving beyond recognizable organizations, institutions, and systems.

Context

Processes of managing and delivering welfare have become increasingly significant in political and policy debates as welfare states have been reformed, retrenched, and reconstructed. As governments seek to create welfare systems that are economical, efficient, and effective they have looked to redesign the organizations through which welfare is delivered. Equally, as they seek to accomplish new policy objectives – for example, activation, empowerment, behaviour change – they have sought to transform the systems and processes through which welfare is delivered. This chapter explores some of the key issues at stake in these developments, beginning from the proposition that 'managing and delivering welfare' is never just a technical matter.

For most of the twentieth century, welfare in the United Kingdom was organized and delivered through professional bureaucracies, in which principles of rational administration (the rules and regulations of bureaucracy) were combined with forms of professional judgement (doctors, teachers, social workers) in the production and distribution of welfare benefits and services. In

The Student's Companion to Social Policy, Fourth Edition. Edited by Pete Alcock, Margaret May, Sharon Wright.
© 2012 John Wiley & Sons, Ltd. Published 2012 by John Wiley & Sons, Ltd.

the last three decades of the twentieth century this model of delivering welfare came under increasing challenge from a number of directions: it was attacked for its cost; for its inefficiency and ineffectiveness; for its concentration of power in the hands of professionals and bureaucrats; for its lack of transparency and accountability; and, above all, as an inappropriate alternative to market dynamics.

The result of these diverse challenges has been a continuing process of reinvention and redesign of welfare provision. In the process, organizational forms, system principles, occupational recruitment, work practices, and the place of service users have been challenged, changed, and changed again. Little of this has been about the technical considerations of how to design effective organizations. Rather, it has been shaped by the changing political objectives and purposes of welfare policy (making people independent, for instance); by commitment to idealized principles of delivering welfare (making it more like a market, for example); and especially by the view that welfare delivery can be improved by the introduction of more and better management.

Making Markets, Making Managers

What has been called the New Public Management (NPM) dominated reforms of public services (including welfare provision) during the past forty years. NPM reforms were intended to create more economical, efficient, and effective organizations for delivering welfare. This often involved introducing markets or market-like mechanisms into services: putting services out to competitive tendering or separating purchasers and providers, or commissioners and contractors. Such market-like mechanisms were supposed to improve efficiency, make services more responsive to customers, and create innovation and improvement. Their actual impact remains much debated, since they also fragmented services, and created extra costs – notably those of *transition* (the costs of changing the system) and *transaction* (the costs of running a more complex system).

The system changes involved in the NPM – towards more dispersed, contractually co-ordinated, and dispersed sets of organizations – also created pressures to find new tools for co-ordinating such systems and ensuring they delivered welfare more efficiently. Some of these new tools involved new technologies (IT systems promised better data, faster information, and the possibility of improved managerial oversight and direction). Other innovations included the separation of strategy and implementation, with implementation (delivery) being organized around the pursuit of centrally set targets (what later became derided as the 'target culture'). So, hospitals were given targets for bed use and waiting list reduction, while police forces were set targets for crime clear up rates and reducing public fear of crime. Targets were central to the process of performance management: providing the framework within which the service, specific organizations within the service, and particular parts of organizations could be directed, judged, and compared with others.

The use of targets as a means of managing welfare organizations was closely linked to a third system of control: the massive expansion of processes of audit, inspection, and scrutiny in the three decades after 1980 (see Chapter 39). Audit, deriving originally from models of financial control and inspection, extended into the business of measuring and evaluating many aspects of organizational performance. At the same time, older models of professional inspection (based in Her Majesty's Inspectors for schools, prisons and so on) were reformed into new types of scrutiny body – most notably in the example of the Office for Standards in Education which visited and judged schools in England, publishing their judgements and constructing league tables of comparative school performance. Such audit and inspection processes both extended forms of central scrutiny and control over welfare providers and produced data intended to help users of such services to be better-informed and more empowered welfare consumers (see Chapter 40).

However, all of these changes to welfare organizations were overshadowed by the commitment to establish more and better management as the co-ordinating principle. Managers were expected to make welfare organizations behave in a more 'business-like way', even if they were not competing in a market place. Managers, it was claimed, could deliver the improved performance that professionals and bureaucrats could not. Managers would be customer centred and performance focused and would ensure that policies, strategies, and targets would be effectively translated into practice. Installing more and better management required managers to be made: some were imported from the private sector; some were converted from existing professionals or bureaucrats; many were sent off for re-education as training courses in public service management flourished.

Doing the Right Thing? Managing Dilemmas

Although the commitment to more and better management was built on the belief that management was a bundle of generic skills that could be applied to any organization to improve its performance, welfare organizations presented a number of distinctive difficulties. Where the 'bottom line' of profit and loss is typically the single most important indicator of organizational success in the private sector, success in welfare provision is subject to competing – and sometimes conflicting – objectives. So, should a service promote active and independent citizens; should it provide choice and control for service users; should it distribute resources equitably; should it reduce costs in an era of fiscal restraint? Where such desired objectives come into conflict: who should set the priorities – and through what means?

Sometimes such priority setting is done politically, nationally, or locally. But more often organizations are confronted with multiple objectives – and instructed to deliver. In such circumstances, management may become the site of trying to reconcile competing objectives and different principles, often in the context of limited resources and increasing demand. Welfare organizations have typically been asked 'to do more with less', making 'efficiency savings' while improving standards and meeting increased expectations. In such circumstances, managers may make judgements about which objectives to pursue – though such choices are constrained: by the prevailing 'targets' or performance standards on which they will be audited, inspected, and judged. But they may also pass on these dilemmas, devolving them to those who work lower

down the organization's hierarchy. Some social policy research explores how 'front line staff' make policy in practice as they try to resolve such dilemmas.

More generally, however, welfare organizations have been confronted with some difficult conflicting pressures: for example, between expanding choices for the public (e.g., patient choice in the NHS) and managing demand and resources (e.g., through rationing and priority setting). They have also been faced with conflicting demands about how they conduct themselves. In the redesigned welfare systems of the twenty-first century, 'success' has usually been assessed in organizational terms: individual schools, hospitals, universities, and so on, are judged and compared. This has promoted a competitive orientation, as each individual organization tries to improve its own performance, manage its own resources, and enhance its own reputation (if necessary, at the expense of its competitors).

Such a competitive model incites competitive calculation and behaviour. As a result organizations have tried to 'cherry pick' their customers (the pupils or parents likely to deliver the best examination performance for schools, for example). They have tried to exclude costly, risky and difficult customers (e.g. people with weight or drug related problems in health care). They have tried to manage their boundaries: does this old person need social care or health care? The decision matters because the old person will be one or the other service's cost. Costs matter: while welfare provision does not take the form of a market in which people pay for services, increased demand usually means increased costs for organizations. Finally, the pursuit of organizational success has led service-providing organizations to narrow their focus onto the limited number of targets against which they will be judged, rather than any wider view of promoting social welfare or well-being.

This competitive model, originating in the market or market-like reforms of the 1980s, has remained a pressure on those managing welfare, but it has been made more difficult by equally powerful imperatives to collaborate: to engage in partnerships, to work together, to build networks, and more. By the end of the 1990s, the pressures to compete *and* collaborate posed major dilemmas for those trying to manage welfare organizations that had to decide when and where to compete or collaborate; with whom or against whom; and about what issues and objectives.

Delivery Problems: Managing People

Delivering welfare involves some complex problems, many of which centre on the processes of managing people – both inside and outside the organization. Although contemporary ideas of management stress the importance of the 'multiple stakeholders' who have an interest in, or are affected by the specific organization, the most critical delivery problems have been associated with those who work in the organization and those who use its services. Given that many welfare organizations used to be professional bureaucracies, many services are still delivered by professionals or semi-professionals (teachers, social workers, doctors, nurses, and other trained specialist staff). As a result, managers have to find a way to both make use of professional expertise and constrain professional autonomy in their attempt to create more efficient and effective organizations. Setting new rules, introducing new technologies, establishing norms of 'best practice', introducing performance-related pay systems based on individual appraisal, and, most importantly, changing working practices to constrain autonomy have all been used in welfare organizations to manage professionals. An alternative has been to turn professionals into managers or, in more recent terms, 'leaders'. In health care, teaching, social care, and elsewhere, career progression has increasingly come to mean moving into management or leadership roles.

Of course, not all welfare workers are professional or semi-professional. Much of the labour of welfare is done by unqualified – and low paid – workers, from cleaners to domiciliary care workers. Much of this work was contracted out from welfare organizations to external agencies (as a way of driving down costs and increasing efficiency). As with other types of work, it has been subject to changing terms and conditions of employment – with a speed-up or intensification of work; more contingent contracting and, often, stricter surveillance. For example, the time allo-

cated to domiciliary care work is rigorously task-defined and often explicitly excludes being sociable with the person receiving the support. It is also worth noting that much welfare work is done by volunteers or by friends, family, or neighbours. It is much harder to subject such 'workers' to forms of labour discipline and control, but volunteers in charities involved in welfare work have often encountered efforts to rationalize, modernize, and manage their work, since voluntary organizations have also been subjected to the same pressures to become more 'business-like'.

Managing people also involves welfare organizations in managing those who use their services. This is the focus of considerable difficulty and ambivalence. The challenges to professional bureaucracies of welfare noted above involved criticisms of the power they exercised; their impersonality; and their exercise of partial and inequitable discretionary judgements. Some of the reforms to welfare services have aimed to make them more accessible, more equitable, and more user-focused. At the same time, limited resources and more conditional access to welfare benefits and services have ensured that aspirations and expectations go unfulfilled. In the process, welfare organizations have to deal with a public that they perceive as more difficult, more differentiated, and more demanding: in total, less willing to defer to the state and its agents. This makes for unstable and tense encounters between welfare providers and those seeking help, assistance and support.

Delivering Welfare

This makes the processes of delivering welfare the focus of macro- and micropolitics. Macropolitics press on delivering welfare in the competing policy objectives; in the recurrently tense relationship between demand and resources; and in the contradictory expectations of a public who would like to see low levels of taxation and high quality public services. They also mark the point where the social relationships of difference and inequality meet the limits of welfare – both in the limits to resources and in the limited commitments to equity, justice, and fairness embedded in the administration of welfare.

At the same time, these large social and political dynamics work themselves out in the micro-dynamics of interactions between those receiving, needing, or demanding welfare and those involved in delivering, managing, and controlling welfare. Welfare organizations work, in part, by assessing people: their eligibility; their needs; their possibilities; their character; and even their deservingness. Particular services use different criteria of value, employ different frameworks for making judgements, and act in specific ways as a consequence. But welfare is rarely a simple transaction between a person with a need and an organization committed to universally providing solutions. This conditionality at the heart of welfare has increased in recent decades across the range of welfare provisions. New frameworks for judging value, merit, and need have appeared (notably how willing is the person to be active and independent?). But assessing people remains central to the business of welfare and it is the focus of tensions between those doing the assessing and those being subjected to such judgements.

These tensions are intensified as people approach welfare with greater expectations or in a more demanding way (as rights-bearing citizens; responsible tax-payers; or insistent choice-making consumers). They are also intensified as welfare policy makes more demands on those seeking welfare. The micropolitics of delivering welfare are, not surprisingly, full of possibilities for antagonism, misunderstanding, and ill-feeling. Power, difference, and inequalities flow across these encounters – and, as governments demand more from citizens, the tensions deepen. The increasingly accepted view that welfare provided by the state should be used to modify people's behaviour adds to the difficult dynamics of managing and delivering welfare. Demanding that those receiving state support sign up to 'contracts' promising to be better tenants, better parents, better dieters, better job searchers, or better citizens has become part of the normal practice of welfare. But it requires those delivering welfare to extend their powers of assessment, judgement, and surveillance of welfare recipients.

One effect of this combination of pressures and tensions in the delivery of welfare is the intensification of what some have called the 'emotional labour' of welfare work. This points to the ways in which delivering welfare is never just a matter of distributing benefits or services to their recipients. On the contrary, welfare work often involves managing the reactions and responses of the recipient: calming or cajoling; repressing or uplifting; encouraging or denying. Although some welfare work explicitly addresses the emotional or psychic state of the recipient (aspects of social work, for example) most other welfare work involves emotional labour, too: whether it involves refusing someone's claim for benefit or reassuring children about their progress in school. Finally, it is worth noting that emotional labour in welfare work also extends to the worker's own emotions: the processes of coping with the anxieties and ambivalence that delivering welfare may create.

Located as they are at the intersection of individuals' lives and needs and the power and authority of the state, welfare services are always likely to be contentious, but the policy and organizational reforms of the past few decades have intensified and extended the possibilities of tensions and troubles.

Emerging Issues

Two recent trends in the processes of managing and delivering welfare may become more significant over the next few years. The first is the increasing concern with making people independent: self-reliant rather than relying on publicly provided welfare. This ambition has involved reducing or withdrawing state support from people, and using welfare provision to encourage or enforce greater independence. It covers a range of policy areas – from getting people off welfare benefits (and into paid work) to creating 'expert patients' who take charge of managing their own illnesses. Given the financial crisis of 2008–10, the economic incentives for governments to reduce 'welfare dependence' are greater than ever. Here again, we might see the role of multiple objectives in shaping welfare delivery: does policy seek to support people being independent, or to reduce the level of public spending on particular social groups? Those involved in managing and delivering welfare may find it hard to tell. They may also find it hard to deliver the 'independence' named in the policy and encounter some difficult reactions as they are expected to both reduce support and police behaviour more closely.

Finally, I have talked about welfare organizations and systems throughout this chapter but the idea of welfare systems is itself being challenged in current (2011) reform proposals, particularly those affecting education and health care. Here we see a concern to 'liberate' welfare services from institutional controls: enabling people to set up new schools outside the state system, but with public funds, or devolving the commissioning decisions for health care to General Practitioners (GPs) instead of regional or local health bodies. Such possibilities might undermine the idea of a health or education *system*, further fragmenting and dispersing welfare organizations. They also concentrate much more power into the hands of central government (as funders and regulators). It is too early to tell what the consequences of this proliferation of providers, purchasers, and decision-makers might be for the tasks of managing and delivering welfare. But it is reasonable to speculate that they might not escape the dilemmas of competing policy objectives; the difficult relationships between welfare, power, and inequality; the recurrent problems of matching need, demand, and resources in equitable ways; and the tensions and troubles of managing the encounters with a diverse and often contentious public.

Guide to Further Sources

J. Clarke, J. Newman, J. Smith, *et al.*, *Creating Citizen-Consumers: Changing Publics and Changing Public Services* (London: Sage, 2007) explores the move to treating the public as 'consumers' of public services. N. Flynn, *Public Sector Management* (5th edn London: Sage, 2007), is a lucid – and regularly updated – introduction to the conditions and problems of managing in the public sector.

S. Morgen, J. Acker, and J. Weigt, *Stretched Thin: Poor Families, Welfare Work and Welfare Reform* (Ithaca, NY: Cornell University Press 2009) is an exceptional ethnography of welfare reform in the United States that examines the impact of policy and organizational changes on welfare recipients, workers, and managers.

J. Newman and J. Clarke, *Publics, Politics and Power: remaking the public in public services* (London: Sage, 2009) examines some of the conflicting efforts to reinvent the public and transform public services in the twenty-first century

and explores some of the changing forms of organization and management in these processes. J. Newman and E. Tonkens (eds), *Summoning the Active Citizen* (Amsterdam: Amsterdam University Press, 2010) is a collection exploring the diverse settings in which European countries attempt to make their citizens active. R. Van Berkel and B. Valkenburg (eds), *Making it Personal: Individualising Activation Services in the EU* (Bristol: Policy Press, 2007) examines how labour market activation policy changes have been entwined with shifts in the organization and management of welfare.

There are several web sites in which debates about managing welfare can be found, including that of the Office for Public Management www.opm.co.uk, the Chartered Institute of Public Finance and Accountancy, which hosts *Public Money and Management* and the Public Management and Policy Association www.cipfa.org.uk and the Institute for Public Policy Research, one of the longest established think-tanks in the field www.ippr.org.uk.

Review Questions

1   In what ways can the processes of managing and delivering welfare be seen as dealing with competing objectives?
2   Why has management been so central to how welfare organizations have been reformed?
3   What means of control have been developed to enable more effective central control over welfare systems?
4   Why might the relationship between welfare service providers and service recipients be difficult?
5   Should welfare be used to make people change their behaviour?

Visit the book companion site at www.wiley.com/go/alcock to make use of the resources designed to accompany the textbook. There you will find chapter-specific guides to further resources, including governmental, international, think-tank, pressure groups, and relevant journals sources. You will also find a glossary based on *The Blackwell Dictionary of Social Policy*, help sheets, and case studies, guidance on managing assignments in social policy and career advice.

39

Accountability for Welfare

Jackie Gulland

██▨▨░██▨██▨▨██▨░▨██▨▨░░▨██▨░██▨██░▨██▨██░██▨██░▨░██▨

Overview

- ■ Accountability is about public bodies *accounting* for their actions: how they collect and spend money, what they do with it, the quality of services provided, and the extent to which policies are followed.
- ■ Accountability is a relational term.
- ■ The 'hollowing out' of the state has made accountability more complex.
- ■ While it is important that state actors should be accountable for their actions, mechanisms for improving accountability also carry disadvantages.
- ■ Accountability is not neutral: it is a normative concept, closely related to issues of power and political priorities.

██▨▨░██▨██▨▨██▨░▨██▨▨░░▨██▨░██▨██░▨██▨██░██▨██░▨░██▨

Accountability as a Normative Concept

When scandals emerge in the press about the misdemeanours of politicians, failed or expensive policies, or stories about people who have died or suffered abuse at the hands of the state, the first call is for someone to be held 'to account'. There are demands for 'more accountability'. Accountability is perceived to be a good thing but it is a normative concept, loaded with many tensions which are usually overlooked in these demands. Accountability is best considered as a *relational* term, concerning the way in which the state interacts with its citizens. Accountability raises questions about wider issues of power and political priorities to which we will return.

Social policy analysts approach the question of accountability by looking at

The Student's Companion to Social Policy, Fourth Edition. Edited by Pete Alcock, Margaret May, Sharon Wright.
© 2012 John Wiley & Sons, Ltd. Published 2012 by John Wiley & Sons, Ltd.

- *What* kind of things should be accounted for?
- *Who* should be held accountable?
- To *whom* should they be held accountable?
- What *mechanisms* are available for ensuring accountability?

What Kind of Things should be Accounted For?

Accountability for finances

Accountability in the public sector has focused primarily on finances. The idea of an 'accountant' as someone who checks financial records is related to this. We can see examples of financial accountability in the National Audit Office, which scrutinizes the public spending of the Westminster government. Other bodies (see Guide to Further Sources) are responsible for the financial auditing of local government and in the devolved administrations. These bodies were originally concerned with scrutinizing the accuracy of records of how public money was collected and spent. However, since the 1980s, financial accountability bodies have extended their remit to looking at whether public bodies provide quality services which represent 'value for money'. This extension of their role expands the concept beyond the apparently objective activities of checking that money has not been misspent or used for the wrong purpose into much more contested areas of policy priorities.

Meeting policy goals

As well as ensuring that money has been well spent and that services are of an acceptable standard, it is reasonable to expect that public services do what policy-makers intend them to do. This is another difficult area, as policies may be in conflict with each other, for example, a general policy of cutting public expenditure may be in conflict with one of improving services. On a wider level, governments may have broad policies promoting equality and human rights which come into conflict with other priorities on public spending or on security. Local authorities also have a range of policy goals which come into conflict with each other. This means that being accountable for meeting policy goals is not an easy task and is a highly political endeavour.

Avoidance of risk

Accountability comes to the fore when things go wrong. When a child dies under local authority supervision, when a hospital is found to have a history of medical mishaps, when a policy 'fails' to meet its objectives, or when budgets are massively overspent, there are demands for improved accountability. One of the disadvantages of the increasing focus on managing and avoiding risk is that it can skew policy priorities in directions led by media scandals.

Who Should be Held Accountable?

In order to understand accountability we have to know who (or what body) is expected to account for their actions. The simplest way to think about this is in a hierarchy, with politicians at the top. As our democratically elected representatives, we expect that politicians, particularly government ministers should be accountable for the actions of government. However, this is not always simple, since day-to-day decisions, as well as broader policy actions, are delegated to senior officials, service managers, and front line staff. Ensuring a hierarchy of accountability so that those at the top can be held responsible for the actions of those at the bottom is a complex and time-consuming activity. This complexity is increased in a system of multilevel governance where devolved and local authorities are responsible for many public services. Other policy decisions are affected by the actions of international bodies such as the European Union (see Chapter 43). This 'hollowing out of the state', along with the practice of outsourcing much of government activity to third party providers, such as the voluntary and private sector, as well as 'arms length' government agencies, has challenged hierarchical notions of accountability.

Whatever the level of governance, there is a question about the extent to which front line service staff are expected to be accountable for their own actions. This varies depending on the nature of the service and the professional status of staff. For example, we would expect different levels of individual accountability from professionals such as teachers and doctors than we would from support workers such as cleaners and receptionists.

Some have argued that accountability does not stop at the front line of service provision, with an increased focus on the responsibilities of service users and the community. Examples of user accountability include the requirement that benefit claimants account for their efforts to look for work, that parents take responsibility for their children's education, and that health service users take greater responsibility for managing their own health. In these cases service users have to *account* for their behaviour in order to qualify for services (see Chapter 40).

Accountability to Whom?

The third aspect of accountability that we have to consider is to whom public services must be accountable. Some writers have conceived of accountability as 'circular', where the agency or public body is in the centre and spokes of accountability radiate out, upwards to parliament, elected representatives, courts and supranational bodies, sideways to colleagues, professional organizations and 'networks' and downwards to the electorate, service users, and other interest groups. Bovens (2005) has described this as 'the problem of many eyes'. This circle of accountability shows how tensions arise depending on where in the circle actors are situated. The upper and lower parts of the circle represent different levels of power, where the higher levels are considered to be more powerful and the lower levels, less powerful. When looking at mechanisms of accountability we can see that different mechanisms are aimed at different parts of this circle. The effectiveness and importance of each mechanism varies depending on the priority given to different parts of the circle.

Most notions of accountability assume that the beneficiary is ultimately the 'public'. Sociologists describe the concept of many 'publics' which can represent both individual and collective interests. The public consists of both the electorate who, in theory, have democratic control over elected bodies, and of people who are directly

affected by public services, some of whom are not able to participate in elections (e.g. children, prisoners, people without citizenship status) and people who may have the right to vote but are unable or unwilling to use it because of other structural disadvantages. People can be affected by public services in several ways: as tax payers, as service users, as potential service users or relatives of service users, as employees and business operators, and as members of the community in which the service operates. Their interests in the provision and cost of services will be very different depending on their perspective. People's relationship with services will also be differentiated according to their gender, ethnic origin, age, and any health problems or disabilities. The concept of 'the public' is not straightforward.

Mechanisms for Accountability

Bovens (2005) describes the process of accountability as having three stages: the person held accountable must feel an obligation (formal or informal) to account for his or her conduct; second, any information provided must be capable of interrogation or questioning; and finally, the people to whom the account is made must be able to pass judgement on the account, by accepting it or denouncing it with appropriate consequences, for example democratic mechanisms, fines, disciplinary action, or informal action such as negative exposure in the press.

Democratic mechanisms

The first stop of accountability is often considered to be to parliament. As the elected body in a democracy, members of parliament should know what is being done in their name and should be able to make changes to policies or practices which appear to be too expensive or to be not working well. Elected members in turn, expect to be held accountable to their electorate or 'the public'. This applies to Westminster politicians, representatives in devolved administrations, local councillors, and other bodies where representatives are elected. The theory is that because elected representatives are accountable to their electorate, the electorate can remove them from power if they are unhappy with their activities. In recent years attempts have been made to make bodies more accountable by having more locally elected representatives. However, democratic mechanisms rely on accountability to the 'public', which we have seen is a contested concept.

Legal mechanisms

Courts can be used to call public service providers to account if they are perceived to fail to meet legal requirements. They can hear claims for personal injury if someone is injured or dies as the result of medical negligence, for example. Judicial review is another legal mechanism which can be used to call public bodies to account if they are alleged to have failed to meet certain standards of administrative law, for example that they have not complied with legislation, that they have been to restrictive in the use of discretionary powers, that they have acted 'unreasonably' or that they have taken action beyond their powers. The grounds for judicial review are complex and it is a technical and expensive processes. Despite this, actions for judicial review have mushroomed in the past thirty years and have led to some important decisions about the operation of public services, for example in relation to housing homeless people, providing social care services, and in relation to the rights of asylum seekers and prisoners. The introduction of the Human Rights Act 1998 has led to many court cases which have raised important new questions about the operation of public services.

Related to courts, public inquiries are another legal mechanism for accountability. Some public inquiries are required by law while others are set up in response to political or public demand after disasters or financial scandals. Public inquiries have been beset with problems relating to their independence, remit, and powers but they continue to remain an important part of the accountability landscape.

Ombudsmen

Sometimes described as 'people's champions', ombudsmen have powers to investigate complaints about 'maladministration' in public services. The first ombudsman in the United Kingdom was the Parliamentary Commissioner for Administration, set up in 1967, specifically to provide an additional measure of accountability to Parliament. This Ombudsman reports to the House of Commons Select Committee on Public Administration and investigates complaints about services which are the responsibility of the Westminster Parliament. Other ombudsmen investigate complaints about the devolved administrations and about the health service and local government in England. Ombudsmen have become increasingly prominent in dealing with problems with public services, seen by many as a cheaper and more user friendly alternative to the courts.

Freedom of information

Freedom of information legislation, introduced from 2000 onwards, has opened up new avenues for accountability, leading to public debate about matters such as the MPs' expenses scandal of 2009. It also has its limitations however and writers have criticized the prevailing culture of secrecy in public bodies as well as the complexities raised by the application of the legislation to privatized and outsourced public services.

Regulation, audit, and inspection

Regulation, audit, and inspection are mechanisms for accountability which have become particularly important since the transfer of many welfare services from the state to private and third sector providers (see Chapter 31). The growth in these mechanisms has been described as the growth of the 'regulatory state' or the 'audit explosion' (Power 2005).

Regulation involves the setting of rules or standards that services are expected to meet and carries along with it sanctions if regulated bodies fail to meet these standards or follow the rules. Inspection often goes along with regulation, as inspectors are appointed to check that standards are being met. Inspection agencies include such bodies as Ofsted which inspects schools in England. Some bodies are both regulators and inspectors while in other services the roles are separate. In order to have any power, regulation and inspection must carry the power to fine service providers for failing to meet standards, to make services change their practices, to publicize poorly performing services, to remove government contracts, and ultimately to close down services. Regulatory and inspection regimes also rely on information which can be considered by independent reviewers. The collection and assessment of information about the activities of public bodies is sometimes known as audit. Traditionally audit concerned mainly financial activities but in recent years has expanded to include wider issues such as service quality and 'value for money'.

Professional mechanisms

Professionals such as doctors, nurses, teachers, and social workers have traditionally relied on self-regulation and professional standards to provide accountability to their fellow professionals. The role of self-regulatory bodies is to use peer or elite knowledge to ensure that the standards of the profession are maintained. Pure self-regulation by the professions has come under increased pressure in recent years as trust in professionals has declined. Pressures have come from both the managerialist suspicion that professionals do not pay sufficient attention to value for money and from the 'user' perspective that professionals do not take sufficient account of user views, combined with a small number of high profile cases such as the murders committed by the GP, Harold Shipman This has led to a decline in self-regulation and an increase in independent or semi-independent regulatory bodies, covering wider areas of professional practice and including more 'lay members'.

Market mechanisms

The market may not seem like an obvious form of accountability but the out-sourcing and privatization reforms of government services relies on the market as a possible mechanism. The theory is that accountability is to the consumer or the purchaser in the market. Since consumer choice in market systems depends on information, choice can be supported by the use of such devices as league tables in health, education, and so on. The introduction of league tables is closely linked to the expansion of regulation, audit, and inspection but the information needed for these mechanisms may be quite different from the information that 'consumers' want or need. Other market mechanisms, such as individual budgets

in social care, turn service users into consumers, who, in theory can hold suppliers to account by exercising greater choice.

User mechanisms

The role of 'consumers' in the provision of public services has been highlighted by both Conservative and Labour governments, with a range of initiatives introduced to try and provide more user accountability. Alongside these top-down managerial reforms, user movements, particularly in the field of health and social care, have demanded more control over decisions about provision of their services. The Citizens Charter initiatives of the 1990s introduced standards and checklists which service users could use to call service providers to account. Alongside these reforms there was a growth in the availability of complaints mechanisms to enable dissatisfied service users to voice their grievances. These are usually accompanied by a rhetoric that public services should 'learn from complaints'. Although some complaints procedures have been effective in bringing problems to light, there is less evidence that public services use them as a mechanism for improving services generally. Other mechanisms for providing user accountability include 'consumer panels', the use of 'lay' and 'user' representatives on decision-making bodies and the expansion of market-type mechanisms discussed above.

Issues Arising From Accountability

Accountability and power

Accountability takes many different forms and is closely related to power. As the circular model of accountability shows, some of the people to whom public services should be accountable are more powerful than others. User movements have tried to increase the power of service users within this model by building into public services accountability mechanisms which include those most directly affected. Critics have argued that much of this is just paying lip service to users and that it will make little difference because of the inherent power differences. Others have argued that increased 'citizen' accountability at the expense of democratic accountability hands power to the more privileged in society, because they are more able to access information and pursue grievances and to participate in such things as the local management of schools and community services.

Costs of accountability

Despite the benefits of increased accountability, accountability also has negative consequences. Accountability mechanisms are expensive: public money is spent on record-keeping, audit, inspection, courts, and ombudsmen at the expense of direct provision of services. Alongside this, research has shown that organizations tend to react to increased monitoring of their activities by partaking in 'game playing', skewing their activities and their records to fit the requirements of the regulators, at the expense of priorities which may be more important. The benefits of increased accountability have to be weighed up against these costs.

Accountability and trust

Accountability is often thought of as being related to legitimacy and trust. Some writers have argued that accountability is more likely to be demanded where trust is low. If we generally trust state actors to get on with the job, we are less likely to demand accountability than if we do not trust them. Writers have argued that the rise in demands for accountability in the past thirty years has gone hand in hand with falling public and political trust in the state. One concern of critics of the increase in accountability regimes is that increase in audit, inspection, and regulation leads to a further decline in trust, which in turn leads to lower employee morale, a fall in professional responsibility, and the stifling of creativity.

Accountability and democracy

Inherent to the explosion of different approaches to accountability is the relationship between the state and its citizens. As we have seen, citizens can relate to the state both in individual and collective ways. Managerialist and consumerist approaches to public services stress individual values and downplay collective values. Outsourcing of services and moves towards community run services removes direct democratic control. Each time that central government has attempted to shift public services out of direct control, there has been a parallel move to increase regulation. This tension between direct control of services and arms length rule making is an intrinsic feature of accountability.

Emerging Issues

New governments coming to power have consistently called for changes to mechanisms for accountability. The incoming devolved administrations in the late 1990s announced that they would increase accountability by reducing the number of unelected public bodies. This proved to be difficult, highlighting some of the inherent contradictions in accountability, such as balancing cost, independence, and democracy. The UK coalition government in 2010 promised a vision of the 'Big Society' in which accountability will move downwards towards citizens and communities. Meanwhile one of its first actions was to cut back the number of publicly funded bodies, in order to save money and to introduce more direct parliamentary accountability. How these policies will develop in practice in Westminster and in the devolved administrations is yet to be seen. While it is likely that cost will be important, the wider debates, tensions, and demands for increased accountability will continue.

Guide to Further Sources

E. Ferlie, L. Lynn, and C. Pollitt (eds), *The Oxford Handbook of Public Management* (Oxford: Oxford University Press, 2005) provides an overview of the issues from a management perspective and includes Bovens and Power's studies. A detailed discussion of the various mechanisms can be found in: C. Harlow and R. Rawlings, *Law and Administration* (3rd edn, Cambridge: Cambridge University Press, 2009); M. Adler (ed.), *Administrative Justice in Context* (London: Hart, 2010) and J. Jowell and D. Oliver (eds), *The Changing Constitution* (Oxford: Oxford University Press, 2007). For discussion of managerialism and the concept of 'publics' see: J. Clarke and J. Newman, *The Managerial State: Power, Politics and Ideology in the Remaking of Social Welfare* (London: Sage and Clarke, 1997); J. Clarke, J. Newman, J. Smith, et al., *Creating Citizen-consumers: Changing Publics and Changing Public Services* (London: Sage, 2007).

For the major audit institutions at the time of writing, see the National Audit Office web site, www.nao.org.uk, and separate web sites for the devolved governments: www.audit-scotland.gov. uk; www.wao.gov.uk; www.niauditoffice.gov. uk. For the main public sector ombudsmen for UK parliament and health in England, www. ombudsman.org.uk; English local government, www.lgo.org.uk; Scotland, www.spso.org.uk; Wales, www.ombudsman-wales.org.uk; and Northern Ireland, www.ni-ombudsman.org.uk.

Review Questions

1   Think about a particular welfare service (e.g. education, health, social care). In relation to this service *who* should be held accountable? and to *whom* should they be held accountable? What tensions arise between the needs of different groups?

2   In relation to a particular welfare service, what accountability mechanisms can you identify? How do these mechanisms overlap? Are any of them in conflict with each other?

3   What are the advantages and disadvantages of increasing accountability?

4   How do democratic and 'user' focused accountability mechanisms conflict with each other? How could mechanisms be improved to take account of both?

5   Identify any recent proposals for increasing accountability and/or cutting the costs of accountability. What implications do these proposals have for the issues raised in this chapter?

Visit the book companion site at www.wiley. com/go/alcock to make use of the resources designed to accompany the textbook. There you will find chapter-specific guides to further resources, including governmental, international, think-tank, pressure groups, and relevant journals sources. You will also find a glossary based on *The Blackwell Dictionary of Social Policy*, help sheets, and case studies, guidance on managing assignments in social policy and career advice.

40

Welfare Users and Social Policy

Marian Barnes

Overview

■ The original 'welfare citizens' were seen primarily in passive terms.

■ The influence of neo-liberal thinking created the identity of 'welfare consumers'.

■ Service-user organizations challenged assumptions of professionally determined service delivery and impacted on policy and research.

■ Both Labour and Conservative governments have promoted the idea of 'active citizens' with responsibility for their own and others' welfare.

■ Mechanisms for user/citizen influence on policy and services continue to change.

Imagining Welfare Citizens

The creation of the welfare state resulted in the creation of welfare citizens. The welfare state imagined by Beveridge in the 1940s envisaged the welfare citizen as white, male, and working to support a wife and children (see Chapter 18). There have been many re-imaginings of welfare citizens or welfare users since. These have been prompted by social and demographic changes – an increasingly diverse population, an ageing population, an increase in female employment, growing diversity in family structures; by an expansion in the scope of the welfare state as well as shifts in its architecture; by politically driven reconfigurations of state/citizen responsibilities; and by challenges coming from welfare users themselves. The focus here is on the impact of the last two of these changes, looking primarily at those taking place in England, although similar shifts in the state–citizen relationship have been evident elsewhere and can be explored in the sources listed in the last section.

The Student's Companion to Social Policy, Fourth Edition. Edited by Pete Alcock, Margaret May, Sharon Wright.
© 2012 John Wiley & Sons, Ltd. Published 2012 by John Wiley & Sons, Ltd.

From Welfare Citizen to Consumer to Commissioner

The creation of the welfare state after the Second World War was an embodiment of the state's responsibilities toward ensuring welfare and social justice. The concept of citizenship was expanded to encompass social citizenship that would have benefits for both individual citizens and for the state itself. While the scope of this was limited – both in relation to the question of who was recognized as a citizen, and the range of services encompassed within it (for example, personal social services did not emerge until the 1970s), the principle underpinning the establishment of the welfare state was that citizens had a right to welfare.

In practice, it has operated primarily on the basis of an assessment of need, providing a safety net for those least able to look after themselves. Resource constraints have always limited the delivery of universal social rights and a major theme of social policy has been how to define and target precisely which citizens will receive help from the state. In this context and during this period welfare users were conceived as recipients of services, there was little expectation that they would play an active role in determining their own needs, let alone shaping policy or service delivery.

The shift that started to occur from the late 1970s in terms of the overall identity of 'welfare users' – from that of citizen to consumer, is arguably more profound than specific decisions about the level of need that will, for example, determine older people's entitlements to social care, or whether certain 'self induced' health problems (resulting from smoking or excessive use of alcohol for example) should preclude access to free health care. However, precisely who could or should determine need has been one focus for challenge from service users.

Neo-liberal arguments in the late 1970s started to influence the architecture of the welfare state in a way that continues today. In the 1980s the emphasis was on encouraging both private and voluntary providers into a welfare market. Labour governments from 1997–2010 encouraged an increased role for the voluntary or 'third' sector, a trend being further developed by the UK coalition government elected in 2010.

Thus, the role of the state has shifted from provider to purchaser to commissioner of services, leaving a much reduced direct provision role (see Chapter 30). In this context the identity of the welfare citizen was first re-imagined as that of welfare consumer 'shopping around' in a welfare market, while the more recent introduction of 'personalization' as the basis on which social and health care are provided has led to service users becoming their own commissioners, using money allocated to them on the basis of assessed need to commission their own support (see Chapter 51).

Key to the identity of welfare users as both consumers and commissioners is the ability to exercise choice about what services they receive. The strength of this shift from viewing recipients of welfare as 'passive' citizens to 'active' consumers reflects users' frustration about being subject to professional assessment and decision-making. The opportunity to shift the balance to 'empower' service users by giving them choice over services was a potent antidote to the sense of powerlessness that was increasingly being expressed by the 1980s.

This was a period in which disabled people and users of mental health services (some of whom identified themselves as 'survivors' not only of mental illness but of oppressive interventions from welfare professionals) created organizations that challenged bureaucratic and professional dominance of welfare services. One aspect of the argument, put forward primarily by people with physical impairments at that time, was that they should be able to make their own decisions about the services they received, rather than be dependent on professional assessment and gate-keeping.

However, the exercise of choice necessitates a range of services from which to choose, as well as the availability of information to assist the process of selection, and the capacity and willingness to make judgements about the best or preferred option. It also assumes that people see their relationship with welfare services in the same way as they see their relationship with private sector goods and services The questionable nature of these assumptions underpinned the many critiques of consumerist constructions of the relationship between service providers and users that emerged during the Thatcher/Major years, and which continued to be voiced as subsequent

Labour governments continued to promote the identity of service user as consumer. Such critiques have become more muted as personalization has been hailed as a force for positive transformation in the relationship between welfare state and citizen, but still endure.

Different mechanisms were put in place through which clients, patients, claimants, and other recipients of welfare services were translated into consumers, stimulated both by the Conservative project of marketization, and by the challenges coming from service user and health consumer groups. In the 1980s market research and consumer satisfaction surveys were introduced to assess how well the NHS was meeting the needs and wishes of its customers and satisfaction surveys have continued to be a regular means of obtaining feedback. The 1990 NHS and Community Care Act introduced the internal market into the NHS, and the Patients' Charter introduced procedural rights for patients, set standards, and published league tables intended to improve accountability. While resistance to a market-based health service has remained strong, the idea that there should be separation between purchasers, and later 'commissioners', and service providers has become broadly established. What is now referred to as 'intelligent commissioning' encourages a proliferation of service providers within the private and the 'third sector' (voluntary sector), and social enterprises. Service users are encouraged to take up direct payments or personal budgets to purchase their own support services directly from a developing social market.

Active, Responsible Citizens

Alongside the encouragement of the active consumer, Conservative governments of the 1980s and 1990s promoted the 'active citizen' – someone who not only took responsibility for demanding value for money from public services, but also took responsibility for looking after their own welfare, that of their families, and the communities in which they live. Once again, Labour continued to promote the importance of active citizens, developing the concept in a more communitarian direction than was evident in Tory discourse. For example, as Home Secretary, David Blunkett promoted the importance of self-

discipline, family life, strong communities, and relationships based on rights and responsibilities, adopting the concept of 'civil renewal' to characterize the changes he sought. His vision for civil renewal encompassed a range of social groups and relationships, including actions to be taken by inward migrants to make a positive contribution to their 'host' country. It was also closely associated with the development of the 'Respect' agenda that targeted perceived antisocial behaviour among young people in order to prevent, encourage, and enforce good behaviour and to create responsible citizenship.

We can identify a number of incarnations of the active or responsible citizen in relation to welfare. For example,

- Community care policy has depended on the preparedness of family members to take on the major responsibility for the care of disabled, ill, or frail relations. Successive governments have recognized the significance of unpaid care to ensuring the well-being of those they support and to protecting the state from demands for welfare it feels unable to meet. Such recognition has led to strategies to support carers to continue to care, but which at the same time reinforce and extend caring responsibilities.
- One responsibility that the 2008 Carers Strategy set out was that carers should look after their own health in order to continue to be able to provide care to others. This emphasis on self-care is explicit in the title of a 2004 Department of Health policy document 'Choosing Health' – responsible citizens should choose to behave in ways that enhance and improve their health, for example by not smoking, taking exercise, and maintaining a healthy diet, in order to reduce the demands on health services.
- Participation in community based action to contribute to community cohesion and regeneration. There are many examples and contexts in which people living in poor communities subject to structural disadvantage and environmental degradation are exhorted or 'empowered' to take action to address the multiple problems they are experiencing. As in the case of carers, we can see conflicting or competing principles at stake – on the one

hand poor communities are recognized as having the capacity to be active agents to make change, on the other they are expected to take responsibility for seeking local solutions to problems that often have macrolevel structural causes

■ Responsible parenting. The identification of antisocial behaviour as a major social problem was associated with an identification of feckless, incompetent parents unable to control their children or act as role models to them. One response was to develop a series of interventions intended both to 'support' parents, but also regulate their parenting practices so that they might raise future responsible citizens.

The identity of the *active* citizen, rather than what came to be seen as a more passive understanding of the citizen as rights bearer, is thus the site of similar contestation to that associated with the 'active consumer'. Both offer recognition of the agency of welfare users, but also impose responsibilities associated with particular types of behaviour.

The proliferation of initiatives though which consumers, citizens, and community members have been invited, encouraged, and exhorted to take part in shaping and delivering social policy through membership of Patient and Public Involvement Forums, Local Involvement Networks, Sure Start Boards, Senior Citizens Forums, and many more, embody different and at times competing ways of thinking about relationships between the welfare state and its citizens. These have been important opportunities for citizens to have their say about policies and practices that affect their lives both individually and collectively, and have impacted both particular social policies (such as personalization) and relationships between welfare professionals and those who use their services. Such developments also represent a substantial shift in the way in which policy-making takes place, and in the practice of democracy. Whether they represent a fundamental change in the balance of power between welfare users and the welfare state is more questionable.

Activists and Experts

Taking part in the 'invited spaces' of public participation and user involvement is only one context in which welfare users have started to shape the welfare system in which they are engaged. Alongside official initiatives to give patients, service users, and citizens a say in policy and service delivery, groups of patients, users, carers and local communities have also organized separately, claimed the right to determine their own identities as well as the support necessary to meet their own needs, and to influence policy and service delivery. In the case of the carer's movement, this has been influential in gaining recognition for the identity of 'carer' as a distinct role and relationship, and in generating a body of policy and practice designed to support caring relationships (see Chapter 34).

Organizations of welfare users have also challenged the way in which knowledge is produced about what it means to live with impairment or mental illness, to grow old, to provide care for a disabled child, or to depend on welfare services to meet basic needs. Thus, the way in which research is carried out and the way in which practitioners are educated and trained has been affected by collective action among service users. Research funders now require consideration of how users are to be involved in the conduct of health and social care research and the training of social workers and other welfare professionals often includes direct input from users.

Assumptions that the only valid form of knowledge comes via professional education can no longer be sustained in the face of recognition of the value of the expert knowledge that comes from lived experience of mental illness, poverty, disability, or other experiences of welfare users. One way in which this has been harnessed is via the 'expert patients' programme. This is an initiative focused on people who live with 'long-term conditions': such as diabetes, arthritis, or cancer, which recognizes that people develop strategies for living with and managing such conditions outwith the advice or expertise of clinicians. The programme offers training by 'expert patients' to support those learning to live with such conditions. Social policy as a discipline has needed to recognize the contributions and critiques of those whose analysis comes from lived experience rather than academic study.

Collective action among users of welfare services has been organized around specific 'conditions': cancer or arthritis for example, through umbrella organizations with a broader remit, such as the Long-term Medical Conditions Alliance; those that relate to specific experiences, such as women who have experienced sexual abuse, groups that focus on reproductive health issues, carers or people who hear voices; those that identify themselves as part of a broader disability movement; and community based groups whose focus is on health inequalities and the availability and quality of generic health services.

These groups vary in political stance, in their preparedness to work with public officials, their national or local focus, and their size and resources. Some have prioritized advocacy or political campaigning, others provide a focus for sharing and exploring experiences, others have developed alternative models of service delivery (such as Independent Living Centres), and some have developed user led research and training.

Both researchers and activists have considered the significance of the collective challenge posed by user groups as evidence that they constitute a social movement or movements. Thus, one of the most significant impacts of the disabled people's movement has been the articulation of the social model of disability. This reframes disability as a socially constructed condition rather than an individual problem or 'tragedy' (see Chapter 57). The solution to the 'problem' of disability thus becomes one of addressing 'disabling barriers' rather than working on the bodies of disabled people. This shift in the way in which social issues or social problems are conceptualized is characteristic of new social movements whose aims focus on the transformation of values and meanings, rather than on redistribution.

Taking part in social movement action has both personal and political value, and has been of particular significance for people, including people with learning disabilities and those who live with mental health problems, whose identity and self-esteem has been undermined by the way they are treated – within the health and social care system and beyond. While many have been sceptical about the extent of the change achieved either through oppositional campaigning, or by working in partnership with service providers, taking part in such action has marked recognition that they have much to contribute and has been a personal transformation for many participants.

There is one way in which the disabled people's movement has made a significant impact on the design of welfare services and that is in the official acceptance of the idea of direct payments within the context of the shift towards personalization and self-directed support. This has also created a key role for what are referred to within official circles as User Led Organizations (ULOs) in supporting service users to exercise choice in how to spend their allocated budget. A key consequence of this is that ULOs are now brought within the welfare system and may be seen to have lost their independence and capacity to offer independent challenge.

Emerging Issues

Relationships between welfare state and welfare users have undergone major changes in the late twentieth and early twenty-first century. This is evident in the face-to-face relationships between those who provide and those who receive services, in the way in which policies are made and services are governed, and in the way in which policy issues are framed and researched. Questions remain about the extent to which this has led to transformational improvements in the lives of those who need welfare services, but it is impossible now to imagine a return to a situation in which people simply 'took what they were given' without question.

The mechanisms for 'user involvement' will continue to change, for example, one of the early announcements of the UK coalition government in 2010 was to abolish Local Involvement Networks and replace them with 'Health Watch' organizations. Another fear in some quarters is that the emphasis on individual choice that is key to the personalization agenda will become stronger under the coalition and will limit the capacity for collective influence exerted by organized user groups. Certainly it is clear that the emphasis on the responsibility of active citizens is being reinforced, in this new context under the rubric of the 'Big Society' in which the responsibilities of the state are balanced by 'what we can do for ourselves' and 'what we can do for others.' Such responsibilities are being promoted in the context of savage public spending cuts which mean even more limited access to state welfare.

The tensions between recognizing the contribution welfare users can make to both policy and service delivery, and the responsibility of the state to ensure the welfare and well-being of its citizens; and between ensuring individually responsive services and enabling opportunities for collective influence on policy and service design, remain key to continuing negotiations between the welfare state and its citizens. But social policy as both discipline and practice can no longer ignore welfare users as active agents within the system.

Guide to Further Sources

M. Barnes and R. Bowl, *Taking Over the Asylum: Empowerment and Mental Health* (Basingstoke: Palgrave, 2001) considers both official initiatives to involve mental health service users and action by users/survivors themselves. M. Barnes, J. Newman, and H. Sullivan, *Power, Participation and Political Renewal. Case Studies in Public Participation* (Bristol: Policy Press, 2007) discusses competing discourses of different 'publics' in public participation, and provides case study examples of these in practice. J. Clarke *et al.*, *Creating Citizen-Consumers* (London: Sage, 2007) is based on research that explores relationships between public services and the public in the context of health, social care, and policing. A. Cornwell and V. Schattan Coelho (eds), *Spaces for Change* (London: Zed Books, 2007) is a collection that that explores the way in which decision-making about health and other services is being opened up to public influence in the global south

as well as the north. A European perspective on active citizenship can be found in J. E. Newman, and E. Tonkens (eds), *Active Citizenship in Europe* (Amsterdam: University of Amsterdam Press, 2011).

The concept of the Big Society is fundamental to the coalition government's thinking in this area www.thebigsociety.co.uk. Relevant web sites include those of the national survivor user network www.nsun.org.uk and the National Centre for Independent Living www.ncil.org.uk.

Review Questions

1   What have been the major drivers for change in relationships between service users and providers?
2   Have these changes contributed to social justice?
3   Is greater influence by service users unambiguously a 'good thing'?
4   Are 'active citizens' and 'active consumers' the same?
5   Can users be influential without independent user groups?

Visit the book companion site at www.wiley.com/go/alcock to make use of the resources designed to accompany the textbook. There you will find chapter-specific guides to further resources, including governmental, international, think-tank, pressure groups, and relevant journals sources. You will also find a glossary based on *The Blackwell Dictionary of Social Policy*, help sheets, and case studies, guidance on managing assignments in social policy and career advice.

41

Local and Regional Government and Governance

Guy Daly and Howard Davis

■■■

Overview

- The analysis of local provision involves the study of both local government and local governance.
- Both are a key element of social policy formation and provision.
- Local government structures are subject to constant reorganization and there is continuous tension between central and local concerns.
- The development of local government is best considered in terms of five stages, the latest involving major changes in its role and resources.
- These are presenting new challenges and questions about the configuration of local governance.

■■■

The Development of Local Government and Local Governance

The local, however that is defined, has helped to shape social policy and provision in the past and continues to do so. As explored elsewhere in this text, social policy may be defined in a traditional Beveridgean manner with a focus on welfare services such as health care, education, housing, personal social services and care, income maintenance, and employment, or via a more expansive definition which also encompasses leisure, transport and the environment, or via more recent constructions which focus on community safety and social inclusion.

Whichever approach is used, local government and local governance are key parts of social policy and provision. These different terms – local government and local governance – are generally used to distinguish between the elected local councils on the one hand and the wider range of local public service bodies on the other.

The Student's Companion to Social Policy, Fourth Edition. Edited by Pete Alcock, Margaret May, Sharon Wright.
© 2012 John Wiley & Sons, Ltd. Published 2012 by John Wiley & Sons, Ltd.

While Britain has a more centralized set of government and governance arrangements than many of its fellow European Union member states, the state at the centre directs and works alongside local, sub-national, and devolved (Scotland, Wales, and Northern Ireland) policy-making and implementation structures (see Chapter 42). Indeed, when UK governmental structures are compared with other European states, it is notable that local government is constitutionally weaker within the United Kingdom and, at the same time, the units of local government are relatively large but have relatively fewer councillors per head.

What this means is, first, that in the UK local government's influence tends to emanate from the scale and nature of its operations rather than through constitutional strength and, second, that UK local government is liable to and has experienced constant reorganization and changes to its responsibilities, structures, and governance arrangements.

History is often an important influence on the way that things are done and the structures and institutions that are in place. The government and governance of local communities is no exception. This history can be traced back for centuries. Present day local government, however, really begins in the nineteenth century and has, in many ways, a strong connection with the progress of the industrial revolution. In particular, as urbanization and industrialization increased, the need for a wider range of services became more apparent.

Sanitation, elementary education, public health, law and order, and physical infrastructure were vital in building successful businesses and economies. In what might be seen as a period of enlightened self-interest by the local 'great and good', local public bodies increasingly took over service provision from private and charitable organizations.

Key dates include the Municipal Corporations Act of 1835, the Poor Law Amendment Act 1834, the Local Government Acts of 1888, 1894 and 1929 – and parallel legislation for London, Scotland, Wales, and Ireland. By the time of the Second World War local councils in urban areas were responsible for, and running, most local public services – literally from cradle to grave. In rural areas this was less the case and local public services were far less developed.

Local governance within the post-Second World War consensus

The period from 1945 up until the election of the Thatcher Conservative government in 1979 is often described as a period of consensus across the major political parties and this is arguably as true for local governance and government as is it was for other social policy arenas. The period was one in which local government was a major partner in building the welfare state, reflected in a significant growth in local authorities' expenditure between 1945 and 1979. Local councils had key responsibilities for providing

- social housing
- education
- personal social services and social care for children and older people
- community based health care until 1974
- public health, and
- public protection – police and fire services, ambulances (until 1974), consumer protection.

Local governance and the New Right

However, during the 1970s the consensual period of expansion and belief in state provision, including through local government, started to be questioned. The period of Conservative government between 1979 and 1997 signalled the definitive break with the post-war consensus. Indeed, it can be argued that local government was one of the prime sites for the New Right reforms in social policy. The Thatcher/Major governments' approach to local government can be typified as

- a period in the early 1980s of focusing on controlling local government expenditure;
- a period in the mid-1980s of restructuring with the abolition of the Greater London Council (GLC) and the metropolitan county councils – and shifts of responsibilities away from elected local government into government appointed local bodies ('quangos');
- a period in the mid- to late 1980s of challenging local authorities' role as the direct providers of services through privatization and the encouragement of local authorities to be enablers of services rather than direct providers;

- a period in the early 1990s of new managerialist approaches, for example, with the promotion of citizen's charters, league tales, inspection, and audit.

All of local government's main services were affected, including

- education – centralization of control including the weakening of local education authorities, the implementation of the national curriculum, local management of schools, and the independence of further and higher education;
- housing – 'right to buy' scheme encouraged tenants to buy their council homes at a discount, transfer of whole estates through the creation of Housing Action Trusts, and in the 1990s the first examples of large scale stock transfer schemes;
- social care – promotion of social services departments as enablers of residential and domiciliary care;
- introduction of competitive pressures into many services through compulsory competitive tendering (CCT) and the purchaser/provider split; and
- the creation of Urban Development Corporations that took over key urban regeneration responsibilities from local government.

All in all, the Thatcher and Major period of government has been depicted as a period in which the local state was 'hollowed out' with the privatization of certain local authority responsibilities, increased central pressure on those services that remained, and the shift of some responsibilities to local quangos.

Even so, the period of 1979–97 was not one of passive acquiescence by local government. On the contrary, perhaps in part as a response to the politics of the New Right, this period saw the emergence of what has been described as the 'Urban Left' in local government. In a number of cities, for example Liverpool, Sheffield, parts of London, and in the Greater London Council, Labour-controlled authorities adopted radical Left agendas, whether in relation to transport, housing, policing, education, jobs and services generally, multiculturalism, or positive action for disabled persons' groups and lesbian and gay groups. Local government was often the site of political dispute between the New Right and the Left, epitomized by the fights over the 'poll tax'.

However, while the Conservative power base in local government had been virtually wiped out by the time Labour came to power in 1997, much of the Urban Left's agenda had been defeated by Conservative central government legislation. Paradoxically, much of the Urban Left agenda (for example rights for disadvantaged groups) has nowadays been absorbed into mainstream social policy. What this also shows is the continual tension between central government and local governance bodies. On the one hand the centre (Parliament) may wish for a universal policy and yet, because for example inequalities are not spatially uniform, at the local level particular solutions may be required to meet specific concerns.

Local governance and New Labour

The Labour administration of 1997 arrived with a huge agenda for change and moved quickly to use the language and rhetoric of partnership between national and local government. It also soon repealed one of the most hated aspects of Conservative local government legislation – the obligation to subject local public services to open competition with the private sector (via CCT) replacing it with a new duty of continuous improvement.

However, it soon became apparent that, like its Conservative predecessor, Labour also had its doubts about local government. There was to be no return to old (pre-Conservative government) ways of working. There was to be no simple undoing of Conservative legislation affecting local government and local public services and the government quickly identified what it saw as a number of problems with local government as it stood.

While many aspects of Labour's aspirations were widely shared its solutions were not always so warmly embraced. Among the more controversial aspects were the requirements on councils to streamline their decision-making arrangements – leading to the separation of executive and representative roles among councillors. This led to the creation of local authority Cabinets and Executives and the concentration of executive powers in fewer hands; something that many in local government regretted. A small number of authorities moved to having directly elected Executive Mayors.

Legislation also gave central government new powers to act on service failures by local councils and introduced the concept of inspection to all local government services. The investment in inspection undoubtedly increased the focus on service improvement and unlocked some long-standing problems in a number of authorities. However, the inspection process came at some cost – a matter of increasing concern to local councils as the regime rolled out and on. There were also arguably diminishing returns. This led in time to moves towards more proportionate and risk-based approaches to inspection; though the controversy about the respective costs and value of inspection continued.

The agenda was two-pronged. On the one hand, there was a considerable investment in key services along with an emphasis by central government on the important role of local government. However, at the same time, Labour also emphasized and enacted major programmes of reform in order to bring about its vision of a revitalized local government.

Challenging the performance management of authorities and services was key to its approach. Central government sought to embed a culture of continuous improvement and innovation across the whole range of local public services. The period might therefore be characterized as one of continuous revolution, in which change management was crucial. As such, the government and governance of local communities were faced with major challenges and change in just about everything done at the local level. Key to this were

- an emphasis on community leadership rather than direct service delivery;
- increased engagement of, and responsiveness to, local communities and service users;
- an emphasis on performance management and increased efficiency in the use of resources;
- an emphasis on impacts and results; and
- pragmatism rather than ideology as to the best ways forward.

In addition, Labour created regional structures in that, alongside the devolved administrations in Scotland, Wales, and Northern Ireland, in England Regional Development Agencies were established to oversee spatial, planning, and regeneration matters.

In part because of Labour's emphasis on 'what works is what counts', local government and governance continued to be conducted within a mixed and changing structural and organizational context.

Localism and the UK coalition government

The UK coalition government that emerged from the 2010 election initially focused principally on a strategy for reducing the UK's budget deficit. However, large numbers of policy announcements followed, often with little initial clarity or detail, affecting the structures and modes of operation of wide swathes of public services. It aimed to create a 'big society' – an empowered society where communities and voluntary action were to the fore – a 'big society' rather than a 'big state'.

In relation to local government and public services at the local level, the UK coalition government defined its priority, in the words of Eric Pickles in 2010, Secretary of State for the Department of Communities and Local Government at the time, as 'localism, localism, localism'. But 'localism' was not simply to be equated with either place (in the geographical sense) or local government. It was seen as a means for pushing power downwards and outwards to the lowest possible level. This includes communities acquiring the right to bid to run services and to save facilities at risk of closure.

The pressures on voluntary and community action are, however, likely to be significant as the freeing-up of local action has to be seen in the context of major reductions in the levels and scope of public spending set in train in 2010 by the UK coalition government's post-election emergency budget and Comprehensive Spending Review and subsequent proposals on local funding. Local government and local public services therefore face a continuing struggle in contending with the largest spending, and staffing, cuts in recent history, while demands for many services, for example, adult social care, continue to increase. This can be expected to lead to continuing pressures on local authorities and other local public services to save money by withdrawing from, merging or sharing service provision, and searching for alternative ways of ensuring front line service delivery.

Local Government and Governance Structures

When it comes to local government structures, most of the UK population is served by so-called unitary local authorities. This is where there is just one local authority for the particular local area providing all or most local government services in that area. These authorities come in a variety of guises and with a variety of titles but all are responsible for the spectrum of local government services – from street scene to lifelong learning, from trading standards to social care.

An exception to this general rule exists in some parts of England outside the main urban areas – the English shires. In these areas a two-tier local government system exists comprising a county council and a number of district councils, with the former responsible for those services thought to need a larger scale for their operation such as lifelong learning, social care, and strategic planning. The district councils on the other hand have responsibility for most local environmental services (such as refuse collection and street cleaning), together with housing, leisure services, and local development control. However, the two tiers are increasingly working more closely together and beginning moves towards a 'virtual unitary' structure where, although the two tiers continue to exist, they may share services and officers and seek to offer seamless service delivery to the public.

All of the councils mentioned above are directly elected by local electors, whether they are in a unitary or two-tier setting. There are though some differences in electoral arrangements between different types of council. In London there exists in addition to the London local authorities (the London boroughs) a directly elected regional authority – the Greater London Authority (GLA) – comprising an Assembly and a Mayor of London. The GLA is responsible for key London-wide functions such as public protection (police and fire), transport, and economic development.

One other tier of directly elected government that needs to be mentioned is the parish. Parish, town, or community councils are a key link in the chain of local representation. They do not exist in all areas – most notably having been absent from the main urban areas – though this is beginning to change. For the most part, they also have powers rather than duties – acting as the voice of villages, small towns, and neighbourhoods – and making that voice heard to other tiers of government as the occasion demands. They have few service delivery responsibilities.

Some important local services are not provided by elected local government at all. Key among them are health services (apart from public health) – which are the responsibility of the various arms and parts of the National Health Service – and policing – which generally comes under a local police authority or police board.

In order to overcome the fragmentation of local public services between local government and other bodies there has, since the 1997 general election, been an increasing emphasis on partnership working. This has continued, though with different emphases, under the UK coalition government. The term 'local governance' is today used to refer to these wider local public service provision and partnership arrangements – distinguishing them from the elected local government (council) structures described earlier.

Under Labour a range of statutory partnerships aimed to bring together all the key local public service bodies in each local authority area – councils, police, health, and so forth – to agree key common objectives and priorities for all the local public services in that area. Typically these included a number of objectives seeking to make their communities healthier, cleaner, greener, and safer – with better education and employment prospects. Under the UK coalition government, the emphasis moved away from statutory partnerships to more voluntary arrangements based on local needs and wishes. However, whatever the political controlling forces, there is inevitably a need for some form of local governance, if not local government, arrangements.

Emerging Issues

As we have seen local government and local arrangements remain important for the shaping and delivery of social policy. From the industrial revolution onwards, as well as during the period of establishing the post-war welfare state, through the periods of Conservative, Labour and, more recently, the UK coalition government, local government has been required to both co-ordinate and deliver key elements of social policy.

However, issues remain around the need for local and sub-national governance arrangements to engage more effectively with social policy agendas, including local inequalities and local needs. Ways of ensuring increased civic engagement and civic renewal – including the greater participation of citizens and service users in local decision-making – are likely to be areas of continuing focus and debate. This extends into questions of where the 'boundary' should properly fall between voluntary and community action and (local) state responsibility, in terms of both the 'staffing' and funding of local services and facilities, especially in an era of tighter public finances.

The wider question of the adequacy or otherwise of the mechanisms for financing local government and local public services can also be expected to be an area of differing views. In addition, ongoing controversy can be anticipated concerning the effectiveness of local government and local governance structures and arrangements, including views on the effectiveness or otherwise of performance and accountability arrangements, and of stronger leadership structures such as elected police commissioners and greater numbers of directly elected city mayors.

Whatever the outcome of these particular debates local government is likely to remain key in attempts to improve the health, education, economic prosperity, housing, environment, safety, and security of their communities. Indeed, it is arguable that without local government to lead on these initiatives, local governance would be even more complicated, disjointed, and fragmented than it is today.

Guide to Further Resources

A useful overview of the management and governance of public services can be found in: T. Bovaird and E. Loffler (eds), *Public Management and Governance* (2nd edn, London: Routledge, 2009). B. Denters and L. E. Rose, *Comparing Local Governance: Trends and Developments* (Basingstoke: Palgrave Macmillan, 2005), is a good introductory text that compares local governance in the United Kingdom with several other European countries, the United States, Australia, and New Zealand. C. Durose, S. Greaseley, and L. Richarson *Changing Local Governance, Changing Citizens* (Bristol: Policy Press, 2009) is a useful exploration of the changing relationship between citizens and local decision-makers.

R. A. W. Rhodes, *Beyond Westminster and Whitehall: Sub-Central Governments of Britain* (London: Unwin Hyman, 1998), remains a seminal text on the nature of the relationships between central government and local governance structures. J. Stewart, *The Nature of British Local Government* (Basingstoke: Macmillan Press, 2000) remains a good source on the historical underpinnings of British local government. D. Wilson and C. Game (eds), *Local Government in the United Kingdom* (5th edn, Basingstoke: Palgrave Macmillan, 2011) also offers a good general introduction to the subject.

Useful web sites include: The Local Government Association, www.lga.gov.uk (there are equivalent sites for Scotland, Wales and Northern Ireland); The Government gateway portal for all public services and government departments, www.direct.gov.uk, and the *Social Policy Digest*, http://journals.cambridge.org.spd/action/home.

Review Questions

1 Do you know which council or councils are responsible for overseeing which services in your locality?
2 Do you know what the political complexion is of your local council(s) and what the electoral arrangements are?
3 What do you think could be done to increase participation in civic engagement and local decision-making?
4 What do you think are some of the advantages and disadvantages of directly elected mayors being in charge of local councils?
5 What do you think of the idea that the 'local state' should do less and citizens should engage more in voluntary action?

Visit the book companion site at www.wiley.com/ go/alcock to make use of the resources designed to accompany the textbook. There you will find chapter-specific guides to further resources, including governmental, international, think- tank, pressure groups, and relevant journals sources. You will also find a glossary based on *The Blackwell Dictionary of Social Policy*, help sheets and case studies, guidance on managing assign- ments in social policy and career advice.

42

Social Policy and Devolution

Richard Parry

Overview

- The United Kingdom is a unitary, London-centred state that has made a political adjustment to the wishes of Scotland, Wales, and Northern Ireland by devolving powers over many areas of social policy.
- England still dominates in both scale and thinking, and retains control over the tax-benefit system.
- The organization of the welfare state within the devolved nations is more coherent than in England.
- The devolved nations have made some interesting policy initiatives, generally in the direction of a more universalist and less privatized welfare state.
- The current arrangements are politically and financially unstable.

Uniformity and Diversity in UK Social Policy

The United Kingdom is a strongly unitary state and lacks a clear concept of regional differences in social policy in terms of formation, implementation, and content. The main source of difference is the status of Scotland, Wales, and Northern Ireland within the United Kingdom, enjoying nationhood but not statehood and since 1999 having their own devolved elected administrations with extensive powers over social policy. The key feature, however, is the dominance of England in the United Kingdom. It accounts for 85 per cent of the population and London, its capital, is the centre of political, governmental, cultural, and media activity. Britain has uniform welfare benefit rates and a lesser sense of systematic multilevel political structure than any country of comparable size. But there is a tension in United Kingdom social policy between tolerating differences on grounds of diversity and choice

The Student's Companion to Social Policy, Fourth Edition. Edited by Pete Alcock, Margaret May, Sharon Wright.
© 2012 John Wiley & Sons, Ltd. Published 2012 by John Wiley & Sons, Ltd.

and resisting them on grounds of uniform citizen rights without 'postcode lotteries'.

Scotland, Wales, and Northern Ireland have distinct historical traditions and political profiles. Scotland was independent until 1707 and the Act of Union preserved its legal system, Presbyterian Church, and local government. It had stronger traditions in education and medicine than did England, and became a United Kingdom leader in these fields. Wales was never a defined independent state but its linguistic and religious pattern was clearly different. The Labour government of 1997 promoted the transfer of the powers of the Scottish Office to a law-making Scottish Parliament, and of the Welsh Office to a National Assembly for Wales administering and financing them within a framework of Westminster legislation.

Both are elected for four-year terms under a system that included a minority of regional seats allocated from party lists to make the overall seat distribution as proportional as possible. Referendums in September 1997 approved the proposals by a strong majority in Scotland (74 per cent) but a bare 50 per cent in Wales. Scotland also voted 63 per cent to give the Parliament limited powers to alter income tax, but this has not been used. Elections were held in May 1999 and the new administrations assumed their powers on 1 July 1999. Labour fell short of overall majorities and (in Scotland from the start and in Wales from October 2000) formed a coalition government with the Liberal Democrats. After the 2003 elections Labour continued in coalition in Scotland but was just able to form a majority administration in Wales on its own. After the 2007 elections, in Scotland the pro-independence Scottish National Party edged ahead of Labour in seats and votes and formed a minority administration; it was able to pass its budgets after deals with the Conservatives but not its proposed referendum on independence. In Wales Labour lost relatively more ground but after an unsuccessful attempt by the other parties to negotiate an alternative coalition it formed a coalition deal with the nationalist Plaid Cymru. After the 2011 elections the Labour-dominated pattern seen in 2003 was resumed.

Ireland had a separate Parliament until 1801, then united with Great Britain but split in 1922 into an independent country (later the Republic of Ireland) and the six counties of Northern Ireland, which remained in the United Kingdom and until 1972 had a local Parliament. Following the Belfast Good Friday agreement of April 1998 a law-making Assembly was elected and an Executive with members of all political parties ran, with interruptions, from December 1999 to October 2002 when it was suspended and direct rule from Westminster reinstated. Political talks in 2006 (the St Andrews Agreement) paved the way for elections in March 2007 that reinforced the position of formerly 'extremist' parties in each community, the Democratic Unionists and Sinn Féin, and in a historic compromise they agreed to work together in the Executive, which was reactivated in May 2007 and took over police and justice powers in April 2010.

Nation-specific Social Policy Legislation

There is a single United Kingdom framework for social security (Northern Ireland has different original legislation but strict parity of structure and rates). Pre-devolution, education and housing legislation was largely the same in England and Wales but different in Scotland and Northern Ireland (especially in the structure of school examinations in Scotland and denominational education in Northern Ireland). These latter two nations also had a distinct tradition in health within the common NHS 'brand'. Outside the area of cash benefits, social policy is largely devolved; exceptions include the health professions, abortion, and drugs policy. But crime, justice, police, and prisons in Wales have always been run on a common basis with England and are not devolved.

Since devolution, the Scottish Parliament is free to legislate in non-reserved areas, and in addition the 'Sewel Convention' allows it to ask Westminster to make changes in statutes in devolved areas as part of UK legislation (used most notably in the 2004 law to institute civil partnerships). The most significant Scottish Parliament social policy legislation includes the Housing (Scotland) Act 2001 which created a single kind of social tenancy and new policies on homelessness; the Community Care and Health (Scotland) Act 2002 to set a framework for non-means tested personal care; and the Anti-Social

Behaviour Act (Scotland) 2004, seen as taking a tougher attitude to youth crime issues. Perhaps the most eye-catching initiative was the ban on smoking in public places in March 2006, over a year ahead of the rest of the UK. Social legislation since 2007 has been less significant because the SNP government lacked a majority – an SNP proposal for minimum unit pricing on alcohol was defeated in 2010 – but one innovation was the piloting of direct elections to two Health Boards in 2010.

The National Assembly for Wales works within a legislative framework set by the Westminster Parliament. Major Wales-only provisions in education and health legislation were passed but the process was slow. The Government of Wales Act 2006 introduced the concept of an 'Assembly Measure' in devolved areas, and further 'legislative competence orders' have in effect given the Assembly powers over education, health, and housing. The Act allowed full law-making powers on the Scottish model after a further referendum. Promotion of a 'yes' vote in this referendum was a key part of the Labour-Plaid Cymru deal and it was secured in 2011.

Northern Ireland's previous devolved government until 1972 maintained religiously discriminatory features in education and housing while seeking parity with mainland standards in health and social security. Later policies emphasized equal opportunities (with explicit legislation against religious discrimination, and Catholic schools funded equally) and left a relatively benign, well-resourced, and non-innovatory climate for social policy. School education retained selectivity on academic grounds long after this ended in the rest of the United Kingdom: a review of post-primary education in 2001 recommended that it should be ended, and direct rule ministers reaffirmed this in 2008. The centrally run eleven-plus test was abolished in 2009 but a variety of quasi-selective transfer arrangements based on parental choice and school decisions remain in place.

The Operation of the Devolved Administrations

The Scottish and Welsh administrations (the Scottish Government (until 2007 called the Scottish Executive) and the Welsh Assembly Government) are descendants of the 'joined-up' former Scottish and Welsh Offices. Since 2007 Scotland has no central departments as such, only groups of directorates serving, in social policy areas, Cabinet Secretaries for Health and Well-being, Education and Lifelong Learning, and Justice. Wales has non-statutory departments serving ministers for Children, Education, and Lifelong Learning; Health and Social Services; and Social Justice and Local Government. In Northern Ireland, social policy departments, which have statutory existence as part of the power-sharing between parties, are Education, Employment and Learning (including post-sixteen education); Health, Social Services and Public Safety; and Social Development (including housing and social security).

All three systems have permanent committees of elected members in the subject-area of each minister that combine the functions of legislative scrutiny and policy investigation. In Scotland the committees have the power to initiate legislation; there is also a Public Petitions Committee to consider petitions from citizens on an issue or grievance. In Wales, the assembly and administration were initially a single legal and corporate entity; assembly clerks were civil servants and ministers sat on committees, but in May 2007 a Westminster-style separation took effect.

The administration of social policy in the four nations of the United Kingdom is summarized in Table 42.1. Scotland (since 2004) and Wales (since 2009) have integrated area Health Boards and have abandoned the trusts found in England. Local government in the three nations is much more neatly organized than it is in England. In 1996, local government in Scotland and Wales was reorganized from two-tier to single-tier (thirty-two and twenty-two authorities). Northern Ireland has had twenty-six districts since 1973 but with education, health, and social services (linked, uniquely in the United Kingdom) and housing administered by appointed bodies. Other functions – roads, water, social security – are administered by agencies of the Northern Ireland Civil Service. A single Health and Social Services Board was formed in 2009 but plans to reduce the number of local authorities from twenty-six to eleven in 2011 were shelved in 2010; a single Education and Skills Authority was

Table 42.1 Who runs United Kingdom social policy 2010 (before NHS reform in England).

	Scotland	Wales	Northern Ireland	England
Health	Scottish Government Health Directorates 14 area Health Boards 8 special Health Boards	Welsh Assembly Government Department for Health and Social Services and Department for Public Health and Health Professions 7 Health Boards	Department of Health, Social Services and Public Safety 4 Health and Social Care Boards 5 Health and Social Care Trusts	Department of Health 10 Strategic Health Authorities 122 Foundation Trusts 252 other trusts 152 Primary Care Trusts
Education	Scottish Government Schools and Lifelong learning directorates 32 local authorities Scottish Funding Council (further and higher education)	Welsh Assembly Government Department for Children, Education, Lifelong Learning and Skills (Education Group) 22 local authorities Education and Learning Wales (within Welsh Assembly Government)	Department of Education/ Department of Employment and Learning 5 Education and Library Boards	Department for Education and Skills Local authorities (27 counties, 56 unitary authorities, 36 metropolitan boroughs, 33 London boroughs) Higher Education Funding Council for England Further Education Funding Council
Housing	Scottish Government Housing and Regeneration Directorate 32 Local authorities Registered Social Landlords (including Housing Associations)	Welsh Assembly Government Department for Environment, Sustainability and Housing) 22 Local authorities Housing Associations	Department of Social Development Northern Ireland Housing Executive Housing Associations	Local authorities (unitary, metropolitan and London boroughs, districts) Housing Corporation Housing Associations
Training	Scottish Enterprise, Highlands & Islands Enterprise 6 areas of the local enterprise network Skills Development Scotland Ltd (publicly owned company)	Education and Learning Wales (within Welsh Assembly Government)	Training and Employment Agency (within Department of Employment and Learning)	Learning and Skills Council 25 Sector Skills councils

Source: Adapted from R. Parry, 'Reshaping structures of government across the UK', in G. Lodge and K. Schmuecker (eds), *Devolution in Practice* (London: Institute for Research on Public Policy, 2010).

agreed in principle by the Executive in 2008 but the transition to it is slow and the five Education and Library Boards remain.

Needs and Resources at Sub-national Level

The United Kingdom's social policy has been underwritten by an implicit north-west to south-east gradient – Scotland, Wales, Northern Ireland, and Northern England were seen as relatively deprived and so could claim additional resources to deal with their problems. These differentials have narrowed, and because house prices are lower and public sector health and education better serviced, the non-English nations may feel better off and rank high in subjective quality-of-life indices.

This provides the backdrop to the position on relative public spending (Table 42.2). Figures for 2009–10 reveal a convergence of spending differentials since devolution started. Northern Ireland leads, at 17 per cent more social expenditure per head than the UK average, but London and the North East are ahead of Scotland and Wales. Housing differentials stand out but public housing expenditure is small. More important is Scotland's advantage in health and education, which is more structural than needs-based.

The convergence of spending reflects the Barnett Formula used for apportioning expenditure to the nations both before and after devolution: put simply, the budget changes year-by-year in step with changes in corresponding English expenditure and is transferred as a block to the devolved administrations who can alter priorities within the block without reference to the Treasury. This avoids constant haggling over items and is meant to converge expenditure over time, because new money is apportioned on a population basis rather than on historic shares. The fact that the differentials are moving only slowly led to repeated calls for more fiscal autonomy for the devolved nations, especially in the report of the Calman Commission on Scottish Devolution (set up by the UK government) in 2009 and implemented by the Scotland Bill 2011, which, after a transitional period, will cut the block grant by the yield of 10 per cent on income tax and force the Scottish Parliament to fix an income tax rate to balance its books.

Flexible Initiatives at Sub-national Level

An important justification for devolution is that it allows for even more flexibility and experimentation within the United Kingdom. In 1968 the

Table 42.2 Spending per head on social policy 2009–2010.

Index: UK = 100	Total social	Social protection	Health	Education and training	Housing and community amenities
Northern Ireland	117	119	98	108	261
North East	112	114	109	111	108
London	110	100	112	120	187
Scotland	109	108	108	107	143
Wales	107	115	102	101	73
North West	105	107	107	100	97
West Midlands	101	103	99	101	77
Yorkshire and the Humber	98	98	98	101	83
South West	94	97	94	89	63
East Midlands	92	93	91	95	64
South East	88	88	92	90	65
East	88	90	89	88	61
(UK av £)	7,153	3,569	1,913	1,413	258

Source: Calculated from HM Treasury, *Public Expenditure Statistical Analyses* (Cm 7890, July 2010) tables 9.15 and 9.16.

Scottish system of children's hearings (non-judicial disposals of the cases of children in trouble) had defined, in contrast to England, the policy area as social work rather than law and order. Scottish school examinations remain quite different, with broadly based Highers rather than more specialized A-levels. The Welsh language is promoted in Welsh schools more than ever before, and post-devolution Wales has moved further towards a distinctive educational policy through the abolition of school tests for 7-year-olds, the elimination of league tables for school examination results, and a 'Welsh baccalaureate' developed from 2003 onwards as an alternative to A-levels.

Since devolution, policy initiatives have tended to greater generosity in Scotland and Wales. The main developments are that Scotland has abolished undergraduate tuition fees for Scottish (and non-UK European Union) students at Scottish universities; Wales made prescriptions and check-ups free for the under-twenty-fives and over-sixties, prior to abolishing them entirely, and introduced a 'learning grant' to provide variable financial support to students in both higher and further education; and Scotland, and to a lesser extent Wales, has moved towards non-means tested personal care for the elderly in assessed need in response to the Royal Commission on Long-Term Care for the Elderly of 1999. Scotland's policy attracted much attention, but caps on the allowable fees and the need for local authority assessment of needs make it less free and universal than it might seem.

Emerging Issues

Devolution has brought into focus two long-standing themes: the uniformity of social security and benefit rules that make it hard to run devolved anti-poverty policies, and the ability of the three non-English nations to do things their own way with relative Westminster indifference. Paradoxically, devolution policies that were meant to leave the territories to take local decisions have highlighted the occasions where the logic of their policy-making differs from that of the UK government and have called into question the historic expenditure advantage of Scotland and Northern Ireland.

The devolved administrations have resisted the targeting and differentiation now found in UK policy. In Wales, free prescription charges became an emblematic policy and were achieved for all in April 2007; Scotland has pursued a more limited route on matters like free eyesight check-ups but plans to phase out prescription charges by 2012; Northern Ireland abolished prescription charges in 2010. Universalist thinking is evident in personal care for the elderly, and to a lesser extent student support.

Divergence in delivery structures has been more of a policy design choice than an adaptation to local circumstances, especially in health service organization (within a common NHS 'brand') and the 'lifelong learning' area (skills training, higher and further education in terms of provision, financing and charging). The devolved administrations have tried to deal with the whole range of social and economic variables in their nations even when lacking powers to address them, as in the SNP government's fifteen 'national outcomes' set in 2007 that structured 'single outcome agreements' with local authorities. Equality provisions (gender, ethnicity, religious community, language) have been taken forward in all three devolved nations with a valuable thinking-through from first principles. But the devolved systems cannot resist UK changes on tax and benefit policy, such as the coalition proposal for a Universal Credit that would incorporate housing benefit.

After the 2010 UK election no party was in power at both the UK and devolved levels. The Conservative-Liberal Democrat coalition had a political legitimacy in Scotland and Wales that would have been denied the Conservatives alone, and set out with an agenda of 'respect' for devolution but a pledge to reform financial arrangements. But the current devolution settlement still seeks to respond in a non-uniform way to political pressures around the United Kingdom without any overall concept of multilevel government. After the North East of England's 78 per cent no vote to a regional assembly in 2004, devolution in England was stalled. A chronic problem is the so-called West Lothian question as MPs from Scotland, Wales, and Northern Ireland sit at Westminster and can vote on England-only legislation in devolved fields.

A decisive factor may be the vulnerability of devolved social policy to spending cuts carried through from the 2010 Spending Review. The devolved systems could opt out of English policy changes in areas like GP commissioning of all health services, removal of fee limits in higher education, and fixed-term social housing tenancies – but the expenditure consequences of the changes will be passed on to them. In non-cash areas the devolved nations may become the last home of the old UK welfare state dismantled in England (especially the NHS), but this will have to be financed. The direction of policy, starting with Scotland, is towards fiscal autonomy where tax levels follow spending decisions. This poses a threat to the divergent social policies that had in fact been more generous and to the stability of devolution as a mid-point between a unitary UK and independence for the nations.

Guide to Further Sources

The best source, a comprehensive and pioneering account, is Derek Birrell, *The Impact of Devolution on Social Policy* (Bristol: Policy Press, 2009). Keeping up with post-devolution developments is not always easy: the best work is that of the Constitution Unit, which publishes quarterly monitoring reports on each of the devolved nations and the English regions, www.ucl.ac.uk/constitution-unit, and regular volumes since 2000, most recently Alan Trench (ed.), *The State of the Nations* (Exeter: Imprint Academic, 2008). A good summary is J. Adams and K. Schmueker (eds), *Devolution in Practice* (London: Institute for Research on Public Policy, 2010). An important comparative study is S. Greer's *Territorial Politics and Health Policy* (Manchester: Manchester University Press, 2005).

Research promoted by the ERRC Devolution and Constitutional Change Programme (2000–6)

is summarized on the Devolution and Constitutional Change web site, www.devolution.ac.uk. Journals like the quarterly *Scottish Affairs* and the annual *Contemporary Wales* are very useful. There is wealth of statistical data in *Regional Trends*, published annually by The Stationery Office for the Office for National Statistics.

Publications of the devolved administrations are available on their web sites: www.scotland.gov.uk, www.wales.gov.uk, and www.northernireland.gov.uk. In Scotland, parliamentary reports are available at www.scottish.parliament.uk, as are Northern Ireland Assembly debates and reports at www.ni-assembly.gov.uk.

Review Questions

1 What areas of social policy have been devolved to Scotland, Wales, and Northern Ireland?
2 How do the devolution arrangements differ between the three nations?
3 What has been the effect of having nationalists in government since 2007?
4 What have been the main social policy divergences and innovations in the devolved nations?
5 How is devolution funded, and how may this change in future economic circumstances?

Visit the book companion site at www.wiley.com/go/alcock to make use of the resources designed to accompany the textbook. There you will find chapter-specific guides to further resources, including governmental, international, think-tank, pressure groups, and relevant journals sources. You will also find a glossary based on *The Blackwell Dictionary of Social Policy*, help sheets, and case studies, guidance on managing assignments in social policy and career advice.

43

Social Policy and the European Union

Linda Hantrais

- Social policy has been on the European agenda since the founding of the European Economic Community (EEC) in 1957.
- The social dimension of the European Union (EU) has been primarily concerned with the social protection of workers.
- The Union has progressively extended its social policy competence and has introduced softer and more proactive instruments for policy-making and implementation.
- The relationship between the European Union and national level governance is interactive, with national governments retaining responsibility for the content, organization, and delivery of social protection systems.
- In a context of population decline and ageing and the aftermath of economic recession, the Union is facing unprecedented challenges to its social model.

Background

The United Kingdom was not one of the six founding member states of the European Economic Community established in 1957 with the signing of the Treaty of Rome. Following accession in 1973, the British government opposed Community action in social areas, resulting in the chapter on social affairs being relegated to a Protocol and Agreement on Social Policy appended to the Maastricht Treaty in 1993. The British government also delayed progress of legislation on workers' rights, arguing that it would impinge on national sovereignty and adversely affect employment. Under the Labour government elected in 1997, the United Kingdom

The Student's Companion to Social Policy, Fourth Edition. Edited by Pete Alcock, Margaret May, Sharon Wright.
© 2012 John Wiley & Sons, Ltd. Published 2012 by John Wiley & Sons, Ltd.

signed up to the Agreement on Social Policy, and the social chapter was incorporated into the Treaty of Amsterdam in the same year, thus lending social policy a stronger legal base. The priority given to employment was endorsed both by the Treaty and the Luxembourg summit in 1997, when the first employment guidelines were adopted.

In the early twenty-first century, as the Union enlarged to the East, a European social model was emerging; enshrined in the Charter of Fundamental Rights of the European Union agreed at the Nice summit in 2000, the model embodied citizenship rights and the core values that all member states were committed to pursue. Faced with the growing threat of population ageing, a trend exacerbated as the baby boom generation approached retirement age, the focus of EU social policy debate shifted following the Hampton Court summit in 2005. By 2010, in the midst of a severe economic recession, employment remained high on the policy agenda, while the Lisbon Treaty (amended Treaty on European Union) confirmed the commitment of member states to the Union's expanded social agenda (see Box 43.1).

Developing the Union's Social Policy Remit

Although, as its name implied, the European Economic Community was essentially an economic community, from the outset it acquired a social policy remit. Articles 117–128 on social policy in the Treaty of Rome advocated close co-operation between member states, particularly in training, employment, working conditions, social security, and collective bargaining; they endorsed the equal pay principle, provided for the harmonization of social security measures to accommodate migrant workers, and the operation of a European Social Fund to assist in the employment and re-employment of workers, and encourage geographical and occupational mobility.

In the post-war context of rapid economic growth, the underlying objectives of European social policy were to avoid distortion of competition and support free movement of labour within the Community. Since the welfare systems of the

Box 43.1 Social Policy in the Lisbon Treaty

- After several failed attempts to introduce a European constitution, the heads of state and government of all twenty-seven EU member states signed the Lisbon Treaty in 2007; it entered into force on 1 December 2009.
- Reiterating statements in previous treaties, the Preamble presents the aim of promoting economic and social progress by ensuring that 'advances in economic integration are accompanied by parallel progress in other fields'.
- Articles 145–164 in Part 3, Titles IX Employment, X Social Policy, and XI Social Fund, confirm the role of the Union in promoting co-operation between member states in areas of social policy by co-ordinating actions designed to encourage a high level of employment, adequate social protection for workers and their families, and the prevention of social exclusion.
- Other titles are devoted to Free Movement of Persons (IV), Education, Vocational Training, Youth, and Sport (XII), Culture (XIII), Public Health (XIV) and Economic, Social, and Territorial Cohesion (XVIII).
- The Charter of Fundamental Rights was not incorporated into the Lisbon Treaty, but Article 6 formally recognizes the rights, freedoms, and principles laid down in the Charter, thereby making it legally binding. Although the Treaty does not create new rights or extend the competences of the Union as defined elsewhere in the Treaties, a Protocol annexed to it affirms that the Charter's justiciable rights do not apply to the United Kingdom, the Czech Republic, or Poland.

founder member states were based largely on the insurance principle, unfair competition might arise if some countries levied higher social charges on employment, leading to social dumping as companies relocated to areas with lower labour costs. The functioning of the common market was expected to result automatically in social development, implying that the Community would not need to interfere directly with redistributive benefits. By the mid-1970s, economic growth was slowing down following the oil crises, and the belief in automatic social harmonization was called into question.

A more active approach to social reform was required. The 1974 resolution on a social action programme proposed that the Community should develop common objectives for national social policies, without standardizing solutions to social problems or removing responsibility for social policy from member states. The 1980s were marked by pressures to develop a 'social space', premised on social dialogue between trade unions and employers (the social partners), enabling them to agree objectives and establish a minimum platform of guaranteed social rights for workers, to be applied by individual member states in an attempt to stimulate convergence.

The problem of agreeing even a minimum level of protection for workers was apparent in the negotiations leading to the 1989 Community Charter of the Fundamental Social Rights of Workers, which did not have force of law. The Charter's action programme recognized the importance of observing national diversity, and the Maastricht Treaty formalized the subsidiarity principle, thereby setting the tone for social legislation in later years. Subsidiarity means that the Union is empowered to act only if its aims can be more effectively achieved at European than national level. Accordingly, opportunities for concerted action among nations in the area of social protection are constrained.

Each of the five successive waves of EU membership made harmonization, or even convergence, of social policy provisions more difficult to achieve. The social protection systems of the six original EEC member states (Belgium, France, Federal Republic of Germany, Italy, Luxembourg, and the Netherlands) were variants of the Bismarckian or continental model of welfare, based on the employment–insurance principle.

The new member states in the 1970s (Denmark, Ireland, United Kingdom) subscribed to social protection systems funded from taxation and providing universal flat-rate coverage. The southern states (Greece, Portugal, Spain) that joined the Union in the early 1980s had less developed welfare systems, whereas the Nordic states (Finland, Sweden) that became members in 1995 shared features with Denmark; Austria was closer to the German pattern. The two island states (Cyprus, Malta) and ten post-Soviet states (Bulgaria, Czech Republic, Estonia, Hungary, Latvia, Lithuania, Poland, Romania, Slovakia, and Slovenia) that acceded to the Union in 2004 and 2007 brought further variants of welfare systems (see Figure 43.1)

The goal of harmonizing social protection seemed to be more pressing with the Single European Market and economic and monetary union. By the 1990s, some convergence was occurring due to the common trend towards welfare retrenchment, made necessary by economic recession, and the shift towards mixed systems of welfare. Enlargement to the East stimulated the search for less formal approaches as an alternative to harmonization.

Social Policy-making Processes in the Union

Despite the relatively limited social policy remit in the founding treaties, after more than fifty years of operation, the Union has developed a multi-tiered system of governance, as instituted under the Lisbon Treaty (see Box 43.2)

Decision-making procedures have also evolved to take account of expanding membership. To facilitate the passage of contentious legislation, the Single European Act of 1986 introduced qualified majority voting (QMV) in the areas of health and safety at work, working conditions, information and consultation of workers, equality between men and women, and the integration of persons excluded from the labour market. The Amsterdam Treaty extended QMV to active employment measures, and the Nice Treaty added anti-discrimination measures, mobility, and specific action supporting economic and social cohesion. The Lisbon Treaty further extended QMV to measures combating climate change, energy secu-

Figure 43.1 The European Union.

rity, and emergency humanitarian aid but retained unanimous voting for any attempts at harmonization in the field of social security and social protection. By applying the co-decision procedure (renamed the 'ordinary legislative procedure') to new areas such as legal immigration, the Treaty further expanded the EP's law-making powers.

The Union's legal sources include primary legislation in the form of treaties and secondary legislation, ranging from regulations, directives, and decisions, its most binding instruments, to recommendations, resolutions, and opinions, which are advisory, or communications and memoranda, which signal initial thinking on an issue. Relatively few regulations apply in the

social field, with the notable exception of co-ordination of social security arrangements for migrant workers and the Structural Funds. Directives, which set objectives for legislation but leave individual states to select the most suitable form of implementation, have been used to considerable effect to promote equal treatment and health and safety at work. Recommendations have played an important role in developing a framework for concerted action and convergence in the social policy field.

The open method of co-ordination (OMC), formally introduced as a means of intervention in employment policies at the Lisbon summit in 2000, offers a soft-law alternative designed to

Box 43.2   The European Union's System of Governance

- The *Council* (of Ministers), which meets twice a year to determine policy directions, is composed of heads of government of member states. As the principal governing body, it represents national interests and is responsible for taking decisions on laws to be applied across the Union. The president of the Council is appointed for a two-and-a-half year term by qualified majority voting, with the possibility of one renewal.

- The *European Parliament* (EP), whose members are directly elected by citizens of member states every five years, has extensive budgetary and supervisory powers on a par with the Council for much EU legislation, although Members of the European Parliament (MEPs) form political rather than national blocks. The EP cannot initiate bills, but it can decline to take up a position on a Commission proposal and can force the Commission to resign.

- The *Commission* formally initiates, implements, and monitors European legislation. Under the Lisbon Treaty, each member state has one Commissioner. Commissioners are political appointees but are expected to act independently of national interests. The directorates general are responsible for preparing proposals and working documents for consideration by the Council; they therefore play an important part in setting the Union's policy agenda. The Lisbon Treaty requires the Commission to monitor and report on the social situation – demographic trends, the development of social policies in member states, and employment data – and draw up guidelines for member states to assist them in drafting employment policies.

- The *Court of Justice*, which sits in Luxembourg, is the Union's legal voice and guardian of treaties and implementing legislation. Its main task is to ensure that legal instruments adopted at European Union and national levels are compatible with European law. Through its interpretation of legislation, the Court has built up a substantial and influential body of case law in the social area.

encourage co-operation, exchange of best practice, and agreement on common targets and guidelines for member states, supported in the case of employment and social exclusion by national action plans. OMC relies on regular monitoring of progress to meet the targets set, allowing member states to compare their efforts and learn from the experience of others.

Today, the Union has available a broad array of multilayered and fragmented policy-making institutions, procedures and instruments, which have gradually extended its area of competence and authority. The policy-making process depends on the ability of national and supranational actors to co-operate in setting objectives, initiating, enacting, and implementing legislation. The sharing of responsibility distinguishes European structures from those of most international organizations. As in federal states, the Union has to act for the greater good of its member states, while not encroaching too far into national sovereignty or infringing the subsidiarity principle. Whereas the Union has not secured full legitimacy as a supranational authority in the social policy field, the competence of member states has undoubtedly been eroded. A delicate balance, therefore, has to be struck between the interests of the different tiers of the Union's institutions, involving a complex process of negotiation and compromise, vested interests, and trade-offs.

European Union Social Policy Intervention

The Union's objective of removing barriers to the free movement of labour served to justify an array of policies for co-ordinating social protection systems, supported by action programmes, networks, and observatories to stimulate initiatives and monitor progress in the social field.

Rather than seeking to change national systems, action in the area of education and training focused initially on comparing the content and level of qualifications across the Community to stimulate transferability between member states. General directives were issued on the mutual recognition of the equivalence of diplomas. From the mid-1970s, the Commission initiated action programmes to develop vocational training, encourage mobility among students and young workers, and promote co-operation between education and industry. In the early twenty-first century, the Commission advocated investment in human resources through quality education and lifelong learning. Co-operation and support for member states are primary concerns in the Lisbon Treaty, while responsibility rests at national level for determining teaching content and the organization of educational systems. The Lisbon Treaty introduced a European dimension in sport, by supporting, co-ordinating, and supplementing the actions of member states.

Several articles in the EEC Treaty were devoted to the improvement of living and working conditions as a means of equalizing opportunities and promoting mobility. Particular attention was paid to health and safety at work, resulting in a large body of binding legislation. The introduction of QMV for health and safety legislation resulted in directives designed to ensure the physical protection of workers, including the protection of pregnant women, control the organization of working time, and expand action in the area of public health. Here, the Lisbon Treaty sought to complement national policies and combat cross-border threats to health.

In line with the priority given to employment policy and working conditions at the EU level, and despite opposition from some member states – notably Denmark and the United Kingdom – wary of the possible impact on employment practices and equal opportunities, the Commission has instigated legislation and set up action programmes to protect women as workers. The policies promoted include directives requiring equal pay for work of equal value,

equal treatment, and employment-related social insurance rights. Increasingly, attention has been paid to measures to reconcile occupational and family life. In the 1990s, gender mainstreaming was introduced to resolve persistent inequalities and, in 2009, the Commission adopted a Women's Charter committed to building a gender perspective into all its policies for five years.

In the 1970s, the impact of economic recession, rising unemployment, and demographic ageing became policy issues. The prospect of greater freedom of movement heightened concern about welfare tourism and the exporting of poverty between member states, if unemployed workers and their families crossed borders in search of more generous provision. The Commission funded a series of action programmes to combat poverty and social exclusion, and the Structural Funds were deployed to underpin regional policy by tackling the sources of economic disparities. The employment guidelines served as a major plank in the Union's strategy to combat labour market exclusion by improving employability through active policy measures, which remain high on the social policy agenda in the post-crisis economy of the 2010s.

Greater life expectancy created heavy demands on pension provision, health, and care services. The Commission was required to monitor provision for older and disabled people, particularly with regard to maintenance and caring, arrangements for transferring the rights of mobile workers and pensioners, and the overall impact of policy on living standards. Communications published in 1999 and 2006 proposed strategies for strengthening solidarity and equity between the generations. By 2010, the main thrust of EU policy had shifted to active ageing as the baby-boom generations reached retirement age.

Despite the considerable body of legislation on freedom of movement, information about intra-European mobility suggests that migration between member states has remained relatively low, although enlargement to the East initially provoked an unprecedented westwards wave of internal migration from Central and East European countries. Progressively, more attention has been paid to the challenges posed by third country migration in co-ordinating national policies and in dealing with refugees and asylum seekers. These concerns were formally recognized when the right to equality of opportunity and treatment, without distinction of race, colour, ethnicity, national origin, culture, or religion was written into the Treaty of Amsterdam, and all discrimination on these grounds was outlawed in the Charter of Fundamental Rights.

While doubts may be expressed about the coherence of the Union's social policy remit, these examples illustrate how its institutions have developed a wide-ranging competence in social affairs to become a major, if disputed, social policy actor. Despite the blocking tactics of some member states, a considerable body of legislation and practice – *acquis communautaire* – has been instituted, requiring compliance from national governments and constraining their domain of action. However, the changes incorporated in the Union's Treaties, combined with the shift towards less binding forms of legislation in the social field, have tended to result in standards being sought that can realistically be achieved by the least advanced countries – the lowest common denominator – leaving individual member states with considerable discretion in policy implementation.

Emerging Issues

In the early 2000s, the Treaties still formally recognized that member states should remain responsible for their own systems of social protection, while advocating closer co-operation as a means of identifying common objectives and solutions. The debates of the 1970s and 1980s over fundamental issues, such as whether or not the Community should have a social dimension, have lost their salience in the face of pressing socio-demographic and economic problems requiring common responses.

Although EU member states often fail to agree about the extent of the Union's involvement in social policy or the form it should take, they broadly agree about the major social problems confronting them in the early twenty-first century. Demographic trends in combination with technological and structural change, the impact of further enlargement, and the extension of the Union's sphere of influence have created new pressures on welfare systems, exacerbated by economic crises. Member states continue to seek

jointly ways of dealing with persistently high levels of unemployment, shortages of skilled labour, long-term old age dependency, and the changing structure of households and gender relations, while struggling to contain the costs of providing high-quality services.

These trends call into question the principles on which national social security systems were founded. EU member states are concerned to ensure the financial viability and sustainability of social protection systems, while safeguarding employment and avoiding social exclusion. Population ageing has raised questions about the conditions governing retirement age and pension rights, while also exacerbating the problems of providing health and social care. Different mixes of solutions are being tried: greater targeting of benefits, the tightening of eligibility criteria and greater emphasis on active measures to move people off benefits and into work, the introduction of social insurance schemes to cover long-term care, the privatization of services, and the promotion of a volunteering culture. The Commission has not lost sight of the need to 'modernize' social protection systems in response to socio-economic and demographic change and further enlargement, while consolidating the European social model and reinforcing intergenerational solidarity at the macro (societal) and micro (family) levels.

Guide to Further Sources

Regular updates on demographic trends, the social situation, social protection, and employment are available on the European Commission's web site, www.ec.europa.eu/social/. The development of the Union's social dimension, its role in setting a European-wide social policy agenda and the impact of its policies at national level are analysed in detail by L. Hantrais, *Social Policy in the European Union* (3rd edn, London: Palgrave and St Martin's Press, 2007). K. Schubert, S. Hegelich, and U. Bazant (eds), *The Handbook of European Welfare Systems* (Oxford: Routledge, 2009) provides a comprehensive overview of the welfare systems in all twenty-seven member states, and examines current debates surrounding their interplay with EU welfare policy.

Review Questions

1   How has the relationship between economic and social policy evolved since the establishment of the EEC in 1957?
2   To what extent has the autonomy of national social protection systems been undermined by the growing EU social policy competence?
3   What has been the impact of different waves of enlargement on the EU social policy remit?
4   To what extent are national social policy models compatible with a European social model?
5   How has the Lisbon Treaty affected the EU social dimension?

Visit the book companion site at www.wiley.com/go/alcock to make use of the resources designed to accompany the textbook. There you will find chapter-specific guides to further resources, including governmental, international, think-tank, pressure groups, and relevant journals sources. You will also find a glossary based on *The Blackwell Dictionary of Social Policy*, help sheets, and case studies, guidance on managing assignments in social policy and career advice.

44

International Organizations

Nicola Yeates

Overview

- International organizations are an important arena of social policy formation.
- A distinction may be made between international governmental organizations and international non-governmental organizations.
- These organizations actively shape the distribution and redistribution of resources within and between countries.
- They are tangibly involved in the financing, regulation, and provision of welfare goods and services.
- Debates about social policy in these organizations reflect different ideologies and perspectives on the best way of promoting human welfare.

International Organizations, Global Governance, and Social Policy

The study of International Organizations (IOs) in relation to social policy has emerged as a major concern within Social Policy (Box 44.1).

IOs are significant sites of transnational collective action and policy-making. They have played an active role in social policy formation in most parts of the world since the early twentieth cen-

tury, but international co-operation and action has expanded and intensified particularly since the end of the Second World War, when the Bretton Woods institutions and an international trade regime (GATT) were established. The number of IOs grew from about seventy in 1940 to more than one thousand by the close of the twentieth century. The intensification of policy co-operation within these spheres of cross-border governance is a key element of political globalization. They lie at the heart of the system of global governance – the

The Student's Companion to Social Policy, Fourth Edition. Edited by Pete Alcock, Margaret May, Sharon Wright.
© 2012 John Wiley & Sons, Ltd. Published 2012 by John Wiley & Sons, Ltd.

Box 44.1 Globalizing Social Policy

- Social policy issues are increasingly being perceived to be global in scope and cause.
- Transnational flows of goods, services, capital, ideas, and people link different welfare systems around the world.
- Transnational forms of collective action have emerged.
- International organizations are tangibly involved in social policy formation.
- These responses have material outcomes and impacts on social groups, policy areas, and welfare provision.

complex legal, institutional, and political framework of public and private international agreements, treaties, regulations, and accords that regulate social, political, and economic life. This system is neither unified, nor coherent, nor complete. But it is key to understanding how territories and populations are governed.

IOs initiate, guide, influence, and determine social policy and development. They underwrite the conditions and patterns of international economic investment, production, and exchange, set the parameters of macroeconomic policy, and promulgate particular policy ideas and initiatives. Through this IOs play a key role in determining how resources are accumulated and distributed within and between countries, and as such they form an important part of any explanation of social inequality and poverty globally. The policies of the World Bank, International Monetary Fund (IMF), and the World Trade Organization (WTO) are held to be particularly significant in this respect because of their role in the diffusion of neo-liberalism.

Types and Kinds of International Organizations

A distinction needs to be made between international *governmental* organizations (IGOs) and international *non-governmental* organizations

(INGOs). IGOs are essentially international fora through which sovereign governments enter into collaborative political and legal relationships, while INGOs are entities through which voluntary, charitable, trade union, professional associations, industry organizations, and business groups operate internationally. Some IOs operate on a worldwide scale, others do so on a sub-global scale. Table 44.1 provides some examples of different groupings operating on global and regional scales.

IOs vary considerably in terms of power and resources (see Table 44.2). A number of INGOs command significant budgets and are better staffed than some IGOs (compare, for example, the WTO's 630 staff with Oxfam's 2,800). Some IGOs have no independent legal force or permanent secretariat; others have the force of international law behind them (WTO, EU, UN) and/or substantial bureaucracies (ILO, WB, EU, UN). Many may be little more than political alliances or 'clubs' comprising a minority of the world's governments without a permanent secretariat (G8, G24, G77).

IOs' Involvement in Social Policy

Substantial and routine international co-operation and co-ordination exists on a range of matters of direct relevance to social policy:

- trade, investment, and macroeconomic policy
- the environment
- employment and livelihoods
- security policy
- education and training
- health and social care
- social security and pensions
- housing
- food and water security
- migration and asylum
- fertility and population control
- humanitarian and development aid.

IGOs

The involvement of IGOs in the regulation, financing, and provision welfare services is substantial (see Table 44.3). There have been important attempts at regulation through international

Table 44.1 Examples of IGOs and INGOs.

IGOs	INGOs
Global	
World Bank (WB)	World Economic Forum
International Monetary Fund	World Social Forum
United Nations	World Water Forum
UN social agencies, e.g. International Labour Organization (ILO), World Health Organization (WHO), Unicef	International Confederation of Free Trade Unions
World Trade Organization	International Planned Parenthood Federation
Organisation for Economic Co-operation and Development	OXFAM, War on Want
G8, G77, G24 etc.	International Pharmaceutical Industries Association
Regional	
European Union	European Services Forum
North American Free Trade Agreement (NAFTA)	European Trade Union Confederation
ASEAN (Association of South East Asian Nations)	European Social Forum
South Asian Area for Regional Cooperation (SAARC)	Asian Social Forum
Mercado Común del Sur (Southern Core Common Market)(Mercosur)	African Social Forum
Caribbean Community and Common Market (CARICOM)	
Southern African Development Community (SADC)	

Table 44.2 Examples of social governance at national, world-regions, and global levels.

	National	EU	Global
Economic stability	Central banks	European Central Bank in Eurozone	IMF / Bank of International settlements?
Revenue	Taxation	Customs revenues, plus Member state donations (note discussion of tax harmonisation)	Mix of UN appeals, ad hoc global funds, multilateral overseas development assistance
Redistribution	Tax and income transfers policy	Structural funds, Common Agricultural Policy	Ad hoc humanitarian relief, special global funds, debt relief, differential pricing of drugs
Regulation	State laws and directives	EU laws, regulations and directives, including Social Charter	UN conventions WTO trade law Corporate codes of conduct
Citizenship rights	Court redress Consumer charters Tripartite governance	Court redress Tripartite governance	UN Commission for Human Rights but no legal redress.

Source: N. Yeates, 'Social policy and supranational governance' in P. Alcock, *et al.* (eds) *The Student's Companion to Social Policy* (3rd edn, Oxford: Blackwell, 2007) adapted from B. Deacon, (2003) 'Supranational agencies and social policy' in ibid. (2nd edn, 2003).

Table 44.3 Examples of IGOs' involvement in welfare provision, finance, and regulation.

	Provision	*Finance*	*Regulation*
Global	Humanitarian relief, population programmes, social development projects, special global (health, social) funds delivered through IGOs and INGOs	Revenue raised from appeals, donations and ODA channelled into ad hoc humanitarian relief, special global funds, debt relief, and differential pricing (drugs)	International labour and social standards through ILO, OECD conventions; human rights through UN; social, health, and education in international trade law, economic fora
Regional (EU)	Human resources/social funds, regional development funds	Revenues raised from customs and government donations (talk of tax) distributed through agricultural and structural funds	Labour and social standards through regulations, directives and agreements

Source: N. Yeates, 'Social policy and supranational governance' in P. Alcock, *et al.* (eds) *The Student's Companion to Social Policy* (3rd edn, Oxford: Blackwell, 2007) adapted from B. Deacon, (2003) 'Supranational agencies and social policy' in ibid. (2nd edn, 2003).

level standard-setting by the UN and its agencies, such as the ILO and WHO. These organizations have also experimented with international financing for welfare services (e.g. ILO's Global Social Trust Fund), as has the World Bank (through its development loans programmes). The WTO is an important actor due to its role in negotiating and implementing international trade treaties, such as the GATS (General Agreement on Trade in Services). Regional formations vary in the extent to which they are active in social policy. The most 'advanced' such formation in these terms is the EU, though other regional formations have also developed or are in the process of developing an active role in social policy.

INGOs

INGOs are involved in all parts of the global policy-making process, from agenda- and norm-setting through to policy implementation. Some enjoy official consultative status, working, for instance, through various UN and World Bank NGO Committees. INGOs play a key role in delivering many IGOs' programmes notably humanitarian aid. They can provide access to areas and groups that IGOs cannot reach. They also fill gaps in provision for poor, rural, and

conflict-ridden communities where political and economic conditions do not attract for-profit providers.

The growing participation of NGOs in global policy formation and implementation is sometimes seen as signifying the emergence of a 'global civil society' and of the democratization and socialization of global politics. For others, though, it is consistent with global neo-liberalism in that voluntary action is equated with values such as self-interest, hard work, flexibility, freedom of choice, private property, and a distrust of state bureaucracy. Many INGOs are associations of industrial, commercial, and for-profit organizations so the trend to enhance NGO involvement in IGO policy formation may be amplifying the power of such organizations to shape the direction of policy. IGOs' encouragement of civil society participation in policy formation may therefore be interpreted as a means of residualizing and privatizing welfare, albeit dressed up in the language of social development, participation, and empowerment.

Impacts of IOs on Social Policy

IOs shape social policy formation in numerous – but not always direct or immediate – ways:

- By providing a forum for mutual education, analysis, and debate. While this may not directly or immediately produce formal agreements or common policy agendas, it promotes shared analyses, beliefs, and concerns that inform policy debate and provide a platform for future collaboration.
- By defining international social standards. The UN's human rights charters, the ILO's Labour Conventions, or the WHO's Health Conventions, for example, all provide a common socio-legal framework within which national social policies must work.
- Through wider market integration processes which generate a need for further regulatory reforms. For example, the creation of a Common Market in Western Europe and Latin America has involved labour and social security measures to promote labour mobility. These wider economic integration processes may have more far-reaching impacts upon the quality of social provision. For example, the creation of international markets in welfare services may undermine cross-class social solidarity that was historically important in the development of welfare states. Similarly, there have been concerns that the 'free' movement of capital may trigger a competitive devaluation of public welfare schemes ('social dumping').

IOs are not universally successful in influencing the course of national social policy development. Their successes vary considerably between different policy areas and countries. Governments often seem able to freely 'pick and mix' among a range of proposals and courses of action offered to them by IOs; at other times they may be strongly 'steered' towards, or seem compelled in some way to accept, certain recommendations through the provision of financial aid or other inducements and benefits.

In sum, IOs do more than form part of the social policy context: they actively participate in the political and policy processes and set (or attempt to influence the setting of)

- the terms of international trade, aid, and development policies;
- the allocation and use of aid, development, and social funds; and
- social standards and norms.

IOs also oversee and are sometimes directly involved in the implementation of social policies and programmes. Through these activities IOs:

- shape the distribution and redistribution of resources worldwide,
- frame social policy debate in national and global spheres of governance, and
- influence the nature of social provision in national contexts.

Social Policy Concepts in a Global Context

Equality, rights, and justice

Equality, rights, and justice have traditionally been examined at the interpersonal or intergroup level within particular national settings. In a global context we might ask to what extent the world is a 'fair' place. Is it 'just' that access to resources, life chances, opportunity, and quality of life determined by which country you happen to be born in or live in rather than by hard work, skill, or merit? What would be a just basis for representation in institutions of global governance? Northern states have more voting rights in Bretton Woods' institutions than Southern ones, while the UN is often also criticized for being Northern dominated. The WTO at least enshrines formal equality even if in practice this is not realized.

We might also consider differences in the extent to which citizenship rights are differentially embodied and guaranteed by global formations. Here, we could contrast European arrangements with the lack of progress at the global level. The Council of Europe provides European citizens the right to equal treatment before the Court of Human Rights in Strasbourg; the UN identifies similar rights through the International Covenant on Economic, Social and Cultural Rights and the Declaration of Human Rights, but it has no mechanism for their legal enforcement nor does it allow individual rights of petition. A further issue is the hierarchy of economic and social rights: some international treaties (e.g. WTOs GATS, North America's NAFTA) have established certain enforceable economic (trade and investment) rights for businesses while eschewing protective social and labour rights for citizens.

One particular issue concerns the extent to which social rights are inherent rights that attach to all human beings irrespective of cultural and economic context. 'Cosmopolitans' argue that some or all of the presently defined labour standards defined by the ILO Philadelphia Declaration (1944) are universal rights. 'Nationalists' advocate a kind of global relativism, arguing that it is for individual countries and communities to decide what constitutes an appropriate set of rights and what mix of rights carry corresponding social obligations.

Efficiency, equity, and choice

In a global context, debates about efficiency, equity, and choice become a discussion about whether global production and trade should be subject to 'social rules'. 'Free' trade advocates argue that international trade is the best way of improving individual and collective welfare, as globally competitive countries, businesses, and labour forces will attract more investment and opportunities. Critics, however, point to how global competition often involves the superexploitation of vulnerable labour forces in poorer countries, and how rich countries like the United Kingdom and the United States maintain protectionist trade regimes while demanding that developing countries dismantle theirs. 'Free trade' policies, it is argued, encourage countries to engage in competitive social deregulation to attract foreign investment or prevent capital flight overseas, measures which produce inefficient, sub-optimal social and economic outcomes.

Some advocates of 'free trade' policies are beginning to appreciate the benefits of certain kinds of social regulation, if only to avoid the damaging effects of consumer activism against products made involving exploited labour. But attempts to establish coherent global social regulation have seen limited success. One unsuccessful attempt in the late 1990s was the 'social clause' campaign which proposed to make market access conditional upon governments meeting 'core' labour standards. This was opposed on the grounds that 'free' trade will 'lift all boats' and that it would reinscribe protectionism by the Global North against the Global South. Recent regulatory measures have shown a tendency towards voluntarism: the OECD Guidelines for Multinational Enterprises set out principles for socially-oriented business practices, but MNCs' observance of them is strictly voluntary. Voluntary codes of corporate conduct have proliferated but monitoring of their implementation rests upon the efforts of resource-limited NGOs.

Altruism, reciprocity, and obligation

Principles of altruism, reciprocity, and obligation are enshrined in many of the policies and programmes of IOs and international agreements. The IMF and World Bank embody these ideas insofar as they provide finance for socio-economic development projects in 'developing' countries; the UNHCR has overall responsibility for the care of refugees worldwide. The specification of a target of 0.7 per cent of Gross National Income that countries should allocate for Overseas Development Assistance (ODA), debt relief packages for low-income highly indebted countries, and the Millennium Development Goals (MDGs) are further examples of recent moves to globalize social solidarity. Other experiments in the international financing of social goods exist, such as the ILO's Global Social Trust in the field of social security. In the health field, examples include international agreements on the differential pricing of drugs and the WHO ethical code of conduct to regulate the international recruitment of medical personnel from developing countries by rich countries.

Alongside IGOs are the efforts of philanthropic and charitable (including faith-based) groups. Northern Foundations (Ford, Volkswagen, Soros, Gates) are involved in funding global programmes of social research and social provision. Many of the recently created global funds and programmes, such as GAVI (the global vaccinations programme) and the GFATM (Global Fund to Fight AIDS, Tuberculosis and Malaria) involve private sector financing. Many of UNICEF's activities and campaigns are funded by charitable and commercial support (through its Save the Children appeals).

One question is whether these apparent expressions of altruism, obligation, and humanitarianism are anything more than disguised self-interest on the part of donors. International loans and other kinds of aid often provide good economic returns to lenders since the granting of aid may be conditional upon the purchase of goods and services of businesses based in the donor country. Another question is whether voluntaristic forms of international action are sufficiently powerful and whether more mandatory and concerted forms of action are needed.

Global Social Reform

Addressing the weaknesses of IOs are an indispensable part of global social policy reform campaigns. One problem with IGOs is that they do not possess state-like powers. There is no centralized international mechanism to negotiate and enforce treaty obligations worldwide and there is no coherent means for legal redress by aggrieved citizens. There is no central bank. IGOs do not have independent revenue-raising powers and are dependent on donor funding. The IMF comes closest to a nascent international state insofar as it carries out a number of state functions, such as the allocation of funds and the regulation of some aspects of international finance, but it lacks the political resources and coercive capacity of states.

A reformed UN system is regarded by some as the best means for developing a more coherent and effective global social policy. UN reform could involve various democratization reforms, providing it with an independent source of funding (perhaps out of global taxes), and a lead role in working with the new Groups of countries, the IMF, World Bank, WTO, and regional formations to institute a planned approach to global social development. Others argue that reforming extant organizations does not go far enough and that new organizations need to be constructed. Either way, there is a good deal of agreement that issues of power imbalances within these organizations need to be addressed, in particular by enhancing the representation of poorer and developing countries in them. While some campaigners look forward to the reinvention of global governmental institutions, others seek an enhanced role for world-regional associations of nations through which to deliver social policy more attuned to the needs of the populations of the region concerned.

Others are sceptical about the extent to which IOs (whether on a global or world-regional scale, new or reformed) can ever be in the long-term interests of social development and instead seek their dismantlement altogether. Such arguments are often advanced in the context of 'deglobalization' initiatives, especially by advocates of localization and self-reliance approaches that aim to promote the viability of smaller-scale, localized, and diversified economies. This alternative global social imaginary involves inventing (or returning to) forms of economic and social organization that are hooked into, but not dominated by outside forces.

Emerging Issues

The role of IOs in bringing about a global economy based on stability and social justice will remain at the foreground of debate. The failure of the global regulatory system to prevent the most recent global financial crisis intensified concerns that the system of global governance was inadequate. The successes and failures of global policy in relation to the Millennium Development Goals will also remain high on political and policy agendas of agencies and organizations concerned with international social development and poverty reduction. With the role of commercial providers and philanthropists in financing and delivering international health and welfare services expecting to be intensified, questions will be asked about the efficiency and effectiveness of private responses to global inequality and poverty. Questions about how social protections can be extended to, and secured for, the greatest number of people worldwide will also remain live issues, together with questions about the scale and nature of international financing needed to foster and secure this provision for the poorest countries and social groups in particular.

Guide to Further Sources

For further discussion of themes and issues covered in this chapter two linked student texts are recommended. The first N. Yeates (ed.), *Understanding Global Social Policy* (Bristol: Policy Press, 2008) provides an accessible introduction to key issues and debates in global health, employment, housing, pensions, corporations, trade, population, and migration policy. The second, N. Yeates and C. Holden (eds), *The Global Social Policy Reader* (Bristol: Policy Press, 2009), brings together key readings charting the concepts, actors and processes constituting global social policy and provides a detailed guide to current debates about global social policy reform.

The journal, *Global Social Policy: Journal of Public Policy and Social Development* publishes articles on a wide range of issues in global social policy; its Digest (also available online) summarizes current policy developments. Extensive online resources have been developed by the SPA's International and Comparative Social Policy group, they include comprehensive links to research and activist organizations' web sites in the field, see www.globalwelfare.net.

Review Questions

1 Why are IOs central to the study of social policy?

2 To what extent are IOs involved in social policy formation?

3 How influential are IOs in matters of national social policy?

4 How might key concepts be adapted to the global context?

5 Summarize the different positions on IOs within global social reform debates.

Visit the book companion site at www.wiley.com/go/alcock to make use of the resources designed to accompany the textbook. There you will find chapter-specific guides to further resources, including governmental, international, think-tank, pressure groups, and relevant journals sources. You will also find a glossary based on *The Blackwell Dictionary of Social Policy*, help sheets, and case studies, guidance on managing assignments in social policy and career advice.

PART VII

Welfare Services

45

Income Maintenance and Social Security

Stephen McKay and Karen Rowlingson

Overview

- Social security represents just under one-third of all government spending. The largest group of benefit recipients are children, 13 million of whom receive Child Benefit, through their parents – though there are plans to remove entitlement from higher earners. Pensioners come next, with 12 million receiving state retirement pension.
- Definitions of social security vary from broad definitions encompassing all methods of securing an income to narrow definitions focusing on state systems of income maintenance.
- Social security systems vary in their aims. The British system focuses on alleviating poverty, hence considerable reliance on means-tested provision. Continental European systems focus more on insurance-based systems.
- State benefits are typically divided into: *contributory benefits* such as the state retirement pension; *means-tested benefits*/tax credits such as income support; and contingent or *categorical benefits* such as child benefit.
- There has been an emphasis from both Conservative and Labour governments in Britain on individual responsibility rather than state provision. This is evident in recent reforms of pensions, disability benefit, and child support.

The Importance of Social Security

The incomes of individuals and families come from several sources – from the private sector through wages/salaries, support from other family members, and often from the state in the form of cash benefits. The discussion of *social security* takes this as its starting point, sometimes looking broadly at the range of income sources, usually looking more narrowly at the role the

The Student's Companion to Social Policy, Fourth Edition. Edited by Pete Alcock, Margaret May, Sharon Wright.
© 2012 John Wiley & Sons, Ltd. Published 2012 by John Wiley & Sons, Ltd.

state plays in maintaining incomes. Different welfare states play very different roles in income maintenance, from minimalist schemes existing only for the poor (if then), to comprehensive systems covering an extensive range of risks to income security, and involving significant redistribution.

This chapter provides an overview of social security in Britain. Most people spend much of their lives either receiving or paying for social security – often both at the same time. However, the system is far from simple and most of us understand very little about what it aims to do, how it operates and its effects. A number of facts illustrate the importance of the social security system in Britain:

- Government spending on social security benefits and tax credits in the United Kingdom in 2009–10 is around £190 billion per year – just under one-third of all government spending and about the same as health and education spending combined. This represents about £3,200 each year for every woman, man and child in the country.
- Some 60 per cent of British households receive at least one social security benefit, with 20 per cent receiving an income-related (means-tested) benefit (FRS 2008/9, http://research.dwp.gov.uk/asd/frs/). Some 57 per cent of social tenants receive at least one means-tested benefit.

The benefits responsible for the greatest spending are the state Retirement Pension, Income Support/Pension Credit, Housing Benefit, Child Benefit, Disability Living Allowance and Incapacity Benefit (the last of these becoming Employment and Support Allowance). Social security benefits are paid mostly from general taxes and from specific contributions for social security – which we know as National Insurance.

What is 'Social Security'?

Social security clearly plays a central role in people's lives. But what is meant by social security? There is no universally accepted neat definition of 'social security', and it may be defined in a number of ways.

Starting with the very widest definition, it is sometimes used to refer to all the ways people organize their lives in order to ensure access to an adequate income. This wide concept includes securing income from all sources such as earnings from employers and self-employment, financial help from charities, money from a family member and cash benefits from the state. If we take the widest definition then the private sector is the foremost provider of income maintenance as earnings from employment and profits from self-employment are the chief source of income for most people of working age, and pensions in retirement are often based on such earnings.

A slightly narrower definition of social security would include all types of financial support, except those provided by the market system. In this way, reliance on the immediate or extended family would still be classed as helping to achieve social security. However, it is increasingly usual to adopt an even narrower definition, and to regard social security as those sources of immediate financial support provided by the state.

This debate about definition is, of course, important across the range of services studied within social policy. The study of health is broader than the activities of the National Health Service, for example, and the provision of care extends well beyond the social services.

The definition of 'social security' as the system of cash benefits paid by the government to different individuals appears to be fairly simple and unproblematic. But it is inadequate not least because some 'benefits' are not paid for by the state, or need not be. For example, statutory sick pay used to be paid by government but, whilst it remains a legal entitlement, it is now mostly a cost met by employers. There are also occupational schemes for sickness, widowhood and retirement that are similar to state benefits, and which have a similar function, but which are organized by employers. One could also envisage the government finding ways to 'privatize' what are currently state benefits, or instigating new compulsory private provision, perhaps for pensions. So, both voluntary employer schemes, and some programmes mandated by government, may also be classed as social security – neither of which neatly fit the above definition.

Another rather grey area is the distinction between cash benefits, systems of tax allowances and, increasingly, 'tax credits' which are the responsibility of Her Majesty's Revenue and Customs (HMRC, formerly the Inland Revenue). Tax credits have become an increasingly important part of the 'social security' system. The government generally prefers to see them as standing apart from social security benefits – in particular, that they are designed for workers, rather than those not in work. There are, however, good reasons for seeing tax credits as very similar to social security benefits as there are important areas where tax credits and benefits perform similar roles.

For the reasons mentioned above, it is difficult to give a precise definition of social security, and different people/organizations will prefer different definitions. In this chapter, we take a fairly pragmatic approach focusing on state systems of income maintenance – largely benefits (administered by the Department for Work and Pensions) and tax credits (administered by HMRC).

The Aims of Social Security

Having defined social security we now ask what are the aims of the system? The answer is complex. Like elsewhere, the system in Britain has evolved over time and so is not what would be designed if policy-makers were now starting from scratch. Furthermore, different parts of the system have different aims and so it is not possible to identify a single or even main aim. With these reservations in mind, Box 45.1 lists some of the possible objectives of social security.

Within these general aims, the British social security system has been designed to achieve the following:

- to maintain incentives for self-provision (through earning and saving);
- to keep take-up of benefits high;
- to counter possible fraud; and
- to ensure that administrative costs are low.

The aims of the British system have traditionally been more limited than those of systems in Europe, if wider than in some parts of the rest of the English-speaking world. The importance of relieving poverty in the British system explains the considerable reliance on *means-testing* in Britain. Receipt of means-tested benefits depends

> **Box 45.1 Possible Aims of Social Security**
>
> - Insuring against the risks of particular events in life, such as retirement, unemployment and sickness.
> - Relieving poverty or low income.
> - Redistributing resources across people's life-cycles, especially from working age to retirement.
> - Redistributing resources from rich to poor.
> - 'Compensating' for some types of extra cost (such as children, disability).
> - Providing financial support when 'traditional' families break down.

on a person or family having resources (typically income, and often savings) below a certain level in order to receive benefits. Means-testing is also common in America, New Zealand and Australia but much less common elsewhere, especially in continental Europe where social security tends to be less centralized and more concerned with income maintenance and compensation.

An Overview of the Current System

The social security system today is a highly complex organism which has evolved over time and which very few people understand in all its detail. For every possible generalization about the system there are myriad caveats which need to be made. It is therefore difficult to give a brief overview without over-simplifying the system and therefore possibly giving misleading information. Nevertheless, there are various ways of classifying the different benefits in the UK system. For example, benefits can be categorized into two dichotomies: universal versus means-tested; contributory versus non-contributory. If we use the rules of entitlement as our yardstick, social security can be divided into three main components: contributory benefits (benefits which rely upon having paid contributions); means-tested benefits and tax credits (benefits which depend upon income); and contingent benefits (benefits which depend upon your position or category).

Contributory benefits

The main root for the current social security system lies in the Beveridge Report published in the early 1940s (see Chapter 18), although insurance-based and other benefits had been introduced well before this time. At the heart of the Beveridge approach – of contributory benefits or 'social insurance' – is the idea that people face a range of risks that might lead to severe reductions in living standards. These include the risk of unemployment, or being incapacitated and unable to work, or retiring, or losing the main income-earner in a family. Some risks are rather uncommon, and relatively unrelated to economic circumstances, such as widowhood. Other risks, such as retirement, are much more widespread and predictable.

The main issues that arise with social insurance include

- Why should the state provide this service, rather than private insurance? What relationship should there then be between state and private insurance?
- What risks should be covered?
- On what basis should contributions be made, or be deemed to be made?

Entitlement to social insurance benefits is based on having paid National Insurance contributions, and being in a risk covered by these benefits (such as unemployment or retirement). These benefits are individualized in that the earnings of a partner do not generally affect entitlement. The main benefit in this group is the State Retirement Pension. Other benefits are the contributory parts of Incapacity Benefit and contribution based Jobseeker's Allowance.

Means-tested benefits/tax credits

Entitlement to means-tested benefits depends on the level of 'family' resources, particularly income and savings. The four main examples in the British system are Income Support/Pension Credit, Working Tax Credit, Housing Benefit and Council Tax Benefit.

The system of benefits based on means-testing, particularly for those on low incomes, is sometimes known as 'social assistance'. In Britain, social assistance is almost synonymous with the benefit Income Support (and its equivalent for older people, Pension Credit), and income-based Jobseeker's Allowance for unemployed people. These benefits are paid to those whose income and savings are below defined levels, taking into account the size and type of family.

Countries differ a great deal in the extent of this type of provision. In Australia and New Zealand, almost all benefits include an element of 'means-testing'. This does not mean that only the poorest may receive benefits – in some instances the aim is to exclude the richest rather than to include only the poorest. Child tax credit plays a similar role in the United Kingdom with most families with children now entitled to it. In much of Northern Europe, social assistance plays a much smaller role, picking up those not covered by the main social insurance system. In addition they are often administered locally, with local organizations having some discretion about the precise rules of entitlement.

Additional conditions are often attached to receiving social assistance. People of working age, without sole responsibility for caring for children or disabled adults, must be able to work, available for work and actively seeking work. In past times, they may have had to enter a workhouse to qualify.

Contingent benefits

These are sometimes referred to as categorical benefits or as non means-tested and non-contributory. Entitlement depends on the existence of certain circumstances (or contingencies) such as having a child (Child Benefit) being disabled (Disability Living Allowance).

In the British social security system, some benefits effectively recognize that certain groups of people face extra costs which the state will share. The clearest example is benefits for dependent children and Child Benefit. There is no test of contributions, and the family's level of income is not taken into consideration (at the present time, though from 2013 it is planned to remove entitlement where a parent pays the 40% income tax rate). There are, however, certain tests of residence that must be satisfied. Disability benefits provide another example, where some elements are purely contingent and reflect neither current means nor previous contributions.

It is worth emphasizing that this division into three groups is something of a simplification of differences between benefits. Means-tested benefits do not just depend on financial resources; they also tend to rely on some combination of being in a particular situation or a particular family type. For example, non-disabled single people without children may only claim Income Support if they meet conditions relating to being unemployed. It is possible for certain sources of income to affect contributory benefits, for example Jobseeker's Allowance and Incapacity Benefit (both contribution-based) can be reduced if a person receives income from a personal or occupational pension.

Alongside benefits for different groups, there are also benefits to help people meet specific extra costs of living. Housing Benefit helps people pay their rent if they are on a low income. The cost of this benefit has increased dramatically in the past three decades because there has been a deliberate policy shift from subsidizing 'bricks and mortar' (in terms of low council rents) to subsidizing individuals (by raising rents and paying benefit to those on low incomes). While low-paid renters can receive help, those with mortgages are mostly denied assistance with their housing costs. Those on low incomes can also receive help with their council tax. The other major benefit to help meet extra costs of daily living is the Social Fund. This is another distinctive feature of the British system although social workers in some other countries can give out money to people in need. The Social Fund is a much-criticized part of the system, particularly as claimants are mostly given loans rather than grants.

How Social Security is Delivered

In 2001, the Department of Social Security merged with parts of the Department for Employment and Skills to become the Department for Work and Pensions (DWP). This reinforced an increasing emphasis on 'work as the best form of welfare'. The new department increasingly differentiates those above and below working age as well as those in paid work and those not. All those claiming benefits who are of working age but not in paid work are given a Work Focused Interview where issues about employment are discussed prior to a claim for financial support being dealt with.

Jobcentre Plus is the agency providing benefit and job search services while the service dealing with pensions and older people is The Pension Service. The Disability and Carers Service provides compensation for disabled people and their carers. The DWP is also currently responsible for the Child Support Agency, though this is in the process of being incorporated into the Child Maintenance and Enforcement Commission (C-MEC). Tax credits are the responsibility of HMRC. Local authorities remain responsible for Housing Benefit and Council Tax Benefit.

Benefit Levels, Poverty, and Adequacy

In the past twenty-five years, expenditure on benefits has risen in both absolute and real terms. But increasing expenditure on benefits has not generally been fuelled by rises in the real levels of benefit and indeed there is widespread evidence that benefit levels are not adequate to meet people's basic requirements. Beveridge initially aimed to set benefits at subsistence levels according to budget studies in the 1930s but there is disagreement about whether he achieved this. Price inflation means that benefit levels have to be raised every year ('uprated') otherwise they are worth less in real terms. There is some evidence that both the initial levels of benefits and the uprating to prices in the 1940s were not set correctly. In more recent years, some benefits have been frozen and others have been linked to price inflation rather than to wage inflation (if it was higher). This means that benefit recipients have become increasingly worse off, relative to workers. Moreover since the early 1980s more benefits have been brought within the scope of income tax, such as state Retirement Pensions, JSA and Incapacity Benefit, and this has affected the relative generosity of these benefits.

Benefits in Cash and in Kind

In most cases the aims of social security are achieved by paying cash benefits. However this need not be the case. Benefits could be provided 'in-kind', either through providing services or vouchers that may only be spent on certain types of good. In the United States, an important method of providing for poor families is through the Food Stamps programme. This pays out vouchers that must be exchanged for food. In Britain, receiving Income Support and some other benefits carries with it rights some services at no charge, such as dental treatment, eye examinations and legal aid ('passported benefits').

The British system developed along two lines: the national social security system generally provided cash benefits to cover some needs such as the need for food, clothes, and money for bills whereas other needs, particularly the need for social care, was covered by local social services departments who provided in-kind services.

Emerging Issues

The past twenty-five years have seen an increasing emphasis from all governments on individual responsibility rather than state provision. This trend looks set to continue with a number of important reforms on the horizon. The 2010 coalition government is seeking major simplification for those of working age, creating a single benefit (Universal Credit) to subsume many existing benefits, and a Work Programme to replace a variety of welfare-to-work schemes.

Individual saving will also be encouraged through the introduction of new personal accounts in the form of the National Endowment Savings Trust (NEST). As far as disability benefits are concerned, incapacity benefit is being scrapped in favour of a new Employment and Support Allowance where, again, individuals will be expected to secure their incomes through the labour market where at all possible rather than through the state. The Child Support Agency is being replaced, with the expectation that individuals will be expected to make their own arrangements where possible.

The 2010 Budget and Comprehensive Spending Review set out a programme of large reductions in the growth of social security spending. The biggest change is to uprate many benefits by the consumer price index, which is generally lower than the retail prices index (or variants of it) that is currently used. There are also reductions in Housing Benefit and in Tax Credits, restricting either the amounts paid or the income levels of eligible families. Some disability benefits are also being reformed with the aim of reducing expenditure.

The British system continues, therefore, to tread a neo-liberal path towards minimal state support in favour of income maintenance through the labour market and individual savings. However, this approach appears doomed to fail to eradicate child poverty by 2020, as mandated by the 2010 Child Poverty Act.

Guide to Further Sources

It is best to start with Jane Millar (ed.), *Understanding Social Security* (2nd edn, Bristol: Policy Press, 2009). This book is an edited collection covering the key benefit groups and general issues in relation to social security. Its focus is the United Kingdom and it provides a user-friendly introduction to the main issues. Robert Walker, *Social Security and Welfare: Concepts and Comparisons* (Maidenhead: Open University Press, 2005) is aimed at those who already have a general understanding of the key issues. It focuses on the objectives and outcomes of social security systems through cross-national comparisons. Another useful introductory textbook (sadly out of print) is Stephen McKay and Karen Rowlingson's *Social Security in Britain* (London: Macmillan, 1999).

Those wanting to keep up to date should read the *Journal of Poverty & Social Justice*, details online at www.policypress.org.uk. The Department for Work and Pensions publishes regular research reports, and press releases at www.dwp.gov.uk. Figures on tax credits may be found on the HMRC web site, www.hmrc.gov.uk. The Institute for Fiscal Studies, www.ifs.org.uk, produces timely commentaries on reform, from an economic perspective.

Review Questions

1 What is the scope of social security?
2 What are the advantages and disadvantages of using means-tested support to alleviate poverty?
3 Is it better to provide people with either vouchers (such as Food Stamps in the United States) or support in the form of cash?
4 Is the wide variety of different benefits justified, or is a move to a 'Universal Credit' to be preferred?
5 Have changes in economic and social conditions rendered obsolete the Beveridge plan for the benefits system.

Visit the book companion site at www.wiley.com/go/alcock to make use of the resources designed to accompany the textbook. There you will find chapter-specific guides to further resources, including governmental, international, think-tank, pressure groups, and relevant journals sources. You will also find a glossary based on *The Blackwell Dictionary of Social Policy*, help sheets, and case studies, guidance on managing assignments in social policy and career advice.

46

Employment

Alan Deacon and Ruth Patrick

Overview

- The UK coalition government has continued and intensified the welfare-to-work programmes introduced by New Labour (1997–2010).
- A central feature of welfare-to-work programmes since 1997 has been the growing use of conditionality.
- The scope of welfare-to-work programmes has been steadily widened in recent years, and they now focus increasingly upon lone parents and disabled people.
- Third sector and private agencies will play an increasing role in the delivery of welfare-to-work programmes.
- The intensification of welfare-to-work programmes has been criticized on the grounds that it devalues unpaid work, especially caring.

Context

Employment policies occupy a central but controversial place in debates about the future of welfare. For millions of people paid employment is not only their major – or sole – source of income, but it is also the basis of their social standing and of their self-esteem. Those without such work are at greater risk of poverty and are more likely to experience ill-health. Moreover, their children are less likely to do well at school and to obtain secure, well-paid jobs. Unemployment is also linked to a range of other social problems. Whatever the precise patterns of causality, it is undeniable that communities in which unemployment is high are also disproportionately affected by crime,

The Student's Companion to Social Policy, Fourth Edition. Edited by Pete Alcock, Margaret May, Sharon Wright.
© 2012 John Wiley & Sons, Ltd. Published 2012 by John Wiley & Sons, Ltd.

family breakdown and antisocial behaviour. For governments, high rates of employment boost tax revenues and cut the cost of benefits; thereby making it easier to reduce overall levels of public expenditure. It is not surprising, then, that so-called welfare-to-work programmes were at the heart of the welfare reforms introduced by New Labour governments between 1997 and 2010, nor that those programmes have been continued and extended by the subsequent UK coalition government.

The term welfare-to-work refers to a range of policies that are intended to encourage, to enable, and at times to compel benefit claimants to seek paid employment. These include measures to increase the job opportunities available to welfare claimants, through job creation schemes or the payment of subsidies to employers who take people directly off the unemployment register. They also include measures to increase the financial incentive to take advantage of these opportunities, either by enhancing the benefits paid to those in low-paid work, or by restricting the benefits they would receive when out of work.

In recent years, however, the primary focus of welfare-to-work programmes has been upon the provision of personal support and advice to claimants. The rationale for this is that at the individual level the effect of particularly long-term unemployment is to de-skill and de-motivate people, and to make them less attractive to employers. Policy-makers argue that the most effective way to help those affected in this way is to provide them with an advisor who will help them to draw up and follow a personal return to work plan, and thereby acquire the skills and motivation that employers require. They further argue that it is reasonable to require claimants to take advantage of the opportunities created by these programmes, or face the possible loss of their benefits. Moreover, this focus on the stimulation of job seeking activity is believed to be of benefit even in a recession, when, if anything, it is even more important to ensure that claimants are equipped to take advantage of the recovery when it eventually arrives.

The purpose of this chapter is to provide a brief introduction to these policy developments and to the academic and political debates around them. Before doing so, however, it is important to note that these developments and debates have taken place during a period of significant change in the labour market.

Unemployment in Britain fell almost continuously from 1993 to 2004, by which time the numbers claiming unemployment benefits had reached a thirty year low. In that year the rate of unemployment averaged 4.8 per cent and this figure was to remain broadly unchanged until the impact of the recession produced a step-change to nearly 8 per cent during 2009. Young people have been particularly hard-hit by the economic downturn, and the rate of unemployment among sixteen- to twenty-four- year-olds stood at nearly 20 per cent at the end of 2010.

Welfare-to-Work Policy 1997–2011

Britain's New Labour government consistently declared its ambition to 'rebuild the welfare state around work' (DSS 1998: 21). This ambition was most often framed as an attempt to move away from 'passive', relatively unconditional benefit provision towards a system which provides support to make the transition from welfare 'dependency' into paid work. Over thirteen years in power, New Labour reformed the welfare state such that all unemployed people and many lone parents and disabled people are now expected to take steps to enter work or risk benefit sanctions. The UK coalition government elected in May 2010 shares New Labour's commitment to reducing the benefit claimant count and ensuring that, for the majority, receipt of out-of-work benefits is explicitly tied to work-related conditions.

Repeatedly, first Blair and Brown, and now Cameron stress that the right to welfare should be conditional on individuals' fulfilling their responsibilities to seek and prepare for paid employment. The contractual binding of rights and responsibilities is a remarkably consistent theme of both New Labour and coalition rhetoric, and is often used to defend sanctions against those who fail to keep their side of the 'welfare bargain'. Indeed, the obligation to work, wherever possible, is construed as the primary responsibility of the dutiful citizen. Furthermore, social inclusion is equated with participation in the formal labour market, with welfare-to-work measures characterized as efforts to promote social inclusion by supporting people into paid work.

Central to New Labour's welfare-to-work strategy was a programme of New Deals that provided work-related support to specific groups of welfare claimants, with varying degrees of compulsion attached to the schemes. Launched in 1998, the flagship New Deal for Young People mandated the participation of all young people on Jobseeker's Allowance (JSA) who had been out of work for six months or more. Participants could choose from the four options of work experience, training, education or participation in an environmental taskforce, but there was no 'fifth option of simply remaining on benefit' (DSS 1998: 25). By contrast, New Deals for lone parents and disabled people were voluntary, although over New Labour's time in office the conditionality attached to these groups of welfare claimants steadily increased (Wright 2009). Shortly before losing power, New Labour started to roll the various programmes of New Deals into one Flexible New Deal designed to offer personalized and flexible support.

Since entering government, the coalition has revealed what it describes as a radical and new approach to welfare reform, promising a welfare state that ends passive welfare dependency and provides meaningful, targeted help to reduce worklessness (DWP 2010). At the heart of this 'new' strategy is the Work Programme, a single programme of welfare-to-work support for all eligible welfare claimants. Due to be launched in Summer 2011, this programme will be delivered by private and voluntary sector providers who will be paid largely on the basis of results achieved in getting their 'customers' off welfare and into sustainable jobs. The government has promised earlier intervention for those requiring the most help, such as disabled people, young people, problematic drug users and ex-offenders. Welfare-to-work providers helping the hardest to reach will receive the largest payments, with a maximum fee of £14,000 per claimant sustained in employment for two years. While packaged as a radical departure, the Work Programme in fact demonstrates marked similarities with New Labour's Flexible New Deal reinforcing the idea that, on

welfare-to-work at least, all three main political parties take a broadly similar approach (Deacon and Patrick 2011).

In its 2010 White Paper on welfare reform, the coalition also announced plans for a programme of compulsory work activity for those on JSA who are judged by Jobcentre Plus staff to need extra 'help' to 'acquire the work habit' (DWP 2010). The Mandatory Work Activity (MWA) programme will require claimants to engage in four weeks unpaid work in the community, or risk the complete suspension of their benefits. The introduction of MWA represents a stepping-up of the level of compulsion and conditionality, although here again it should be noted that New Labour had plans in place to launch a similar scheme (called Work for Your Benefits).

Policy Trends 1997–2011

Taking the period of 1997–2011 as a whole it is possible to trace four key policy trends in the welfare-to-work arena, trends which seem to continue relatively unaltered following the transition from New Labour to coalition government. First, there has been a consistent and increasing stress on attaching conditions to benefit receipt, such that those on out-of-work benefits must participate in welfare-to-work programmes and related activities or risk reductions in benefits or their complete suspension. This approach, championed in the New Deal for Young People, has been steadily extended to incorporate a greater proportion of welfare claimants alongside parallel steps to increase the level of sanctions threatened for non-engagement. In their December 2010 White Paper, the coalition announced a new regime of conditionality, which includes the threat of a maximum penalty of three years without benefits for those who three times fail to apply for a job, accept a job offer or participate in MWA (DWP 2010). Furthermore, the level of conditionality applied to those on disability benefits has also been extended, and those on Employment and Support Allowance (ESA) judged to have some capacity to work now face benefit suspension for failure to participate in work-related activity.

Second, governments have increasingly looked beyond the traditional target group for welfare-to-work policies, the unemployed, to focus on the broader economically inactive population, with a particular emphasis on increasing the employment rates of lone parents and disabled people (Wright 2009). This has been an ongoing project, with the past fourteen years seeing the obligations and expectations placed on these groups gradually extended. From December 2011 all lone parents whose youngest child is aged five or over will only be able to claim JSA and will thus be subject to substantial welfare conditionality.

Disabled people will also be subject to increasing conditionality, as the coalition presses ahead with New Labour proposals to migrate all Incapacity Benefit claimants onto the relatively new ESA. The ESA aims to focus more on what people can do, rather than what they cannot, and is linked to a Work Capability Assessment (WCA) that determines benefit eligibility. Those judged to have some capacity to work are placed in the 'employment' group of ESA, where they are expected to participate in the Work Programme and associated work-related activity or risk benefit sanctions. Only those with the most severe impairments receive ESA unconditionally and are placed in the 'support' group. Figures for the operation of the WCA between October 2008 and May 2010 show that the majority were found fit to work (65 per cent), and thus transferred onto JSA and subject to work-related conditionality. One-quarter were placed in the 'employment group', with only 10 per cent allocated into the 'support' group (DWP 2011). There have long been concerns regarding the operation of the WCA, with particular fears that it is incorrectly finding people fit to work. These concerns are likely to intensify from March 2011 when the WCA will be used to reassess some 1.5 million disability benefit claimants at a rate of 10,000 assessments a week.

A third discernable policy trend is the continued attempt to 'make work pay', and to increase the incentives attached to paid work. New Labour sought to achieve this objective through the introduction of a National Minimum Wage and a new series of in-work benefits called tax credits (see Chapter 45). The early pronouncements of

the new coalition government similarly emphasized the need to make work pay, and it has outlined plans for a potentially radical reform of the benefits system through the introduction of a single Universal Credit. This Universal Credit will seek to integrate out-of-work benefits with in-work tax credits, and thereby to strengthen work incentives by reducing the rate at which tax is applied and benefits withdrawn as people move off welfare and into work (DWP 2010).

This may not be the whole story, however, as it was noted in the introduction that work incentives can be increased by either improving the rewards attached to paid work or by reducing those attached to benefit receipt. It is possible that the coalition will opt more for the latter approach. Indeed, both the emergency budget of June 2010 and the spending review announced in the following October included measures to reduce the value and availability of benefits. In particular, they included plans to reduce the rate of housing benefits paid to those on JSA for twelve months or more and to restrict the length of time ESA could be received by those who had been assessed as having some capacity to work (Deacon and Patrick 2011).

The fourth and final trend relates to the reliance on the private and voluntary sector for the delivery of welfare-to-work programmes. The coalition has continued the trend for the delivery of welfare-to-work programmes to be contracted out to a rapidly expanding welfare to work industry. Increasingly, payments will be made on the basis of results, with contractors paid only where they successfully assist claimants in making the welfare-to-work transition. Proposals are in place for welfare-to-work programmes to be partially funded on the basis of planned future benefit savings accrued when a claimant enters work. Ethical concerns have been raised here regarding the expansion of the 'welfare-to-work industry' and how far companies motivated primarily by profit maximization will act in the best interests of welfare claimants.

A New Welfare Settlement

As a former New Labour Minister James Purnell has observed there is now 'a covert consensus in

Britain on welfare' (cited in Deacon and Patrick 2011). Indeed, it is possible to outline a welfare settlement that sees the three main parties in broad agreement regarding the purpose, nature and objectives of effective welfare-to-work policies. This new settlement is underpinned by three important assumptions. The first is that paid employment has the potential to transform people's lives in ways which go beyond relief from poverty to improvements to self-esteem, family life, mental health and well-being. The second assumption is that if 'work is what works' in welfare reform, then it follows that it is fair and reasonable to expect benefit claimants to take advantage of welfare-to-work programmes and for governments to impose penalties and sanctions upon those who fail to do so. The third assumption is that welfare-to-work programmes will be more effective and more cost-efficient if they are delivered by third and private sector agencies.

Given the extent and reach of this settlement it is important to consider the concerns that have been raised about the validity of the assumptions that underpin it, and to discuss the criticisms that have been made of welfare-to-work programmes under both New Labour and the coalition.

Emerging Issues

The first of these criticisms relate to the effectiveness of the programmes in helping people make a sustainable transition from welfare into work. While there is some evidence that the New Deals did increase levels of employment, this took place in a climate of economic growth and the approach remains relatively untested in times of public sector job losses and *rising* unemployment. Further, there are questions regarding the nature of the employment opportunities open to those coming through the welfare-to-work regime, with particular concerns regarding the seeming dominance of low-paid, unskilled and often temporary jobs.

A second criticism is that the focus of the programmes upon the need to enhance the skills and employability of those referred to them inevitably means that the problem is seen to lie with the individual rather than with the labour market. This in turn leads to a neglect of the structural

barriers that claimants may face, such as an absence of suitable jobs or a lack of suitable child-care. Applying conditionality to disabled people, for example, suggests that they require the threat of sanctions to encourage them to improve their employability and enter work. It has been argued that is to ignore evidence of structural barriers to disabled peoples' full and equal participation in the labour market, which include physical barriers of access and endemic discrimination and employer prejudice (Piggott and Grover 2009).

A third criticism is that, while the impact of sanctions on encouraging people to take steps to enter work remains fairly ambiguous, there is well documented evidence regarding the hardship faced by those experiencing sanctions (Peters and Joyce 2006). These negative impacts often extend beyond financial hardship to worsening mental health, strains on family life and physical health problems.

Finally, and more broadly, there has long been concern regarding the emphasis which welfare-to-work measures place on work as the primary duty of the responsible citizen. Constantly stressing the value of paid work and, in particular, requiring lone parents to seek work as a condition of benefit receipt, may seem to suggest that to make a socially valuable contribution it is necessary to engage in the formal labour market. This in turn raises still more profound questions about whether paid work is indeed the only, or even the primary way, in which citizens can contribute to the common good. It has been argued that to see only paid work as the marker of adult citizenship is to devalue other forms of contribution such as volunteering, parenting and other forms of informal care. Moreover, this is at a time when there is an ever growing need for such informal care work to meet the demands of an increasingly ageing population. In this context, some would argue that to equate financial self-sufficiency with independence, as successive government documents seem to do, reflects too narrow an understanding of the meaning of self-reliance (Young 2002). Such critics would call instead for employment policies that begin with the recognition that everyone is dependent upon others at some point in their life, and which attempt to strike a more even balance between work and care.

Box 46.1 Timeline of Key
Welfare-to-work Policies, Britain
1997–2011

1998 New Deal for Young People, New
      Deal for Lone Parents and New Deal
      25 Plus all launched (additional New
      Deals followed later)
1999 National Minimum Wage intro-
      duced, alongside system of Working
      Family Tax Credits and Childcare
      Tax Credits
2001 New Deal for Disabled People
      introduced
2001 Lone parents whose children aged
      between five and sixteen required
      to attend Work Focused Interviews
      as condition of benefit receipt
2002 Jobcentre Plus established, combin-
      ing the Benefits Agency and the
      Employment Service into a single
      point of access
2003 Pathways to Work piloted (particular
      package of employment support
      for disabled people) which includes
      compulsory Work Focused Inter-
      views
2008 Pathways to work rolled out nation-
      ally
2008 Disability benefit, Employment and
      Support Allowance, introduced for
      new claimants
2009 Flexible New Deal piloted in parts
      of the United Kingdom
2010 Migration of existing Incapacity
      Benefit Claimants onto Employ-
      ment and Support Allowance com-
      mences with pilots
2010 Coalition government announce
      plans for a new Universal Credit,
      due to come into operation between
      2013–17
2011 Work Programme launched
2011 All lone parents whose eldest child
      is five or over migrated onto Job
      Seeker's Allowance (n.b. this is a
      gradual process that has been ongoing
      since 2008, when the age was first
      reduced from sixteen to twelve)

Guide to Further Sources

A. Deacon and R. Patrick's 'A New Welfare Settlement? The Coalition Government and Welfare-to-Work', in H. Bochel (ed.), *The Conservative Party and Social Policy* (Bristol: Policy Press, 2011), pp. 116–79, provides a more detailed analysis of the coalition government's policies, and of the 'new welfare settlement'.

An early statement of New Labour's aims in welfare reform and of the 'mutual obligations' of government and claimants can be found in: Department of Social Security (DSS), *A New Contract for Welfare*, Cm 3805 (London: HMSO, 1998).

The coalition government's first White Paper on welfare reform was: Department for Work and Pensions (DWP), *Universal Credit: Welfare that works*, Cm 7957 (London: HMSO, 2010). The DWP's web site, www.dwp.gov.uk, includes relevant statistics, ministerial speeches, and policy papers. This is an invaluable resource which is updated daily.

A valuable report on the impact of sanctions upon those claiming Job Seekers Allowance can be found in M. Peters and L. Joyce, *A Review of the JSA Sanctions Regime: Summary Research Findings*, Research Report No 313 (London, DWP, 2006).

The introduction of the ESA is critically discussed in L. Piggott and C. Grover, Retrenching incapacity benefit: employment support allowance and paid work, *Social Policy and Society* 8/2 (2009): 159–61.

S. Wright, 'Welfare-to-work', in J. Millar (ed.), *Understanding Social Security: Issues for Policy and Practice* (2nd edn, Bristol: Policy Press, 2009), pp. 193–212, gives a more detailed account and critique of the development of welfare-to-work policies under New Labour. In particular it explains more fully how the focus of such polices widened from the unemployed to those termed 'economically inactive', especially lone parents and disabled people.

I. M. Young, 'Autonomy, Welfare Reform and Meaningful Work', in Kittay, E. F. and Feder, E. K. (eds) *The Subject of Care: Feminist Perspectives on Dependency* (Lanham, MD: Rowman and Littlefield, 2002): 40–59, is a powerful critique of the assumption that personal autonomy is dependent upon financial self-sufficiency, or that all paid work is necessarily meaningful.

Review Questions

1 What arguments are used to justify conditionality in welfare-to-work programmes?
2 What underpins the growing consensus on welfare-to-work?
3 In what ways has the scope of welfare-to-work widened in recent years?
4 What criticisms can be made of welfare-to-work programmes?
5 Is it possible to reconcile welfare-to-work policies with rising levels of unemployment and growing demands for informal care?

Visit the book companion site at www.wiley.com/go/alcock to make use of the resources designed to accompany the textbook. There you will find chapter-specific guides to further resources, including governmental, international, think-tank, pressure groups, and relevant journals sources. You will also find a glossary based on *The Blackwell Dictionary of Social Policy*, help sheets, and case studies, guidance on managing assignments in social policy and career advice.

47

Health Care

Rob Baggott

Overview

- Health care issues are prominent in most industrial societies. Health care takes up a large proportion of the taxpayer's money and attracts considerable media attention.
- The medical profession remains a powerful influence within the health care system, although the perspectives of patients, users, and carers are increasingly acknowledged.
- Three main models of health care funding exist – tax-based, state insurance, and private insurance. The United Kingdom is mainly a tax-based system. Large sums of money have been committed to the NHS in recent years, but financial problems and inequities in funding remain.
- There is increasing plurality in service provision, encouraging the private and voluntary sector into the NHS 'market'.
- Renewed efforts have been made to encourage partnership working between the NHS, local government, voluntary groups, and the private sector.

The Importance of Health and Health Care

In modern societies, the state accepts much responsibility for the health of its citizens. This is reflected in the high level of public expenditure on health services in most industrialized countries. The state also takes steps to protect and promote the health of the public. Indeed, governments are aware of the health effects of people's socio-economic circumstances, environment, and lifestyles (see HM Government/Department of

The Student's Companion to Social Policy, Fourth Edition. Edited by Pete Alcock, Margaret May, Sharon Wright.
© 2012 John Wiley & Sons, Ltd. Published 2012 by John Wiley & Sons, Ltd.

Health 2004; Strategic Review of Health Inequalities in England 2010).

Health care is not like most other goods or services. Supply tends to create demand. Hence a technological breakthrough – such as a new breast-cancer drug – generates demand from people who believe it will save their lives, even if this turns out to be misplaced. Moreover, people lack the specialized, technical knowledge needed to purchase health care appropriately. Furthermore, a health care market based on private purchasing power tends to discriminate against the very people that need treatment. Poorer people, people with disabilities, children, and elderly people have the greatest health needs, but are the least able to afford private health insurance or to pay directly for care services.

In most industrialized societies, many believe that health care is a promoter of social solidarity and citizenship, and should be regarded as a basic human right. Although economic and social inequalities are tolerated, there is a strong feeling that good health should be available to all and that people's health should not be determined by their socio-economic circumstances or where they live.

Health services absorb a large amount of taxpayers' money. They employ huge numbers of people (the NHS is the second largest employer in the world after the US company 'Walmart'). Health issues are often highly emotionally charged, attract considerable media attention and are the subject of single-issue pressure group campaigns. Moreover, the policy arena is inhabited by powerful interest groups, such as the medical profession and the drugs industry, which are highly skilled in influencing the political agenda. In addition, health issues are a major concern for voters and an important focus for party political debates.

What is Health? What is Health Care?

Health can be seen in a negative way, as the absence of disease (Aggleton 1990). This is associated with the 'biomedical' approach to health, dominated by scientific enquiry into the causes of disease and the effectiveness of treatment. In contrast, the positive approach to health focuses on the promotion of health and well-being in a wider sense, encapsulated in the definition of health produced by the World Health Organization in 1946: 'a state of complete physical, mental and social well-being and not merely the absence of disease or infirmity.'

Health care can be divided into primary, secondary, and tertiary care. Primary care is provided by GPs and other professionals in practices, clinic, and community-settings (including the patient's home). Around 90 per cent of contacts between the public and the health services take place here. Primary care includes activities such as preventive services (immunization, screening, health promotion), care (such as changing dressings and monitoring health), and treatment (prescribing and administering drugs, minor surgery). Secondary care refers to the range of acute and specialist services provided by hospitals. Highly specialized services – known as tertiary services – deal with very complex conditions. Despite these distinctions, the boundary is shifting. Treatment is increasingly provided in community settings and this is expected to increase in the future (HM Government/Department of Health 2006).

Health care is often defined by the boundaries of professional work. The health professions, particularly the medical profession, are traditionally very powerful. They have shaped services to reflect their own expertise and interests. As a result, services have developed in a paternalistic way. However, there are countervailing forces. A substantial amount of care is provided by volunteers and informal carers. There are around 7 million carers in Britain. People also engage in self-help and self-medication (for example, buying medicines over-the-counter) and chronically ill people with long-term conditions increasingly self-manage their illnesses. Indeed, people with conditions such as asthma, arthritis, and diabetes are increasingly acknowledged as 'expert patients', managing their health in partnership with professionals. Some patients have been given individual care budgets, initially for social care, now being extended to health care. More generally, there is a greater emphasis nowadays on the perspectives and preferences of patients, users, and carers. The professions increasingly identify the patient as a partner in the process of health care. Nonetheless, professions remain powerful both in individual clinical encounters and within the health care system. They can exert influence in many ways, such as the control of information and the shaping of values and ideas about health and health care.

Funding Health Services

The amount of funding needed for future health services is likely to be affected by the underlying health of the population (Wanless 2002). The level of lifestyle-related disease, for example that associated with smoking, alcohol misuse and obesity, is therefore of great concern. The growing elderly population is likely to increase pressures on health budgets, though no one knows by how much. It is possible that tomorrow's elderly population may be fitter and healthier than today and might not require as much health care. Another factor is new technology, which could lead to the development of more effective interventions. Although this is likely to increase costs, at least in the short term, new techniques can offer the prospect of greater cost-effectiveness overall. For example, endoscopy, once a 'new technology' has facilitated significant growth of day surgery, contributing to a reduction in average in-patient costs.

In the United Kingdom, recent Labour governments granted large funding increases to the NHS. From being one of the most miserly health care systems in the industrialized world, the United Kingdom is now spending close to the OECD average. Yet in spite of this generosity, many parts of the service remain in financial difficulty. The imperative for efficiency savings will exacerbate this further. The continuing shortage of funds has led some to consider alternative sources of funding.

In essence there are three main models of health care funding. Tax-based systems, state insurance systems, and systems based on private insurance. The United Kingdom falls mainly in the first category, though a minority of the population – over one-tenth – have private health insurance. There are also co-payments – in the form of prescription charges for example, and other charges (for example, hospital car parking). Moreover, many people choose to pay directly for health care (such as alternative therapies, over-

the-counter prescriptions and in some cases, hospital treatment). Additional health care funding comes from the National Lottery and from other charitable sources.

The allocation of funding within the NHS is an important issue. Historically, budgets were allocated to health authorities on the basis of previous allocations adjusted for inflation. Following criticism that this system did not reflect variations in health needs across the country, new formulae were devised. These have since been revised on several occasions. The current approach is to give local health authorities (known as Primary Care Trusts) a budget with which to commission health services for local people. Their budgets are in turn determined by a formula which reflects needs (such as the age of the population, deprivation, and so on). Despite these changes, considerable inequalities remain in access to treatment between different local areas and between different socio-economic groups. There is also a perennial problem of unmet health care need. Cases of people unable to access treatments, often new and expensive therapies are common in the media. However, such cases of 'rationing' are not unique to the United Kingdom, or to tax-based health care systems. All health care systems to some extent have to prioritize and restrict treatments within the context of budgetary pressures.

Organization, Planning, and Commissioning

Reorganizations of the NHS have been undertaken to promote a more coherent and uniform service. This has strengthened the power of the centre (i.e. the Department of Health) over the local NHS. However, more recently, reforms have proclaimed a desire to a return to a more localized approach.

The NHS in different parts of the United Kingdom varied, even prior to the devolution of powers to Wales, Scotland, and Northern Ireland. Devolution has encouraged further diversity. Scotland for example dispensed with NHS trusts, bringing services under local health boards. It introduced free sight tests and dental checks for all and decided to phase out prescription charges. Scotland also introduced free long-term personal

care for elderly people. Wales introduced free prescriptions for all and gave more generous entitlement to free eye and dental checks than in
England. Important variations in how health
services are managed and regulated are evident
between the countries of the United Kingdom,
with Northern Ireland, Wales, and Scotland
adopting different systems of performance management from England. In addition there have
been differences in policy, with much less support
outside England for extending private health care
provision and using market forces.

Currently, the NHS in England is overseen by
the Department of Health and the Strategic
Health Authorities (SHAs). Within each SHA
area, Primary Care Trusts (PCTs) are responsible
for commissioning services from trusts. These
include specialist trusts (such as those providing
ambulance and mental heath services); Care
trusts (which provide health and social care to
particular groups, such as people with learning
disabilities); NHS trusts (which provide a range
of hospital and specialist services); and foundation trusts (which have been given powers of self-
management). However, this structure will
change. A change in government in 2010 led
to proposals from the Conservative–Liberal
Democrat coalition to abolish PCTs and SHAs
within the next couple of years (Department of
Health 2010). Commissioning will be undertaken
by consortia of GPs. All trusts will be expected to
become foundation trusts.

One of the key buzzwords today is 'plurality'.
Recent governments wanted to encourage competition between the NHS and the private sector
(and increasingly, the voluntary sector). The Blair
government established new independent sector
treatment centres (ISTCs) to deliver non-urgent
surgical care, paid for by the NHS. Commercial
interests also got involved in the NHS through
Public-Private Partnerships (PPP) consortia for
the building of hospitals and primary care facilities, by taking on primary care services on behalf
of the NHS, and as a result of contracting out
NHS support services. The private sector was also
stimulated by measures to allow patients to
choose where they would be treated, options
including private providers as well as NHS hospitals. These trends will continue, with
Conservative–Liberal Democrat coalition government proposing a 'level playing field' for

private and voluntary sector operators wishing to
compete for NHS work.

Over the past few decades, the NHS in England
has become more subject to market forces, irrespective of private sector involvement. The
Thatcher and Major governments presided over
the introduction of an internal market in the
NHS. This involved the identification of purchasers (GP fundholders and health authorities)
and providers (trusts) who would agree contracts
to deliver care. Although financial flows were
expected to follow these contracts, the government intervened in the market because of its side
effects (notably inequalities, inefficiencies, and
the political consequences of hospitals closures).
Initially, the Blair government abolished this
market, only later to introduce a similar system.
Payment by Results rewarded hospitals and other
service providers for the treatment they provide.
At the same time GPs acquired powers to run
budgets, though with less scope and freedom as
under the fundholding system.

Management and Regulation

Recent governments have sought to strengthen
NHS management. This has taken the form of
appointing individuals with a key remit for
achieving aims and objectives (chief executives
and chairs of health bodies); tougher performance targets (such as reducing waiting times,
reducing hospital infection rates); and new performance assessment systems.

At the same time, NHS organizations were
required to improve management processes.
Health authority structures introduced in the
1990s, modelled on corporate boards, were
retained by Labour. After 2003, amid much controversy, the Blair government created foundation
trusts. These new organizations, while remaining
part of the NHS, were promised greater autonomy, particularly in financial matters, in organizing and managing their activities, and in setting
their priorities. They were also expected to be
more accountable to local people. However, the
autonomy and local accountability of Foundation
trusts has been less than expected. Public participation is low and managers retain significant
power. Moreover, Foundation trusts are regulated
by a national body (known as Monitor) which

sets the terms on which they are established and can intervene if they fail to comply. Furthermore, foundation trusts must meet NHS standards as well as some national agreements (such as those on pay and conditions).

Despite rhetoric about decentralizing health services and giving more autonomy to local NHS bodies, there was in fact substantial centralization. From 1997 a number of new regulatory bodies were established. These included the Healthcare Commission, which set standards of care and management in England, inspected NHS organizations, and produced performance ratings. It also investigated serious service failures. This body was later merged with the social care regulator, to become the Care Quality Commission. Another important body is the National Institute for Health and Clinical Excellence (known as NICE) which issues guidance to the NHS in England and Wales on the cost-effectiveness of interventions. It also now issues guidance on public health interventions (such as smoking cessation and the prevention of alcohol misuse).

Following a series of scandals – including the GP Harold Shipman (who murdered many of his patients) and the Bristol Royal Infirmary case (involving poor standards of surgery in children with heart problems) – the system of regulation for health care professions was reformed. A new body was established to oversee the systems of professional self-regulation. The General Medical Council (GMC) was reformed, increasing representation of lay people and extending its powers to suspend doctors. A system of licensing was introduced for doctors, which will be accompanied by a system of revalidation, requiring doctors to demonstrate continued competence to practice.

In response to criticisms that NHS reforms had over-centralized decision-making and reduced professional autonomy, the Brown government established a review by Lord Darzi, a prominent surgeon and health minister. His view was that the NHS must be fair, personal, effective, and safe (Department of Health 2008). Darzi backed the idea of an NHS constitution, explicitly setting out its principles and values, alongside commitments and rights for patients, public, and staff. Subsequently, the NHS constitution was given legal foundation. Darzi's review empha-

sized the need to work with professionals and local people in order to bring about improvements in care. He urged greater choice and information for patients, more powerful incentives to improve the quality of service, a key role for local NHS bodies in leading service improvements and greater empowerment of front-line staff. Although there has since been a change of government, Darzi's agenda remains relevant and the key principles of reform he identified will continue to feature in policy.

Partnerships

Effective health care depends heavily on other services such as social care, transport, and housing. In general, though with some local exceptions, the relationship between the NHS and social care providers has been poor. This has arisen from financial, organizational, and cultural differences between the NHS and local government.

Many efforts have been made to address this problem, including joint planning and financial arrangements. In the late 1990s, a statutory duty of partnership was imposed on the NHS and local government. Other changes since include the introduction of 'pooled budgets' between the NHS and local councils and a closer alignment of local authority boundaries with PCTs. For specific client groups receiving health and social care, Care Trusts have been created in some local areas. Such arrangements, in effect merging health and social care functions in one body, are rare.

Government redoubled efforts to improve joint working through more joint appointments, the creation of integrated teams of staff from the NHS and local authorities, integrated planning, and common systems of performance assessment (see HM Government/Department of Health 2006). As part of wider efforts to create more 'joined up' government, local area agreements (LAAs) were introduced. These, along with stronger partnerships at local level (in the form of local strategic partnerships – which include organizations such as the NHS, local government, other statutory bodies and the voluntary and private sectors) are entrusted with achieving priorities for each local area.

Partnerships are also a means of improving public health. Local authority responsibility for public health was strengthened after 2000 and councils now have powers to improve community well-being. Building on previous and current partnership arrangements (such as Health Action Zones, which targeted health inequalities; and Sure Start, which aims to help families with very young children), the NHS is expected to work much more closely with local authorities and other partners to address issues such as smoking, alcohol abuse, obesity, sexual health, and health inequalities. Interestingly, the coalition government has proposed substantially increasing local authority responsibilities and powers in public health (HM Government 2010), taking over some functions from the NHS.

Emerging Issues

All major industrialized democracies face similar problems in health policy and are engaged in reform. The United Kingdom is no exception.

First, health care systems must satisfy demands for health services while controlling costs. Although the Cameron government stated that the NHS will receive real term increases in each year of the present Parliament, the service will be under pressure from increasing demands and efficiency targets (HM Government Comprehensive Spending Review 2010). Increasingly the focus will be improving cost-effectiveness, by concentrating on interventions of proven effectiveness, using cost-saving and quality enhancing technologies (including information technologies), limiting entitlement to those who can gain benefit, and by clearer specification of health service priorities. This will also require better data on outcomes and costs, and improved utilization of this information by managers and clinicians.

Second, we need to respond more effectively to the choices and views of service users and the wider public. It is acknowledged that health services should no longer be delivered in a paternalistic way. Service planners, managers, and professionals must be more responsive to the preferences of the public and individuals. But greater voice and choice must be introduced carefully. Not all people have the same capacity and resources to make choices or participate in decision-making. It is important that the exten-

sion of voice and choice does not lead to greater inequalities.

Third, the modern health service includes many stakeholders. The potential for fragmentation is real and this must be avoided. It is important that pluralism in health services does not undermine the fundamental ethos of the health care system. More specifically, the presence of a larger number of organizations delivering services under the banner of the NHS provides a substantial challenge for regulators.

Finally, health must not be seen as purely the responsibility of the health care system. With regard to the United Kingdom, it is important to strengthen the contribution of other agencies and organizations (such as other government departments, local government, and the voluntary sector) and to build effective partnerships geared to health improvement. Individual responsibility is also important. However, it is also necessary to acknowledge the influences on individual health, such as the media and business corporations. Above all, the socio-economic and environmental factors that affect health must be fully acknowledged and addressed.

Guide to Further Sources

For a general overview see Rob Baggott, *Health and Health Care in Britain* (Basingstoke: Palgrave, 2004), *Understanding Health Policy* (Bristol: Policy Press, 2007) and Chris Ham, HM Government/Department of Health 2006 *Health Policy in Britain* (Basingstoke: Palgrave, 2009). Aggleton discusses the meaning of health in *Health* (London: Routledge, 1990). *Public Health: Policy and Politics* by Rob Baggott (Basingstoke: Palgrave, 2010) gives a thorough account of public health issues. Inequalities and how to address them are discussed by the Marmot Report (Strategic Review of Health Inequalities in England), *Fair Society: Healthy Lives* (London: Department of Health, 2010). Important Labour government documents include HM Government/ Department of Health, *Choosing Health: Making Healthy Choices Easier* (London: The Stationery Office, 2004) and HM Government/Department of Health, *Our Health Our Care, Our Say* (London: The Stationery Office, 2006). The NHS next stage review, setting out the Brown government's approach, was outlined in Department of Health, *High Quality Care for All* (London: The Stationery Office, 2008). The Cameron government's reform programme is set out in Department of Health, *Equity and Excellence: Liberating the NHS* (London: The Stationery Office, 2010). Its plans for public health are set out in HM Government 'Healthy Lives, Healthy People' (London: The Stationary Office, 2010). HM Government 'Comprehensive Spending Review 2010', www.hm-treasury.gov.uk/spend_index.htm. See also D. Wanless, *Securing our Future Health: Taking a Long-term View: Final Report* (London: HM Treasury, 2002).

Review Questions

1 Why is health and healthcare a prominent political issue?
2 Why is it important for government to have a role in (a) promoting health and (b) ensuring access to health care?

3 To what extent has health policy changed in recent decades? What are the continuities in policy?
4 Should we spend more on health care? If so, how should these resources be generated?
5 Why are partnerships important in providing health care and promoting health?

Visit the book companion site at www.wiley.com/go/alcock to make use of the resources designed to accompany the textbook. There you will find chapter-specific guides to further resources, including governmental, international, think-tank, pressure groups, and relevant journals sources. You will also find a glossary based on *The Blackwell Dictionary of Social Policy*, help sheets, and case studies, guidance on managing assignments in social policy and career advice.

48

Education in Schools

Anne West

▪▪

Overview

- The school systems in the United Kingdom have differing legislative frameworks and policies. School structures, funding, curriculum, and assessment vary.
- Choice, diversity, and market-oriented policies have a high profile in England but not in the rest of the United Kingdom.
- Across the countries of the United Kingdom, there has been a focus on increasing the achievement levels of children from disadvantaged backgrounds. Approaches to tackle the attainment gap vary between countries.
- Across the United Kingdom, there is an entitlement to part-time preschool education for three- and four-year-old children, and in England and Wales an extension to some disadvantaged two-year-olds.

▪▪

Context

The importance of education, particularly in terms of increasing human capital and economic competitiveness, is acknowledged at national and supranational levels. Education also plays a crucial role in terms of cognitive and skill development and personal and social development. It is significant for society more broadly given its role in socialization, fostering social justice, and

enhancing social cohesion. This multiplicity of purposes and its compulsory nature means that politicians and policy-makers have given education a high priority.

This chapter is concerned with schooling in the United Kingdom. It focuses on England, but reference is made to other countries and in particular to Scotland. The first section presents a brief historical context and an overview of current school systems in the United Kingdom. The

The Student's Companion to Social Policy, Fourth Edition. Edited by Pete Alcock, Margaret May, Sharon Wright.
© 2012 John Wiley & Sons, Ltd. Published 2012 by John Wiley & Sons, Ltd.

second section focuses on two current issues: choice, diversity, and market-oriented policies; and reducing the achievement gap between different groups of pupils. The final section concludes and highlights some emerging issues.

Schooling in the United Kingdom: Past and Present

Different trajectories in educational provision have been followed in the countries of the United Kingdom, but the churches have historically played an important role. In England and Wales, the Elementary Education Act of 1870 aimed to provide schools in order to fill the gaps in existing provision made by the Church. Subsequently, the 1902 Education Act established local education authorities together with a system of secondary education. With the 1918 Education Act, fees for elementary schools were abolished and education became compulsory until the age of fourteen. In Northern Ireland, the school system, which developed along denominational grounds, goes back to the 1830s. In Scotland, legislation dating to the seventeenth century and before had established a parochial school system. This was extended from the 1830s until the 1872 Education (Scotland) Act created a Board of Education and education became the responsibility of local elected bodies with funding coming from the local property tax. Although fees were charged initially, free primary education was introduced in 1890, and in 1901, education became compulsory until the age of fourteen.

In England and Wales, the 1944 Education Act set up a universal system of free, compulsory schooling from age five to fifteen (sixteen from 1972) with state-funded schooling being provided by local authority and church schools. The 1944 Education Act did not prescribe the structure of secondary education, but enabled the implementation of a 'tripartite' system, comprising grammar schools, technical schools, and 'secondary modern' schools. The 1947 Education Act (Northern Ireland) was similar to the 1944 Act.

Following the introduction of a selective system in England, concerns emerged, as the main beneficiaries of grammar schools were the middle classes. During the 1960s, there was a policy shift, and in 1965 the Labour government

requested local education authorities to submit plans for the introduction of comprehensive education. A broadly comprehensive ('all ability') system of education was eventually introduced across much of England and Wales and in Scotland, while in Northern Ireland a selective system was retained (Eurydice n.d.).

Major changes in education policy took place under Conservative administrations (1979–97). Parental choice of school had a high political profile. In England and Wales, the 1980 Education Act enabled parents to express a preference for the school of their choice for their child; similar legislation was enacted in Northern Ireland. In Scotland, following the 1981 Education (Scotland) Act, parents had the right to nominate a school they wished their child to attend (make a 'placing request'), if they wanted him or her to attend a school other than the local school.

Subsequently, school diversity emerged, at least in theory, as a key policy issue in England, Wales, and Scotland. Following the 1988 Education Reform Act in England and Wales, and the 1989 Self-Governing Schools (Scotland) Act, schools could opt out of local authority control. They became funded by the government and had more autonomy than previously. The vast majority of schools that opted out were in England.

In England, there was further diversification, with fifteen independent city technology schools being set up: their capital funds were intended to be met by private sector sponsors, with revenue costs being met by the government.

In England and Wales, the 1988 Education Reform Act introduced formula funding, whereby individual school budgets were determined predominantly on the basis of the number of pupils on roll (a quasi-voucher system). Official school 'league tables' of public examination results were also introduced and published. Incentives were thus created for schools to maximize their income and their pupils' examination results via the newly created quasi-market (Le Grand and Bartlett 1993). Underpinning the reforms was the view that parents would choose the 'best' schools for their child, based on the information available – in particular, examination results – and that the ensuing competition between schools would result in educational standards increasing. Concerns were, however, raised about the crude nature of the published examination results.

Because of the link between socio-economic background and attainment, schools with more advantaged intakes in general obtain higher results than those with less advantaged intakes. However, in terms of school quality, the value added by the school over and above social background factors is important. There were also concerns raised about 'cream skimming' by certain schools, in the main church and grant-maintained schools (with control over admissions), selecting pupils likely to do well academically and enhance the school's league table position (see West 2007).

Private and State-Maintained Schools

In the United Kingdom, the vast majority of pupils of compulsory school age are educated in state-maintained schools, although fewer in England (93 per cent) than in the other countries of the United Kingdom. The remainder are in independent (private) schools, many of which charge high fees, thereby restricting access to these schools by those from poorer backgrounds.

The state-maintained school systems in the United Kingdom vary. England and Wales have a similar legislative framework and that for Northern Ireland is also broadly similar. In Scotland, the legislative context is different, and some changes have also taken place since devolution.

Compulsory education begins at the age of five, except in Northern Ireland, when it begins at four. Secondary school starts at eleven except in Scotland, when it starts at twelve. Across the United Kingdom, compulsory education ends at sixteen. Post-compulsory secondary education for sixteen- to nineteen-year-olds is provided in schools, sixth form colleges, and further education colleges.

Primary schools cater for children of all abilities. However, at secondary level, systems and structures differ. In Scotland and Wales, there is a comprehensive system. In England, the system is broadly comprehensive, although around 5 per cent of secondary schools are fully academically selective grammar schools. Further, a significant minority of nominally comprehensive schools, predominantly those that control their own admissions, use a variety of different methods that are to some degree selective (e.g. selecting a proportion of pupils on the basis of aptitude/ability in a subject area) and virtually all religious schools give priority to children on the basis of their religion (see West 2007). In Northern Ireland, selection is no longer supported by the Northern Ireland Department of Education, but is not prohibited and many secondary schools continue to select pupils on the basis of academic ability (Eurydice n.d.).

Curriculum and Assessment

The 1988 Education Reform Act introduced a national curriculum and programme of assessment in England and Wales, as did the 1989 Education Reform (Northern Ireland) Order 1989. In Scotland, there are curriculum guidelines for pupils aged from three to eighteen, but the curriculum is not prescribed by statute. A random survey of pupils evaluates overall pupil attainment (Scottish Survey of Achievement).

At the end of compulsory and post-compulsory secondary schooling there are public examinations across the United Kingdom; these vary between countries (Box 48.1). In England, performance tables ('league tables') are published by the government and in the press. The key indicator is the percentage of pupils obtaining five or more GCSE passes (or equivalent) at grades A* to C including English and mathematics. This is an important indicator as this level is generally needed for progression to academic courses post-sixteen (GCE Advanced levels) which are normally needed for entry to higher education. The Conservative–Liberal Democrat government has also introduced a new award the English Baccalaureate awarded to those who obtain GCSEs (grades A* to C) in English, mathematics, the sciences, a modern or ancient foreign language, and a humanity (e.g. history or geography). Performance tables include the proportion of pupils attaining this award.

School Management, Governance, and Inspection

Local management of schools was introduced in England and Wales following the 1988 Education Reform Act (it was also introduced in Northern

Box 48.1 Public Examinations in the United Kingdom

England, Wales, and Northern Ireland

■ GCSE or International GCSE examinations (or pre-vocational equivalent) taken in individual subjects by most pupils (sixteen years);
■ GCE Advanced Subsidiary levels (seventeen years);
■ GCE Advanced levels may be taken (eighteen years); generally required for entry to higher education;
■ Wales: Welsh Baccalaureate (or Welsh Bac) includes qualifications such as AS and A levels and a 'core' of key skills of varying types.

Scotland

■ Scottish Certificate of Education examinations Standard Grade (sixteen years);
■ Higher Grade examinations: age seventeen years;
■ Higher Grade/Advanced Higher Grade examinations (eighteen years) (generally required for entry to higher education).

Box 48.2 School Inspection

England: Office for Standards in Education (Ofsted).
Wales: Estyn (HM's Chief Inspector of Education and Training).
Scotland: HM Inspectorate of Education.
Northern Ireland: Education and Training Inspectorate.

(Parental Involvement) Act, parent councils replaced school boards, which had some similarities with school governing bodies; these are responsible for helping to improve the quality of education and to develop children's potential. Inspection bodies in each country have responsibility for ensuring that schools are providing an acceptable quality of education (see Box 48.2).

Current Issues

Two current issues are of particular interest from a policy perspective. The first is that of choice, diversity, and market-oriented reforms. The second issue relates to reducing the achievement gap between different groups of pupils.

Choice, diversity, and market-oriented policies

Grant-maintained schools were abolished by the UK Labour government (1997–2010). In England and Wales, following the 1998 School Standards and Framework Act, their status changed, in the main to foundation schools, although some became voluntary schools. In Scotland, the 2000 Standards in Scotland's Schools etc. Act abolished self-governing status. Other aspects of policy in relation to choice and diversity have diverged, particularly since devolution. The divergence is clearest when England and Scotland are compared.

In England, market-oriented reforms have continued. Official school performance tables are published by the government and in the media as 'league tables'. There has also been an increase in school diversity. A small number of new faith schools have also become part of the

Ireland). Schools became responsible for deciding how the school budget from their local authority (determined largely on the basis of pupil numbers) should be spent. In Scotland, local authorities decide on the level of support to be given to schools: most local authorities distribute their agreed budgets to schools on a formula basis, with pupil roll being the main determinant measure used. Individual schools are responsible for managing their own day-to-day expenditure via devolved school management, but, unlike in England, the school's 'normal complement' of staff is paid by the local authority (Eurydice n.d.).

Governing bodies of schools that are funded by local authorities (as opposed to academies) in England, Wales, and Northern Ireland include parents and representatives of the school and local community; they have a strategic role, including managing the school's budget. In Scotland, following the 2006 Scottish Schools state-maintained system. Most significantly, independent 'academies' have been introduced. Under the Labour government the main goal was to improve the quality of education in disadvantaged areas, with many such schools being set up in disadvantaged areas. Under the Conservative–Liberal Democrat government the goals are to increase diversity and school autonomy. Local authority maintained schools are now able to convert to academy status and new 'free' schools can be set up by sponsors such as groups of parents. In all cases, revenue funding is provided by the government. The governance of academies differs from that of local authority maintained schools and the national curriculum does not need to be followed.

Legislation has sought to allay concerns about cream-skimming by schools; the 1998 School Standards and Framework Act and the 2006 Education and Inspections Act, along with a School Admissions Code, can be seen as an attempt to regulate the admissions system.

Whilst league tables and school diversity remain high on the political agenda in England, the situation in the other countries of the UK is different. No official school performance tables are now published in Wales, Scotland or Northern Ireland. Moreover, in the case of Scotland, the 2000 Standards in Scotland's Schools etc. Act gave greater powers to local authorities in relation to restrict choice by refusing 'placing requests'. Significantly, there are no policies in place to increase parental choice of schools (see Box 48.3).

There are only limited data available comparing educational outcomes across the United Kingdom. However, the results of the Programme for International Student Assessment (PISA) (OECD 2010) revealed that the mean scores for reading, mathematics, and science were broadly similar for England, Northern Ireland, and for Scotland, suggesting that the different education systems perform similarly even though their policies in relation to school choice and diversity differ; the results for Wales were lower. This implies that other factors are responsible for differences in achievement.

Reducing the achievement gap

A major area of concern across the United Kingdom relates to differences in the levels of

Box 48.3 Comprehensive Schools in Scotland

Our comprehensive system is right for Scotland and it performs in the top class on the world stage. The comprehensive schools we want to see are rich, colourful, and diverse, offering choice for pupils and with ambition for themselves and for every one of their pupils. No one is Scotland should be required to select a school to get the first rate education they deserve and are entitled to. Choice between schools in Scotland is no substitute for the universal excellence we seek and Scotland's communities demand (Scottish Executive, *Ambitious, Excellent Schools*, 2004: 1).

achievement of children from different social groups. The association between poverty and low educational achievement is an important and persistent concern across the United Kingdom. In England, for example, pupils from low-income families perform less well, on average, in public examinations than do others: according to DfE figures in 2010, 31 per cent of children eligible for free school meals obtained five or more GCSE examination passes including English and mathematics at grades A* to C, compared with 59 per cent of those not eligible.

There are also differences in terms of the achievement of girls and boys, with more girls than boys achieving five or more GCSEs at grades A* to C including English and mathematics. Differences are also apparent outside the United Kingdom. In 2009, the PISA results revealed that girls outperformed boys in reading in every participating country (OECD 2010). Differences are clearest when comparing the proportion of boys and girls who perform at the lowest reading proficiency levels; the low levels of achievement for some boys are a significant challenge for education policy. Interestingly, in relation to mathematics and science, there was variation between countries in terms of the performance of boys and girls.

The evidence relating to the educational performance of children from different ethnic groups, most of who live in England, is complex. DfE data show that more pupils of Chinese and Indian origin achieve 5 or more A*–C grades at GCSE or equivalent including English and mathematics GCSEs. More generally, pupils of any white background achieved in line with the national level, those of any black background achieved below the national level and those of any Asian background performed above the national level.

The overall differences are associated with disadvantage. Other groups of children also fare poorly, in particular those with special educational needs and those in care.

The question arises as to how these achievement gaps are to be reduced. In England, funding has traditionally been greater to local authorities with higher levels of disadvantage. The Conservative–Liberal Democrat government is to introduce a new 'pupil premium', which provides additional funding linked to the number of pupils from disadvantaged backgrounds enrolled at a school (this has been set at £430 for each child known to be eligible for free school meals or in care). However significant amounts of money have been, and continue to be, targeted by central government on disadvantaged local authorities; the amount that is added by the pupil premium is only a small proportion of what is already allocated to local authorities with high proportions of children from disadvantaged backgrounds, such as London. However, this situation may change as the coalition government is also to consult on a new national funding formula.

In addition, there has been a United Kingdom-wide focus on the provision of free early years education. There are benefits of high-quality preschool educational provision to a range of cognitive outcomes (Sylva *et al.* 2004). There is an entitlement to free part-time early education for 3- and 4-year olds. In England and in Wales there has been an extension to certain disadvantaged two-year-olds. The details and implementation vary between the countries of the United Kingdom, although voluntary and private providers have had a key role to play in the expansion of preschool provision. The evidence suggests that quality is higher in certain types of provision; this is likely to be related to the differing staff qualifications (with those employing qualified teachers being more likely to provide higher quality provision).

Emerging Issues

Policy in relation to schools varies between the countries of the United Kingdom. However, there are common objectives in relation to increasing human capital and economic competitiveness, by improving overall attainment, and to reducing achievement gaps. The means by which these are to be achieved differ. In England, choice, diversity, and increased competition are seen as being of key importance in terms of raising standards, with the role of independent academies set to increase markedly; in other countries of the United Kingdom this is not the case. In relation to seeking to reduce achievement gaps, major initiatives were introduced under the Labour government across the United Kingdom, in particular, an entitlement to part-time preschool education. This is to set to continue under the Conservative–Liberal Democrat government and indeed legislation in England is planned to ensure that disadvantaged two-year-olds receive fifteen hours a week of free early education from 2013.

Perhaps the most significant issue affecting school-based education is retrenchment: there has been some protection for schools, but reductions are being made. How these will affect provision remains to be seen.

Guide to Further Sources

The Department for Education (DfE) publishes education statistics and commissioned research on its web site, www.dfe.gov.uk.

For example: DfE (2010) GCSE and Equivalent Attainment by Pupil Characteristics in England, 2009/10, www.education.gov.uk/rsgateway/DB/SFR/s000977/index.shtml;

The Eurydice Network provides information on European education systems and policies: http://eacea.ec.europa.eu/education/eurydice/index_en.php; Eurybase is a database on education systems in Europe: http://eacea.ec.europa.eu/education/eurydice/eurybase_en.php.

Detailed information on the structure of education systems can be found on the following web sites: England, http://eacea.ec.europa.eu/education/eurydice/documents/eurybase/structures/041_UKEngland_EN.pdf; Northern Ireland, http://eacea.ec.europa.eu/education/eurydice/documents/

eurybase/structures/041_UKNorthern%20 Ireland_EN.pdf; Scotland, http://eacea.ec.europa. eu/education/eurydice/documents/eurybase/ structures/041_UKScotland_EN.pdf; Wales, http: //eacea.ec.europa.eu/education/eurydice/ documents/eurybase/structures/041_UKWales_ EN.pdf.

J. Le Grand and W. Bartlett (eds), *Quasi-Markets and Social Policy* (London: Macmillan, 1993) discusses quasi-markets. A. West, 'Schools, Financing and Educational Standards', in J. Hills, J. Le Grand and D. Piachaud (eds), *Making Social Policy Work: Essays in Honour of Howard Glennerster* (Bristol: Policy Press, 2007), pp. 85–108, examines expenditure and standards in schools in England.

Scottish Executive, *Ambitious, Excellent Schools: Our Agenda for Action* (Edinburgh, 2004) sets out the reform agenda for Scotland's schools and *A Curriculum for Excellence* (Edinburgh, 2004) is central to this.

Organisation for Economic Co-operation and Development (OECD), *PISA 2009 at a Glance* (2010) presents the 2009 PISA results at www.oecd.org/dataoecd/31/28/46660259.pdf.

Findings from a key evaluation of preschool education in England are presented in K. Sylva *et al.*, *The Effective Provision of Pre-school Education (EPPE) Project: Effective Pre-School Education, Final Report 1997–2004* (London: DfES, 2004), available online at www.education.gov.uk/children andyoungpeople/earlylearningandchildcare/ a0068162/effective-provision-of-pre-school-education-eppe.

Preschool provision in England is examined in A. West, J. Roberts, and P. Noden, 'Funding Early Years Education and Care: Can a Mixed Economy of Providers Deliver Universal High Quality Provision?' *British Journal of Educational Studies*, 58/2 (2010): 155–79.

The concept of 'underachievement' is examined in A. West and H. Pennell, *Underachievement in Schools* (New York: Routledge Falmer, 2003).

Review Questions

1 How do the school systems across the United Kingdom vary?
2 What market-oriented policies have been implemented?
3 Why is there a concern about achievement levels?
4 What approaches have been adopted to try and reduce the achievement gap?
5 Why is preschool education considered to be important?

Visit the book companion site at www.wiley.com/go/alcock to make use of the resources designed to accompany the textbook. There you will find chapter-specific guides to further resources, including governmental, international, think-tank, pressure groups, and relevant journals sources. You will also find a glossary based on *The Blackwell Dictionary of Social Policy*, help sheets, and case studies, guidance on managing assignments in social policy and career advice.

49

Lifelong Learning and Training

Claire Callender

Overview

- Lifelong learning includes people of all ages learning in a variety of contexts. It is an idea informing post-compulsory education and training policies, prompted by globalization and changes in the labour market.
- These policies are important for economic growth and the wellbeing of society but their economic objectives are prioritized.
- Policies focus on improving the skill levels and mix of the existing and future workforce so there is a balance in the supply of, and demand for, skilled labour.
- Between 1997 and 2010, the Labour government tried to increase the supply of skilled workers by expanding post-compulsory education, encouraging greater participation, and getting people to take more and higher qualifications. The new coalition government plans to increase the demand for skilled worker by focusing on skills rather than qualifications.
- The UK coalition government announced public expenditure cuts on post-compulsory education in 2010, shifting more of the costs onto learners and employers.
- Participation in post-compulsory education remains unequal, with those from disadvantaged backgrounds in greatest need but missing out. Inequality begets inequality and cumulates across the life cycle.

The Student's Companion to Social Policy, Fourth Edition. Edited by Pete Alcock, Margaret May, Sharon Wright.
© 2012 John Wiley & Sons, Ltd. Published 2012 by John Wiley & Sons, Ltd.

What is Lifelong Learning?

Central to lifelong learning is the idea that learning should take place at all stages in a person's life – from the cradle to the grave, and be embedded in their lives. The learning can take place anywhere – in schools, colleges, universities, at work, at home, or in the community but focuses mainly on adults.

Lifelong learning requires an education system that gives everyone opportunities to learn at all levels, whenever they need to learn rather than because they are a certain age. These opportunities need to cater for: people with university degrees and those without any qualifications; those in highly skilled jobs wanting professional development; people in unskilled jobs or without a job experiencing difficulties reading and writing; people who have retired; and those who just want to learn something new. This is a very different way of thinking about education and training which in the past was restricted to formal learning in specialized educational institutions, aimed mostly at school leavers and young people at the start of their working life.

Everyone can benefit from lifelong learning and the diverse learning involved means there is no single policy covering all aspects of lifelong learning. Instead, there is a collection of policies and strategies, which together contribute to the *goal* of lifelong learning. Lifelong learning, therefore, is an *idea* informing and underpinning education and training policies. It captures an approach to a set of policies.

The policies most associated with lifelong learning focus on the period after the end of compulsory schooling, currently at age sixteen. However, the 2008 Education and Skills Act increased the minimum age at which young people in England can leave learning, requiring them to continue in education or training to 17 from 2013 and to 18 from 2015. This stage, after compulsory participation in education or training, is called post-compulsory.

Post-compulsory education and training can be delivered by a wide variety of providers – by the state in schools, sixth form colleges, further education colleges, and universities; by the growing private and voluntary sector; and by employers through work-based learning.

Unlike compulsory education, post-compulsory education is non-statutory. Individuals, rather than the state, take responsibility for their own education except for the unemployed where the state often intervenes. Currently, most post-compulsory education takes place in further education colleges and universities, and is funded by central government and taxpayers. In future, more learners will pay for their learning or contribute more towards its costs. Employers also provide and pay for work-related training. This can be on-the-job and undertaken at an employer's premises, or off-the-job and happens at a college or university, or it can be on- and off-the-job.

Qualifications higher than 'A' Levels such as undergraduate and postgraduate degrees or certificates are usually associated with post-compulsory education. However, for people who did not get 'A' Levels at school, or left without qualifications, their lifelong learning may entail taking lower-level qualifications. They may take vocational qualifications, which are work-related and involve learning practical skills and competencies aimed at preparing people for particular jobs. In contrast, academic qualifications usually require learning about things that are unrelated to a specific job. Some lifelong learning focuses on basic skills such as learning how to read and write. Other lifelong learning may be undertaken purely for pleasure.

Why did Lifelong Learning Come About?

The late 1980s and 1990s saw a global radical rethink about post-compulsory education with the emergence of the term 'Lifelong Learning' on the policy agenda. This was driven by globalization and labour market changes. These developments help explain why lifelong learning policies were introduced, and the nature of these policies, which since devolution now differ in different countries within the United Kingdom.

Globalization (Chapter 53) has had a profound effect on Britain's economic and social policies, including education. Britain, as a result, has shifted towards what is called a knowledge-economy based on high skills and high knowledge work. Now knowledge rather than land, labour, or capital is considered the most important factor shaping production and economic development. Therefore, skills and knowledge are essential for Britain's ability to compete in the global economy and to drive economic growth. Certain types of knowledge are particularly valued, especially theoretical knowledge. This helps explain the current global concern about developing skills in science, technology, engineering, and mathematics (STEM subjects), which are considered critical to economic prosperity.

Globalization, increasing competition, and rapid scientific and technological advances also are leading to changes in the workplace, how work is organized, and the nature of jobs. Few people today can expect to stay in the same job for life. Instead, they are likely to have discontinuous and less secure work patterns over their lifetime, especially in an economic recession with job cuts and high unemployment.

These developments affect the qualifications, skills, and competencies workers need to perform their jobs, to keep them, and to get new jobs. Some skills are redundant while new skills are required. Learning is now not confined to one point in a working life, typically after leaving school. Instead, many people will need to reskill or upskill during their working lives and study part-time which they can fit around existing family and work commitments.

The Ideology of Lifelong Learning

Economic prosperity and social inclusion were key goals of the 1997–2010 Labour Westminster government's social policies, especially in post-compulsory education. Labour believed that Britain's success in a 'knowledge economy' depended first, on technological improvement and innovation; and second, on a well-educated, highly skilled, adaptable, and flexible labour force.

For Labour, skills were the key lever to improve workplace productivity. The most common measures of skills were qualifications. For a successful knowledge-economy, people needed qualifications. With good qualifications, gained through post-compulsory education, individuals could get well-paid secure jobs and reap the wider social and personal benefits of learning (Schuller and Watson 2009). The Labour government recognized that education was the main route for

increasing social mobility and social justice while employment was a means of promoting social inclusion and tackling poverty.

Labour's post-compulsory education policies between 1997 and 2010 in England had both economic and social goals, which brought together market principles and the idea of equality of opportunity. However, most of their lifelong learning policies focused on the economic imperatives of lifelong learning – developing a more productive and efficient workforce. There was a considerable discrepancy between Labour's rhetoric about lifelong learning with its emphasis on its social and civic benefits, and the reality of their policies, which focused on the economic benefits.

The Conservative–Liberal Democratic coalition government, which came to power in England in 2010, also see skills as vital to the economy and for stimulating economic growth and recovery. They too think skills and training are central to employment and productivity in a knowledge driven economy and that post-compulsory education is an important driver for social mobility. Just like their predecessor, the new coalition's policies are dominated by the skill needs of the economy and of employers.

There are differences as well as continuities between the new coalition government's approach to post-compulsory education and the previous Labour government's approach. First, the economic climate in which the coalition is operating is very different because of the global recession. The coalition has cut public expenditure on post-compulsory education to help reduce the fiscal deficit and stimulate economic growth. However, some of these cuts are ideological – driven by their beliefs and ideas about the role of the state, the market, and of citizens. By contrast, under Labour public expenditure on post-compulsory education increased between 1997 and 2010.

Second, the ideology and philosophy of the English coalition differs from Labour's. The coalition's vision is one of open markets, democracy, the 'Big Society', and devolution of power to citizens. Their values include: freedom from the state and government intervention; fairness; and that individuals should take responsibility for their lives and not rely on the state. They are not as supportive as the previous Labour government of central government planning and intervention. They want less 'big' government and less spending on the welfare state. The coalition also think that market forces and principles should play a larger role in shaping the scale, nature, and distribution of welfare provision including post-compulsory education and training. This requires creating more competition between educational providers, encouraging increased private provision, and encouraging more people to pay for services.

The main principles driving the English coalition government are putting the consumer at the heart of decision-making through giving them more choice by encouraging more competition between education providers; empowering and trusting educational providers, which means only light-touch regulation is required and focusing on outcomes instead of targets; and finally delivering more for less. All these ideas are encapsulated in their post-compulsory education policies.

Lifelong Learning, Training, and Skills Policies

The number of unskilled jobs requiring low or no qualifications is shrinking while skilled jobs needing higher-level qualifications are growing. Most governments in advanced industrialized countries believe that to secure economic growth they must improve the skill levels of workers and ensure the workforce has the right type and level of skills needed by the economy and employers. The overall objective of most post-compulsory education and training policies, therefore, is to balance the supply of, and demand for, skilled workers. These policies have to make sure the skill levels of the workforce meet employer needs, and the supply of skills reflects market demand so that there are no skill shortages or skill gaps.

There are, however, different approaches to raising the skills of the future and current workforce and ensuring the right skills mix. The Labour government in England between 1997 and 2010 believed the best way was to increase the number of people with qualifications. They encouraged more participation in post-compulsory education because of its key role in providing higher-level skills and vocational education for the existing and future workforce. They thought qualifications were a good proxy or measure of our country's skills and that improving the workforce's qualifications in line with our interna-

tional competitors would solve our skill and training needs and foster economic growth.

The coalition in England and others have criticized this approach. They acknowledge the need for a skilled workforce, but question whether people need more and higher qualifications because they believe qualifications are not a good proxy for skills – that skills and qualifications are two different things. People can acquire skills without taking a qualification for example, through on the job training at work. They argue that informal learning undertaken at work or elsewhere can be just as valuable as learning undertaken as part of a formal qualification and the stress on qualifications undervalues informal incrementally gained knowledge (Wolf, Jenkins, and Vignoles 2006). The coalition also argue that Labour's focus on improving people's qualifications has led to a system governed by top-down supply. Instead, they want a skills system, which is demand-led and responds to the demand of employers and individuals.

Policy Challenges in England

Lifelong learning, training, and skills policies can be divided into two: policies aimed at improving the skills of the *future* workforce, and those aimed at raising the skill levels of the *current* workforce. Education is a devolved power in some parts of the United Kingdom and so there are divergent policies, for instance in Scotland. Here we focus on policies in England.

Improving the qualifications and skills of the future workforce

Policies for sixteen- to eighteen- year-olds   The goal of policies for sixteen- to eighteen- year-olds is to encourage more young people to stay in, or go back into, education and training so they have the qualifications and skills to progress further in education or the labour market. Those who leave full-time education without any qualifications, or good qualifications, come disproportionately from disadvantaged backgrounds. They have far less chance of finding rewarding employment, or any employment.

In 2009, 45 per cent of eighteen-year-olds were in full time education, 33 per cent were employed, 7 per cent on government supported training, and 15 per cent were not in education, training, or employed (NEET). Those from the lowest socio-economic groups were least likely to be in full-time education (34 per cent) and most likely to be not in education, training, or employed (21 per cent).

In 2009, nearly a quarter of people in England had not attained a Level 2 qualification (equivalent to 5 GCSEs A*–C) by the age of 18, and over a half had not gained a Level 3 qualification (two 'A' Levels or equivalent). Again, those least likely to have achieved these qualifications came from the lowest socio-economic groups – 72 per cent of young people from routine socio-economic groups had not achieved a Level 3 qualification compared with 30 per cent in the higher professional group.

Higher education Governments see higher education (HE) playing a major role in meeting the labour market's growing need for highly skilled workers. In 2007/08, 37 per cent of seventeen- to thirty-year-olds in England entered university for the first time. However, access to university is unequal. Young people from high-income families are five times more likely to go to university than those from low-income families, and to go to the best universities. Labour's policies focused on widening HE participation and combating the inequalities in access but the coalition in England see these problems in terms of social mobility.

The growing importance of, and demand for, HE along with its expansion since the mid-1980s has increased its costs. Governments have tried to reduce these costs by shifting more of them onto students and their families and away from government and taxpayers. They have done this in England by increasing tuition fees because they believe that those who benefit financially from HE should contribute to most of their learning costs. Labour first introduced fees in the 1998 Teaching and Higher Education Act, and then increased them to £3,000 a year in the 2004 Higher Education Act. The Westminster coalition are raising fees to a maximum of £9,000 from 2012/13, and withdrawing the funds they give universities to teach arts, humanities, and social science courses so that these courses will be funded solely through tuition fees. Once students

rather than the state become responsible for paying for their education, HE becomes a private investment rather than a public good funded mainly by the government.

The coalition also wants to create a market in HE. They believe consumer demand, in the form of student choice, should determine what course universities offer. Theoretically, students will have greater choice as new providers enter the market competing on price, which is meant to improve efficiency and drive up quality. Universities and courses attracting high student demand will be able to charge higher fees and to expand. Those that cannot recruit adequate student numbers will have to reduce their fees or shut down unpopular courses, or close completely.

HE will remain free at the point of access because students will get subsidized loans and grants to pay for their fees and living costs. However, it is unknown what impact these reforms will have on student behaviour, their HE choices, their perceptions of the affordability of HE, and crucially on HE participation, especially among the poorest.

Improving the qualifications and skills of the existing workforce

People in work need access to learning as much as those entering the workforce. Policies for adults focus first on those with limited skills or poor basic education who are economically marginalized, find it difficult to get work, or well-paid secure jobs. The second focus is on existing workers who need to update their skills or learn new skills to meet the changing requirements of their employers and the labour market.

The Labour government introduced the first ever national 'skills strategy' for adults with low-level or no qualifications. It gave an entitlement to free training for all adults to gain their first Level 2 qualification, and for nineteen- to twenty-five-year-olds a free entitlement to a Level 3 qualification. However, the coalition government has withdrawn the entitlement to free training for a first Level 2 for those over twenty-five, and those over twenty-four will have to pay fees for a Level 3 qualification. Consequently, large numbers of adult learners will have to pay tuition fees for the first time, or pay higher fees, which could affect opportunities for lifelong learning.

Employers are central to improving their employees' skills. The policy challenge is increasing employers' ambition, engagement, and investment in skills. The coalition government, like those before them, will try to persuade more employers to train more of their workforce.

There is unequal access to employer training, just like other forms of post-compulsory education. Low-skilled employees and those in lower status occupations receive less training, as do older workers compared with younger workers, and employees in small- and medium-sized enterprises compared with those in large companies. Those most in need of training are least likely to receive it – illustrating the continuing inequalities in access to lifelong learning. Continuing education and training does not succeed in making up for skills gaps emerging from compulsory schooling but tend to reinforce disparities resulting from school education. Consequently, educational inequalities accumulate over people's lifetime.

Emerging Issues

While compulsory education is seen as failing to deliver the skilled workforce the economy needs, governments are likely to continue to use the post-compulsory sector as a means of redress. They are likely to introduce further reforms to encourage more employer involvement in skills training. Other future issues include whether the proposed reforms to HE funding are sustainable and reduce public expenditure, whether they lead to a market and greater privatization, whether most universities in England end up charging tuition fees of £9,000, and how potential student react to these changes. Questions about the roles and responsibilities of individuals, the state, and the private sector, including employers, in post-compulsory education provision and funding will continue well into the future.

Guide to Further Sources

Compare: A Journal of Comparative and International Education, 36/3 (2006) is a special issue that focuses on lifelong learning in various countries.

The Department for Education web site has sections on all aspects of post-compulsory education policies plus government and research reports, statistics at http://publications.education.gov.uk/ and www.education.gov.uk/rsgateway/.

An examination of how lifelong learning policies have resulted in inequalities and do not fulfil their aims can be found in K. Evans, Learning Work, and Social Responsibility (Dordrecht: Springer, 2009).

A. Furlong and F. Cartmel, Higher Education and Social Justice (Buckingham: Open University Press/McGraw Hill, 2009) explores unequal access to higher education and why low-income groups are disadvantaged.

The rise of lifelong learning across Europe and polices trends is examines in 'The many faces of lifelong learning: recent educational policy trends in Europe' Journal of Education Policy 17/6 (2002): 611–26, by A. Green.

A review of UK's long-term skill needs and how to achieve them is contained in the UK Commission for Employment and Skills', Ambition 2020: World Class Skills and Jobs for the UK (London: UKCES, 2009), online at www.ukces.org.uk/.

T. Schuller and D. Watson, Learning Through Life: Inquiry into the Future of Lifelong Learning (Leicester: National Institute of Adult and Continuing Education, 2009) presents an overview of the current state of lifelong learning and how it should be reformed.

A. Wolf, A. Jenkins and A. Vignoles, 'Certifying the workforce: economic imperative or failed social policy?' Journal of Education Policy, 21/5 (2006): 535–65, questions the assumptions underpinning the government's skills strategy and its reliance on targets and qualifications and whether they have been successful meeting the government's objectives.

Review Questions

1 Who should have access to lifelong learning?
2 Who should pay for post-compulsory education and training – the government and taxpayers or individual learners and employers?
3 Is post-compulsory education and training a private good or a public good?

4   Who should decide what post-compulsory education and training course are available?
5   What effect are recent reforms likely to have on who goes to university and the choices they make about where, what, and how to study?

Visit the book companion site at www.wiley.com/go/alcock to make use of the resources designed to accompany the textbook. There you will find chapter-specific guides to further resources, including governmental, international, think-tank, pressure groups, and relevant journals sources. You will also find a glossary based on *The Blackwell Dictionary of Social Policy*, help sheets, and case studies, guidance on managing assignments in social policy and career advice.

50

Housing

David Mullins and Alan Murie

■■■

Overview

- Housing policy has played an important part in the welfare state, involving fiscal, tax, and regulatory policies, but there has never been monopoly provision of state housing.
- Between 1919 and 1979 council housing became a significant and desirable housing tenure. Since 1979 it has narrowed its focus, lost subsidy, and become less popular. By 2010 less than one-quarter of social housing was directly provided by local authorities.
- After 1979 supply-side subsidies (for housing construction) were a key target for public expenditure reductions but expenditure on demand-side subsidies (to enable tenants to pay rents) continued to grow.
- Policies on homelessness and access to social housing have important social policy dimensions with a shifting emphasis between local discretion and national direction and between social and private provision.
- Housing loomed large in public spending reductions under the Conservative led-coalition government; this time there was attention to reducing demand-side as well as supply-side subsidies, alongside promotion of localism and reduced regulation.

■■■

Context

Housing plays a central part in debates about social policy and welfare. It involves the market, state, and third sector and processes of production, exchange, ownership, and control. Unlike some areas of social policy, housing has never been a state monopoly, but responses to housing problems have involved a significant role for governments. Council housing was for most of the twentieth

The Student's Companion to Social Policy, Fourth Edition. Edited by Pete Alcock, Margaret May, Sharon Wright.
© 2012 John Wiley & Sons, Ltd. Published 2012 by John Wiley & Sons, Ltd.

century the main mechanism for improving housing conditions in the United Kingdom. Recently housing has formed a major element in the provision of public services by third sector organizations (housing associations). Housing has been subject to fiscal, tax, subsidy, legislative, and regulatory interventions by the state.

As direct state provision has declined there has been an ongoing tension between market and community influences on housing. Housing policy and legislation have diverged at times between England, Scotland, Wales, and Northern Ireland, for example, in relation to homelessness. This chapter provides a historical overview that broadly applies across the United Kingdom covering tenure changes, homelessness and access, the contemporary situation, and emerging issues following the election of a Conservative-led coalition government in May 2010.

The Historical Legacy

The origins of housing policy in the United Kingdom were in response to problems caused by nineteenth-century industrialization. Public health measures introduced in a market dominated by private landlordism were intended to control threats to the health of the whole population but also made private investment in housing less attractive than in other economic sectors. Attempts to meet housing needs through philanthropic effort alone were insufficient and, before the outbreak of the First World War, there were proposals to introduce supply-side subsidies to enable local authorities to build affordable housing for working class families. War-time rent controls were introduced to prevent exploitation, and the post-war pledge to provide 'homes fit for heroes' led to policy reforms.

The key development in housing policy was the introduction, in 1919, of Exchequer subsidies for council housing. Over the next sixty years, local authorities had an expanding and pivotal role in the provision of housing. Over the same period the private rented sector declined and private provision switched towards home ownership – more rapidly for some regions and more affluent households.

The Second World War halted housing construction, and damage to property resulting from air raids left a serious housing problem. This was addressed by cross-party support over the following two decades for policies to increase supply. Nonetheless, housing was not reorganized after the Second World War to the same extent as other parts of the welfare state. There was no National Housing Service and local authorities remained the key providers of state housing in a system dominated by private ownership. Housing as a result has often been regarded as a neglected service and the 'wobbly pillar' of the welfare state. However, Beveridge had recognized 'squalor' as one of the five evils to be tackled: 'dealing with squalor means planning town and countryside and having many more and better homes' (Beveridge 1943: 86). The post-war welfare state Beveridge inspired included a stronger planning system and new towns programme, along with private rent controls. Local authorities and new towns received subsidies to build housing on an unprecedented scale.

Between 1919 and 1979 council housing and owner occupation grew while private renting faced long-term decline. Governments consistently encouraged home ownership, and undermined private renting by reintroducing rent control in1939 and later through slum clearance. Furthermore, as more affluent groups moved into home ownership, and as a subsidized council sector developed, rents that people were prepared to pay made investment in private rented housing unattractive.

From 1970 policy was influenced by the view that the housing supply problem was largely solved and political parties competed to champion home ownership. The 1979 Conservative government introduced the 'Right to Buy' resulting in over 2 million dwellings (out of 6.5 million) being sold to sitting tenants. The government's view of council housing had shifted. Significant building by local authorities was no longer supported, and smaller-scale funding for housing associations only partly filled this gap. Deregulation of private renting and changes in housing finance accelerated the shift from a managed to a market-based system.

The last quarter of the twentieth century saw social housing transformed from state to third sector provision. Housing associations, independent, non-profit bodies, became the preferred providers for new social rented housing. Stock transfers of rented homes to housing associations started in 1988 and by 1996 had overtaken the Right to Buy as the main mechanism reducing the number of council homes. Many local authorities sold their housing stock to housing associations and were left with a strategic housing role. After 2002, a million further homes were transferred to Arms Length Management Organisations (ALMOs) while councils retained ownership of the assets. By 2008 just 24 per cent of social housing stock was still owned and managed by councils, 26 per cent was held by stock transfer, 27 per cent by traditional housing associations, and 23 per cent was managed by ALMOs.

Privatization can be seen as a shift in the boundaries of the welfare state. Many more affluent tenants bought their council dwellings under the Right to Buy with substantial discounts. Tenants who had already benefitted from subsidized rents for the best council homes were multiple beneficiaries when enabled to buy these appreciating assets. Stock transfer also redrew boundaries with non-profit distributing providers regulated and part-funded by the state but initially highly indebted to private funders. This led to strategy and operations being dominated by business plans. While not in itself privatization, stock transfer has been seen as a possible staging post to a social housing system more embedded in the market.

Tenure Changes

A nation of private tenants has become a nation of home owners, with a transitional period in between with a more mixed tenure structure (see Table 50.1). These national figures obscure considerable variation between the four UK jurisdictions, and enormous local differences, with some localities dominated by social housing and others by home ownership.

As tenures grew or declined, so their characteristics changed. By mid-century, the private rented sector comprised increasingly dilapidated stock housing a residual population of elderly long-term tenants and a more mixed, transient population. After 1999 long-term decline was reversed by 'buy to let' investors saving for retirement, the quality of the sector improved, and there was growing demand from 'in-betweens',

Table 50.1 Housing tenure in the United Kingdom, 1914–2007 (%).

	Public rented		Owner occupied	Private rented[a]
1914	<1		10	90
1945	12		26	62
1951	18		29	53
1961	27		43	31
1971	31		50	19
	LAs	HAs[b]		PRS only[b]
1981	30	2.2	58	11
1991	21	3.1	66	9
2001	15	6.4	69	10
2007	10	8.4	70	12

Notes: [a] To 1971 including housing associations (which then formed less than 2% of all dwellings. [b] From 1981 HAs shown separately.
Sources: D. Mullins and A. Muric, *Housing and Construction Statistics*, (London: HMSO, 2006); H. Pawson and S. Wilcox, *UK Housing Review 2010 Briefing Paper* (published online, 2010) <www.cih.org/policy/fpp-UKHR2010-Briefing-Paper.pdf>.

households unable to access home ownership but ineligible for social housing.

Home ownership and council housing had developed in the 1920s to cater for young families, but later changed and diverged. The home ownership sector continues to house the most affluent sections of the population; however, it also houses poorer households including older and unemployed people. It has generally been associated with wealth accumulation but values have sometimes declined (e.g. in the early 1990s and late 2000s). Access to mortgages for house purchase generally became easier until the credit crisis of 2007–9, which originated in high risk loans to marginal purchasers. After the credit crisis more cautious lenders demanded higher deposits, thereby preventing potential first-time buyers from benefiting from historically low interest rates. The entry age for first-time purchase grew steadily.

The council and housing association sectors are now referred to as social housing. Accounting for nearly one-third of all dwellings at its peak in 1979, when it housed some people from the highest income decile; this sector now caters more exclusively for low-income groups. Tenants are no longer predominantly young families but include older people, people with long-term illnesses and disabilities, and lone-parent households. Rationing of access has left those with least bargaining power in the least desirable housing. Research on housing of minority ethnic groups evidences discriminatory outcomes of formal and informal rationing processes. These changes – with the poorest sections of the population becoming more concentrated in social rented housing and especially in the least attractive stock – have been referred to as residualization. This links with government concerns about worklessness among social housing tenants, and to the Conservative-led coalition's view that social housing should provide a 'springboard' to other options rather than lifetime tenancies.

Homelessness and Access to Social Housing

A long-standing social policy dimension of housing concerns homelessness and access to social housing. Changing policies in these areas help to explain the changing composition of the tenure. Council housing initially housed the better-off working class who had stable incomes and were able to afford the rents. The emphasis on housing need increased as policy focused first on slum clearance and then on homelessness with the 1977 Housing (Homeless Persons) Act. Local discretion over lettings has operated within statutory and regulatory guidance; the latter has increased in situations of shortage and in recognition of problems of discrimination and discretion. Homelessness is one of a number of 'reasonable preference' criteria defined by legislation which lettings strategies must have regard to. However, the operation of local criteria such as residence points, 'sons and daughters' policies and local lettings schemes have balanced local concerns (e.g. for community sustainability) with housing need.

After 2000, the adoption of 'choice-based lettings schemes' placed a greater onus on applicants to bid for properties. Concerns about concentrations of 'worklessness' on housing estates led to policies favouring mixed-tenure and mixed-income communities, although this was hard to achieve through allocation policies alone. The

2010 government's proposals for 'a fairer future for social housing' included reducing security of tenure and increasing rents for new tenants and giving local authorities and landlords greater flexibility in allocation policy. They envisaged that flexibility would be used to exclude households with low housing needs from waiting lists but to increase mobility options for existing tenants. Centrally imposed reasonable preference criteria would continue to limit local discretion in some respects (e.g. limiting eligibility of foreign nationals).

Research on homelessness has identified the risks faced by ordinary families of becoming homeless because of the operation of the housing market. Other risks relating to personal factors such as drug and alcohol problems, unemployment, ex-offending, and military service have been significant among single homeless people. This has led to social policy initiatives to tackle 'street homelessness', to develop supported hostel accommodation as 'places of change' and pathways of support into housing and employment including social enterprise solutions. These initiatives are reported to have reduced the incidence of 'rough sleeping'. Rough sleeper counts in major cities showed general declines between 1998 and 2009.

Homelessness is a good example of policy divergence across the United Kingdom. The Scottish Parliament introduced legislation widening eligibility for assistance, and committing to 'permanently house every homeless person by 2012'. These provisions saw official levels of homelessness acceptances increase in Scotland (from 31,141 in 2003 to 36, 643 in 2009) at the same time as they fell in England (from a peak of 148,000 in 2003 to 49,000 in 2009). The use of temporary accommodation also diverged, almost doubling in Scotland from 5,400 to 10,100 while almost halving in England from 95,000 to 53,000 (Pawson and Wilcox 2010). The very different trend in England was associated with a 'prevention agenda', provision of 'housing options' advice and steering potentially homeless people into private renting. However, where households were accepted as homeless the duty to provide accommodation was met through private tenancies in only 7 per cent of cases compared to social housing in 70 per cent. In 2010, the government proposed greater flexibility for

English authorities to meet these homelessness duties through private sector offers within their district and 'suitable' in terms of size, condition, location, and affordability. This extended the previous government's direction but applicants' agreement would no longer be required for 'suitable' offers.

The Contemporary Housing Situation

By 1997 there was no longer a major new-build programme of housing for general needs or for lower-income households and the governance of housing was increasingly fragmented. Policy had shifted towards dismantling state intervention, relying on the private market to provide housing funded through welfare benefits. There were growing problems of social polarization, including racial segregation, urban crime, and inequality that were dysfunctional socially and economically. New problems in the owner-occupied sector were associated with older and low-income households and those affected by family or employment crises, over-extended borrowing, and personal debt.

The early years of New Labour continued with low levels of housing investment, accelerated transfer of council housing to housing associations, and promoted home ownership (including the Right to Buy). Nonetheless, the intention to address social exclusion and to achieve neighbourhood renewal was announced by the incoming prime minister on a large housing estate (the Aylesbury Estate in south London), leading to a national strategy for neighbourhood renewal and area based initiatives such as New Deal for Communities. A ten-year programme of stock transfer and area regeneration was a cornerstone of the Labour government's measures to raise social housing conditions to a new Decent Homes standard by 2010.

A more systematic attempt to reorientate English housing policy came later. The Communities Plan (ODPM 2003) sought to reverse under-investment in housing and regional divergence in economic performance and housing need. It developed different policies for different markets. In the Midlands and the North this included Housing Market Renewal Areas to address housing market decline. In the South-East continuing housing shortages, difficulties in labour force recruitment, and heightened affordability problems led to public expenditure targeted upon growth areas and key workers. The Barker Review (2004) advised the Treasury on improving responsiveness of the new build housing market to rising house prices and tackling undesirable economic consequences of rising house prices driving up the 'affordability threshold', leakage of equity into consumer spending, and associated problems in controlling the money supply and inflation. The government accepted recommendations to change the planning system and to find additional funds for new housing.

As a result of these policies, the latter years of New Labour saw a reversal in the long-term decline in planned investment in new social housing (£8.4 billion was planned for 2008–11, the highest level of investment since the early 1990s). This was partly dependent on cross-subsidies through housing for sale, 'planning gain' whereby private developers were expected to provide a proportion of social housing in new developments. Both of these policies were adversely affected after 2008 by the credit crisis and recession. However, the Labour government supported a 'kickstart' programme to maintain construction, shifting temporarily from housing for sale back to rented housing. While this enabled much of the planned social housing programme to proceed, albeit with a different tenure mix, it could not prevent overall construction of new homes in 2009 falling to the lowest level since the 1920s.

Emerging Issues

The election of a Conservative-led coalition government in May 2010 and its policy imperative to address the public finances following the credit crisis, the bailing out of the banks, and the pursuit of counter-cyclical investment challenged assumptions of previous housing policies. As in earlier crises, housing loomed large in public spending reductions; but this time there was greater attention to reducing demand-side as well as supply-side subsidies. There were emerging conflicts between these policies and new themes to promote localism and 'the Big Society' and to reduce regional and central direction.

The Comprehensive Spending Review halved the housing capital budget and introduced a new investment framework to achieve an estimated 150,000 affordable homes from the reduced spend. All new social homes would be let at 'affordable rents' of up to 80 per cent of market rents (compared to 55–75% in 2007/8). Housing associations would fund new development by charging higher rents for all new homes and some re-lets. All new social housing tenants would have 'flexible' (less secure) tenancies, which might be reviewed as often as every two years, to encourage those perceived as no longer in need of subsidized housing to move on. Later in became apparent that associations might further reduce grant requirements by subsidizing development from sales of existing assets and changes in tenure and rents of existing properties.

Stemming the growth in demand-side subsidies through the housing benefit system, promised even greater savings – at £22 billion housing benefit spend was three to four times greater than the housing capital budget. For private tenants housing benefits would be capped in each area and restricted to the bottom third of local market rents. Further limits were proposed on the total of all welfare benefits paid to individual households and single people under thirty-five were to be restricted to a single-room rent. In the longer term it was proposed that housing benefit would be phased out to become part of a simpler universal credit scheme for low-income households.

The government's expectation was that caps would place a downward pressure on private rents. However, private claimant numbers were increasing due to unmet demand for social housing and increased use of the private sector to meet homelessness duties. Many high rent London Boroughs have very limited private rentals within eligible benefit levels, raising several issues. First, that existing private tenants on benefit might be forced to move, described by the Conservative Mayor of London as 'Kosovo style social cleansing' (Evening Standard October 2010). Second, that there were problems in finding temporary accommodation for homeless households – several London Boroughs were looking at lower rent areas outside London. Third, in obtaining private sector offers to discharge homelessness duties if these had to be 'local'. Meanwhile, higher rents for new social

housing and re-lets might also be inconsistent with containing housing benefit.

There were also to be major changes to the institutional landscape, including the dismantling of the regional housing and planning infrastructure, reduced top-down targets and regulation (abolition of regional spatial strategies and housing targets, and closure of the main housing regulators). In their place came new arrangements (neighbourhood plans, community land trusts, and a community right to build) designed to promote 'new localism' and community involvement. A key challenge to stimulate house building without regional housing targets was tackled through a 'new homes bonus' – a five year subsidy payable to local authorities towards local service costs, matching council tax receipts of each new home (and possibly empty homes brought into use). The extent to which these measures would reverse a seventy-year low in new construction to be reversed is debateable.

Many of these reforms were presented as being about localism – e.g. giving local authorities and social landlords the flexibility to make best use of social housing. However, while they shift decision-making from regional to local (e.g. from regional targets to neighbourhood plans), key elements of national steering are maintained (e.g. restrictions on rehousing foreign nationals). How will markets and communities respond to a further decline in the role of the state in housing? The increased exposure of both social and private tenants to market pressures, the erosion of security of tenure for new social housing tenants and reduced resistance to social polarization between high and lower rent areas are consistent with a market-based neo-liberalism. The rhetoric of localism suggests greater community influence; however, the extent to which local institutions will build social solidarity required for a 'Big Society' remains to be seen. Increased churn and social segregation resulting from housing benefit and social housing reforms will make this harder to achieve.

Guide to Further Sources

Inside Housing provides weekly news and features. Academic journals include *Housing Studies, Housing Theory and Society, International Journal* of *Housing Policy* and *Journal of Housing and the Built Environment*.

An introduction to housing policy in the United Kingdom referring to historical developments, principal tenures and key policy issues is given in D. Mullins and A. Murie's *Housing Policy in the UK* (London: Macmillan, 2006).

D. Mullins and H. Pawson's *After Council Housing. Britain's New Social Landlords* (Basingstoke: Palgrave Macmillan, 2010) is a comprehensive account of the causes and impacts of the transfer of Britain's council housing to new social landlords.

A historical account of the changing role of housing within the welfare state can be found in *Housing and the Welfare State: The Development of Housing Policy in Britain*, by P. Malpass (Basingstoke: Palgrave Macmillan, 2005).

See also the annual publication *UK Housing Review*, by S. Wilcox (University of York: Chartered Institute of Housing and Centre for Housing Policy), www.york.ac.uk/res/ukhr/index.htm. This gives the latest facts and figures on housing finance, tenure, and recent developments in UK housing. The web site includes updated compendium and briefing papers.

Other sources include: K. Barker, *Review of Housing Supply, Delivering Stability: Securing our Future Housing Needs* (HMSO, London, 2004); W. Beveridge, *Pillars of Security* (London: Allen and Unwin, 1943); ODPM, *Sustainable Communities: Building for the Future* (London: ODPM, 2003).

Review Questions

1   How does housing fit in the UK welfare state?
2   How do supply-side and demand-side subsidies affect the roles of private landlords and social housing?
3   Is the transfer of social housing to third sector providers equivalent to privatization?
4   Do homelessness statistics follow homelessness policies or vice versa (considering recent Scottish and English experience)?
5   How will 'localism' and the 'Big Society' affect future housing policies?

Visit the book companion site at www.wiley.com/go/alcock to make use of the resources designed to accompany the textbook. There you will find chapter-specific guides to further resources, including governmental, international, think-tank, pressure groups, and relevant journals sources. You will also find a glossary based on *The Blackwell Dictionary of Social Policy*, help sheets, and case studies, guidance on managing assignments in social policy and career advice.

51

Social Care

Jon Glasby

▪▪

Overview

- The origins of current social care in nineteenth-century philanthropy and in different understandings of the best way to respond to poverty.
- The changing ways in which social care has been delivered over time.
- The relationship between social care and other services such as health care and education.
- Key changes under the New Labour governments of 1997–2010.
- Emerging issues such as investing in prevention and the advent of direct payments and personal budgets.

▪▪

Context

In 1942, William Beveridge's report on *Social Insurance and Allied Services* set out a blueprint for post-war welfare services (see Chapter 18). One of the most quoted sections of the report is Beveridge's description of 'five giants' or social problems which future services should seek to tackle. While these are couched in very 1940s language, they nevertheless map across to current social issues and even to some current government departments (see Table 51.1). Thus, as an example, a 1940s 'giant' such as 'want' becomes poverty or social exclusion and has traditionally fallen under the remit of the social security system. Although other chapters cover these various different services (see Chapters 45 to 52), a key gap in Table 51.1 is social care and social work. Is social care responding to a sixth giant that Beveridge failed to identify? Is it the glue that holds the other five together? Or is it a crisis service that works with people who fall through the gaps in other services?

The Student's Companion to Social Policy, Fourth Edition. Edited by Pete Alcock, Margaret May, Sharon Wright.
© 2012 John Wiley & Sons, Ltd. Published 2012 by John Wiley & Sons, Ltd.

Table 51.1   UK welfare services.

Beveridge's giants	Modern equivalent
Want	Social security
Disease	NHS
Ignorance	Education/lifelong learning
Squalor	Housing/regeneration
Idleness	Employment/leisure

Social Care

Crucial to an understanding of social care is the distinction between several key terms which are often used interchangeably. 'Social care' is an overall description for a range of services and workers who support both adults and children who are facing difficult changes in their lives. While this is a broad description, the focus has often been on providing practical support for a range of specific service user groups, including children at risk of abuse, frail older people, people with mental health problems, people with learning difficulties, and disabled people. By the early twenty-first century there were some 1.6 million people using social care services, with some 1.4 million people working in the social care workforce. While this is more than the entire NHS workforce, social care staff are employed by some 30,000 public, private, and voluntary agencies. Social services also spend around £16 billion per year, with many people using social care services funding their own care.

In contrast, 'social worker' is the name for trained professionals (the social care equivalent of doctors, nurses, or teachers) who are now degree-trained, registered with a formal professional 'Council', and governed by codes of professional conduct. Following the community reforms of 1990, social workers are typically responsible for assessing the needs of individuals, and arranging services to meet those needs from a range of social care providers from across the public, private, and voluntary sectors. Many have been traditionally employed in local authority 'Social Services Departments', although these have since been split into new children's and adults' services in England (see below for further discussion). Of the 1.4 million social care work-force, around 60,000 people are qualified social workers.

The History and Evolution of Social Care

While the history of social care is complex, a key contribution comes from a series of nineteenth-century voluntary organizations and philanthropists. Prior to this, much social support had been provided (as is still the case today) by families and local communities. In Tudor times, much of the assistance available was religious in nature and delivered via the monasteries. Following the dissolution of the monasteries and stimulated by rapid urbanization and industrialization, a number of more formal services began to develop via the now notorious Poor Law. While this included outdoor relief (payments to people in financial need), the main source of 'support' was typically the workhouse, with conditions deliberately made as harsh as possible so as to ensure that only the most needy applied for state help (an approach known as 'the workhouse test' and the principle of 'less eligibility'). Over time, workhouses became increasingly focused on different groups of people, with different approaches emerging for the able-bodied poor (often seen as lazy and capable of supporting themselves), for frail older people, people with mental health problems, and people with learning difficulties (who were increasingly seen as not to blame for their plight and hence deserving of assistance).

During the latter part of the nineteenth century, two prominent voluntary organizations were important in developing new approaches to the alleviation of poverty and in pioneering many of the approaches that later became associated with modern social work:

1   Founded in response to a proliferation of almsgiving following the depression of the late 1860s, the Charity Organization Society (COS) promoted principles of 'scientific charity' – assessing those in need and providing charitable support only to those deemed deserving (with those deemed undeserving left to rely on the Poor Law and the workhouse). In this way, COS hoped to co-ordinate the provision of financial support and to give individuals an incentive to be self-sufficient (guarding against the danger that generous support would only encourage the feckless and thriftless). In many ways, similar notions

underpin current debates about whether or not to give to people begging on the street – does this support those in need or does it encourage people to be dependent on this form of assistance?

2   Founded in 1884 with the creation of Toynbee Hall in Whitechapel, the Settlement movement had considerable overlaps with COS (and the same individuals were often involved in both movements) but diverged increasingly over time. Settlements were colonies of educated people living in poor areas of large cities, with the dual purpose of using the education and privilege of 'settlers' to help the poor, but also of getting to know the poor as neighbours and hence understanding more about the nature of poverty. Over time, it became increasingly apparent to many settlers that poverty was not the result of individual failings, but the product of wider social forces, and a number of settlers (e.g. Clement Attlee and William Beveridge) made significant contributions to the advent of a welfare state.

In many ways, these different perspectives continue to influence current practice, with social work approaches such as care management (see below for further discussion) continuing to focus on the assessment of individual need to ascertain entitlement to support, and community development and neighbourhood renewal focusing much more on community empowerment and on the individual in a broader social context. Both movements were also influential in the development of early social work, working with leading universities to help found early social work courses and provide placements for students.

Following the Second World War, an increasing amount of social work activity came to be subsumed within two local government departments: specialist children's departments and health and welfare departments. These were later combined into generic social services departments (SSDs) following the 1968 Seebohm report. By bringing together a range of adults' and children's social care services, Seebohm argued, there was scope to create a more comprehensive and co-ordinated approach, to attract greater resources, and to plan ahead to identify and meet the needs of a local area more effec-

tively. SSDs were soon boosted by a growing national infrastructure, including a more unified system of social work education (advocated in various reports by Eileen Younghusband), and the creation of a new National Institute of Social Work Training (which was later subsumed into a new Social Care Institute for Excellence).

In many ways, this system was to remain intact until the late 1980s, when a review of community care services by Sir Roy Griffiths (managing director of Sainsbury supermarket) led to the 1990 NHS and Community Care Act. Henceforth, social workers were to be 'care managers', responsible for assessing individual need and arranging care packages from a combination of public, private, and voluntary services. Consistent with the ideological commitments of the then Conservative government, this changed social workers into 'purchasers' rather than providers, and much of the new funding that accompanied the changes was to be spent in the independent sector.

Since 1997, much of this ethos has remained, but with a growing emphasis on modernization (often portrayed as a 'Third Way' between the market-based ideology of the New Right and the public sector values of Labour). Unfortunately, such a concept tends to be better at defining what a Third Way is not (i.e. not the market and not the state), and the result has arguably been a rather eclectic series of different policies and approaches. However, central to recent policy has been an emphasis on

- Greater *choice and control* (with people using services having greater say over what they receive and how money is spent on their behalf). Perhaps the best example is the increasing role played by direct payments, with social care service users receiving the cash equivalent of directly provided services with which to purchase their own care or hire their own staff.

- Greater *partnership working* (with health and social care in particular becoming increasingly interrelated over time). In 2000, this led to the announcement of a new form of organization (in England) – the Care Trust – which was seen as a vehicle with which to integrate health and social care fully. While this model has not proved popular in practice, policy has continued to stress the importance of joint working between health and social care.

■ A stronger emphasis on *citizenship* and *social inclusion* (with a growing tendency – slow at first – to look beyond traditional health/ social care to more universal services, and various attempts to tackle discrimination and promote human rights). As an example, the learning disability White Paper, *Valuing People*, stressed four overarching principles (rights, inclusion, choice, and independence), viewing social care and health in terms of what they can contribute to the lives of people with learning disabilities rather than as an end in themselves.

In structural terms, the key change under New Labour has been the abolition (in England) of generic SSDs, and the creation of new integrated services for children and for adults. Thus, new Directors of Children's Services are now responsible for both education and children's social care, bringing together wider partners via Children's Trusts. Similarly, Directors of Adult Social Services are charged with developing partnerships with NHS colleagues and broader services, and often oversee both adult social care and other services (such as housing, leisure, or adult education). In recognition of such changes, many English SSDs have split into a Directorate of Children's Services and various configurations of adult care (termed 'Social Care and Health', 'Social Inclusion and Health', Social Care and Housing', 'Adults and Communities' etc.). Similar changes have also taken place elsewhere in the system, with English policy increasingly diverging between the Department of Health and the Department of Education. In many ways, this takes social care back to pre-Seebohm days (without necessarily stating why the need for generic SSDs which Seebohm placed at the heart of his vision for social care is now no longer relevant). In recent years, it has also been difficult for some of the national social care bodies to retain a generic approach to social care issues, working across the children and adult divide. This has been particularly the case since the tragic death of 'Baby P', with a series of more recent reforms seemingly driven primarily by a need to reform child protection services rather than to

develop social care and social work careers and values more generally.

Emerging Issues

Always something of a crisis service for those in need, social care and social work have had a chequered history. While there has always been a need to support the most vulnerable in society, there has always been uncertainty over the best way to do this, from the different notions of poverty underpinning the voluntary action of the nineteenth century, to the different visions of Beveridge, Seebohm, Griffiths, New Labour, and the 2010 coalition government. With increasing financial and demographic pressures, however, previous approaches are increasingly strained, and considerable uncertainty remains as to how best to refocus services towards a more preventative approach, secure added value through more effective inter-agency working and place the people who use services at the centre of decision-making. Whatever happens, history suggests that the imperative to support those most in need in society – be they adults or children – is unlikely to go away, and that some form of social support – whatever it is called and wherever it sits – seems as essential now as ever. This seems particularly the case following the 2010 Spending Review – with the risk of rising need and less resource with which to work.

In the early twenty-first century, social care faces a series of challenges as it seeks to respond to a combination of social, economic, and demographic changes. First and foremost, an ageing population, medical advances, and changes in the availability of family support mean that there are more and more very frail older people in need of support, and a growing number of younger people with very profound and complex physical impairments and learning disabilities. With a very challenging financial context, fundamental change may be required to meet new demands, and a range of government policies emphasize the need to move from a system of crisis support to one based much more around prevention and promoting well-being. Quite how to do this in practice (and how to invest in long-term prevention while also continuing to meet the needs of those in crisis) remains unresolved. In recent years, this has also led to a growing debate about how best to fund long-term care for frail older people, with New Labour launching a national consultation (the 'Big Care Debate'), a Green Paper, and a subsequent White Paper exploring the scope to develop more of a 'National Care Service', similar in some respects to the National Health Service. In Scotland, a policy of free personal care has adopted a proposal of the 1999 Royal Commission on Long Term Care but rejected by Whitehall – and only time will tell whether this proves sustainable and produces helpful policy learning for other parts of the United Kingdom. Whatever happens, the funding of long-term care seems likely to remain controversial and the political consensus needed to develop such an approach has seemed unlikely amid heated debates about possible funding mechanisms.

Allied to this, many public services are becoming more focused on the issue of outcomes, asking increasingly difficult questions about the extent to which current activity adds value or achieves anything different for service users. This is a hard concept in several public services, where the emphasis has traditionally been on issues of input, process, and output (that is, focusing on what we do in social care, not on whether any of it makes any practical difference). In principle at least, an outcomes-based approach to inspection and performance management could lead to some searching questions about the contribution of social care and to a move away from notions of equality of input (treating everyone the same) to equality of outcome (working with different groups differently to achieve similar outcomes). An outcomes-based approach is now being adopted more generally by the coalition government, although some early insights are available from Scotland's attempts to develop a joint outcomes framework for health and social care.

Also linked is the increasingly central role of partnership working, with social care, health, education, and other local services increasingly asked to work together to meet the needs of people with complex, cross-cutting needs. For all this seems like common sense, working with multiple partners and reconciling different priorities and cultures is extremely labour intensive, and questions remain as to the best way of developing effective inter-agency partnerships, the cost of partnership working, and the extent to which

new relationships are seen to add value to existing single agency approaches. At the same time, structural changes in children's and adults' services in England have arguably left social care feeling very fragile and vulnerable, with a risk of being dominated by larger, better resourced, and more publicly popular services (such as the NHS or education). However, the same seems to be true at a practice level in Northern Ireland – with fears that social care remains a junior partner despite a much longer history of integrated health and social care. Partnership working may also become more difficult in Wales in the medium-term (following significant NHS reorganization and less certainty about future social care structures) and in England (following the emphasis of the 2010 White Paper on GP-led consortia). Of course, whether the partnership agenda is a threat or an opportunity depends on your point of view, and this can equally be seen as a chance to take what is important about social care values and principles and mainstream them. As children's and adults' services increasingly diverge in England, moreover, it may be difficult to retain a sufficient focus on the whole family, with inter-agency children and inter-agency adult services creating a new barrier for situations where there is a young carer or a disabled parent (and with scope to learn lessons from the different structures in different parts of the United Kingdom).

Finally, the initial concept of direct payments has been developed by the more recent advent of personal budgets (sometimes described as part of a wider 'personalization' agenda). Under this system, service users are assessed (or indeed self-assess) and are immediately given an indication of the amount of money to which someone with their level of need might be entitled. They can then choose how this is spent – whether in the public, private, or voluntary sector, via direct services or direct payments, or via some sort of combination of any of the above options. In principle this is a bold and radical change to current practice and to the current balance of power, and could herald one of the most profound changes in social care since the advent of the Charity Organization Society. Such an approach is now being rolled out rapidly in adult social care, with government policy stressing that all adult social care will be provided through a personal budget in future (except in an emergency). Historically, such approaches have tended to spread more quickly in some parts of southern England, with a number of political concerns in some more traditional 'old' Labour areas in parts of Scotland, Wales, and the North-East – although such differences are perhaps starting to fade as the debate develops.

Over time, this could lead to a very different relationship between the state and the individual away from the 'professional gift' model of the 1940s (where the individual is a passive recipient of other people's services) to a 'citizenship' model (where the person is an active participant in designing and co-producing their own support). Similar approaches are also being piloted in disabled children's services and in some forms of health care, and there is growing interest in combining different funding streams (including social care, social security, equipment and adaptations, employment support, etc.). In future this might lead to a situation where disabled people experience greater financial transparency and greater flexibility, with the right to control the various public resources to which they are entitled. However, this agenda remains fragile at the time of writing, with the opportunity to promote more of a citizenship-based approach but an equal risk that social care could simply allow the old system to reassert itself under the guise of the new language. Following the 2010 Spending Review there is also a danger that the government adopts the language of choice and control as a smokescreen for fundamental cuts rather than out of a genuine commitment to citizenship.

Guide to Further Sources

Useful web sites

For details on services and policy in different parts of the United Kingdom, see:

■ www.dh.gov.uk and www.education.gov.uk/childrenandyoungpeople/safeguarding (England) – see also www.education.gov.uk/swrb/ for details of work of the Social Work Reform Board; http://wales.gov.uk/topics/health/socialcare (Wales) – see also the recent Independent Commission on Social Services www.icssw.org; www.dhsspsni.gov.uk (Northern Ireland), for integrated health

and social care – see also the Office for Social Services www.dhsspsni.gov.uk/index/ssi/ssi-organisation.htm; (Scotland) www.scotland.gov.uk/Topics/Health/care (community care) andwww.scotland.gov.uk/Topics/People/Young-People (young people) – see also www.scotland.gov.uk/Publications/2006/02/02094408/0 for details of Scotland's twenty-first century Social Work Review

For details of the Social Care Institute for Excellence (SCIE) which identifies and disseminates good practice in children's and adult social care in England, Wales and Northern Ireland, see SCIE's Social Care Online is a large (and free) database of relevant research and other publications www.scie.org.uk.

For more on the development of direct payments and personal budgets, see

The Centre for Welfare Reform www.centreforwelfarereform.org; In Control www.in-control.org.uk; The National Centre for Independent Living www.ncil.org.uk.

For introductory reading see Community Care is the standard trade publication, with up-to-date news, views, research and policy analysis.

For recent social care history, see

■ R. Means and R. Smith, From Poor Law to Community Care (Basingstoke: Macmillan, 1998); R. Means, H. Morbey and R. Smith, From Community Care to Market Care? The Development of Welfare Services for Older People (Bristol: Policy Press, 2002); M. Payne, The Origins of Social Work: Continuity and Change (Basingstoke: Palgrave, 2005).

For specific service user groups, see: D. Kirton (2009) Child Social Work: Policy and Practice (Sage: London, 2009). This provides an overview of child care policy and practice in the United Kingdom aimed at social work students and practitioners; M. Lymberry (2005) Social Work with Older People: Context, Policy and Practice (London: Sage, 2005). An introduction to key policy and practice dilemmas, with a helpful consideration of links between social care and health); R. Means, S. Richards, and R. Smith, Community Care: Policy and Practice (4th edn, Basingstoke: Palgrave Macmillan, 2008) is a regularly updated textbook and one of the best introductions available to community care services for a range of adult service user groups; M. Oliver and B. Sapey, *Social Work with Disabled People* (3rd edn, Basingstoke: Palgrave, 2006) is a classic textbook critiquing traditional social work practice; H. Lester and J. Glasby, *Mental Health Policy and Practice* (2nd edn, Basingstoke: Palgrave, 2010) is an introductory textbook on mental health services, with an inter-agency focus.

For direct payments, see J. Leese and J. Bornat (eds), *Developments in direct payments* (Bristol: Policy Press, 2006) or J. Glasby and R. Littlechild, *Direct Payments and Personal Budgets: Putting Personalisation into Practice* (2nd edn, Bristol: Policy Press, 2009).

Review Questions

1   How can social care be encouraged to work effectively with other services (such as educa-tion or health) without losing its distinctive contribution and values?

2   How can services carry on meeting the needs of people in crisis while also trying to invest in longer-term preventative approaches?

3   What impact will personal budgets have on the nature and delivery of social care?

4   How can policy best promote inter-agency services without creating a split in services for children and for adults?

5   How fit for purpose does social care feel in the early twenty-first century, and what needs to change moving forwards?

Visit the book companion site at www.wiley.com/go/alcock to make use of the resources designed to accompany the textbook. There you will find chapter-specific guides to further resources, including governmental, international, think-tank, pressure groups, and relevant journals sources. You will also find a glossary based on *The Blackwell Dictionary of Social Policy*, help sheets, and case studies, guidance on managing assign-ments in social policy and career advice.

52

Criminal Justice

Tim Newburn

Overview

- Traditionally, criminal justice and penal policy have not been greatly studied by social policy scholars; this is now changing markedly.
- The main institutions of our 'modern' system of criminal justice came into being during the nineteenth and early twentieth centuries.
- A profound shift in emphasis away from welfare and rehabilitation occurred in the final three decades of the twentieth century.
- The dominant features of contemporary criminal justice have been punitiveness, politicization, and populism.
- The late twentieth century has seen a remarkable growth in the use of imprisonment and other forms of penal surveillance.

Criminal Justice and Social Policy

In the main, scholars of social and public policy have tended to ignore the area of criminal justice. Compared with, say, health, education, welfare, and culture, criminal justice has been relatively invisible. Yet, as Max Weber identified, the creation and maintenance of systems for protecting against the breakdown of internal social order is generally thought to be among the key characteristics and functions that define the modern nation-state. The period since the Second World War has seen a substantial increase in crime (though with a more recent down-turn) and a growing sense that this is one of the more pressing political and policy issues of the times.

The past two centuries or so have seen the progressive rationalization and bureaucratization of criminal justice and penal processes. From localized, community-based systems of policing and punishment there have developed huge state-

The Student's Companion to Social Policy, Fourth Edition. Edited by Pete Alcock, Margaret May, Sharon Wright.
© 2012 John Wiley & Sons, Ltd. Published 2012 by John Wiley & Sons, Ltd.

managed apparatuses, and vast bodies of laws, rules and regulations, aimed at controlling crime. The first thing to note is that there is no single system of criminal justice in the United Kingdom. There are three distinctive systems: in England and Wales, in Scotland, and in Northern Ireland. My focus here is primarily upon England and Wales. The criminal justice system is made up of the following major agencies and organizations:

Police – forty-three constabularies in England and Wales (a further eight regional forces in Scotland, together with a single Police Service of Northern Ireland).

Crown Prosecution Service – established in 1985 and currently administered in forty-two areas, contiguously with police force areas.

Magistrates' Courts and the *Crown Court* – the vast majority of cases (generally the less serious) are heard in Magistrates' Courts whereas the more serious are heard in the Crown Court in front of judge and jury.

National Offender Management Service (NOMS) – an executive agency of the Ministry of Justice which brings together HM Prison Service and the National Probation Service (which is responsible for the supervision of offenders in the community and the provision of reports to the criminal courts)

Crime and Disorder Reduction Partnerships – established by the Crime and Disorder Act 1998, these are multi-agency partnerships involving representation from police, local authorities, probation, health, and so forth, and are tasked with monitoring local crime problems, and publishing and overseeing plans for local crime reduction.

Patterns of Crime

Broadly speaking there are two main methods used for measuring and tracking trends in crime. One is taken from data collected routinely by law enforcement agencies concerning crimes reported by the public or otherwise coming to the attention of the authorities. In Britain such data are collected by the police and are generally referred to as *recorded crime statistics*. The second uses survey methods to elicit information from a representative sample of the population about their experiences of crime – primarily as victims wherever this is the case – usually over the previous twelve months. In England and Wales this is the British Crime Survey (BCS), first undertaken in 1981 and which has run intermittently since then but is now an annual survey.

Both sources of data have their shortcomings. Recorded crime statistics can tell us little about those 'crimes' that are never reported to the police – estimated to be at least one-half of all offences. By contrast, the BCS doesn't cover all crimes (including corporate or organized crime and 'victimless' crimes such as drugs possession). It is generally advisable to consult and compare both sources when attempting to understand and track levels and trends in crime.

It is widely believed that we live in times of unprecedented levels of crime. Whether such beliefs are accurate rather depends on the timeframe being utilized. It is certainly the case compared with, say, the 1940s, 1950s, or 1960s that current levels of crime are very high. However, if we take a longer historical perspective then there is rather reliable evidence to suggest that previous eras were characterized by very high levels of crime and disorder, even by contemporary standards. It appears to have been in the mid-1950s that crime began to increase markedly, with recorded crime rising by almost three-quarters between 1955 and 1960. Why might this be so? Well, one important point to note first is that this period saw a very substantial increase in the availability of mass market consumer goods, many of which were portable. Second, changes in the labour market saw a substantial increase in the proportion of women going out to work with the consequence that houses were left empty for considerably longer period than had previously been the case. Third, it is also likely that the police became more assiduous in their recording of crime during this period. As can be seen from Figure 52.1 crime continued to rise fairly markedly and consistently from that period on, all the way through to the mid-1990s when it began to fall.

Figure 52.1 shows levels of recorded crime over the past three decades. Police-recorded crime data show crime rising relatively steadily during the 1980s and then increasing markedly from toward the end of the decade until 1992. From that point recorded crime rates declined

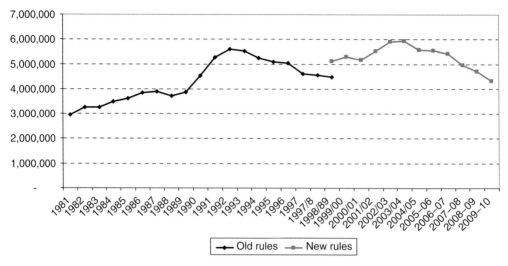

Figure 52.1   Overall recorded crime rate, England and Wales, 1981–2010.
Source: Based on Flatley *et al.* (2010).

until 1998/9 when new 'counting rules' (ways in which the police record crime) were introduced. As the gap between the two sets of 1998/9 figures illustrate, the new counting rules produced an immediate increase in the number of offences recorded and, thereafter, appear to show crime increasing again until 2003/4, whereupon crime begins to decline.

Data drawn from the various British Crime Surveys in many ways match the general trend visible from police-recorded statistics in the 1980s and early 1990s, though they depart quite significantly in the period since the late 1990s. BCS data, like police-recorded crime, show crime rising into the 1990s – in this case to 1995 – and then falling. By contrast with police-recorded crime, the downturn measured by the BCS continues almost uninterrupted since 1995. Indeed, according to this measure, BCS crime was estimated to be 50 per cent lower by 2010 than the peak in 1995 (see Figure 52.2).

A Brief History of Criminal Justice

Though the death penalty was the focus of the penal system in medieval times, and levels of capital punishment were high, executions underwent something of a brief boom in the second half of the seventeenth century. Much of the eighteenth century was characterized by a search for viable secondary punishments. Transportation (whereby prisoners were taken by boat to serve their sentences in penal colonies, mainly in America and Australia) was the other major form of judicial punishment in Britain and by the 1760s transportation to the colonies accounted for at least 70 per cent of all sentences at the central criminal court in London. From this point on, however, transportation declined and the use of imprisonment began to grow.

The system of punishment in Victorian Britain differed quite significantly from that of the late eighteenth century. The use of the death penalty declined markedly throughout the 1800s, public ceremonies of execution ceased in 1868 and corporal punishment of adults was rare by the second half of the century. Put simply, imprisonment moved from being merely a repository for those awaiting trial, sentence, or death in the sixteenth and seventeenth centuries to a site where punishment was inflicted on an increasingly wide range of offenders during the course of the eighteenth and nineteenth centuries.

In the preindustrial era, 'policing' was a community-based, less formal set of activities. In the United Kingdom the establishment of formal policing was preceded by community-based systems such as the 'hue and cry' in which local

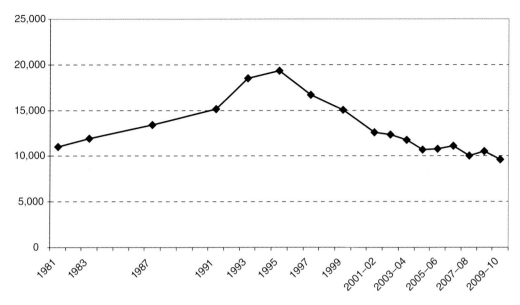

Figure 52.2   All crime (British Crime Survey) 1981–2009/10.
Source: Based on Flatley *et al.* (2010).

citizens took responsibility for raising the alarm and for chasing down the offender. Eighteenth century England was characterized by increasing concerns about crime. By the mid- to late eighteenth century, crime and disorder was perceived to pose a threat to social stability and it was around this time (in 1829 in London) that what we now understand as 'the police' emerged.

The nineteenth and early twentieth centuries saw the creation of the fundamental institutions of the modern criminal justice system: the prison, the police, the courts and related systems of criminal prosecution, probation and, in due course, an increasingly complex array of non-custodial penalties (fines, probation, community service etc.). Toward the end of the nineteenth century separate systems for dealing with juvenile offenders also emerged. The first half of the twentieth century saw the consolidation and reform of the modern criminal justice system. This period drew to an end around the middle of the twentieth century and was the era in which the 'solidarity project' – in which the state was the guarantor of full citizenship and security for all – was increasingly eclipsed by market forces. Recent decades have seen the emergence of a rapidly expanding mixed economy in many areas of criminal justice and, crucially, what also to many appears to be a

decisive shift in what are believed to be the purposes and ambitions of our criminal justice and penal policies.

The Aims of Punishment

In preindustrial/colonial times much punishment was public in character and, as such, was designed to shame, to bring forth expressions of guilt, remorse, and repentance. Loss of freedom – through imprisonment – was far from a common response to criminal infractions and was not assumed, as yet, to be an effective method for stimulating reform. By the middle of the nineteenth century this had all changed and in the United Kingdom a major public debate about the prison system was underway. The system, it was suggested, was failing in its objective of deterring criminals while simultaneously being too harsh. What emerged was a new system of punishment in which, while *deterrence* remained, an important goal of criminal justice policy, reform, and *rehabilitation* lay at its heart. The range of sanctions available to criminal courts expanded markedly, probation and other forms of training became established, and a range of new institutions were established or consolidated, many of which were conceived as direct alternatives to imprisonment.

The penal-welfare strategies that developed in the late nineteenth century reached their high point a little after the mid-twentieth century. However, there has been a radical restructuring and reorientation since that period. At the heart of this shift has been declining trust in the welfare and rehabilitative functions of criminal justice and the gradual rise to dominance of a set of discourses and practices that are more punitive, more politicized, and more populist. By the late 1970s there was a clear loss of faith in the power of the state to reform and, through reform, to reduce crime.

Criminal justice policy in this period was caught up in the battle between two competing versions of the role of the state. The first emphasized welfare and civil rights, and the reduction of social inequalities. The other railed against 'big government' and sought to limit state intervention in citizens' lives in most areas – with the exception of criminal justice. In this second model the state has a much diminished role in managing and protecting social welfare, something increasingly left to the market, but has an increasingly enhanced role in the management of social order. Indeed, for commentators such as Charles Murray, rising crime and disorder were precisely a product of welfare dependency.

As a consequence effective criminal justice and penal policy 'came to be viewed as a matter of imposing more controls, increasing disincentives, and, if necessary, segregating the dangerous sector of the population' (Garland 2001: 102). Over the course of the past twenty years such punitiveness has become the standard political position on crime and order for politicians of all hues. Thus, the other great change in this field concerns the politicization of criminal justice.

Criminal Justice and Penal Politics

Crime is now a staple of political discourse and of electoral politics. While this may not feel surprising it is, in fact, a relatively new political phenomenon. Until the early 1970s in the United Kingdom, for example, criminal justice policy barely featured in major elections and certainly

was far from the 'wedge issue' it has often been since.

In the criminal justice arena, politicians' concern with how they are likely to be perceived has had a profound effect on policy-making in recent times. Crucially, as numerous commentators have noted, by the 1990s the old divisions between 'conservative' and 'liberal' political positions on crime had disappeared, and had been replaced by what appeared to be a straightforward 'tough on crime' message. The past two decades have seen a progressively intensifying battle by the major political parties to be seen as the party of law and order. A 'tough on crime' stance has come to be associated with electoral success and its opposite, being 'soft on crime', with electoral failure.

The lengthy political dominance of Conservatism during the 1980s in the United Kingdom led to vociferous debates within the British Labour Party over the possible sources of electoral success in what were clearly changed times. The Labour Party sought to dump its various hostages to fortune, not least of which was its previously more liberal policies on crime control. 'New Labour' in the United Kingdom embraced so-called third-way politics. In the criminal justice arena this meant attempting to modify the old-fashioned liberal penal-welfarism that the party had largely clung to throughout the 1980s and into the 1990s by adding into the mix what was by now considered the *sine qua non* of successful electoral politics: a healthy dose of punitive rhetoric and the promise of similarly punitive policies. This mixture has never been more successfully captured than in Tony Blair's 1993 soundbite, 'tough on crime and tough on the causes of crime'.

Contemporary Penal Policy

The clearest change in penal policy can be seen in relation to the use of imprisonment. Figure 52.3 shows the prison population in England and Wales for the past half-century or so. The prison population stood approximately 20,000 at the turn of the twentieth century, the prison population declined from the First World War through the Second World War and then began to rise. It reached its turn of the century levels again by the

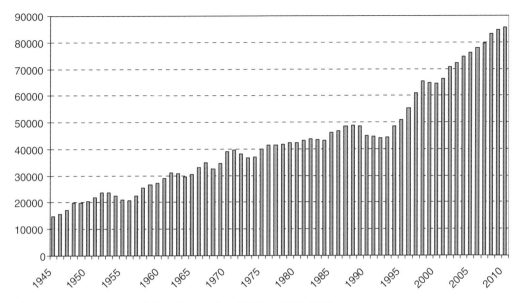

Figure 52.3 Prison population, England and Wales, 1945–2010.
Source: Newburn (2007), updated from HM Prison Services Statistics.

late 1950s and by the early 1980s reached a historic high in the low 40,000s. The population was reaching 50,000 by the end of the decade, at which point various strategies were employed, successfully, to begin to reduce the numbers incarcerated. At roughly the point that crime reached its peak in England and Wales the prison population once again began to rise, and to do so markedly more quickly than at any point since the Second World War.

The reasons for the expanding prison population are complex. There are three main possibilities: an increase in the numbers being caught and sentenced; an increase in the seriousness of the crimes being prosecuted; and, an increase in sentence severity. There is little or no evidence that the changes reflect an increase in the numbers of offenders being caught or convicted – these have remained relatively stable. Indeed, there does not appear to have been any substantial increase in the seriousness overall of the offences before the courts. Rather, the greatest change seems to have been in the severity of the sentences being passed by the courts: with prison sentences becoming more likely for certain offences, and also being imposed for longer periods of time than previously.

If punitiveness is one of the defining features of recent criminal justice policy then a further trait that can be identified, and one that is shared with other areas of public policy, is *managerialism*. There has been a progressive shift away from a simple concern with policy outputs and a move toward policy outcomes. As part of this an enormous architecture of performance management has been created, visible in probation, prisons, and policing. The 1998 Crime and Disorder Act brought in a raft of changes in youth justice, three of which have been central to recent Labour administrations' emphasis on outcomes. It introduced an overriding aim for the youth justice system, created the Youth Justice Board (YJB), a non-departmental public body responsible for monitoring performance, and created multi-agency Youth Offending Teams responsible for working with young offenders subject to penalties other than imprisonment. Similarly, though in a different area, the Act also introduced multi-agency Crime and Disorder (Reduction) Partnerships with responsibility for conducting local crime audits and publishing plans for local crime reduction, against which performance is assessed. Finally, there have been successive changes to policing which, again, have sought to increase government control over the management and delivery of criminal justice services.

As well as a range of measures to increase the severity of the penalties attaching to criminal offending, Labour governments between 1997 and 2010 invested considerable energy on what has come to be termed 'antisocial behaviour'. Antisocial behaviour orders (ASBOs) were introduced in the 1998 Crime and Disorder Act, though initially there was considerable reluctance in most parts of the country to use them. A dedicated unit was created within the Home Office in 2003 to promote local activism, and considerable further legislation (the Criminal Justice and Court Services Act 2000, the Criminal Justice and Police Act 2001, the Police Reform Act 2002 and, in particular, the Anti-Social Behaviour Act 2003) has added a raft of additional powers which the authorities have been encouraged to use vigorously. ASBOs have proved controversial for a number of reasons, not least that they are civil orders that can result in criminal convictions if those subject to them fail to comply with their conditions. Side by side with the increasing use of formal criminal sanctions such as community and custodial penalties, there has been a considerable spread of this new form of contractualized social control with consequent dangers of drawing yet more people into the criminal justice system.

Emerging Issues

In 2010 a coalition government came to preside over criminal justice and penal policy for the first time for over half a century. Already some mixed messages have emerged. Most newsworthy arguably has been the policy shift in the Ministry of Justice which has questioned the wisdom of short prison sentences, has set targets for the reduction the overall number of people in prison, and argued for a return to a greater emphasis on rehabilitation (Ministry of Justice 2010). For students of penal politics this signalled something of a sea-change. Here was a Conservative Justice Secretary eschewing the tough political rhetoric that had become the staple form of discourse in the past twenty years. Furthermore, the main critics of the proposals turned out to be a combination of those on the Right of the Conservative Party, together with ex-Labour Home Secretaries. It does not appear to be politics as usual.

What the future will bring is difficult to assess. The grim financial climate and the budget cuts outlined in the Comprehensive Spending Review mean substantial reductions to a number of criminal justice budgets – including both prisons and probation, and especially in relation to policing. There is also the 'Big Society' agenda which, although its core features are rather unspecified, is likely to mean increasing emphasis on the role of the third sector, together with initiatives which are argued to give greater voice to local citizens and community groups such as the proposal to introduce directly-elected 'police and crime commissioners'. As yet it is far from clear what this next phase of criminal justice and penal policy will look like. Given the rather predictably punitive flavour of much of the past two decades, however, the very fact that general trend of penal policy no longer feels set in stone marks something of a departure.

Guide to Further Sources

There are numerous very helpful information sources on the web. Both the Home Office and Ministry of Justice web sites contain a lot of material.

On the Home Office site, http://rds.homeoffice.gov.uk/rds/pubsintro1.html, you can find the data from which Figures 52.1 and 52.2 were created. You will find the 2010 Ministry of Justice White Paper, *Breaking the Cycle: Effective Punishment, Rehabilitation and Sentencing of Offenders*, on the government's justice web site: www.justice.gov.uk/about/publications.htm.

Crime in England and Wales 2009/10 by J. Flatley *et al.* (2010), /www.homeoffice.gov.uk/publications/science-research-statistics/research-statistics/crime-research/hosb1210/hosb1210?view=Binary, provides further details. The International Centre for Prison Studies runs a web site that contains a lot of useful data on trends in the use of imprisonment around the world: www.kcl.ac.uk/schools/law/research/icps.

The most influential book in recent years in this area is D. Garland, *The Culture of Control* (Oxford: Oxford University Press, 2001) which explores the changing nature of crime and penal policy and culture in America and Britain. A weighty, but definitive, volume is M. Maguire,

R. Morgan, and R. Reiner (2007) (eds), *Oxford Handbook of Criminology* (4th edn, Oxford: Oxford University Press, 2007). This is an edited textbook with contributions from many leading criminologists covering their particular areas of expertise. In particular, those wishing to read more about penal politics should read the following chapter: D. Downes and R. Morgan, 'No Turning Back: The Politics of Law and Order into the Millennium'. An introductory textbook which covers the bulk of criminological topics, aimed at the new undergraduate student is T. Newburn, *Criminology* (Cullompton: Willan, 2007). Finally, a provocative, thoughtful, and persuasive book in which the reasons for the changing nature of crime control in contemporary Britain are explored is: R. Reiner, *Law and Order: An Honest Citizen's Guide to Crime Control* (Cambridge: Polity Press, 2007).

Review Questions

1 What are the two main sources of data about crime?

2 What has been the general trend in crime over the past thirty years?

3 How might the dominant characteristics of criminal justice policy over the same period be described?

4 What explains the rise in the prison population between 1990 and 2010?

5 In what ways have penal politics changed in recent times?

Visit the book companion site at www.wiley.com/go/alcock to make use of the resources designed to accompany the textbook. There you will find chapter-specific guides to further resources, including governmental, international, think-tank, pressure groups, and relevant journals sources. You will also find a glossary based on *The Blackwell Dictionary of Social Policy*, help sheets, and case studies, guidance on managing assignments in social policy and career advice.

PART VIII
Services for Particular Groups

53

'Race' and Social Welfare

Lucinda Platt

Overview

- The United Kingdom's minority groups make up a small, but growing, section of the population.
- Race relations policies developed in tandem with immigration controls to promote the incorporation of minorities in contrast to the exclusion of non-citizens.
- There is great diversity in history and current experience between the United Kingdom's minority groups.
- Nevertheless, all non-white minorities have typically faced racism and exclusion from services, as a result of racialized conceptions of belonging, rights, and citizenship.
- The United Kingdom's ethnic minority groups show great diversity in outcomes across policy areas, though they share the experience of disadvantage relative to their skills and experience.
- Policy has had a role in both creating inequalities across social welfare domains, and in addressing them.

Context

The United Kingdom has traditionally been a country of immigration and the population of the United Kingdom is multi-ethnic. As well as the different nationalities – English, Scottish, Welsh, and Irish – associated with the different countries of the United Kingdom, in 2001 around 8 per cent of the population belonged to a non-white minority ethnic group. The classification and policy consideration of British minorities has typically focused on non-white minorities; and

The Student's Companion to Social Policy, Fourth Edition. Edited by Pete Alcock, Margaret May, Sharon Wright.
© 2012 John Wiley & Sons, Ltd. Published 2012 by John Wiley & Sons, Ltd.

racism within society and within service provision was previously regarded as the primary challenge for policy development and delivery. However, diversity within the minority population is now widely acknowledged, as well as the particular needs of certain white minority populations and sub-populations; and there is consequent demand for responses which go beyond a unifying anti-racism and recognize the complex role of different histories and backgrounds in determining people's needs for and access to social welfare.

Issues of 'race' and ethnicity cut across areas of social welfare. Thus, they have a bearing on many of the chapters in this book that treat distinct policy areas. However, ethnic minorities are also the objects of policy. This chapter treats the development of 'race relations' policy and the way it articulates with conceptions of citizenship, before discussing the ways in which issues of race and ethnicity have shaped both social policy needs and policy responses, using examples from housing and employment. It begins with a consideration of the language of 'race' and ethnicity.

Concepts and Terminology

The language of 'race' is both emotive and contested. While it is recognized that races do not exist in any meaningful biological sense, the terminology of 'race' is embedded within both popular discourse and policy and people act as if the notion of race had meaning, including through racism. Racism is behaviour that uses physical markers of difference such as skin colour as the basis of assumed inferiority and as a justification for hostility and unfavourable treatment.

In Britain and Europe the language of ethnicity has generally replaced that of race. However, the two terms continue to be tied together since ethnic minority groups are typically racialized and subject to racism. It has been argued that paying attention to ethnicity – and religion – allows recognition of 'cultural' racism, which goes beyond the emphasis on skin colour associated with 'race'.

Ethnicity is a self-conscious and claimed identity that is shared with others on the basis of a belief in common descent, and may be linked to country of origin, language, religion, or customs,

and may also be shaped by contact with others and experiences of colonization or migration. Ethnicity tends to assume a notion of a group to which belonging is asserted or ascribed. While everyone in principle belongs to an ethnic group, ethnicity is often regarded as being salient predominantly for those of minority ethnicity, and, typically for those of non-white ethnicity. Nevertheless it is inaccurate to conflate ethnicity and ethnic groups with minority ethnicity.

Minority ethnicity and minority religion often overlap, and in addition there has been an increasing recognition of the racialization of religion, as well as of the way that religious affiliation itself can result in prejudicial treatment. This has been particularly noted in relation to Islam and the experience of Muslims, though is not restricted to Islam, and has long been a feature of community relations in Northern Ireland. Religious affiliation does not, however, subsume or substitute for ethnic difference. A focus on ethno-religious groups may, therefore, prove most pertinent for policy and service delivery in the future.

The Development of Policy on 'Race' and Social Welfare

Race Relations policy developed as part of an approach to citizenship that constructed external exclusion as being the price to pay for internal harmony. The development of race relations policy was seen as a means of justifying the introduction of residence restrictions on those who were, nominally at least, British citizens but had been resident in former colonial countries. Thus, somewhat paradoxically, the United Kingdom was foremost in Europe in the development of anti-discrimination legislation while also imposing greater restrictions on entry than many other countries.

This association between 'good race relations' and immigration control was premised on a racialization of belonging: it was only non-white immigration that was identified as problematic. The formulation of policy that was 'internally inclusive but externally exclusive' contributed to the construction of resident minorities as the source of pressure on public services, rather than recognizing the need for an appropriate policy response to deal with changes in demand across the population as a whole.

Race Relations Policy

Race Relations Acts in 1965 and 1968 with modest provisions were followed by a more comprehensive Act in 1976. The 1976 Race Relations Act outlawed direct discrimination, indirect discrimination (where a requirement or restriction disadvantaged a member of one group more than another and could not be justified on other grounds), and victimization (where complaining about discrimination resulted in less favourable treatment). It covered employment, education, and the provision of services. It also established the Commission for Racial Equality (CRE). Under the Act it was unlawful to discriminate against anyone on grounds of race, colour, nationality, or ethnic or national origin. Nevertheless, the impact of this Act was limited to those cases where individuals brought complaints to Tribunal. It was unable to recognize or tackle structural aspects of disadvantage; and while the CRE could investigate institutions where systematic discrimination seemed to be occurring (for example, school exclusions or housing allocations), it could not enforce recommendations.

The 1976 Act remained the primary race relations legislation until 2000. Following the conclusions of the Macpherson Inquiry and its findings of 'institutional racism', an overhaul of Race Relations legislation was considered necessary. The 2000 Race Relations (Amendment) Act increased the power of the CRE in that its recommendations were now enforceable. The 2000 Act also put greater onus on public services to scrutinize their own practices and policies for potential discriminatory effects through the publication of Race Equality Impact Assessments. Following from the growing recognition of religious disadvantage and discrimination, in 2006 the Racial and Religious Hatred Act created new offences of stirring up hatred against persons on religious grounds. This law provided possibilities of legal redress for religious minorities not covered by the Race Relations Act.

From 2007, the CRE and its powers were incorporated into the Equalities and Human Rights Commission (EHRC), established by the 2006 Equality Act. The EHRC brought together those organizations that were responsible for monitoring and tackling discrimination across sex, race and ethnicity, and disability, and added responsibilities relating to age, sexual orientation and religion and belief, as well as a wider human rights agenda. With the 2010 Equalities Act, protection across the different equality strands was streamlined, and, in some areas, extended. The EHRC became the key national organization responsible for challenging racial and religious discrimination.

We can see in these developments that a concern with institutional practice and rights of citizens to fair treatment has been ongoing. However, in recent years it has been accompanied by a parallel policy focus which emphasizes the responsibility of individuals to 'earn' their citizenship rights. A series of disturbances in Northern English towns in the Summer of 2001 led to a concern with 'community cohesion'. The concept of 'community cohesion' was often interpreted as an injunction for minorities to 'integrate', and received further emphasis following the July 2005 London bombings. It was questioned whether certain sectors of the population truly 'belonged' and demonstrations of assimilation to posited British values and standards were demanded. In this newer model, then, citizenship is constructed as a contingent rather than an absolute right.

Immigration Policy

This emphasis on earned citizenship is also reflected in the development of immigration law from the early 2000s. Home Office policy has stressed the importance of national cohesion and shared values. A points system identifies the English speaking and highly skilled top tier migrants as suitable for settlement. This has been accompanied by a naturalization process including an oath and a test of cultural knowledge that came into place with the 2002 Nationality, Immigration and Asylum Act. On the other hand, asylum seekers and low-skilled labour migrants have been increasingly problematized, though the major increase in migration from Eastern Europe following A8 accession in 2004 complicated the racialization of labour migrants. The populist appeal of immigration restrictions, and the fear of cultural and racialized others has been a feature of policy since the 1962 Immigration Act; and controls and legislation have proliferated in recent decades. There is now a cross-party consensus on the need to 'talk tough' about immigration, in language that is linked to both economic imperatives and preservation of 'values'.

However, it is not just the policies that are targeted at minority groups and at the promotion of race relations that shape the experience and outcomes of those of different ethnicities. Unique histories of groups both in relation to pre-migration context, settlement in the United Kingdom, and subsequent experiences, and the adequacy of policy responses across a range of areas, have resulted in particular relationships with policy and particular social needs. This chapter considers housing and employment as two examples of the complex relationship between policy and minority group experiences. Exploration of social security, education, and health policy would similarly enable consideration of the diversity of ethnic groups' experience and its intersection with policy.

Minority Histories and Social Welfare

The 2001 Census for England and Wales specified sixteen options for its ethnic group question. Scotland and Northern Ireland had their own versions of the question. As well as a number of 'other' options and four 'mixed' groups, which enabled people to acknowledge mixed parentage or identification, the specified groups were White British (88 per cent of the population of Great Britain), White Irish (1.2 per cent), Indian (1.8 per cent), Pakistani (1.3 per cent), Bangladeshi (0.5 per cent), Black Caribbean (1 per cent), Black African (0.8 per cent) and Chinese (0.4 per cent). Two further categories added in 2011 are Arab and Gypsy or Irish Traveller. Each of the ethnic groups has distinctive migration history and settlement patterns and subsequent experiences of employment, housing, health, and so on. Pre-migration backgrounds and histories also influenced the resources that migrant groups brought with them or could call on, which are relevant to outcomes across the generations.

While there were minority groups present in the United Kingdom in the first half of the twentieth century and before, the development of the United Kingdom as a multi-ethnic and multicultural society can be dated to the post-war period. Britain was facing acute employment shortages and opened its borders to subjects from (former) colonies, as well as Europe. Minority settlement tended to be in areas of high employment, but consequently high levels of housing competition. Jobs on offer were often those that were the least desirable and the most precarious, leaving ethnic minority employees more susceptible to unemployment. Areas of settlement also reflected industries in which the different groups found, or could create, a particular niche. Thus, for example, Caribbean men often worked in the construction industries, settling in both London and the Midlands, while many Caribbean women were recruited to the new National Health Service. In 2001 over 60 per cent of Caribbeans lived in London. Pakistanis, whose period of migration peaked in 1961, tended to settle in the Northern industrial towns and the Midlands and worked in the textile industries, which later suffered from de-industrialization. They also worked in the motor industries, where the decline was later and longer-run. Some Indians from the migration of the 1950s also worked in the Midlands textile plants, but they also settled in London, finding work in the service and health sectors. More recent Indian migrants have been heavily concentrated in health professions. In 2001 40 per cent of Indians lived in London and a further 30 per cent in the West and East Midlands, in particular in Leicester. East African Asians, who typically define themselves as ethnically Indian, largely come from Kenya, where they suffered from the introduction of discriminatory laws in 1967, and Uganda, where they were expelled from in 1972. They typically came as families and though they had often lost their assets they frequently brought with them, and subsequently exploited, business skills. With these skills and with fluent English their situation was different from that of the Vietnamese refugees (largely ethnically Chinese) who arrived in Britain as part of a negotiated settlement, who often lacked English language and other transferable qualifications, as well as historical links to the United Kingdom. Mainland and Hong Kong Chinese, however, had different experiences, many coming as students, particularly among more recent migrants, while older Chinese migration patterns have focused around catering opportunities in the first generation, leading to relatively dispersed patterns of settlement.

The introduction of immigration controls after 1962 (the Nationality Act of 1948 had granted entry to anyone with a British passport) resulted in systems of sponsorship and chain migration, as well as in the longer term shifting the nature of migration towards family reunification and asylum. Chain migration has tended to foster replication of settlement patterns even as minorities show a tendency to move away from areas of concentration over time and across generations. Bangladeshi chain migration, following on from a period of primary immigration in the 1970s and 1980s, has focused around the catering and food industries, in which over half of Bangladeshis work, and is associated with high local residential concentrations in parts of London, where over 50 per cent of Bangladeshis lived in 2001. Black Africans are a heterogeneous group of relatively recent immigrants with their origins in a range of different countries and with different reasons for migration – asylum, education, and employment. They have high average levels of qualifications, which are not typically reflected in the employment they achieve, and settle overwhelmingly in London (nearly 80 per cent lived in London in 2001), often finding work in the low-paid service sector.

These different group histories and features have resulted in very different housing and employment careers and distinctive relationships with policy both across policy fields and across ethnic groups.

Housing

Areas of employment demand which sought migrant workers in the post-war period were also areas of housing shortage. Housing that was available to post-war immigrants was often that which had been designated for clearance, but local authorities, reluctant to rehouse what they deemed as a 'stranger' population, would often take the decision not to clear the properties. The net result was that the visible immigrant popula-

tions tended to be concentrated in areas of housing decline in the poorest parts of cities. One solution to housing pressure was to use community resources to buy cheap housing and let it to other migrants. In some cases, local authorities provided support for mortgages for these purposes. Such owner occupation could have a very different status from the privilege typically associated with that form of tenure, with much higher levels of housing problems, such as damp, lack of amenities, and overcrowding for these minority group owner occupiers. Additionally, owner occupation could tie individuals and families to a particular location even after the jobs were gone. Thus, local housing policies have had long-term consequences for residence, health, and employment opportunities

There were early attempts to limit access of minority groups to local authority housing, through, for example, residence requirements. Investigations throughout the 1970s and 1980s revealed evidence of discriminatory housing policies across a number of local authorities. This meant that those who did access local authority housing often ended up in worse stock. This had further ramifications for its value following the introduction of 'Right to Buy' legislation in 1980, and the transition of local authority housing to a residual housing tenure. With their later period of primary migration and the tendency to settle in London, Bangladeshis are the greatest current users of local authority housing of any ethnic group. They are moreover more likely to face housing stress than others in local authority housing, and changes to social housing policy and to housing benefits proposed at the time of writing are likely to impact particularly heavily.

Employment

All minority groups, and both men and women, face higher rates of unemployment than the average, and this is true across United Kingdom born as well as foreign born minority groups (see Figures 53.1 and 53.2). Moreover, rates of economic inactivity can represent non-employment stemming from discouragement as well as ill-health or family and caring responsibilities. Recent estimates of differential unemployment only partly incorporate the impact of the current

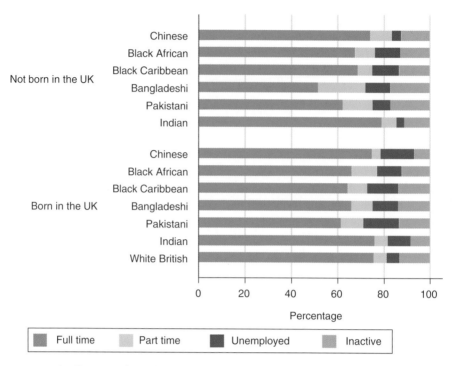

Figure 53.1 Distribution of employment, unemployment, and economic inactivity among the working age by ethnic group and whether UK born, men.
Source: Labour Force Survey 2006 Quarter 4 to 2010 Quarter 3, pooled (weighted). Based on data from the Office for National Statistics made available through the UK Data Archive. Contains public sector information licensed under the Open Government Licence v1.0. Note: full-time students are excluded.

recession, but it is know that recession tends to hit minority groups harder.

A major study of ethnic minorities in the Labour Market carried out by the prime minister's Strategy Unit in 2001, explored the causes of the employment differentials and possible policy solutions. It also led to the establishment of a cross-departmental Ethnic Minority Employment Task Force to address the labour market position of minority ethnic groups, and to help achieve a reduction in the employment gap between minorities and majority, a reduction that formed an explicit policy target.

Analysis has shown that absolute differences in employment chances between ethnic groups are partly susceptible to explanation in terms of differences in qualifications, age, experience, sector of employment, rates of illness, and region of residence, many of which are embedded in groups' migration and settlement histories, and in policy responses to these. However, discrimi-

nation also contributes to differential outcomes across groups.

Policy attempts to address employment differentials have included generic policies focusing on skills and on making work pay through such measures as the minimum wage and tax credits, and child-care policies. They have also included targeted measures focusing on understanding – and tackling – discrimination, job search support through ethnic minority outreach, incorporating partners into new deal initiatives through partners outreach and focusing initiatives on areas with high rates of minorities. In 2008, the National Audit Office found evidence that some of the specific programmes had been effective, even if there had been little time to evaluate them prior to changes in organizational structure, which discontinued them.

Overall, there was evidence that the employment rates of ethnic minority groups did increase over the ten-year period from 1997, and some of

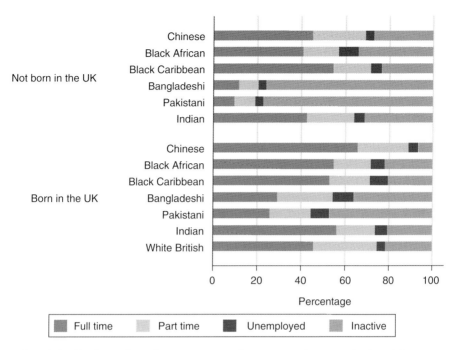

Figure 53.2 Distribution of employment, unemployment, and economic inactivity among the working age by ethnic group and whether UK born, women.
Source: Labour Force Survey 2006 Quarter 4 to 2010 Quarter 3, pooled (weighted). Based on data from the Office for National Statistics made available through the UK Data Archive. Contains public sector information licensed under the Open Government Licence v1.0. Note: full-time students are excluded.

this does appear to have stemmed from policy interventions, generic as much as specific, accompanied by the benefits of a buoyant economy. However, ethnic minorities are known to be more vulnerable to job loss in a recession and the relative gains may be undone in the current economic climate.

Moreover, the implementation of the budget cuts announced by the United Kingdom coalition government in the 2010 Spending Review, alongside those already in place, will impact key areas that are significant for minority groups and are likely to have implications for equalizing their opportunities. These areas include the skills agenda, the removal of the Education Maintenance Allowance that supported less well-off students to continue in post-compulsory education, and the shift of the majority of higher education funding from central support to individual students, and changes to equalities bodies. In addition, changes to in-work as well as out-of-work

and family related benefits are likely to disproportionately affect some minority groups. Such changes are likely to present major challenges for the relative social welfare of minority ethnic groups in the future.

Guide to Further Sources

There is an extensive literature on ethnicity and housing, of which P. Somerville and A. Steele (eds), 'Race', Housing and Social Exclusion (London: Jessica Kingsley, 2002) provides a good example. A recent account of ethnicity and employment, as well as other areas of ethnic inequality can be found in L. Platt, Understanding Inequalities: Stratification and Difference (Cambridge: Polity, 2011). The 2010 EHRC report, How Fair is Britain? Equality, Human Rights and Good Relations in 2010 (London: Equality and Human Rights Commission) also provides an account of inequalities and policy implications across equality domains and a range of policy-relevant fields. The Parekh Report still offers a wide-ranging discussion of issues relating to social welfare in a multi-ethnic society: B. Parekh, *The Future of Multi-Ethnic Britain* (London: Profile Books, 2000). The discussion of immigration and race relations policy in this chapter draws on C. Joppke, *Immigration and the Nation-State: The United States, Germany, and Great Britain* (Oxford: Oxford University Press, 1999) and H. Goulbourne, *Race Relations in Britain since 1945* (Basingstoke: Palgrave Macmillan, 1998).

Review Questions

1 How does the concept of ethnicity improve upon a focus of race in social policy?

2 What are the main features of British race relations policy?

3 At what points does social policy intersect with 'race' and ethnicity?

4 What has been the role of policy in contributing to housing inequalities?

5 Why do employment rates differ across ethnic groups?

Visit the book companion site at www.wiley.com/go/alcock to make use of the resources designed to accompany the textbook. There you will find chapter-specific guides to further resources, including governmental, international, think-tank, pressure groups, and relevant journals sources. You will also find a glossary based on *The Blackwell Dictionary of Social Policy*, help sheets, and case studies, guidance on managing assignments in social policy and career advice.

54

Children

Tess Ridge

Overview

- Children are key recipients of welfare services across a wide range of policy areas, and their lives are considerably shaped by the type and quality of welfare services available.
- Modern childhood is undergoing considerable social and economic change and children of the twenty-first century live increasingly complex lives in a range of diverse family settings.
- Child welfare policies change over time, and depend on fluid and changing assumptions about the needs and rights of children, the needs and rights of parents, and the role of the state in children's lives.
- There is increasing recognition in policy that children are social actors and bearers of rights. There is also a trend towards 'social investment policies' which focus on children as 'citizen workers' of the future.
- The chapter examines a key policy area for children, the issue of child poverty. It explores the Child Poverty Act and looks at the impact on children of a range of policy initiatives and the implications for children of changes and continuities in policy when there is a change of government.

Introduction

In the United Kingdom in 2010 there were just under 12 million children under the age of sixteen and they represented about 19 per cent of the population. The majority of these children were living in a family setting with their welfare needs being met by a range of informal and formal provision. Social policies for children need to be understood within the context of this informal/

formal welfare mix. Children are often the target of policies and they are also important consumers of welfare. They are key recipients of welfare services across a range of policy areas including education, health, housing and the environment, child-care, social services, and financial support through the social security and tax system.

Children rely very heavily on welfare services for their present and future well-being, and their lives are affected by policies at local, national (including devolved administrations), and transnational levels. Undoubtedly, areas such as education, child-care, and health policies and services have clear implications for children's well-being, but in other areas too, for example, the environment and transport, there can be intended or unintended impacts on children's lives. The ways in which children are treated by policy-makers is also dependent on how childhood is perceived at any one time. This chapter will examine how changing conditions of childhood may affect policies, and highlight some of the key debates and developments in this area.

Changing Conditions of Childhood

To understand how policy can affect children's lives, it is first important to recognize that childhood, as we know it, is a relatively modern social construction, which changes over time. Harry Hendrick (2005) traces the development of child welfare over time and identifies the1830s as a key period for the development of interest and intervention in child welfare. Growing concerns regarding children's labour, their education, juvenile delinquency, and children's protection led to a range of interventions. Although the role of state in child welfare was not fully developed at that time, rather 'welfare interventions' were informed by diverse perspectives including philanthropy and reforming evangelism which focused on 'rescuing' children from their labour, the streets and their perceived 'undesirable' parents (see Hendrick 2005; Cunningham 2005). The late 1880s and the early 1900s saw a shift in balance between philanthropic/evangelical activities and the state which signalled the beginning of state welfare policies which were informed by the work of a growing band of professionals and 'experts' in childhood and children's lives.

Hendrick argues that what followed was a far more complex notion of childhood and child welfare which 'looked to children's physical and mental development, to their education, their protection from uncivilized and neglectful behaviour and to their instruction in matters of hygiene, personal responsibility and 'citizenship' (Hendrick 2005:34). These developments laid the foundations for much of the modern suite of social policies that affect children today including health, education, and social care.

Twenty-first Century Childhood

In the twenty-first century, childhood in the United Kingdom is undergoing a further period of considerable social and economic change. These changes impact the way that policies are developed for children and their families.

Demographic and social changes in the second half of the twentieth century have also wrought considerable transformations in family formation and structure. Trends toward reduced fertility and later child-bearing have led to an overall reduction in the number of children being born in economically developed Western societies. Increasing instability in family life has led to a growth in cohabitation and rising rates of family dissolution, and this in turn has resulted in great diversity and complexity in family forms. As a consequence, children's lives are increasingly multifaceted and they can live in a variety of family settings. Clearly, it is difficult for the state to provide effective universal or targeted policies for children who are living increasingly diverse and complex lives.

Children, Family, and Social Policy

Like childhood, child welfare policies have also changed over time, and depend on fluid and changing assumptions about the needs and rights of children, the needs and rights of parents, and the role of the state in children's lives. They are also affected by the political economy of welfare and different perceptions and ideologies of childhood that prevail at the time. The state's value position in relation to childhood and family life has been an important factor when it comes to shaping policies. Historically, children's needs and interests have remained hidden within the private sphere of the family and as a result they have tended to be invisible in the policy process. Their interests have been mainly served by social policies which are directed at the interests of the family. This 'familialization' of children has meant that policies which directly respond to children's needs were unlikely to be developed. This is apparent, for example, in the provision of child-care which has rarely been provided from the starting point of what is best for children, but rather as an important service for families, and in particular as a means to encourage mothers back into the labour market.

The assumption that children's best interests are consonant with their family's best interests is problematic and, as a result, their needs and concerns are always in danger of being subsumed by the needs and interests of the family and of the state. There are also considerable 'tensions and contradictions' in the relationship between the state and the family and this reflects an ongoing debate between the rights and responsibilities of parents for their children and the obligations of the state to provide services for children and intervene in their lives when they are deemed to be at risk. Underpinning these tensions lays the fundamental issue of whether children are seen as a private good or whether society has a legitimate collective interest in investing in them and ensuring their well-being.

Children's Rights

The issue of children's rights is an important one for social policy. There is increasing recognition, in social policy, that children are social actors and bearers of rights, this is part of a new trend towards including the voices of service users in policy and the increasing participation of children in research, practice, and policy formulation. The United Kingdom has a series of rights based legislative acts – such as The Children's Acts of 1989 and 2006 – and wider international conventions – such as the United Nations Convention on the Rights of the Child (UNCRC). In line with changing expectations regarding children's interests and well-being Children's Commissioners have been appointed, with the devolved administrations leading the way with Wales first in 2001 and finally England in 2005. Children's Commissioners have responsibility for promoting the views and interests of all children and young people at a national and devolved level within a rights-based framework informed by the United Nations Convention on the Rights of the Child (UNCRC).

However, despite these advances there are still considerable areas of tension within policy regarding the rights of children. For example, although there is a positive policy to eradicate child poverty in line with the Articles 26 and 27 of the UN Convention on the Rights of the Child, marginalized children, such as children of asylum-seekers, tend to have far less attention paid to their welfare rights.

Devolution has resulted in a diverse range of policy developments across the difference nations of the United Kingdom with policies for children and young people particularly likely to show divergence. Increasingly where you are born in the United Kingdom will affect the policies and laws that will have an impact on your childhood and by extension your future adulthood. These changes are also informed by different notions of children as rights bearers and citizens (see Box 54.2).

Children as a 'Social Investments'

Although children's needs have historically been hidden within the family, the position of children and families in welfare policy is changing. Ruth Lister argues that 'we are witnessing a genuine, unprecedented attempt to shift the social priorities of the state and nation to investing in children' (in Hendrick 2005: 455). This signals a profound shift in the position of children and families in the welfare mix as the state moves towards the development of a 'social investment state'. The 'social investment state' entails a movement away from traditional welfare policies towards policies built on investment in social and human capital. In this welfare strategy, children are central to future economic success; they are the 'citizen-workers of the future' (ibid.). In the 'social investment state' children are valued for the adults they will become and policies are explicitly targeted towards ensuring that their potential is developed to ensure the economic prosperity of the country in the future in order to maintain national economic prosperity in a competitive global market. Therefore, childhood and the development of healthy and educated/ skilled children are too important for the economic future of the country to be left solely in the hands of parents.

> **Box 54.2** Children's Citizenship, Rights, and Entitlements across the Devolved Authorities
>
> Children's rights and entitlements are linked to citizenship.
>
> - In England children's rights are linked with duties rather than citizenship entitlements and children are seen as in need of protection. Until they reach independence, any citizenship is 'by proxy' through their families.
> - In Scotland, welfare rights are important but children are in effect 'citizens in the making'.
> - Northern Ireland has a rights-based approach but an outcomes model that sees citizenship not as entitlement but as 'the by-product of good provision'.
> - In Wales, children's entitlements are strong, the Welsh Assembly has accepted the UNCRC as the fundamental underpinning for all its work with children and young people. Children are conceived as citizens in their own right
>
> (Clutton in Invenizzi and Williams 2008:179)

The development of social investment policies has, in many ways, been beneficial to children's interests in the United Kingdom. For example during the recent UK Labour government of 1997–2010 there was a significant increase in investment in children through policies to eradicate child poverty (see below). However, despite such improvements, there is a tension between policies that focus on children as future adults and the quality of life that they experience in childhood. This highlights a key debate about whether children are treated in policy as 'beings' (children in childhood) or as 'becomings' (future adults and citizen workers). As Prout argues (in Hendrick 2005), too strong a focus on children as future adults is unbalanced without an equal concern for the well-being of children in childhood, and the quality of their social lives and opportunities for self-realization.

Policy in Action – Ending Child Poverty

We now turn to examine the issue of child poverty a key policy area for children where recent policy strategies have had a profound impact on how policies have been developed for children. This policy issue reflects very well some of the tensions outlined above and involves policy-making across a range of welfare providers including education, health, social security, and personal social services.

Children are particularly vulnerable to poverty, and fiscal support for them and their families through the tax and social security system plays a vital role in their protection, especially for children who live in lone-parent households and/or where there is unemployment, low pay, or long-term sickness and disability. The level of support provided by the state can be crucial in securing the economic well-being of children.

In 1999, faced with a child poverty rate of over 4 million, the Labour government pledged to eradicate child poverty within a twenty-year period (see Box 54.3). To do so, it developed a major programme of welfare reform which had three key interrelated components, making work possible and making work pay, improved financial support for families with children and investment in children.

The tensions between children as 'beings' and as 'becomings' are evident in Labour's Early Years programme, which included Sure Start in areas of deprivation and Children's Centres to deliver child-care and a range of parental support. These policies were formulated in recognition that early interventions in children's lives could be highly effective in preparing them for school and as such had a strong 'social investment' agenda. However, there can be real tensions between Early Years initiatives and the government's welfare to work policies, and it is not always clear whether the focus is support for parents and children or the pursuit of wider economic issues and concerns.

The Labour government struggled and ultimately failed to meet its poverty reduction targets

> **Box 54.3** Child Anti-poverty
>
> Labour's child anti-poverty policies included
>
> - Early Years investment – including Sure Start, Children's Centres, family support and advice
> - Education – tackling exclusions and truancy; improving literacy and numeracy.
> - Increased financial support through the tax and benefit system – tax credits for low-income working families and increased payments for children through Child Benefit and Child Tax Credit.
> - Employment related policies including welfare-to-work policies like New Deal for Lone Parents and the minimum wage.
> - Improved child-care – National Childcare Strategy for children from birth to fourteen.

and in what turned out to be one of it's final acts in power brought in unique legislation that bound all future governments of whatever hue to keep the child poverty pledge and eradicate child poverty by 2020. The Child Poverty Act 2010 set out a range of duties that required future governments to develop a child poverty strategy, present it to Parliament every three years, and report every year on their progress (see Box 54.4).

Critics of Labour's anti-poverty programme pointed to the dominance of the welfare-to-work agenda that underpinned much of the policy. For example, policies that encourage mothers, especially lone mothers, into employment will have an impact on children's lives. The intention is that children will experience increased financial security through their mother's income from work; however, the balance of work and care within families is affected, and as a result so too are children's experiences of child-care and after-school care, as well as the length and quality of time that they are able to spend with their mothers. Others have argued that greater redistribution of income

> **Box 54.4** The Child Poverty
> Act 2010
>
> Purpose of the Bill:
> - To enshrine in law the UK govern-
>   ment's commitment to end child
>   poverty by 2020.
>
>   Key elements:
> - Every future government is required
>   to produce a child poverty strategy
>   directed towards 2020 and due every
>   three years. The strategy is to be placed
>   before Parliament.
> - Annual report of progress towards
>   target set before Parliament – inten-
>   tion to hold governments to account.
> - Independent Child Poverty Com-
>   mission set up to advise policy and
>   monitor government progress.
> - Duty placed on Local Authorities,
>   devolved authorities and their part-
>   ners to tackle child poverty

from rich to poor would have been necessary to lift poorer families out of poverty.

The new UK coalition government while bound by the Child Poverty Act has adopted a very different approach to child poverty arguing that a transfer of income is not necessarily the route they wish to take to reduce child poverty. The first Child Poverty Strategy has been developed in the midst of severe austerity measures and significant cuts in social security and housing support for low income families. Independent research has showed that these cuts will disproportionately impact low-income children and their families. In the context of changing economic, social, and political values the future well-being of low-income children will depend very heavily on what economic and social welfare provision is made for them in the years ahead.

Emerging Issues

Childhood is undergoing considerable transformation, as social, demographic, and economic changes impact upon the everyday lives of children and their families. Formulating adequate and effective social polices that respond to children's needs and concerns have presented considerable challenges for governments as they seek to reconcile the often divergent needs of the state, families, and children. Despite the Child Poverty Act and the legal binding on future governments of whatever political hue to eradicate child poverty by 2020 it is likely that the experience of poverty and disadvantage will continue to remain a severe problem for many children over the foreseeable future. The adequate provision of benefits and state support for families in employment and – most critically – out of employment will be a key concern. These are very sensitive policy issues that cut right to the heart of the child/parent/state welfare triangle. Income support policies for children reflect the tensions between the duties and responsibilities of parents and the duties and responsibilities of the state for ensuring children's well-being.

At the start of the twenty-first century the interests of children slowly came in from the margins to the very heart of policy. However, there is no guarantee that their needs and concerns will stay at the centre of policy. Children are highly vulnerable to changes in government and the attendant potential for new policy directions driven by new political priorities.

Guide to Further Sources

A key text that introduces child policy issues is H. Hendrick's, *Child Welfare and Social Policy, An Essential Reader* (Bristol: Policy Press, 2005) for a further historical insight see also H. Cunningham, *Children and Childhood in Western Society since 1500* (Harlow: Pearson Education, 2005). C. Hallett and A. Prout, *Hearing the Voices of Children* (London: Routledge/Falmer, 2003) draws on the new social studies of childhood; it is a sociological approach but is focused on social policy and, in particular, on the emergence of children's voices in policy domains. Valuable texts about children's rights and citizenship are H. Montgomery and M. Kellett (eds), *Children and Young People's Worlds: Developing Frameworks for Integrated Practice* (Bristol: Policy Press, 2009) and A. Invernizzi and J. Williams, *Children and Citizenship* (London: Sage, 2008).

R. Eke, H. Butcher, and M. Lee, *Whose Childhood is it? The Roles of Children, Adults and Policy Makers* (Continuum: London, 2009) provide a valuable insight into Early Years policies, the debates about 'being' and 'becoming' and their implications for children.

Government web sites including the Child Poverty Unit, the Department for Work and Pensions and the Department for Education are valuable sources of policy documents and research. Further information about child poverty see J. Waldfogel, *Britain's War on Poverty* (New York: Russell Sage Foundation, 2010) and look at the Child Poverty Action Group (CPAG) web site www.cpag.org.uk, which has a regular update on child poverty statistics. The Child Poverty Act is also available at www.legislation.gov.uk/ukpga/2010/9/contents.

On a wider stage the UNICEF web site, www.unicef.org, carries information about the UN Convention on the Rights of the Child and many other issues that affect children.

Review Questions

1 How has childhood changed in Britain over the past thirty years?
2 What role do children's rights play in policy?
3 What is the Child Poverty Act 2010, and what are the implications for children of this legislation?
4 How has devolution in the United Kingdom affected policies for children?
5 What are social investment policies and how do they affect children?

Visit the book companion site at www.wiley.com/go/alcock to make use of the resources designed to accompany the textbook. There you will find chapter-specific guides to further resources, including governmental, international, think-tank, pressure groups, and relevant journals sources. You will also find a glossary based on *The Blackwell Dictionary of Social Policy*, help sheets, and case studies, guidance on managing assignments in social policy and career advice.

55

Young People

Bob Coles

Overview

- This chapter starts with a brief discussion about what we mean by 'youth' and 'young people'.
- It describes the emergence of youth policy in Britain in four main phases:
    - The first covers the arrival of youth policy in the period 1997–2000, mainly under the influence of the Social Exclusion Unit. This saw the first Minister for Young People.
    - The second period (2000–5) saw the birth, life, and 'demise' of the 'Connexions Strategy' described at the end of 1999 by the prime minister as 'our front line policy for young people'. Yet by 2005 no-one spoke of this 'strategy' at all.
    - During the (overlapping) third period, youth policy became submerged in policy for 'children-and-young people' under the predominant discourses of the 2003 Green Paper *Every Child Matters* and further enmeshed following a 2005 Green Paper *Youth Matters*.
    - Finally, we describe some of the issues which are beginning to emerge as the coalition government, elected in 2010, begins an era of austerity.

Context

In the mid-1980s half a million sixteen-year-olds were denied unemployment benefits and recruited onto the Youth Training Scheme (YTS). In those days policy was set by separate govern- ment departments responsible for the big institu- tions of the welfare state (social security, health, education, and the Home Office) and we had nothing which could be described as a coherent approach to youth policy. Youth unemployment was at record levels but was seen as an unavoidable

The Student's Companion to Social Policy, Fourth Edition. Edited by Pete Alcock, Margaret May, Sharon Wright.
© 2012 John Wiley & Sons, Ltd. Published 2012 by John Wiley & Sons, Ltd.

consequence of addressing wider economic problems. Any attempt to develop an integrated approach to meeting young people's needs was not developed until after the first New Labour government in 1997. By then, the 1980s were regarded as an era when, shamefully, youth had been abandoned to market forces with only discredited training schemes acting as a safety-net against mass youth unemployment.

Perspectives on Youth and Youth Transitions

'Youth' is often described as an interstitial phase in the life course between childhood and adulthood and 'young people' those at this phase in the life course. Different social science emphasize different aspects of this. The term 'adolescence' is often used in psychology describing biological and psychological aspects of physical, emotional, and sexual maturation associated with the teenage years. Sociologists have more often defined youth as associated with institutional transitions, three of which predominate. The first involves completing education and entering the labour market – the school-to-work transition. The second involves attaining (relative) independence of families of origin (including partnering and family formations) – the domestic transition. The third involves moving from the parental home, sometimes initially involving temporary transitional accommodation, but eventually achieving a 'home' independent of parents – the housing transition. Political scientists and others have focused on the ways in which different rights and responsibilities accrue to young people during their teenage years. Indeed some analysts have talked about youth citizenship as being distinctive from the full citizenship of adults. As an applied social science, social policy draws on all of these perspectives in order to provide a critical appreciation of how, to what degree, and in what ways the needs of young people are met.

The Polarization of Youth Transitions

The 'youth transition model' has proved especially useful in helping understand the 're-structuration' of youth that occurred in the final quarter of the twentieth century and continued into the twenty-first. It helps highlight the ways in which 'traditional transitions' have been replaced by 'extended' and 'fractured' transitions. 'Traditional transitions', commonplace until the mid-1970s, involve young people leaving school at minimum school leaving age and almost immediately and unproblematically obtaining employment. As young people worked in their late teenage years, they continue to live in the parental home, they saved, formed partnerships, got engaged, then married, and on marriage, moved to their own home and start a family, and usually in that order. In the twenty-first century, although significant numbers of young people still attempt some of the major transitions in their teenage years, traditional transitions have been largely replaced by 'extended transitions'. These involve longer periods spent in post-16 and higher education, longer periods of family dependency, later parenting (the average age of a woman having her first child is now over twenty-six), more complex partnering (often including cohabitation) and more complex and extended periods living in 'transitional housing'.

'Fractured transitions' refer to young people leaving school without securing a job or training, or leaving home without attaining a stable home of their own, and so experiencing various forms of youth homelessness. 'Fractured transitions' often involve drop-out from families as well as drop-out from education, training, or employment. Longer periods of family dependency assumed by extended transitions occur at the very time when many family relationships proved brittle and some families unable to cope. By the age of sixteen only around a half of young people are living with both biological parents, many have experienced the divorce or separation of their parents and significant numbers live with step-parents. 'Fractured' school-to-work transitions are also associated both with previous experiences of disadvantage (either in education, family life or both) and with other transition experiences – such as becoming a teenage parent, leaving home (often for negative reasons such as family disputes), or being involved in crime, drug misuse, and/or the criminal justice system. This involved what governments since 1997 have referred to as 'social exclusion'.

The Emergence of Youth Policy in the UK 1997–2000

Before the first New Labour government in 1997, it could easily be argued that Britain did not have a youth policy. Previous governments took the view that youth-related issues were best dealt with by the great departments of state (education, social security, health, etc.). Some academics had argued passionately for the development of more coherence, illustrating how failure to co-ordinate policy left the different departments pulling in contradictory directions. Education policy had presided over a staggering increase of permanent exclusions from school (450 per cent between 1990 and 1997) and exclusions from school were known to be strongly connected with involvement in youth crime. The withdrawal of benefits for sixteen- to eighteen-year-olds, in 1988, was intended to drive young people into training or post-16 education. Instead an estimated 160,000 young people did nothing instead – another path associated with youth crime, drug misuse and teenage pregnancy – problems for the Home Office and the Department of Health. Youth crime and drop-out were also known to be hugely expensive to the exchequer as well as damaging to young people's welfare.

The chief instigator of youth policy in the early years of the first Blair government was the Social Exclusion Unit (SEU) set up shortly after the election. The Unit, part of the Cabinet Office, fulfilled tasks set for it by the prime minister and reported directly to him. It was used to address issues around 'social exclusion' – recognized as a complex, multifaceted syndrome of disadvantage, the responsibilities for which spanned different government departments. 'Joined-up problems' were increasingly recognized as requiring 'joined-up solutions'. Before the end of the century the SEU had produced five major reports, all on predominantly youth-related issues:

- truancy and school exclusion;
- rough sleeping (including youth homelessness);
- poor neighbourhoods;
- teenage pregnancy; and
- sixteen- to eighteen-year-olds not in education, employment, or training (NEET).

Not all these reports can be described in detail here but the third and fifth reports, in the above list, were to change the landscape of youth policy in England. The third report was on spatial clusters of disadvantage in poor neighbourhoods and the challenges faced by neighbourhood renewal. As the topic was so large and complex, after the report, eighteen Policy Action Teams (PATs) were set up further to develop policy in more detail. PAT 12 focused on Young People. The report pointed out that Britain was alone in Europe in not having a Minister, a Ministry, a parliamentary committee, or indeed any vehicle for cross-ministerial discussion of youth matters. As a consequence there was a mixture of duplication of effort in some communities, and deserts of no provision in others, with projects emanating from eight government departments, six units, and ten other agencies. It produced a radical new vision for better co-ordination of youth policy across government. This involved a Minister for Young People, a Children and Young People's Unit (CYPU) to further develop and co-ordinate policy, and a high powered cross-departmental Ministerial Group. England finally had mechanisms for the co-ordination of youth policy.

The Connexions Strategy in England 2000–2005

The fifth report from the SEU *Bridging the Gap* published in 1999 concerned young people aged sixteen to eighteen who were not in any form of education, employment or training (NEET). The report confirmed that being disengaged at the ages of sixteen and seventeen was a good predictor of later unemployment and also closely linked to educational disaffection and disadvantage prior to the age of sixteen. It was also correlated with an involvement in crime, misuse of drugs, and teenage pregnancy. Other categories of young people which predominated among those who were NEET included care leavers, young carers, young people with mental health problems, and young people with disabilities and special educational needs. So, although responsibilities for NEET fell to the then DfES, many of the issues connected with NEET remained the responsibility of other departments. The SEU report suggested the development of a new multi-professional

Box 55.1 Connexions

The Connexions Service in England aimed to offer a *universal* service to all young people and a *targeted* service offering intensive support to a minority of young people facing complex problems. One of the biggest challenges facing the new service was to provide both through a national network of Personal Advisers (PAs). The Connexions Strategy remit was much broader than that of the old careers services which it absorbed or replaced. It aimed to provide (through sub-regional Connexions Partnership Boards) the co-ordination of support and services across a range of different agencies. This included health agencies (including the drug prevention and advisory service, and teenage pregnancy and motherhood), education (including educational welfare and the youth service as well as schools and colleges), social services (including leaving care teams), youth justice (including the police and youth offending teams), housing departments, and the voluntary sector (including youth homelessness projects). The Connexions Strategy anticipated it would deal with three tiers of need. Most young people would only require information, advice, or guidance on their education and learning, careers, or personal development. Others, at risk of disengaging, needed in-depth support and guidance and help to assess their needs, to develop and support action plans, and to monitor progress. A smaller group needed specialist assessment and support which may require services being 'brokered' from other specialist services. Connexions PAs were also expected to act as 'advocates' for young people, ensuring that appropriate services and benefits were obtained, playing the role of a 'powerful friend' where agencies were failing to comply with their duties and responsibilities.

service to help give guidance, advice and support for young people between the ages of thirteen and nineteen – a Connexions Strategy with, at the heart of that, a new Connexions Service. While Scotland, Wales, and Northern Ireland did not have a Social Exclusion Unit, nor develop a service badged as 'Connexions', similar issues were addressed there, and similar patterns of multi-agency working were developed in those countries too. (See Box 55.1.)

The majority of Connexions PAs, provided careers education and guidance in the same way they had before and schools and colleges saw little change, except perhaps that PAs were spread even more thinly. Each PA providing the universal entitlement may have had up to around 800 young people to serve. PAs addressing more complex need often came from a different professional background, often youth work or work in the voluntary sector. Indeed many retained their original base. Yet other PAs worked within specialist teams working with young offenders, care leavers, or young people with special educational needs or disabilities.

Although the Connexions Strategy was intended to be *the* joined-up strategy for work with young people, in practice, until 2005 'joined-up' patterns of support were also being promoted independently by other government departments and agencies. Two deserve special mention. Addressing the extent, the expense, and the ineffectiveness of responses to youth crime had been on the policy agenda for some time after a critical report by the Audit Commission in 1996 – *Misspent Youth*. In opposition, New Labour spent a great deal of effort planning its proposals for change. The reforms of the youth justice system which followed the 1999 Crime and Disorder Act saw the creation of multi-agency youth offending teams (YOTs) in all local authorities, drawing together police, probation, social services, and others in a concerted attempt to address and reduce youth crime (see Chapter 52).

Young people leaving care (usually at around the age of sixteen before 2001) were hugely over-represented among some 'youth problem' groups. The care system was the subject of a thorough and far reaching review commissioned by the

Conservative government. The new government's response proposed different forms of inspection, quality assurance, and standards of care under a *Quality Protects* initiative. Arrangements for young people leaving care were initially reformed under the *Children (Leaving Care) Act of 2000*. One of the issues being addressed was that, although the majority of young people not in care experienced extended youth transitions and longer periods of family dependency, care leavers were moved to forms of independent living as early as the age of sixteen. This was both unsettling and often resulted in disastrous consequences. Finally a further Green Paper *Care Matters* was published in 2006 leading eventually to the raising of the age at which young people left care.

Everybody Matters (but some more than others)

In September 2003 the government published the Green Paper *Every Child Matters* which was to have immense significance in policy development on Children and Young People. Although it was ostensibly a follow-through of an enquiry into child abuse, it signalled a reconfiguration of the structures of policy at both national, local authority, and community levels. Following the consultation on the Green Paper, the Children Act 2004 also heralded the appointment of a Children's Commissioner for England to act as an independent champion for children. When appointed, the position was used to comment on the conditions and services offered to vulnerable groups such as young asylum seekers, and failures to adequately respond to the needs of children and young people, such as those with mental health problems. The second Minister for Youth (John Denham) had resigned in the run up to the Iraq war. After the war the new minister appointed was given the title of Minister for Children, Young People, and Families, invariably referred to as the Minister for Children, signs that youth issues were becoming marginalized. The 2004 Act further widened the responsibilities of the Minister to deal with youth issues previously dealt with by the DoH (teenage pregnancy, the looked after children system, and family law, but interestingly *not* at the time youth offending).

From 2007–10 all these responsibilities were located within a new Department for Children, Schools, and Families. At a local authority level too the Act required co-ordination of services and responsibilities with local authorities to have a single Director of Children's Services. This new post was accountable for education *and* social services and the integration of all associated activities. This was accomplished through another new body – Children's Trusts combining the local authority and health services and which had charge of the commissioning of Connexions and Youth Offending Teams. At a community level a range of services for children and young people were to be co-located in Sure Start Children's Centres and Full Service Extended Schools.

Given this new constellation of structures for children and young people, it was clear that some reconfiguration of the Connexions Strategy would have to occur. During the summer of 2004 the DfES held three (separate) inquiries which prefaced a Youth Green Paper and these signalled a change in direction. One involved a 'top to bottom' review of careers education and guidance. Many careers companies felt threatened and marginalized by Connexions where the universal service of advice and guidance for the majority of pupils in schools and colleges received less priority than targeted services for those at risk of disengaging. Schools too thought the service they were receiving had declined and, in that they were embracing a wider 'full service' role for the welfare of pupils, thought this was to be extended to information, advice, and guidance too.

The second review concerned a review of 'activities' for young people: 'things to do; places to go' became a mantra which recognized the need to address decades of decline and neglect in youth work. The youth service had been 'transformed' (in theory) by reviews in the late 1990s, but on the ground many youth workers found themselves starved of resources, limping from year to year on short-term contracts and constantly juggling their priorities to meet policy fads and funding opportunities.

Finally, the third review examined services and support for vulnerable young people. This suggested that the bold ambitions of the Connexions Strategy were deemed to be failing. Indeed, no one talked about a Connexions Strategy any more, only a service, and the Minister for Children was on record as suggesting that the days on the Connexions Service may be numbered. Why it was deemed a failure remains a mystery. Most evidence was positive about its achievements especially in supporting vulnerable young people.

Under proposals made initially in the 2005 Green Paper *Youth Matters* local authorities were left to decide whether or not to keep Connexions or their own version of a youth support system. Whatever their choice, local authorities were once again put in control, this time through Children's Trusts who received all government funding for services for children and young people. The old sub-regional Connexions Partnership Boards were abandoned. Careers education and guidance (CEG) was broadened to 'Information, Advice and Guidance' (IAG) with promises of a mixed media service (including new technologies such as the Internet and help-lines), quality standards, and opt-out permissive powers for schools. On targeted support for vulnerable young people, government promised multi-agency working, a Lead Professional, a Common Assessment Framework and new patterns of information sharing – all of which seemed strangely like the abandoned Connexions Strategy. In the event, many local authorities retained some form of a youth support service and addressing NEET was a key performance indicator for them.

Coalition Government, Recession, Austerity, and Back to the Future

In 2010, the new Conservative–Liberal Democrat coalition government was formed with a strong commitment to reduce urgently the deficit in public finances. On its first day, the government replaced the Department for Children, Schools and Families with a new Department of Education, a title not seen since the 1970s. The school building programme, instigated by the previous government (as part of Keynesian economics stimulus measures) was also cut almost immediately. The Audit Commission produced a report which indicated that, between 2002 and 2009 the lifetime, public finance cost of NEET had risen from £8 billion to £13 billion. It argued that much of this could be avoided by investing

in well-targeted youth projects funded by local authorities at a cost of only a few thousand pounds each. Yet, in anticipation of the autumn 2010 spending review, local authorities started to cancel youth project contracts and issued redundancy notices to youth workers. The research for the Audit Commission, however, pointed out, the big multibillion pound costs of NEET accrued to central government through the costs of unemployment and criminal justice. But the government was determined to cut 'waste' (especially Quangos) and ironically this including the Audit Commission itself. 'Necessary savings' seemed the order of the day.

In 2010, university graduates faced an employment market in the midst of recession with rumours there were seventy graduates chasing every single graduate job. Entry to university in 2010 was the toughest on record with more than a hundred thousand well qualified applicants left without places. The government talked up alternative (non-graduate) routes to work, the need for better CEG for would-be undergraduates, and alternative routes into the labour market at the age of eighteen. Yet it cancelled the extension to the Future Jobs Fund (for eighteen- to twenty-four-year-olds) from March 2011 and made only a very modest commitment to apprenticeships. Widespread youth unemployment seemed once again to be the major issue for youth policy. It all seemed like the 1980s coming round again.

Guide to Further Sources

The Audit Commission, *Against the Odds* (London: Audit Commission, 2010) provides a thorough investigation of NEET. Includes separate analyses of the constituent categories, the public finance costs, and what policy initiatives were deemed successful in addressing them. It is also a good example of the interface of biography and social policy, see www.audit-commission.gov.uk/nationalstudies/localgov/againsttheodds/Pages/default.aspx.

A biannual compilation of useful statistics on young people is given in J. Goleman and F. Brookes, *Key Data on Adolescence 2009* (7th edn, Brighton: Trust for the Centre for Adolescence, 2009).

The DfES' Green Paper proposing fundamental reform to youth policy *Youth Matters*. Cm 629 (London: HMSO, 2005) is available online at www.education.gov.uk/publications/standard/publicationDetail/Page1/Cm6629, as is the DfES, *Youth Matters: Next Steps* (London: HMSO, 2005) at www.education.gov.uk/publications/standard/publicationDetail/Page1/DFES-0261-2006. These were key policy documents of the late New Labour years.

A. Furlong and F. Cartmel (2006) *Young People and Social Change* (second edition, Buckingham: Open University Press, 2006 is a rewritten version of a very influential text.

Linked to *Against the Odds* is S. Henderson *et al.*'s *Inventing Adulthoods: A Biographical Approach to Youth Transitions* (London: Sage, 2006) a theoretical 'break-through' exploring the interface between biography and structure – just add in the social policy. A largely conceptual book based upon up-to-date studies is G. Jones, *Youth* (Cambridge: Polity, 2009).

G. Jones and R. Bell's *Youth Policies in the UK*, www.keele.ac.uk/depts/so/youthchron/index.htm, is a web site which provides details of specific policy developments.

A report on a specific study conducted in the north east, but containing excellent reviews of debates around young people, the underclass, and social exclusion can be found in *Disconnected Youth. Growing Up in Britain's Poor Neighbourhoods* (Basingstoke: Palgrave, 2005) by R. MacDonald and J. Marsh.

Review Questions

1 What are the key stages in youth policy development described in the chapter and what are the key features of each stage?
2 What were the main reasons for the development of a more holistic approach to youth policy after 1997?
3 What is meant by 'social exclusion' and what were the main categories of young people thought to be at risk of social exclusion?
4 Why do you think 'NEET' became such a predominant policy concern after 1997?
5 How has youth policy changed since the 2010 election?

Visit the book companion site at www.wiley.com/go/alcock to make use of the resources designed to accompany the textbook. There you will find chapter-specific guides to further resources, including governmental, international, think-tank, pressure groups, and relevant journals sources. You will also find a glossary based on *The Blackwell Dictionary of Social Policy*, help sheets, and case studies, guidance on managing assignments in social policy and career advice.

56

Older People

Kirk Mann and Gabrielle Mastin

Overview

- Demographic changes mean that older people are a major focus of debate within social policy.
- The United Kingdom (along with many countries) is an ageing society with a 'dependency ratio' increasing, due to improved life expectancy and decreasing fertility rates.
- Funding adequate retirement incomes for older people is a major concern that raises fundamental issues regarding the responsibilities of government, employers, and individuals.
- Younger people are likely to have to work longer than their parents' generation. The concept of retirement and what a working life should consist of is being questioned.
- Older people are the largest consumers of health and social care services, and share many needs with disabled people (see Chapter 57).

Context

The focus of this brief overview of policies and issues affecting older people is on current and prospective debates. First, it is important to recognize that older people are not a homogenous group and the experience of ageing varies enor-

mously – people do not reach a certain age and suddenly become 'older persons'. Here we are referring to people over the age of fifty, a definition that is consistent with that used by most academics and governments. We could have taken the State Pension Age (SPA) as our definition but that would overlook the fact that the

The Student's Companion to Social Policy, Fourth Edition. Edited by Pete Alcock, Margaret May, Sharon Wright.
© 2012 John Wiley & Sons, Ltd. Published 2012 by John Wiley & Sons, Ltd.

impacts of ageing affect people differently. The crucial question is how society responds to this.

Older people are major welfare service users in terms of sheer numbers, disparate needs, and resource implications. The success of health and welfare policies in the twentieth century means people are living longer and have higher lifestyle expectations than in the past. In 2006 the Organization for Economic Co-operation and Development (OECD) produced a report whose title claimed to both identify a major social problem and proposed a simple solution 'Live Longer, Work Longer'. In many countries increased longevity has prompted governments to raise the state pension age, to change funding arrangements for health and care services and alter pension rights. An increasing number of older people will need care and support services and a major issue is who will provide and pay for these. It is likely that young people today will have to work longer and save more – than previous generations – before they retire.

Population Change and Older People

Population ageing is a feature of all developed and many developing countries. Although life expectancy has increased for both men and women, and across all social classes, it remains the case that women in general live longer than men and that people living in poverty have the shortest life expectancy. One consequence of this and the fact that women have tended to marry men who are slightly older than them is that there is a clear gender dynamic in older age. After the age of seventy-five the proportion of women to men increases markedly, although it is discernible even from the age of sixty.

Population ageing is not just a consequence of people living longer, although that is a key factor. Fertility rates have fallen in all OECD countries and very steeply in some. This means there are fewer young people in relation to older people and fewer people in the paid labour market but more retired people (see Table 56.1).

In this context the OECD (2006) urged national governments to consider whether 'the dependency ratio', which is the proportion of the population who rely on public welfare in relation to the proportion who are of working age, is sustainable in the near future. Although an ageing population plays a part in the 'dependency ratio' numbers in higher education and the unemployed, among other factors, also influence it. The phrase 'dependency ratio' is viewed by some as negative because it implies older people are a burden. Nevertheless, the evidence of an ageing population is quite clear. In the short to medium term the impact of the 'baby boom' generation (born 1946–54) who are now approaching retirement is seen to be particularly problematic for countries like the United Kingdom that have a 'Pay As You Earn' (PAYE) state-funded pension system. This funds current pensioners from revenues paid by current workers. If the ratio of people in the paid labour market to those on state

Table 56.1 Projected population by age, United Kingdom, 2008–2033 in millions.

Ages	2008	2013	2018	2023	2028	2033
Under 16	11.5	11.7	12.2	12.6	12.7	12.8
Working age[a]	38.1	39.4	40.8	41.8	43.1	43.3
Under 40	19.8	20.1	20.6	20.9	20.9	21.0
40 & over	18.3	19.4	20.3	20.9	22.1	22.3
Nos of SPA[a]	11.8	12.4	12.6	13.4	14.0	15.6
Old age support ratio [b]	3.23	3.19	3.25	3.11	3.07	2.78

Notes:
[a] Working age and pensionable age populations based on state pension age (SPA) for given year.
[b] The ratio of working age to numbers of SPA.
Source: Office for National Statistics 2009: 3. Contains public sector information licensed under the Open Government Licence v1.0.

pensions falls, as predicted, then taxes and National Insurance (NI) contributions could increase.

Older People and the Labour Market

Since the Old Age Pension Act 1908 there has been an expectation that most people will exit paid labour at SPA. Many employers supported a SPA because it enabled them to shed older workers and many employees embraced the idea of 'enjoying their retirement'. Recently, however, many governments, including the United Kingdom's, have scrapped a set retirement age. Other countries have raised the SPA (in France in 2010 there were demonstrations against raising this to sixty-two) and in the United Kingdom it will be sixty-six for both men and women by 2020 and sixty-eight by 2046, although this process could be accelerated.

Older workers are also being encouraged to stay in paid work with financial incentives (e.g. higher state pensions and tax allowances for those who work beyond SPA), and more flexible attitudes to part-time work after SPA. The New Deal 50+ was introduced to help older workers get back into the paid labour market and to develop some of their basic skills. This initiative came in just before the financial crisis of 2007 and with unemployment rising and the prospect of spending cuts it is unlikely to have done much to increase the employment rate of older workers. It will be important to monitor the labour force participation rate of older workers as it may indicate whether age discrimination in the labour market is occurring irrespective of the legislation and government policy.

Despite the recent emphasis on encouraging employment for older people, many are still excluded from the labour market when they reach a certain age. Whether or not this is viewed as a form of age discrimination is a moot point. In 2006 the Equal Employment (Age) Regulations came into force in the United Kingdom (many other countries have had similar legislation for many years), which made age discrimination in employment unlawful. These regulations outlawed age discrimination in recruitment, dismissal, and workplace opportunities and granted

employees the 'right to request' work beyond retirement age, but employers can refuse such requests without giving a reason. These regulations are important but it remains to be seen whether they tackle ageism in the workplace in more testing times.

The motives of those seeking to increase the labour force participation of older workers are varied. Addressing economic concerns, such as the 'dependency ratio' and fears of labour shortages (prior to 2007), are clearly factors. Others point to the benefits of remaining in work for older people in terms of their income and general well-being. Some sociologists have suggested that the very idea of a fixed age of retirement produces a ghetto for older people that is a legacy of mid-twentieth century thinking. The shift in policy-making circles over the past twenty years or so has generally been toward greater conditionality and fewer citizenship rights and in this context that means that a fixed SPA and existing pension rights are being eroded.

In contrast many older people have strong feelings about their right to a decent retirement income and a period in their lives when they can escape from paid work. Some employers feel restrained by age discrimination legislation believing that younger workers are more efficient, cheaper, or more competent with new skills and technologies. Some sociologists suggest that attempts at tying older people to paid work are a feature of mid-twentieth century modernist thinking and out of step with a more consumerist and leisure focused society. There have also been claims that we should see the young old (fifty to seventy) and those who enjoy being free of responsibilities for dependents and of paid work as part of a 'third age' era of learning, leisure, and relative good health.

Older People and Retirement Incomes

Retirement income in most OECD countries usually consists of at least two types of pension; state funded and occupationally related. In the United Kingdom, the Basic State Pension (BSP) is paid to everyone who has made the required number of NI contributions. It is often described as a universal benefit but because some people have not paid the full NI contributions (often women who have had care responsibilities or people who have been unable to work for long periods of time) not everyone over SPA gets the full amount. The state safety net is meant to be the Pension Credit, which is higher than the BSP and is means tested. However, around one-third of pensioners who are entitled do not claim it and about 40 per cent of pensioners entitled to Council Tax Benefit do not claim that either. Consequently, despite some progress, pensioner poverty continues to be a major policy issue with 1.8 million pensioners still below the poverty line and certain groups – for example older pensioners, those living alone, women and ethnic minority households – at greater risk of low income.

Occupational pensions have traditionally been Defined Benefit (DB) or Final Salary schemes with the pension based on former earnings and time served in the scheme. These have been a key factor in the increased income of many pensioner households. However, in the private sector many employers have recently closed their DB schemes or made them far less generous, offering instead access to Defined Contribution (DC) schemes. These rely on the contributions made by employer and employee and on stock market performance to generate a pension fund. The financial crisis since 2007 has hit individuals with a DC fund hard and some will have had to revise their retirement plans. In the public sector controlling the costs of DB schemes is likely to heighten tensions between trade unions seeking to protect their pension rights and employers wanting to reduce liabilities. (See also Chapter 32.)

Between 2012 and 2017 a new Personal Accounts employer based (DC) pension is being introduced in Great Britain. Effectively all employees between the age of twenty-two and SPA will be automatically enrolled unless they opt out or their employer offers a better scheme. This is intended to promote private pension saving among mid- to low-income earners and will do nothing to assist older people in the short to medium term. There is also some doubt whether the low contribution rates will provide a sufficient fund in the longer term for those in lower income brackets.

What stands out regarding future retirement income in the United Kingdom (but also in other countries) is a shift away from pension rights that the state and employers guarantee towards individual responsibility. How capable individuals or indeed finance markets and pension fund managers are in assessing the risks associated with pension saving is a crucial question, one that we will be unable to answer for many years.

Older People and Social Care

The great majority of older people (fifty plus) do not need care services and many provide care for partners and grandchildren. Social care for older people covers a range of services including day care centres, residential care homes, meals, and domiciliary services. These can be provided directly by local authorities or facilitated by them through direct (cash) payments and delivered by voluntary and private (for profit) organizations. Unlike the National Health Service (NHS) which provides services for all free at the point of use, social care services are subject to formal assessments. In England, an individual's 'risk to independence' is categorized against a system known as FACS (Fair Access to Care Services), and is financially assessed through means and assets tests which limit free access to services. Scotland uses a similar system and since 2006 introduced a national tool known as SSA IoRN (Single Shared Assessment – Indicator of Relative Need) to group older people's needs from low to high. The social care system in Scotland, unlike the rest of the United Kingdom, changed in 2002 through employing a system of free personal domiciliary care for older people, and offering local social work authorities various discretions to abate or waive other social care charges.

Since 2002, the whole of the United Kingdom has supported free nursing care for older people in care homes, however the associated costs of social care remains a very real and emotive concern. For home owners on a modest pension this can mean borrowing against the capital in their home or in some circumstances having to sell it. This has been, and will remain, an emotive issue. Interestingly, all three main political parties in the United Kingdom promised (in 2010) to end the practice of forcing elderly people to sell their homes to pay for care. For those without assets or resources social care services are an essential 'safety-net' measure. Exactly how the state and the individual should address the care needs of elderly, often frail, people is one of the major social policy issues of the next few years. As older people are the largest consumers of health and social care, the combined and escalating costs of state pensions, health, and social care have encouraged some policy commentators to talk of the 'burden of ageing'. Others, however, have countered this view in light of longer and healthier lives being a positive achievement due in part to social policies in the previous century.

Nevertheless the negative idea of a 'burden of ageing' has driven policy in the past and may do so again in the near future. The 1990 NHS and Community Care Act could be seen as an early indicator that the negative language was suppressing the positive. This Act sought to bring about change by introducing competition through market forces, which it was thought would drive costs down while giving service users more 'choice'. Subsequently, there has been an emphasis on 'personalized' services and non-institutional care. The role of the NHS as a provider of long-term care has decreased, with social care services increasingly taking its place with a commensurate emphasis on self-care, prevention, and low cost interventions by family and friends.

It is likely that the structure of social care delivery will change once again within the next five years. In England, options are being reviewed and one suggestion is that all older people with a care need above a particular threshold should receive some public funding for their needs, with a means-tested sliding scale that would ensure the poorest had their full costs met and even the richest getting something towards their care costs. To fund this there are proposals for voluntary or compulsory insurance schemes but concern has been expressed that the cost of care services are rising steeply, at a time when local authorities are under pressure to reduce expenditure and raise revenues. (See too Chapter 51.)

Many of the care needs of older people are the same as those of disabled people, for example the desire for independent living and control over service outcomes, but the delivery differs markedly (see Chapter 57). Whereas (working-aged) disabled people are now receiving record amounts of Direct Payments (cash payments in lieu of social care services), these, most notably home care, are significantly under-claimed by older people. There is also evidence of a degree of age discrimination in the types of benefits available to older people. For example, Disability Living Allowance is only available to first time claimants aged under 65 whereas the equivalent for older people – Attendance Allowance – is paid at a lower rate and is less flexible.

The issue of age discrimination within health and social care services was highlighted by the 'Older Person's National Service Framework' (DoH 2001). This identified service 'standards' and the need to 'root out age discrimination' in both access to, and quality of, services. Subsequently the publication of 'Opportunity Age' (DWP 2005) established some laudable aspirations for meeting the needs of an ageing population. In some respects these are restating the objectives set by the NHS in terms of offering patients treatment on the basis of clinical need irrespective of age. It is unlikely that any government in the near future would publicly renege on this objective but how the service needs and costs of an ageing society will be addressed by the 'Big Society', in an era of public spending cuts, will be a major question in the next few years.

The tendency to associate older people with illness, decline, and institutionalized care has been challenged and there are now more active models, encouraging independent living, choice, and community care. If services are to respond to the needs of older people they will have to pay close attention to what users want and they are unlikely to all want the same.

Emerging Issues

In this chapter we have outlined some recent key policy issues and developments. Currently these are being debated by policy-makers in many countries. Defining how long a working (and caring) life might be and whether there should even be a set retirement age is one key issue.

Central to how we address many of the challenges that an ageing society poses will be a concern with collective rights and individual responsibilities. In the areas of retirement saving and social and health care needs, this question of rights and responsibilities will continue to be hotly contested. Governments are emphasizing individual responsibility for needs that will arise for most people many years ahead. However, long-term planning and saving is frustrated by immediate needs (e.g. mortgage/rent, children etc) and inadequate income. We have also identified the possibility of tensions in what governments say they want older people to do and the realities older people confront in the paid labour market and in seeking social care. Age discrimination may be unlawful but like other forms of discrimination it may persist with employers, service providers, and ageist social attitudes excluding older people by more subtle means. The unemployment and labour force participation rates of older people in a period of economic difficulty will be important indicators.

Pensions and pensioner poverty will continue to be major social policy challenges. Means and asset testing and cuts in welfare expenditure and services will be felt hardest by the poorest. Simultaneously as employers reduce entitlements many older people will approach retirement with a lower occupational pension than today's retirees. While the tax subsidies to top earners (those in the 40 per cent band) persist, they are likely to continue to use pension saving as a tax avoidance mechanism and can look forward to much higher retirement incomes. The prospect of wider social divisions between older people is very real.

Diversity will increasingly be a feature of the older population and that will provide additional challenges to systems that have tended to regard older people as a homogenous social group. The personalization of services offers a way of addressing diversity but may also undermine a rights based approach by market driven 'choices' that individualize older people.

Guide to Further Sources

Readings for ageing, care, and income support tend to deal with each of these separately. Consequently we have identified some of the texts that are accessible in each of the areas. A good book for students interested in ageing and social care generally, offering a good introduction to both social policy and social work students is K. Crawford and J. Walker, *Social Work with Older People* (2nd edn, Exeter: Learning Matters, 2008). A good comparative study of ageing is provided

by V. Timonen, *Ageing Societies: A Comparative Introduction* (Buckingham: Open University Press, 2008). For a comprehensive review of pension provisions see M. Hill. *Pensions* (Bristol: Policy Press, 2007). Whereas J. Vincent, *Old Age* (London: Routledge, 2003) provides a sound overview of the key themes and issues relating to ageing.

To check your current SPA go to the Direct Gov web site at http://pensions.direct.gov.uk/en/state-pension-age-calculator/home.asp.

Other government publications are: Office for National Statistics, *National Population Projections* (published online, 2009 at www.statistics.gov.uk/cci/nugget.asp?id=1352); OECD, *Live Longer, Work Longer* (online, OECD, 2006 at www.oecd.org/dataoecd/54/47/35961390.pdf); Department of Health, *Older Person's National Service Framework* (online, 2001 at www.dh.gov.uk/en/Publicationsandstatistics/Publications/PublicationsPolicyAndGuidance/DH_4003066); and Department of Work and Pensions, *Opportunity Age* (online 2005 at www.dwp.gov.uk/docs/opportunity-age-volume1.pdf).

Review Questions

1   What are the key factors that contribute to an ageing society and should we be concerned or celebrate these?
2   If people are living longer should we expect them to work longer?
3   How should we pay for pensions? Should it be a matter for individuals, employers and/or the state?
4   Should older people be able to decide how their care needs are met?
5   If older people have a good pension and assets should they use these to pay for their care needs?

Visit the book companion site at www.wiley.com/go/alcock to make use of the resources designed to accompany the textbook. There you will find chapter-specific guides to further resources, including governmental, international, think-tank, pressure groups, and relevant journals sources. You will also find a glossary based on *The Blackwell Dictionary of Social Policy*, help sheets, and case studies, guidance on managing assignments in social policy and career advice.

57

Disability

Mark Priestley

Overview

- There has been growing interest and development in disability policy since the 1970s.
- Disability is more and more seen as an issue of human rights, citizenship, and equality rather than one of care and rehabilitation.
- The claims and voices of the disabled people's movement have been instrumental in bringing about this change.
- Disabled people have become more active welfare consumers, taking control of resources to manage the support they need in place of traditional services.
- More countries have introduced policies to counter disability discrimination, based on civil and human rights, but legislation is not enough to guarantee full citizenship.
- Transnational governance has become more important through institutions like the European Union and the United Nations.

Context

Disability became increasingly prominent in policy debates during the second half of the twentieth century, both in the United Kingdom and globally, culminating with agreement in 2006 on a United Nations Convention to protect the rights of disabled people throughout the world. The rising prominence of disability has been characterized by three significant themes. First, there has been a dramatic shift in policy thinking. Where 'disability' was once seen as a deficiency within the person it is now more likely to be viewed as a form of discrimination arising from deficiencies

The Student's Companion to Social Policy, Fourth Edition. Edited by Pete Alcock, Margaret May, Sharon Wright.
© 2012 John Wiley & Sons, Ltd. Published 2012 by John Wiley & Sons, Ltd.

in society. Second, there has been a corresponding move from policies for care and compensation towards policies to ensure equal rights and the removal of barriers to social inclusion. Third, and underpinning these developments, there has been a groundswell of self-organization among disabled people themselves, leading to greater representation in policy claims and greater involvement in the production of welfare.

Taking the first of these themes, most contemporary debates begin from a distinction between different models of disability, or different ways of thinking about the needs of disabled people. Traditional policy approaches often treated disability as an individual problem caused by physical, sensory, or cognitive impairment. The solution was either to treat the person (through improved medical and rehabilitation services) or to compensate them for their 'limitations' (by arranging less valued social roles, such as sheltered employment, residential care, social security payments, and so on). Thus, both the assumed cause of the problem and the policy response focused on the individual. The alternative approach, usually termed the 'social model of disability' sees the disadvantage experienced by disabled people as caused by limitations in society. As Oliver (1996: 33) puts it,

> disability, according to the social model, is all the things that impose restrictions on disabled people; ranging from individual prejudice to institutional discrimination, from inaccessible buildings to unusable transport systems, from segregated education to excluding work arrangements, and so on. Further, the consequences of this failure do not simply and randomly fall on individuals but systematically upon disabled people as a group who experience this failure as discrimination institutionalized throughout society.

Until the 1990s, this kind of thinking remained a fringe concern in policy-making – strongly advocated by disability activists (nationally and internationally) but at the margins of the policy community. Nowadays, the 'social model' and human rights are often referred to by policymakers at national and international level. However, disability continues to raise a number of very challenging and controversial policy debates.

The Historical Context: Disability as an Administrative Category

Some understanding of history is essential in grasping the relationship between disabled people, social policy, and the state. Today, in the United Kingdom and other developed economies, almost all aspects of disabled people's lives are subject to some kind of distinctive public policy (for example, there are specific policies concerning disabled people's education, health, housing, transport, employment, welfare benefits, family life, and civil rights). Yet, prior to the emergence of the welfare state, people with significant impairments remained largely undifferentiated from the greater mass of 'the poor'. A key point then is to understand why disabled people exist as a separate category for policymakers at all.

Within critical disability studies, social model theorists evoked a broadly materialist account of British history to show how the growth of urban industrial capitalism created disability as a welfare 'problem' for the state. These arguments suggest that the emergence of competitive wage labour markets and factory production methods excluded many people with impairments from paid work and consigned increasing numbers to lives of poverty and economic dependency. As other policy historians have shown, the state's role in facilitating early industrial capitalism involved vigorous social measures to control the labour force and to remove incentives for idleness among the mass of the population. In this context, a key development for disabled people was the distinction made between the 'impotent' and the 'able-bodied' poor (or the 'deserving' and 'undeserving'). While the idle poor were rigorously disciplined those deemed 'unable to work' were identified for the provision of limited welfare. The earliest English definitions of those 'not able to work' made no mention people with impairments but by the time of the first Poor Law, in 1601, it was already clear that a new category of disabled people was emerging – and that *inability to work* would become the key to deciding who was, and who was not, 'disabled'.

Policing this distinction, and thereby entitlement to public assistance, required a whole new system of surveillance, regulation, and control, which brought responsibility for disabled people's welfare from the private into the public domain. It is not necessary to chart this history in detail here and some of the key reading at the end of the chapter provides excellent overviews (for a British history, see Borsay 2005). Stone (1984) shows how disability functioned as an important administrative category in the control of labour and in access to public welfare. In particular, she highlights the policy challenges in providing any fixed definition of who disabled people really are. A key problem here is that the kind of disability definitions developed in countries like the United Kingdom, Germany, or the United States have been interpreted differently over time.

A useful example is to consider why large numbers of disabled people considered 'unable to work' during times of high unemployment (like the 1930s) were quickly drafted into the labour force at times of greater need (for example, in munitions factories during the Second World War). Similar patterns are evident if we look at those deemed 'unable to work', and claiming disability benefits, in the lean times of the late 1970s and early 1980s who were then targeted in vigorous back-to-work policies under New Labour after 1997 and in the austerity measures introduced by the coalition government from 2010. Thus, it is important to see disability as a flexible policy category, determined more by economic and political circumstances than by biology.

Policy Claims: The Disabled People's Movement

Although state responses to the needs of disabled people have been driven by economic and political forces they have also been shaped by the policy claims of disabled people themselves. Such claims and protests have a long history but the modern disabled people's movement emerged from the growing political consciousness of the late 1960s and 1970s. Since the early 1980s disability activists have organized globally under the umbrella of Disabled Peoples' International (with national and regional assemblies representing 135 countries) and in Europe via the European Disability Forum.

The development of disabled people's organizations in the United States, the United Kingdom and parts of mainland Europe has been well documented in the disability studies literature (see Campbell and Oliver's 1996 book for some fascinating insights into developments in Britain). Initiative like the 'European Year of Disabled People', in 2003, and the African and Asia-Pacific 'Decades of Disabled People' provided opportunities for self-advocacy and awareness raising that impacted regional policy-making.

The claims of disabled people's organizations have influenced both the content of policies and the processes of policy-making. Four underlying principles are worthy of note. First, there has been strong advocacy for the principle of 'nothing about us without us' (see Charlton 1998) to ensure that disabled people have a voice in policy discussions that affect them. Where such debates were once dominated by medical and rehabilitation professionals, or welfare charities, it is now rare to find disability policy forums that do not involve disabled people as significant actors. Second, there have been demands to focus policy investments on creating greater accessibility (for example, in the built environment, transport, or information technologies). Third, there has been strong advocacy for non-discrimination laws based on equality and human rights. Most countries now have such laws in place (like the disability provisions of the Equality Act in Britain), supported by similar provisions in the Treaty on the functioning of the Europe Union and by the United Nations Convention on the Rights of Persons with Disabilities. Finally, there have been claims to the greater involvement of disabled people in producing their own welfare solutions, resulting in policy changes towards greater choice and control in everyday life. The latter two themes merit some further discussion.

Independent Living: New Modes of Welfare Production

The concept of independent living has been a prominent theme in disabled people's policy claims. The key struggles have aimed at freeing disabled people from oppressive long-term residential institutions and developing new mechanisms to support community living. In Britain, as in many other countries, there have been significant closures of traditional institutions and the widespread implementation of 'community care' since the 1990s. The movement for independent living has been a key voice, challenging traditional models of 'care' and offering alternatives to support disabled people in practical ways. Here, the key aim has been to place more resources in the hands of disabled people themselves to organize and purchase their own support for daily living rather than relying on predefined 'services' (for example, by employing personal assistants to help with everyday tasks and activities rather than attending a day centre or receiving home help and social services). Early independent living projects in Britain, Scandinavia, and the United States were often run and controlled by disabled people themselves and provided new ways of thinking about welfare – blurring the traditional boundaries between purchasers, providers and consumers (see Barnes and Mercer 2005).

The success of such schemes, in offering disabled people more choice and control, gave rise to the emergence of new policies for 'direct payments' from 1996 and 'personal budgets', allowing people to arrange and purchase their own support in place of the services they might be otherwise entitled to. Direct payments have brought new opportunities for self-determination and independent living and have found favour in British government strategy. Take-up still varies greatly in different parts of the country but has increased and there are ambitious expectations within government that individualized budgets can become the mechanism of choice for people who want support to live independently. This, in combination with radical public sector spending cuts since 2010, raises considerable questions about the future of traditional 'services' and the viability of some public services and institutions.

Non-discrimination: Policies for Civil Rights

As highlighted earlier, the rapid development of civil rights and anti-discrimination legislation has been a key feature of policy development, although different countries have taken different approaches. While non-discrimination legislation was secured in the United States in 1990 (via the Americans with Disabilities Act) there was resistance to similar policies in Britain, especially

from those concerned that providing equal rights for disabled people might impose unbearable costs on employers and service providers and thereby undermine national economic competitiveness. However, there was also mounting evidence that disabled people experienced discrimination institutionalized throughout society and, in 1995, a Disability Discrimination Act was passed.

From the outset it became illegal for employers to discriminate against disabled employees or for service providers to treat disabled customers less favourably but only insofar as this might be seen as 'reasonable' or 'justified' (see, Lawson 2008). Over time, the legislation was strengthened and extended to cover discrimination in education, business premises, and transport. In 2006, a more general equality duty was placed on public authorities, mirroring policies to tackle institutional racism and gender inequalities. All public bodies (like government departments, local authorities, hospitals, schools and colleges, etc.) have a duty to promote positive attitudes and equality and to eliminate disability discrimination.

The mere presence of anti-discrimination legislation has little impact without enforcement. In Britain, this began with a Disability Rights Commission (DRC), established in 2000, as an independent body to promote disability equality in England, Scotland, and Wales (in Northern Ireland a single body covered disability equality and other dimensions of discrimination, such as racism and gender equality). The 2006 Equality Act paved the way for the abolition of the DRC and its incorporation within a general Commission for Equality and Human Rights. The 2010 Equality Act then consolidated non-discrimination legislation across all areas. In 2009, the UK government ratified the UN Convention on the Rights of Persons with Disabilities and its Optional Protocol, requiring the maintenance of independent mechanisms of monitoring and appeal.

The legalistic rights-based approach to policy shares much in common with the social model of disability discussed earlier but, on its own, it offers a less radical strategy. The social model (as defined by its early authors) focused on the structural basis for disabled people's oppression, arising from the social relations of production and reproduction in modern capitalist societies. The implication was that real change could not be achieved without political struggle to challenge the infrastructure of disabling societies and institutions. By contrast, the campaign for legal rights drew more on a 'minority group approach' that emphasized claims within existing legal frameworks and constitutional law. Both social model and rights-based approaches recognize disability as a human rights issue but a social model interpretation suggests that disability requires more far reaching structural change to solve the problems that disabled people face.

Globalization and Governance: United Nations and European Union Influences

There are at least half a billion disabled people in the world – one in ten of the population – and this number is set to rise dramatically. Although the issues in rich technological countries, with developed welfare provision, are often different from those in poorer countries, disabled people remain among the poorest of the poor throughout the world. Access to resources is highly gendered, and the needs of disabled women and girls merit specific attention. Generational issues are also important and reduced life chances for disabled children and disabled elders are evident. Global problems demand global responses and the increasing significance of transnational policy-making is particularly evident in the European Union and the United Nations.

It was in 1975 that the UN made its first Declaration on the Rights of Disabled Persons and 1981 was proclaimed International Year of Disabled Persons. In 1985, the Universal Declaration of Human Rights was extended to include disabled people and work began on a longer-term strategy under the slogan 'towards a society for all'. The adoption in 1993 of international Rules on the Equalization of Opportunities for Disabled Persons led more and more states to introduce anti-discriminatory legislation and, eventually, to agree a more binding and comprehensive human rights Convention on the Rights of Persons with Disabilities in 1996.

At the EU level, there was little early evidence of critical debates, although the mid-1970s saw some limited action programmes on vocational and social integration and a review of national policies. By the early 1980s there were signs of a broader socio-economic understanding (including acknowledgement that disabled people are among those most adversely affected by the economic cycle of a capitalist free market). The development of EU policy in the 1990s was then marked by the emergence of a legal rights-based approach, focused initially on employment rights. After pressure from disability organizations, disabled people were made 'visible' as European citizens in the Amsterdam Treaty of 1997 (now recognized in Article 19 of the Treaty on the functioning of the European Union). While EU policy has tended to focus more on market regulation than redistribution attention has shifted towards the social model agenda and structural investment in the creation of barrier-free environments. The European Disability Strategy 2010–2020 takes a broad approach and articulates its key principles in terms of accessibility, participation, and equality (with policy action across a range of fields such as employment, education and training, social protection, and access to health).

Emerging Issues

Enactment of the UN Convention, from 2008, has raised expectations and placed new responsibilities on states to ensure greater participation and equality of disabled people in society. There has been much goodwill from governments but major questions about the policy implications remain. The claims of the disabled people's movement have been fundamental to changing the way we think about disability policy. Yet, despite the successes, or perhaps because of them, there are uncertainties about the future. As disability is mainstreamed within the single equality agenda there may be fewer 'places at the table' for disabled people in the policy-making process. While there are genuine public commitments to the human and social rights of disabled people, their realization is threatened by economic challenges. In resource-poor countries the enormity of needs for poverty reduction and human development means that disabled people are often overlooked in policy investments. In richer welfare states there have also been intense financial pressures arising from economic downturn and financial crisis.

Governments in European welfare states have become concerned about the number of people out of work and claiming disability benefits (e.g. with around 2.6 million people on incapacity benefits in Britain in 2010) and sought to 'help' them into work through policy change. Following the election of a Centre–Right coalition government in 2010, and implementation of its Comprehensive Spending Review, there have been significant changes. The personalization agenda in health and social care, including personal budgets, continues but austerity cuts have targeted disability benefits in particular, and reduced some benefit payments. Public sector cuts, particularly in local government, have impacted on the availability of many services used by disabled people. There has been a limiting of eligibility to out of work disability benefits with the introduction of tighter medical and 'work capability' testing. The aim is clearly to reduce the number of people receiving disability benefits while being seen to offer some support for those judged more 'severely' disabled (reinforcing the arguments made at the outset about the 'flexible' nature of disability as a policy category in changing economic conditions).

Guide to Further Sources

For historical discussion of disability policy in modern welfare states, it would be useful to look at both D. Stone, *The Disabled State* (Philadelphia, PN: Temple University Press, 1984) and A. Borsay, *Disability and Social Policy in Britain since 1750: A History of Exclusion* (Basingstoke: Palgrave Macmillan, 2005). The former is helpful in understanding the relationship between disabled people, welfare and the state while the latter provides an itemized history of policy development in Britain. A. Lawson *Disability and Equality Law in Britain: The Role of Reasonable Adjustment* (Oxford: Hart Publishing, 2008) provides an excellent analysis of the principles behind non-discrimination policies. S. Shah and M. Priestley, *Disability and Social Change: Private Lives and Public Policies* (Bristol: Policy Press, 2011) examine key policy changes in Britain since the establishment of the modern welfare through the lived experience of disabled people.

D. Mabbett, 'The development of rights-based social policy in the European Union: The example of disability rights', *Journal of Common Market Studies*, 43/1 (2005): 97–120, shows how disability emerged in European policy-making. The following three books all provide important insights into the emergence of disabled people's self-organization and the development of user-led policy alternatives to support independent living: J. Charlton, *Nothing About Us Without Us: Disability Oppression and Empowerment* (Berkeley, MA: University of California Press, 1998); J. Campbell and M. Oliver, *Disability Politics: Understanding Our Past, Changing Our Future* (London: Routledge, 1996); C. Barnes and G. Mercer, *Independent Futures: Creating User-led Disability Services in a Disabling Society* (Bristol: Policy Press, 2005) all provide important insights into the emergence of disabled people's self-organization and the development of user-led policy alternatives to support independent living.

M. Oliver, *Understanding Disability: From Theory to Practice* (Basingstoke: Palgrave Macmillan, 1996) is useful as an introduction to different models of disability and their connection to theory and policy. The book also provides useful pointers to some of the influential ideas and writings that influenced policy change.

The academic journal *Disability & Society* and *The Yearbook of European Disability Law* are excellent sources. Online, the Disability Archive UK provides free access to several hundred papers by disability activists and researchers at www.leeds.ac.uk/disability-studies, and the ANED web site provides reports on disability policies throughout Europe at www.disability-europe.net. In the United Kingdom, current policy details are available on the Direct Gov web site www.direct.gov.uk/en/DisabledPeople/, and the government Office for Disability Issues also publishes useful information and key equality indicators at www.officefordisability.gov.uk/.

Review Questions

1   What is the difference between 'individual' and 'social' models of disability and what are the implications for social policies?

2 How convincing is the argument that 'disability' and 'disabled people' are flexible or fluid administrative categories that change in response to market conditions?

3 How are disabled people and their organizations represented in the policy process and how influential have their voices been?

4 What combination of regulatory and redistributive policies is most likely to deliver equality and full participation for disabled people?

5 To what extent are national disability policies now influenced by compliance with European and global governance?

Visit the book companion site at www.wiley.com/go/alcock to make use of the resources designed to accompany the textbook. There you will find chapter-specific guides to further resources, including governmental, international, think-tank, pressure groups, and relevant journals sources. You will also find a glossary based on *The Blackwell Dictionary of Social Policy*, help sheets, and case studies, guidance on managing assignments in social policy and career advice.

58

Migrants and Asylum Seekers

Alice Bloch

Overview

- Britain has a long history of migration and ethnic diversity.
- People migrate for economic, social, and familial reasons and/or to escape persecution, human rights abuses, war, and conflict.
- Immigration and asylum policy has been concerned with curbing immigration and is racialized.
- The links between immigration and social welfare became established as early as 1905 and are still interconnected.
- Immigration and asylum policy has resulted in a hierarchy of rights where some groups are included while others have been increasingly excluded from society.

Context

The term migrant is used to describe both internal and international migrants. Internal migrants move within the borders of a state while international migrants cross international borders. This chapter focuses on international migration and social policy responses to migration and migrants. Though migration is often portrayed as a relatively recent phenomenon, Britain has a long history of migration and of ethnic diversity. Due to limitations in transportation technologies, early migration tended to be from other European countries, although as early as the sixteenth century, Africans were brought to Britain as slaves. Some migrants came to Britain for economic reasons, some, like the French Huguenots, came as a consequence of religious persecution while others came to Britain to join family members. During the nineteenth century, most migration to Britain continued to be from Europe. Migrants from Ireland formed the largest

The Student's Companion to Social Policy, Fourth Edition. Edited by Pete Alcock, Margaret May, Sharon Wright.
© 2012 John Wiley & Sons, Ltd. Published 2012 by John Wiley & Sons, Ltd.

minority group with migration from Ireland growing rapidly during the potato famine in the mid-nineteenth century. Britain attracted migrants because it was the first industrial country and the growing economy provided economic opportunities. By the start of the twentieth century, there were small numbers of Chinese, African, Indian, and Caribbean migrants who had come as students, seafarers, performers, and business people, as well as a diverse European migrant population with the greatest numbers coming from Ireland, Germany, Poland, and Russia. There was also emigration from Britain triggered by industrialization and empire. People emigrated to America in the nineteenth century (1800–60) and Canada in the later in the same century. Throughout the nineteenth and into the latter part of the twentieth century Britons moved to Australia and New Zealand as part of colonial settlement. There was also emigration to other countries of the British Empire including India and Kenya.

A greater diversity of origin among migrants really began after the Second World War with migrants from colonial and commonwealth countries coming to Britain for employment and then family reunion. Contemporary migration is a global phenomenon facilitated by globalization and improvements in transportation technologies. Global inequalities, the needs of the global economy, changing family structures including transnational families, war, conflict, and human rights abuses all contribute to migration. The consequence has been increasing numbers of global migrants and greater ethnic diversity in countries of migrant settlement; Britain is no exception to this global trend. In Britain most migrant workers settle in large towns and cities including London, Birmingham, Glasgow, and Edinburgh and work in the service sector, construction, administration and food processing, though some migrants live in rural areas and work in agriculture. There is a particular demand for migrant labour in rural areas of Scotland, to compensate for the declining population.

Exploring the relationship between migration and social policy is complex because the interaction between changing patterns of migration and social policy responses creates a rapidly changing policy environment. In the United Kingdom there have been eight immigration acts since 1993

and traditional migrant entry routes such as targeted labour market gaps, seeking asylum, and family reunion have been severely constrained by policies of deterrence and restrictionism. Migration and migrants have become increasingly problematized as a challenge to the idea of national identity, social cohesion, and security in public and official discourse. This chapter will define key terms relating to migration and asylum, will explain the main reasons why people migrate, and then consider the way in which responses to migration including immigration controls and welfare provision, have shifted in response to different patterns of migration and cohorts of migrants. The chapter will conclude by identifying emerging issues in the social policy of migration and asylum.

Definitions

The term migrant is often used generically but for social policy analysis it is important to understand who migrants are and the differing categories they fall into, because this is linked to a set of legal and welfare rights entitlements. The term immigrant is used from the perspective of the receiving country to describe someone who is free to enter, work, and settle in a country without any restrictions. Until 1962 British subjects, who were citizens of the United Kingdom and its colonies and those who were Commonwealth citizens such as people from the Indian sub-continent and the Caribbean, could enter and settle in the United Kingdom without restrictions. Free entry and settlement in the United Kingdom is extended to citizens from countries in the European Union with the exception of Romanian and Bulgarian nationals who are free to enter Britain but are restricted in terms of employment and are not entitled to settle permanently.

There is also a category of temporary migrants, and this includes people on temporary work schemes and student visas. Under these schemes entry and/or permission to stay in the United Kingdom is dependent on obtaining a visa. Temporary migrants often face restrictions to the type of employment they can occupy and restricted access to social services and benefits including social security and housing provision.

From the late 1980s, refugees and asylum seekers attracted the most political, public and policy attention though more recently undocumented or irregular migrants have been high on the agenda. Britain has a long history of granting refuge to those experiencing persecution and is a signatory to the 1951 United Nations Convention on the Status of the Refugee (Geneva Convention). Under the 1951 Convention, a *refugee* is defined as someone who, 'owing to a well-founded fear of being persecuted for reasons of race, religion, nationality, membership of a particular social group or political opinion, is outside the country of his nationality and is unable, or owing to such a fear is unwilling to avail himself of the protection of that country'. In the United Kingdom people can arrive as programme refugees meaning they have refugee status on arrival or they can come to the United Kingdom and seek asylum. An asylum seeker is someone who has applied for refugee status in the United Kingdom and is waiting for a Home Office decision on their case.

Refugees have the same rights to welfare, employment, and family reunion as United Kingdom citizens and until August 2005 were given indefinite leave to remain. However, since September 2005 refugees have been granted leave to remain for just five years which will have longer term consequences for settlement as temporary leave to remain leaves people insecure and that impedes settlement and integration. Asylum seekers have very few rights and entitlements, are not legally entitled to work, and are excluded from mainstream social security. Destitute asylum seekers are offered housing, on a no choice basis regardless of their existing social networks and community structures, in five regions around the United Kingdom: North West, Midlands, North East, Wales, and Scotland.

In addition to those with recognized statuses, some people enter the United Kingdom clandestinely as undocumented migrants or become undocumented (or irregular) by for example, not leaving the country once their visa has expired or when their asylum case is rejected. Controlling or managing migration is one of the main concerns of successive UK governments and now only a minority can enter and settle in the United Kingdom without restrictions.

Why Do People Migrate?

Employment and economic opportunities are two of the key factors influencing any decision to migrate. In the period following the Second World War Britain experienced labour shortages and so migrant workers were actively recruited from Ireland, the Caribbean as well as Eastern Europeans who had been displaced during the war. The 1950s was a key decade of labour migration to the United Kingdom from Commonwealth countries first from the Caribbean and then from the Indian sub-continent preceding increasingly restrictive immigration controls that began in the early 1960s.

People also move to join family members and these kinship networks have been an important facilitator of migration. The term chain-migration is used to describe the pattern of South Asian migration to Britain. Chain migration is where a migration chain emerges. First, one family member arrives in the United Kingdom, secures accommodation and a job and sends for the next family member providing accommodation on arrival and often locating a job too and this carries on. The family and community are crucial in migration chains and often provide the financial and cultural capital that facilities it. Once started, migratory movements often become self-sustaining and extended as spouses and children migrate to be reunited with their family.

Civil war, conflict, political oppression, discrimination, and human rights abuses can also result in migration and it is these motivations for leaving a country of origin that are most associated with refugees and asylum seekers. Immigration controls and pre-embarkation checks make it difficult to enter the United Kingdom as an asylum seeker legally while the closed borders surrounding the European Union means that increasingly people who want to seek asylum find themselves dependent on people smugglers who plan their flight and often provide false documentation. The 1951 Geneva Convention was developed in response to conditions in post-war Europe and the limited grounds for claiming refugee status in the Geneva Convention means that poverty, generalized violence, and displacement due to development projects or environmental disaster do not meet the international refugee definition. It is these factors, which are associated with economic and/ or social disruption, that result in the migration of people from the global South and East to the highly developed countries of the North and the West.

It is increasingly recognized, though not in the bureaucratic categories used by governments and policy-makers, that people often have more than one reason for migrating – or mixed motives – and that the reasons why refugees and asylum seekers leave their country of origin overlap with the migration choices made by others.

The United Kingdom is a signatory of the Geneva Convention and has to meet international obligations. However successive governments have also been under pressure at different times to control migration. Since the late 1980s the focus has been on asylum seekers and more specifically border controls, restricted rights, and enforcement (detention and deportation) strategies. The public discourse has revolved around the dichotomy of 'deserving' refugees and 'bogus' or 'undeserving' asylum seekers who are portrayed as coming to the United Kingdom to exploit the supposedly generous welfare system and employment opportunities. It is because of this that the rights of asylum seekers have been gradually eroded.

British Policy: Past and Present

Immigration policy has developed incrementally with trends in different periods best understood in the context of migration flows, the economic situation, and public discourse. Policy can be divided into four main phases: the control of mostly Jewish aliens from Europe, 1905–45; the racialized control of immigration from commonwealth countries, 1960s to the 1980s; the control of asylum, late 1980s to 2000; and from 2000 managed migration and the social cohesion agenda. In order to manage migration, capping the numbers of non-EU migrants allowed into the United Kingdom has been introduced though areas that need migrant labour, particularly Scotland, are now contesting Whitehall policy.

The first period, from 1905, was important because the links between immigration and welfare were clearly made. Under the 1905 Aliens Act, entry could be refused if a migrant had no means of subsistence or they could be deported if they were in receipt of Poor Relief within one year of entering Britain. In 1914, the Aliens Restriction Act was passed in response to anti-alien feeling, especially anti-German, generated by the outbreak of the First World War. Under this Act, aliens had to register with the police and the Home Secretary and immigration officers were given powers to control entry, deportation, and employment. The 1919 Aliens Restrictions (Amendment) Act extended the terms of the 1914 Act to peacetime and included restrictions on employment even for some naturalized citizens.

The next major piece of legislation was the 1948 British Nationality Act which gave British subjects, who were citizens of the United Kingdom and Colonies (UKC), and Commonwealth citizens, the right to enter, settle, and work in Britain. It also created a third category of citizens of Eire. These were neither aliens nor subjects but held all the rights and duties of UKC citizens.

The second main phase of immigration controls started with the 1962 Commonwealth Immigrants Act and ended with the Immigration Act, 1988. This period was concerned with curbing immigration from countries of the Commonwealth and New Commonwealth and brought primary migration among black commonwealth citizens virtually to an end; though significantly not among white Commonwealth citizens, demonstrating the racialized nature of these controls. The context for the second phase of immigration controls was the increase in numbers of people arriving from British colonies and Commonwealth countries in the period after the Second World War and the arrival of refugees from independence struggles and post-colonial conflicts.

In 1945 Britain needed labour to rebuild the country. Eastern Europeans from displaced persons camps were recruited, followed by migrants from the Caribbean and the Indian sub-continent. Amid public concerns about immigration the 1962 Commonwealth Immigration Act was passed. This Act was significant because for the first time restrictions on entry and settlement were placed on UKC subjects not born in the United Kingdom.

The 1968 Commonwealth Immigrants Act was rushed through Parliament in three days amid fears that east African Asians, as UK passport holders, would exercise their right to come to Britain in the face of post-colonial Africanization policies. UK passport holders were subject to immigration controls unless they had a parent or grandparent born, adopted, registered, or naturalized in the United Kingdom. The Act effectively excluded east African Asians from entering the United Kingdom but not those of UK descent living in east Africa. The 1971 Immigration Act introduced the concept of partials and non-partials and in effect changed the status of Commonwealth citizens to aliens by allowing the right to abode only among those born in the United Kingdom or with a parent born in the United Kingdom. The 1981 British Nationality Act removed the right of citizenship to those born in the United Kingdom and only those able to satisfy the partial rule were automatically entitled to citizenship. The 1988 Immigration Act introduced the public funds test for dependents of people who had settled in Britain before 1973, All British and Commonwealth citizens who wanted their dependents to join them had to sponsor them and prove that they could do that without recourse to public funds.

This third phase of immigration control focused on limiting the entry of asylum seekers and their exclusion from social and economic participation in society. Since 2000 policy has been concerned with managing migration and social cohesion. Table 58.1 shows the Acts from 1993 and their main effects.

The cumulative effect of successive Acts has been first, the curtailment of the social, economic, and welfare rights of asylum seeking individuals and families and their exclusion from mainstream welfare support. Second, greater control over who enters the country and greater stipulations regarding citizenship to reflect the social cohesion agenda.

The European Union

The European Union has been gradually harmonizing policy. The focus has been border controls, information sharing, procedures for determining which asylum cases are eligible for refugee status, as well as the standards for the protection and treatment of asylum seekers. With the expansion of Europe, securing borders has become more difficult as some migrants enter clandestinely with the assistance of smugglers or are trafficked for the purposes of exploitation.

At Tampere in 1999 a timetable was agreed for a common European asylum and migration policy. It made progress on asylum issues – directives covering minimum standards on reception, asylum procedures, and a revision of the Dublin Convention (specifying which Member State is responsible for examining an asylum application to prevent refused asylum seekers from moving to another member state) are now in place. The Stockholm Programme, agreed in 2009, has been adopted by EU member states for the period 2010–14. The programme is concerned with ensuring the European Union manages migration, combats trafficking and that migration policy is both dynamic and sustainable.

Emerging Issues

Emerging issues in migration and asylum policy will centre on increasing external and internal controls. Biometric documents, greater surveillance, and a points based immigration system will exclude all but those migrants deemed most desirable for the UK economy. A cap has also been placed on migration and included are students from outside the European Union.

The relationship between citizen entitlements, language skills, and knowledge of the United Kingdom will exclude some, especially women from countries where there have been fewer opportunities for formal education than among their male counterparts. Among those entitled to stay in the United Kingdom the emphasis will continue to be on integration, social cohesion, and national identity.

The increased control of borders both at the EU level and in the United Kingdom will mean that the role of smugglers in the migration process will continue and is likely to expand. This will result in more clandestine entrants and greater numbers of people without any legal right to be in the United Kingdom who are vulnerable to workplace exploitation and are without access to basic social rights.

Table 58.1 Immigration and asylum legislation since 1993.

Legislation	Effect
1993 Asylum and Immigration Appeals Act	Local authorities no longer have to provide housing to asylum seekers.
1996 Asylum and Immigration Act	This Act contained the Social Security (Persons from Abroad) Miscellaneous Amendment regulations which removed the entitlement of social security benefits for asylum seekers who applied for asylum within the United Kingdom – that is in-country – rather than at the port of entry. In-country applicants received in-kind support from local authorities, under the 1948 National Assistance Act, often in the form of vouchers.
1999 Immigration and Asylum Act	Asylum seekers removed from the mainstream benefits system and the National Asylum Support Service (NASS) was introduced to administer a virtually cashless voucher system, at less than the value of income support. The dispersal of asylum seekers on a no-choice basis to locations around the United Kingdom was also introduced.
2002 Nationality, Immigration and Asylum Act	Introduced Section 55 which allowed the Home Office to withdraw access to NASS support from those who do not apply for asylum 'as soon as reasonably practicable'.
2004 Asylum and Immigration Act	A failed asylum seeker with a family can now have their support withdrawn if the person has failed without 'reasonable excuse' to leave the United Kingdom voluntarily. Local Authorities have a duty to provide for children under eighteen under the Children Act 1989 and if necessary children will be separated from their family.
2006 Immigration, Asylum and Nationality Act	Asylum seekers unable to travel to their home countries due to medical situations or there being no safe route home are given board, lodgings, and vouchers instead of cash.
2007 UK Borders Act	Increases power of immigration officers to detain, to enter, and search homes and to search and arrest in relation to illegal working. Provides for biometric immigration documents and allows the Border and Immigration Agency (BIA) to require anyone granted limited leave to enter and remain to report to the BIA or stipulate address of residence.
2009 Borders, Citizenship and Immigration Act	Increased the residence period required prior to naturalization from five to eight years though it can be reduced to six through voluntary work known as 'active citizenship'. Refugees will have to meet the language proficiency requirements and/or Knowledge of Life in the UK test before being granted citizenship.

Guide to Further Sources

General texts on migration and policy responses in the United Kingdom are: R. Sales, *Understanding Immigration and Refugee Policy: Contradictions and Continuities* (Bristol: Policy Press, 2007);

J. Solomos, *Race and Racism in Britain* (3rd edn, Basingstoke: Palgrave, 2003); S. Cohen, B. Humphries, and E. Mynott, E. (eds), *From Immigration Controls to Welfare Controls* (London: Routledge, 2003) focus on the links between immigration control and welfare.

S. Castles and M. J. Miller, *The Age of Migration: International population movements and the modern world* (4th edn, Basingstoke: Palgrave, 2009) is an invaluable resource about global migration and migrant settlement.

Analysis of refugees in the United Kingdom is provided by: T. Kushner and K. Knox, *Refugees in the Age of Genocide* (London: Frank Cass, 1999); A. Bloch, *The Migration and Settlement of Refugees in Britain* (Basingstoke: Palgrave, 2002).

A helpful guide to the European Union is A. Geddes (2009) *Migration as Foreign Policy? The External Dimension of EU Action on Migration and Asylum* (Issue 2, Stockholm: Swedish Institute for European Policy Studies); The edited collection by C. Jones Finer, *Migration, Immigration and Social Policy* (Oxford: Blackwell, 2006) explores key areas in migration and includes social policy case studies from Europe and the European Union.

Government web sites, the Border Agency, at www.ukba.homeoffice.gov.uk and National Statistics at www.statistics.gov.uk, contain useful policy documents, research reports, and statistical data. The Refugee Council web site, www.refugeecouncil.org.uk/, provides up-to-date information on asylum policy, asylum statistics as well as briefings on key topics.

Review Questions

1 Why do people migrate?
2 What are the different categories of migrant?
3 What have been the main policy responses to migration and what factors drive policy?
4 Giving examples, in what ways have immigration, asylum, and welfare policies intersected?
5 What have been and are likely to be the main areas of EU policy?

Visit the book companion site at www.wiley.com/go/alcock to make use of the resources designed to accompany the textbook. There you will find chapter-specific guides to further resources, including governmental, international, think-tank, pressure groups, and relevant journals sources. You will also find a glossary based on *The Blackwell Dictionary of Social Policy*, help sheets, and case studies, guidance on managing assignments in social policy and career advice.

PART IX

International Issues

59

Comparative Analysis

Margaret May

Overview

- Comparative analysis is a crucial constituent of social policy.
- Its development reflects shifts in the discipline and national welfare strategies.
- Comparative enquiry raises distinct conceptual and methodological issues.
- Cross-national comparisons can be framed in various ways.
- There is a range of explanations for variations in country welfare mixes.

Context

The study of welfare provision necessarily involves some form of comparison between current practice and past or alternative ways of meeting need or improving existing policies. The comparisons may not always be explicit and value bases may differ. But they are central to a discipline geared to evaluating welfare arrangements and ascertaining the factors that drive their design and varying, often conflicting, purposes and outcomes. Increasingly for analysts across the globe addressing these issues effectively requires cross- as well as intra-national research.

Whatever the cultural or geographical starting point, this enables not only the appraisal of welfare arrangements through other lenses but

the identification of commonalities and differences and their implications. It also opens up questions about the genesis of welfare systems, the nature and direction of change in national social policies, the influence of different drivers and constraints and what these might tell us about likely developments. Considering these questions feeds into what is for many the overarching value of comparative analysis, its potential for enhancing provisions in one country by drawing on and 'learning' from the experience (and 'failures') of others. Such borrowing may, however, simply be a way of legitimizing desired change. It thus raises further questions regarding the selectivity and diffusion as well as the feasibility and effectiveness of policy transfers.

The Student's Companion to Social Policy, Fourth Edition. Edited by Pete Alcock, Margaret May, Sharon Wright.
© 2012 John Wiley & Sons, Ltd. Published 2012 by John Wiley & Sons, Ltd.

Research on these issues is far from new, but until recently focused primarily on 'western' societies. Over the past two decades though it has extended internationally, prompted initially by an awareness of the extent to which governments in these countries seemed to be facing common problems and reconfiguring their policies in similar ways.

Pre-eminent were the many processes associated with globalization and the related threats to national autonomy and social expenditure (see Chapter 22). Conjoined were other new challenges to the post-war welfare order, especially those posed by rising consumer expectations, growing diversity, demographic ageing, and new social risks stemming from shifting employment and family patterns. Policy design moreover appeared to be increasingly moulded not only by the operation of global markets but the widening remit of international governmental organizations (IGOs) such as the European Union, the OECD, and the World Bank (see Chapters 43, 44). Adding to this, governments too were extending their investment in comparative policy formation. In the United Kingdom this was partly driven by Labour's commitment to evidence-based welfare. However, it also reflected the wider spread of welfare benchmarking as a lever for change.

The resultant welter of statistics and league tables demanded careful appraisal, as did the many proposals for policy importation, their take-up, and correlation with other international pressures. The deregulation of national financial markets, for instance, meant pension, mortgages, and other services in many countries were increasingly provided by local subsidiaries of multinational conglomerates, with administration often outsourced elsewhere. Other organizations including higher education and social care providers also moved into a global market (see Chapter 31). The spread of new information and other technologies hastened these processes, as did the spread of an international labour market for welfare personnel and new forms of transnational welfare lobbying.

Concern over these developments intensified following the 2008–10 banking crisis. In highlighting the scale and instabilities of economic internationalization, it also raised awareness of the related geo-political shifts and the growth of a multipolar global economy powered by China and other emerging economies. Together with another round of welfare restructuring in parts of Europe, these added a further dimension to debates about the nature and outcomes of social policy cross-nationally.

Approaches to Comparative Analysis

In addressing these issues comparative analysts use a range of approaches. Some concentrate on country-specific studies, detailing provisions but leaving the tasks of comparative evaluation to the reader. Others, while adopting an overt comparative approach, start from different points on the policy compass, examining particular sectors, 'programmes, problems', user needs, or policy processes and attitudes, usually in countries with broadly similar socio-economic and political structures. Whatever the focus these 'domain-specific' studies potentially involve comparing a number of interrelated elements (Box 59.1).

Box 59.1   Key Issues in 'Domain-Specific' Comparative Analysis

- scale and nature of the 'need'/'problem'
- range of provision
- overall welfare context
- policy-making processes
- aims of a particular programme(s)/ service(s)/benefit(s)
- programme origins and development over time
- entitlement criteria
- provider structure (statutory/non-statutory/mixed)
- resource structure
- regulatory structure
- administrative structure
- delivery/allocation processes
- 'efficacy'/'outcomes' of current provision
- pressures for change
- policy proposals.

Box 59.2 Key Issues in 'Whole System' Comparative Analysis

- general welfare milieu
- policy-making 'styles' and processes
- key forms of welfare 'input' or 'effort'
- predominant patterns of welfare production
- predominant processes of welfare allocation
- main welfare output(s)
- major welfare outcome(s).

Other analysts adopt a broader, macro approach, engaging in 'whole system' comparisons across a range of societies, often over time, entailing a consideration of key signature issues (Box 59.2).

Research Dilemmas

Researching these phenomena within one's home country is far from straightforward. Cross-national study, particularly of 'whole systems' is even more problematic and ensuring like-for like comparisons presents major conceptual and methodological challenges, not least those of selecting the countries and their number or the policies for analysis. Social policy researchers are neither 'culture-free' in their interpretations or research remits. Superficially similar terms can carry very different meanings and local practices are easily misread. The constructs 'welfare state' and 'social policy' for instance are far from synonymous or similarly understood. Notions of 'social needs' and 'risks' may differ and are highly contested. Indeed, one salutary feature of comparative study is the extent to which burning issues or 'social problems' in one society may be differently perceived or discounted elsewhere.

Adding to these issues benefit and welfare programmes may have several, possibly conflicting, aims and inputs. Providers may be governmental, non-statutory or, 'mixed'. Resource structures too may vary in terms of funding (national or local taxation, direct and indirect; compulsory or private insurance; charges; or combinations of these) and staffing, as may organizational arrangements, management cultures, and informal 'street-level' practices. 'Domain' level appraisal, whether of take-up relative to 'need', enhanced individual well-being, decreased inequality, cost-effectiveness, or other possible criteria is also highly value-laden and far from straightforward and evaluating outcomes at a macro level is particularly problematic (see Chapter 60).

In many ways the techniques utilsed are those deployed in 'within-country' research and demand similar caution. But comparativists confront additional dilemmas. The well-documented limitations of official statistics, for instance, are compounded by differing national conventions that may pre-empt direct comparison. Sources, categories, and formats may differ. There may be gaps in coverage, changes in definition, or methods of gathering and classifying data, which are often designed for other purposes. In many parts of the world welfare-related information may not be available or only in aggregate form. The challenges are not only a matter of accessing, standardizing, or collecting empirically comparable data, but those posed by differing investigative rules and epistemological traditions and, increasingly, moving beyond a Euro-American methodological base.

Considerable effort has been invested in surmounting these problems. 'Safari' surveys of one or more countries by teams from another have given way to collaborative multinational projects designed to enhance cross-cultural 'literacy' and combine differing research styles. Greater use is being made of multi-method strategies, sophisticated quantitative and qualitative techniques, and cross-disciplinary investigations. Fuller, more robust data sets and parallel national panel studies have also been developed by IGOs, governmental and non-governmental bodies, along with measures to improve access to microdata and online facilities. Given the cost of alternative studies comparative enquiry remains highly reliant on such databases, particularly that of the OECD. Though widely used even this may not readily relate to some policy concerns or allow for particular comparisons (see Chapter 60) while study of non-OECD countries still demands considerable ingenuity. Nonetheless considerable advances have been made, extending the comparative radar and ways of addressing the core debates within it.

Typologies and Regimes

One key issue is the use of classificatory frameworks to characterize and explicate the social policy landscape cross-nationally. The most influential early taxonomies were those advanced in the wake of the post-war welfare settlements by the Americans, Wilensky and Lebeaux and Titmuss in the United Kingdom. The former distinguished two 'models of welfare', to which Titmuss (1974) added a third ideal-type:

1 *The Residual Welfare Model* (typified by the United States) marked by extensive non-state, market-based provision and selective, means-tested 'safety net' public benefits and services, widely perceived as stigmatizing.
2 *The Institutional Redistributive Model* (typified by Sweden) marked by universal, rights-based, non-stigmatizing, redistributive state benefits and services, viewed as a 'normal' function of industrial society.
3 *The Industrial Achievement-Performance Model* (typified by the former West Germany) marked by work-based benefits and services, with state welfare functioning as an adjunct to the economy.

Current theorization, however, is dominated by debates over the similar but fuller categorization developed by the Danish analyst Esping-Andersen (1990). Covering eighteen OECD countries and based on largely post hoc analysis of three international data sets, this encompassed not only differences in public provision, but political and class formations. Unlike earlier modelling it also incorporated consideration of the distribution as well as levels of social spending. Surveying these allocative issues he suggested welfare states varied along three interwoven dimensions:

- *Decommodification* – the extent to which the state frees individuals from market forces and enables them to lead socially acceptable lives independent of the labour market.
- *Stratification* – the extent to which state welfare differentiates between social classes and promotes equality and social integration.
- *The public–private mix* – the relative roles of the state, market, and family in supplying welfare.

To plot these Esping-Andersen devised decommodification indices, measuring the scope and generosity of three crucial benefits (pensions, sickness, and unemployment). His analysis led him to distinguish three ideal type 'welfare regimes'.

- *Social-Democratic regimes*, characteristic of Scandinavian countries, where a coalition of labour organizations and small farmers secured a state committed to full employment and generous, redistributive, universalist welfare benefits, incorporating both middle- and working-class interests.
- *Conservative/Corporatist regimes*, characteristic of continental Europe where occupationally segregated benefits were introduced by conservative-dominated governments to secure working- and middle-class support.
- *Liberal Welfare Regimes*, characteristic of English-speaking countries, where, in the absence of stable cross-class alliances, state welfare operated mainly on selective lines as a residual safety net for the poor.

As with any ideal-type framework, some nations fitted these constructs more easily than others. However, Esping-Andersen concluded that the welfare systems of advanced economies could be subsumed within this trichotomy, which also had a predictive value, indicating different regimes moved along distinct trajectories.

This analysis prompted a flood of research, becoming a reference point for comparative study, much of which is still framed by the controversies it triggered. While covering numerous theoretical, methodological, and substantive concerns, these centre on the representativeness of his typology, the value of welfare modelling more generally, and his explication of regime differentiation.

For his critics Esping-Andersen's focus on benefits and class rather than other divisions masked the range of variations within and between societies, casting doubt on his typology and country allocations. Feminist studies, for instance, challenged his neglect of gender and care issues and its salience for women. Research into ethnic, faith-based and other divisions also questioned aspects of his study, as did that on his policy canvass. This was extensively criticized as overly narrow and statist, belying the often different dynamics and impacts of public services, other forms of state intervention and non-governmental provision.

Consideration of these, it was argued, could alter country 'placings' within his regimes. Public services did not always map neatly onto his classification, while some national patterns appeared to be programme-specific. When gender, other dimensions, non-statutory provision, or other governmental policies were factored in the picture could change again, repositioning some countries and making it difficult to allocate others. As fundamentally it appeared his focus on social protection marginalized the productivist role of social policy and the ways in which it was used to drive economic modernization. Beyond these opinion also varied on ways of formulating and measuring the impact of different systems and countries' relative welfare 'performance' and 'generosity' (see Chapter 60).

For some analysts these and related methodological complexities meant the most fruitful approach lay with domain-specific comparison rather than further modelling which, in their view had limited descriptive and forensic power. While recognizing in-country policy variations, others saw typologizing as a valuable heuristic tool, enabling them to capture and compare a country's welfare 'DNA'.

Research from this 'helicopter' perspective posited a more complex scenario encompassing further welfare worlds such as those of the Antipodes, the Mediterranean, Eastern Europe, East Asia, and 'outliers' or 'sub-categories' within regimes (see Chapters 62 and 63). It also led to attempts to extend regime analysis to the developing world, most notably by Gough and colleagues' concept of global or metawelfare regimes.

Their studies initially identified three such regimes, to which subsequent analysis added two sub-categories (Abu Sharkh and Gough 2010).

Looking at an 'extended welfare mix' (including external aid and remittances from overseas workers as well as governmental and non-governmental arrangements) and key welfare outcomes in sixty-five non-OECD countries, this distinguished between

- 'proto-welfare state regimes'
- 'informal security regimes' ('successful' and 'failing'), and
- 'insecurity regimes'.

The first comprises a cluster of countries (mainly in the ex-Soviet Union and southern South America), where state provisions and welfare outcomes resemble OECD welfare states. The others differ starkly in terms of state spending and programmes, external resourcing, and the nature and stability of employment, social networks and governments. Those in 'successful Informal Security regimes' (China, much of East Asia, the rest of South-Central America, Iran, Turkey, Tajikistan) are characterized by relatively good outcomes despite low state inputs and external flows. Outcomes in 'failing Informal Security regimes' (mainly in the Indian sub-continent, southern, and eastern Africa) are far lower and in 'Insecurity regimes' (mainly in Sub-Saharan Africa) contingent on unsustainable informal support and the vagaries of external aid.

Like Esping-Anders's triad this global schema is seen as a means not only of encapsulating deep-seated cross-national variations and groupings, but their policy implications. In line with earlier research it also allows for further distinctions such as those between the 'productivist' East Asian, 'clientistic' Latin American, and 'residual' South Asian welfare orders.

The myriad questions it raises are only beginning to be addressed. But in pointing to the need for a fully international conspectus it has added a further dimension to another debate over regime theorization, that over the roots and durability of welfare formations.

Convergence and Divergence

Here policy analysts divide again, differing over the factors powering cross-national variation, continuity and change, signs of convergence or divergence and the applicability of studies of western welfare states to other regions. Schematically there appear to be seven main schools of thought on these issues, each with many permutations.

First, a long-standing body of thinking upholds the key role of *economic influences* in the patterning of social policy in western societies. Many early comparativists saw welfare statism as the concomitant of urban-industrialization, necessitated by the destabilization of traditional forms of social protection, the new needs and problems it generated and the social infrastructure required for growth. Together with the wealth generated these pressures were believed to make for continuing welfare expansion and country convergence as differences in the timing of industrialization ironed out.

Subsequent surveys, critical of its functionalist base, questioned this view of the linear growth of welfare states and it has given way to more nuanced accounts of the interplay between economic change and social policy (Chapter 22). It was echoed, however, in early studies of the impact of globalization, which saw it as forcing downward neo-liberal style convergence as governments strove to maintain economic competitiveness. The evidence for this, however, was far from clear-cut, with later research emphasizing re-engineering rather than retrenchment, but again differing as to whether this was unidimensional and reactive or reflective of other factors.

Among these a second school of thought singles out *socio-structural influences* as contributing to both common trends and national variations. Similarities in population profiles, composition, and family patterns, such as demographic ageing or increased single-parenting for instance, prompted analogous though not identical policy developments. More contentiously studies from this perspective also highlighted the influence of social composition, suggesting that, as in the United States, public provision was more constrained in diverse societies.

Many comparative analysts, however, uphold *political influences* as the prime determinants of welfare mixes and variations cross-nationally. Historically this third school of thought emphasized the correlation between the spread of democracy, working class mobilization, and collectivism. Marxist writers in particular saw state welfare as the product of class struggle in industrial-capitalist societies, although also stressing its role in enforcing labour discipline and social stability.

For other researchers, including Esping-Andersen, conflict between different social groups and the power resources they bring to bear explain not only the genesis of western welfare states, but elemental differences between them. Residual regimes, for instance, reflected weak, often disempowered working-class organizations; others very different power balances, bargaining, and compromises. Studies in this vein also drew attention to the impact of feminist and other social movements. But what in essence this line of thinking argues is that 'politics matter' and that partisan configurations and political choices decide social policy, maintaining cross-national variation despite other pressures.

This case is aligned to the fourth, which highlights *institutional influences*. These range from prerequisites for public welfare such as strong administrative systems, to fundamental differentiators, particularly constitutional and electoral structures, the 'veto points' these entail and the 'long shadows' or 'path dependencies' cast by initial collectivist provision. These, it is argued, account for the resilience of welfare formations, with measures once in place, and provider and beneficiary support for them, constraining paradigm change.

While some studies suggest incremental innovation can, over time, be 'path-breaking', this position has been attacked for underestimating endogenous policy or regime shifts. It does, however, tie in with another line of thinking, emphasizing *welfarist ideological influences*. Embedded here is the contention that welfare states reflect historically rooted differences in public beliefs, value systems, cultures, and religious affinities that can override internal political divisions and maintain general tendencies towards, for instance Scandinavian universalism or Anglophone selectivism.

Coming full circle to the seventh school of thought these may be pliable in the face of exogenous *transnational influences*, particularly in the face of downward economic imperatives. Concern here currently centres on the purveyance of pan-global ideologies, the role of IGOs, other powerful advocacy groups, and policy entrepreneurs in promoting particular, especially neo-liberal strategies (see Chapters 44 and 61) and the processes involved. Compared to the global south, traditional welfare states may be more resistant to such diffusion, raising questions about other influences on social policy. For example public provision in some countries is the product of non-democratic administrations, while in many emerging economies it is seen as a lever for development, with governments investing primarily in workforce training and support.

Emerging Issues

In many ways this and the other issues touched on above will continue to dominate comparative analysis. Three concerns will, however, take centre-stage. Debate will, first, centre on the ongoing challenge of accessing and generating reliable comparable data, especially for non-OECD countries and, more generally, of minimizing the inherent difficulties of cross-cultural research. Second, it will focus on the fall-out from the banking crisis and its impact on the sustainability of traditional welfare states and social provision across the globe. The most pressing issue though is the global challenge of climate change. This is just filtering into comparative discourse. But with its profound implications for individual well-being, social justice, and notions of citizenship, it opens up fundamental questions about the assumptive bases of social policy that demand extended comparative study and look set to prompt the development of new interventions and analytical approaches.

Guide to Further Sources

Many of the issues outlined here are taken up in subsequent chapters. P. Alcock and C. Craig (eds) (2009) *International Social Policy* (2nd edn,

London: Palgrave Macmillan, 2009) provides a stimulating introduction to comparative analysis along with a number of country surveys. More detailed coverage can be found in R. Titmuss, *Social Policy* (London: Allen and Unwin, 1974); G. Esping-Andersen, *The Three Worlds of Welfare Capitalism* (Cambridge: Polity Press, 1990); M. Abu Sharkh and I. Gough, 'Global regimes: A cluster analysis', *Global Social Policy*, 10/27 (2010): 27–58; F., Castles *et al.* (eds), *The Oxford Handbook of the Welfare State* (Oxford: Oxford University Press, 2010); and L. Hantrais, *International Comparative Research* (Basingstoke: Palgrave Macmillan, 2009). Current developments can also be tracked through the *Social Policy Digest* (http://.journals.cambridge.org) and the links on the SPA, OECD, and UN web sites www.spa.org.uk, www.oecd.org, and www.unrisd.org.

Review Questions

1 How would you account for the growing interest in comparative social policy?
2 What are the main methodological problems faced in comparative policy research?
3 Taking any two countries and a social policy issue of your choice what factors would you include in a comparative study?
4 What are the main drawbacks of using typologies in comparative analysis?
5 What factors might explain cross-national variations in social policy?

Visit the book companion site at www.wiley.com/go/alcock to make use of the resources designed to accompany the textbook. There you will find chapter-specific guides to further resources, including governmental, international, think-tank, pressure groups, and relevant journals sources. You will also find a glossary based on *The Blackwell Dictionary of Social Policy*, help sheets, and case studies, guidance on managing assignments in social policy and career advice.

60

Social Policy in Europe

Jochen Clasen

░■

Overview

- ■ European countries have consistently been the highest spenders on social policy within the economically advanced groups of Organisation for Economic Co-operation and Development (OECD) countries.
- ■ European countries provide the most generous benefit levels within the OECD.
- ■ Typically European (but not British) is the use of employment protection as a mechanism for securing income for wage earners.
- ■ Typically European (but not British) is the involvement of social partners in social policy-making.

░■

What is Europe?

Geographically, Europe is a rather vague entity. Its eastern border in particular is ambiguous. Russia is a European country, but is all of Russia part of Europe? Is Turkey European or Asian, or both? Politically, things are not much simpler. The idea that 'Europe' can somehow be regarded as synonymous with the European Union is unduly reductionist. Even if, in 2010, the European Union covers twenty-seven countries and thus repre-

sents most people who live in Europe, it excludes not only very small states such as Liechtenstein or Andorra, but politically important countries such as Norway and Switzerland.

From a British perspective, 'Europe' is often portrayed as both different from the United Kingdom and homogenous in its non-British character, as popular references to things 'European' with regard to food or football indicate. In some respects, the former notion might have some substance given the linguistic and

I should like to thank Evgeniya Plotnikova for her excellent research assistance. *J.C.*

The Student's Companion to Social Policy, Fourth Edition. Edited by Pete Alcock, Margaret May, Sharon Wright.
© 2012 John Wiley & Sons, Ltd. Published 2012 by John Wiley & Sons, Ltd.

partly cultural affinity of the United Kingdom with the United States, Australia, Canada, and New Zealand as the economically advanced English-speaking 'family of nations' (Castles 1993). As for the latter point, however, culturally, linguistically, and socio-economically Europe is rather heterogeneous. Since this applies to social policy too, it is rather difficult, if not impossible, to capture the variation of 'social policy in Europe' within the space constraints of this short chapter.

European Social Policy: Does It Exist?

Is there such a thing as European social policy, or, more precisely, within the set of economically advanced countries in the world, is it possible to identify characteristics which are typical of social policy in Europe? Asking a similar question, and applying financial, institutional and ideological criteria, Baldwin (1996) firmly arrived at a negative conclusion. Indeed, using a perspective of public social spending as a point of departure, the range of social policy effort across European (and even European Union) countries was very wide indeed in the 1980s and early 1990s. Equally, there was hardly any distinctively European pattern in which resources were distributed, that is, as universal, insurance-based or means-tested support. Equally, the level of benefits, such as public pensions or unemployment compensation, was neither consistently higher nor lower in European countries than in other OECD countries.

On average, Baldwin conceded, welfare spending might be more generous in European than in non-European countries, but he questioned how much, with so broad a range within the European social systems. Similarly Alber (2010) questions the notion of 'residual' US social policy which often tends to be contrasted with a more generous or comprehensive European idea of social protection. Indeed he shows that in some areas, such as public pensions, US social policy is more generous and redistributive than many European countries. If anything, he argues, European countries have become more 'American' in recent years due to a dominant discourse on 'activation' at the expense of 'social protection', while US social policy has become somewhat more European with respect to the debate on health care.

How could we broadly assess these arguments made by Baldwin (1996) and Alber (2010)? If we take the European Union as a point of departure, the processes of enlargement in 2004 (adding ten countries) and 2007 (another two) have certainly created more rather than less diversity in the scope, depth, and institutional range of social policy provision. However, if we consider the level of public social expenditure as a proportion of national income as a measurement of the relative emphasis countries put on social policy and assess the thirty economically most advanced countries in the world (OECD-30), European nations have consistently been the highest spenders on social policy since 1980, with Sweden invariably at the top of the table.

Similarly, throughout the past two decades there has always been a gap between the economically advanced European countries and the richer non-European countries such as the United States, Canada, Australia, New Zealand, and Japan. Aggregate public social expenditure across the EU-15, that is, member states prior to the European Union expansion towards Central and Southern Europe in 2004, has been consistently higher than aggregate spending in these five non-European countries. Moreover, in 2005 each EU-15 country spent at least 20 per cent of their GDP on social protection, except for Ireland, where strong economic growth depressed the relative effort in public social spending (OECD 2009a). By contrast, no economically advanced country outside Europe reached this mark. Perhaps as a corollary, the average total revenue from tax and social insurance contributions as a percentage of GDP is significantly higher in European countries than in non-European OECD countries (OECD 2009b).

Of course, there are questions of comparability. Some social policy domains (such as education for example) are often excluded from aggregate social spending and, while taking account of different sizes of national economies, measuring social expenditure as a share of GDP is always liable to fluctuations in national business cycles. Ideally, differences between such demographic patterns or unemployment levels should be considered in order to arrive at 'adjusted' levels of spending (Siegel, in Clasen and Siegel 2007). Moreover, recent analyses of 'net' social spending have pointed out that cross-national differences are less marked once the effects of taxation on benefit income, indirect taxation on consumption financed by benefits, as well as tax breaks are considered (Adema and Ladaique 2009). If, in addition, voluntary social spending is considered, the variation in levels of net 'total' social expenditure between European and non-European OECD countries narrows considerably.

However, such a broad measure might be less useful since it conceals redistributive efforts, which is a major objective of social policy (on this see Castles and Obinger 2007). Thus, taking account of the effect of taxation, but leaving aside voluntary spending, differences between the higher European spenders and lower spending non-European countries remain distinctive. However, using 'net publicly mandated social spending' as an indicator suggests that continental European countries, such as France and Germany, are top of the OECD table as a result of the fact that tax systems in countries usually ranked at the top, such as Denmark and Sweden, claw back more money handed out for social purposes.

How could we assess whether European countries are more generous than other countries? One indicator is the so-called net replacement rate, that is, the level of net benefit income in relation to previous net earnings. The OECD provides such calculations for different risks (such as unemployment, sickness, etc), income levels and family constellations (OECD 2010). A quick glance at, in this case, unemployment compensation during the first phase out of work indicates a significant degree of variation and, at first sight, little sense of a European pattern. However, it is noticeable that across eighteen different combinations of family types and earnings levels, the five most generous countries (out of thirty OECD countries) are always EU-15 member states (or Switzerland), albeit not always the same five. By contrast, while European countries, including the United Kingdom, can sometimes be found among the least generous five countries, this group is generally dominated by non-European countries.

Another often assumed trait of social policy in Europe is the emphasis on a broad rather than narrow notion of social citizenship. For example, in 2005 the vast majority of European countries distributed more than 90 per cent of their total cash transfers without an income test. By con-

trast, close to 80 per cent of cash benefits in Australia were income-tested, half in Canada, and close to 40 per cent in New Zealand (Adema and Ladaique 2009: 27). However, the picture is less than perfect given that means-testing is less prevalent in the United States (16 per cent) than in European countries such as Ireland (31 per cent) or the United Kingdom (26 per cent).

The role of publicly provided rather than privately purchased social policy is yet another characteristic associated with European social policy. In fact, the picture is much more blurred, which is partly due to the problem of delineating public (and thus assumed to be mandatory) and market-based private (and thus voluntary) social spending. The OECD makes a distinction between voluntary private and mandated private protection expenditure, but difficulties remain. Nominally, private occupational pensions based on collective agreements, for example, can be fairly comprehensive and regulated in a way which makes them all but mandatory. Equally, sickness or disability benefits provided by employers are generally categorized by the OECD as private mandatory social spending, but not in all cases, thereby creating anomalies (De Deken and Kittel, in Clasen and Siegel 2007).

This has considerable consequences, as the case of the Netherlands demonstrates, which the OECD (2009a) deems to have the second highest level of private voluntary social spending across thirty OECD countries, surpassed only by the United States. Other authors, however, consider the OECD's categorization of Dutch spending as a 'misnomer' (De Deken and Kittel, in Clasen and Siegel 2007). In short, in the absence of satisfactory conceptual clarity and good comparable data, it is difficult to substantiate the OECD's claim that market-based voluntary social protection is as relevant in some European countries (the United Kingdom, the Netherlands and also France) as it is outside Europe.

Turning to outcome measures of (not only) social policy, a consistent pattern emerges which indicates that some, but not all, European countries are maintaining relatively low levels of poverty and income inequality. Defining poverty as the proportion of individuals with below a certain percentage of median disposable income, say 50 per cent of the median, OECD data (2009a) indicate that the four Nordic countries, but also

West (Benelux, Austria, Switzerland, France) and Central European countries (the Czech Republic, Slovakia, Hungary) performed best across thirty-one economically developed countries.

The picture is similar for inequality (of disposable income; i.e. after tax and benefits), with North and West European countries, such as Denmark, Sweden, and the Netherlands, having the lowest levels of inequality of all OECD countries. At the same time, however, there are several European countries, including the United Kingdom, Ireland, Italy, and Spain, which have levels of inequality that are above the OECD average and as high as in several economically advanced countries outside Europe (OECD 2009a).

Baldwin (1996) pointed to institutional cross-national variation in, for example, the organization of health care or the role of family allowances. Here, his assessment of the absence of a European identity remains valid because of continuing diversity across and within countries, as well as within individual social policy arrangements. This is perhaps most visible in pension systems which tend to be multi-tiered, with or without a minimum public pension, at times means-tested but often not, and supplemented by mandatory or voluntary occupational systems (see also Alber 2010). Categorizing health care systems too, a range of regulatory and financial models can be found across the OECD, but no distinctively European identity.

In sum, from a macro-perspective, social policy in Europe is distinctive in the sense of relatively high levels of public social spending, a broad notion of social citizenship and benefit rates which are typically, but not in all cases, more generous than in other economically advanced countries. Several European countries come out top in terms of reducing poverty and containing income inequality. However, there is no European social policy identity in the ways in which social protection is organized or in the mix between public and private provision.

Typically European and/or Typically British?

There is too much diversity of social policy arrangements even within the EU member states for it to be possible to postulate any sense of uniformity. However, while diverse in settings and outcomes, there are social policy characteristics which are either exclusively, or predominately, found in Europe. In the remainder of this chapter I shall address some of these and, in this context, reflect on the relative position of British social policy as typically (or atypically) European.

Social policy needs resources that are collected via direct and indirect taxation or social security contributions, sometimes referred to as 'payroll tax'. Typically European countries devote a greater role to contributory (social insurance) as opposed to tax funding of the welfare state, as indicated by the combined (employee and employer) share of social security contributions. In 2007 social security contributions in European countries typically amounted to between 10 and 16 per cent of GDP, but were well below 10 per cent in all non-European OECD countries (except for Japan). However, there are exceptions such as Denmark, Ireland, Switzerland, and the United Kingdom (OECD 2009b).

Applying a broader understanding of social policy, typically European is the use of employment protection as a mechanism of providing income security to workers. Across nineteen EU countries for which data exist, the United Kingdom had the lowest level of employment protection in 2008 (OECD 2009a), followed by Ireland. Denmark too provides relatively little employment security but this is compensated by generous unemployment benefits and a strong profile of active labour market policies such as training. By contrast, the United Kingdom spends considerably less on active labour market policies than almost all other EU-15 countries (OECD 2009a).

Equally, the United Kingdom and Ireland focus benefit support on low-income groups and are significantly less generous to middle- and higher-income groups. This is also reflected in the relative scope of means-tested benefits, which in Ireland and the United Kingdom is significantly above the EU average as indicated earlier (Adema and Ladaique, 2009: 27). A quick glance at the generosity of benefits (such as unemployment protection and public pensions) underlines the fact that average and better income groups are invariably better protected in Northern and particularly in Western continental European countries compared with the United Kingdom (see OECD 2010). In short, low levels of both job and income security, which are due to an only weakly regulated labour market, make the United Kingdom (and Ireland) somewhat atypically European and puts the countries firmly within the camp of economically advanced 'liberal market economies' otherwise found outside Europe – in the United States, Canada, Australia, and New Zealand.

In many European countries, trade unions and employers have long played pivotal roles in the administration of social policy, and in particular social insurance programmes, such as pensions, unemployment, injury, or sickness insurance. The actual range and scope of involvement differs, of course. For example, employers and trade unions in Germany collaborate within quasi-public but legally independent and financially separate organizations of social insurance, at times joined by state officials. Social partners in Austria, Belgium, the Netherlands, and Switzerland play similar roles. In France, employees and employer are jointly in charge of social insurance schemes such as the unemployment benefit and pension funds. In Sweden, Denmark, and Finland trade union affiliated organizations are solely responsible for administering unemployment insurance.

Related to this, the idea of social security acting as a form of 'social wage', that is, reflecting former earnings as a way of at least partially preserving accustomed living standards, is common in most European countries. In the United Kingdom, neither such arrangements nor the notion of social policy as part of industrial relations applies. Finally, collective bargaining is another important social policy instrument which Central and North European countries, but much less so the United Kingdom or Ireland, rely on as a means for securing not only income but regulating working conditions.

In sum, in the context of economically advanced countries in the European Union, the United Kingdom (and Ireland to a lesser degree) is somewhat atypical in a European sense because of a notion of social policy which is narrowly focused on the redistribution of market income via taxation and benefits and services (Bonoli, in Clasen and Siegel 2007), as opposed to a broader understanding which pursues social policy goals also via channels such as employment protection or collective agreements.

Emerging Issues

There is no European welfare state and there is no distinctive European social policy identity. But Europeans engage more in social policy than countries in any other region of the world and, typically, apply a broader and more generous notion of social citizenship. Not all European nations are successful in combating poverty or containing income inequality, but the best performing countries in both respects are European. Not least as a result of improved efforts in some areas (such as education and health), the United Kingdom has moved from the edge to the middle of the range of European social policy as far as expenditure is concerned. However, in many other respects, and particularly with regard to the link between social policy and other policy fields such as industrial relations and employment protection, British social policy remains somewhat atypically European.

A European outlook serves as a reminder that social policy can (and perhaps should) be regarded from a broad perspective, involving more policy areas than the conventional welfare state domains. Similarly, more nuanced data on social spending are gradually becoming available which, despite methodological challenges, allow for more meaningful cross-national comparisons within and beyond social policy in European countries (see Chapter 59).

Guide to Further Sources

For the debate on which indicators of social spending are most suitable for comparisons, see F. G. Castles and H. Obinger, 'Social expenditure and redistribution', *Journal of European Social Policy* 17/3 (2007): 206–22 and W. Adema and M. Ladaique, 'How expensive is the welfare state? Gross and net indicators in the OECD Social Expenditure database', *OECD Social, Employment and Migration Working Papers*, 92 (Paris: OECD, 2009). J. Clasen, and N. A. Siegel (eds), *Investigating Welfare State Change. The 'Dependent Variable Problem' in Comparative Analysis* (Cheltenham:

Edward Elgar, 2007), includes several contributions which reflect on the problems of conceptualizing and empirically comparing national social policy arrangements.

The two studies mentioned which deal with the distinctiveness of European versus US social policy are J. Alber, 'What the European and American welfare states have in common and where they differ: Facts and fiction in comparisons of the European Social Model and the United States', *Journal of European Social Policy*, 20/2 (2010): 102–25 and P. Baldwin (1996) 'Can we define a European welfare state model?' in B. Greve (ed.), *Comparative Welfare Systems: The Scandinavian Model in a Period of Change* (Basingstoke: Macmillan, 1996), 29–44. F. G. Castles (ed.), *Families of Nations: Patterns of Public Policy in Western Democracies* (Aldershot: Dartmouth, 1993) provides further insights.

Both Eurostat (www.epp.eurostat.ec.europa.eu/portal/page/portal/statistics/themes) and the OECD (2009a) (http://stats.oecd.org/Index.aspx) are indispensable for data on social policy, and this chapter has also used data from OECD, *Revenue Statistics 1965–2008* (OECD: Paris, 2009b) and OECD (2010) *Net Replacement Rates during the Initial Phase of Unemployment 2001–2008* (OECD: Paris, 2010).

For more information on social policy in European countries, ESPAnet (the European Social Policy Analysis network) provides links to relevant national social policy associations, organizations and research centres at www.espanet.org. The European Data Center for Work and Welfare is a web portal with direct links to information on quantitative and qualitative comparative and national data at www.edacwowe.eu. For EU social policy the Directorate General for Employment, Social Affairs and Equal Opportunities is a good starting point: http://stats.oecd.org/Index.aspx.

Review Questions

1 Is there such a thing as 'European social policy'?
2 Does it make sense to contrast US with European social policy?
3 What is typical for European welfare states?
4 In what sense is the United Kingdom a typical European welfare state?
5 In what sense is the United Kingdom different from most other European welfare states?

Visit the book companion site at www.wiley.com/go/alcock to make use of the resources designed to accompany the textbook. There you will find chapter-specific guides to further resources, including governmental, international, think-tank, pressure groups, and relevant journals sources. You will also find a glossary based on *The Blackwell Dictionary of Social Policy*, help sheets, and case studies, guidance on managing assignments in social policy and career advice.

61

Social Policy in Liberal Market Societies

Michael Hill

Overview

- Liberal market societies are defined as ones where social policy development has been particularly inhibited by political value systems that see it as a threat to the working of capitalist markets.
- While the United States is seen as the archetypical example of a liberal market system, social policy 'regime theory' identifies a group of nations with similar characteristics including the United Kingdom and other predominantly English speaking nations.
- There is a range of approaches to social policy within liberal market regimes.
- Discussion is complicated by the dominance of liberal market approaches in the management of the economy in many parts of the world.
- The debate over liberal market social policy regimes forms part of a wider controversy about the likelihood and characteristics of a single global social policy agenda.

Characterizing Liberal Market Societies

In exploring what is meant by 'liberal market societies' there is a need to clear out of the way potential misunderstandings about the use of the word liberal in this context, as it is used in many different ways. One of the usages of liberal carries the particular connotation of freedom, but when linked in this way to the world market it is only the freedom of markets that is being signified. The reference here is then to liberal economic ideas which see the free market as the ideal device for allocating life chances, and the primary role for the state as being to enhance economic efficiency. It is also important to bear in mind that the usage here is not the same as the US usage of liberal to convey a progressive approach to social policy.

Accordingly when we look at social policy in liberal market societies we are looking at an approach to social provision in which interference with the free working of the market has been kept to a relatively low level. This is, of course, in the modern world, in comparison with the other social policy models.

The point about comparison is, obviously, important. This label is being used in comparative discussions of social policy to designate a particular social model or regime type distinguishable from others (see Chapter 59). The most influential contemporary usage is in the work of Esping-Andersen where it designates a kind of welfare state in which means-testing is widespread, social insurance is little used, and there is little redistribution through social policy. It may also be noted that there are comparable efforts by other writers to contrast the extent of government intervention in respect of industrial relations and the management of the economy as a whole.

Social Policy in the United States

The United States is often seen as the archetypical liberal market society. Its performance in respect of social policy – expressed either in terms of levels of expenditure or in terms of the incidence of poverty, inequality, and ill-health – is markedly inferior to other societies of comparable prosperity (see Chapter 60). In dominant US political discourse public social policy (often identified as 'welfare' with that term being given a special connotation to refer to reluctantly provided means-tested relief) is seen as a costly imposition upon citizens and upon the economy. As a consequence, while the relief of extreme poverty is not entirely neglected, most social support is only provided under conditions in which the behaviour of those getting it is regulated. In particular there are expectations that efforts will be made to find paid work, and failure to do so may result in the termination of benefits.

There are some slight exceptions from that picture of social policy in the United States. In the

1930s limited social insurance systems were developed providing pensions and some disability and unemployment benefits. But these were linked to regular employment through strong contributory systems to provide benefits for the relatively economically secure white working class. Moreover they were not consolidated, as most European systems were, after the Second World War, rather they have experienced attrition. Rates of income replacement are low. There are no family allowances and European developments in respects of rights to support for disabled people or for parenthood find no real echoes in the United States.

The other respect in which the United States has stood out from other nations of comparable prosperity has been the absence of a comprehensive health care system. Measures enacted in the 1960s provided some state support for health care for elderly people (Medicare) and for the very poor (Medicaid). But there remained serious gaps in the system, such that many people were driven into poverty by high health expenses. In 2010 President Obama succeeded in getting Congress to pass reform to health insurance aimed at plugging the gaps in the system. At the time of writing it is too early to judge how this complex legislation, much compromised to get it through the legislature, will work out in practice.

Other Liberal Market Regimes

In his regime typology, Esping-Andersen also links Australia, New Zealand, Canada, Ireland, and the United Kingdom with the United States as liberal market social policy regimes. It may be noted that these are all societies in which English is the dominant language. The liberal market systems are sometimes referred to as 'Anglo-Saxon' regimes, an unfortunate usage as the term is a pseudo racial one unacceptable to the Irish or to many residents of these multi-ethnic societies. On the other hand it is reasonable to accept that there are shared cultural influences across these Anglophone societies.

These other countries differ from the United States inasmuch as comprehensive health care systems have been developed. They have also been reluctant to introduce welfare to work policies that may entirely eliminate support for some of the poor. Australia and New Zealand have been characterized in the past as 'wage earners welfare states' with high levels of male employment and strong benefits linked to employment. The feminist attack on male dominance, coming as it has in a period of welfare state retrenchment, has not really led towards more universalist policies.

There are other societies that some writers also include in the category. This brings us to a crucial point about the identification of liberal market social policy systems. In many respects the whole comparative social policy discourse is about the extent to which, in a wide range of modern societies with democratic systems of government, capitalist economic institutions are dominant and social policy involves a relatively marginal set of government interventions to modify its impact upon the welfare of citizens. In which case, why are some systems described as liberal market ones while others are labelled differently? Can we actually draw clear distinctions between regime types?

The crucial starting point for regime theory is an argument that, while in all democratic societies (indeed nearly all societies) governments give some attention to unmet needs (if only through Poor Law systems), in some societies redistribution of resources outside the market on the basis of need goes much further. Esping-Andersen explicitly explains this in terms of the significance of political movements, and describes the effects upon social stratification as reducing the effects of market processes, using a special term: 'decommodification' (see Chapter 59). However, this is just referring to a tendency, shared by many societies and in practice the boundaries of the liberal market category are hard to define, particularly since (as shown above) while Esping-Andersen highlights the absence of 'universal' (meaning the incorporation of all citizens) transfer systems in liberal market regimes, social insurance is in fact found in some liberal market societies, but in modified and rather limited forms.

More difficult is the fact that there is not necessarily a clear link between the use of social insurance as a key social policy device and effective redistribution. While it has been argued that social insurance makes redistribution politically easier because everyone has a stake in the system, some social insurance systems redistribute very little. Moreover in certain circumstances direct

tax funding of a universal system may be a more effective redistributive device. This observation is particularly pertinent for some problems about the inclusion of the United Kingdom in the group of liberal market social policy regimes. As far as health care is concerned the universally available tax-funded NHS stands out as the key example of a social policy in the United Kingdom that largely frees health care from market forces, and has a potential to address health inequalities more effectively than an insurance-based system.

Something of the same kind may be said about pension provision, though this is more complicated and therefore controversial. Many of the biggest and most comprehensive social insurance based pension systems are not particularly redistributive. A feature of highly developed social insurance systems is that what pensioners get is principally determined by their previous labour market positions. Hence, even though the state may play a big role in making the system secure, it may have done very little to mitigate the effects of market forces. This means that we have to look for other, often more difficult to measure, indices of redistribution. Crucial here are

- whether there is a guaranteed minimum (provided on a residency or citizenship basis regardless of previous employment);
- whether that minimum is set at a relatively generous level; and
- whether access to this minimum is governed by means-tests of any form.

Hence the UK system satisfies the first two of those tests: there is a universally guaranteed minimum and that minimum is relatively generous (at least by the standards of other countries). This benefit is however a means-tested benefit (pension credit). However, even the countries with strong social insurance pension schemes underpin them in various ways with means-tests. Then the extent of that generosity depends upon the rules applying to those means-tests.

It is thus important to explore relationships between income differences in societies *before* government interventions and *after* them, suggesting that it is the size of the 'gap' between rich and poor and the extent to which policies close that gap that needs to be the object of attention rather than simply aggregate expenditure. Then income transfer policies may be examined in terms of their contribution to *both* the reduction of inequality and the eradication of poverty; these are alternative social policy goals that need to be interpreted in their wider political contexts. Income transfer systems may be compared in terms of *efficiency* (the relationship between outputs and inputs) and *effectiveness* (the actual redistributive outcomes). This raises questions about the wide range of influences on incomes, and the variety of policy options available to political actors who want the state to try to change income distribution. Accordingly attention has been drawn by critics of Esping-Andersen's approach to

- the pursuit of equalization through the achievement of equality in pre-tax, pre-transfer incomes, and the prevention of unemployment; and
- the use of rights-based means tests to effect substantial redistribution.

At times, in the histories of social policy in the United Kingdom, Australia, and New Zealand, policies in these categories have been important.

Why the Liberal Market Categorization Raises Important Questions

It is probably the case that by now some readers will be concluding that what we have here is an academic game in which scholars compete to offer alternative lists of nations. Such categorization can be important for theory building, and in this case there are some crucial questions for social policy analysis about the extent to which the working of the market is, and can be, modified in the interests of welfare and redistributive goals. There is much contemporary debate about the viability of social policy arrangements that are not market based. For example, in the area of pensions' policy international organizations like the World Bank have argued strongly for a model in which, beyond a state guaranteed minimum, pensions should be provided through contributions to private marketized organizations. Justifications are offered for this in terms of the prime importance of tying social policy to eco-

nomic goals. Nations looking to develop or strengthen pension systems (for example in East Asia – see Chapter 62 – South America and Eastern Europe) are urged to adopt this model. That approach is also challenged by a social insurance model (particularly developed in Continental Western Europe but now also in Japan and South Korea). Significantly the argument then centres not only on social goals but also on arguments about whether privatized pensions make the economic contributions claimed for them.

Were the United States a smaller and less influential country the characteristics of its social policy would not require so much attention. But US 'experts' (particularly economists) have taken a message around the world that freedom should involve minimum intervention into markets, and therefore residual social policy designed only to prevent serious deprivation. They have had a strong influence upon the advice given by international organizations like the World Bank and the International Monetary Fund. This takes us to an important contemporary question about the role of the state in economic management, one that has serious implications for social policy development.

Arguments For and Against the Liberal Market Model

It is important to recognize that we have here not merely a set of arguments about competitiveness but also a conflict of discourses. The liberal market model embodies a set of principles: about the superiority of market arrangements, about the importance of growth, about the virtues of employment. These are strongly defended by powerful actors – the beneficiaries of capitalist economic arrangements globally and within the most powerful nation in the world – against alternative discourses.

There is, however, another view that, although the evidence so far does not show that regimes with strong social policy systems cannot compete, the trends towards lower wages (and lower wage related costs – such as social insurance contributions from employers) across the world will gradually eliminate the economic advantages of the economies with strong social policy systems. New competitors, particularly China and India, are also developing trained and highly adaptive labour forces, at much lower wage costs. The arguments for the liberal market approach to social policy are being taken very seriously by many nations, not solely those labelled in these terms by regime theory. Hence we have observed cuts to Dutch welfare benefits, earlier categorized by very high levels of income replacement, proclaimed as generating a 'Dutch miracle' of improved competitiveness. And even in Sweden there have been changes to the pensions' system involving the creation of a funded layer in which compulsory contributions go into private pension schemes. Traditional European welfare systems are on the defensive, making changes that may perhaps engender greater longer term changes.

An important facet of the argument between the alternative social policy models concerns the impact of them upon competitiveness in the global economy (see Chapter 22). In fact there is an absence of strong evidence that the liberal market systems compete more effectively than others. Consider Esping-Andersen's list of nations in that category. There are many simplistic journalistic assertions on this theme, many seeming to have cogency at one point in time but then losing force as nations rise and fall in the economic performance league. Efforts to test hypotheses about the impact of social policy upon economic growth run into considerable difficulties because of the multiplicity of factors that influence the latter.

Esping-Andersen's more recent work, building on his original theory, suggests that the nature of economic activity within a society is likely to be a crucial intermediary factor between social policy and growth. Where the neo-liberal model (see Chapter 8) suggests that competitiveness can be achieved only through the driving down of wages and the removal of social protection it is argued there is an alternative that involves a focus upon preserving a highly trained and adaptable labour force. Social policy can make a contribution to this. Moreover, inasmuch as social protection systems contribute to social harmony they generate a commitment to national problem solving. Finally, since the welfare state is a system for the sharing of costs within a society, then where it is absent the costs of economic change fall elsewhere with possibly more damaging consequences for the society (a key example here is of course the existence of high crime rates). Hence the relationship between social policy and growth is not as simple as neo-liberal theory suggests. Moreover, even if there is such a relationship the evidence on inequalities within the world's most economically advanced nations (particularly the United States) and on the social problems that seem to stem from those inequalities offer reasons for arguing that advancing social policy is more important than promoting growth.

Emerging Issues

The banking crisis of 2007/8 seemed initially to reinforce the critique of the neo-liberal model, as it became apparent that minimally controlled financial markets had run into serious problems. However, the crucial policy development across the world was measures to prevent the collapse of the banking system, involving extensive new public expenditure. Furthermore the recession that followed the crisis produced a fall in government income from taxation and increases in expenditure on existing social welfare measures. The result was that by the end of 2009 governments throughout the world were seeking to curb public expenditure. Hence at the time of writing far from seeing a retreat from the liberal market model there is a quest for new ways to limit social policy expenditure. The dominant view, evident even in those nations where social policies have historically diverged from the liberal market model, seems to be that long-run economic recovery depends upon freeing the market from the burden of an expensive state. There is however a minority view that this response will ultimately deepen the recession. If the latter view is right it may ultimately lead to the revival of a more positive approach to social expenditure.

Hence it is still the case that the era of an influential alternative social democratic discourse challenging the liberal market one seems to be coming to an end. Contemporary developments in social policy reflect the search for a compromise between the two discourses. There has been a strong shift, right across the world, towards policies that are seen as enhancing employment. There is also, in the face of the ageing of the population in all the developed nations, a strong liberal market challenge to public pensions' systems where benefits are guaranteed and contribution funds have not been built up (as in private 'defined contribution' systems).

Guide to Further Sources

The nature of comparative social policy analysis is that classification systems explore individual type or regime categories in terms of their relationships to the alternatives. Hence this chapter inevitably poses questions about contrasts. It is not possible then to direct readers to a literature on liberal market regimes and *nothing but* those regimes. The key sources for the exposition of the characteristics of the liberal market model of social policy are thus G. Esping-Andersen, *The Three Worlds of Welfare Capitalism* (Cambridge: Polity Press, 1990), and R. E. Goodin *et al.*, *The Real Worlds of Welfare Capitalism* (Cambridge: Cambridge University Press, 1999) which, as well as offering a comparative analysis, explores the characteristics of one liberal market regime, the United States.

Many of the ensuing and still ongoing debates can be pursued in M. Hill, *Social Policy in the Modern World* (Oxford: Blackwell, 2006) the contributions to Part VII of G. Castles *et al.* (eds), *The Oxford Handbook of the Welfare State* (Oxford: Oxford University Press, 2010) and P. Alcock and G. Craig (eds), *International Social Policy* (2nd edn, Basingstoke: Palgrave Macmillan, 2009) which also has a chapter by J. Clarke on the United States.

Review Questions

1 How is the word 'liberal' being used in the categorization of societies as liberal market ones?

2 What seem to have been the distinguishing characteristics of social policy in the United States?

3 How important would you expect social insurance to be in liberal market societies?

4 How important would you expect means tests to be in liberal market societies?

5 What are the forces that are tending to spread liberal market oriented social policies around the world?

Visit the book companion site at www.wiley.com/go/alcock to make use of the resources designed to accompany the textbook. There you will find chapter-specific guides to further resources, including governmental, international, think-tank, pressure groups, and relevant journals sources. You will also find a glossary based on *The Blackwell Dictionary of Social Policy*, help sheets, and case studies, guidance on managing assignments in social policy and career advice.

62

Social Policy in East Asian Societies

Michael Hill

Overview

- The growing importance of East Asian societies in the global economy has stimulated interest in their social policy arrangements.
- Social provision in these societies is highly variable but also differs from that in other regions.
- There are various ways of characterizing and explaining social policy in East Asian societies.
- Studying welfare systems in East Asia raises wider questions about comparative policy theorization.
- Social provision in these societies is facing new challenges arising from a combination of economic and demographic change.

Context

Until the 1970s the English language literature paid little attention to social policy developments in East Asia. Only Japan had developed welfare institutions broadly comparable to those of the West. In China social welfare protection depended largely upon a person's attachment to an economically secure work unit. Elsewhere social welfare policies were rudimentary. Since that time there have been significant developments in social policy in East Asia, and a growing interest in those developments within the social policy literature. There has been a flow of students from East Asia, eager to contribute and make sense of developments in their own countries, writing theses in English or other European languages.

Inevitably questions have arisen about the distinctiveness of these East Asian developments and whether a policy learning process is occurring, questions that in turn raise issues for comparative theory (see Chapter 59). The early comparative

The Student's Companion to Social Policy, Fourth Edition. Edited by Pete Alcock, Margaret May, Sharon Wright.
© 2012 John Wiley & Sons, Ltd. Published 2012 by John Wiley & Sons, Ltd.

social policy theory embodied a strong determinist element, suggesting the growth of state social policy can be explained by industrialization, urbanization, and democratization (in linked combinations). Such thinking implied that differences across the world would be eroded by these processes. Later theory gave more attention to political differences between states, stressing differences in the extent of social policy development and the forms it takes. Much of that later theory involves attempts to establish a typology, implying that each system will belong to one of a finite number of 'regime' categories. Hence a question that has been addressed is whether such regime theory can be applied in East Asia, and if so how?

What Countries Are We Talking About?

There is an arbitrary character to any attempt to divide the world into regions for a discussion like this. Those divisions moreover tend to have an ethnocentric character; societies that are seen to be alike to Western eyes are put together. The East Asian nations are, of course, the nations on the western side of the Pacific Ocean. The northeastern Asian nations are the ones that attract most attention from social policy scholars. Among them there is one massive nation (China), another large one (Japan), and the divided nation of Korea (with important social welfare development in South Korea, and – as far as social policy scholars are concerned – no attention given to North Korea). There are two cities that were European colonies and are now quasi-autonomous Special Administrative Regions of China – Hong Kong and Macao. The latter is very small and has been little studied, though it is interesting to note as having an embryonic welfare system largely funded by taxes on gambling. Finally, in the northern group there is Taiwan, an island with a population of over 20 million claimed by China but operating as an independent state, now with a democratic form of government and extensive social policies.

The nations to the south of that group have secured much less attention, with the exception of the city-state of Singapore. A scrutiny of an atlas suggests there is no good reason to exclude

discussion of Vietnam, Laos, Cambodia, Thailand, Malaysia, Borneo, and the Philippines from consideration here (and we could look even further south) (see Figure 62.1). In practice, they have received little attention, with the partial exception of Malaysia, where limited developments have occurred along lines not unlike Singapore's. This may largely be explained in terms of the limited development of formal social policy.

So it has been the social policy systems of Japan, South Korea, Hong Kong, Singapore, and Taiwan that have secured most of the consideration in the discussions of social policy in East Asia. China has secured less attention. That is all changing now. This discussion therefore starts there.

Social Policy in China

Two threads in Chinese history merit attention for social policy. One is the very long-standing Confucian tradition in the government of that vast country which saw welfare as a decentralized matter, with the extended family in a key role for individual welfare backed up by localized granaries to deliver exceptional assistance. The other is the apparent sweeping away of Chinese tradition by the Communist movement, led by Mao Zedong, after the Second World War. While the actual manifestation of this was often confusing, at the heart of Maoist social welfare policy was the notion of the all-providing work unit to which all citizens should be attached (sometimes called 'the iron rice bowl' providing for a unit's young and sick and even its pensioners).

Since Mao's death, while the central political dominance of the Communist Party has been maintained economic development has been pragmatic, involving a slow move away from explicit state ownership and centralized planning. The consequence of this has been the establishment of a whole range of new economic enterprises, including many foreign owned companies, and the decline of state entities. In respect of the latter a particular concern has been to enable the elimination of those that are no longer profitable.

The significance of this for Chinese social policy has been that there has had to be a search for alternatives to the work unit based 'iron rice

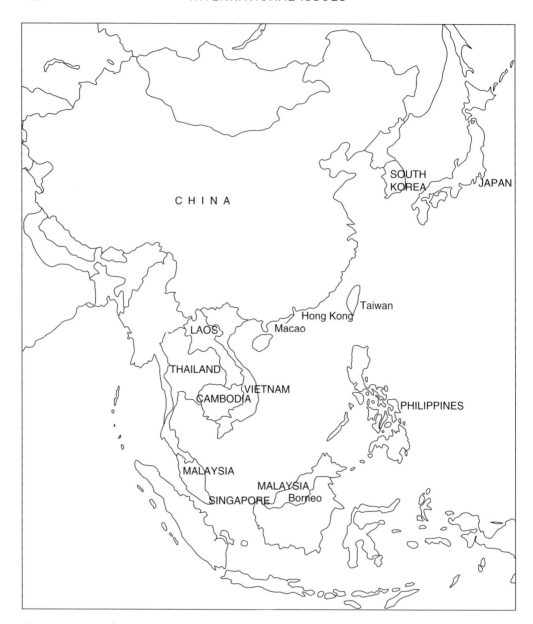

Figure 62.1   South East Asia.

bowl'. What has transpired is complex and often confusing. In urban areas social insurance policies have been developed to provide pensions and health care. In rural areas a variety of direct state subsidized health services continue. But there are many gaps in the system. The older policies were developed for a static society in which people remained in their villages or work units all their lives. Citizen registration remains based upon

such an assumption. The reality is massive internal migration, with migrants to cities neither protected through workplace participation nor through local institutions. In respect of much social need the older Confucian tradition is evident in the application of expectations that help is not provided if extended families can do so.

It would be rash to try to predict how Chinese social policy will develop. What is evident is two themes in development that also feature in the wider debate about social policies in East Asian societies. One of these is the notion that developments are likely to occur in a rather different cultural context than those in the West, involving a stress on Confucian ideologies. The other is the suggestion that 'productivism' – putting economic development before social development – is characteristic of social policy change.

Confucian Social Policy?

As noted above the suggestion is that Confucian family ideologies lead to a greater delegation of welfare responsibilities to the family and extended family. However, wider problems about this argument are that (a) in any underdeveloped income maintenance system the family will *faute de mieux* have to take on greater responsibilities, and (b) the use of Confucian 'type' ideologies as a justification for inaction by the political elite is not evidence that political demands can and will be damped down in this way in the absence of evidence of the acceptance of that reasoning by the people. It must also be said that the label Confucian is not really appropriate outside the Chinese societies.

Productivist Welfare Capitalism in East Asia?

It is suggested that social policy in East Asia can be described as involving productivist welfare capitalism in which the orientation towards growth has been of key importance for social policy development. The difference here from the liberal market regimes, which that term seems also to describe (see Chapter 61), is that the governments of the East Asian societies have been seen to be engaged in harnessing social policy effort particularly to the aspiration to ensure rapid economic growth. Hence, for example, while education policy has been stressed, governments have argued against rapid expansion of social care policies on the grounds that this could hinder the development project.

The very active state driven developments (particularly characteristic of South Korea, Taiwan, and Singapore) have rather specific implications for social policy. The groups who first secured social protection in these societies were the military and civil servants. This was followed by measures to extend some insurance based benefits to industrial workers. Securing the support of the emergent industrial 'working class' was important for the state-led growth – very significant in these societies. Hence inasmuch as governments secured social support they did it through their success in generating rapid income growth for the majority of the people.

Is Western Developed Regime Theory the Most Useful Approach to Analysing East Asian Social Policy?

As already noted, among the East Asian nations Japan clearly has the most developed system. It features in many world scale comparative analyses. In recent years good comparative data has emerged on developments in South Korea too. Developments in Taiwan have quite a lot in common with those two, with all three nations using social insurance extensively.

Hong Kong and Singapore are small, though rich, and their social policy development has had some special features. In Hong Kong's case its colonial status meant that the United Kingdom encouraged some basic welfare development but kept costs low and did not let it develop social insurance. Singapore developed a rather distinctive approach of its own – a 'providence' fund – involving forced government protected saving for social policy purposes.

So the debate about the characteristics of East Asian social policy is above all a debate about what is going on in Japan, South Korea, Taiwan, Hong Kong, and Singapore, with some references to complex and hard to classify developments in China.

Recent comparative theory has centred on Esping-Andersen's three-regime model (see Chapter 59). In his work one East Asian nation is included – Japan – and is seen as belonging to his 'conservative' category alongside European nations such as France, Germany, Austria, and Switzerland. Esping-Andersen's original conclusions on Japan were challenged and he later defended his view, arguing that it is not helpful to multiply the number of specific regime categories. However, he conceded that Japan is a marginal case between the conservative and liberal market. Esping-Andersen went on to stress the ways in which the pulls between the two alternatives draws attention to strains and pressures within the Japanese system (particularly those relating to the role of the family in welfare). In that sense one of the cases for regime theory is that it helps the analysis of these.

It is not surprising, given the controversy about Japan that a rather similar argument has arisen about South Korea. That society is interesting inasmuch as there seems to be a struggle occurring around differing perspectives on welfare that correspond with all three of the alternatives in Esping-Andersen's model. There has been a strong emphasis upon the need to protect the market economy. There has been an emphasis upon the role of the family in welfare, and a strong interest in the use of social insurance, two characteristics of the conservative model. But there have also been significant advances towards universal and redistributive policies in relation to both pensions and health care.

There has been consideration of the extent to which Taiwan shares the 'conservative' regime characteristics while Singapore and Hong Kong have been categorized as rather more like liberal market regimes.

Rejection or Revisions of Regime Theory?

It has alternatively been argued that the whole regime approach is inapplicable because it embodies 'Western' ethnocentric assumptions about the role of the state and welfare development as a product of what has been described as 'the truce' between capital and labour. Support for that perspective is perhaps offered by the fact that the politics of China is not normally analysed in these terms. However, regime models now can be applied to the transformation of China described above. Is what is going on in China in the evolutionary terms outlined above actually involving choices between the conservative and the liberal market models?

What may be problematical is not regime theory as a starting point but efforts to follow it

too closely in an analysis of contemporary developments (a conclusion that may apply to other societies as well as to the East Asian ones). Three modern theoretical developments that deserve further consideration here are

- Institutional theory (stressing that there may be crucial points in the evolution of systems where institutional choices are made).
- The impact of policy learning and policy borrowing when those choices are made.
- The 'pathways' set up by those initial choices that have a key impact upon subsequent developments.

In all the nations discussed here, apart from Japan, key decisions about approaches to social policy were made (or in the case of China, are being made) in pre-democratic political systems. Moreover even in the Japanese case some institutional arrangements imposed upon that country after defeat in war have been important. Elsewhere authoritarian governments struggled with problems of securing or maintaining relatively high levels of popular support while at the same time facilitating economic growth. Social policy institutions were a specific product of decisions made outside democratic arenas, but making extensive use of expert advice.

The stories of Singapore and Taiwan show similar features, while in Hong Kong the issues were about maintaining British rule in a colony with economic opportunities but also massive social problems associated with the inflow of population from China (with accordingly large-scale social housing projects as a key social policy).

Taiwan provides an interesting case. The ruling group in pre-democratic Taiwan, the KMT, legitimized its policies in terms of the efforts of Dr Sun Yat-Sen, the leading ideologist in China in the 1920s after the Emperor was overthrown, to fuse Confucian ideas with Western republican and socialist ones. This led to the establishment of a cluster of separate social insurance schemes.

The Taiwan story also illustrates the second theme, policy borrowing from Europe. Initially this can be seen in terms of the central conflict explored in Chapter 61 between liberal market approaches and the more state-led ideas (including in particular social insurance). Subsequently the newly industrialized and increasingly democratic East Asian nations had the opportunity to observe the strengths and weaknesses of European policies adopted earlier in time and to learn from them selectively. They have, inevitably, been drawn into the new global debate about the economic costs of generous welfare benefit systems and have wanted to draw their own conclusions.

Early choices have a substantial subsequent impact, particularly in providing 'pathways' that constrain changes of direction. Social insurance is particularly significant in this respect, in setting up long run commitments and expectations. Japan, South Korea, and Taiwan stand out as having gone down the social insurance road so that it subsequently influences later developments. A key Japanese example is the way it has moved on from some cost problems in its health insurance system to a form of care insurance (as has Germany). That topic is now on the Taiwan agenda. In the Chinese case social insurance for state enterprise employees is a logical step forward from the work-unit model for welfare since it offers a way to collectivize risks that can no longer be carried by individual enterprises. So as far as new private enterprise is concerned the agenda is open, though market solutions to welfare problems are inevitably attractive.

Emerging Issues

In exploring emerging issues the comments above about existing pathways are important. However, in East Asia there are two developments that may shift some or all nations dramatically away from any identified pathways. These are first, economic and second, demographic.

The very rapid economic transformation of China poses social policy issues not just for that country but also for its neighbours. In China the dual system described above, of developing welfare institutions in the urban areas and a residual system in the rural areas, is threatened by both the intrusion into the former of foreign economic enterprises eager to operate with a minimum of constraints and the massive migration of rural workers to emergent jobs in the cities. The weakening central state apparatus is torn between aspirations to encourage growth without 'strings' and concern to maintain social

welfare institutions. Any effort to forecast what will happen has to take on the difficult task of predicting how this vast society will democratize.

Outside China itself it is important not to underestimate the impact of Chinese economic change on its near neighbours. A large adjacent growing low wage economy threatens the standards of living in its neighbours, and consequently also social welfare provisions that impose tax costs. The Chinese challenge can be observed most directly in Hong Kong, now a Special Administrative Region belonging to China.

The economic crisis that emerged in 2008 contributed to a highlighting of the economic relationship between China and the West. Not only is it evident that China's production and export performance is a threat to earlier established economies, but the crisis also reinforced attention to the way in which investment of Chinese surpluses had made it easier for people in the United States and the United Kingdom to live beyond their means. This had made a significant contribution to the instability of Western economies. Some Western experts suggest it would benefit us all if China spent more of its surplus on welfare!

In respect of demographic change what is special about East Asia is that the worldwide demographic shift towards 'ageing societies' consequent upon the combination of falling birth rates and death rates is particularly dramatic. Currently the most dramatic changes are occurring in Japan and South Korea, but in due course (as a consequence of its one child policy) China's transformation will be massive. We see thus both falling populations and a rapid growth in the number of elderly people relative to the numbers of prime age adults.

In Japan, South Korea, and Taiwan debate about this phenomenon centres upon issues about female roles. There are two traditional expectations of women – to bear children and to care for older people (generally their in-laws) – and a modern one of increased labour market participation. Ironically, inasmuch as there is a concern about insufficient prime age adults to meet the needs of the labour market, married women are the main source of extra labour. While politicians may exhort – as controversially has been the case in Japan – women to fulfil roles of child bearers and carers, this surely can have little effect without attention being given to *either* securing new labour from other countries *or* policies to reduce the pressures upon female labour market participants.

These alternatives imply social policy changes. Those related to migration are complex and these countries are very reluctant to open their frontiers to migrant workers. Those relating to family life (which surely must be addressed since it seems unlikely that government's can repress new female aspirations anyway) seem likely to engender new government initiatives in relation to social care at both ends of the life cycle. In respect of care of older people Japan is already leading the way in this direction with the initiation of social care insurance.

These two emerging trends will of course interact very substantially, since what happens to the economy of the region will have a variety of impacts upon national labour markets and on the demand for female labour. However, studies of family policy suggest that while governments may succeed in reducing birth rates they have considerable difficulty in increasing them. In any case the oppression of women consequent upon the combination of the three pressures discussed above is surely one that social policy needs to address.

Guide to Further Sources

I. Peng and J. Wong, 'East Asia' in F.G. Castles *et al.* (eds), *The Oxford Handbook of the Welfare States*, Oxford: Oxford University Press, 2010), pp. 656–70 offers a larger overview of the issues explored here. C. K. Chan, L.N. King, and D. Phillips, *Social Policy in China* (Bristol: Policy Press, 2008) is the best source on developments in China. For comparative accounts of developments in the other nations see A. Walker and C-K. Wong (eds), *East Asian Welfare Regimes in Transition* (Bristol: Policy Press, 2005) and M. Ramesh, *Social Policy in East and Southeast Asia: Education, Health, Housing and Income Maintenance* (London: Routledge Curzon, 2004). Recent developments in East Asia are reviewed in H-J. Kwon, 'The reform of the developmental welfare state in East Asia', *International Journal of Social Welfare*, 18/1 (2009): 12–21. A bibliographic essay by X. Shang and R. Gleeson, 'Some useful sources on Chinese Social Policy', *Social Policy and Society*, 10/1 (2011): 117–21, supplements these references for China and other Chinese societies.

Review Questions

1 What impact has it been suggested Confucianism may have on social policy in East Asia?
2 What do you understand by the notion of 'the iron rice bowl'?
3 Why is China moving away from' the iron rice bowl' approach to welfare?
4 What are the features of social policy development in Japan, South Korea, and Taiwan that have led some writers to see them as rather like the conservative regimes of continental Europe?
5 Why is it particularly important to pay attention to the impact of demographic change upon social policy in East Asia?

Visit the book companion site at www.wiley.com/go/alcock to make use of the resources designed to accompany the textbook. There you will find chapter-specific guides to further resources, including governmental, international, think-tank, pressure groups, and relevant journals sources. You will also find a glossary based on *The Blackwell Dictionary of Social Policy*, help sheets, and case studies, guidance on managing assignments in social policy and career advice.

63

Social Policy in Middle Eastern Societies

Rana Jawad

Overview

■ Social policy in Middle Eastern countries can be broadly characterized as corporatist/residual.

■ In the absence of adequate empirical research, the Rentier state concept has dominated academic discourse – especially in relation to the Arab countries.

■ A major challenge facing the formulation of social policy in the region is the lack of adequate definitions and empirical data (apart from Turkey and Israel).

■ International organizations exercise a major influence on social policy agendas in the Middle East.

■ Arab governments are beginning to formulate social vision statements that emphasize economic development but have yet to clearly articulate the roles of citizenship and social rights in their societies.

Reinstating Social Policy in the Middle East

This chapter provides a historical and analytical perspective on social policy in Middle Eastern societies: Does it exist? What does it mean? How does it operate? Who provides it and who uses it? These questions underpin this chapter since it will clear be from very early on that the study of social policy in the Middle East is somewhat new,

even though in practice, governments and civil society organizations have been engaged in social welfare activities since the 1940s (the time of state independence in the region). As Figure 63.1 indicates, the Middle East extends from Morocco to Turkey along the southern and eastern shores of the Mediterranean, as far east as Iran and south to Sudan, Saudi Arabia, and Yemen. The region has a population of half a billion that is Muslim in the majority, but as it is home to the

The Student's Companion to Social Policy, Fourth Edition. Edited by Pete Alcock, Margaret May, Sharon Wright.
© 2012 John Wiley & Sons, Ltd. Published 2012 by John Wiley & Sons, Ltd.

Figure 63.1　The geographical area known as the Middle East.
Source:　R. Jawad, *Social Welfare and Religion in the Middle East* (Bristol: Policy Press, 2010).

world's three largest monotheistic religions, it continues to have substantial Christian and Jewish populations.

It is worth noting that this is a region still very much in the making: disputes over territorial borders, recognition of ethnic minority status, and concerns with nation-building remain alive, with very real implications for whose interests social policy represents. From a Western perspective, the overriding public perception of the Middle East as a place of backward social and economic practices and extremist religious ideologies makes it harder to discuss the existence and role of social policy there.

However, the academic and policy tides are changing, and somewhat like the turning of a large freight ship, this chapter seeks to dispel some of the myths that surround the study of social policy in the Middle East and to provide some useful first understandings of what it means and how it works. Moreover, it argues that social policy as a subject area can greatly contribute to academic knowledge and public understandings of socio-political dynamics in the Middle East. This is because the key units of analysis in social policy such as social welfare, citizenship, equality, poverty, rights, and a mixed economy of welfare and human well-being can offer an alternative view of Middle Eastern societies whereby contemporary examples of positive social action can be better appreciated and the sense of this region being an exception to global trends de-emphasized.

A Historical Overview: Oil, Independence, and Lost Opportunities

With the aims of nation-building and state legitimization as their primary objectives, Middle Eastern states have pursued various policies in the era of independence (1940s). These had a redistributive character as follows:

- nationalization of foreign assets and large domestic enterprises such as the Suez Canal in Egypt;
- land reform;
- mass education and, in some cases, secularization of the education system; and
- support of low-income groups through direct financial transfers by the state (with Turkey leading the way).

The 1940s and 1950s in the Middle East were therefore deeply imbued with secular and socialist sentiment, the vestiges of which can still be found in countries such as Egypt, Syria, and Iraq. Until the 1980s, the Middle East experienced immense social transformations, due almost entirely to the sudden oil windfall. This was used to establish and fund state social services such as guaranteed government employment for graduates; new labour legislation (favouring workers in large public enterprises) such as health insurance, retirement pay, maternity pay; free education; free hospital care; and basic consumer subsidies, the most important of which were food and housing. Urbanization and economic development were accompanied by significant attainments in education and enhanced female labour participation.

But, this was a short honeymoon. The easy access to capital that resulted from oil revenues concentrated wealth among the urban elite, and left the majority of the populations poorly skilled and ruled primarily via patrimonial and tribal structures. This reliance on natural resource rents for social spending has earned the welfare regimes of the Middle East the label of 'Rentier'.

Theoretical Overview: A New Ethic of Welfare Beyond Rentierism

'Rent' is not 'an earned income' like wages and profit because it does not depend on reward for participation in the process of economic production; it is a gift resulting from ownership of natural resources. Four key characteristics define the Rentier state:

- rent income dominates the economy;
- the rent comes from outside the country;
- rent wealth is generated by a minority group in the population but distributed and utilized among the majority; and
- the government is the main receiver of external rent.

Thus, oil-producing economies such as Saudi Arabia and Kuwait are the characteristic examples of Rentier economies. But there is also a Rentier mentality in the region whereby the state becomes a provider of favours and benefits as opposed to the upholder of citizenship rights and obligations. Rentier behaviour can be found in the form of dependence on military or political aid, workers' remittances and tourist expenditure, all of which are forms of external rent.

However, both empirically and analytically, the Rentier concept is deficient as a classification concept for social policy in the Middle East. It misses the way in which the social order is itself negotiated and how the state also exercises influence on the formation of national identity and its symbols. Indeed, a more culturally sensitive analysis of social policy would suggest that non-state actors especially in the form of religious movements have a large stake in the social welfare settlement in the Middle East (see Chapter 23).

Beyond the concept of the Rentier state, the welfare regime approach propagated by Esping-Andersen (see Chapter 59) may help to provide some tools for classifying social policy in the Middle East. These include: the notion of a 'regime' of welfare; the departure from social welfare expenditure as the key denominator of social policy classification; the emphasis on a 'welfare mix' which highlights the role of non-state actors especially the market; and third the political economy approach which allows analysis of power structures and social norms. With regard to the discussion of welfare regime types in developing country contexts, the Middle East has tended to be missed from discussion though new research publications show this situation to be changing. We should also not forget the issue of terminology, Middle Eastern countries tend to speak of an ill-defined 'social sphere' or 'social strategies' as opposed to a fully fledged welfare state and social policy. Government policies also prefer using the term social development since this assumes economic progress and modernization.

A Brief Socio-Economic Profile of the Middle East Region

The region (see Figure 63.1) has diverse socio-economic profiles with per capita income levels ranging from over US$25,000 to below US$1,000. The first Arab Human Development Report (2002) described the Arab region in particular as being 'richer than it is developed', with its oil-driven economic policies resulting in substantial social and economic volatility. There is also limited availability of poverty statistics. The region has made some progress in reducing absolute poverty over the past two decades, with the 2009 Arab Human Development report (www.arab-hdr.org) estimating a fall in the percentage of the population in the Middle East and North Africa living on less than two dollars a day from 26.7 per cent in 1981 to 16.9 per cent in 2005. Extreme poverty is especially acute in the low-income Arab countries affecting around one-third of the population. A distinctive demographic feature with important social policy implications is the region's 'youth bulge' with around 60 per cent of the population under the age of twenty-five.

The data on regional poverty cited above need to be read with caution, as poverty is a multidimensional phenomenon. There are, therefore, a variety of social problems which Middle Eastern countries today are grappling with namely, unemployment particularly among the youth, population growth, adult illiteracy, high school drop-out rates, lack of access to universal health care, and social, income, and gender disparities.

Revitalizing Social Policy in the Middle East: The Contemporary Context

Today, most Middle Eastern countries have income transfer policies that are employment-based only and favour security forces and public sector workers. There is also a gap in state-provision of social care services since this is traditionally left to the realm of the family. A key shortcoming of all major social policies in the region is their urban bias that means that unionized workers in industry, construction, and trade tend to be among the best protected.

The question then of how much weight and importance social objectives are accorded is important. Social concerns appear to play a subsidiary role. While Middle Eastern countries profess to respecting core values of human development, justice, and prosperity for all their citizens, their social policy objectives point to a primary concern with economic development and national wealth creation. On the ground, social inequalities as well as inadequate access to vital social services remain key features of many countries such as Lebanon, Egypt, and Morocco. This so-called productivist approach to social policy can be explained as follows (see also Chapter 62).

Configuration of social policy provision

In the absence of comprehensive and concrete social policies in the Middle East, it is more apt to a certain extent to argue that these countries have social strategies in place. Thus, they are following a combination of medium- and short-term social strategies aimed at alleviating the negative effects of public policies geared primarily towards economic growth, and to a lesser degree spreading the fruits of development where possible. Table 63.1 shows the breakdown of social protection and pro-poor growth strategies that are proposed by Middle Eastern countries. It is complemented by Table 63.2, which shows the kinds of formal contribution-based social insurance schemes that Middle Eastern countries have. Taken together, they summarize the situation of social policy in the Middle East.

Table 63.1 Social policy strategies in fifteen Arab countries complied by the author and based on national government strategies.

Policy	Social Protection/Basic Needs Satisfaction								Social Protection/Social Assistance				Pro-Poor Growth/Strategies		
Country	Social safety nets (cash transfers, food aid)	Contribution-based social security	Social care and social work	Expansion of basic education services	Expansion of basic health services	Health insurance for all citizens	Affordable housing	Food and/or utilities subsidies	Zakat and social funds, civil society, charities	Employment training services	Trading co-operatives	Citizenship education	Small enterprise development	Employment promotion in industrial and macro-economic policies	Rural development
Bahrain	X	X		X	X	X	X		X	X					
Egypt[a]	X	X	X	X	X	X	X		X				X	X	
Iraq	X	X		X	X			X		X					X
Jordan	X	X		X	X	X	X			X					
Kuwait	X	X	X	X	X		X		X		X				X
Lebanon	X	X	X	X	X	X			X			X			
Oman	X	X		X	X				X						
Palestinian Territories	X	X	X	X	X	X	X			X	X		X	X	X
Qatar	X	X		X	X	X			X			X	X		X
Saudi Arabia	X	X	X	X	X		X		X				X	X	X
Sudan	X	X	X	X	X										X
Syria	X	X		X	X					X					
Tunisia[a]	X	X	X			X	X	X	X	X			X	X	X
UAE	X	X		X	X				X						
Yemen	X	X		X	X										X

[a] A note on Egypt and Tunisia: At the time of writing, both the governments of Egypt and Tunisia are in transition and have yet to articulate their new social and political priorities. The data on Egypt which are shown in the table date back to the pre-revolution government but have not been overturned by the new government. The data provided for Tunisia come from available information from the ministries that have social policy responsibilities in the new post-revolution government.

Table 63.2 Available data on formal contribution-based social security schemes, 2010.

Scheme Country	Old age	Disability and survivors	Work injury	Unemployment	Sickness	Maternity	Family
Bahrain	X	X	X	X			
Iraq[a]	X	X	X	X	X	X	X
Jordan	X	X	X				
Kuwait	X	X	X				
Lebanon	X	X	X			X	X
Oman	X	X	X				
Saudi Arabia	X	X	X		X	X	
Syria	X	X	X				
Yemen	X	X	X		X[b]	X[b]	
Turkey	X	X	X	X	X	X	
Israel	X	X	X	X	X	X	X

Notes: [a] Information on Iraq is more than ten years old.
[b] Public sector employees only.
Source: Adapted from International Social Security Association country profiles, www.issa.int/Observatory/Country-Profiles.

The strategies shown in Table 63.1 are grouped into three categories:

1 social protection aimed at needs satisfaction;
2 social protection in the form of safety nets and social assistance services; and
3 pro-poor growth strategies and social development programmes.

As Table 63.1 shows, the bulk of the strategies proposed by Middle Eastern countries fall under the category of what we may call social protection schemes with a limited range of economic growth policies that seek to minimize the impact on the poorest members of the population, if not improve their situation (i.e. pro-poor policies). The policies shown cover the full range of social, industrial, and macroeconomic policies. The emphasis on private sector investment and employment-based social insurance in the Middle East is also made clearer when we look at what kinds of social security legislation are available in the region (Table 63.2).

Table 63.2 shows what data are available via the International Social Security Association web site on the kinds of social security schemes provided by Middle Eastern Countries. These are all employment-based schemes and are primarily restricted to old age, disability, and work injury. Thus, the basic social policy approach of Middle Eastern countries may be summed up by Figure 63.2 where the levels of protection offered to the population are weak and more likely to deal with the symptoms of poverty.

Based on the above analysis, the institutional mix of social policy in Middle Eastern countries relies heavily on the market, the family, the charitable and religious welfare sector, and finally a state role that is primarily in the form of financing and less in terms of direct provision.

A residual/productivist and corporatist approach to social policy

In terms of welfare regime analysis, we may pitch Middle Eastern countries somewhere between

Private sector-led economic growth and capital investment	+	social safety nets and 'affordability' programmes	+	limited contribution-based social security

Figure 63.2 A model of social policy in the Middle East.

residual and corporatist models. With some minor exceptions of countries with long socialist traditions such as Syria and Egypt, most countries are now adopting a strong neo-liberal stance whereby the private sector is the main engine of social and economic prosperity, the state provides social safety nets for poor and vulnerable groups, and the family (mainly the nuclear family) and charitable/religious organizations are expected to play a role in offering social support services. This exemplifies the classic definitions of residual or 'productivist' social policy where economic growth is given priority over more equitable mechanisms of redistribution and universal non-contributory coverage.

The Gulf States have traditionally occupied the category of Rentier economies whereby social welfare provision is primarily funded by oil revenues and is divorced from notions of citizenship rights and obligations. There is evidence of positive intentions in some of the Gulf States to diversify their economies in view of the eventual disappearance of oil and hydrocarbon resources. Indeed positive moves in societal security in these countries may be found in Bahrain, which has now implemented an unemployment scheme.

There is also a difficulty in the region in relation to the basic intellectual groundwork and policy evaluation process. With the exceptions of Turkey and Israel perhaps, most governments of the Middle East do not have clear definitions of poverty, nor have they developed adequate statistical data to analyse the problem of poverty in their countries. There is a general lack of harmonized social welfare expenditure data. Moreover, the definition of social welfare is based primarily on the fulfilment of human needs as demonstrated by the precedence given to social safety nets in social policy. Thus, Middle Eastern countries are far away from the discourse of social rights and citizenship that is more familiar in the West. Yet, the focus on needs and social safety nets contradicts government policy rhetoric in some Middle Eastern countries that seeks to 'help citizens achieve their full potential'. Thus, Middle Eastern countries remain socially conservative societies where it is envisaged that the family will play the central role in issues of moral and social identity.

In conclusion, Middle Eastern governments have two overarching tendencies in social policy:

on the one hand, they are focused on employment-based social security which means that formally employed private sector workers and public sector workers are most likely to receive protection (such as through end of service indemnity pay). On the other hand, this partial corporatist tendency is supported by a parallel welfare approach of residual and productivist social policy which sees Middle Eastern states prioritizing economic growth, contracting out social welfare services to private providers, and offering social safety nets that merely alleviate the problem of poverty. Middle Eastern governments thus continue to promote patrimonial social structures that give precedence to the family and the religious community in social welfare initiatives.

Emerging Issues

It is an important time for social policy in the Middle East both as a field of study and also as a legitimate arm of state action. Some key emerging issues are: Many governments are now producing social policy vision statements which attempt to set out the kind of societies that they aim to construct. Though modest, and in all cases favouring a private sector-led economic development path, government policy discourses are addressing the significant socio-economic challenges and problems their societies now face. Political will and an articulate plan for social policy have yet to be formulated by most of the Arab countries. Indeed, political instability in the region stands in the way of social policy: countries such as Lebanon and Iraq are in the throes of economic reconstruction; and emergency relief often impedes social policy development.

Of paramount importance is how countries move beyond oil revenue to finance social services for the future. Iran and the other Gulf countries are keen to find alternative ways of diversifying their economic bases further. But the lack of reliable data needs to be dealt with. It is therefore, important to conduct further quantitative and qualitative research to produce a classification of the welfare systems in the Middle East and to study the extent to which Turkey and Israel compare and contrast with European welfare regimes.

European Union accession for Turkey will matter a great deal in this respect and a heavy reform process is underway. Moreover, in Turkey, the ruling AKP party has followed a strong neo-liberal path that is creating a more society-based and religion-friendly climate for social welfare provision. Thus, as things take their course we should not quite expect to see a social policy revolution in the Middle East, but rather a redressing of dispassionate social scientific analysis that offers a more balanced view of Middle Eastern societies and public policies.

Guide to Further Resources

R. El-Ghonemy, *Affluence and Poverty in the Middle East* (London: Routledge, 1998) provides a comprehensive account of political, economic, and social factors that have produced the contemporary social inequalities in the region. M. Loewe, 'New avenues to be opened for social protection in the Arab world: The case of Egypt', *International Journal of Social Welfare*, 13/1 (2004): 3–14, critically explores the social security system in Egypt. G. Luciani (ed.), *The Arab State* (London: Routledge, 1990), though out of date, provides an authoritative original analysis of the nature of the Arab state including Rentierism. R. Jawad, *Social Welfare and Religion in the Middle East: A Lebanese Perspective* (Bristol: Policy Press, 2009) gives a detailed empirical analysis of social policy in the Middle East based on a case study of the Lebanon (and supplementary research on Egypt, Iran, and Turkey) with special focus on the role of religion.

The contributors to M. Karshenas and V. M. Moghadam (eds), *Social Policy in the Middle East: Economic, Political and Gender Dynamics*, United Nations Research Institute for Social Development (Basingstoke: Palgrave Macmillan, 2006) discuss social policy from a development perspective in various countries in the Middle East. B. Yakut-Cakar, 'Turkey', in B. Deacon and P. Stubbs (eds), *Social Policy and International Interventions in South East Europe* (Cheltenham: Edward Elgar, 2007), pp. 103–29 gives an overview of social

policy in Turkey and compares it to Southern European welfare systems

Policy developments and up-to-date statistical information on social, economic, and political trends can be found on the World Bank's Middle East and North Africa web site http://web.world bank.org/WBSITE/EXTERNAL/COUNTRIES/ MENAEXT/0,,menuPK:247603~pagePK:158889 ~piPK:146815~theSitePK:256299,00.html, the United Nations Development Programme Arab Human Development Reports (including 2002) http://hdr.undp.org/en/reports/regionalreports/ arabstates/name,3140,en.html, and the International Social Security Association Country Profiles www.issa.int/Observatory/Country-Profiles.

Review Questions

1   What is a Rentier state? Does the concept help or hinder the classification of social policy in the Middle East?

2   Why is it important to consider the role of international development institutions when analysing social policy in the Middle East?

3   How well does Esping-Andersen's typology of welfare regimes help us understand the nature and scope of social policy in the Middle East?

4   What are the shortcomings of a state-centred approach to social policy in the Middle East?

5   In what ways do Middle Eastern countries demonstrate corporatist and residual social policies?

Visit the book companion site at www.wiley.com/ go/alcock to make use of the resources designed to accompany the textbook. There you will find chapter-specific guides to further resources, including governmental, international, think-tank, pressure groups, and relevant journals sources. You will also find a glossary based on *The Blackwell Dictionary of Social Policy*, help sheets and case studies, guidance on managing assignments in social policy and career advice.

64

Social Policy in Developing Societies

Patricia Kennett

Overview

- The study of welfare arrangements in developing societies is a relatively new and expanding domain within mainstream social policy.
- A range of classification systems have been devised to explore and account for these arrangements.
- International institutions and overseas development assistance play a key role in shaping social policy in developing societies.
- There is growing recognition of the need for more predictable, sustainable forms of social protection and the expansion of social assistance programmes.

Context

An understanding of social policy in any part of the world can most successfully be achieved through analyses that incorporate historical, political, economic, as well as social dimensions. This is particularly the case when attempting to understand social policy in less industrialized societies, where the experiences of colonialism, independence and nation-building, the degree of influence exerted by international financial institutions, and the extent and nature of poverty and inequality have had a major impact on shaping social policy debates and systems of welfare.

There has often been a lack of a clear identity for social policy in such countries and a much greater emphasis on the broader notion of social development. Since the 1950s the main tenet of development thinking has been premised, either explicitly or implicitly, on the role of modernization as a vehicle for facilitating economic growth through urbanization, industrialization, and capital investment. The phrase itself and the perceived strategies for achieving it, have implied the

The Student's Companion to Social Policy, Fourth Edition. Edited by Pete Alcock, Margaret May, Sharon Wright.
© 2012 John Wiley & Sons, Ltd. Published 2012 by John Wiley & Sons, Ltd.

desirability of adopting a unilinear and universal development trajectory replicating and perpetuating the structures and systems dominant in Western industrial countries to the developing world. The development discourse has, until recently, tended to subordinate or subsume social policy within economic policy and to focus on homogeneity across developing societies, rather than diversity. This chapter looks first at these conceptual distinctions before considering social policy in a development context focusing specifically on Latin America and Africa.

Concepts and Categories

A variety of imprecise and inconsistent conceptual distinctions have been used to categorize and differentiate areas of the globe, such as First/ Third World, Developed/Developing, North/ South, industrialized/less industrialized, which have usually involved poorer countries being contrasted, negatively, with the more developed, advanced, industrialized, richer countries of the North.

The World Bank's main criterion for classifying countries is the size of their economy measured by gross national income (GNI) per capita, with every country classified as either low, middle (sub-divided into lower middle and upper middle), or high income. There are currently forty low income countries with a 2009 GNI of $995 or less, fifty-eight lower middle income countries with a GNI of between US$996 and US$3,945, forty-eight upper middle income countries with a GNI of between US$3,646 and US$12,195, and sixty-nine with a GNI of US$12,196 or more. Those counties classified as low or middle-income countries are generally understood to be 'developing societies'. In 1971 the United Nations established the Least Developed Countries (LDCs) group when twenty-four countries were identified as having a low per capita income, a low level of human resource development based on indicators of nutrition, health and education and adult literacy, and a high degree of economic vulnerability. In 2009 forty-nine countries were designated by the United Nations as the Least Developed Countries, of which thirty-three were in Africa, fifteen in Asia and the Pacific, and one in Latin

America and the Caribbean, representing a total population of 815.16 million people in 2008.

Since the 1990s the United Nations Human Development Index (HDI) has provided a different approach to categorizing and ranking countries through the use of composite indices based on educational attainment, health and survival, economic resources and standard of living. The world average HDI rose to 0.68 in 2010 from 0.47 in 1990 and 0.48 in 1970. In 2010, the HDI provided a relative ranking of 169 countries based on their average achievements, with forty-two countries categorized as having very high human development, forty-three high human development, forty-two with medium human development, and forty-two with low human development.

Diversity in Social Expenditure and Social Policy Instruments

The developing world incorporates a range of diversity in terms of colonial history, political profile, social structure, levels of development, and state and institutional capacity. Social policy instruments are wide-ranging and as well as more traditional welfare measures have come to include land reform, food and water subsidies, and the regulation of the private sector. The choice and combination of instruments is likely to be unique to each country, as it involves the interplay of a range of forces, including ideological predisposition, institutional structures, and the political and economic context.

A major factor impacting the structures of provision and choice of social policy instruments has been the history and current context of geopolitical relationships between the North and the South which have manifested through imperialism, colonialism, the institutionalization of relations of political and economic dependency, and development strategies and programmes which have in combination aggravated and perpetuated ethnic and religious tensions and conflict, and contributed to many of the negative aspects of social life in Africa, Asia, and Latin America.

Figure 64.1 provides an overview of total public social expenditure by region of the world. It highlights the wide disparities in social sector spending between different regions. Western European countries spend an average of 25 per

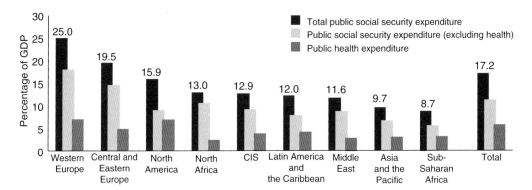

Figure 64.1 Total public social expenditure, regional estimates weighted by GDP, latest available year between 2002 and 2007 (percentage of GDP)
Source: Figure 2.7. Extending Social Security to All: A Guide through challenges and options, p.29.
© International Labour Organization: Geneva, 2010.

cent of GDP on the social sector, compared with 12 per cent in Latin America and the Caribbean (LAC), and 8.7 per cent in Sub-Saharan Africa. The widest disparities in expenditure are found in the area of social protection, which includes pensions, unemployment, and disability benefits. In Western European countries approximately 18 per cent of GDP is spend on social security, compared with approximately 8 per cent in LAC and approximately 6 per cent in Sub-Saharan Africa. The development and maintenance of social security systems requires, in the first instance, an appropriate and complex infrastructure, state capacity, and a formal labour market through which to raise and collect taxes to finance and implement social sector programmes.

Poorer countries are usually characterized by limited state capacity and infrastructure, and budget and policy restrictions particularly from International Financial Institutions (IFIs). In addition traditional labour structures, and massive and chronic levels of poverty and inequality, have mitigated against the evolution of social security systems. The disparities in health spending are not so great, but there is still variation between different regions of the world as Figure 64.1 shows. The pattern is a little different in the case of education. In 2004, for example, low income countries allocated a higher proportion of their GDP (5.3 per cent) to education than upper-middle income (4.9 per cent) and lower-middle- income countries (4.6 per cent). This

highlights the trend towards growing investment in education in poorer countries.

Policy Issues and Regimes

While the aggregate data introduced above provides a useful starting point for analysing social policy in less developed countries, more important is an appreciation of the structures of welfare, its composition and the complex and changing patterns of relationships between different producers. Although patterns of social policy across the South vary depending on each country's distinctive historical pathway, focusing on Latin America and Africa, it is possible to identify two broad categories of social policy and welfare system which can be characterized as clientelistic and residual (see Chapter 59). These different models can be linked to the levels of regulatory and institutional capacity achieved by particular states and the ways in which society has been organized.

■ *The clientelistic model*, predominant in Latin America, emerged as a consequence of the power of elites and interest groups and their ability to 'colonize' the state apparatus. Welfare systems developed relatively early in Latin America compared to other developing regions and, by the 1980s many countries in the region had long-standing, and in some cases well-developed formal welfare. Formal social insurance programmes were introduced during the first half of the twentieth century and focused on providing insurance for specific groups of workers through earnings related contributions. Barrientos (2004) highlights the importance of the extensive array of employment protection regulation, a particularly important component of the Latin American 'welfare mix'. While there have been aspirations towards the universal provision of education and health care the adverse economic conditions in the 1980s curtailed this ambition and significant gaps and inequalities in provision remain. The clientelistic model of welfare, which he categorizes as 'a liberal-informal welfare regime' can be characterized as occupationally stratified in terms of social insurance and employment protection and highly segmented in health insurance and health care provision.

For the most part, this model benefits only a small proportion of the population who are in privileged positions in the formal sector. The majority of those in rural areas and those who attempt to earn a living in the urban informal sector and their households (approximately 52 per cent of the population in Latin America) are excluded. Thus, the majority of the population has relied on informal support networks to protect them against social risk, and the sparse networks linked to national and international non-governmental organizations.

■ *Residual* social policy and welfare systems are most evident across much of Africa, particularly Sub-Saharan Africa, the origins of which can be located in the history and experience of colonial rule through which the first limited social services were introduced. It has been argued that the expansion of formal social policy under the colonial administration was largely determined by economic factors and the exploitation of the resources of the colonies, as well as the maintenance of social order. Social policy provision was minimal, residual, and discriminatory and more concerned with providing for the needs of, and thus support-

ing, the colonial administration. Following independence in the 1960s and 1970s social policy was to play an important role in legitimizing many post-colonial governments, with the development of social programmes in education, housing, health, and price subsidies and controls. This was supported by the Keynesian model of development, dominant up until the 1970s. Social policy measures were seen as appropriate and desirable and, in tandem with economic growth, were key instruments for social development and the elimination of poverty.

The United Nations, and other international organizations including the International Labour Organization (ILO), the World Health Organization (WHO), and the World Bank supported community-based projects concerned with, for example, health care and education. However, by the end of the 1970s it appeared that this strategy was unsustainable. Political instability, drought, a drop in the price of primary commodities, defaults on loans, and corruption brought the African state to crisis point. Social services and the social infrastructure decayed from sheer neglect and where they existed in rudimentary forms were appropriated by local barons and misused for political patronage. This resulted in a drastic reduction in expenditure and in public sector expenditure.

Development, International Institutions, and Social Policy

By the early 1980s the perception that the relationship between macroeconomic policy and social policy could be a positive one had been completely rejected and devalued. Most countries in Latin America and Africa were experiencing a decline in economic growth rates, high inflation levels, a growing debt burden, and an increasingly competitive international environment compared to the 1970s. The Debt Crisis and economic decline became the key issues across the globe, and rolling back the state, reducing public expenditure, privatization, the elimination of subsidies and opening up economies became fundamental components of the development paradigm.

The dominant discourse emerging at the global level was that the problems of development were primarily ones of economic (mis) management, inefficiency, and state corruption. From this perspective improvements in social policy could only flow from improved economic performance. This was a reflection of the new economic orthodoxy emerging in the North which was subsequently transmitted to developing societies through the influential IFIs and promoted monetarist economic policy, deregulation, and privatization. These themes were reflected at the global level and a consensus emerged on the most appropriate model of economic and political management for developing countries including the privatization of state run organizations, liberalization of the economy, the free market, and retrenching of the public sector.

There was also the commitment to channel aid through non-governmental organizations, rather than through country governments (see Chapter 44). This package of measures has often been termed the 'Washington Consensus', a phrase coined by Economist John Williamson in 1990 when referring to appropriate development strategies for Latin America. Its strategies were promoted by global institutions and the most powerful state players and took the form of structural adjustment programmes through which loans to poor countries were conditional on policy changes proposed by the World Bank.

By the end of the 1990s there was recognition that structural adjustment had done little to improve the economic circumstances and social well-being of people in less industrialized countries. A radical rethink of the national and international policies needed to tackle the problems of poor countries that were failing to prosper was called for by civil society organizations and national governments in both the North and the South. There was a shift in the terrain of intervention from the economic to the political sphere as the term 'governance' became a dominant theme in international institutions. There was also a growing recognition and the emergence of a global discourse that social rights should be respected in the development process and that poverty reduction should be adopted as a central objective of international development co-operation.

More recently IFIs, such as the World Bank, have begun to incorporate much more explicit references to poverty reduction and social development in their approach to concessional assistance to low-income countries and in 2000 189 UN member states agreed a set of specific targets for reducing poverty, hunger, disease, gender inequality, illiteracy, and environmental degradation which were incorporated in the Millennium Development Goals.

Many developing countries, particularly the LDCs are highly dependent on external resources. However, there has been increasing concern that the amount of aid from richer countries is failing to reach specified targets or to match pledges made by national governments. In addition to concerns about the quantity of aid, the quality of overseas development aid has also been called into question. Aid is often unpredictable, has numerous strings attached, and usually involves the recipient incurring transaction costs. According to the UN, international aid continues to be underused, inefficiently targeted, and in need of repair. The practice of tied aid, linking development assistance to the provision of supplies and services provided by the donor country, remains widely prevalent, as does the economic conditionality imposed by IFIs.

Extending Social Protection

More recently there has a growing interest in the provision of social protection in developing countries, accompanied by an interest in the potential of cash transfer programmes to alleviate poverty and as an instrument through which to achieve the Millennium Development Goals which is cost-effective and fiscally sustainable. The system originated in Brazil in 1995 but has expanded through Latin America and the Caribbean, and to Africa where the National Social Protection strategy incorporates the commitment to the provision of basic social assistance through cash transfer programmes. Over forty national cash transfer programmes have been established globally, and cover three-quarters of a billion people in the South. The expansion of these programmes has, in part, been a result of the recognition of the need for regular and predictable social protection programmes, rather than dependency on repeated humanitarian intervention, and intermittent and unpredictable aid.

Cash Transfer programmes vary in their scope, aim to protect the very poorest in a society, and promote human capital development. Conditional Cash Transfer programmes impose certain requirements on potential beneficiaries, such as school attendance, immunization, and visits to health clinics and are more fully developed in Latin America than sub-Saharan Africa. While initial evaluations have shown positive results in terms of school enrolment, levels of immunization, and attendance at health centres, there is some concern regarding the quality and quantity of education and health services received by recipients and their long-term impact. While the impact and extent of these programmes should not be over-stated, nor problems with implementation and conditionality overlooked, cash transfers could be viewed as the foundation of a broader commitment to strengthening systems of social protection in less-developed countries.

Emerging Issues

The focus of this chapter has been on developing societies, a contested concept and a category that incorporates enormous diversity and heterogeneity. Nevertheless, the recent financial crisis, combined with rising food prices and concerns regarding the impact of global warming has highlighted the inadequacies of the existing development paradigm and its inability to enhance and sustain well-being for a substantial proportion of men, women, and children living in the South. Historically, the highest levels of income inequality have been found in Africa and Latin America, a situation that worsened during the 1980s and 1990s. In Latin America in the 1990s wealthier households accounted for more than 30 per cent of total income, while the poorest 40 per cent of households received only 9 to 15 per cent of total income. The largest income gap is in Brazil, and the lowest levels of income inequality can be found in Uruguay and Costa Rica.

Of the world's population (2.5 billion people) 40 per cent live on less than $2 a day. However, there has been a downward trend in the poverty rate in all regions of the word except for sub-Saharan Africa, a part of the world which accounts for a rising share of the world's poorest 20 per cent. One in two people in sub-Saharan Africa is now located in the poorest 20 per cent of the world income distribution. The Chronic Poverty Research Centre estimates in its 2008–9 Report that between 320 and 440 million people are trapped in chronic poverty, defined as those people who 'remain poor for much or all of their lives, many of who will pass on their poverty to their children, and all too often die easily preventable deaths'. Being in chronic poverty is not just about having a low income it is about multidimensional poverty: hunger, illiteracy, dirty drinking water, no access to health services, social isolation, and exploitation. Around one-quarter to one-third of the people living on less than US$1 per day are chronically poor. Sub-Saharan Africa has one of the highest levels of chronic poverty.

While recognizing the specificity of individual developing counties, the chapter has also considered more general trends in social policy development, particularly in terms of the relationship between North and South and the role of international institutions. The challenge for the international community, national governments and civil society is overcoming the democratic deficit evident in international institutions, strengthening the voice of developing country representatives, reforming the aid infrastructure and exhibiting a genuine commitment to social policy and sustainable development. A deepening and widening of appropriate country-owned social protection programmes, combined with an improvement in access to, and quality of, health and educational services, as well as labour market opportunities would provide the multidimensional framework through which to support human security and sustainable development. Social policy not only has the capacity to contribute to social capital and social cohesion but can also play a significant role in reinforcing the legitimacy of the political order and contributing to political stability.

Guide to Further Sources

Issues and debates touched on in this chapter are explored in T. Akin Aina, 'West and Central Africa: Social Policy for Reconstruction and Development', in D. Morales-Gomez (ed.), *Transnational Social Policies. The New Development Challenges of Globalisation* (London: Earthscan,

1999), pp. 69–88. I. Gough and G. Wood with A. Barrientos *et al.* (2004) *Insecurity and Welfare Regimes in Asia, Africa and Latin America* (Cambridge: Cambridge University Press, 2004) this includes A. Barrientos' chapter 'Latin America: A liberal-informal welfare regime?' referred to here. For a comprehensive account of social transfer programmes in less-developed countries see J. Hanlon, A. Barrientos, and D. Hulm, *Just Give Money to the Poor* (Sterling, VA: Kumarian Press, 2010).

The United Nations Development Programme (UNDP) (www.undp.org), The United Nations Research Institute for Social Development (www.unrisd.org), the World Bank (www.worldbank.org), the International Labour Organization (www.ilo.org), and the World Health Organization (www.who.int), as well as Oxfam International (www.oxfam.org) and Save the Children (www.savethechildren.org) produce substantial amounts of material on developing societies much of which is relevant to the study of social policy.

Review Questions

1   Is the conceptual distinction between different parts of the world useful for understanding social policy in developing countries?

2   What are the key factors that have shaped social policy in developing countries?

3   What are the potential threats to human security in developing countries and what role can social policy play in protecting households against these threats?

4   Has intervention by international institutions encouraged or inhibited the development of social policy in developing countries?

5   What is the potential for Cash Transfer Schemes to provide the foundation for more comprehensive systems of social protection in developing countries?

Visit the book companion site at www.wiley.com/go/alcock to make use of the resources designed to accompany the textbook. There you will find chapter-specific guides to further resources, including governmental, international, think-tank, pressure groups, and relevant journals sources. You will also find a glossary based on *The Blackwell Dictionary of Social Policy*, help sheets, and case studies, guidance on managing assignments in social policy and career advice.

Appendix: The Social Policy Association (SPA)

The SPA is the professional association for academics, researchers, and students in social policy and administration. As an academic association in the social science field it is a member of the Academy of Learned Societies for the Social Sciences and it has close collaborative links with other professional associations in cognate fields, such as the British Sociological Association (BSA) and the Social Research Association (SRA). It also has close associations with SWAP, the subject centre for social policy and social work, one of the Higher education Academy's twenty-four discipline-based subject centres. The SPA works closely with SWAP and has been active in the development of the social policy benchmark statement, the range of which is reflected in the *Companion*.

The SPA is a membership organization and membership is open to all students, teachers, and others with work in the social policy field. All members pay an annual fee, with the cost of membership varying according to income bands. The benefits of membership are

- Free subscription to the leading policy journals, the *Journal of Social Policy* (four issues per year) and *Policy and Society* (four issues per year).

- Free copy of *Social Policy Review*, published annually by the Policy Press – an edited collection of articles reviewing developments and debates in social policy in Britain and internationally.

- A small grants scheme to support the setting up of seminars and conferences for members.

- *Policy World*: A popular newsletter published twice a year.

- Subgroups for postgraduate students, international and comparative social policy analysts.

- An Annual Conference held in July each year in the United Kingdom.

- Discounts on subscriptions to other leading academic journals – *European Journal of Social Policy*, *Policy and Politics*, and *Social Policy and Administration*.

The majority of members of the SPA live and work in the United Kingdom, but the Association also has active embers all over the world, including in particular Europe, North America, the Far East, and Australia. The Association has growing links with social policy associations and scholars throughout the world.

The Student's Companion to Social Policy, Fourth Edition. Edited by Pete Alcock, Margaret May, Sharon Wright.
© 2012 John Wiley & Sons, Ltd. Published 2012 by John Wiley & Sons, Ltd.

The Association is managed by an Executive Committee made up of members elected at the Annual Conference, with members serving on the committee for periods of three years at a time. In addition there are officers – Chair, Secretary, and treasurer – also elected and serving on a three-year basis. Students of social policy are encouraged to join the Association and contact staff members in their departments, schools, or faculties. The SPA can be contacted through its web page (www.social-policy.com).

Index

The Student's Companion to Social Policy, Fourth Edition. Edited by Pete Alcock, Margaret May, Sharon Wright.
© 2012 John Wiley & Sons, Ltd. Published 2012 by John Wiley & Sons, Ltd.

Index compiled by Neil Manley